ADVANCED
PERSONALITY

THE PLENUM SERIES IN SOCIAL/CLINICAL PSYCHOLOGY

Series Editor: C. R. Snyder

University of Kansas
Lawrence, Kansas

ADVANCED PERSONALITY

EDITED BY

DAVID F. BARONE

Nova Southeastern University
Fort Lauderdale, Florida

MICHEL HERSEN

Pacific University
Forest Grove, Oregon

AND

VINCENT B. VAN HASSELT

Nova Southeastern University
Fort Lauderdale, Florida

PLENUM PRESS • NEW YORK AND LONDON

Library of Congress Cataloging-in-Publication Data

ISBN 0-3064-8435-8

CONTRIBUTORS

RICHARD D. ASHMORE, Department of Psychology, Livingston College, Rutgers University, The State University of New Jersey, New Brunswick, New Jersey 08903

GONZALO BACIGALUPE, Graduate College of Education, University of Massachusetts–Boston, Boston, Massachusetts 02125

DAVID F. BARONE, Center for Psychological Studies, Nova Southeastern University, Fort Lauderdale, Florida 33314

LEONARD BERKOWITZ, Department of Psychology, University of Wisconsin at Madison, Madison, Wisconsin 53706

MADELON Y. BOLLING, Department of Psychology, University of Washington, Seattle, Washington, 98195-1525

DANIEL CERVONE, Department of Psychology, University of Illinois at Chicago, Chicago, Illinois, 60607-7128

PAUL T. COSTA JR., Gerontology Research Center, National Institute on Aging, National Institutes of Health, Baltimore, Maryland 21224

EDWARD DIENER, Department of Psychology, University of Illinois, Champaign, Illinois 61820

SEYMOUR EPSTEIN, Department of Psychology, University of Massachusetts, Amherst, Massachusetts 01003

CHRISTOPHER J. FLEMING, Department of Psychology, Rutgers University, The State University of New Jersey, New Brunswick, New Jersey 08903

W. BRADLEY GOELTZ, Center for Psychological Studies, Nova Southeastern University, Fort Lauderdale, Florida 33314

STEVEN N. GOLD, Center for Psychological Studies, Nova Southeastern University, Fort Lauderdale, Florida 33314

LESLIE S. GREENBERG, Department of Psychology, York University, North York, Ontario M3J 1P3, Canada

ROBERT J. KOHLENBERG, Department of Psychology, University of Washington, Seattle, Washington 98195-1525

KATHRYN D. KOMINARS, Student Counseling Center, Florida International University, Miami, Florida 33199

ROBERT C. LANE, Center for Psychological Studies, Nova Southeastern University, Fort Lauderdale, Florida 33314

ROBERT McCRAE, Gerontology Research Center, National Institute on Aging, National Institutes of Health, Baltimore, Maryland 21224

DANIEL M. OGILVIE, Department of Psychology, Rutgers, The State University of New Jersey, New Brunswick, New Jersey 08903

CURIE PARK, Department of Psychology, University of Michigan, Ann Arbor, Michigan 48109-1346

CHAUNCY R. PARKER, Department of Psychology, University of Washington, Seattle, Washington 98195-1525

GRETA E. PENNELL, Department of Psychology, Rutgers, The State University of New Jersey, New Brunswick, New Jersey 08903

CHRISTOPHER PETERSON, Department of Psychology, University of Michigan, Ann Arbor, Michigan 48109-1346

BADY QUINTAR, Center for Psychological Studies, Nova Southeastern University, Fort Lauderdale, Florida 33314

ANDREA D. SEWELL, Department of Psychology, Livingston College, Rutgers University, The State University of New Jersey, New Brunswick, New Jersey 08903

HOWARD SHEVRIN, Department of Psychiatry, University of Michigan Medical Center, Ann Arbor, Michigan 48105

JEANNE C. WATSON, Department of Applied Psychology, The Ontario Institute for Studies in Education, Toronto, Ontario M5S 1V6, Canada

THOMAS A. WIDIGER, Department of Psychology, University of Kentucky, Lexington, Kentucky 40506-0044

S. LLOYD WILLIAMS, Department of Psychology, Lehigh University, Bethlehem, Pennsylvania 18015-3068

MARVIN ZUCKERMAN, Department of Psychology, University of Delaware, Newark, Delaware 19716-2577

PREFACE

Having taught a personality course in a master's-level professional program for many years, we know the difficulty of finding a text written at the right level for our students. Personality texts are too elementary, and personality handbooks are too advanced. This text seeks to fill the gap between the two. It provides an advanced treatment of personality for upper-level undergraduates and entry-level graduate students in psychology, education, social work, and related fields. Given our participation in academic and professional education, we have constructed a text to meet the needs of both kinds of training.

Instructors of personality courses debate how much theory, research, and current controversy should be included. The field of personality comprises all three; all three are covered in this text. The field of personality has historical roots in the clinic as well as in academic studies, so theory and research from both sources are included. We know from experience that this particular mix of information is palatable to our students. We include tables that students have found helpful as organizing schemes and study aids.

We are pleased that authors with great expertise in personality theory and research agreed to participate in this project. We appreciate their commitment and forbearance. Given that the theories and research are so diverse, we chose not to constrain coverage with a common format. We invite out readers to share the authors' enthusiasm and deep understanding of personality. We also wish to acknowledge our friend and editor at Plenum Press, Eliot Werner, for his continuing support. We are especially appreciative of the technical efforts of Maura Sullivan and Carole Londereé.

DAVID F. BARONE
MICHEL HERSEN
VINCENT B. VAN HASSELT

CONTENTS

PART I

INTRODUCTION

CHAPTER 1

INTRODUCTION TO PERSONALITY STUDY

DAVID F. BARONE AND KATHRYN D. KOMINARS

A CONCEPTUAL FRAMEWORK

KNOWLEDGE AS DIFFERENT ANSWERS TO DIFFERENT QUESTIONS

It is customary to introduce a subject by defining it. The study of personality, however, is so diverse that one can define it only with alternative, seemingly unrelated statements: personality as the integrated functioning of psychological components, personality as individuals' differing dispositions, and personality as processes involved in integrated functioning. More basic than the definition of *personality* is the question, how do we understand the diversity of the field of personality? To answer it, we need to venture into the philosophy and history of science.

Logical empiricism (originally called logical positivism) is a philosophy of science that has been taught to generations of psychology students. It portrays research as having been derived from theory, data gathering as being free of theoretical bias, and knowledge as being cumulative and ever converging on truth (Toulmin & Leary, 1985/1992). An alternative understanding of science was posited almost a century ago by John Dewey and William James, early philosopher-psychologists (Barone, 1996; Barone, Maddux, & Snyder, 1997).

DAVID F. BARONE • Center for Psychological Studies, Nova Southeastern University, Fort Lauderdale, Florida 33314.
KATHRYN D. KOMINARS • Student Counseling Center, Florida International University, Miami, Florida 33169.

Advanced Personality, edited by David F. Barone, Michel Hersen, and Vincent B. Van Hasselt. Plenum Press, New York, 1998.

In their philosophy, called *pragmatism,* inquiry is prompted by an unresolved concern, knowledge is the current best solution to that concern or problem, and the value of knowledge is demonstrated in outcomes made possible by its predictions. Thus, a subject matter may be approached in very different ways and the resulting knowledge may be incommensurable (i.e., noncomparable). The recent postpositivist philosophies of science make most of the same points, although the terms and emphases may be different (e.g., Caprara & Van Heck, 1992; Cook, 1985; Gholson & Barker, 1985; Kaplan, 1964; Rychlak, 1968). Especially since Kuhn's (1970) theory, science has been construed less idealistically and as being invested with the personal and social agendas of scientists.

In Kuhnian terms, inquiry in personality can be construed as being in a pre-paradigmatic phase, which occurs in young fields before there is agreement on basic questions, definitions, and research paradigm. The study of personality is not a simple story of a subject that has been consenually defined and knowledge of it that has accumulated. Instead, it is a complex story of how multiple traditions, schools, and theories have emerged in response to different questions and have coexisted—whether indifferently, hostilely, or synergistically. Despite calls to slight the history and systems of personality study (Kuhn, 1970, chap. 5; Mendelsohn, 1993), knowledge of them can guide the emergence of consensus around topics that need to be addressed and the pros and cons of how to do so. We will consider three primary traditions—clinical, psychometric, and experimental—and the schools and theories that have developed within them. The differing concerns and methods of inquiry in these traditions have resulted in the three different definitions of personality noted earlier: personality as system (the integrated functioning of psychological components), personality as structures (dispositions differing between individuals), and personality as functions (the processes involved in integrated functioning).

MULTIPLE TRADITIONS AND SCHOOLS OF PERSONALITY STUDY

Modern personality study began with the work of Freud. He and his colleagues in psychiatry sought a theory to help them understand the problems of their patients. The physiological knowledge that they acquired during medical training was inadequate to this purpose. Their proposed theories were built on an empirical basis: clinical interviews of their patients. Their models of biologically based intrapsychic events detailed structures (psychoanalysis), processes (psychodynamics), and resulting personality types, traits, and styles. Their unit of study was the whole person, but the idiographic understanding of the individual depends on nomothetic knowledge of lawful psychological processes. Many of the clinicians who came after Freud were convinced of the importance of what happened between persons as well as within them, and of the importance of aspirations and healthy functions as well as pathology. The resulting schools of thought formulated lawful interpersonal and family processes and processes of personal growth.

The first three chapters in Part II of this text present theories in the clinical tradition within the psychoanalytic, interpersonal and systemic, and humanistic and experiential schools of thought. The clinical tradition of personality study began outside of psychology. It does not conform to the notion that science equals concrete measurement and experimentation. Its historic separation from academic psychology's inquiry into personality and other psychological processes is not as wide as it had been. Nevertheless, the clinical tradition continues to offer comprehensive answers to questions of concern to mental health professionals, including questions about maladaptive personality functioning that are not easily answered by laboratory research (Erdelyi, 1985; Westen, 1991; 1994; 1995).

Another tradition of personality study—the psychometric tradition—began before Freud with the work of Francis Galton, a cousin of Charles Darwin (chap. 6, this text; Fancher, 1990). He was committed to measuring genetrically based individual differences that accounted for people's different degrees of success in a competitive world. In the beginning, low-level psychomotor skills were measured, but it soon became clear that more accurate predictions were made possible with the measurement of more complex, high-level integrated functions. Included were personality characteristics as found in everyday language. (As early social cognitive theorists would later argue, people are naive scientists who gain prediction and control by inferring regularities in others and themselves [Heider, 1958; Kelly, 1955].)

The most common methodology of the psychometric tradition gathers people's reported judgments of self and others and analyzes them with bivariate and multivariate statistics. The trait school, covered in detail in Chapter 5, combines features of the other two traditions: a standardization of the interview technique established in the clinical tradition, and a mathematical analysis of results that is typical of scientific inquiry. However, the approach of the trait school is like a descriptive biological taxonomy rather than experimental interventions of explanatory scientific inquiry. From Galton on, the psychometric tradition has also assessed the heritability of traits by natural experiments, comparing identical with fraternal twins, and twins reared together with those reared apart, for example. In recent years, much additional work on the biological bases of personality has been done; the psychobiological school, as discussed in Chapter 6, may have to be considered an emergent additional tradition (Buss, 1995). The psychometric tradition is part of academic psychology's study of personality (as evidenced by part of a heading in the *Journal of Personality and Social Psychology:* "Individual Differences"). Despite claims of its hegemony in the field, it remains a part, not the whole, of personality study (Epstein, 1994; Pervin, 1994; Westen, 1995).

As psychology developed into an experimental science studying perception, learning, cognition, development, and social interaction, its theories and findings addressed questions asked by Freud and others about complex human functioning. Out of such inquiries came new hypotheses and the experimental research that tested them, such as that on conflict, social learning, and social development (Barone *et al.* 1997). Unlike clinicians, who must deal with the whole person, experimental scientists can select for inquiry one aspect of human functioning, controlling or holding the rest constant. Their research yields statements of lawful causal relationships found valid among people in general, in contrast to the psychometric interest in describing differences between people. The results of their research are empirically validated minitheories of specific personality processes, rather than the more comprehensive but less verifiable personality theories of the clinicians. Of particular interest to those working in the experimental tradition have been social-interactional and self-referential processes (Chapters 7 and 8, which present the learning and social cognitive schools of personality). The experimental tradition has increasingly taken on issues associated with the clinical tradition, and recent cognitive theories (such as discussed in Chapter 9) add coverage of affective processes. This experimental tradition is a recognized part of academic psychology's study of personality (as evidenced by the other part of a heading in the *Journal of Personality and Social Psychology:* "Personality Processes").

The different traditions of personality study have been long recognized and are now supported by research. Early presidents of the American Psychological Association (APA), such as John Dewey (1900/1976), addressed the pros and cons of the clinical method of scientific practitioners and the experimental method of laboratory scientists (Barone, 1996; Barone et al., 1997). At midcentury, the distinction between the two methods was being discussed more technically in terms of maximizing internal validity (experimental method) or external validity (clinical method) (Campbell, 1957). Also, a distinction between experimental researchers' focus on central tendency and psychometric researchers' focus on individual variation was being drawn (Cronbach, 1957).

Recent empirical work on a taxonomy of personality study provides support for the primacy of the clinical, experimental, and psychometric traditions, but not for a particular breakdown of schools. Rosenberg and Gara (1983) had experts rate the work of 61 prominent contributors to personality and social psychology. Three groupings emerged from statistical analysis of the ratings. The primary dimension found included the attributes of holism and case study method at one end, and experimental methodology, observable behavior, and statistical analysis at the other. This dimension distinguishes the clinical tradition from the academic. A taxonomic mapping by hierarchical clustering divided the latter into psychometric and experimental traditions. (Recent research on personality theorists employing the citation method utilizes this tripartite categorization [Mayer & Carlsmith, 1997]).

Working our way down the hierarchy of personality study, we label the next level as schools; there is no empirical support for any particular number of schools. The seven schools that we present are commonly acknowledged (see Table 1.1), but a different number of schools and different labels for them can be found elsewhere. Each chapter in Part II covers many of the individual theories of personality found within these seven schools.

CHARACTERISTICS OF PERSONALITY THEORIES

Traditions and schools of personality study differ on many specific characteristics (Emmons, 1995; Mayer, 1995). Table 1.1. includes eight of the characteristics that we believe are especially useful in distinguishing among the seven theoretical approaches covered in part II. The following discussion presents our rationale for evaluating each school of thought on each characteristic. We are confident in our conclusions but acknowledge that some are disputable. Our goal is to stimulate thinking and discussion about how theories are similar to and different from one another (cf. Hall & Lindzey, 1978, p. 692). Where a characteristic is challenged by a particular theory, we have placed it in parentheses.

The first two characteristics involve method. The three schools in the clinical tradition rely on case studies, whereas the four schools in the academic tradition rely on correlational and experimental research. However, clinical schools have increasingly added experimental research (Chapters 10, 13, 15, this text; Erdelyi, 1985). The empirical basis of theories in the clinical tradition includes self-reports by patients-clients, and clinicians' observations of client behavior during sessions with them. Trait theories collect judgments about typical behavior, whether reported by self or others. The other three theories rely primarily on observations of behavior (including physiological changes), although social cognitive theories also collect self-reports about internal events.

The remaining characteristics involve subject matter, the first three of which distinguish among the three traditions. Clinical theories primarily study pathology, although the _method_ _Subject matter_ _Causality_

TABLE 1.1. Characteristics of Personality Theories

School	Case Study/Research *	Self-Report/Behav.Obser.	Pathology/Normality	Function/Structure	Whole/Parts	Mind/Behavior/Physiology	Conscious/Unconscious	Self/Inner/Outer Deter.
Clinical								
• Psychoanalytic	C, R	R, B	P	F, S	W, P	M	U, C	I
• Interpersonal/Systemic	C, R	R, B	P	F, S	W	B, M	U, C	O
• Humanistic/Experiential	C, R	R, B	P, N	F	W	M	C, U	S
Academic								
• Trait	R	R	N	S	P	M, B, P	C	I
• Psychobiological	R	B	N, P	F, S	P, W	P	U	I
• Operant/Learning	R	B	(N, P)	F	P	B	(U)	O
• Social Cognitive	R	B, R	(N, P)	F	P, W	B, M	C, U	S, O

Note. Boldface letters are used to indicate which characteristics apply in each column; if more than one applies, the primary one is given first. Parentheses indicate that a characteristic is disputed by a particular theory.

humanistic/experiential theories also study normalcy. The remaining theories focus on normalcy, although most have an ancillary interest in pathology. Because operant/learning and social cognitive theories have challenged the notion that normalcy and pathology are discontinuous (Chapters 8, 14, this text; Ullmann & Krasner, 1969), their evaluations on this disputed dichotomy are in parentheses. Most of the theories are interested in the processes by which personality functions; trait theories are the clear exception; they seek to describe the structure of individual differences. Psychoanalytic and interpersonal systemic theories are also interested in (psychic) structure and personality types, while psychobiological theories are interested in (physiological) structure and genetically based types. Clinical theories maintain a focus on the whole personality, whereas academic theories focus on parts in pursuit of analytic understanding. Psychoanalytic theories (as the name indicates) also analyze personality into lower-level components while psychobiological and social cognitive theories also consider integrated functioning and "middle-level" units that combine basic processes for adaptive, integrated functioning (Buss & Cantor, 1989; Cantor, 1990; Cantor & Kihlstrom, 1987).

Other characteristics involve the domains of subject matter that theories study and identify as causes. The study of mind/behavior/physiology is such a daunting enterprise that most personality theories focus on just one or two of these events. Only trait theories that deemphasize personality processes attempt to integrate mind, behavior, and physiology: "A trait is, then, a *neuropsychic structure having the capacity to . . . initiate and guide . . . adaptive and expressive behavior*" (Allport, 1961, p. 347, italics in the original). Originally, psychology was the study of mind; in today's reformulation, it is the study of cognitive and affective processes. Most of the theories focus on these processes. The exceptions are psychobiological theories, which focus on physiological events, and operant/learning theories, which focus on behavior. Behavior is also the primary focus of interpersonal/systemic and social cognitive theories. For them, social adaptation, which occurs through behavior, is the goal, while cognitive and affective processes are the means to that end. Psychological processes can be presented as occurring unconsciously, not only as construed psychoanalytically, but also as a result of physiological and affective processes and conditioning. They also can be presented as occurring consciously, as in ego functioning, self-concept, trait judgments, or social cognitive processes. Despite the commitment of early social cognitive theories to consciousness, recent theories include a consideration of unconscious cognitive and affective processes (Chapter 9, this text; Barone *et al.,* 1997). The parentheses in operant/learning theory indicate that, because this theory rejects the study of mind, this distinction is moot. The final characteristic involves whether conscious self-processes have a causal role, or whether personality is determined by other inner or outer factors. The humanistic/experiential and social cognitive theories allow for personal (self) agency; in contrast, psychoanalytic, trait, and psychobiological theories primarily attribute personality to inner (nonself) forces. Operant/learning and interpersonal/systemic theories primarily attribute it to outer forces.

These characteristics themselves can be a topic of consideration in personality study (e.g., Mayer, 1995; Pervin, 1978). Controversies often involve dialectical, either-or formulations, such as whether personality is intrapsychic or interpersonal, an expression of internal dispositions or external situations, a result of nature or nurture, characterized by stability or change, and so on. These controversies are addressed throughout this text. One enduring issue in personality—that of unconscious and conscious functioning—is addressed at length in Part III because of the accumulation of experimental demonstrations of unconscious processing and the new formulation of this old distinction in terms of explicit and implicit cognitive functioning (Barone *et al.,* 1997; Kihlstrom, 1990).

From the small set of characteristics discussed, it is apparent that each school of personality theory can be considered a separate "species." Schools within a tradition, as well as theories within a school, share some but not all characteristics; thus, categorization is based not on absolute criteria but on family resemblance (Wittgenstein, 1953/1968). Theories from different schools may converge on certain characteristics, such as the focus on behavior by interpersonal and social cognitive theories as animal species from different families converge on a common characteristic, such as fish and porpoises having fins, and birds and bats having wings. Given that each personality theory has a unique set of characteristics, it is worth studying individually. This has always been personologists' attitude toward individual human beings (Allport, 1937, 1961). Perhaps it is because of this special interest in the idiographic (individual), as well as the nomothetic (generic), that the field of personality has been so tolerant of multiple theories. Perhaps it is also because personality is such a complex phenomenon that each theory can apprehend only a part of it. Until we achieve the grail of the all-encompassing integrative theory, we benefit from studying the variety of theories of personality that have addressed significant concerns and have advanced our understanding (Maddi, 1993; Rychlak, 1993).

CHRONOLOGY OF PERSONALITY THEORISTS

Understanding personality study, like understanding an individual, includes not only abstract analysis and categorization, but also narration of a history. The history of personality study is not a simple story of sequential, cumulative development, so understanding can be aided by a chronological table. Table 1.2a,b lists major personality theorists, including some not covered in depth in this text. The selections are meant to be instructive rather than all-inclusive; it is possible to debate at length who should and should not be included. The theorists in the table are organized into five groups: the three schools within the clinical tradition, and the two academic traditions. A thin line runs from each theorist's birth date to the date of his or her first influential publication (not necessarily the most famous one). To indicate the period of influence of each theorist, a thick line goes from the date of publication to the date of his or her death or to the present. (Note that studies of commonly cited works—e.g., Mayer & Carlsmith, 1997—may use slightly different time periods.)

Within a given school, it is likely that earlier theorists influenced later ones and that contemporaries interacted. With the exception of Freud's universal influence, the multiple traditions and schools of personality study developed in parallel, often without much mutual influence or interaction. This symbolic isolation of cultures located in the same space and time also appears in the general study of history and culture. Familiar examples of such isolation include adjoining neighborhoods divided by class or ethnicity, and departments and schools that share the same university campus. The following are historical comments relevant to the table; they supplement coverage found throughout this book (Allport, 1961; Hall & Lindzey, 1978; Pervin, 1990).

Studying the table reveals the generational structure of personality theory. First-generational theorists were born before 1880, were educated in the 19th century, were publishing by the turn of the century, and died by the mid-20th century. The large number of second-generational theorists were born in the late 19th and early 20th centuries (1800–1909), were edu-

TABLE 1.2A Chronology of Personality Theorists (with Dates of Birth, First Major Work, and Death) from Schools within the Clinical Tradition

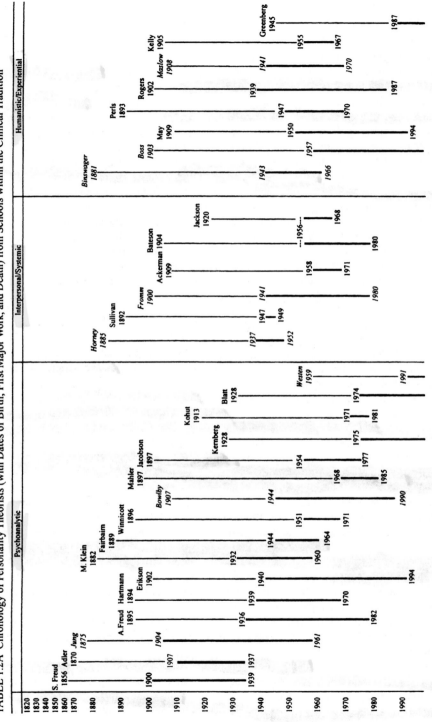

Note: Theorists in italics are not covered in subsequent chapters.

TABLE 1.2B Chronology of Personality Theorists (with Dates of Birth, First Major Work, and Death) from the Two Academic Traditions

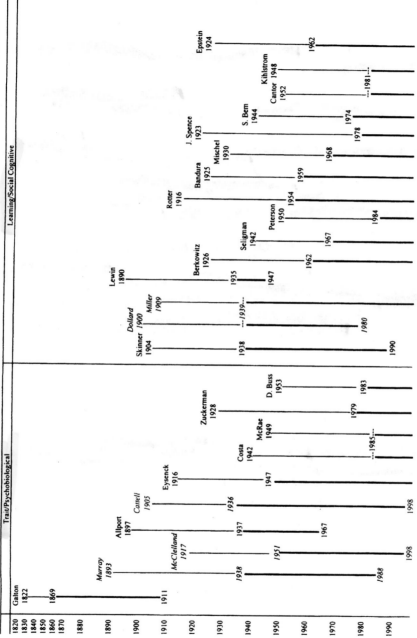

Note: Theorists in italics are not covered in subsequent chapters.

cated in the early decades of 20th century when the first generation's publications were available, began to produce major publications of their own from the 1930s to 1950s, and have mostly died or are very elderly. (It was during the second generation that the identity of personality study was established—Allport, 1937; Murray, 1938—so that some chronologies consider everything up until this time to be first generation or consider Freud, Galton, and other early theorists as precursors to personality study.) Third-generational theorists were born during the period from prior to World War I to the beginning of World War II (1910–1940), had access to the first and second generations' publications, began their own publishing sometime from the late 1940s through 1970s, and are now late in their careers. The fourth generation is primarily made up of postwar "baby boomers" who were born from 1941 to 1965. They were educated in the 1960s through the 1980s and had the work of three generations available to them. The fourth generation began to publish major works in the 1980s, and its members are in the prime of their careers. (The fifth generation of personality study is among those reading this text and being educated in the 1990s and beyond. The names of those who eventually make major contributions will be added to chronologies like this one in the future.)

Within the psychoanalytic school, Sigmund Freud is the firstborn as well as most influential. He was second author of *Studies on Hysteria* with Joseph Breuer (1895/1955), but his first major work was *Interpretation of Dreams* (1900/1953). Freud's younger colleagues, Alfred Adler and Carl Jung, were also beginning to publish at this time. Although Adler and Jung made an impact on personality theory and psychotherapy, Freud disaffiliated with both of them, and they often are not included in orthodox psychoanalytic histories (Chapter 2, this text). Adler, however, has been embraced as a precursor of social cognitive theory (Chapter 12, this text; Barone *et al.*, 1997). Other psychoanalytic theorists are well-covered in Chapter 2 except for John Bowlby, another thinker who went beyond the psychoanalytic tradition to draw on systems theory and ethology (the latter a kind of psychobiological theory) in formulating his attachment theory. Table 1.2a,b includes many major psychoanalytic theorists from the first two generations of personality study but only a few from the last two; this accurately represents the early and middle part of this century as the period of greatest activity for this school. Recent psychoanalytic theorists such as Sidney Blatt and Drew Westen connect with other schools, especially social cognitive theory, while social cognitive theorists, for example, Seymour Epstein and John Kihlstrom, have in turn connected to psychoanalytic theories.

Early theorists in the interpersonal/systemic school were educated in Freud's theory, but departed from it even more radically than object/relations theorists. Karen Horney, Erich Fromm, and Harry Sullivan (the last of whom is discussed in Chapter 3) all drew on work in the social sciences and advocated a more cultural and interpersonal approach to personality. Also included in the table are three major theorists involved in founding the interpersonal/systemic approach during the second and third generations of personality study. (Some of the other major theorists in this school from these generations are not included in the table: Murray Bowen, Jay Haley, Theodore Lidz, Salvador Minuchin, Virginia Satir, and Carl Whitaker [Levant, 1984; Nichols, 1984].) After a period of vigorous theorizing that stretched from the late 1930s to 1980, this school has tapered off as many of those trained in it have drifted in a postmodern, constructivist direction, as discussed in Chapter 3. Interpersonal and cultural construals of the self are increasingly a concern in personality study, especially in the social cognitive school (Chapters 15 and 16, this text; Banaji & Prentice, 1994; Markus & Cross, 1990).

Early theorists in the humanistic/experiential school were first educated in the psychoanalytic school but were also influenced by European existential philosophy, phenomenology, Gestalt psychology, and by American pragmatic philosophy and functional psychology. Existential theorists include Ludwig Binswager and Medard Boss, Swiss psychiatrists who studied with Freud and Jung, and Rollo May, an American, who is covered in Chapter 4. Gestalt psychology influenced personality study through the very different theories of the clinician Fritz Perls and the social cognitive experimentalist Kurt Lewin. Carl Rogers and Abraham Maslow, along with Rollo May, founded the Association for Humanistic Psychology. Rogers, who is covered in Chapter 4, and Maslow (1954) switched the emphasis from pathology to human potential. George Kelly, like Rogers, was a psychotherapist influenced by the pragmatic philosophy and functional psychology of John Dewey (Barone, 1996) as well as by the constructivism of Jean Piaget. (His role as a progenitor of social cognitive personality theory is noted in Chapter 15; see also Barone *et al.,* 1997; Cantor & Kihlstrom, 1987). Like the interpersonal/systemic school, the humanistic/experiential school was a second-generational reaction against Freud; its time of greatest activity was the 1950s through the 1970s. (Only Leslie Greenberg is included in Table 1.2a as a more recent theorist in this school of personality study.) Many of its ideas are continued in the work of social cognitive theorists, such as Albert Bandura, Seymour Epstein, Christopher Peterson, and Martin Seligman.

Trait and psychobiological theories of personality, such as those of Hans Eysenck and Marvin Zuckerman, are foreshadowed in the work of Galton (Chapter 6). Gordon Allport articulated the trait approach to personality and the value of studying individuals (Chapter 9). His contemporary Henry Murray and others such as David McClelland, who are not covered in this text, provided a theory of needs influenced by psychoanalytic theories. Dispositional theories based on motivational constructs have declined in the last generation. Motivation is increasingly studied by the social cognitive school, whereas the focus of dispositional theorizing has been on descriptive traits. Raymond Cattell (1946), who is mentioned only in passing in subsequent chapters, developed one the first comprehensive psychometric trait theories of personality. The trait and psychobiological schools of thought is currently very active, as seen in the five-factor trait theory of Paul Costa, Jr. and Robert McRae (Chapter 5) and the development of an evolutionary theory of personality by David Buss and others (as well as much of the current research reported in Part IV, this text).

The operant/learning and social cognitive schools of personality study have a long history and are currently very active (Barone *et al.,* 1997). Behavioral theories of learning based on laboratory research with animals were applied to human personality by B. F. Skinner (1953; Chapter 7, this text) and John Dollard and Neal Miller (1950; Miller & Dollard, 1941). The latter, who are not covered in this text, addressed many of the issues raised by Freud and added human research to support the hypotheses in their social learning theory. Kurt Lewin, another member of the second generation, together with social psychologist Fritz Heider, founder of attribution theory, contributed social Gestalt theories to the developing social cognitive school of thought. Another tradition that contributes to this school is constructivism, as found in the work of Jean Piaget and Frederic Bartlett (discussed in Barone *et al.,* 1997). Albert Bandura (Chapter 8) and Leonard Berkowitz (Chapter 11) pursued topics such as the frustration-aggression hypothesis and added cognitive and social considerations. Berkowitz is more associated with social psychology, but work within the social cognitive school now spans personality and social psychology. The phenomenon of learned helplessness was discovered in the animal learning laboratory by Martin Seligman and others, and it was applied, with infusions of attribution theory, to human depression by Seligman, Christopher Peterson, and others (Chapter 12). Julian Rotter continued the development of social learning theory with infusions of ideas from Lewin (Chapter 12), and Bandura has advanced from social learning to social cognitive theorizing. Walter Mischel set off the person-situation controversy (Chapter 11) by challenging traditional dispositionist personality theories with a contextualist approach consistent with interpersonal/systems, behavioral, and social psychological theories. Mischel's (1973) theorizing carried on the cognitive constructivist interest of his teacher, George Kelly (Chapter 12). Nancy Cantor (Chapters 8 and 13) has continued to advance this line of theorizing and, with John Kihlstrom, developed a theory of social intelligence. How people construct their gender identities has been the subject of the theories of Janet Spence and Sandra Bem. The last theorist in this school is Seymour Epstein (Chapter 9), whose wide-ranging interests and writings span many of the schools (Epstein, 1997). A source of strength for the social cognitive school is its incorporation of ideas and methods from other schools; for example, Rotter, Epstein, Seligman, and Peterson not only provide experimental research on causes of phenomena of clinical concern but also provide psychometric research on individual differences in these phenomena.

PERSONALITY RESEARCH IN THEORETICAL CONTEXT

Personality study includes a growing body of research to supplement and validate its theories. Although research may be based explicitly on hypotheses from one personality theory or school, contemporary personality research increasingly draws on various schools of thought. Thus, covering current research topics as derivative of particular theories or schools fails to appreciate the full range of influences on such research and the integration achieved by pursuing a variety of questions using a variety of methods. Research that is derived from particular schools is presented along with the theories in Part II of this text. Research derived in part from psychoanalytic theories is presented in Part III with reference to the special issue of conscious and unconscious processing. Other broad-ranging, current research topics in personality are presented in Part IV.

Table 1.3 provides an evaluation of the extent to which schools of personality study (as presented in Part II) are involved in the formulation of research topics. A school may be central (C) to the formulation of a research topic; a school may be peripheral (P) in that it is alluded to or drawn on in a limited way; or finally, a school may have no involvement in the research as presented. Table 1.3 is intended to be read from research topics to theories (left to right). Reading down the columns does not provide a valid indication of the amount of interest that schools have in a certain topic, for example, psychoanalytic theories and subjective well-being (SWB), but it does provide an indication of how important the various schools of thought are to current research. The table reveals that trait theories are central to every research topic presented, that social cognitive theories are central to all but two, and, that at the low end, humanistic/experiential and operant/learning theories are central to one each. In the text that follows, we provide our rationales for the evaluations given; as with Table 1.2a,b we are confident in most of our judgments, while acknowledging that some are disputable. Our goal in presenting Table 1.3 is to stimulate thinking about the connection between research and theory. Our contention is that most research in personality today is theoretically eclectic—another justification for studying the diverse array of personality theories.

TABLE 1.3. Involvement of Personality Theories in Research Topics

Research topics	Psychoanalytic	Interpersonal/ Systemic	Humanistic/ Experiential	Trait	Psychobiological	Operant/ Learning	Social Cognitive
Aggressive personalities	C	P	P	C	P	P	C
Helplessness/ Explanatory style	P	P	P	C	P	C	C
Subjective well-being (SWB)	—	P	C	C	C	P	P
Personality disorders	C	P	P	C	P	P	P
Self-with-Other representations (SWORs)	C	C	P	C	—	P	C
Sex/Gender and the individual	P	C	P	C	C	P	C

Note. Each theory's involvement in a particular research topic as presented is evaluated as C = central or P = peripheral. When we feel involvement is absent, the space contains a dash.

The theoretical bases of the research on aggressive personalities presented in Chapter 11 are in psychoanalytic, learning (more social cognitive than operant), and trait theories. The research focuses, respectively, on hostile and affective aggression (connected historically with the frustration-aggression hypothesis [Berkowitz, 1989]); the situational and cognitive bases of aggression; and the generality of aggression across situations. The topic as developed connects with three other schools: the humanistic/experiential (interaction of affect and cognition), psychobiological (anger-in and heart disease), and interpersonal/systemic theories (instrumental aggression and bullying). Thus, as research has proceeded, a topic originating in the psychoanalytic school has been influenced by all of the subsequent schools presented.

Learned helplessness (Chapter 12) is another research area arising from the experimental learning tradition. The study of conditioned helplessness in dogs (operant/learning school) gave rise to the study of people's explanations when faced with aversive events (social cognitive school). Subsequent research on the consistency of explanatory style strongly connects this topic as developed with the trait school. The focus on people's interpretations of their experiences connects with phenomenological humanistic theories and ego-psychological psychoanalytic theories. Recent research on the heritability of explanatory styles connects with the psychobiological school, and research on their sociocultural context connects with the interpersonal/systemic school. Again, we see that a topic based in one school (learning) has connected with all the others.

Subjective well-being (SWB; Chapter 13) is about phenomenological experience, which is the subject matter of humanistic/experiential theories. The research on this topic has proceeded from the psychometric assumption that psychological phenomena can be assessed from self-reports. The research presented has sought to demonstrate that SWB is a stable, consistent, inherited disposition, thus connecting it strongly with trait and psychobiological theories. Other research connects it peripherally with three other schools: research on sex differences with the larger cultural context (interpersonal/systemic theories), research on life tasks and goals with social cognitive theories, and research on density of reinforcement with operant theory. Affective experience is of central importance to psychoanalytic theories, but this school is not referenced; the topic's focus on positive experience expresses the humanistic/experiential reaction against psychoanalytic preoccupation with pathology. The study of SWB has gone from its home base (humanistic/experiential school) to connect with all other schools except the psychoanalytic.

The research presented in Chapter 14 connects personality disorders strongly with the five-factor personality model, thus making the trait school central. The typology of personality disorders was derived from clinical diagnostic work informed by psychoanalytic theories (e.g., Kernberg), thus making this school also central to the topic. Construing personality disorders as disturbances in interpersonal relationships and raising the issue of their social construction connect this topic peripherally with the interpersonal/systemic and social cognitive schools. Also involved peripherally are the humanistic/experiential school (the issue of pathologizing modes of adaptation) and operant/learning school (the impact of situational context on a behavior's adaptiveness). The topic connects peripherally with the psychobiological school; data on the heritability of personality disorders are lacking despite positive results for associated traits.

Self-with-other representations (SWORs; Chapter 15) are people's knowledge structures about themselves in relational context, thus making the social cognitive and interpersonal/systemic schools central to this topic. That this knowledge is to some (great) extent implicit also connects this theory strongly with the psychoanalytic school, especially with regard to object relations and attachment theories. That SWORs occur stably within a relationship and consistently across relationships, have a hierarchical structure, and are identified via multivariate statistical techniques demonstrate the centrality of the trait school to this topic. SWORs are subjective constructions, which also connects them peripherally with phenomenological (humanistic/experiential) theories. Although operant theory is not referenced in chapter 15, it is connected peripherally to SWORs elsewhere (Ogilvie & Rose, 1995). There is no connection made with psychobiological theories. As other accounts also demonstrate (Barone et al., 1997), SWORs is a research topic that is now of interest across many schools of personality study.

The final topic, sex/gender and the individual (Chapter 16), concerns a biologically based difference about which there are social and individual cognitive constructions. Thus, the psychobiological, interpersonal/systemic, and social cognitive schools are central to the topic. Sex is construed as a type (group difference), while masculinity, femininity, and androgyny are construed as traits; thus, the trait school is also central to this topic. That these constructions are part of a person's self-concept makes a peripheral connection with the humanistic/experiential school. Although this topic obviously was of special importance to Freud, the psychoanalytic school is only peripherally connected with the topic, as is operant/learning theories, through research on the processes of sex-role identification and sex-role learning.

CHAPTER SUMMARIES

THEORIES OF PERSONALITY

Part II presents seven chapters (2–8) on different schools of personality. The diversity of the theories is shown by the differing emphases given to theory or data, the clinic or research as an empirical basis for the theory, past or present work, and comprehensive or selective coverage of personality.

Chapter 2, "Psychoanalytic Theories of Personality," begins with a biographical sketch of Sigmund Freud. Bady Quintar, Robert Lane, and W. Bradley Goeltz present his concepts and theory by exploring the various models that he used to create an organized and comprehensive representation of the human psyche as a system. Those models include the topographical, psychoeconomic and psychodynamic, structural, and psychogenetic. The chapter goes on to examine subsequent psychoanalytic theories and the contributions of the major figures associated with each: ego psychology (Anna Freud, Heinz Hartmann, and Erik Erikson), object relations (Melanie Klein, W. Ronald Fairbairn, Donald Winnicott, Margaret Mahler, Edith Jacobson, and Otto Kernberg), and self psychology (Heinz Kohut). The chapter concludes with the dialectic of structural versus interpersonal theories and the issue of research on psychoanalysis.

In Chapter 3, "Interpersonal and Systemic Theories of Personality," Steven Gold and Gonzalo Bacigalupe explore a constellation of approaches that share the basic concept that the self is a product of social experience. Harry Stack Sullivan addressed factors such as anxiety and mothering, and their impact on the development of the self. The family therapy movement identified family interaction as the source of personality disturbance and focus of intervention. The chapter covers systems theory, the philosophical basis of this movement, and various theories within this movement. It concludes with an examination of the recent influence of social constructionism. The inclusion of concepts such as socialization and enculturation as areas of interest for these theoretical approaches brings cultural considerations into the discussion of personality.

In Chapter 4, "Humanistic and Experiential Theories of Personality," Jeanne Watson and Leslie Greenberg cover person-centered, gestalt, existential, and experiential theories. They present each theory's epistemological assumptions, ontological assumptions about the development of self, and formulation of personality functioning. Although these theories are distinct, they share two common assumptions: an emphasis on subjectivity and the construal of the individual as a self-reflective agent. According to this school, dysfunction occurs when people lose touch with their feelings and values. Experiential theories emphasize the integration of emotion and cognition and the function of emotion in communication.

Paul Costa and Robert McCrae argue for the centrality of traits to an understanding of personality in Chapter 5, "Trait Theories of Personality." They discuss the issue of the cross-situational consistency of personality traits. They explore the significance of trait theory as a "universal personality structure." Costa and McCrae have been the primary developers of the five-factor model of personality traits. Here, they introduce the five factors: neuroticism, extraversion, openness to experience, agreeableness, and conscientiousness. They also review research that indicates that these factors are heritable and supports the existence of this model in all cultures studied. Additionally, they present their own research, which demonstrates the stability of these factors during adulthood. They criticize theories that do not integrate what is known about traits as outdated. Finally, they show how traits fit into a comprehensive model of a person, and how this model can be used to guide theory and research in personality.

Marvin Zuckerman begins Chapter 6, "Psychobiological Theories of Personality," with a discussion of the connection between modern psychobiological theories of personality and older theories of temperament. This historical background provides a useful foundation for the subsequent description of the current state of the psychobiological approaches to personality theory. For example, Zuckerman draws connections between humors and neurotransmitters and between phrenology and neuropsychology. The chapter includes discussions of cortical excitation and inhibition, arousal and other relevant concepts, and findings about heritability of personality traits. Zuckerman analyzes personality in terms of levels—from supertraits through cognitive-behavioral and emotional mechanisms to psychophysiology, hormones, and neurotransmitters.

In Chapter 7, "Operant Theory of Personality," Chauncey Parker, Madelon Bolling, and Robert Kohlenberg reject the concept of personality as an entity while providing their understanding of what is referred to as *personality*. The authors examine characteristics essential to understanding personality, such as consistency, uniqueness, and the quality "within." They also discuss operant conditioning, contingencies of reinforcement, and functional analysis, using these constructs to account for the consistency and inconsistency of behavior in borderline personality disorder. Development of the sense of self is addressed and serves as the foundation for understanding the quality "within" that is intrinsic to personality (although they locate the root of behavior in the environment).

S. Lloyd Williams and Daniel Cervone present ideas developed especially by Bandura, about the reciprocal interaction of personality, behavior, and the environment, and about the centrality of cognition in adapting to the world and in regulating and developing oneself in Chapter 8, "Social Cognitive Theories of Personality." According to the authors, people use their symbolizing capabilities to learn from others' actions and verbal communications and to predict and plan for possible future events. People guide their own behavior and development by setting goals and standards, monitoring their performance, and rewarding themselves. Of special significance are people's beliefs about their own capacity to act effectively, that is, their perceived self-efficacy and control. Self-efficacy and other social cognitive personality variables are construed in specific contexts rather than as generalized traits.

SPECIAL ISSUE: CONSCIOUS AND UNCONSCIOUS FUNCTIONING

Part III includes two chapters on an issue of special current interest: conscious and unconscious functioning. Chapters 9 and 10 present recent theories on this topic and lines of research supporting the theories.

In Chapter 9, "Cognitive-Experiential Self-Theory," Seymour Epstein presents an eclectic theory of personality that focuses on a person's implicit self-theory rather than the explicit self-theory central to other social cognitive theories. This theory draws on recent research that supports knowing not only through a rational (cognitive) system but also through an emotional (experiential) system, the latter a reformulation of the psychoanalytic unconscious. It posits four basic needs and individual differences in beliefs related to them. The theory explains maladjustment as dissociation between and within systems, as conflict between need fulfillments, and/or as problematic beliefs. The author presents research on heuristic processing, basic beliefs, and individual differences in processing modes to support the theory.

Howard Shevrin, in Chapter 10, "Why Do We Need to Be Conscious? A Psychoanalytic Answer," pursues other recent theory and research on unconscious and conscious functioning. He begins by considering contemporary philosophy of the mind relevant to the question. He discusses Freud's various views on consciousness, none of which satisfactorily answers the question, why do we need it? He also argues that cognitive psychology's identification of consciousness with controlled processing does not satisfactorily answer the question posed. Shevrin then introduces two recent theories of consciousness. Building on Freud's ideas, B. Opatow theorizes that consciousness develops out of negation of primary process and the infant's primitive hallucinatory wish fulfillments, connecting wishes to reality-based fulfillments. G. M. Edelman theorizes that consciousness is an evolutionary advance that discriminates the difference between memory and perception, so that value-free data unbiased by stored knowledge is more possible. Shevrin's own views are similar and are supported by research on subliminal perception and implicit memory.

CURRENT RESEARCH TOPICS IN PERSONALITY

Part IV presents six areas of current research in personality. Each area draws in varying degrees on the theories presented in Part II.

In Chapter 11, "Aggressive Personalities," Leonard Berkowitz defines common terms for discussing aggression and discusses the use of self-report inventories to assess aggression. He elaborates four characteristics of aggression: hostile attitude, proneness to anger, reactivity to provocations, and aggressive behavior. He reviews evidence for the consistency and long-term stability of aggressiveness, as suggested by childhood conduct disorder and adult antisocial personality; he also reviews evidence for their inconsistency. Finally, Berkowitz presents his own theory on the importance of the automatic activation of aggression by anger-provoking stimuli.

Christopher Peterson and Curie Park review the original animal research on learned helplessness and extensive human research on explanatory style in Chapter 12, "Learned Helplessness and Explanatory Style." Explanatory style is defined as a cognitive individual difference, that is, a traitlike tendency to explain events on a dimension from pessimism to optimism. Peterson and Park note predecessors of the cognitive-motivational perspective, such as Alfred Adler, Kurt Lewin, Fritz Heider, Julian Rotter, and recent social cognitive theorists. The authors present various current measures of explanatory style, review research on its origins in children, and consider cultural influences on explanatory style.

Research on the phenomenological experiences of positive and negative affect, which are relatively independent of each other, is reported on by Ed Diener in Chapter 13, "Subjective Well-Being and Personality." Diener notes that subjective well-being (SWB) is related to inherited temperament, is stable across time, and consistent across situations. He provides further evidence that SWB is a traitlike personality variable in its low correlation with nonpersonality and situational variables like income and health status. Of the Big Five personality traits, the author relates extroversion to positive affect, and considers neuroticism as identical to negative affect. He relates other personality variables, such as self-esteem, optimism, and agency, to SWB. Diener concludes that the various process theories that connect SWB to personality involve density of reinforcements, person-environment fit, memory, baseline temperament, life tasks, and goals.

In Chapter 14, "Personality Disorders," Thomas Widiger discusses the difficulty of labeling a cluster of characteristics as inflexible, maladaptive, and personally distressing. By questioning the clear distinction between normal and disordered personalities, he is able to combine research on normal personality with work on clinical diagnosis. He then evaluates five personality disorders in terms of the Big Five Factors and their various facets. Borderline personality disorder exhibits extreme neuroticism. Schizoid personality disorder is characterized by extreme introversion, but without the neuroticism found in avoidant personality disorder. Histrionic personality disorder involves extreme, maladaptive extraversion. Schizotypal personality disorder is the most difficult to account for with the five-factor model; it includes introversion, neuroticism, antagonism (low agreeableness), and possibly extreme, maladaptive openness. Obsessive-compulsive personality disorder appears to include extreme, maladaptive conscientiousness, but research support for this conclusion is weak. Given that the five-factor model was developed for a normal range of functioning, the discussion reveals the challenges involved in extending it to extreme maladaptive personalities.

In Chapter 15, "Self-with-Other Representations," Daniel Ogilvie and Christopher Fleming present research on a quantitative method of describing how individuals implicitly organize their relational schemas, that is, how they represent themselves with others. According to script theory, such schemas develop out of affectively charged experiences with certain sequences of relational events, which the person comes to expect, seek out, and create. These schemas produce recurrent (traitlike) experiences in the person that are nonetheless tied to situational (interpersonal) events. Displaying implicit cognitive structures draws on the clinical tradition of George Kelly's Repertory Grid method and the psychometric tradition of multivariate analysis. The "June" case study reveals the method's utility as an idiographic approach in contributing to self-knowledge. The method is applicable to nomothetic research when common trait ratings are provided.

Richard Ashmore and Andrea Sewell recognize the conjunction of biological aspects of male and female behavior (sex) and sociocultural construction of these behaviors (gender) in Chapter 16, "Sex/Gender and the Individual." One way to approach this topic has been to focus on psychological differences correlated with biological sex (that is, group rather than individual differences). In contrast to some claims of maximal or minimal sex differences, the authors argue that no simple summary statement of the findings is possible. Another approach to the topic is to focus on gender as a traitlike personality variable that may be ascribed to others and to oneself. Masculinity and femininity can be construed as poles of a single dimension or as two independent constructs, the latter giving rise to the notion of androgyny. The third approach covered in the chapter treats sex/gender as a social category. A society's division of labor by gender influences the qualities and behavior most commonly enacted by men and women, and thus is associated with different expectations of them.

REFERENCES

Ackerman, N. W. (1958). *The psychodynamics of family life*. New York: Basic Books.

Adler, A. (1917). *Study of organ inferiority and its psychical compensation*. New York: Nervous and Mental Disease Publishing. (Original work published 1907).

Allport, G. W. (1937). *Personality: A psychological interpretation*. New York: Holt.

Allport, G. W. (1961). *Pattern and growth in personality*. New York: Holt, Rinehart & Winston.

Banaji, M. R., & Prentice, D. A. (1994). The self in social contexts. *Annual Review of Psychology, 45*, 297–332.

Bandura, A., & Walters, R. H. *Adolescent aggression*. New York: Ronald Press, 1959.

Barone, D. F. (1996). John Dewey: Psychologist, philosopher, and reformer. In G. A. Kimble, C. A. Boneau, & M. Wertheimer (Eds.), *Portraits of pioneers in psychology* (Vol. 2, pp. 46–61). Washington, DC: American Psychological Association.

Barone, D. F. (1997). Introduction to symposium on constructing self with others. *Review of General Psychology,* 323–325.

Barone, D. R., Maddux, J. E., & Snyder, C. R. (1997). *Social cognitive psychology: History and current domains*. New York: Plenum Press.

Bateson, G. Jackson, D., Haley, J., & Weakland, J. (1956). Toward a communication theory of schizophrenia. *Behavioral Science, 1*, 251–264.

Bem, S. L. (1974). The measurement of psychological androgyny. *Journal of Consulting and Clinical Psychology, 42*, 165–172.

Berkowitz, L. (1962.) *Aggression: A social psychological analysis,* New York: McGraw-Hill.

Berkowitz, L. (1989). The frustration-aggression hypothesis: An examination and reformulation. *Psychological Bulletin, 106*, 59–73.

Binswager, L. (1963). *Dasein [Being in the World]*. New York: Basic Books. (Original work published 1943)

Blatt, S. J. (1974). Levels of object representation in anaclitic and introjective depression. *Psychoanalytic Study of the Child, 29*, 107–157.

Boss, M. (1982). *Psychoanalysis and daseinanalysis*. New York: Simon & Schuster. (Original work published 1957).

Bowlby, J. (1944). *Forty-four juvenile thiefs: Their characters and home life*. London: Bailliem, Tindal & Cox.

Breuer, J., & Freud, S. (1955). Studies on hysteria. In J. Steachey (Ed. and Trans.), *The standard edition of the complete psychological works of Sigmund Freud* (Vol. 2). London: Hogarth Press. (Original work published 1895)

Buss, D. M. (1983). Evolutionary biology and personality psychology: Implications of genetic variability. *Personality and Individual Differences, 4*, 53–61.

Buss, D. M. (1995). Evolutionary psychology—A new paradigm for psychological science. *Psychological Inquiry,*
    6, 1–30.
Buss, D. M., & Cantor, N. (1989). Introduction. In D. M. Buss & N. Cantor (Eds.), *Personality psychology: Recent*
    trends and emerging directions (pp. 1–12). New York: Springer-Verlag.
Campbell, D. T. (1957). Factors relevant to the validity of experiments in social settings. *Psychological Bulletin,*
    54, 297–312.
Cantor, N. (1990). From thought to behavior: Having and doing in the study of personality and cognition. *Ameri-*
    can Psychologist, 45, 735–750.
Cantor, N., & Kihlstrom, J. F. (Eds.). (1981). *Personality, cognition, and social interaction.* Hillsdale, NJ: Erlbaum.
Cantor, N., & Kihlstrom, J. F. (1987). *Personality and social intelligence.* Englewood Cliffs, NJ: Prentice-Hall.
Caprara, G.-V., & Van Heck, G. L. (1992). Personality psychology: Some epistemological assertions and histori-
    cal considerations. In G.-V. Caprara & G. L. Van Heck (Eds.), *Modern personality psychology: Critical re-*
    views and new directions (pp. 3–26). New York: Harvester Wheatsheaf.
Catell, R. B. (1936). *A guide to mental testing for psychological clinics, schools and industrial psychologists.* Lon-
    don: University of London Press.
Cattell, R. B. (1946). *Description and measurement of personality.* New York: World Book.
Cook, T. D. (1985). Postpositivist critical multiplism. In R. L. Shotland & M. M. Mark (Eds.), *Social science and*
    social policy (pp. 21–62). Beverly Hills, CA: Sage.
Costa, P. T., Jr., & McCrae, R. R. (1985). *The NEO Personality Inventory Manual.* Odessa, FL: Psychological As-
    sessment Resources.
Cronbach, L. J. (1957). The two disciplines of scientific psychology. *American Psychologist, 12,* 671–684.
Dewey, J. (1976). Psychology and social practice. In J. A. Boydston (Ed.), *The middle works of John Dewey,*
    1899–1924 (Vol. 1, pp. 131–150). Carbondale, IL: Southern Illinois University Press. (Original work pub-
    lished 1900)
Dollard, J., & Miller, N. E. (1950). *Personality and psychotherapy: An analysis in terms of learning, thinking, and*
    culture. New York: McGraw-Hill.
Dollard, J., Miller, N. E., Doob, L. W., Mowrer, O. H., & Sears, R. R. (1939). *Frustration and aggression.* New
    Haven, CT: Yale University Press.
Emmons, R. A. (1995). Levels and domains of personality: An introduction. *Journal of Personality, 63,* 341–364.
Epstein, S. (1962). Theory and experiment on the measurement of drive and conflict. In M. R. Jones (Ed.), *Ne-*
    braska symposium on motivation (pp. 127–206). Lincoln, NE: University of Nebraska Press.
Epstein, S. (1994). Trait theory as personality theory: Can a part be as great as the whole? *Psychological Inquiry,*
    5, 120–122.
Epstein, S. (1997). This I have learned from over 40 years of personality research. *Journal of Personality, 65,* 3–32.
Erdelyi, M. H. (1985). *Psychoanalysis: Freud's cognitive psychology.* New York: Freeman.
Erikson, E. H. (1940). Studies in the interpretation of play: Clinical observations of play disruption in young chil-
    dren. *Genetic Psychology Monographs, 22,* 557–671.
Eysenck, H. J. (1947). *Dimensions of personality.* London: Routledge & Kegan Paul.
Fairbairn, W. R. D. (1954). Endopsychic structure considered in terms of object relationships. In *An object-rela-*
    tions theory of the personality (pp. 82–136). New York: Basic Books. (Original work published 1944)
Fancher, R. E. (1990). *Pioneers of psychology* (2nd ed.). New York: Norton.
Freud, A. (1966). *The writings of Anna Freud: Vol. 2. The ego and the mechanisms of defense* (Rev. ed.). New York:
    International Universities Press. (Original work published 1936)
Freud, S. (1953). The interpretation of dreams. In J. Strachey (Ed. and Trans.), *The standard edition of the complete*
    psychological works of Sigmund Freud (Vols. 4–5). London: Hogarth Press. (Original work published 1900)
Fromm, E. (1941). *Escape from freedom.* New York: Rinehart.
Galton, F. (1972). *Hereditary genius.* Gloucester, MA: Peter Smith. (Original work published 1869)
Gholson, B., & Barker, P. (1985). Kuhn, Lakatos, and Laudan: Applications in the history of physics and psychol-
    ogy. *American Psychologist, 40,* 755–769.
Greenberg, L. S., & Safran, J. (1987). *Emotion in psychotherapy: Affect, cognition and the process of change.* New
    York: Guilford Press.
Hall, C. S., & Lindzey, G. (1978). *Theories of personality* (3rd ed.). New York: Wiley.
Hartmann, H. (1964). *Ego psychology and the problem of adaptation.* New York: International Universities Press.
    (Original work published 1939)
Heider, F. (1958). *The psychology of interpersonal relations.* New York: Wiley.

Horney, K. (1937). *Neurotic personality of our times*. New York: Norton.

Jacobson, E. (1954). The self and the object world. *Psychoanalytic Study of the Child, 9,* 75–127.

Jung, C. G. (1973). Experimental researches. In H. Read, M. Fordham, & G. Adler (Eds.), L. Stein (Trans.), *The collected works of C. G. Jung* (Vol. 2). Princeton, NJ: Princeton University Press. (Original work published 1904–1909)

Kaplan, A. (1964). *The conduct of inquiry: Methodology for behavioral science*. San Francisco: Chandler.

Kelly, G. A. (1955). *The psychology of personal constructs* (Vols. 1–2). New York: W. W. Norton.

Kernberg, O. (1975). *Borderline conditions and pathological narcissism*. New York: Aronson.

Kihlstrom, J. F. (1990). The psychological unconscious. In L. A. Pervin (Ed.), *Handbook of personality* (pp. 445–464). New York: Guilford Press.

Klein, M. (1975). *The psychoanalysis of children*. London: Delocarte Press. (Original work published 1932)

Kohut, H. (1971). *The analysis of the self*. New York: International Universities Press.

Kuhn, T. S. (1970). *The structure of scientific revolutions* (2nd ed.). Chicago: University of Chicago Press.

Levant, R. F. (1984). *Family therapy: A comprehensive overview*. Englewood Cliffs, NJ: Prentice-Hall.

Lewin, K. (1935). *A dynamic theory of personality: Selected papers*. New York: McGraw-Hill.

Maddi, S. R. (1993). The continuing relevance of personality theory. In K. H. Craik, R. Hogan, & R. N. Wolfe (Eds.), *Fifty years of personality psychology* (pp. 85–101). New York: Plenum Press.

Mahler, M. S., & Furer, M. (1968). *On human symbiosis and the vicissitudes of individuation*. New York: International Universities Press.

Markus, H., & Cross, S. (1990). The interpersonal self. In L. A. Pervin (Ed.), *Handbook of personality* (pp. 576–608). New York: Guilford Press.

Maslow, A. H. (1954). *Motivation and personality*. New York: Harper & Row.

Maslow, A. H., & Mittelmann, B. (1941). *Principles of abnormal psychology: The dynamics of psychic illness*. New York: Harper.

May, R. (1950). *The meaning of anxiety*. New York: Ronald Press.

Mayer, J. D. (1995). A framework for the classification of personality components. *Journal of Personality, 63,* 819–877.

Mayer, J. D., & Carlsmith, K. M. (1997). Eminence ratings of personality psychologists as a reflection of the field. *Personality and Social Psychology Bulletin, 23,* 707–716.

McClelland, D. C. (1951). *Personality*. New York: Holt, Rinehart & Winston.

Mendelsohn, G. (1993). It's time to put theories of personality in their place, or Allport and Stagner got it right, why can't we? In K. H. Craik, R. Hogan, & R. N. Wolfe (Eds.), *Fifty years of personality psychology* (pp. 103–115). New York: Plenum Press.

Miller, N. E., & Dollard, J. (1941). *Social learning and imitation*. New Haven: Yale University Press.

Mischel, W. (1968). *Personality and assessment*. New York: Wiley.

Mischel, W. (1973). Toward a cognitive social learning reconceptualization of personality. *Psychological Review, 80,* 252–283.

Murray, H. A. (1938). *Explorations in personality*. New York: Oxford University Press.

Nichols, M. P. (1984). *Family therapy: Concepts and methods*. New York: Gardner Press.

Ogilvie, D. M., & Rose, K. M. (1995). Self-with-others representations and a taxonomy of motives: Two approaches to studying persons. *Journal of Personality, 63,* 643–679.

Perls, F. S. (1947). *Ego, hunger and aggression*. London: Allen & Unwin.

Pervin, L. A. (1978). *Current controversies and issues in personality*. New York: Wiley.

Pervin, L. A. (1990). A brief history of modern personality theory. In L. A. Pervin (Ed.), *Handbook of personality: Theory and research* (pp. 3–18). New York: Guilford Press.

Pervin, L. A. (1994). A critical analysis of current trait theory. *Psychological Inquiry, 5,* 103–113.

Peterson, C., & Seligman, M. E. P. (1984). Causal explanations as a risk factor for depression: Theory and evidence. *Psychological Review, 91,* 347–374.

Rogers, C. R. (1939). *The clinical treatment of the problem child*. Boston: Houghton Mifflin.

Rosenberg, S., & Gara, M. A. (1983). Contemporary perspectives and future directions of personality and social psychology. *Journal of Personality and Social Psychology, 45,* 57–73.

Rotter, J. B. (1954). *Social learning and clinical psychology*. Englewood Cliffs, NJ: Prentice-Hall.

Rychlak, J. F. (1968). *A philosophy of science for personality theory*. Boston: Houghton Mifflin.

Rychlak, J. F. (1993). A suggested principle of complementarity for psychology: In theory, not method. *American Psychologist, 48,* 933–942.

Seligman, M. E. P., & Maier, S. F. (1967). Failure to escape traumatic shock. *Journal of Experimental Psychology,* *74,* 1–9.

Skinner, B. F. (1938). *The behavior of organisms.* New York: Appleton-Century-Crofts.

Skinner, B. F. (1953). *Science and human behavior.* New York: Macmillan.

Spence, J. T., & Helmreich, R. L. (1978). *Masculinity and femininity: Their psychological dimensions, correlates, and antecedents.* Austin, TX: University of Texas Press.

Sullivan, H. S. (1947). *Conceptions of modern psychiatry.* Washington, DC: William Alanson White Psychiatric Foundation.

Toulmin, S., & Leary, D. E. (1992). The cult of empiricism in psychology, and beyond. In S. Koch & D. E. Leary (Eds.), *A century of psychology as science* (pp. 594–617). Washington, DC: American Psychological Association. (Original work published 1985)

Ullmann, L. F., & Krasner, L. (1969). *A psychological approach to abnormal behavior.* Englewood Cliffs, NJ: Prentice-Hall.

Westen, D. (1991). Social cognition and object relations. *Psychological Bulletin, 109,* 429–455.

Westen, D. (1994). Toward an integrative model of affect regulation: Applications to social-psychological research. *Journal of Personality, 62,* 641–667.

Western, D. (1995). A clinical-empirical model of personality: Life after the Mischelian ice age and the NEO-lithic era. *Journal of Personality, 63,* 495–524.

Winnicott, D. W. (1958). Transitional objects and transitional phenomena. In *Through pediatrics to psycho-analysis: Collected papers* (pp. 229–242). New York: Basic Books. (Original work published 1951)

Wittgenstein, L. (1968). *Philosophical investigations* (3rd ed.) (G. E. M. Anscombe, Trans.). New York: Macmillan. (Original work published 1953)

Zuckerman, M. (1979). *Sensation seeking: Beyond the optimal level of arousal.* Hillsdale, NJ: Erlbaum.

PART II

THEORIES OF PERSONALITY

The seven theories in this part of the book reflect the diversity of the field of personality discussed in Chapter 1 and analyzed in Table 1.1. We begin with three theories that emerge from clinical practice and conclude with four theories tied to empirical research in psychology. (See Table 1.2a,b for their chronology.)

Psychoanalytic theories (Chapter 2) are based on the practice of psychotherapy and attempt to provide a comprehensive understanding of intrapsychic functioning and the development of different personality styles. This "first force" in personality and psychotherapy represents a 100-year tradition that began with Sigmund Freud and subsequently developed in a social (object relations) and cognitive (ego psychology) direction. Psychoanalytic theories have been formulated primarily by medically trained psychiatrists, and this tradition has remained in large part outside of the tradition of academic psychology.

Interpersonal and systemic theories (Chapter 3) draw on the psychoanalytic and other traditions, such as the turn-of-the-century symbolic interactionism of G. H. Mead and the systems theory of von Bertalanffy. These theories contextualize persons and seek to understand them not as separate from, but as parts of larger, social systems, especially the family. Beginning with the clinically informed theory of Sullivan and continuing with theories of contemporary family therapists, personality formation and disturbance and therapeutic intervention have been located within the family rather than the person. Whereas the psychoanalytic school is tied to psychiatry, the interpersonal/systemic tradition increasingly distanced itself from medical thinking and connected instead with critical thinking in the social sciences and humanities, including, most recently, social constructionism.

Aspects of human experience neglected in mechanistic theories of psychoanalysis and learning are the focus of the "third force" in theories of personality and psychotherapy (Chapter 4). The therapy-based theories of Rogers, Perls, and the existentialists draw on psychoanalytic theories, as well as on humanistic theorizing as exemplified by Maslow. Contemporary developments in this tradition are found in the experiential theory of personality and psychotherapy, which hold that persons are agents, that personality becomes a self-creating act rather than a thing determined by biology and/or culture. These theories, often referred to as phenomenological, encompass not only cognitive but also affective experiences and the integration of the two.

That personality is (a) a set of stable response dispositions and (b) derives from biological endowment are two of the oldest beliefs about personality, shared by the ancient Greeks and Freud. Trait theories of personality (Chapter 5), first articulated by Allport, continue to support the usefulness of the notion of enduring personality dispositions. This school built on the psychometric measurement and statistical strategies of Galton and Pearson, has always had a strong quantitative research base. It has emphasized description rather than explanation and sought to identify the basic structure of personality. The five-factor model currently receives the most support from contemporary research.

Whereas Freud could only wish to pursue a project for a scientific psychology based on knowledge of physiology and psychology, today's psychobiological theories of personality (Chapter 6) have 100 years of such knowledge and research methodologies on which to build. Most recently, there has been a renewal of interest in temperamental types; current research supports these as being inherited. Such research provides a biological explanation for the basic structure of personality as identified by trait theorists. Further, it increasingly reveals the specific biological mechanisms by which traits affect behavior.

American psychology from James to the present has been first and foremost a functional psychology: psychological processes are best understood as they function to enhance environmental adaptation. "Second force" theories of personality and psychotherapy include functional theories derived from laboratory-based operant learning theory (Skinner) and lab- and clinic-based social learning theories (Dollard and Miller, Rotter). The operant theory of personality (Chapter 7) is especially provocative; its premise is that there is no such thing as personality. Despite the large body of empirical support for an operant theory of animal learning and research on successful operant interventions for psychological problems, there is a paucity of personality research based on this perspective.

Researchers studying social cognitive theories of personality (Chapter 8), derived from earlier social learning theories, are vigorously providing data to support their hypotheses about personality and the applicability of these hypotheses to cognitive-behavioral interventions. Social cognitive theories have absorbed the cognitive revolution in American psychology and have developed further the ideas of earlier cognitive approaches to personality, such as that of George Kelly. They connect to the study of information processing in cognitive psychology and the study of social cognition in social psychology. The social cognitive school also addresses social and cognitive concerns of other theories of personality: the interpersonal context of personality and self-beliefs as an influence on behavior. (For a broader view of social cognitive psychology, which also includes trait, biological, and unconscious aspects of personality, see Barone, Maddux, & Snyder, 1997).

REFERENCE

Barone, D. F., Maddux, J. E., & Snyder, C. R. (1997). *Social cognitive psychology: History and current domains.* New York: Plenum Press.

CHAPTER 2

PSYCHOANALYTIC THEORIES OF PERSONALITY

Bady Quintar, Robert C. Lane, and W. Bradley Goeltz

Prior to the emergence of psychoanalysis as a promising science, the zeitgeist was dominated by materialist biology and the natural sciences. Toward the middle of the 19th century, the scientific circles were challenging the basic assumptions of the naturalistic and speculative philosophy that dominated the intellectual community. The 19th-century concept of energy, the new discoveries in neurology, and the Darwinian theory of evolution were highly influential in the development of psychoanalysis as a new science. Holtzman (1995) states,

> The Darwinian influence can be seen in Freud's ideas of the development of infantile forms of sexuality into mature adult sexuality or of their failure to develop, as exemplified by disordered or "perverse" behavior. The epigenetics of sexuality, the idea that sexuality in its mature genital form does not appear suddenly *de novo* but emerges from an orderly developmental sequence beginning in infancy, was perhaps as revolutionary as Darwin's idea of the phylogenetic descent of man and the origin of species. Indeed, this revolutionary view of sexuality was directly derived from Darwinian thought. (p. 16)

At present, the term *psychoanalysis* refers to (a) a procedure for investigating mental processes, (b) a form of psychotherapy, and (c) a theory of personality development.

Bady Quintar, Robert C. Lane, and W. Bradley Goeltz • Center for Psychological Studies, Nova Southeastern University, Fort Lauderdale, Florida 33314.

Advanced Personality, edited by David F. Barone, Michel Hersen, and Vincent B. Van Hasselt. Plenum Press, New York, 1998.

SIGMUND FREUD: A FATHER FIGURE

LIFE

Sigmund Freud was born on May 6, 1856, in Friberg, Austria. He was the first of six children of Jacob Freud, a strict authoritarian father and a successful wool merchant, and Amalie, a young, attractive, loving mother who had a very close relationship with her son whom she inspired greatly. At the age of 17, Freud, who was an outstanding student, entered medical school at the University of Vienna and, after eight years, finished his medical training. Rather than practicing medicine, he was interested in engaging in scientific research and would eventually discover the analgesic properties of cocaine, a substance that he used for several years. Though a neurologist by necessity (for it was one of the few professions open to a person of the Jewish faith living in an anti-Semitic monarchy), his real interests were literature, art, and psychology.

In 1880, he began working with a kindly, caring, Viennese psychiatrist, Joseph Breuer, who had attained remarkable success in treating hysteria with hypnosis. Upon receipt of a small grant, Freud traveled to Paris where he spent approximately five months studying hypnosis with Charcot. Discouraged with the results, he eventually abandoned hypnosis and discovered the technique of *free association*, which came to be known as the *fundamental rule of psychoanalysis*. In 1855, Breuer and Freud published *Studies on Hysteria* in which they reported on their treatment of several cases of hysteria and outlined, for the first time, the techniques that characterize psychoanalytic treatment. In 1886, Freud married Martha Bernays with whom he had six children, the youngest of whom, Anna, followed in her father's footsteps and became a famous psychoanalyst. After the death of his father in 1896, Freud became very depressed and, in the following year, began his self-analysis. The insights he arrived at after analyzing his own dreams and those of his patients resulted in the publication of what many consider his masterpiece, *The Interpretation of Dreams,* in 1900.

In 1923, it was discovered that Freud had cancer of the jaw. For the next 16 years, a period in which he underwent 33 operations, he continued to work tirelessly despite constant pain. Freud loved Vienna, where he had lived for approximately 80 years, and was reluctant to leave it even after it was invaded by Nazi forces. It was Ernest Jones, an old friend and more recently his biographer, who convinced him to move to London after the house of his daughter Anna was overrun repeatedly, and after she was arrested. One year after moving to London, Sigmund Freud, the patriarch of psychoanalysis, died on September 23, 1939.

FREUDIAN CONCEPTS AND THEORY

Due to the complexity of the human psyche, Freud developed a number of hypothetical "models"—ways of conceptualizing the manner in which the mind works. Freud's use of models was in the interest of promoting a common language, and therefore an understanding, of the human mind.

The Topographic Model

Although Freud was not the "discoverer" of the *unconscious,* he established it as a scientific construct and charted its previously obscure and mysterious territory. Never accessible to direct observation, the unconscious is explored and understood via inferences derived from the presence and content of dreams, neurotic symptoms, parapraxis (i.e., misactions such as the infamous "Freudian slip"), and posthypnotic suggestions. The unconscious is distinguished by *primary process* and consists of concrete ideas of things and representatives of instincts. What we actually observe are the psychic manifestations, such as emotions, which link themselves to ideas and give birth to wishes. The unconscious also contains representations of the objects to which the affect is related—they are stored in the form of ideas or memory traces of one's perceptions of objects.

The unconscious may be regarded as the bulk of the individual's psychic self. The aspect of the self that is most readily available, the *conscious,* is topographically the "smallest" portion of one's mental existence ("the tip of the iceberg," the thin, uppermost layer of one's psyche). Adjacent to that "region" is the *preconscious,* which is not immediately available to our conscious awareness, but could become so when one is in a state of relaxation of controls. These concepts—the conscious, preconscious, and unconscious—comprise Freud's *topographic model* of the mind (Brenner, 1973).

In working with patients, Freud realized that dreams were a highly revealing source of information of patients' personality structures and dynamics. The insights he arrived at by analyzing his own dreams and those of his patients led him to the formulation of his views regarding dream interpretations, which became the centerpiece of his psychological theory. He realized that dreams were the "royal road" to the understanding of the dreamer's unconscious. He was convinced that certain daily concerns or preoccupations find their way into the dream (e.g., dreamer sleeping in a cold room may dream of ice skating). This aspect of the dream is referred to as the *day residue.* The *manifest content* of the dream refers to the conscious, surface aspect of it—the dream as told by the dreamer. The *latent content* refers to the covert, hidden, unconscious meaning of the dream, which may be discovered through the interpretation of the dreamer's manifest content and associations. The procedure used in converting the disguised images of the manifest content into the corresponding hidden needs and wishes is known as the *dream work.*

The Psychoeconomic Model

The *psychoeconomic model* assumes that each individual has a given amount of psychic energy available, and that the probability that a certain response can occur depends on the quantity of energy invested in such a response. Furthermore, as more energy is required to fight encroaching pathology, less is available for adaptive, creative, or sublimating activities (Brenner, 1973).

The Psychodynamic Model

The *psychodynamic model* assumes that behavior is a compromise between instinctual, or inborn, drives and counterinstinctual, or reality-oriented forces, each of which is invested with a given amount of psychic energy. Originally, Freud (1916–1917/1963) proposed a dualistic model of the instincts: *ego instincts,* which have to do with the preservation of the individual, and *sexual instincts,* which promote the preservation of the species. Freud then attempted to revive his instinct theory by combining the idea of self-love and self-preservation (i.e., *ego libido*) with love of others and species-preservation (i.e., *object libido*). In 1917, he subsumed aggressive motivation under the instinct of self-preservation. Finally, Freud proposed the dual instinct of life and death. The life instinct, which combined both ego and object libido, he named *Eros,* after the mythical Greek god of love. The death instinct, represented in Greek mythology as a winged spirit in the underworld, to which he assigned the name *Thanatos,* combined aggression directed toward both the self and others. Despite the controversy surrounding the Eros-Thanatos dichotomy, Freud fervently adhered to his dual instinct theory (Brenner, 1973).

In his paper "Instinct and Their Vicissitudes," Freud (1915/1957b) viewed an instinct as a mental representation of a bodily need. He understood it as a "frontier concept" on the border of both the psyche and the soma. Inherent in the concept of instinct is the notion that it is an inflexible, inherited, all-or-none, permanent behavior that occurs universally in all members of the species. Freud used the term *Trieb* (what others translated as "instinct") because *Trieb* is more flexible, lacks the notion of permanence, and is changed under the impact of environmental pressures in both aim and object. Some authors prefer the term *drive* as a more accurate translation of *Trieb* than that of instinct. Under certain conditions, normal physical impulses, in response to heightened tension, can press for immediate discharge in accordance with the *pleasure principle* (i.e., the individual's instinct to seek pleasure). Often, such impulsive discharge seems momentarily comforting; however, in the long run, the consequences of such behavior may become maladaptive, requiring the institution of a new and better regulatory principle that functions to reduce tension and thus brings about a more mature, adaptive, and realistic solution. This new principle, the *reality principle,* makes greater demands on the individual's judgment, reality testing, reasoning, and the ability to delay the discharge of tension until it becomes better organized.

Freud (1900/1953b), in his *Three Essays on the Theory of Sexuality,* described the following four characteristics of an instinct: source, impetus, aim, and object. The *source* is found in the physical, biochemical processes of the body. Any temporary alteration or deficiency may create the kind of tissue need that will press the organism to take action to regain homeostatis. *Impetus* reflects the strength of the demand made by the instinct. All instinctual impulses seek satisfaction or tension reduction in the quickest, most direct manner, which is the *aim* of the instinct. Initially, Freud, coined the term *object* to refer to that which will satisfy a need. His first usage of the term occurred when he discussed the early dyadic relationship between mother and infant.

The Structural Model.

The *structural model* assumes that the psychic apparatus is comprised of three highly interactive systems: the id, the ego, and the superego. The *id,* the most primitive aspect of the mind, represents instinctual energy and exists entirely on an unconscious level. When bodily needs arise, the id, which cannot tolerate the tension produced by bodily needs and which is governed entirely by the pleasure principle, demands the immediate removal of such tension. It utilizes two methods to reduce or eliminate such tensions: *reflex action* and *wish fulfillment.* Thus, when individuals feel cold, their bodies automatically begin to shiver to generate heat which will lower the level of tension. Other bodily needs, such as hunger, lead the organism to produce a mental image of food—the image of the desired food is capable of temporary, partial satisfaction of the need in question. However, with the passage of time, the still unmet needs will intensify, requiring more satisfactory action to be taken to reduce the level of mounting tension.

One aspect of the individual's psyche called the *ego* resorts to thinking, remembering, planning, and executing the necessary actions to obtain the need-gratifying object. The ego, which operates in accordance with the *reality principle,* attempts to match the mental image of the desired object with a comparable object in the external environment. The realistic manner in which the ego operates in satisfying the biological needs of the individual is called *secondary process*. The ego is best understood as that aspect of the psyche that acts as a mediator between the primitive, animalistic, primary process of the id and the individual's perception of external reality.

The third component of the personality, referred to as the *superego,* comes into being when the individual, in the process of socialization, internalizes the values, norms, or beliefs of parents or caregivers. Once the parental and societal rewards and punishments are internalized, the superego is said to be well developed in that external controls are largely replaced by self-control. The superego has two components: the *conscience,* which represents the internalized experience of being punished, and the *ego-ideal,* which stands for the internalized experience of being rewarded. The ego, as the executive agency of the personality, has to mediate constantly between irrational forces in the form of the superego striving toward unattainable perfection and the id's drives toward immediate gratification and avoidance of tension. If, on the other hand, the desired object conflicts with basic beliefs, values, or moral stances of the individual, an anticathexis toward the object is formed, and a less anxiety-revoking, need-satisfying object is substituted. Thus, whenever possible, the ego attempts to control the level of anxiety by resorting to whatever is necessary to facilitate the normal functioning of the individual (Brenner, 1973).

Anxiety, a pivotal concept in psychoanalysis, refers to an unpleasant affect or emotional state characterized by feelings of imminent threat to one's sense of security and integration. The physiological responses to this feeling of anticipated danger include sweating, tremors, accelerated pulse, increased heart and breathing rates, muscle tension, and disturbances in the gastrointestinal or urinary systems. The psychological correlates include feelings of helplessness, decreased ability to concentrate, self-absorption, perceptual hyperalertness, and, at times, even feelings of estrangement, depersonalization, or derealization.

Fear is a response to external and realistic danger, whereas anxiety may be conceptualized as one's response to the threat that unacceptable feelings previously repressed are now at the verge of becoming conscious. Freud distinguished three kinds of anxiety. *Reality anxiety,* or fear, is the result of an objective source of danger in the environment. It is from this basic type of anxiety that the other two types are derived. *Neurotic anxiety* occurs when the instinctual impulses of the id are of such intensity that they threaten to overwhelm the ego and cause individuals to perform acts for which they will be punished. *Moral anxiety,* or guilt feelings, occurs when people entertain thoughts or behave in a way that conflicts with their internalized values, beliefs, or ethical conduct.

Freud understood neurotic symptoms as attempts to minimize the painful experience of anxiety. The symptoms "bind" anxiety that would otherwise be "free floating." Freud originally attributed the emergence of anxiety to disturbances in sexual functioning; indeed, he assumed that libido when not satisfactorily discharged will be transformed into anxiety. Anxiety was then perceived to be the cause of sexual repression, and the lifting of that repression should eliminate anxiety. Since clinical data does not consistently support such a conclusion, he formulated his second theory of anxiety, the *signal theory* (S. Freud, 1926/1959). This theory suggests that anxiety emerges in anticipation of danger rather than as a result of danger, and that it signals the ego to guard its integrity by mobilizing its defenses. Freud's shift from his first to his second theory of anxiety represents his movement from a physiological to a psychological point of view, as well as his increased focus on the central role of the ego in the functioning of the mental apparatus.

Defense mechanisms is a modicum degree of anxiety is helpful in that it warns individuals of impending danger; however, if the threat is not warded off by anticathexis, (i.e., an emotionally charged counterforce), the ego resorts to the use of a variety of defenses. All ego defense mechanisms have two characteristics in common: (a) they falsify or deny reality, and (b) they operate unconsciously (i.e., the person is not aware of using them). These defense mechanisms have adaptive as well as defensive functions. Such defenses include the following:

- *Repression* is a basic defense by which the ego maintains anxiety-provoking thoughts, fantasies, or ideas within the unconscious. This repressed ideation nevertheless exerts considerable influence. The study of free associations, parapraxis, symptom formation, and dream analysis is an attempt to discover repressed ideas and their impact on personality functioning.
- *Denial* is the blocking of threatening external stimuli from entering into awareness.
- *Projection* refers to the unconscious attribution of anxiety-provoking, ego-dystonic (unacceptable to ego) material onto others.
- *Undoing* occurs when a person tries to "cancel" ego-dystonic thoughts or unacceptable acts by "taking it back" or by performing certain rituals or magical gestures.
- *Reaction formation* refers to the management of the original anxiety-provoking impulses by expressing, in an exaggerated manner, diametrically opposite ones.
- *Rationalization* involves fabricating what appears to be a rational, logical response to explain away anxiety-provoking behavior or thought.
- *Displacement* is the substitution of a less threatening behavior for a more anxiety-generating one.
- *Sublimation* refers to transformation of anxiety-arousing or unacceptable impulses into a socially acceptable or culturally valued activity.
- *Introjection* refers to the internalization of values, beliefs, or attitudes of a valued external object or person.
- *Identification* denotes the wish to become like another person through the internalization of that person's values, beliefs, or other characteristics for the purpose of enhancing self-esteem or minimizing the threat of a feared person or object.
- *Regression* refers to primitivization of behavior or to the return to an earlier stage of development in the face of intense stress or heightened anxiety.
- *Intellectualization* points to the tendency to avoid anxiety-arousing situations or events by stripping away the emotional factor and focusing on sterile, intellectual speculations, explanations, or esoteric verbiage.

Arlow and Brenner (1964) state that, while there is a tendency to use interchangeably the topographic and structural models of the mind, the two are indeed different. Freud's attempts to replace the topographic theory with the structural theory stemmed from the need to be able to account more accurately for conscious awareness. Indeed, under the right conditions both the instinctual and the anti-instinctual can be conscious or unconscious.

In a situation of conflict, the instinctual material is kept out of awareness by anti-instinctual forces, such as repression or other defense mechanisms. The structural theory views repression as one of many ego defense mechanisms that protects the integrity of the psychic apparatus. The topographic theory assumes that when repression fails to assume its function, the repressed libido emerges in the form of neurotic anxiety. The structural theory, on the other hand, assumes that anxiety signals the ego to utilize defensive measures to bring about and maintain a measure of psychic equilibrium (Freud, 1926/1959).

The Psychogenetic Model

Freud's *psychogenetic model* describes his theory of psychosexual development. His perception of individual development is one "of emerging sexual and aggressive instincts, unavoidable frustrations, anxieties, and defenses centered on crucial pleasure-seeking, tension-reducing prototypes at different ages" (Monte, 1995). In this model, individuals negotiate a series of five stages—*oral, anal, phallic, latency,* and *genital*—during the course of development. Freud was convinced that children's experiences during these stages are highly significant in shaping their adult personalities. Each of the stages is named after its identifying *erogenous zone* (i.e., that area of the body that predominates children's pleasurable interactions with their environment). Undue gratification or frustration at a particular erogenous zone brings about *fixation* of *libido.* That is, development from one stage to the next is interrupted or delayed if children's experiences of the earlier stage are of extreme pleasure and contentment or of inordinate frustration and displeasure. Thus, either overindulgence or intense frustration may disrupt normal personality development—the ideal state is one of *optimum frustration,* a condition in which children experience a developmental stage as pleasurable and safe, but also as possessing a certain level of dissatisfaction. Such frustration can motivate individuals to seek new paths as they try to maximize the pleasure obtained in their interactions with others. Freud's psychogenetic stages and the character traits expected to result from inadequate negotiation of each stage are as follows:

Oral Stage (birth–18 months). During the first year of life, children are highly dependent on their mothers for their very existence. Their earliest interactions center on the nursing process. The erogenous zone during this stage is the oral cavity. In the early months of the first year, organismic pleasure and tension reduction are associated with sucking, swallowing, and ingesting. Freud suggested that children who are fixated at this early oral stage derive considerable pleasure (reduce stress) in adulthood by resorting to overeating, smoking, drinking, kissing, or sucking their thumbs as well as in taking in knowledge, sceneries, compliments, and so on. Such individuals are frequently referred to as *oral-incorporative* or *oral-ingestive* characters.

While teething, children release tensions and experience pleasure by biting or chewing the things they put in their mouths. Fixation at this point is later manifested by activities such as nail biting or chewing on objects as well as being sarcastic, critical, cynical, and insulting. These activities seem to be rooted in the second half of the oral stage, the oral-biting period. Those fixated at this level are often referred to as *oral-aggressive* or *oral-sadistic characters.*

Anal Stage (18 months–3 years). During the second and third years of life, the anal region and bowels become the dominant erogenous zones. Pleasure or tension reduction in this stage is associated with the ability to control the retention or expulsion of feces. At this time, toddlers move about and explore their environment, often in spite of parental restrictions or restraints. They try to meet the demands of the parents, on whom they depend for support and protection, while simultaneously experiencing the urge to become increasingly self-assertive and autonomous beings. The parents' struggle to exert control over their children's increasing autonomy is eventually met with the children's willful "No!" utterance. While this "No!" represents a significant phase in the toddler's ego and superego developments, the parents are frequently exasperated with what they perceive as negativism and stubbornness and often react with more stringent attempts to control them. Fixation at this stage may be manifested later on by those who derive pleasure from spending money and giving away material possessions (*anal-expulsive characters*), or by those who are characterized as being stingy, parsimonious, stubborn, and orderly (*anal-retentive characters*).

Phallic Stage (3–5 years). Prior to the phallic stage, boys and girls have had a very intimate relationship with the mother, who has ideally met their needs for nurturance, support, protection, safety, and security in addition to being instrumental in helping them acquire a sense of self and an *ego identity*. Indeed, both boys and girls take their mothers as their first *love object*. During the three years of intimate relationship with their primary caregivers, children explore their immediate surroundings, including their bodies. Boys and girls discover that they can derive a certain degree of pleasure by touching and manipulating their genitals and the surrounding areas. Additionally, they become increasingly aware that the mother's attention and soothing ministrations must be shared with their siblings and the father. They resent and become jealous of these interlopers, who demand the mother's exclusive care and devotion.

Freud assumed that during this phase of development boys become increasingly attached to their mothers; they monopolize her affection and wish to possess her. Simultaneously, they fear the retaliation of the "omnipotent father" who will punish them for their transgressions. Freud called this imagined fear of punishment, *castration anxiety*. To protect themselves from such anxiety, boys identify themselves with the perceived aggressor. This identification with father contributes to the crystallization of the psychic structure of the superego and provides the child with a vicarious possession of the mother through identification with the father. Freud named the boy's desire to possess mother sexually by getting rid of his father, the *Oedipus complex*—after the ancient Greek play by Sophocles, *Oedipus Rex,* in which Oedipus unwittingly killed his father and married the king's wife, who turned out to be his natural mother.

Freud felt that for girls the phallic stage followed a very different course—called by him the *Electra complex*—after Sophocles's play, *Electra,* in which Electra sent her brother to murder her mother, who had killed her husband, Electra's father. According to Freud, the girl resents her mother for bringing her into this world without a penis. She rejects her mother and secretly finds herself becoming increasingly attracted to her father, who possesses the sexual organ that she lacks—Freud referred to his as *penis envy*. Eventually, the female wishes to repair the damage of being born without a penis or with a defective one (i.e., the clitoris) by giving birth to a baby boy, thus, symbolically obtaining a penis.

Positive resolutions of the Oedipus and the Electra complexes are brought about by the repression of unacceptable incestuous urges, positive identification with parents of the same sex, and the covert wish to find persons who share some characteristics of the parents of the opposite sex. Negative resolutions of both complexes occur when boys or girls identify themselves with parents of the opposite sex, resulting in attractions to same-sex *love-objects*. Fixation at this stage of development may express itself in overconcern with virility, masculinity, "machoism," and other phallic-intrusive activities in men and seductiveness, exhibitionism, and sexual promiscuity in women.

Latency Stage (6–approximately 12 years). Freud believed that the basic foundation of the adult personality is achieved by the end of the phallic stage. Additionally, he was of the opinion that disturbances in *infantile sexuality* (i.e., the oral, anal, and phallic stages) are at the core of *psychoneurosis* and other forms of psychopathology. He felt that sexual impulses are rechanneled during the period of latency, that is, they are displaced onto nonsexual activities, such as academic learning, athletic performance, social development, and peer-group affiliation.

Genital Stage (13–adulthood). The pregenital stages of infantile sexuality are characterized by what Freud termed *primary narcissim,* which is the pleasure that arises from self-stimulation (e.g., thumb-sucking, control of feces, and masturbation). After latency, the sexual instinct becomes more outwardly focused as the age of reproductive ability becomes imminent. The genital stage is characterized by an increased investment of libido in the opposite sex and in a wider range of *object choices* rather than the primary narcissim of the pregenital stages.

The Seduction Hypothesis. In treating his patients, Freud observed that the theme of childhood sexual seduction was invariably present in their free associations. He recalled that Breuer, Charcot, and the gynecologist Chorbak also commented on the place of early sexual experiences in neurotic disorders; however, they later tried to deny such statements (Jones, 1953, p. 248). Freud initially believed that such seduction must have actually occurred. But when his patients traced their sexual experiences to early ages (when they were sexually immature—physically and emotionally—and thus unable to effect powerful repression), he had to radically alter his *seduction theory.*

On September 21, 1897, Freud wrote to Fliess that his patients' reports of childhood seductions were products of their fertile imaginations rather than faithful accounts of real events. Later he stated, "If hysterical subjects trace back their symptoms to traumas that are fictitious, then the new fact which emerges is precisely that they create such scenes in phantasy, and this physical reality requires to be taken into account alongside practical reality. This reflection was soon followed by the discovery that these phantasies were intended to cover up the autoerotic activity of the first years of childhood, to embellish it, and raise it to a higher plane. And now, from behind the phantasies, the whole range of a child's sexual life came to light" (1954, pp. 215–217). Jeffrey Masson (1984) suggested that Freud's abandonment of the seduction hypothesis was based primarily on Freud's needs to protect his professional reputation and to enhance his practice rather than on conviction borne out of clinical empirical evidence.

EGO PSYCHOLOGY

As the discipline of psychoanalysis developed, there arose an early group of theorists who began to shift their focus from the role of the id in psychic life to that of the ego as the primary means of understanding the individual. With this shift from a mere explanation of pathology to a more general theory of mental life, proportionally more attention came to be focused on the ego as that aspect of the psyche that is perceived as the individual, the self, the "I." The development of *ego psychology* is best reflected in the works of the following three primary theorists: Anna Freud, Heinz Hartmann, and Erik Erikson.

Anna Freud, the Loyal Daughter

Apart from the usual child–parent love, there was an extraordinary bond between Anna and Sigmund Freud. Anna's relationship with her mother was largely devoid of the affection expected in a traditional mother-daughter relationship. Both emotionally, as his daughter, and intellectually, as his student, Anna's whole life was centered around her father. With no formal training in either medicine or psychology, Anna began her training with her father while she was in her early twenties. She attended Freud's lectures and joined the prestigious Wednesday seminars of the Vienna Psychoanalytic Society (Freud's most trusted colleagues, his "inner circle"). Anna's theoretical and clinical contributions, particularly in the area of child analysis, never deterred her from caring for her father, even as he lay stricken with cancer and on his deathbed. From 1922 to 1982, the year of her death, she devoted herself to widening the scope of psychoanalysis by building on her father's discoveries and by modifying orthodox psychoanalytic techniques in working with children and adolescents.

Anna Freud (1945) noted, "In childhood there is only one factor of such central importance that its impairment through a neurosis calls for immediate action; namely, the child's ability to develop, not remain fixated at some stage of development before the maturation process has been concluded" (p. 17). Thus, not only a full-blown childhood neurosis, but potential or actual fixation at a phase of development was sufficient to warrant psychoanalytic treatment. Based on the conviction, borne out of years of experience that to engage a child in analytic treatment a period of preparation is necessary to help the child see the need for treatment, she found it necessary to modify traditional analytic technique and to add to it elements that take into consideration the child's wish to grow, mature, and deal effectively with the demands of reality. To prepare the child for treatment, the analyst must come to be accepted as a useful, knowledgeable, helpful, and trustworthy person, one who is more powerful than the parents. During this preparatory phase, children become aware that, in certain aspects, they are vulnerable and in need of help from their therapists, whom they have grown to perceive as indispensable helpers, *ego ideals.* In the context of this intense positive transference, children will become increasingly willing to receive the assistance of their trustworthy analyst. The establishment of this helpful but lengthy preparatory procedure led to the development of a systematic way of assessing children at the onset of the treatment. The *metapsychological profile* was the method Anna Freud originated to provide such a systematic assessment (1965a, pp. 138–147). The content of this profile included the reason for referral, descriptions of the child and the family, environmental influences as well as an assessment of the development of libidinal and aggressive drives.

In evaluating ego strength, Anna Freud turned her attention to the description of how the ego masters problems posed by life. She introduced the concept of *developmental lines*—an original contribution to psychoanalysis focused on the ego's capacity to deal with life's demands. The developmental lines describe a maturational sequence from dependence to a sense of autonomy.

Anna Freud's attempts to shorten the diagnostic stage of the preparatory period led her to examine closely the ego defenses. In *The Ego and the Mechanisms of Defense* (1936/1966), she stated, "If we know how a particular patient seeks to defend himself against the emergence of his instinctual impulses, i.e., what is the nature of its habitual ego resistances, we can form an idea of his probable attitude towards his own unwelcome affects" (p. 32).

An investigation of ego defenses promotes a better understanding of how the ego developed and how successful it has been in mastering the patient's needs, wishes, and desires. Anna Freud outlined 15 defenses, including those of her father—plus asceticism, altruistic surrender, turning against the self, reversal, and identification with the aggressor.

By building on her father's achievements, she expanded the boundaries of classical psychoanalysis, stimulated interest in ego functioning, adapted analytic therapy for children, and lessened the stress on biological factors, while assigning considerable importance to the impact of the environment. Additionally, she viewed the human being as a masterful creature rather than the victim of internal conflicts or external demands.

HEINZ HARTMANN, THE FATHER OF EGO PSYCHOLOGY

A noteworthy synthesizer and theoretician, Heinz Hartmann was successful in expanding psychoanalytic theory into a general psychology of human behavior. He brought together concepts from various disciplines including biology, psychology, sociology, and medicine, and organized them in such a way that he expanded psychoanalytic conceptualization.

Hartmann became interested in exploring the origin and the development functions of the ego, noting that, "We must recognize that though the ego certainly does grow on conflicts, these are not the only roots of ego development. Not every adaptation to the environment, or every learning and maturation process, is a conflict. I refer to the development *outside of conflict,* of perception, object comprehension, thinking, language, recall phenomena, productivity, to the well-known phases of motor development, grasping, crawling, walking, and to the maturation and learning process implicit in all these and many others" (Hartmann, 1939/1964a, pp. 7–8; italics in original).

Rather than accepting Freud's view that the ego differentiated from the id, Hartmann proposed that initially there is an undifferentiated matrix of innate biological equipment. Parts of this innate biological equipment are the drives or instincts out of which the id emerges. Other parts of this innate equipment are what he called *inborn ego apparatus.* The id and the ego are products of differentiation from this inborn matrix (Hartmann, 1939/1964a, pp. 102–103). Thus, contrary to the classical Freudian view, Hartmann believed that the ego does not develop out of the id, but that it develops from its own biological roots. He postulated two kinds of ego autonomy: *primary autonomy* and *secondary autonomy.* Primary autonomy refers to the inborn biological ego apparatus that develops within the *conflict-free orbit.* The ego can assume a secondary autonomy when the functions it performed that were developed in conflict with the id are later used for adaptation (Hartmann, 1950/1964b, p. 105).

Hartmann's original and highly useful concept of *neutralization,* which refers "to the change of both libidinal and aggressive energy away from the instinctual and toward a non-instinctual mode" (Hartmann, 1955/1964c, p. 227), contributes to our understanding of how this deinstinctualized energy could be used for the purpose of adaptation. According to Hartmann, "the observation underlying the concept of 'adaptation' is that living organisms patently 'fit' into their environment" (Hartmann, 1955/1964c, p. 227). Thus, he understood adaptation to be a reciprocal relationship between the self and the surrounding environment, one in which change must occur both within the self and within the environment if the existence of the individual is to continue.

Erik Erikson

Life

Erik Erikson, the son of Danish parents, was born in Frankfurt, Germany, in 1902. His father abandoned his mother before Erik was born. Three years later, Mrs. Erikson married Dr. Theodore Homberger, Erik's pediatrician. Dr. Homberger's dark hair and eyes stood in sharp contrast to Erik's blond hair and blue eyes. Furthermore, Erik's biological parents were Christian while his stepfather was Jewish. In school, he was often referred to as either "the Jew" or "the *goy*" (a Yiddish word for gentile, sometimes derogatory). Erikson's later consuming interest in *identity crisis, ego identity,* and related issues seem to stem from his early concerns with his own identity.

Erikson was trained as a psychoanalyst by Anna Freud and was highly influenced by her teachings and ideas and those of her father. He was a very creative person who broadened Freud's emphasis on the role of instincts or biological drives to include the importance of psychosocial aspects in human development. Concerned about the interactions of children with their caretakers (usually the mothers), Erikson turned his attention to the investigation of child-rearing practices in various societies. He was deeply interested in cultural norms and rituals as well as the values, beliefs, and expectations that are imparted to children throughout the period of socialization. Indeed, by bringing together biological, social, psychological, ethical, and cultural perspectives, he enriched our understanding of human development more than any other psychoanalyst. In an attempt to organize his views regarding personality development, Erikson added his own conceptualization to the already established Freudian instinctual framework.

Theory

Central to Erikson's formulation was the notion of ego identity. He stated, "I can attempt to make the subject matter of identity more explicit only by approaching it from a variety of angles. . . . At one time, then, it will appear to refer to a conscious *sense of individual identity;* at another, to an unconscious striving for a continuity of personal character; at a third, as a criterion for the silent doings of *ego synthesis,* and, finally, as a maintenance of an inner *solidarity* with a group's ideals and identity" (1959, p. 102). Erikson's concern with ego development and functioning led him to the conclusion that during the course of human development, the ego progresses through a sequence of eight stages. At each specific stage, the ego is confronted with a psychological crisis that is unique to that particular stage. These eight phase-specific stages of human development, referred to by Erikson as the "Life Cycle," have their positive and negative aspects.

Erikson insisted that for healthy development a person must incorporate in his/her ego identity the positive and negative aspects, but that the *ratio* of positive to negative aspects must lean toward the positive, or the person will become vulnerable, relatively defenseless, and prey to victimization by others. The positive resolution of each psychosocial crisis energizes the ego and subsequently facilitates its management of the challenges of the following psychosocial crisis. With the resolution of every crisis, the ego acquires an additional measure of strength or what Erikson calls *virtue* (derived from the Latin *virilitas,* meaning "virility" or "strength"). Erikson stated, "I will call 'virtue', then, certain human qualities of strength, and I will relate them to the process by which ego strength may be developed from stage to stage and imparted from generation to generation" (1964, p. 113). With every psychosocial crisis, the ego uses certain strategies to orient itself and deal with biological and social realities. These strategies include *ritualization*—the positive and culturally sanctioned ways of doing things—and *ritualism*—the negative or stereotyped, mechanical and meaningless, routinized behaviors. The life cycle, with its eight psychosocial crises, ego development (virtue), and ritualizations follows:

Trust versus Mistrust (first year). Successful resolution of this psychosocial crisis leads to the acquisition of basic trust, the virture of *hope*, and the ritualization of *numinous* (hallowed) ideas of the mother's presence. Failure to achieve numinous ritualization, leads to *idolism*—an unreal, illusory image of perfection created between mother and infant (Erikson, 1964, p. 115).

Autonomy versus Shame and Doubt (second year). Favorable resolution of the psychosocial crisis at this age results in the establishment of a sense of autonomy and the virtue of *will*. The ritualization has to do with the ego's ability to differentiate right from wrong. Erikson referred to this ritualization as *judicious*, differentiating it from the ritualism of *legalism*, which refers to the victory of the letter over the spirit of the word and the law.

Initiative versus Guilt (third through fifth years). "During this period of time, children tend to be action-oriented. They play, explore, learn to manipulate, and create activities in collaboration with others. The virture acquired following the successful resolution of this psychosocial crisis is *purpose*. The ritualization in this stage is *authenticity*, and *impersonation* is the corresponding ritualism" (Erikson 1964, p. 122).

Industry versus Inferiority (sixth year through puberty). Successful resolution of this crisis leads to the ego's development of the virtue of *competence. Formality* is the ritualization associated with this psychosocial crisis, describing the child's ability to enjoy learning, be industrious, and master the task. *Formalism* by comparison is a ritualism that focuses primarily on technique and efficiency with very little concern for the meaning or significance of that to which the child is exposed (Erikson, 1964, p. 124).

Identity versus Role Confusion (adolescence). The resolution of the psychosocial crisis at this stage results in the emergence of the virture of *fidelity*. The ritualization corresponding to this psychosocial stage is *ideology*—the adolescent develops a clear sense of ego identity, work ethics, and moral values. *Totalism*, the ritualism of this stage is "a fanatic and exclusive pre-occupation with what seems unquestionably ideal within a tight system of ideas" (Erikson, 1968, p. 96).

Intimacy versus Isolation (early adulthood). "The virtue that emerges with the favorable resolution of the psychosocial crisis at this stage is *love*, the desire to share, to complement each other, and to contribute to each other's welfare is the *affiliative* ritualization of this stage, and *elitism*, which is characterized by social isolation and inflated self-regard, is the ritualism associated with this crisis" (Erikson, 1964, p. 129).

Generativity versus Stagnation (middle age). "The positive resolution of this crisis leads to the acquisition of the virtue of *care. Generation* is the ritualization that characterizes this period, in which mature adults care and transmit societal values to offsprings, and *authoritism*, or the irrational imposition of authority, is the ritualism corresponding to the poor management of the crisis" (Erikson, 1964, p. 131).

Ego Integrity versus Despair (old age). "The virtue of this final stage in the life cycle is *wisdom* and the corresponding ritualization is *integration,* its corresponding ritualism is *salietism,* 'the unwise pretense of being wise'" (Erikson, 1964, p. 133).

Erikson, who is regarded as a bona fide ego psychologist, shares many commonalities with *object relations* theorists, particularly because of the emphasis he places on mother–infant interactions and the biopsychosocial perspectives of his developmental theory. Furthermore, he enriched and broadened our knowledge of ego psychology by ascribing to it additional qualities, including hope, will, purpose, competence, fidelity, love, care, and wisdom, all of which form an integral part of ego strength.

OBJECT RELATIONS

Object relations may be understood as the internalized representations of the earliest interpersonal relationships. Freud originally coined the term *object* to refer to that which will satisfy a specific need. All object relations theorists study the impact of early mother-infant interactions on the individual's current interpersonal relationships. A person's interpersonal relationships represent a compromise between the actual, objective individual to whom the person is relating and the internalized psychic representation of that person. For example, when a young man meets an older woman, his perception of her is determined by both the actual, objective person that she is and a psychic representation that is often distorted by the needs, wishes, fears and expectations that the young man brings with him from his early relationship with his mother. Object relation theorists differ frequently among themselves; however, they all agree on the primacy of mother-infant relationships over the classical Freudian concept of innate instinctual drives. The shift of emphasis from inherent biological factors to the importance of object relationships in shaping personality has brought several important changes into focus, including the emphasis on preoedipal development and the importance of sociopsychological factors. Object relation theorists stress the importance of environmental influences on personality formation and consider the importance of biological factors in providing a very rough blueprint by which development will proceed.

British School of Object Relations

Melanie Klein, a Mother Figure

Born in Vienna in 1882, Melanie Klein studied art and history before marrying and giving birth to three children. She then resumed her studies and eventually specialized in the psychoanalysis of children. In 1926, she moved to London and continued to work, write, and teach until her death in 1960. She was a psychoanalyst who has influenced many followers in Europe and the Americas with her creative and innovative work. Klein remained generally faithful to classical theory, frequently endorsing and occasionally amending or modifying some aspects of basic psychoanalytic views.

In working with troubled children, Klein developed the new technique of *play therapy* through which children express their thoughts, feelings, and their abundantly rich *fan-*

tasies. She relied heavily on Freud's theories and insights, but since she worked directly with children, she became convinced that children have greater ability to develop insight into their behaviors than do adults (Strean, 1994, p. 63). Following Freud's ideas, she concluded that the child's inner world of fantasy is filled with terror, murderous impulses, cannibalistic tendencies, sadistic urges, and raw erotic wishes (Strean, 1994, p. 54). She also observed that children are less defensive than adults, and that the connections between the conscious and the unconscious are closer in young children than in adults. The early defense mechanisms that infants use to control these intense impulses, terrors, and urges are primarily projection, introjection, splitting, and *projective identification,* which refers to "imaginatively splitting part of oneself and attributing it to another for the sake of controlling the other" (St. Clair, 1996, p. 220).

For Klein, infants control their inner needs, establish object relations, and build an inner world of fantasy through constant cycles of projection and introjection. Through introjection, infants establish an inner, psychic world that bears a considerable similarity to the external world, and the projection of children's inner feelings onto objects in the external world plays a significant part in shaping their perceptions of the external world. Klein assigned more importance to the inner world of fantasies than to external reality, and more to the instinctual aspects than the environmental ones. The content of the inner world of fantasies is stored in the psyche, remaining active and exerting its influence on the individual's emotional life and overall psychological functioning.

Klein believed that object relations exist from birth, and that infants are born into a social context. The first object to which infants relate is the mother's breast (part-object). This early relationship is crucial and contributes substantially to the gradual development of the infant's ego and superego. The ego, according to Klein, is present at birth, but goes through substantial development as the infant internalizes the good part-object with which the ego identifies—the nurturing breast.

Klein viewed the *death instinct* as the cause of the child's inner anxieties and felt that the primary aim of therapy is to lower the level of anxiety and modify the harshness of internalized persecutory objects. Her keen insights into the early mental life have widened the scope of psychoanalytic theory, and her shift of emphasis from the triadic oedipal relationship to the dyadic mother-child relationship has enriched our understanding of childhood development. Furthermore, by viewing instincts as connected with objects and drives as being relational, she laid a solid foundation for the British school of object relations.

W. R. D. Fairbairn, the First Pure Object Relations Theorist

Fairbairn (1946/1954b) introduced what he called a "pure" (i.e., strictly psychological) object relations model. He rejected Freud's biological emphasis and advanced the theory that people have a fundamental drive toward relating to each other, than the libido is object seeking, and that the ego strives for a relationship with an object, and not just for pleasure or tension reduction. Furthermore, by locating the libido in the ego, he suggested that the ego has its own energy (p. 150).

Fairbairn's object relations theory helps us understand the intricate relationships between the ego, internalized objects, and the external world. The ego is conceptualized as a dynamic structure that is constantly seeking relationships and interactions with people. If the interactions are gratifying, the ego's integrity is maintained. He postulated that internalized objects become dynamic structures, and that the ego, by being linked to objects, forms an inseparable dynamic structure capable of initiating psychological activity within the psyche. He reasoned that when infants are confronted with frustrating objects, they try to cope with this noxious experience by mentally splitting the object into part-objects, that is, the good and bad aspects. Subsequently, they perceive the environment or others as good, internalize the bad part-object, and view themselves as bad. He reasoned it is safer for them to perceive themselves as bad than to view the external world as bad, threatening, and uncontrollable. These bad part-objects often become intolerable and hence are repressed. Fairbairn held the major goal of therapy to be the release of bad part-objects from the unconscious. If such a transformation is to occur, the therapist must be a caring, *good-enough object* who offers the patient a secure, nonjudgmental environment.

Fairbairn (1944/1954a) suggested that in the course of normal development, the ego splits into three separate components, each relating to different aspects of the object. He called this dynamic multiple substructure of the ego the *endopsychic situation* (p. 112). All infants experience a certain amount of frustration in their relationships with their primary caregivers. Infants subsequently establish safeguards to defend themselves against such frustrations. These safeguards are internal structures that bring about some measure of harmony or equilibrium to infants' psychic organization. When mothers fail to meet the needs of their infants with the promptness that the infants anticipate, they become frustrated and often experience the mothers' behavior as punitive and rejecting. Defensively, the infant splits the mother into two part-objects: the satisfying aspect of mother remains as the good part-object, and the frustrating component becomes the bad part-object, which the infant attempts to control through internalization. However, the internalized bad part-object continues to be frustrating. Fairbairn refers to these internalized bad part-objects and the corresponding part of the ego as *endopsychic structures*. Fairbairn assumed that since these inner objects both tempt and frustrate infants, they subsequently become repressed. The *libidinal ego* corresponds to the exciting part of this bad object, and the *antilibidinal ego* (also known as the internal saboteur) is associated with the rejecting aspects of the internalized bad object. Psychopathology, he assumed, results from the operation of the bad internal objects within the ego.

The ego, in normal development, splits into the following three constituents, each relating to different aspects of an internalized object: *central ego, libidinal ego* and *antilibidinal ego.* The central ego, which comprises conscious and unconscious elements, relates to people and their social environment. It protects its own integrity by repressing the other two subsidiary egos. The libidinal ego is the part of the self that feels needed yet attacked or persecuted. The antilibidinal ego stands often in opposition to the libidinal ego; in many respects, it functions in a way similar to the Freudian superego (Fairbairn, 1944/1954a, p. 89).

Fairbairn's views regarding developmental stages and object relations are very different from the Freudian model. He stressed the nature of the objects and the quality of their relationships, while the Freudian model emphasizes how people obtain satisfaction, and how the libido is manifested in the various erogenous zones of the body. Fairbairn's developmental theory proposes the following three stages in the development of object relations: *infantile dependence stage, transitional stage,* and *mature relational stage.* The infantile dependence stage is characterized by identification with the object; the transitional stage is a period of time when individuals feel their dependency needs and yet long to become autonomous. In the mature relational stage, the quality of the relationships is of the utmost importance. Mutual respect, reciprocity between differentiated persons, and a sense of autonomy are the hallmarks of a mature relationship.

D. W. Winnicott, a Perceptive Contributor

Winnicott began his career as an English pediatrician and later became an outstanding child psychoanalyst and theorist. He devoted many years of his productive life to paying special attention to important areas of child development: dyadic therapeutic relationships, the child's interaction with the immediate social environment, and the emerging sense of self. In focusing on the mother-infant relationship, he stressed repeatedly the importance of the *facilitating environment*—the impact of the mother on the development of her infant. Winnicott (1959/1965b) coined the term *good-enough mother* to describe the kind of dynamic relationship in which the mother offers her infants whatever is needed to insure that they are adequately cared for, and yet she provides a level of frustration that is adequate to encourage the children to progress to more mature levels of development (pp. 124–139).

Winnicott believed that the world of infants is a world that has little relation to reality. To meet their needs, they have to depend almost entirely on their mothers. When hungry, for example, infants fantasize about nursing and may even hallucinate the presence of the breast. When their fantasies or hallucinations occur almost simultaneously with the appearance of the breast, they assume that they possess magical powers to alter certain aspects of reality whenever they so desire. With maturation, children become more reality oriented, and their subjectively felt omnipotence gives way to realistic thinking, planning, and autonomous functioning. Winnicott suggested that, if there is a good-enough mother during the maturational process, then children will react in a spontaneous manner and feel real and genuine in their relationships with others. If children do not have good-enough mothers and are made to comply to their mothers' wishes and live according to their demands and expectations, then they will live socially isolated lives or relate to others in a nongenuine, unrealistic manner. In fact, the presence of a *false self* may result in persons who are unable to get in touch with their own real feelings. A good-enough mother not only fosters the emergence and crystallization of a true self, but also contributes to the child's eventual capacity to be alone and to enjoy solitude.

An original and valued addition to object relations theory is Winnicott's notion of the *transitional object*, typically an inanimate but highly valued object that is the first of the earliest "not-me" possessions. Transitional objects, such as a soft blanket, a cloth doll, or a diaper offer the infant certain feelings of comfort, security, and tranquility. Winnicott (1961/1989b) suggested that the transitional object serves as a comforting maternal breast that is under the control of the infant.

With respect to the developmental process, Winnicott acknowledged that within the context of a facilitating environment of good-enough mothering, the child develops from a relatively unintegrated state to a fairly structured integration with the capacity for meaningful object relations. As the infant passes through absolute dependence to relative dependence to independence, the corresponding roles of parental care: "holding." "mother and infant living together," and "mother, infant, and father living together." Winnicott used the term *ego-relatedness* in discussing the relationship between the infant and the mother in which the infant's ego immaturity is buttressed by the ego support of the mother. With the progressive establishment of good objects in infants' psyches, they will develop the capacity to be alone (Winnicott, 1958/1965a).

Winnicott understood therapy to be as similar to the mother process and felt that the goal of therapy should be to foster the patient's regression (i.e., the reestablishment of the early dependency relationship) in order to relieve, in the context of the transference relationship, earlier infantile deficits that have contributed to the presence of the false self.

AMERICAN SCHOOL OF OBJECT RELATIONS

Margaret Mahler, the Infant–Mother Relationship

Born in Vienna, Margaret Mahler, a physician and child psychoanalyst, came to the United States in 1938, and became a consultant to the Children's Service of the New York State Psychiatric Institute. After a few years of practice, she embarked on a very ambitious task, namely, to study child–mother interactions during the first three years of life. She observed and documented the interactions of mothers with their babies at the Master's Children's Center in New York City. From such observations, she was able to infer the preverbal psychological development of the child. Her description of the process of *separation* (the intrapsychic sense of separateness from mother) and *individuation* (the awareness of being an entity) that take place between the child's fourth month and thirty-sixth month has been a timely and needed contribution to the field of child development. These processes have two separate but complementary and interactive tasks that lead eventually to the development of differentiated self- and object-representations (Mahler, Pine, & Bergman, 1975, p. 63).

From direct observations of mother–infant interactions, Mahler constructed a developmental theory about the psychological birth of the human infant. Her theory had three continuous and overlapping developmental phases: *normal autism, normal symbiosis,* and *separation–individuation.* This last phase, separation–individuation, is further subdivided into the following subphases: *differentiation* and body image, *practicing, rapprochement,* and *consolidation of individuality.*

Normal Autism Phase (birth–1 month). During the first month of life, infants are in a state of absolute primary narcissim. They are unable to differentiate themselves from others. The primary achievement of this phase is the gradual attainment of a homeostatic equilibrium outside the mother's womb. Gradually, infants become dimly aware that the satisfaction of some of their needs comes from external sources. Such budding awareness marks the beginning of the normal symbiotic stage.

Normal Symbiosis Phase (1–4 months). Mahler borrowed the biological term *symbiosis* to describe the state of undifferentiation between mother and infant. It is as though both are "fused" together and exist as a dual entity within a psychologically enclosed "symbiotic shell" (Mahler *et al.,* 1975, p. 44). The mother's reactions to the infant's needs gradually shapes the infant's ability to distinguish satisfying (good) experiences from frustrating (bad) experiences. Infants at this age begin to sense that some of their needs are met by something outside of themselves. With such a development, the objectless primary narcissim of the autistic phase gives way to the gradual development of secondary narcissim, in which the infants' emotional investments shift from themselves to the need-satisfying mothers (Mahler & Furer, 1968, p. 10; Mahler *et al.,* 1975, p. 47).

Differentiation and Development of the Body Image Phase (5–9 months). With the formation of an inner core of self achieved through the experience of having one's needs met by the mother, the process of individuation and separation proceeds vigorously. At the peak of symbiosis, the gradual maturation of the sensorimotor apparatus permits the infant to engage in behaviors that will eventually culminate in the simultaneous process of individuation and separation from the mother. This phase is characterized by the infant's need to physically break away from mother, a process that Mahler refers to as a "hatching process" or "psychological birth." These toddlers spend most of their waking hours exploring their environment, particularly the mother's face. As they explore, they become aware of the similarities and differences between their mothers and others. At about this time, the infant develops *stranger anxiety* (Mahler *et al.,* 1975, p. 56). In the process of exploration, the infant touches, tastes, smells, inserts objects in his mouth, and so on. The differential reactions or sensations that infants experience by interacting with parts of their bodies, the bodies of others, and objects in their environment help them develop primitive mental images of their bodies.

Practicing Phase (10–14 months). This period is characterized by the infants' greater ability to move about freely and to venture away from their mothers. Along with their expanding locomotor capacities, their egos have developed the cognitive and perceptual capacities that enhance their reality testing. Toddlers at this time begin to depend less on their caregivers and more on their developing skills to move about and familiarize themselves with the environment. Intermittent failures to achieve such goals motivate the toddlers consistently to return physically to their mothers for a sort of emotional "refueling" (Mahler *et al.,* 1975, p. 68). Toward the end of this phase, they become increasingly mobile and enjoy freedom of movement and exploration. Their intrapsychic developments often fail to keep pace with their physical progress. The building of a resistance to the fear of separation from the mother is a major achievement during this subphase as the infant vigorously explores the immediate physical, social, and interpersonal world (Mahler & Furer, 1968, p. 22).

Rapprochement Phase (14–24 months). This phase is characterized by the infant's increased awareness of the separateness from the mother. Enjoying the closeness to her, the toddler tries to preserve the symbiotic bond by demanding increased amounts of mother's time and attention. Simultaneously, the child feels the urge to separate from her and to develop further the nascent sense of autonomy and individuality. The toddlers try to distance themselves from the mother by refusing to obey her, by frequently saying "No" to her, or by turning away from her—by pursuing the attention of the father, who is less enmeshed in the symbiotic union of mother and child (Mahler *et al.,* 1975, p. 91).

The intensification of anxiety associated with the ambivalent wish to be autonomous and the pressing underlying need to be closely dependent on mother is referred to as the rapprochement crisis (Mahler & Furer, 1968). At this stage, the ego develops the ability to integrate and synthesize contradictory feelings and perceptions into a unified, synthetic whole. However, should fixation occur at this time, the child's integrative ego functions will not develop sufficiently, and splitting mechanisms will result in serious developmental arrest, often contributing to the development of borderline or narcissistic personality disorders.

Consolidation of Individuality Phase (24–36 months). The primary achievement during this period is the formation of emotional object constancy, a stable self-concept, and the child's self-perception of uniqueness and separateness from others (Mahler *et al.,* 1975, p. 109). The child's internalization of a comforting, dependable, warm, caring, and soothing mother contributes substantially to the achievement of emotional object constancy, the ability to maintain an image of a comforting, loving, and protective mother even when she is not physically present (Mahler *et al.,* 1975, p. 110).

Edith Jacobson, Integrationist

Edith Jacobson received her medical and psychoanalytic training in Germany in the 1930s, began her private practice in New York City in 1940, and in 1942 worked as a training analyst at the New York Psychoanalytic Institute. Her major contribution to psychoanalysis was her attempted integration of the drive and structural points of view into object relations theory. She demonstrated the close and highly complex interaction of instincts, object relations, and the psychic apparatus. She understood maturation as the movement from an utter lack of differentiation to the establishment of organized and delineated structures and processes.

Jacobson proposed that growing infants are relatively helpless and vulnerable and are in need of maternal support to meet their needs and to protect them from excessive gratification or frustration—either of which can lead to regression to a primitive level of functioning in which there is a loss of boundaries between self- and object-representations. This regressive re-fusion can interfere with the development of both ego and superego. As the ego matures, it develops the ability to establish better boundaries between the self- and object-representations. Clearly defined boundaries work against the re-fusions of self-representations and object-representations (Jacobson, 1964).

With the passage of time, infant–mother contacts increase. In the process of nursing, the mother's touch, sight, voice, and emotional expressions serve to stimulate the development of her child's ego and other psychic structures. At approximately three months of age, infants begin to perceive other objects or part-objects (mother or aspects of her) as different from themselves. Repeated experiences of gratification and frustration, when accompanied by normal maturation of the ego, will lead to the development of a greater capacity for discrimination between self-representations and object-representations. After the third year, children try to imitate the behavior of their admired parents. At this time, although there is a fairly clear demarcation between self-image and object-image, the boundaries are still weak and vacillating. A similar lack of stability in libidinal and aggressive drives is noted as children's attitudes shift from dependency yearnings to strivings for autonomy.

As the ego matures, many of its functions become increasing efficient and differentiated. The child's self- and object-representations become progressively realistic; the earlier wish for merger with the parents gives way to a more realistic self-image and a firmer sense of personal identity. According to Jacobson, the beginning of object relations is made possible when the boundaries between self-representations and object-representations are clearly established.

Jacobson assumed that superego development occurs roughly from the beginning of the second year through the seventh year of life. Furthermore, she understood the structure of the superego as comprising the following three aspects: (a) the primitive, punitive images; (b) the ego ideal; and (c) the realistic moderate identifications. The first aspect is composed of the primitive, sadistic, and punitive object-representations that occurred when there was a lack of adequate boundaries between self- and object-representations. The second aspect of superego development takes place when the ego has become more mature, functions according to the reality principle, and has established a more realistic view of object relations. The third aspect consists of the internalization of values and standards of the parents, and of a realistic, mature identification with them. Hence, it replaces the more primitive fantasies of merger with the loved objects (Jacobson, 1964).

Otto Kernberg, Further Integration

A native Austrian who received his medical education in Chile, and later psychiatric training at the Menninger Foundation, Kernberg is one of the most influential contemporary psychoanalysts. He is an original thinker who, like Jacobson, attempted to integrate object relations theory with drive theory. He assumed that psychic structure is achieved as the result of a continuous process of internalizing units of object relations, which include self-representations, object-representations and the feelings associated with them (Kernberg, 1976, p. 33). He assumed that three levels of internalization—introjection, identification, and ego identity—are instrumental in the establishment of psychic structure. Kernberg suggested that some ego functions, such as perception and memory, are innate potentials that exist from birth and play a crucial role in the introjection of object relations. Initial positive mother-infant interactions (particularly during nursing) are introjected and become good internal objects despite the fact that the object relations unit of self-image and object-image are still undifferentiated and fused together. These positive introjects give rise to a primitive ego core. Conflictual mother-infant interactions may result in the internalization of a disturbed object relations unit that becomes defensively split off and paves the way for the eventual emergence of serious difficulties in psychic organization (Kernberg, 1976, p. 36–38).

Around the second year of life, children demonstrate the desire to "declare their independence" from their parents. This wish is facilitated by the increasing development of their cognitive, perceptual, and motor functionings. In their interactions with others, children come to realize that there are certain rules and norms that they must observe. The internalizations of values, norms, and beliefs contributes to further development of the psychic structure, particularly if associated with satisfactory or pleasurable experiences.

Ego identity, which is the highest level of internalization, occurs when the ego organizes and synthesizes all its identifications and introjects in such a way that the child has a sense of continuity of self. Nevertheless, the internal world of object representations differs somewhat from the corresponding external world of actual people. This discrepancy is attributed to the powerful and lasting influence of primitive object images that remain repressed in the unconscious (Kernberg, 1976, p. 32–33).

In addition to proposing that internal object relations develop into the id, ego, and superego, Kernberg believed that psychic structure is formed along five developmental stages. The first stage (birth–1 month) is characterized by the fusion of self and objects and the gradual emergence of self- and object-representations (Kernberg, 1976, p. 60). The second stage (2–8 months) is identified by the formation and consolidation of "good," yet undifferentiated, self–object-representations, out of which the ego will form. In the third stage (8–36 months), differentiation of self-representations from object-representations within the core "bad" self–object-representation takes place (Kernberg, 1976, p. 64). This stage ends with the gradual integration of good and bad self-representations into a self-concept, the integration of good and bad object-representations into a "whole" object-representation, and the achievement of object constancy. The fourth stage (3–6 years of age) consists of the integration of partial images into whole ones; consolidation of id, ego, and superego as intrapsychic structures; establishment of ego identity; and increased organization of the inner world of object representations. Kernberg (1976) believes that the ego and id develop out of a common matrix (p. 69). He advanced the view that the structure of the ego precedes that of the id, and that the integration of the superego as an autonomous intrapsychic structure is achieved during this stage. Kernberg's fifth stage of psychic structural development begins in later childhood and is characterized by the completion of superego integration, greater positive alliance between the ego and superego, consolidation of ego identity, and the eventual reshaping of the self-concept (Kernberg, 1976).

HEINZ KOHUT AND SELF PSYCHOLOGY

LIFE

Heinz Kohut was born in 1913, in Vienna, and received his medical degree from the University of Vienna in 1938. He spent most of his professional life in America, where he was a teacher and a training psychoanalyst at the Chicago Institute for Psychoanalysis. While in the United States, he became increasingly dissatisfied with Freudian drive theory and began to focus his attention on an aspect of the psyche that he called the *self*. Kohut's conceptualized the self in a narrow *and* a broad sense. In the narrow sense, he understood it as a specific structure of the mind; in the broader sense, he viewed the self as the center or the "scepter of the individual's psychological universe" (Kohut, 1977, p. 311). In this second connotation, the self is the whole individual being—as such, one can never completely "know" the self—although with introspection and empathy, a clearer understanding could be gained. Kohut (1977) described the self as "a unit, cohesive in space and enduring in time, which is the center of initiative and a recipient of impressions" (p. 99). In addition to viewing the self as the "locus of relationships," it performed functions frequently assigned to the ego.

With the publication of *The Analysis of the Self* (1971), Kohut laid the foundation of his *self psychology* and began the move away from strict classical drive theory. By 1977, with the publication of *The Restoration of the Self,* he no longer spoke of libido, and only with considerable hesitancy did he make reference to the ego or the superego. Kohut did not reject drive theory; rather, he questioned its usefulness in explaining psychopathological conditions other than the *neuroses*. Classical drive theory views psychopathology as resulting from repressed, unresolved conflicts primarily of an oedipal nature. Furthermore, it assumes that neurotics experience *interstructural conflict* (i.e., conflict between the id, ego, and superego). Kohut, who did much of his work with narcissistic patients, postulated that these patients have some basic defects in the psychological structures. While he did use drive model concepts and language in the early 1970s, by the end of the decade Kohut moved beyond those concepts and introduced new terms to explain his clinical findings and theoretical assumptions. Through his clinical work, *narcissism* became one of the central concepts in Kohut's self psychology. He felt that narcissim is not only a possible aspect but also a necessary aspect of health.

THEORY

Kohut's views regarding the genesis of the self as an active functional agent take into consideration children's innate abilities and the immediate social environment with which they interact and on which they depend for their very survival. The infant's rudimentary self is fragile, amorphous, vulnerable, and without a stable structure of continuity over time.

Hence, it requires the support of others to help develop a more stable, cohesive structure. These others, most often initially the infant's mother and father, are *selfobjects*. Because at this point in development infants are unable to differentiate themselves from the external world, the selfobjects are perceived as aspects of the infants' selves, whose primary functions are to soothe, care for, protect, support, and stimulate the infants' development. If the selfobjects possess a stable, cohesive, well-developed psyche, they will empathically respond to the children's needs. This responsiveness, although not perfect, is "good-enough" in helping to establish a more stable, clearly defined, and cohesive infantile self (Kohut, 1977, p. 87).

Kohut stated that "the child's rudimentary psyche participates in the selfobject's highly developed psychic organization. The child experiences the feeling states of the selfobjects as they are transmitted to the child via touch and tone of voice, and perhaps by still other means—as if they were his own" (Kohut, 1971, pp. 50, 64). Kohut called this process *transmuting internalization*. Although, normally, parents try to anticipate the needs of their infants and try to meet those needs immediately, gratification can never be perfect. Children, feeling frustrated, try to rely on their own inner resources, those aspects of the selfobjects that have already been internalized as parts of their selves. Thus, with *optimal frustration*, children take in the soothing, comforting aspects of the selfobjects and build their inner structures, which will function in place of those selfobjects when they are unavailable.

The pristine, fragile nuclear self that originally comes into being through the process of transmuting internalization is a highly vulnerable and unstable structure that requires a warm, emphatic, and responsive relationship to stimulate further integration. To fortify the nuclear self, a child seeks two vital relationships, which satisfy basic narcissistic needs. By receiving the approval, admiration, and continual reinforcement from the selfobjects (the parents), the child develops what Kohut called a healthy sense of grandiosity and omnipotence. The infant's sense of narcissim or grandiosity is reinforced by the selfobjects (parents), who *mirror* the child's feelings of vitality, self-esteem, healthy self-assertiveness, and ambitiousness. The *grandiose self* develops as the infant's narcissim is mirrored and or reinforced by the behavior of the selfobjects who value and treasure the infant. The experience of the grandiose self might be expressed as, "I am wonderful. I am perfect. Look at me!" In addition to the grandiose, exhibitionistic self, Kohut spoke of a second constituent of the nuclear self—the *idealized parental imago*. Despite the occasional disappointment that is experienced as the selfobject fails to respond without frustration of the infant's needs and desires, the parental selfobject is perceived by the infant as being omnipotent, caring, and vastly capable. The experience of the idealized image might be expressed as, "You are perfect and I am part of you." As parental imperfections become obvious to the child, the idealized parental imago is *introjected* (i.e., internalized, taken in as part of the self) in the attempt to preserve them as ideals.

Kohut referred to the grandiose self and the idealized parental imago as the *bipolar self*. This rudimentary self becomes organized into a cohesive self toward the end of the first and the beginning of the second year of life. In normal development the exhibitionistic, grandiose self becomes integrated into the personality and contributes to feelings of well being, elevated self-esteem, enjoyment of activities, and so on. The idealized parental images are integrated into the child's personality as the idealized superego structure, one that regulates tension, provides idealism, and promotes higher social values. As the person develops, the now integrated grandiose self becomes the source of ambition, while the idealized parental imago becomes the seat of ideals. Kohut conceptualized the interaction between ambitions and ideals as a *tension arc,* along which there is a constant flow of energy that stimulates action. In addition to the bipolar self, Kohut eventually included a third constituent of the self, one which involves the *alter ego* or *twinship needs.* This third constituent underscores the need to be with another alike person.

Kohut's work may be differentiated from classical drive theory in that Freud understood narcissim as a stage through which one moves toward object-relatedness. Kohut, however, believed that narcissim continues throughout a person's life, with continuing development contingent on one's movement to a more sophisticated level of narcissim. Kohut deviated from Freudian theory not only in his understanding of narcissim, but also in that he encouraged the abandonment of the idea of drives and de-emphasized the Oedipus complex. Kohut's relational model bears many similarities to the British and American schools of object relations, and it may be understood as a continuing search for a more complete understanding of human experience.

STRUCTURAL THEORY AND RELATIONAL THEORY: COMPETING OR COMPLEMENTARY?

Freud's structural and subsequent relational models (i.e., those stressing the importance of the dyadic relationship between patients and their analysts) are important; both nature and nurture play a significant role in the development of personality, and one is not superior to the other. Many relational theorists minimize the importance of Freudian drive theory and the classical approach to psychoanalysis, stating that they place too great an emphasis on bodily urges, biology, natural science, internal structures, the intrapsychic, past relationships, fantasy, conflict, defense mechanisms, and resistance. Relational theorists regard classical psychoanalytic theory as positivistic, asocial, and as a one-person psychology that neglects the importance of the interaction, such as that which comprises the therapeutic relationship (i.e., transference and countertransference).

The relational model stresses the interpersonal, the experiential, intersubjectivity, object relations and interaction with the external world, reality, the here-and-now, constructionism, the social environment, and a two-person psychology. The classical Freudian drive model is perceived as emphasizing the psychology of the individual, the private autonomous self, while the relationists focus on the dependent, social aspect of self and personality and group psychology. Freudian psychoanalysts study the methods the patient uses to satisfy instinctual drives and concern themselves primarily with the influence of internal determinants, while relational theorists are more interested in the interpersonal relationships, the influence of external forces.

Gill (1955) noted that, in addition to the points just discussed, there are a number of important philosophical differences between the ways that classical theorists and relational theorists understand human existence. Importantly, classical theory proposes the innate as the primary determining factor in psychic development—one's experiential interaction with the world is determined (shaped) by predisposing innate factors (i.e., those qualities, drives, abilities, and shortcomings with which one is born). The relational theorist, however, would argue that one's experience—one's necessary participation in the environment—is responsible for the development of those qualities that are so closely identified with the individual that they appear to be innate or inborn. Gill also pointed out that classical drive theorists feel that the present is determined by the past, that the individual one becomes is the direct and unavoidable effect of the causal web of one's history. On the other hand, the relationists, agreeing that the past is a powerful determinant in the individual's current life, contend that one is much more independent of the past than a strict determinist philosophy will allow. They understand the past as an "illumination" of the present. A third basic philosophical difference between the two approaches, Gill proposed, is the fact that the relationists understand the current nature of the patient's interpersonal relationships as being the primary agent of change, while the classical theorists emphasize the importance of insight in the psychoanalytic process.

Contemporary structuralists (i.e., modern day classical theorists) offer a series of criticisms regarding current relational theory. For example, they accuse the relationists of minimizing the importance and relevance of Freud's writings without having bothered to read the original works, which, they suggest, leads to inaccurate or even blatantly incorrect interpretations of basic Freudian theory. They also feel that the relationists tend to focus too exclusively on current reality and the immediate implications of the therapist-patient relationship, and in so doing so overlook the curative aspects of the transference neurosis.

As in any debate, the criticism is not at all one-sided. The relationists argue that the structualists' focus on conflict minimizes the understanding of pathology in terms of deficit, the underdevelopment of intrapsychic structure. Additionally, they regard the positivism, objectivism, and psychic determinism of the classical theorists to be limiting when compared with the relational perspective of a subjective reality. The relationists emphasize the mutual impact of the patient and analyst on one another and propose that the structuralists do not appreciate the complexity of the transference-countertransference relationship.

Despite the fact that it is vital to understand the implications of the basic philosophical differences that pervade current clinical practice and theory, many of the adherents of each of these two apparently dichotomous models of the mind behave as if their philosophies are mutually exclusive, and thus discourage movement toward an integrated and complementary perspective, in which the goal is understanding rather than personal or philosophical pride. For example, if one emphasizes the present to the neglect of the past, it is likely that patterns of interpersonal interaction may be overlooked. If, on the contrary, one minimizes the influence and importance of the present in favor of an exclusive focus on the past, the immediate implications of continuing patterns will be neglected. Obviously, in order to function effectively as a clinician, one must accept that the dichotomy presently apparent in psychoanalytic theory is akin to the metaphor of the five blind men each of whom on touching the trunk, ear, tusk, leg, and hide of an elephant, is adamant about the nature of the whole of the creature at hand and disagrees with the interpretations of the other four. Any theory, scientific or philosophical, represents mankind's attempt to explain the minute aspects of an infinitely complicated universe that we are ultimately incapable of comprehending.

PSYCHOANALYSIS AS A RESEARCH PROCEDURE

Research in psychoanalysis differs from research in other areas of psychology. In most cases, we are dealing with case studies of patents' narratives. Academic psychology's emphasis on the experimental and scientific method for evaluating psychoanalysis reveals insufficient understanding of psychoanalysis. Psychoanalysis engages in observation during the interpersonal relationship between patient and therapist, attempts to reconstruct childhood from adult narratives, and engages in clinical systematic examination of the behavior of infants and toddlers in the presence and absence of their mothers. Recording is often objected to by patients, as is note taking, and process notes written from memory at the end of the hour or later may be too subjective. Recording influences therapeutic behavior, while videotaping tends to encourage exhibitionism and superficiality. The number of variables in a single therapeutic session are almost incalculable. The measurement and collection of data in general is enormously difficult and depends on such factors as the nature of the relationship, the type of questions asked, and how and when they were asked. Defining the exact nature of interventions and the impact of interpretation is indeed very difficult.

According to Fisher and Greenberg (1977), there have been more studies on and scientific evaluation of psychoanalysis than any other school of psychology. These studies indicate the effectiveness of psychoanalysis in treating certain pathologies that are resistant to other forms of therapy. Outcomes studies on the effectiveness of psychoanalysis have been based primarily on individual practitioner reports, or case studies, which are plentiful but difficult to verify. The practice of utilizing individual case reports, which is characteristic of clinical psychoanalytic practice and research, is discouraged by cognitive behavioral theorists and is regarded by many as unscientific. If quantification is the standard by which outcomes studies are regarded as "scientific," then the bulk of psychoanalytic clinical research will not and cannot qualify under this standard.

Despite these difficulties, studies on the treatment of certain types of pathology; on the relationship between early history and later pathology; on the effectiveness of treatment and outcome studies in general; on the nature of cure; on anxiety, depression, and other forms and degree or intensity of affect and pathology; and on defenses are increasing in numbers. The experimental designs and research of Sidney Blatt and his associates (Blatt, 1992; Blatt, Cornell, & Eshkol, 1993) at Yale University have received considerable attention.

Blatt has been committed to the study of therapeutic change, the validation of psychoanalytic theory, and the investigation of the benefits of intensive, psychodynamic treatment. He has emphasized the role of the "person" and individual differences in therapeutic change, and has established two types of patients, the anaclitic and the introjective. The *anaclitic* or dependent personality style is characterized by fears of being abandoned. These individuals, often lonely and helpless, have a desperate need to be loved, cared for, nurtured, and protected. Desperate to avoid endangering interpersonal relationships, they avoid conflicts and seek fusion, synthesis, and harmony on emotional, intellectual, and interpersonal levels. They tend to use avoidant defenses (e.g., denial and repression) and are very aware of and focused on their environment. By way of contrast, the *introjective* or self-critical personality style values individuality and self-control. Interpersonally aggressive and self-assertive, they emphasize a sense of identity: achievement, power, prestige, and perfection. They are logical thinkers, introspective, ruminative, autonomous, self-critical, and tend to utilize counteractive defenses, such as projection, isolation, intellectualization, and overcompensation. Blatt has demonstrated experimentally that each type changes in specific ways and is more responsive to particular types of treatment—the anaclitic to psychoanalytic psychotherapy and the introjective to psychoanalysis. Blatt emphasizes the importance of the interpersonal and interactional relationship between patient and therapist and the structure and content of their basic cognitive exchanges when assessing therapeutic alterations, in addition to noting symptomatic shifts with therapy.

Psychoanalytic judgment is highly subjective and not readily amendable to statistical analyses. What is important is the "individual" patient. When the importance of statistical validity replaces clinical truth, the person is lost in the shuffle. Bringing individual psychoanalytic cases that differ in countless ways together and then pooling the data statistically because of common traits—symptoms or diagnoses—often produce negative findings that are all but meaningless. Also, asking analysands to fill out paper-and-pencil rating scales or questionnaires (after the therapeutic frame has emphasized confidentiality) completely ignores the concept of the unconscious, which is implicit in psychodynamic psychotherapy. We must focus on the therapeutic relationship and the clinical experience and judgment of the psychoanalyst-therapist, who has many sources of data to draw from. Outcome studies often ignore the important questions of degree of pathology, the type of personality we are dealing with, the preferred method of treatment for that particular type of personality, and the time necessary to elicit change.

The meaning of any sign or symptom can only be understood in light of the total situation, including the many qualitative variables that might possible impinge on the total situation. The same symptom/syndrome might emerge from a constellation of factors that have a major similarity (i.e., oral deprivation), but possess a host of other unrelated traits. Statistical analysis should assist the clinician in evaluating data but never be used to replace clinical judgment.

Problems in the field of psychoanalytic research include the difference between conscious and unconscious feeling and thought, the ever-changing symptom picture, the nature of the problem as influenced by the reporter, the nature of maladaptive behavior and the definition of what is maladaptive, difficulty in accumulating an adequate sample, and difficulty in attaining a pure representation of any diagnostic category (different symptoms, different meanings of symptoms, different perceptions of the problem).

Bornstein (1996) points out that "a great deal of cutting-edge research in cognitive, social, personality, and developmental psychology today is based on psychoanalytic theory" (p. 3). He goes on to say, "However, more often than not the psychoanalytic roots of these research programs are never acknowledged" (p. 3). He uses as an example the concept of "object representation," which Greenberg and Mitchell (1983) pointed out has played a central role in psychoanalysis for nearly a century. Bornstein (1996) continues, "Variations on this concept have been 'discovered' independently by developmental, cognitive and social psychologists—who invented their own terms . . . *schema, self-representation,* and *internalized working model* (italics added), all of which describe similar (though not identical) theoretical constructs" (p. 3).

REFERENCES

Abraham, K. A. (1953). A short study of the development of libido, viewed in light of mental disorders. In D. Bryan (Ed.) & A . Strackey (Trans.), *Selected papers on psychoanalysis* (pp. 418–501). New York: Basic Books. (Original work published 1924)

Arlow, J., & Brenner, C. (1964). *Psychoanalytic concepts and the structural theory.* New York: International Universities Press.

Blanck, G., & Blanck, R. (1974). *Ego psychology.* New York: Columbia University Press.

Blatt, S. J. (1992). The differential effect of psychotherapy and psychoanalysis on anaclitic and introjective patients: The Menninger psychotherapy research project revisited. *Journal of the American Psychoanalytic Association, 40,* 691–724.

Blatt, S. J., Cornell, C. E., & Eshkol, E. (1993). Personality style, differential vulnerability, and clinical course in immunological and cardiovascular disease. *Clinical Psychology Review, 13,* 421–450.

Bornstein, R. F. (1996). Psychoanalytic research in the 1990s: Reclaiming what is ours. *Bulletin of the Psychoanalytic Research Society, 5,* 3–4.

Brenner, C. (1973). *An elementary textbook of psychoanalysis.* (Rev. ed.). New York: International Universities Press.

Erikson, E. H. (1959). *Identity and the life cycle.* New York: International Universities Press.

Erikson, E. H. (1963). *Childhood and society* (2nd ed.). New York: Norton. (Original work published 1950)

Erikson, E. H. (1964). *Insight and responsibility.* New York: Norton.

Erikson, E. H. (1968). *Identity: Youth and crisis.* New York: Norton.

Fairbairn, W. R. D. (1954a). Endopyschic structure considered in terms of object relationships. In *An object-relations theory of the personality* (pp. 82–136). New York: Basic Books. (Original work published 1944)

Fairbairn, W. R. D. (1954b). Object-relationships and dynamic structure. In *An object-relations theory of the personality* (pp. 137–161). New York: Basic Books. (Original work published 1946)

Freud, A. (1945). *The writings of Anna Freud: Vol. 4. Indications for child analysis.* New York: International Universities Press. (Original work published 1969)

Freud, A. (1954). *The psychoanalytic treatment of children.* London: Imago.

Freud, A. (1965a). *The writings of Anna Freud: Vol. 5. Metapsychological assessment of the adult personality: The adult profile.* New York: International Universities Press. (Original work published 1969)

Freud, A. (1966). *The writings of Anna Freud: Vol. 2. The ego and the mechanisms of defense* rev. ed. New York: International Universities Press. (Original work published 1936)

Freud, A. (1992). *The writings of Anna Freud: Vol. 1. Beating fantasies and daydreams.* New York: International Universities Press. (Original work published 1922)

Freud, S. (1953a). The interpretation of dreams. In J. Strachey (Ed. and Trans.), *The standard edition of the complete psychological works of Sigmund Freud* (Vol. 4–5). London: Hogarth Press. (Original work published 1900)

Freud, S. (1953b). Three essays on the theory of sexuality. In J. Strachey (Ed. and Trans.), *The standard edition of the complete psychological works of Sigmund Freud* (Vol. 7, pp. 125–243). London: Hogarth Press. (Original work published 1900)

Freud, S. (1954). *The origins of psychoanalysis: Letters to Wilhelm Fliess, drafts and notes, 1987–1902.* (Bonaparte, M., Freud, S., & Kris, E. (Eds.). New York: Basic Books.

Freud, S. (1955). Beyond the pleasure principle. In J. Strachey (Ed. and Trans.), *The standard edition of the complete psychological works of Sigmund Freud* (Vol. 28). London: Hogarth Press. (Original work published 1920)

Freud, S. (1957a). On the history of the psychoanalytic movement. In J. Strachey (Ed. and Trans.), *The standard edition of the complete psychological works of Sigmund Freud* (Vol. 14). London: Hogarth Press. (Original work published 1914)

Freud, S. (1957). Instincts and their vicissitudes. In J. Strachey (Ed. and Trans.), *The standard edition of the complete psychological works of Sigmund Freud* (Vol. 14). London: Hogarth Press. (Original work published 1915)

Freud, S. (1957). The unconscious. In J. Strachey (Ed. and Trans.), *The standard edition of the complete psychological works of Sigmund Freud* (Vol. 14). London: Hogarth Press. (Original work published 1915)

Freud, S. (1958). A note on the unconscious in psychoanalysis. In J. Strachey (Ed. and Trans.), *The standard edition of the complete psychological works of Sigmund Freud* (Vol. 13). London: Hogarth Press. (Original work published 1912)

Freud, S. (1959). Inhibition, Symptoms and Anxiety. In J. Strachey (Ed. and Trans.), *The standard edition of the complete psychological works of Sigmund Freud* (Vol. 20, pp. 77–175). London: Hogarth Press. (Original work published 1926)

Freud, S. (1962). The neuro-psychoses of defense. In J. Strachey (Ed. and Trans.), *The standard edition of the complete psychological works of Sigmund Freud* (Vol. 3). London: Hogarth Press. (Original work published 1894)

Freud, S. (1963). Introductory lectures on psychoanalysis. In J. Strachey (Ed. and Trans.), *The standard edition of the complete psychological works of Sigmund Freud* (Vol. 15–16). London: Hogarth Press. (Original work published 1914–1917)

Freud, S. (1964). An outline of psychoanalysis. In J. Strachey (Ed. and Trans.), *The standard edition of the complete psychological works of Sigmund Freud* (Vol. 23). London: Hogarth Press. (Original work published 1940)

Gill, M. (1995). Classical and relational psychoanalysis. *Psychoanalytic psychology, 12*(1), 89–107.

Greenberg, J. R., & Mitchell, S. A. (1983). *Object relations in psychoanalytic theory.* Cambridge: Harvard University Press.

Hartmann, H. (1964a). *Ego psychology and the problem of adaptation.* New York: International Universities Press. (Original work published 1939)

Hartmann, H. (1964b). Psychoanalysis and developmental psychology. In H. Hartmann, *Essays on ego psychology.* (pp. 99–112). New York: International Universities Press. (Original work published 1950)

Hartmann, H. (1964c). Notes on the theory of sublimation. In H. Hartmann, *Essays on ego psychology.* (pp. 215–240). New York: International University Press. (Original work published 1955)

Holzman, P. S. (1995). *Psychoanalysis and psychopathology.* New York: Aronson.

Jacobson, E. (1964). *The self and the object world.* New York: International Universities Press.

Jones, E. (1953). *The life and work of Sigmund Freud: Vol. 1. The formative years and the great discoveries.* New York: Basic Books.

Kernberg, O. (1976). *Object relations theory and clinical psychoanalysis.* New York: Jason Aronson.

Kohut, H. (1971). *The analysis of the self.* New York: International Universities Press.

Kohut, H. (1977). *The restoration of the self.* New York: International Universities Press.

Mahler, M. S., & Furer, M. (1968). *On human symbiosis and the vicissitudes of individuation.* (New York: International Universities Press.

Mahler, M. S., Pine, F., & Bergman, A. (1975). *The psychological birth of the human infant.* New York: Basic Books.

Masson, J. M. (1984). *The assault on truth: Freud's suppression of the seduction theory.* New York: Farrar, Straus & Giroux.

St. Clair, M. (1996). *Object relations and self psychology* (2nd ed.). Pacific Grove, CA: Brooks/Cole.

Strean, Herbert S. (1994). *Essentials of psychoanalysis,* Vol. 2. New York: Brunner/Mazel.

Winnicott, D. W. (1965a). The capacity to be alone. In *The maturational processes and the facilitating environment* (pp. 29–36). New York: International Universities Press. (Original work published 1958)

Winnicott, D. W. (1965b). Classification: Is there a psycho-analytic contribution to psychiatric classification? In *The maturational processes and the facilitating environment* (pp. 124–139). New York: International Universities Press. (Original work published 1959)

Winnicott, D. W. (1965c). Ego integration in child development. In *The maturational processes and the facilitating environment* (pp. 56–63). New York: International Universities Press. (Original work published 1962)

Winnicott, D. W. (1965d). The theory of the parent-infant relationship. In *The maturational processes and the facilitating environment* (pp. 37–55). New York: International Universities Press. (Original work published 1960)

Winnicott, D. W. (1971). Mirror-role of mother and family in child development. In *Playing and reality* (pp. 111–118). New York: Basic Books.

Winnicott, D. W. (1989a). The fate of the transitional object. In C. Winnicott, R. Shepard, & M. Davis (Eds.), *Psychoanalytic explorations.* (pp. 53–58). Cambridge: Harvard University Press. (Original work published 1959)

Winnicott, D. W. (1989b). Psycho-neurosis in childhood. In C. Winnicott, R. Shepard, & M. Davis (Eds.), *Psychoanalytic explorations* (pp. 64–72). Cambridge, MA: Harvard University Press. (Original work published 1961)

CHAPTER 3

INTERPERSONAL AND SYSTEMIC THEORIES OF PERSONALITY

STEVEN N. GOLD AND GONZALO BACIGALUPE

CONCEPTIONS OF PERSONALITY

The spectrum of theories of personality represents a range of accounts and explanations of the phenomena constituting personality development, processes, and functioning. Even more fundamentally, however, each personality theory differs in its conception of what personality *is*. Certain theoretical viewpoints even question or dispute whether personality, in the sense of a force that controls and directs intentions and actions, *exists*. Perhaps the best known instance of such a perspective is that of B. F. Skinner (1957, 1971), who argued that behavior is controlled not by the person or personality, but by the environmental consequences of the person's behavior.

The interpersonal and systemic constellation of personality theories has, throughout its evolution, explicitly questioned the notion of personality as a force that guides, shapes, and explains behavior. Interpersonal and systems theorists maintain that human behavior is not adequately accounted for solely by the workings of the personality of the individual. They have argued that forces beyond the personality and outside the control of the individual either contribute to, or more or less exclusively direct, behavior. More specifically, interpersonal and systems theorists contend that behavior is controlled, at

STEVEN N. GOLD • Center for Psychological Studies, Nova Southeastern University, Fort Lauderdale, Florida 33314.   GONZALO BACIGALUPE • Graduate College of Education, University of Massachusetts–Boston, Boston, Massachusetts 02125.

Advanced Personality, edited by David F. Barone, Michel Hersen, and Vincent B. Van Hasselt. Plenum Press, New York, 1998.

least in large part, by the social environment in the form of interpersonal influences and social systems

This chapter will delineate the conceptions of personality proposed by interpersonal and systems theories by tracing their historical development. The evolution of these theories is marked by an ongoing dialectical controversy regarding the relative degree of causation attributable to interpersonal and interactional as opposed to individual forces in determining behavior. All interpersonal and systems theorists claim that, at least to some extent, interactions with others and with various social systems direct behavior and shape experience. At the extreme, some of these thinkers have argued that personality and personal individuality are not useful clinical constructs (Haley, 1980, 1987; Minuchin, Montalbo, Guerney, Rosman, & Schamer, 1967; Sullivan, 1950; Watzlawick, Beavin, & Jackson, 1967) and are psychological fictions or illusions.

HARRY STACK SULLIVAN'S INTERPERSONAL THEORY

Harry Stack Sullivan is, in many respects, one of the most mysterious and curious figures in the history of personality theory. His contribution to basic issues in personality is one of major importance, and his contemporaries were in awe not only of his ability as a theorist but also of his perceptiveness and skill as a therapist (Havens, 1983; Kvarnes & Parloff, 1976; Perry, 1982). However, much of his private life and personal history have remained obscured by his own seclusiveness and secrecy (Perry, 1972, 1982). As early as the 1920s, Sullivan was forging a conceptual transition in explaining behavior, from the personality of the individual to interaction among persons. Despite his psychiatric training in medical and psychoanalytic concepts, his theory drew most heavily on formulations from the emerging social sciences. The social science perspective, exemplified by the work of Cooley (1902), Mead (1934), and Sapir (1921), viewed the individual's sense of self as being the product of social interactions and experiences.

Others more extensively trained in a psychoanalytic framework than Sullivan, such as Karen Horney (1937, 1939, 1950) and Erick Fromm (1941, 1962, 1970), were similarly shifting their focus from intrapsychic forces to interpersonal forces. Sullivan, however, most closely anticipated and most directly influenced the conceptual frameworks developed further by systems theorists in the 1970s and 1980s (Hoffman, 1981; Reiss, 1981; Rosenblatt, 1994; Selvini-Palazzoli, Cecchin, Prata, & Boscolo, 1978), which continue to guide clinical research through the present day (Selvini-Palazzoli, Cirillo, Selvini, & Sorrentino, 1989; Stanton, Todd & Associates, 1982). We have chosen to focus on Sullivan's model, therefore, not only because it exemplifies interpersonal theories, but also because it is most directly connected to later systems theories.

PERSONAL INFLUENCES

Sullivan's emphasis on the role of interpersonal experience in the development of personality was related to significant restrictions in his own social background and functioning (Perry, 1982). Sullivan was frank in acknowledging his interpersonal awkwardness and social discomfort. Several early life circumstances contributed to major gaps in Sullivan's knowledge of social conventions and in his acquisition of social skills. He grew up on a relatively isolated family farm in upstate New York with no siblings and with parents who were, for that era, unusually late in child bearing. His mother was thirty-nine years old when he was born and had given birth to two older sons each of whom died well before their first birthdays. Other than contacts with relatives, his parents seemed to be segregated to a considerable degree from the larger, primarily Protestant, community by virtue of their humble social status as Irish-Catholic immigrants of modest financial means. By the time Sullivan entered grade school at the age of five and one-half, his Irish brogue, bookishness, and limited previous contact with other children severely hampered his acceptance by schoolmates and assimilation into the community of other children. Consequently, Sullivan's alienation from others persisted throughout his childhood and adolescence.

Even in adulthood, his discomfort with social situations contributed to an interpersonal distance from others and was exacerbated by his homosexuality (Perry, 1982) in an era when homosexuality was considered a diagnosable psychological disorder. Influenced by the conventional wisdom of his era, Sullivan viewed his own sexual preference as pathological and an impediment to full adaptive functioning and integration into adult society. His low estimation of himself, exacerbated by his negative attitudes about his own sexuality, along with his escape into extensive hours of work contributed to his maintaining a relatively isolated lifestyle.

Yet another personal influence on Sullivan's work, apparently, was his own experience with psychological disturbance. Although not widely known, even among his close colleagues, as a young man he had suffered a schizophrenic breakdown and had been hospitalized (Perry, 1972, 1982). This is particularly significant since Sullivan's early work as a psychotherapist through which he came to prominence was with schizophrenic young men seen in a hospital setting. Apparently his first-hand encounter with and resolution of a schizophrenic breakdown provided him with special insight into these patients, the origins of their problems, and how to help them overcome their difficulties (Kvarnes & Parloff, 1976; Perry, 1982; Sullivan, 1974).

It may seem paradoxical that someone who acknowledged his own considerable interpersonal limitations and difficulties devised a theory that emphasized the crucial role of interpersonal experience and functioning in personality development and adaptation. In fact, there is substantial evidence that it was Sullivan's very awareness of his own deficits in personal and social functioning, and his attribution of these difficulties to his restricted exposure to interpersonal learning experiences during his growing up years, that led him to emphasize the importance of the interpersonal realm in his theory of personality (Perry, 1972, 1982). In his writings, sometimes in disguised and other times in direct fashion, he employed examples from his own life to illustrate how psychological problems originate in and are perpetuated by unfortunate, inhibiting, or restrictive interpersonal experiences.

BASIC CONCEPTS IN SULLIVANIAN INTERPERSONAL THEORY

Interpersonal Conception of Personality

Sullivan's theoretical work represents a perspective that was not only vastly different from the way personality was viewed by most of his contemporaries, but also is at variance with conventional conceptions of personality that continue to dominate current popular culture. When we think of personality, we are in the habit of thinking in terms of the individual person. The biases of thought and perception prevalent in our society lead us to think of people as being self-directed individuals, choosing and being responsible for their own beliefs, attitudes, motivations, actions, and feelings.

Interpersonal theories of personality explicitly contradict these assumptions. They contend, based on several lines of reasoning, that personality is properly understood as an area of study not of individual persons but of *interpersonal situations* (see, e.g., Sullivan, 1930–1931, 1948, 1950). *Personality* from this perspective is defined by Sullivan (1953a) as *"the relatively enduring pattern of recurrent interpersonal situations which characterize a human life"* (pp. 110–111; italics in original). Alternately stated, he conceived of personality as being composed of the consistent ways in which an individual *interacts with other people* over time.

Sullivan proposed that personality (a) develops primarily in response interactions with other people, (b) is only observable as it manifests itself in interpersonal situations (i.e., interpersonal interactions), and (c) can only be effectively understood through observation of and participation in interaction in the interpersonal realm. Humans, Sullivan (1950, 1953a, 1956, 1972) argued, are born human *animals* and only full develop into human *beings* through the assimilation of culture via interpersonal interaction. He emphasized that it is through the acquisition from others of language, customs, traditions, conventions, expectations, viewpoints, and so on, that a human infant develops into, learns to function as, and becomes recognizable as a *person*. Moreover, he contended that even after it is achieved, maintaining "personhood" is dependent upon continued interaction with the social environment in a manner analogous to the dependence of the body on a particular physiochemical environment for biological survival (Sullivan, 1950). He pointed out in this regard the deterioration of uniquely human capacities that occurs even in relatively capable and well-adapted people in response to social isolation. *"A personality,"* Sullivan (1953b, p. 10; italics in original) stated, "can never be isolated from the complex of interpersonal relations in which the person lives and has his being."

From this perspective, idiosyncratic differences in personality are primarily a reflection of the unique set of socialization and acculturation experiences encountered by each individual. Sullivan (1953a) emphasized the many local variations that exist within the larger culture. Each particular family, for example, transmits its own unique set of customs, traditions, and viewpoints to its members. The corresponding diversity in socialization experiences results in a wide range of possible patterns of personality functioning within the same culture.

However, Sullivan (1950, 1953a) seemed to have felt that there was an excessive and unproductive preoccupation on the part of psychiatrists and personality theorists with studying individual differences. He strongly believed that human functioning was most productively understood by studying what individuals have in common rather than idiosyncratic differences among them. This perspective is summed up in what Sullivan (1953a) referred to as his one-genus postulate, that is, that *"everyone is much more simply human than otherwise"* (p. 32, italics in the original).

A related concern of Sullivan's was his conviction that much of personality theory was marked by unscientific conjectures about the private experiences of the individual. To the extent that the study of personality aspired to be scientific, he insisted, it must concern itself with phenomena that are observable. He claimed that the proper realm of study for those wishing to investigate personality was the public realm of interpersonal interactions

(Sullivan, 1953a). Implicit in this viewpoint is the assumption that it is erroneous to believe that one can observe interpersonal interaction in a disengaged way; the interpersonal realm can only be studied, Sullivan asserted, through interaction itself. He referred to this method of investigation as *participant observation.*

The Role of Anxiety in Personality Functioning

In interpersonal theories, socialization, the process by which the human infant develops into a person, is inextricably intertwined with the experience of anxiety. It is primarily in order to avoid the distress associated with the experience of anxiety that the individual is motivated to incorporate and subscribe to the viewpoints, tenets, expectations, and abilities endorsed and transmitted by the larger society, according to Sullivan. Sullivan (1948, 1953a) proposed the existence of a continuum of experience, the hypothetical end points of which are *euphoria*—the absence of anxiety—and *uncanny emotion*—intense pervasive anxiety. He employed the term *uncanny emotion* to indicate that experiences colored by the most extreme forms of anxiety are so overwhelming that they cannot adequately be conveyed in words. This is a crucial observation, he indicated, because a cardinal characteristic of anxiety is that it disrupts concentration and awareness. Consequently, anxiety tends to interfere with clearly identifying the circumstances that provoked it, which in turn impedes effectively relieving anxiety. The more sudden and severe anxiety is, the more likely it is to disrupt the capacity to remove it.

Sullivan believed that anxiety has its origins early in life in the infant's interactions with its primary caretaker, using his term, with the *mothering one.* While acknowledging his inability to adequately account for the mechanisms by which it occurs, he proposed that *"the tension of anxiety, when present in the mothering one, induces anxiety in the infant"* (Sullivan, 1953a, p. 41; italics in the original). He refers to this phenomenon as *empathy.* He grounded this conjecture in the observation that when the primary caretaker is distressed, even when that distress is not directed at the infant, interaction between the mothering one and the infant culminates in observable signs of emotional disturbance and behavioral disorganization in the infant.

Sullivan (1950, 1953a) suggested that disapproval of the infant's behavior by the mothering one comes to be associated with anxiety by the infant. He pointed out that much of the mothering one's behavior in relation to the infant is governed by cultural expectations that have been conveyed to her regarding her social responsibilities to the child (Sullivan, 1953a). She adheres to these expectations due to concern that failure to do so will earn the disapproval of others. In situations in which she anticipates that others may disapprove of her handling of the infant, she is likely to become anxious. Because her anxiety empathically induces anxiety in the infant, the mothering one's concern about being disapproved creates anxiety in the infant. The disruptive effect of anxiety on the infant's functioning makes the mothering one more anxious that she will be criticized about her handling of the baby, which in turn increases the likelihood of her expressing disapproval toward the infant.

In this fashion, during the course of development, anxiety comes to be associated with the disapproval of those (referred to by Sullivan as *significant others*) whose esteem is important to one. Consequently, the process of socialization is fueled by the infant's, and later the child's, desire to avoid the disapproval of significant others in order to be spared the discomfort of anxiety. By adulthood, the anticipation of disapproval by significant others comes to be the more common source of anxiety. Anxiety, therefore, in marked contrast to Freud's formulation, is located in interpersonal relationships rather than intrapsychic conflicts.

The Function of the Self-System

The concept of the self proposed by Sullivan differs in several respects from the conventional, common notion of self and from that found in many other theories of personality. Although in earlier forms of his theory he employed the term *self* (Sullivan 1972), he later replaced this with the term *self-system* (Sullivan, 1953a; 1953b; 1956). The adoption of the term *self-system* more explicitly conveys his notion that the self is not a static entity, structure, or being, but rather an active process, or *dynamism* (Sullivan, 1953a; 1956; 1972). At earlier points in the development of his theory, therefore, the term *self-dynamism* was used by Sullivan (1953b) to refer to the same construct that he subsequently came to call the self-system.

Sullivan's concept of the self, or self-system, contains an inherent paradox. We tend to think of the self as the aspect of personality that most distinctly embodies the *unique* identity of the *individual.* According to Sullivan (1950; 1953a), however, the self, including the sense individuality and uniqueness, is a product of interpersonal experience and social influence. The self-system is constructed out of our perceptions of other people's reactions to us or, to use the term Sullivan (1953b) borrowed from Mead (1934), from *reflected appraisals.* One can think of the term *reflected* as implying that other people function in effect as mirrors that provide us, through their reaction to us, with various images of ourselves. This idea is very closely related to the notion that the human animal becomes a human being as a result of socialization or interaction with others. While it may seem strange at first to consider that the aspect of personality that we think of as being most unique and individualized—our sense of self—is a product of social experience, it becomes clearer when one tries to imagine developing a self-concept and a sense of self in the absence of social interaction. It is difficult to identify a component of what one would consider the self—beliefs, attitudes, goals, perspectives, habits, patterns of behavior—that is not in some fashion learned from or influenced by other people. Moreover, the term *appraisals* indicates that it is what we perceive as others' evaluations or estimations of us, that is, the degree to which they approve or disapprove of us and our behavior, that shapes the self-system, how we view ourselves.

As already discussed, Sullivan proposed that anxiety is elicited primarily by the anticipation of disapproval by significant others. He used the term *security* to refer to the relative absence of anxiety, making it in effect a shorthand term for *interpersonal security,* because it reflects the degree to which one feels free of concern at any given moment that one will encounter disapproval. However, Sullivan (1953a) also stated that "by security I mean one's feeling of self-esteem and personal worth" (p. 267). Probably in order to convey that *interpersonal security* and *self-esteem* refer to the same phenomenon, Sullivan often used the term *prestige* almost interchangeably with these two terms. What we consider most unique, individual, and separate about a person—the self—is for Sullivan (1950, 1953a) not individual but interpersonal in nature. The self-system is shaped by the approval and disapproval of significant others, and its function is to maintain self-esteem by avoiding anxiety.

There are two major strategies through which the self-system avoids the experience of anxiety (Sullivan, 1953a). The first, and more obvious one, is to avoid what one anticipates will elicit the disapproval of significant others and to do what one believes will win their approval. This is the process that mobilizes socialization—the acquisition of values, beliefs, behaviors, roles, and so on, endorsed by the larger society. The second more subtle but strikingly pervasive way in which the self-system avoids anxiety is by not allowing those things that might elicit disapproval to fully register in awareness. In this manner, aspects of personality that would challenge one's view of oneself and thereby threaten one's self-esteem elude recognition. As a result, the self-system is relatively impervious to change.

Sullivan (1953a, 1956) used the term *selective inattention* for the self-system process that most commonly is invoked in controlling awareness. It is very different from Freud's concept of repression (Sullivan, 1956) because selective inattention is a more complex and subtle process than forgetting or blocking material from awareness. It is a matter of directing the focus of concentration. Rather than constituting not knowing, it is a phenomenon of not noticing. Sullivan (1953a, 1956) emphasized that we are actually aware of events that are subjected to selective inattention. However, when something is selectively unattended to, it does not register in focal awareness. As a result, the implications and significance of the event are overlooked. Such paradoxes of simultaneously knowing and not knowing were beginning to be studied in Sullivan's day in the New Look in perception, and are addressed contemporarily by work on implicit cognition (Barone, Maddux, & Snyder, 1977; see Chapters 9–10.) Sullivan (1953a) used the following anecdote about a soda fountain clerk at a drugstore that he frequented to illustrate these features of selective inattention:

> He showed a very rare collection of hostilities to customers, so that whatever you asked for, he would dutifully, when he got around to it, bring you something else. Having suffered from this repeatedly, I was extremely unpleasant on one particular occasion and said, "What is that, huh?" And he said, "Water. Didn't you ask for it?" And I said, *"Get me what I asked for!"* Whereupon the poor bird tottered off under the unpleasantness and got me what I had asked for. But the great joker [sic] is that the next time I saw him he grinned at me and immediately got me what I asked for. (pp. 319–320; italics in the original)

This story nicely depicts the paradoxical quality of selective inattention: When an event is subjected to selective inattention, one is in some sense genuinely not cognizant of it, or at least oblivious to its significance, but is as the same time in a very real sense aware of it. This dual quality of incidents to which selective inattention is applied accounts for the remarkable regularity with which the clerk managed to bring customers the wrong item, apparently without recognizing this to be the case.

In rarer instances an even more extreme and extensive process than selective inattention, *dissociation,* is employed by the self-system to avoid anxiety (Sullivan, 1953a, 1953b; Mullahy, 1953b). In contrast to material that is subjected to selective inattention, incidents that are dissociated *are* excluded from awareness. Items to which selective inattention has been applied can enter focal awareness under certain conditions, for example, when mentioned at an opportune moment by a trusted person whose intentions are perceived as benevolent. Dissociated material, however, is not recognized as part of the self-system even when one is confronted with evidence of its existence. It arouses a much greater level of distress than the anxiety that selectively inattended material elicits, discomfort at the level of uncanny emotion. Dissociated experiences, therefore, are even more unlikely to be acknowledged and reintegrated into the self-system than experiences to which selective inattention has been applied.

Due to the effects of selective inattention and dissociation, the self-perceptions that comprise the self-system are highly resistant to modification (Sullivan, 1948, 1950, 1953a). Having arrived at a perception of oneself that one is convinced will meet with the approval of the significant others in one's life, one clings tenaciously to this self-image in order to avoid anxiety. The sense of uniqueness, individuality, and power invoked by the use of the word *I*, the felt need to protect one's self-esteem, the desire to preserve the prestige and respect one believes one receives from others, all contribute to the determination with which one maintains one's current view of oneself. The self-system in attempting to elude the disapproval of significant others and therefore to avoid the discomfort of anxiety inhibits opportunities to recognize and benefit from observations that would lead to improvement in one's ability to function effectively in interpersonal relations.

For Sullivan (1953a), the self-system's efforts to avoid anxiety constituted a mixed blessing. On one hand, the desire to receive the approval of significant others and avoid their disapproval is the major force that motivates the individual to undergo the intricate learning processes comprising socialization and acculturation. Just how crucial this mechanism is becomes clear when one considers that these processes include the assimilation of language and all the other complex performances required to respond effectively to the appreciable demands of functioning within a particular human society. As with other knowledge structures, such as Piaget's (Piaget & Inhelder, 1969, 1971) *schemas* and Kelly's (1955) *constructs,* another aspect of the self-system's concern with avoiding anxiety is that it can have a significant inhibitory effect on learning. It tends to screen out recognition of data inconsistent with its current understanding and perspective or when assimilating such data to distort it. Sullivan (1953a) invoked this tendency, which he refers to as the *theorem of escape,* to account for the observation that people often persist in the same patterns of behavior despite the fact that they have repeatedly proven to be ineffective, and that efforts to intervene by directly pointing this out to an individual rarely are productive because they are likely to be ignored, discounted, or explained away. Dollard and Miller (1950), George Kelly (1955), and other personality and clinical theorists of the time employed terms such as *the neurotic paradox* and *the impereability of constructs* to refer to this phenomenon.

The Developmental Eras

The strength of the tendency of the self-system to avoid change is considerable but far from absolute. The countervailing tendency of the self-system to develop in response to socializing influences is most powerful with the press of newly matured needs or capacities that signal entry into each new developmental stage or eras (Sullivan, 1953a, 1953b, 1972). Although his names for these eras imply their correspondence to chronological periods (e.g., infancy, childhood, early adolescence), he explicitly pointed out that a particular individual who is chronologically an adult can function primarily at an "earlier" era. Although the preoccupations and patterns of behavior of each era initially arise at the chronologically labeled period, failure to master an era's interpersonal skills significantly hampers advancement to subsequent levels of functioning despite progression in chronological age. Sullivan (1953a) indicated that "arrest in the juvenile era is not by any means an extraordinarily unusual developmental disorder among people in this culture and in these times" (p. 279).

Sullivan's (1953a, 1953b, 1972) detailed account of how the self-system develops from infancy through adolescence is a cornerstone of his theory. It is through the interpersonal influence of significant others that one evolves from human animalhood and acquires the innumerable patterns of behavior that characterize a human being's later development. His description of this process provided many specific examples of how he applied the theoretical constructs discussed thus far to understanding the individual as a product of social interaction indivisible from his or her interpersonal environment.

Although Sullivan (1953a) provided a more intricate description of infancy than any of the subsequent development eras, we will not cover it in detail here because the concepts he introduces in discussing this period are too intricate to adequately explain in this chapter. In infancy, interpersonal interaction is governed by the principle labeled by Sullivan (1953a) the *theorem of tenderness*, which proposes that the manifestation of needs (e.g., to be fed, diapered, and soothed) by the infant elicits *tender cooperative behavior* on the part of the mothering one. Her ministrations constitute the infant's first interpersonal experiences and the foundation for its transformation from human animal to human being. The emergence of the subsequent developmental era, however, represents a momentous shift in the very nature of interpersonal interaction.

The Childhood Era. From childhood onward, social interaction is no longer guided by the interpersonal patterns encompassed by the theorem of tenderness. Sullivan (1953a, 1953b) equated the onset of childhood with the emergence of language. With this growing capacity for communication, the child is more accessible to social influences; a new principle of interpersonal interaction, Sullivan's *theorem of reciprocal emotion*, becomes predominant. This theorem, also termed the *theorem of reciprocal motivation*, states that *"integration in an interpersonal situation is a reciprocal process in which (1) complementary needs are resolved, or aggravated; (2) reciprocal patterns of activity are developed, or disintegrated; and (3) foresight of satisfaction, or rebuff, of similar needs is facilitated"* (Sullivan, 1953a, p. 198; italics in the original). This theorem makes explicit that activities and outcomes in interpersonal encounters are not under the control of any of the participants but rather are a function of the interactive, reciprocal processes between them.

As the child progresses through this era, an increasing degree of active cooperation is expected from him or her—initially by the mothering one, later by other family members, and still later by others outside the family as the circle of social contacts widens—in mastering the numerous prescriptions of the culture in which he or she is growing up. Sullivan (1950, 1953a) emphasized that as a group these cultural prescriptions are extremely complex, are not logically deducible from a single or a few guiding principles, and are often mutually inconsistent or contradictory. Even those prescriptions for which there is a logical basis are inculcated in the child long before he or she has the capacity to fathom the reasoning underlying them.

Since the acquisition of these principles is motivated by the desire to win the approval and avoid the disapproval of significant others, the child learns early on how to conceal transgressions from authority figures and thereby deceive them. Most remarkably, the ability to deceive authority figures is often taught to the child by the authority figures themselves in the form of verbalisms and personae. These are, respectively, statements and self-presentations that are ingenuous but enable one to avoid the disapproval of others and therefore the consequent anxiety (Sullivan, 1953a). A common example of a verbalism is the statement that children are commonly taught to make, "I'm sorry." Children are routinely and explicitly taught to make this statement long before they are capable of grasping its meaning. They do learn, however, that making it at the appropriate time will regularly allow them to avoid the disapproval of authorities.

The Juvenile Era. The transition from childhood to the juvenile era is signaled by the emergence of the need for interaction with peers (Sullivan, 1953a, 1953b, 1972), which coincides approximately with the age at which formal school begins. One of the most important aspects of this era is its potential to act as a corrective for potentially problematic patterns of interpersonal interaction acquired within the family. Indulged children, for example, who do not readily attend to others' needs and wishes and who expect others to cater to them, often learn to adjust these expectations in the company of peers during the juvenile era. Moreover, exposure to peers and the opportunity to "compare notes" with them during this era promote the realization that there are many variations in perspective and prescribed behavior beyond those learned in one's particular family. In this way, the particular rules and viewpoints transmitted in one's family can be more readily recognized and questioned.

Two major patterns of interpersonal interaction pervasive in social dealings in the school years are learned in one's dealing with peers in the juvenile era: competition and compromise. Sullivan (1953a) notes that people whose functioning remains "chronically juvenile" in character tend to approach interpersonal situations by reflexively attempting either to get the advantage of other people or to win their approval.

The Preadolescent Era. Entrance into the preadolescent era is marked by a shift in one's interpersonal orientation away from preoccupation with getting one's own needs met in one's dealing with others to concern with the needs and sense of well being of a particular same-sex peer, the *chum* (Sullivan, 1953a, 1953b, 1972). Sullivan identifies this shift as the first approximation of love, a relationship in which the needs and emotional comfort of another valued person take on more or less equal importance with one's own. An important developmental aspect of the chum relationship is its promoting validation of personal worth in each of its participants through their mutual identification of self-interest and self-evaluation with the interests and valuation of the other. Individuals who enter preadolescence with considerable difficulties but who manage to enter into a chumship can leave this era with a markedly increased capacity for effective interpersonal relating.

The Early Adolescent Era. Sullivan (1953a) defines the early adolescent as beginning with the emergence of the capacity for lust (i.e., genital sexuality) at puberty and culminating in the establishment of a patterning of sexual behavior. With the dawning of the capacity for lust, attention shifts from chumship to members of the opposite sex. Implicit in this assertion is Sullivan's assumption, pervasive in his era, that homosexuality constituted a form of maladjustment. For Sullivan, homosexuality represented a failure to make a developmental progression onward to a heterosexual orientation.

Sullivan (1953a) described in detail the many factors that complicate and form impediments to the early adolescent's efforts to achieve an adequate capacity for emotional intimacy and sexual adjustment with the opposite sex. Prominent among these obstacles he identified are those endemic to American culture, such as the double standard of morality and widespread prohibitions against sexual experimentation among adolescents. These cultural factors compound the inherent complexity of sexual adjustment created by the many ways in which the needs for the satisfaction of lust, of intimacy, and security can "collide" with each other. Achieving a workable pattern of sexual behavior, in other words, requires doing so in a way that simultaneously promotes closeness without arousing appreciable anxiety—a considerable challenge. This challenge is frequently further compounded when early sexual encounters between relatively inexperienced adolescent partners go poorly, increasing their anxiety, lowering their self-esteem, and augmenting the probable development of various patterns of sexual dysfunction.

The Late Adolescent Era. Sullivan (1953a) stated that the culmination of early adolescence and progression into late adolescence occurs when a person arrives at a preferred patterning of genital activity, that is, "when he discovers what he likes in the way of genital behavior and how to fit it into the rest of his life" (p. 297). He refers to the status attained when one has transcended late adolescence as maturity. Although he does not make the point explicitly, his use of the term *maturity* seems to refer to the capacity to function effectively on an adult level as distinguished from the chronological attainment of adulthood. Psychological adjustment is equated with the degree to which one's level of development is consistent with one's age, and developmental level is above all reflected in one's level of interpersonal functioning. Sullivan (1953a) contended, therefore, that "each of the outstanding achievements of the developmental eras that I have discussed will be outstandingly manifest in the mature personality" (p. 310). Among the more conspicuous aspects of maturity noted by him are well-developed capacities for intimate and collaborative relations with others. A hallmark of maturity is sufficient self-esteem and freedom from anxiety to enable attentiveness and responsiveness to the insecurities and divergent perspectives of one's intimate and associates. Moreover, the mature person's comparatively high degree of security allows for interests to be explored and extended relatively unhampered by a concern with maintaining the current status of the self-system to avoid the anxiety that might be aroused by changes in perspective.

SULLIVAN'S INFLUENCE

Sullivan's interpersonal theory represents a dramatic shift away from Freud's intrapsychic model of personality. Our emphasis here has been on the ways in which it constituted a precursor to later systems theories. However, Sullivan's contribution to contemporary psychology is much more extensive and multifaceted. By explicitly delineating processes extending beyond infancy and childhood, he anticipated subsequent extensions of developmental theory to adolescence, adulthood, and aging. His recognition of the influence of relationships outside the family, particularly friendships, on the developing personality of the child prefigured contemporary research in that area (e.g., Youniss, 1980). Moreover, his emphasis on the role of interpersonal as opposed to intrapsychic forces in individual psychotherapy foreshadowed very recent trends in psychoanalytic and psychodynamic theory and practice (see Chapter 2).

FROM INTERPERSONAL TO SYSTEMS THEORY

Sullivan emphasized the interpersonal nature of psychological problems in his theory. However, he continued to rely on individual psychotherapy, the dyadic interaction between therapist and client, as his primary mode of intervention. Several years after his death many of the implications of his interpersonal model for the practice of psychotherapy was more fully explored by what would come to be known as the *family therapy movement.* This group of therapists and theorists, some inspired by Sullivan (Broderick & Schrader, 1991) and others by cybernetics and other systems theories that originated outside of psychology, developed radically new approaches to treatment.

Several founders of the family therapy movement, although not directly influenced by Sullivan, shared with him having had substantial exposure to schizophrenic disorders. Through this experience, they arrived at the conclusion, as had Sullivan, that interpersonal forces play a major role in the development of personality and psychological problems. Carl Whitaker, one of the early and most creative innovators in the field of family therapy, also had been schizophrenic as a young adult (Neill & Kniskern, 1982). Whitaker (1958) and other pioneers in the family therapy movement had in common with Sullivan the experience of working extensively with schizophrenic individuals in a hospital setting. In an attempt to account for their observation that the functioning of some schizophrenics improved markedly while in the hospital only to deteriorate rapidly after discharge (Ruesch & Bateson, 1951), they began meeting with the patients along with their families (see, e.g., Jackson, 1968a, 1968b). They concluded that disordered modes of interaction and communication within the family created and maintained many schizophrenics' difficulties. (This interpersonal formulation of a generation ago has been eclipsed by the position in contemporary psychology that schizophrenia is caused by biochemical rather than social forces [e.g., Gottesman, 1991; Lindenmayer & Kay, 1992; Weiner, 1985].)

Family therapists concur with Sullivan's view that interpersonal contexts play a key role in the formation and functioning of the personality. However, they differ with Sullivan in focusing more on the interactions among people than on the impact of those interactions on the individual. Consequently, they hold a more optimistic view of the human condition (Neill, 1982) than Sullivan's description of human development as a process culminating in personality patterns that are strongly resistant to change. They intervene to transform the family system's existing patterns of interaction rather than the individual's historically determined patterns of behavior. What follows is an overview of the evolution of family and systems theories that centers on how the origins and main assumptions of these models challenge the usefulness of concepts such as personality and individual personhood in explaining behavior in general and mental disorders in particular.

Systemic family therapists focused on the family rather than on the personality of an individual as the unit of analysis and intervention. Mainstream psychological concepts such as personality traits and the entire notion of personality were rejected in some of the early systemic theories. In its place, the interactions among the members of systems were employed as explanatory constructs. Family therapists have employed this level of analysis to account for the existence of patterns of behavior and their resistance to change. In addressing the issue of behavioral stability within the family, systems theory parallels personality theory's attempts to account for continuity in an individual's behavior patterns over time.

GENERAL SYSTEMS THEORY

General systems theory was the result of efforts by biologist Ludwig von Bertalanffy (1968) and sociologist Walter Buckley (1967) to investigate the principles common to all complex entities. It is the transdisciplinary study of how a phenomenon is organized independent of its specific components and location (Heylighen & Joslyn, 1992). Von Bertalanffy and Buckley postulated that an observer could formulate the rules that account for the functioning of interconnected parts. "This thinking represents a fundamental change from focusing on content, material substance, and the distribution of physical energy to considering pattern, process, and communication as being the essential elements of description and explanation" (Guttman, 1991, p. 42).

Systems are open organizations in continuous interaction with their environments. A family can be represented as a system, its parts being the individual members who create a whole by virtue of their interaction. Through the lens of systems theory, a family is viewed as a network of interactions among its members rather than as an aggregation of individual member's characteristics. Von Bertalanffy (1968) contended that the way the parts are organized determines the system's identity, which is independent of the particular characteristics of each part. A system's identity is created by the interaction of its parts rather their individual content.

Systems do not exist in a vacuum. Families, for example, are in constant engagement with larger systems, such as the local community, the educational system, the legal system, and the state (Auerswald, 1968; Imber-Black, 1988; Schwartzman, 1985). Families, like all systems, have boundaries that protect them from being disrupted or destroyed. Boundaries are defined by family rules and determine who is part of a family and who is not. They govern the incoming information and the communications transmitted outside the system. What is known about the family by nonmembers and shared with each member within it, for instance, will be affected by the family's boundary-regulating function.

Systemic theories are critical of approaches to the mind, such as the individual personality theory, that reduce it to an independent entity. Initially, interpersonal theorists emphasized the interactive nature of human behavior. Members of a system were seen as constantly affecting and being affected by each other in a mutual, multidirectional fashion. This point of view automatically called into question the justification for assuming that any particular member's perspective is more accurate or legitimate than any other member's. Bateson (1972) said, "The observer must be included within the focus of observation, and what can be studied is always a relationship or an infinite regress of relationships. . . . Never a 'thing'" (p. 246). Bateson's remark is reminiscent of Sullivan's concept of participant observation.

In the early systemic writings, the observer is still perceived as being able to detect an objective reality existing independent of him or her. In the second wave of systems theory, the observer is conceived of as creating his or her viewpoint via interaction with the observed rather than as a neutral, external, objective witness who takes note of the interactions between others (Bateson, 1979; Maturana & Varela, 1984; von Foerster, 1981). Later developments in systems theory have questioned viewing personality as an independent entity that can be captured in language by an objective observer. Systems theorists argue that language is not a passive representation of an external objective reality. It constitutes, rather, an active creation of socially defined reality. "Reality" from this vantage point is built up through negotiation among people, resulting in the creation of multiple social realities in which people participate (Gergen, 1994).

In contrast to mainstream psychology's view of individuals' personalities as being independent and relatively constant entities, systems thinking views individual behavior as being shaped by the dynamics of the family system. Variations in the person's behavior are seen as a function of the interactional and contextual environment in which the person is positioned. Frequently, the most important life context for persons is the family of origin or their current family situation. In a systemic framework, a person is not seen as a "freestanding" and constant entity; constancy reflects the degree of consistent patterns of interaction within the system (Rosenblatt, 1994). Description of these interactions, as opposed to account of their potential effect on the individual's behavior or identity, predominates in the writings of systemic authors. In a clinical context, a systemic practitioner may prefer to describe a clinical problem, such as an eating disorder, by describing family process and structure and the functional familial aspects of the disorder rather than personality characteristics of the person exhibiting the eating disorder (e.g., Minuchin, Rosman & Baker, 1978).

Systemic theorists contend that human interaction is complex and cyclical, and that individuals attribute diverse meanings to communicational events occurring in their families. Systems theory explains behavior in a cyclical as opposed to a linear, cause-and-effect fashion. People attribute meaning to their behavior and that of others. This attribution of meaning, called *punctuation,* varies depending on the point in the interaction where the person chooses to focus her or his attention. This process highlights the cyclical characteristic of any interactive process. From a systemic perspective, what other theories would consider an individual's "personality" is a reflection of the patterned interaction among family members (Watzlawick, Beavin, & Jackson, 1967) and the punctuation of others (Keeney, 1982; Watzlawick *et al.,* 1967). During a family conflict, for example, each participant in the family (or therapeutic system) will adopt a divergent perspective and thus describe and/or explain the problems differently and act accordingly. The systemic perspective construes these punctuations as being a function of the part the person is playing in the family. This approach also assumes that human beings have the capacity to analyze the context in which interactions occur. Consequently, people have the capacity to *metacommunicate* or make comments about their own communication and punctuation.

FAMILY THERAPY FOUNDERS

Family therapy as a treatment modality and a philosophical viewpoint has relied heavily on systems theory for a conceptual framework. The family therapy movement grew out of mounting frustration among some clinicians with what they perceived as limited effectiveness of individual-oriented psychotherapies. The family context was considered by them to provide a better perspective from which to understand the development of psychological difficulties. This perspective tends to view the personality of the individual as a product of the interactive workings of the family. In this respect, family therapists adopted the idea of circularity as a central guiding construct in assessing and resolving problems that had traditionally been attributed to the workings of personality. Hoffman (1981) wrote:

> If one saw a person with a psychiatric affliction in a clinician's office, it would be easy to assume that he or she suffered from an intrapsychic disorder arising from the past. But if one saw the same person with his or her family, in the context of current relationships, one began to see something quite different. One would see communications and behaviors from everybody present, composing many circular causal loops that played back and forth, with the behavior of the afflicted person only part of a larger, recursive dance. (pp. 6–7)

Circularity in communication was among the fundament concepts derived from observations made in the study of families that had a member diagnosed as schizophrenic. Family therapists came to perceive the disordered behaviors constituting schizophrenia as emerging from dysfunctional patterns of interactions within the family. In contrast to the long-standing focus of the mental health field in the Western world on the inner workings of the individual psyche, the new family therapy field focused on communication as behavior among family members. This conceptual shift has been described as a transition from psyche to system (Neill & Kniskern, 1982).

During the 1950s, several therapists across the United States began working within this framework. The most influential groups were those inspired by the work of mental health professionals such as Nathan Ackerman and Don Jackson and social scientists such as Gregory Bateson (Gurman & Kniskern, 1981, 1991). Ackerman, a child psychiatrist, began to meet with families and educate others about the advantages of seeing the family when there was a child with behavior problems or psychological difficulties. The most influential journal in the field, *Family Process,* grew out of collaboration between Ackerman on the East Coast and in the Midwest and Jackson on the West Coast.

Ackerman and Psychoanalytically Influenced Family Therapy

Ackerman (1970) differentiated psychoanalytic and family therapy treatment without rejecting either, highlighting the pragmatic aspects rather than theoretical implications of the newly emergent family therapy approach. He criticized the biological biases and mechanistic and genetic reductionism of individually oriented psychoanalysis and relocated pathology in interactions between family members rather than the individual. This conceptual change removed conventional individual therapy's isolation of the patient from the family and of the family from the analyst. The psychoanalytic approach, Ackerman wrote, "focuses on the internal manifestations of disorder of the individual personality . . . [while] family treatment focuses on the behavior disorders of a system of interacting personalities, the family group" (p. 7). His stance was consistent with systemic theory's focus on interactional patterns among family members generated by their relationships as opposed to an emphasis on the personality characteristics of each member. He proposed that in their interaction family members not only learn specific values and norms of the system but also *learn how to learn* them. Human beings, then, learn how to learn in the context of interaction, a concept that Bateson (1958, 1972) used prominently and developed further in his early theorizing. The central role of this process parallels the function of socialization as highlighted by Sullivan and other interpersonal theorists (Fromm, 1941; Horney, 1937).

Ackerman (1970) sought to integrate his psychodynamic practice with family therapy; he asserted that a shift toward health in family relationships is not an inevitable product of psychoanalytic treatment. "In fact, it is by no means rare that following psychoanalytic treatment of one family member, there occurs a paradoxical worsening of family relationships" (Ackerman, 1970, p. 8). While behavioral change in one family member could elicit positive changes in other members, it more than creates a context within which they discount the change and subtly coerce the changing individual to return to previous patterns of behavior. A family system creates an identity or organization that is ultimately beyond the control of the particular individuals, even though they may have helped create or modify the system to which they belong. Ackerman wrote that if therapeutic gains were to stabilize, the whole family system would have to modify its ways of behaving, thinking, and feeling about a problematic situation.

Although the unit of analysis changed from the individual to the family, mental thinking about cure and psychopathology did not change dramatically except that now there might be more than one individual in the therapy room. Ackerman and other *transgenerational family therapists* (Boszormenyi-Nagy & Spark, 1973; Bowen, 1978; Framo, 1976;

Whitaker, 1958) have emphasized the evolving nature of family systems, and how family organizations transcend the therapeutic focus on the present interaction. If systems are constituted and maintained through time, pathology is "contagiously passed down from one generation to the next" (Ackerman, 1970, p. 8). Pathology is transmitted across generations via the system's enduring influence over its members' patterns of behavior. For this reason, Ackerman and other transgenerational family therapists suggested that clinicians be alert to the movement of a "pathogenic conflict" or disorder across three generations.

Ackerman started to use systemic ideas while retaining psychodynamic concepts in his model of treatment. For instance, he wrote about the mechanism of defense, a psychoanalytical concept that originated in individual psychotherapy. However, Ackerman introduced the idea of defense as operating the level of the system to explain how families protect themselves from the anxieties arising from conflict. He believed that defenses emerging from the inner psyche of an individual interrelate with those generated in the family context. Family defenses are a shared form of avoiding conflict, a diversion from the group task of facing anxiety. If the defenses break down, the essential family functions become progressively and selectively disabled. Within this framework, families develop selective ways of confronting their developmental tasks and conflicts that may include the deployment of defenses. If those defenses are not available, the conflict can erupt, destroying the overall family organization. A family member in individual therapy would not be able to override the family system's defenses; the individual's identity is so intimately tied to the family's organization that he or she could not maintain individual gains.

For example, a misbehaving child could be seen from a systemic viewpoint as fulfilling a need on the part of the family to project "badness'" or "rebelliousness" onto a particular member so that the rest of the system can disown those qualities. Evidence of improvements in the individual child's behavior would tend to raise anxiety in the family system and therefore be ignored. Instead of recognizing and acknowledging positive changes, the family would continue to search for opportunities to perceive and label the child's behavior as negative. If this strategy failed, another member of the family would be assigned the role of the "scapegoat" or "black sheep."

Ackerman (1970) formulated a series of therapeutic guidelines that highlighted the use of the therapist's self as a fundamental clinical tool. His explicit use of the concept of the therapist's self links interactional-system theories with the interpersonal model postulated by Sullivan. Acknowledging the existence of the therapist's self implies a recognition of the individual personality as a single entity, even in the context of a systemic framework. In Ackerman's perspective, a therapist utilizes his or her own self to foster healthier relationships among family members. The therapist "mobilizes those forms of interaction that maximize the opportunity for undoing distorted percepts of self and others, for dissolving confusion, and clarifying the view of the salient conflicts" (Ackerman, 1970, p. 12). The therapist "injects into the family something new, the *right* emotions and the *right* perceptions in place of the wrong ones. Crucial to the entire effort is the breaking down of anxiety-ridden taboos against the sharing of vital family problems" (Ackerman, 1970, p. 12). Ackerman (1981) advocated that the therapist inject into the family more honest, meaningful, and genuine kinds of interactions, both verbal and nonverbal. These "right" feelings and analytical observations would give the family a new way of releasing some of its emotions in a safe context via "selective gratification of valid emotional needs" (Ackerman, 1981, p. 17), conflict resolution, and expanding the repertoire of interpersonal abilities.

Ackerman considered psychoanalytic treatment a more specialized approach because of its "unique access to disturbances which have their source in the unconscious mental life" (1970, p. 14). Family therapy, in contrast, approaches conflict by considering it in the broader context of multiple and embedded relationships. In delineating psychological problems and treatment, Ackerman breached the self-referential features of psychoanalytic dogma by adding (as did Sullivan) interpersonal events—the conscious organization of experience, reality, the present, and the group—to the explanatory concepts of intrapsychic dynamics, unconscious forces, fantasy, the past, and the personality of the individual. Family therapy provides strategies for assessment and treatment of "interacting personalities."

Traditional psychoanalysis has dealt with the patient as an isolated, individual personality. The psychotherapist working in this tradition believes that healthy readaptation occurs as a consequence of transforming the inner workings of the individual personality. The family therapist emphasizes moving from the outside inward, changing the context in which interactions occur and expecting that changing those interactions will elicit changes in the individual's patterns of behavior. The psychoanalytically oriented therapist focuses on moving from the inside outward: the therapeutic change in the inner dynamics of the personality are expected to impact favorably on the individual's interpersonal relationships.

Jackson, Bateson, and the Palo Alto Group

Jackson (1970), the founder of the interactional school of family therapy, believed that "individual personality, character, and deviance are shaped by the individual's relations with his fellows" (p. 111). From a vantage point similar to Ackerman's, Jackson wrote:

> Symptoms, defenses, character structure and personality can be seen as terms describing the individual's typical interactions which occur in response to a particular interpersonal context. Since the family is the most influential learning context, surely a more detailed study of family process would yield valuable clues to the etiology of such typical modes of interaction. (p. 112; italics added)

Jackson, a psychoanalyst by training who was supervised by Sullivan for three years, redefined in communicational terms the notion of "ego function" as the "capacity to discriminate communicational modes" (Sluzki & Ramson, 1977, p. 45). For instance, in the case of a person diagnosed as schizophrenic, the capacity to interpret internal and external messages is weakened. The person's symptoms are "learned in the same way that people with more ordinary habits appropriately learned theirs, accommodating to the interactional demands of family life" (Sluzki & Ramson, 1977, p. 46). Therefore, the unit of diagnosis must include the interpersonal environment in which the identified patient lives and cannot be limited to a particular behavior. To accurately evaluate a particular behavior, Jackson, argued, as did Sullivan and Ackerman, that one must take into consideration the interpersonal milieu in which it occurs. Jackson's (1968b) writings about family homeostatis, the tendency to find equilibrium through maintenance of the status quo, described the capacity of systems to maintain stability even if their members attempt changes. Families may attempt to maintain a balance by resisting change or countering changes with dramatic shifts, thus preventing the evolution of a more adaptive or creative pattern. A family therapist could detect a particular family dysfunction and aim to catalyze change at the level of the system while taking into account the context in which it exists. A classical example is the one in which a young adult develops schizophrenic symptoms at the time of departing from home to lead an independent life. From a systems perspective, the schizophrenic symptoms emerge in order to maintain stability in the family. This conjecture is supported by the observation that the parents who have been in conflict and on the verge of separating routinely come together to help the "ill" offspring. When their child starts to recuperate, the parents threaten to separate, and the cycle starts all over again, unless there is an intervention that highlights the developmental context in which the "symptoms" appear.

Gregory Bateson, an anthropologist, was a communication researcher with whom Jackson began to collaborate in 1954 (Bateson, Jackson, Haley, & Weakland, 1976). From 1952 to 1962, the Bateson communication project contributed to a new understanding of schizophrenia, which made a lasting impact on the emerging family therapy field. Bateson (1958) in his book, *Naven,* explored the perpetuation of a culture, a concept analogous to the continuity of personality over time or a family's continuing organizational stability. Bateson was also interested in how logical classes and paradoxes operate in interpersonal communication. For instance, the sentence "I am lying" provides serious difficulties in interpretation if no other frames are offered from which to evaluate its "truthfulness." As Haley (1976) explained, "a particular center of controversy was whether the question of truth and untruth, so dear to the logician's heart, was relevant to the analysis of human communication" (p. 61). The metacommunicative difficulties of discussing "crazy" communications like "I am lying" were compared to the difficulty schizophrenics might have in dealing with others while maintaining schizophrenic behaviors.

Jackson studied schizophrenia as a communication pattern rather than as an intrapsychic characteristic. Jackson founded the Mental Research Institute in Palo Alto, California, collaborating with several others who became pioneers in the family therapy movement, including Bateson, Jay Haley, Virginia Satir, and John Weakland (Sluzki & Ramsey, 1976). Jackson was recruited by Bateson, Haley, and Weakland as a clinical consultant on the basis of his experience working with schizophrenic clients. Although Bateson was always associated with the Mental Research Institute, he maintained his independence because of the clinical emphasis the Mental Research Institute had from the beginning. Jackson's interest in the interpersonal aspects of schizophrenia contributed to the formulation of an interactive theory to explain the maintenance of schizophrenic behaviors.

The primary explanatory hypothesis that the Palo Alto group developed was the *double bind* construct. The *double bind,* a term coined by Bateson in 1954 before it was tested, is a hypothesis about what could have happened in the family life of the schizophrenic to account for his or her confusion about the meaning of family communications. It posits that this confusion emerges in an emotionally significant relationship from recurrent experiences in which the receiver of the message has been (a) exposed to two contradictory messages about the same behavior, (b) cannot leave the situation, and (c) is prevented from commenting about it. For example, the patient may repeatedly be told to be quiet about a family secret, not to lie when outsiders ask about the family, and not to comment on the contradictory nature of the message, while being forced to remain in the situation. In sum, whatever the client does will be seen as faulty and deviant. The concept of double bind came to be used to analyze many forms of communicational pathologies and difficulties besides schizophrenia (Jackson, 1968a, 1968b; Watzlawick, Beavin, & Jackson, 1967).

Bateson's work in conjunction with that of the Mental Research Institute redefined schizophrenia as being comprised of patterns of interactions within families as opposed to an illness of an individual person. Schizophrenia was conceptualized by them as "an attempt to cope with ongoing family communication characterized by recurring double binds" (Segal, 1991, p. 172). Although the Bateson's group emphasized the interactive aspect of human communication, they also wrote about the "ego function" as the "process of discriminating communicational modes either within the self or between the self and others" (Bateson *et al.,* 1976, p. 44). Constant exposure to double bind communication would prevent a person from accurately assigning the correct communicational mode to messages received from other persons and to the inner workings of the shelf.

Bateson, Jackson, Haley, & Weakland (1976) emphasized the idea of communicational context as a guide to discriminating normal from abnormal. This concept permeated the discussion of systemic therapists for decades following their seminal work. In 1962, at the end of the research project, they were cautious about the capacity of the double bind hypothesis to explain schizophrenia: "The double bind is a necessary but not sufficient condition in explaining etiology" (Bateson *et al.,* 1975, p. 42). However, their emphasis on relational context rather than on the perception and affective states of the individual has been lasting. It was a ground breaking study in its understanding of how human behavior is interactionally created and maintained.

CONCLUSION: FROM SYSTEMS THEORY TO SOCIAL CONSTRUCTIONISM

Interpersonal and systemic approaches constituted critical reactions to the modern Western notion of personality as a stable structure that can be discovered, isolated, described, and analyzed through psychological evaluation or treatment. The contemporary notion that the self can be objectively investigated is the culmination of a very long and complicated historical process (Foucault, 1979). Interpersonal theorists and systemic family therapists reacted against the assumption of the existence of a unified personality that controls and directs behavior. They anticipated the *postmodern* sensibility that views the self as continually changing in response to constantly shifting relational contexts. These postmodern perspectives view the self as being redefined through a continuous revision of the story about who we are, where we come from, and how we experience other people. These viewpoints, referred to as constructivist theories, challenge to some degree the possibility of having access to an objective reality that exists independently of the observer. Constructivists are more interested in the practical utility of personal constructions than in identifying an objective reality "out there" (von Glaserfeld, 1987). This position was influenced by family therapy research—in part due to its use of the one-way mirror to observe families and clinicians interacting during therapy sessions. This procedure helped teams of observers to "step outside" of these interactions and identify processes at the systemic level, promoting the development of a stance that stressed the necessity of external observers in order to capture accurately the relationship between the system and its context.

Constructive perspectives have evolved into diverse branches that include cognitive constructivist and social constructionist theories. These theories have emphasized the observer as creator of the reality he or she is investigating (Bateson, 1979; Maturana & Varela, 1984; von Foerster, 1981). One form of constructivism emphasized developmental processes of the individual and intersects with Kegan's (1982; Rogers & Kegan, 1991) self-object relations theory and Piaget's (1970) cognitive developmental theory. From their perspective, at different stages in people's development, they evolve new cognitive structures that redirect their mode of interaction with the context in which they live. Knowledge structures are transformed as part of the interaction between the individual and the environment, and as more complex forms of observation are developed. As a result, the person continues to construct "more epistemologically powerful (i.e., inclusive, viable or integrated) ways of making sense out of the world" (Lyddon, 1995, p. 79).

The origins of several family therapy developments have been linked to the ideas of the so-called radical constructivists. Included are some of the family therapy founders, such as Watzlawick (1990), who pose the idea that "no reality extends beyond the individual's experience" (Rosen, 1996, p. 6). Family therapists influenced by this approach have concluded that no independent objective family system exists. Any given family is not an objective entity but a construct whose membership, rules, and other dimensions of identity, organization, and functioning will be viewed divergently by various individuals and clinicians. This position differs from other constructivists (e.g., Kelly, 1955; Mahoney, 1991) who acknowledge the existence of a world and "how we arrive at that knowledge" (Rosen, 1996, p. 11). Constructivists in the family therapy field assume that "to understand any realm of phenomena, we should begin by noting how it was constructed, that is, what distinctions underlie its creation" (Keeney, 1982, p. 21). For instance, Jorgenson (1991) found that families in an interview with a researcher "fashion an identity for the interviewer" (p. 210). At the same time that the therapist develops notions about the family that affect their response to him or her, the family is creating a view of the therapist that similarly shapes his or her behavior and, therefore, their ongoing relationship.

Social constructionists focus on the processes by which people come to describe, explain, or otherwise account for the world (including themselves). This theoretical approach attempts to clarify how people understand the past, present, and future in the context of history and their life circumstances (Gergen, 1985); that is, they focus on people's stories about others and themselves. Therefore, in this framework, our personalities, frequently conceptualized as socially defined *identities*, emerge through a process similar to the one authors engage in when they produce a written text. For social constructionists, knowledge is actively built up by interacting communities rather than passively encountered and observed by isolated individual persons. These ideas bring forth a salient distinction between cognitive constructivists and social constructionists. For social constructionists, assumptions about the nature of being (ontology) and the nature of knowledge (epistemology) are construed in the relationship among individuals, not in the structure of the mind or the "reality" of the world.

The social constructionist turn emphasizes the *storied* nature of human beings (Sarbin, 1986). Our lives are permeated by the process of meaning making through language and by our engagement with others in a continuous process of "storying" the world and ourselves. Story making has pragmatic implications since it is in conversations that we coordinate actions and collectively create and manage social realities (Pearce & Cronen, 1980). These ideas have been particularly useful in reformulating therapeutic practices and escaping from the deterministic metaphors employed by the early systemic theorists. Soon after pioneers established the field of family therapy, systemic family writers rejected the notions of personality, the person, and individuality as the product of the inner workings of the psyche in interaction with its environment. Personality traits were construed as one element of the interactive process that shaped families. Today, the social constructionist framework has moved some authors (Combs & Freedman, 1996; Friedman, 1995; Martin, 1994; Rosen & Kuehlwein, 1996) to reaffirm the value of the concept of personhood and the constitution of selves by grouping them in the context of relationships.

In the 1990s, family therapists have been adopting ideas that emphasize how selves are constructed through discourse. This emphasis can be traced back to early efforts, such as those of Sullivan and systemic theorists, at conceptualizing the observed and the observer as components of an interactive process. From a social constructionist perspective, then, the person can encompass many "I," "you," "he," or "she" positions rather than being equated with a unitary stable position, an approach consistent with the focus on context and interaction in the family systems models. To summarize, the incorporation of interpersonal, systemic, and constructionist sensibilities in a study of personality highlights the view that personality is a construct that we continuously negotiate and redefine. Paraphrasing postmodern authors, this perspective has *decentered* the primacy of the individual self and recognized its existence within the context of evolving stories.

REFERENCES

Ackerman, N. J. (1970). Family psychotherapy and psychoanalysis—Implications of difference. In N. J. Ackerman (Ed.), *Family process* (pp. 5–18). New York: Basic Books.

Ackerman, N. J. (1981). The functions of the family therapist. In R. J. Green & J. L. Framo (Eds.), *Family therapy: Major contributions* (pp. 317–342). Madison, CT: International Universities Press.

Auerswald, E. H. (1968). Interdisciplinary versus ecological approach. *Family Process, 7,* 202–215.

Barone, D. F., Maddux, J. E., & Snyder, C. R. (1997). *Social cognitive psychology: History and current domains.* New York: Plenum Press.

Bateson, G. (1958). *Naven: A survey of the problems suggested by a composite picture of the culture of a New Guinea tribe drawn from three points of view.* Stanford, CA: Stanford University Press.

Bateson, G. (1972). *Steps to an ecology of mind.* New York: Ballantine Books.

Bateson, G. (1979). *Mind and nature: A necessary unit.* New York, Dutton.

Bateson, G., Jackson, D. D., Haley, J., & Weakland, J. (1956). Toward a theory of schizophrenia. *Behavioral Science, 1,* 251–264.

Bateson, G., Jackson, D. D., Haley, J., & Weakland, J. (1976). A note on the double bind (1962). In C. Sluzki, & D. Ramsey (Eds.), *Double bind: The foundation of the communicational approach to the family* (pp. 39–42). New York: Grune & Stratton.

Bertalanffy, L. von. (1988). *General systems theory.* New York: Braziller.

Boszormenyi-Nagy, I., & Spark, G. M. (1973). *Invisible loyalties: Reciprocity in intergenerational family therapy.* Hagerstown, MD: Harper & Row.

Bowen, M. (1978). *Family therapy in clinical practice.* New York: Jason Aronson.

Broderick, C. G., & Schrader, S. S. (1991). The history of professional marriage and family therapy. In A. S. Gurman & D. P. Kniskern (Eds.), *Handbook of family therapy* (Vol. 2, pp. 3–40). New York: Brunner/Mazel.

Buckley, W. (1967). *Sociology and modern systems theory.* Englewood Cliffs, NJ: Prentice-Hall.

Combs, G., & Freedman, J. (1996). *Narrative therapy: The social construction of preferred realities.* New York: Norton.

Cooley, C. H. (1902). *Human nature and the social order.* New York: Scribners.

Dollard, J., & Miller, N. E. (1950). *Personality and psychotherapy: An analysis in terms of learning, thinking, and culture.* New York: McGraw-Hill.

Foerster, H. von. (1981). *Observing systems.* Seaside, CA: Intersystems Publications.

Foucault, M. (1979). *Discipline and punish: The birth of the prison.* New York: Vintage.

Framo, J. (1976). Family of origin as a therapeutic resource for adults in marital and family therapy: You can and should go home again. *Family Process, 15,* 193–210.

Friedman, S. (Ed.). (1955). *The reflecting team in action: Collaborative practice in family therapy.* New York: Guilford Press.

Fromm, E. (1941). *Escape from freedom.* New York: Avon Books.

Fromm, E. (1962). *Sigmund Freud's mission: An analysis of his personality and influence.* New York: Simon & Schuster.

Fromm E. (1970). *The crisis of psychoanalysis.* New York: Simon & Schuster.

Gergen, K. (1985). The social constructionist movement in modern psychology. *American Psychologist 40,* 266–275.

Gergen, K. (1994). *Realities and relationships: Soundings in social construction.* Cambridge, MA: Harvard University Press.

Glaserfeld, E. von. (1987). *The construction of knowledge: Contributions of conceptual semantics.* Seaside, CA: Intersystems Publications.

Gottesman, I. I. (1991). *Schizophrenia genesis: The origins of madness.* New York: W. H. Freeman.

Gurman, A., & Kniskern, D. (Eds.). (1981). *Handbook of family therapy* (Vol. 1). New York: Brunner/Mazel.

Gurman, A., & Kniskern, D. (Eds.). (1991). *Handbook of family therapy* (Vol. 2). New York: Brunner/Mazel.

Guttman, H. A. (1991). Systems theory, cybernetics, and epistemology. In A. Gurman & D. Kniskern (Eds.), *Handbook of Family Therapy* (Vol. 2, pp. 41–64). New York: Brunner/Mazel.

Haley, J. (1976). Development of a theory: A history of a research project. In C. Sluzki & D. Ramsey (Eds.), *Double bind: The foundation of the communicational approach to the family* (pp. 59–104). New York: Grune & Stratton.

Haley, J. (1980). *Leaving home: The therapy of disturbed young people.* New York: McGraw-Hill.

Haley, J. (1987). *Problem solving therapy* (2nd ed.). San Francisco: Jossey-Bass.

Havens, L. (Ed.). (1983). *Participant observation: The psychotherapy schools in action.* Northvale, NJ: Jason Aronson.

Heylighten, F., & Joslyn, C. (1992, November 1). What are cybernetics and systems science? *Principia Cybernetica Web* [On-line].http://pesprhc1.vib.acbe/:/webSTRVET.html.

Hoffman, L. (1981). *Foundations of family therapy.* New York: Basic Books.

Horney, K. (1937). *The neurotic personality of our time.* New York: Norton.

Horney, K. (1939). *New ways in psychoanalysis,* New York: Norton.

Horney, K. (1950). *Neurosis and human growth.* New York: Norton.

Imber-Black, E. (1988). *Families and larger systems: A family therapist's guide through the labyrinth.* New York: Guilford Press.

Jackson, D. D. (Ed.). (1968a). *Communication, family, and marriage* (Vol. 1). Palo Alto, CA: Science and Behavior Books.

Jackson, D. D. (Ed.). (1968b). *Communication, family, and marriage* (Vol. 2). Palo Alto, CA: Science and Behavior Books.

Jackson, D. D. (1970). The study of the family. In N. J. Ackerman (Ed.), *Family process* (pp. 111–130). New York: Basic Books.

Jorgenson, J. (1991). Co-constructing the interviewer/co-constructing "family." In F. Steier (Ed.), *Research and reflexivity* (pp. 210–225). Newbury Park, CA: Sage.

Keeney, B. (1982). *Aesthetic of change.* New York: Guilford Press.

Kegan, R. (1982). *The evolving self.* Cambridge, MA: Harvard University Press.

Kelly, G. A. (1955). *The psychology of personal constructs* (Vols. 1–2). New York: Norton.

Kvarnes, R. G., & Parloff, G. H. (Eds.). (1976). *A Harry Stack Sullivan case seminar: Treatment of a young male schizophrenic.* New York: Norton.

Lindenmayer, J. P., & Kay, S. R. (Eds.). (1992). *New biological vistas on schizophrenia.* New York: Brunner/Mazel.

Lyddon, W. J. (1995). Forms and facets of constructivist psychology. In R. Neimeyer & M. J. Mahoney (Eds.), *Constructivism in psychotherapy* (pp. 69–92). Washington, DC: American Psychological Association.

Mahoney, M. J. (1991). *Human change processes: The scientific foundations of psychotherapy.* New York: Basic Books.

Martin, J. (1994). *The construction and understanding of psychotherapeutic change: Conversations, memories, and theories.* New York: Teachers College Press.

Maturana, H., & Varela, F. (1984). *El arbol del conocimiento* [The tree of knowledge: The biological roots of human understanding]. Santiago, Chile: Editorial Universitaria.

Mead, G. H. (1934). *Mind, self, and society.* Chicago: University of Chicago Press.

Minuchin, S., Montalbo, B., Guerney, B., Rosman, B., & Schamer, F. (1967). *Families of the slums.* New York: Basic Books.

Minuchin, S., Rosman, B., & Baker, L. (1978). *Psychosomatic families: Anorexia nervosa in context.* Cambridge: Harvard University Press.

Mullahy, P. (1953b). A theory of interpersonal relations and the evolution of personality. In H. S. Sullivan (Ed.), *Conceptions of Modern Psychiatry* (pp. 239–294). New York: Norton.

Neill, J. (1982). Biographical introduction to the work of Carl Whitaker. In J. Neill & D. Kniskern (Eds.), *From psyche to system: The evolving therapy of Carl Whitaker* (pp. 1–20). New York: Guilford Press.

Neill, J., & Kniskern, D. (Eds.). (1982). *From psyche to system: The evolving therapy of Carl Whitaker.* New York: Guilford Press.

Pearce, B., & Cronen, V. (1980). *Communication, action and meaning: The creation of social realities.* New York: Praeger.

Perry, H. S. (1972). Introduction to H. S. Sullivan, *Personal psychopathology* (pp. ix–xxiii) New York: Norton.

Perry, H. S. (1982). *Psychiatrist of America: The life of Harry Stack Sullivan.* Cambridge, MA: Belknap Press.

Piaget, J., & Inhelder, B. (1971). *Mental imagery in the child.* New York: Basic Books.

Reiss, D. (1981). *The family construction of reality.* Cambridge, MA: Harvard University Press.

Rogers, L., & Kegan, R. (1991). Mental growth and mental health as distinct concepts in the study of developmental psychology: Theory, research, and clinical implications. In D. P. Keating & H. Rosen (Eds.), *Constructivist perspectives on developmental psychopathology and atypical development* (pp. 103–147). Hillsdale, NJ: Erlbaum.

Rosen H. (1996). Meaning-making narratives: Foundations for constructivist and social constructionist psychotherapies. In H. Rosen & K. T. Kuehlwein (Eds.), *Constructing realities: Meaning-making perspectives for psychotherapists* (pp. 3–51). New York: Jossey-Bass.

Rosen, H., & Kuehlwein, K. T. (Eds.). (1996). *Constructing realities: Meaning-making perspectives for psychotherapists.* New York: Jossey-Bass.

Rosenblatt, P. C. (1994). *Metaphors of family systems theory.* New York: Guilford Press.

Ruesch, J., & Bateson, G. (1951). *Communication: The social matrix of psychiatry.* New York: Norton.

Sapir, E. (1921). *Language, an introduction to the study of speech.* New York: Harcourt, Brace.

Sarbin, T. R. (Ed.). (1986). *Narrative psychology: The storied nature of human conduct.* New York: Praeger.

Schwartzman, J. (Ed.). (1985). *Families and other systems: The macrosystemic context of family therapy.* New York: Guilford Press.

Segal, L. (1991). Brief therapy: The MRI approach. In A. Gurman & D. Kniskern (Eds.), *Handbook of Family Therapy* (Vol. 2). (pp. 171–199). New York: Brunner/Mazel.

Selvini-Palazzoli, M., Cecchin, G., Prata, G., & Boscolo, L. (1978). *Paradox and counterparadox.* New York: Jason Aronson.

Selvini-Palazzoli, M., Cirillo, S., Selvini, M., & Sorrentino, A. M. (1989). *Family games: General models of psychotic processes in the family.* New York: Norton.

Skinner, B. F. (1957). *Verbal behavior.* New York: Appleton-Century-Crofts.

Skinner, B. F. (1971). *Beyond freedom and dignity.* New York: Knopf.

Sluzki, C., & Ramsey, D. (Eds.). (1976). *Double bind: The foundation of the communicational approach to the family.* New York: Grune & Stratton.

Stanton, M. D., Todd, T. C., & Associates. (1982). *The family therapy of drug abuse and addiction.* New York: Guilford Press.

Sullivan, H. S. (1930–1931). Socio-psychiatric research: Its implications for the schizophrenia problem and for mental hygiene. *American Journal of Psychiatry, 87,* 977–991.

Sullivan, H. S. (1931). Environmental factors in etiology and course under treatment of schizophrenia. *Medical Journal and Record, 133,* 19–22.

Sullivan, H. S. (1948). The meaning of anxiety in psychiatry and life. *Psychiatry, 48,* 1–13.

Sullivan, H. S. (1950). The illusion of personal individuality. *Psychiatry, 13,* 317–332.

Sullivan, H. S. (1953a). *The interpersonal theory of psychiatry.* New York: Norton.

Sullivan, H. S. (1953b). *Conceptions of modern psychiatry.* New York: Norton.

Sullivan, H. S. (1956). *Clinical studies in psychiatry.* New York: Norton.

Sullivan, H. S. (1972). *Personal psychopathology.* New York: Norton.

Sullivan, H. S. (1974). *Schizophrenia as a human process.* New York: Norton.

Watzlawick, P. (1990). *Munchausen's pigtail or psychotherapy and "reality."* New York: Norton.

Watzlawick, P., Beavin, J., & Jackson, D. D. (1967). *Pragmatics of human communication.* New York: Norton.

Weiner, H. (1985). Schizophrenia: Etiology. In H. Kaplan & B. Sadock (Eds.), *Comprehensive textbook on psychiatry* (pp. 650–680). Baltimore: Williams & Wilkins. New York: Norton.

Whitaker, C. (Ed.). (1958). *Psychotherapy of chronic schizophrenic patients.* Boston: Little Brown.

Youniss, J. (1980). *Parents and peers in social development.* Chicago: University of Chicago Press.

CHAPTER 4

HUMANISTIC AND EXPERIENTIAL THEORIES OF PERSONALITY

JEANNE C. WATSON AND LESLIE S. GREENBERG

INTRODUCTION

Personality has been defined as the state of being a person, possessing traits or character. Alternatively, it is said to refer to the physiological, intellectual, emotional, and physical characteristics of the individual, especially those that are seen by others. Humanistic theories of personality include person-centered gestalt, and existential approaches. While each of these schools of thought is quite distinctive in many ways, there are a number of fundamental epistemological and ontological assumptions that they share that characterize them as humanistic. These are first (a) the emphasis on subjectivity and (b) the emphasis on people as self-reflective agents (Heidegger, 1962; Jaspers, 1963; Perls, 1973; Polster & Polster, 1973; Rice & Greenberg, 1992; Rogers, 1965; Schneider & May, 1995; Taylor, 1975; Tiryakian, 1962).

The emphasis on subjectivity refers to the validity of people's phenomenological reality as well as to the importance of feelings and moods in apprehending reality. According to

JEANNE C. WATSON • Department of Applied Psychology, The Ontario Institute for Studies in Education, Toronto, Ontario, M5S 1V6, Canada   LESLIE S. GREENBERG • Department of Psychology, York University North, York, Ontario M3J 1P3, Canada.

Advanced Personality, edited by David F. Barone, Michel Hersen, and Vincent B. Van Hasselt. Plenum Press, New York, 1998.

Charles Taylor (1975), people are beings who are capable of symbolizing their experiences and for whom things matter and have significance. The importance of things or their significance is revealed by their feelings and desires. It is through their feelings that people come to understand the impact of their experiences, gain an understanding of how they need to act in response to that impact, and communicate with others (Greenberg, Rice, & Elliott, 1993; Rogers, 1959; Taylor, 1975; Watson & Greenberg, 1996).

The emphasis on people as self-reflective agents refers to people's capacity for choice and self-determination, as well as their ability to represent experience symbolically and to reflect on and evaluate that experience in terms of higher order values and goals (Fagan, 1974; May & Yalom, 1989; Perls, 1973; Taylor, 1975; Tiryakian, 1962). From this perspective, there is a dynamic interaction between language or other forms of symbolic expression and feelings such that as each is formed it influences the other in an ongoing spiral (Gendlin, 1981; Taylor, 1975; Watson & Greenberg, 1996). Moreover, there are two ways of evaluating experience: (a) in accord with one's immediate needs and desires and (b) in accord with another framework that has the capacity to override more immediate concerns and assess them in terms of higher order values (Taylor, 1975).

Humanistic personality theories emphasize that dysfunction occurs when people lose touch with their innermost feelings, desires, goals, and values. The objective of these therapeutic approaches is to restore people's access to disowned or isolated aspects of themselves, which enables them to make more authentic, honest, and satisfying choices for living. Under the rubric of humanistic theories, we will cover person-centered, Gestalt, and existential approaches and then show how different ideas from these three streams of thought converge in experiential theory and practice. We will present person-centered theory first, followed by gestalt and existential theories. Subsequently, we will explicate an experiential theory of personality. In doing so, we will examine each theory's model of personality development, its structural components, characteristics of healthy functioning, and sources of dysfunction.

PERSON-CENTERED THEORY

Initially, Carl Rogers was not concerned about developing a theory of personality. He was focused more on how clients change in therapy and on isolating those factors and variables that make change possible (Meador & Rogers, 1979; Raskin & Rogers, 1989; Rogers, 1959; 1961). As a result of his work with clients who were struggling with painful aspects of their experiences, Rogers suggested that behavior could best be understood in terms of how people perceive reality. People's perceptions of the world and the people with whom they come into contact have considerable influence on how they will respond. If I perceive my infant's crying as naughty and demanding, my response is likely to be very different from the way I would respond if I perceive the infant as crying from pain or hunger. Each person's view of reality is highly subjective, informed by one's own perceptions, and past and present experiences. In therapy, Rogers struggled not only to understand and access the inner worldview of the other, but also to communicate implicitly to clients that the possibility of change lay in the very subjectivity of their perceptions, thereby suggesting the possibility of multiple views of the same phenomenon.

While Rogers emphasized that the person is the primary source of experiencing, he recognized that the individual exists in a social and physical environment to which he or she must continually respond and adapt. A basic assumption of person-centered theory is that organisms respond as organized wholes to the demands of their environments. The primary objective of the organism is to actualize, maintain, and enhance itself. According to this view, people are forward looking, motivated by future concerns and anticipations as well as by current needs and desires. Their behavior and actions are attempts to meet current needs as they experience them in the environment as they perceive it (Rogers, 1959).

Within a person-centered framework, people's attempts to adjust and adapt to the demands of their environments are facilitated by their feelings, a synthesis of emotion, and cognition. Feelings inform them of the impact of their environment and the action tendencies that they need to pursue as a result of that impact and enable them to communicate with others. The intensity of their emotions informs them of the significance or importance of various experiences. Some theorists have suggested that within a person-centered framework personality traits are action strategies or ways of acting in certain situations that have a consistency over time (Bohart, 1995). These strategies are sometimes referred to as personal styles (Rice, 1974; Taylor, 1975; Watson, 1992).

EPISTEMOLOGICAL ASSUMPTIONS

Rogers saw development as an ongoing process; individuals continually change and adapt to meet the demands of their environments. He stressed people's creativity and openness to experience. Rogers's view of personality development emphasized people's capacity to learn from experience, to change, and grow. At birth, the infant enters the world as an active, curious, exploratory being, capable of learning about and experiencing the world and of developing and using its innate capacities (Bohart, 1995; Rogers, 1959). The capacities that are fundamental to personality development include the concept of experiencing, the tendency to actualize the organism and the self, and various cognitive abilities.

The concept of *experiencing* has been defined by Gendlin (1981) as a felt sense or an inner barometer that provides information and guides people in determining the accuracy of their representations or are those aspects of experience to which they are trying to give form either symbolically—as in play, language, art, music, algebra—or in some other aspect of their physical development, for example, learning to talk or walk. According to Gendlin (1981), people can often sense more complex patterns than they can put into words. This capacity has also been referred to as the ability to subceive or to discriminate stimuli without conscious awareness. It is this capacity to experience the world subjectively that facilitates people's growth and development and their interactions with their environments, allowing them to act on their experiences in ways that will enhance their survival and functioning.

A second innate capacity that Rogers identified is the tendency to actualize the organism and the self; this capacity is also called the *growth tendency.* Rogers assumed that humankind has an inborn tendency to grow and develop if conditions for doing so are adequate. This tendency can be thwarted and even reversed altogether if certain conditions are not present at birth (Bowlby, 1982; Field *et al.,* 1986; Harlow, 1959). Bohart (1995) defined the growth tendency as the capacity to develop more differentiated and integrated life structures. We can see this tendency operating at the individual and the social level. The idea that people have the capacity to realize their potential or to actualize themselves is equated with optimal, healthy functioning.

A third capacity that Rogers explored had to do with people's cognitive abilities, which include attentional processes, awareness, perception, and the skills necessary to plan and to symbolize experience, construct meaning, and learn and make choices about actions.

While these capacities are central to Rogers's theory, they are never clearly explicated. Rather, they must be inferred from Rogers's view of the change process and his representation of healthy functioning. Later person-centered theorists, drawing on information-processing theory, emphasized these abilities in their accounts of the change process in psychotherapy (Toukmanian, 1986; 1992; Wexler & Rice, 1974).

ONTOLOGICAL ASSUMPTIONS: THE DEVELOPMENT OF SELF

Rogers distinguished between the organism and the self. He referred to the entire person as the organism, while noting that the self structure consists of all the experiences, memories, feelings, and knowledge that an individual accrues over his or her life span. This gestalt, as described by Rogers is available to awareness but not necessarily in awareness at all times. There are two parts to the self that develop over time: the *ideal self* and the *self-concept*. The ideal self according to Rogers is that aspect of the person that represents how the person would like to be and act. It consists of those aspects of experience that we value most highly. The self-concept, on the other hand, refers to how the person actually views himself or herself. These two aspects of self may be quite similar and consistent or incongruent and at odds with one another. For example, there may be gaps between the ideal self and the self-concept such that while an individual might value integrity, he might feel that he often compromises himself for fear of confrontation with others.

The *self* was defined by Rogers (1959) as the "organized, consistent conceptual gestalt composed of perceptions of the relationships of the 'I' or the 'me' to others and to various aspects of life together with the values attached to these perceptions" (pp. 200). Thus, the self is the way that people view and evaluate their own unique personal qualities. Moreover, Rogers conceived of the self as a process in relationship with the world at large. He observed that early on the infant begins to differentiate himself or herself from the environment, and that this differentiation provides the infant with the beginnings of a self-structure. Thus, it is as a result of interactions with the environment (particularly interactions in which the person is being evaluated by others) that the self is formed.

In addition to the innate capabilities that people have available to them to enhance their functioning and survival, Rogers emphasized the role of attachment in his theory of personality development. As the infant and child are initially dependent on others for support and survival, their need to obtain and maintain the nurture and protection of significant others is central to Rogers's conception of development. Attachment to others is facilitated and maintained by an inborn need for the positive regard of those on whom we are dependent. It is as a result of this need for positive regard that children learn and come to internalize the values, standards, and expectations of significant others in order to insure their physical and psychological survival.

Values and expectations that are internalized from significant others are called *conditions of worth*. These are the rules that people infer or that they are taught directly about what is prized or valued by significant others. As examples, we learn from significant others whether displaying anger is acceptable, whether it is a hindrance that we are girls rather than boys, whether we are valuable members of the family, or whether we should be ambitious. It is from these internalized conditions of worth that individuals come to develop a sense of self-regard. People value themselves as they have been valued. They evaluate themselves in terms of the values and standards that they have internalized from significant others; their self-regard depends on the degree to which they perceive themselves as measuring up to those internalized standards. A person's organismic experience may at times conflict with internalized conditions of worth developed to maintain the regard of another. At these times, the need for positive regard takes precedence to such a degree that the organism becomes invested in maintaining the self-concept and will distort or deny awareness of any experience that is perceived as threatening to the self-concept. Rogers believed that people were capable of changing their conditions of worth and altering their self-concept if they were exposed to a nurturing, nonevaluative environment where they could safely acknowledge organismic experiences that were at odds with their self-concept.

Thus, there are two types of values that individuals incorporate as a result of their experiences with their environments. There are those values that are consistent with the organism and those that are not. The values that are part of the self-structure and that are congruent with the organism are experienced as coming from within. These values are owned and adhered to by the individual and serve as guides to action and criteria for evaluating experience. In contrast, other values that are incorporated or introjected from others may not be congruent with the organism, although they also will be perceived as coming from within (Bohart, 1995).

PERSONALITY FUNCTIONING

Rogers identified three possible modes of functioning or being in the world: (a) to symbolize, perceive, and organize experiences into some relationship to the self; (b) to ignore experience because it appears to have no relationship to the self-structure; or (c) to deny or distort experience because it is viewed as discordant with the self-structure. Typically, the individual behaves in ways that are consistent with his or her concept of self. When an individual behaves in ways that are inconsistent with the self, this behavior may be the result of organic needs that have not been symbolized in awareness, in which case the behavior is typically not owned.

The cornerstone of healthy functioning according to Rogers is an openness to experience, resulting in a state of congruence. As Lietaer (1991) made clear congruence does not mean a state of harmony; rather it is a way of being that is characterized by flexibility, openness, and the ability to hold concepts of the real and ideal self tentatively so that they can be accessible and receptive to new information and experience and subject to change if necessary. Thus, perceptions are accurate and open to corroboration or disconfirmation, depending on the evidence at hand. If people are functioning optimally, experiences are seen as limited and differentiated; they are accurately located in space and time and dominated by facts that can be evaluated in multiple ways. Moreover at this level of functioning, people are aware of different levels of abstraction and are able to test inferences and abstractions against reality (Meador & Rogers, 1979; Rogers, 1959). According to this view, the well-adjusted person experiences in a comprehensive and thorough manner. She or he leaves open the possibility of synthesizing different aspects of experiencing to form an organized whole in ways that are satisfying and consistent with his or her current values, desires, needs, and the specific demands of the environment.

The fully functioning person trusts his or her feelings, viewed here as the integration of emotions with cognitively felt meanings (Bohart, 1995; Rice, 1974; Rogers, 1965). This view does not hold that people should follow their feelings blindly; rather, the information imparted by one's feelings should be available to awareness and used as a guide in determining future actions. People are thought to display mature behavior when they perceive in a comprehensive and thorough manner; are nondefensive; accept responsibility for their behavior; accept responsibility for being differentiated from others; make evaluations in accord with the information from their own senses and organismic valuing, accept others as unique; and prize themselves and others (Meader & Rogers, 1979; Rogers, 1959).

Rogers viewed healthy functioning as fluid, malleable, and evolving. In contrast, dysfunction is characterized by rigidity and a state of incongruence. Rogers used *incongruence* to refer to discrepancies that occur between the self as perceived and experienced. If people adhere rigidly to a specific views of themselves, then experiences that challenge or contradict those views may be perceived as threatening. When such discrepancies arise, the organism may deny or distort sensory and visceral experience so that it cannot be symbolized in awareness and reorganized to form a new gestalt within the self-structure. Thus, Rogers saw maladjustment as the blocking or closing off of some aspects of experience in order to maintain a self-structure that is discordant with the organismic valuing process.

Maladjustment reflects defensive functioning or a restricted manner of experiencing that is characterized by overgeneralization of experience, a poor concept of time, and poor reality testing. People demonstrate restricted experiencing when they confuse fact and evaluation and use abstractions rather than reality testing (Rogers, 1959). Rogers suggested that restricted and maladjusted experiencing can only be reduced and altered when people are in safe environments. In safe, unthreatening contexts people may be able to examine the threatening aspects of their experiences and replace their introjected value systems with their own organismic valuing process, which is open to information from a variety of sources and leaves individuals free to behave and experience in more open and comprehensive ways.

GESTALT THEORY

There are many similarities between gestalt and person-centered theory. Like the latter, gestalt theory emphasizes awareness, subjective experiencing, and the assimilation of introjects. However, gestalt theory casts a slightly different emphasis and provides an often unseen perspective on the same landscape, providing a breadth to person-centered theory that can enrich and enliven the view. Like Rogers, Fritz Perls (1969, 1973) was more concerned with explicating the change process and those factors that contribute to impaired functioning than he was with developing a theory of personality.

As does person-centered theory, gestalt theory emphasizes the interaction between the individual and environment; however, the interaction between the two is more focal in Perls's work as both are seen as inseparable. According to Perls, experience occurs at the boundary between the organism and its environment where contact is made. Exploration and promotion of contact between individuals and their environments is the essence of gestalt therapy. Gestalt theorists believe that it is over their manner of making contact with their environment that people have most control in influencing how their needs and goals are met. Consequently, gestalt therapists are concerned with the attention that people pay to the field, how they negotiate their interactions with it, and the types of contact that people make with their environments. While emphasizing existence as it is experienced, Perls also emphasized the notion of homeostasis and people's capacity for self-regulation, growth, and healing. Like the existentialists, Perls, more than Rogers, emphasized that people are moral agents. He explicated the notion of personal responsibility and the idea that people are accountable for their choices and actions. The stress on personal responsibility in gestalt and existential theory is perhaps not surprising, given the devastating post–World War II context in which the writings of many of these theorists were emerging. In contrast, Rogers was the child of a more benign political environment.

EPISTEMOLOGICAL ASSUMPTIONS

Perls (1969, 1973) saw people as endowed with certain capabilities, including awareness, experiencing, a drive to health as well as needs and desires, and healthy aggression, in order to assimilate new experiences from the environment. By awareness, Perls was referring to people's capacity to perceive their environments and themselves in terms of gestalts or figure–ground relationships. People are continually organizing their experiences according to the demands of their inner environment—their needs, desires, and goals—and the demands of their outer environment. It is by becoming aware that people demonstrate responsibility and choice. Echoing the existentialists, Perls saw lack of awareness as resulting in self-deception and inauthentic existence.

In gestalt theory, experience has two components: that which is subjectively felt and that which is objectively observed (Yontef & Simkin, 1989). This definition of experience acknowledges people's inner subjective, visceral reality, as well as the reality of the external world they observe and know through their senses. Perls stressed that it was people's capacity for experiencing that provided them with knowledge about the world and themselves, and it was awareness of this capacity that he sought to foster in psychotherapy (Polster & Polster, 1973). Perls saw emotion as being made up of physiological responses and cognitions in a specific environmental context (Perls, Hefferline, & Goodman, 1951). Emotions maintain individuals' contacts with reality and alert them to changes in homeostasis that require attention. They provide indispensable but not complete knowledge of the environment; thus, they are seen as important guides along with reason and deliberation to future action. People's capacities to think abstractly and manipulate symbols were also seen as important aspects of human functioning that helped individuals to grow and adapt to new situations (Perls, 1973).

ONTOLOGICAL ASSUMPTIONS: THE DEVELOPMENT OF SELF

In gestalt theory, the self is seen (a) as an agent that creates experience and (b) as a process that comes into being at the moment of contact between individuals and their environments (Latner, 1992; Yontef, 1991). Gestalt theory sees the self as constantly in process as it interacts with its environment. The self is analogous to Rogers's concept of the organism (Latner, 1992; Yontef, 1991). It represents the whole person and is the part of the personality that integrates experience and initiates change (Latner, 1992).

Perls (1973) posits a number of structures in the development of the self, some of which are innate and others acquired in interaction with the environment. The structural components that we will look at shortly include contact boundaries, fields, and introjects. Perls saw the field as being differentiated according to boundaries, which may be either rigid or permeable. Boundaries represent the points of contact between the individual and the field. They have a dual function: (a) they connect individuals with one another, and (b) they preserve individuals' autonomy and separation (Yontef, 1991). Separation insures protection from potentially harmful contacts. People meet their needs and realize themselves through contact with others and their environments. They grow and develop as they encounter new experiences. Boundaries provide a sense of self in so far as they enable the individual to distinguish self from other. Perls *et al.* (1951) wrote that "all contact is creative adjustment of the organism and environment" (p. 230). However, while Perls saw adjustment as important, he recognized that individuals need to act on their environments in order to realize their needs and goals (Yontef, 1991). Regulation of the contact boundary is central to people's psychological health and well-being. For example, the manner in which people make contact with their environments, either aggressively (taking too much) or timidly (taking too little), has important implications for their functioning and survival.

Like Rogers, Perls stressed the importance of attachment and early relationships in the formation of the developing child's sense of self. He believed that children need parental relationships that are characterized by warmth, the space to struggle and grow, and clearly defined limits. Yontef sees this relationship as ideally having an organismic, environmental, and ecological balance (Yontef & Simkin, 1989). As children interact with their environments, they begin the process of assimilating their experiences, including their parents' value systems. The criterion used to determine whether experiences are assimilable or not is whether they are nourishing or toxic. According to Perls, people have an innate capacity to discriminate experience on these grounds. During the course of development and in the process of becoming moral agents, individuals need to establish a balance between their own organismic needs and desires, those values that they have assimilated into their self-structure, and the demands of their environments. This process of self-regulation is vital to healthy functioning.

A concept that is central to a gestalt theory of personality is that of *introjects*. Introjects are values that are not assimilated as part of the self-structure. Such values are not owned and may conflict with an individual's own organismic needs and desires. If experience is to be owned and incorporated as part of the self-structure, it needs to be examined critically and evaluated before it can be assimilated. Just as we need to eat, chew, and digest food before we can derive nourishment, so too we have to digest information, facts, and values that we are exposed to in our environments. If the latter are absorbed without being assimilated, they are experienced as introjects and may give rise to conflicts to the extent that they are irreconcilably different. In contrast to other psychological theories that held introjection to be a necessary part of development, Gestalt therapists view all introjection as unhealthy.

PERSONALITY FUNCTIONING

Healthy functioning from a gestalt perspective is based on two assumptions: (a) the relationship between the organism and its environment is a patterned, dynamic whole; and (b) the interaction between the organism and the environment is regulated according to the principle of homeostatis (Carmer & Rouzer, 1974; Perls, 1969). People organize experiences according to their needs, which may be either physical or psychological (Perls, (1973). It is the ability of individuals to know, accept, and meet such needs within the constraints of their current environments that reflects healthy functioning.

According to gestalt theory, a gestalt—otherwise defined as a pattern or configuration—is organized in terms of figure and ground. The *figure* is that which is salient or stands out from a specific context or conglomerate of experience. That part of experience that is not figural becomes *ground* and recedes into the background or field. That which becomes figural is dictated by our needs, desires, and interests at any given moment. It is likely to remain figural until the desire or need is satisfied or some experience of greater salience is identified, at which point experience is once again reconfigured into a new gestalt. If a need is not satisfied, the gestalt is said to remain unfinished, claiming the person's attention until some sort of closure can be achieved.

In order to adequately meet their needs, individuals have to be aware. Gestalt theorists define *awareness* as "the experience of heightened differentiation between organism and environment so as to facilitate the satisfaction of the predominant need" (Carmer & Rouzer, 1974; Melnick & Nevis, 1992; Yontef, 1991). This awareness is best understood as a gestalt in which the need predominates, orienting the individual to seek satisfaction in the field. There are four stages in the creation and satisfaction of a need. These stages, known as the experience cycle (Yontef, 1991), are awareness, excitement, action tendency, and contact or need satisfaction (Carmer & Rouzer, 1974; Melnick & Nevis, 1992; Zinker, 1977). Initially, a person becomes aroused or experiences a state of inner tension that alerts that person to the presence of some inner need pressing for satisfaction. Once he or she becomes aware of the need and differentiates it from the field, he or she then becomes activated to meet that need in the current context. The person is aroused to action and seeks to contact the environment in such a way as to insure the satisfaction of the inner need. Thus, the gestalt can achieve closure and the individual is free to move on to other needs and encounters with the environment.

Central to the notion of meeting one's needs is the concept of *homeostais* or self-regulation. Perls (1969) believed that homeostatis was the individual's way of maintain equilibrium. Stewart (1974) conceived of homeostatis as a zero point around which the individual experiences neither pleasure nor pain. However, when the balance is disrupted, as when the individual experiences thirst or the need for affection, then the organism strives to satisfy the need so as to return to the original state of equilibrium.

Like Rogers, Perls saw individuals as oriented toward growth and the satisfaction of their needs. Healthy individuals, according to gestalt theory, trust their own natures and capacities and allow themselves to become in the process of being. Thus, healthy individuals are not bound by unnecessary rules and constraints but rather are able to function in fluid and permeable ways. For Perls and Rogers, healthy functioning is characterized by flexibility and the capacity to adjust and adapt to new situations and needs as they emerge and become figural in the moment (Yontef & Simkin, 1989). Healthy individuals know how to be autonomous and self-supporting as well as dependent on their environments for the satisfaction of their needs (Perls, 1973; Yontef & Simkin, 1989). According to Perls, flexibility, cohesion, stability, and minimal conflict are essential to healthy functioning.

By contrast, dysfunctional behavior is characterized by blocked awareness and disturbances in people's interactions with their environments. When individuals' contacts with their environments are disturbed, they may attempt to meet their needs too quickly or too slowly. In either case, they have demonstrated their inability to adequately differentiate themselves from their environments or to form gestalts of the environment–organism field that would facilitate satisfaction of their needs. Like Rogers, Perls (1973) saw dysfunction as resulting when people were out of touch with their own organismic needs and desires.

There are several processes that may contribute to the development of dysfunctional behavior: (a) impaired contacts with an environment within which individuals are too confluent or isolated, (b) the development of introjects and projections, and (c) the processes of retroflection and deflection (Perls, 1973; Polster & Polster, 1973). Confluence occurs when individuals are inadequately differentiated and feel no separation between themselves and their environments. The parts are indistinguishable from the whole (Perls, 1973). According to Perls, infants are confluent with their environments; they have to learn to differentiate themselves from others. Moreover, even as adults, there are times when we still experience confluence—for example, when engrossed in a novel or engaged in some ritualistic activity that allows us to feel at one with the larger group. However, these moments are transitory; they become dysfunctional when they become enduring and chronic. People who are chronically confluent find it difficult to tolerate differences; moreover, they confuse their needs and desires with those of the group.

The opposite of confluence is isolation. In this state, individuals are totally withdrawn from their surroundings. They are unable to reach out to establish contact to meet their needs. While there are times when all of us may withdraw from the group—when we need to protect ourselves or when we need to refresh and recharge ourselves, for example—isolated individuals regularly engage in this mode of being.

As posited by Rogers, introjects are similar to conditions of worth. According to Perls, introjects consist of the fact and the values—including aesthetic, moral, and ethical—that we encounter. If these are internalized without being properly assimilated, they are experienced as oppressive and alien. Values have to be owned through a process of critical examination and evaluation and assimilated into existing frameworks if they are to be integrated into the personality. Perls (1973) identified two problems that resulted from the internalization of introjects: first, individuals are unable to discover their true selves as their introjects limit their behaviors and consequently their ability to develop to their fullest potential. Second, introjects can lead to disintegration of the personality to the extent that they result in individuals holding incompatible concepts and values that are difficult to reconcile. The opposite of introjection is projection, that is, the attempt to see in the environment what is in the self. Here we are speaking of disowned parts of the self and the blurring of boundaries between self and other.

Retroflection is the process by which individuals do unto themselves that which they would like to do unto others (Perls, 1973). Instead of trying to change the environment, individuals who are retroflecting channel their energies into changing themselves. Thus, individuals who retroflect may try to give to themselves that which they have been unsuccessful at acquiring from environments; alternatively, they may punish themselves instead of other people. Retroflections often consist of aggressive needs that the individual cannot express. All these processes result in a breakdown or interruption between the dynamic, fluid relationship between figure and ground that is so necessary to healthy functioning.

EXISTENTIAL THEORY

Existentialist theory posits a dynamic model of human functioning (Bugenthal & Sterling, 1992; May & Yalom, 1989). Like Freud, existentialist theorists assume that people balance and juggle conflicting conscious and unconscious forces. However, in the existential model the conflict that is at the core of human existence does not involve sexual and aggressive impulses; rather, it is between the individual and the givens of existence (May & Yalom, 1989; Tiryakian, 1962). Yalom identifies four basic concerns that define the human condition and with which everyone struggles. These are concerns with death, freedom, isolation, and meaninglessness.

From the existential standpoint, the core conflict that human beings experience is that between the wish to live and the inevitability of death (i.e., being and the threat of nonbeing). It is posited that from an early age people are consumed by the fear of death and obliteration and must struggle to cope with it using defenses (for example, denial).

The second conflict identified by the existentialists is that between freedom and the limits of one's existence. Freedom is defined as the capacity for choice (Schneider & May, 1995). Conflict occurs between individuals' awareness of freedom balanced against the need for structure and groundedness (May & Yalom, 1989). Existentialists assume that individuals are responsible agents capable of choosing and directing the course of their lives. Individuals who exercise choice and responsibility are said to be authentic. However, there is great variability among individuals in the degrees to which they may be willing to assume responsibility for their lives. For example, some people present themselves as victimized by the world—quite helpless in the face of occurring events. Yet, others are more willing to assume responsibility for their decision, life course, and well-being and do not see themselves as flotsam tossed around on the sea of life.

The third conflict identified by existential theorists pertains to existential isolation, which they distinguish from interpersonal and intrapersonal isolation. Interpersonal isolation refers to the distance between people that occurs as a function of poor social skills and psychopathology. Intrapersonal isolation refers to the split-off and isolated aspects of people's experience that are out of conscious awareness. Existential isolation refers to people's capacity to become self-aware and reflective. With this knowledge comes an understanding that one can never share one's consciousness with another. The intense loneliness that follows this awareness is in conflict with our need to be connected and protected by the other.

The fourth dynamic conflict or ultimate concern involves the meaninglessness of existence. Because of their tendency to organize experiences, existential theorists assume that individuals have an innate desire for meaning and order. This need is severely challenged as people confront the inevitability of death, isolation, and what at times may seem like a chaotic, random universe. In existential theory, developing a sense of meaning is an important life task because it forms the basis for the value systems that individuals construct to guide the way they live. It is these value systems that inform people's choices and determine the course of their lives.

EPISTEMOLOGICAL ASSUMPTIONS

Existential theorists have suggested that there are several factors that determine the development of personality, including awareness, embeddedness, finitude, agency, autonomy, and separateness (Bugenthal & Sterling, 1992). The authors of this chapter refer to awareness as the innate human capacity that enables people to attend to their inner affective and physiological experiences as well as to their outer environments. Moreover, people are born with capacities to perceive and reflect about themselves and the world.

The second important dimension of people's lives with regard to shaping their personalities has to do with the embeddedness of existence. Embeddedness refers to the limitations imposed on them by their human form. People are limited to hearing and seeing only those aspects of the world that are available to their senses. Moreover, they are susceptible to illness, aging, and death. The finiteness of being is the third important aspect of existence. The inevitability of death and the limits of existence give rise to an omnipotent impulse as people try to compensate for the reality of their corporeality.

The fourth, fifth, and sixth dimensions of existence emphasize that we are social agents. As social agents, we are responsible for our actions; we have the capacity to formulate moral frameworks and apply these to our lives (Bugenthal & Sterling, 1992). While individuals are autonomous, separate entities, it should be emphasized that they are also relational beings for whom intersubjectivity and connections with others are important.

ONTOLOGICAL ASSUMPTIONS: THE DEVELOPMENT OF SELF

Existential theorists see people from infancy onward as being engaged in a process of discovery and invention (Bugenthal & Sterling, 1992). As with other humanistic theories, existential theory assumes that one of the tasks individuals need to perform is to differentiate their experiences. Primarily, they need to distinguish between what is bad and what is good about their experiences. In this process, people's subjectivity, defined as their ability to attend to their perceptions, feelings, and intentions, is emphasized. Bugenthal and Sterling (1992) saw the self as an evolving process and people as capable of learning and growing throughout their lives. According to their model, experience is continually in flux, and people are continually organizing and revising it.

Existentialist theorists are more concerned with the process of living than with identifying specific personality structures. Bugenthal and Sterling (1992) suggested that people develop self and world construct systems as they encounter experience—grow and develop. As we interact with the world, we are engaged in creating ways of making sense of our experiences and of forming identities that will enable us to differentiate selves from others. We need to develop a sense of how to survive and learn what is satisfying or painful, gives support and protection, and what makes us feel powerful and competent. Burgenthal and Sterling write: "As we form these views we are continually developing, revising, and living out our notions of ourselves—of what are our strengths, our gifts, and our vulnerabilities; of how we handle certain recurrent situations, and of what are deepest strivings seek" (1992, p. 232). According to their view, we are constantly engaged in creating our lives and world afresh each moment. Moreover, our constructs act like a lens focusing on certain aspects of experience while screening out and distorting others.

PERSONALITY FUNCTIONING

The core of healthy functioning according to the existentialist perspective is the integration of freedom—characterized by will, creativity, and expressiveness—and limitation—characterized by natural and social restraints, vulnerability, and death (May, 1969; Schneider & May, 1995). There are six realms or dimensions of experience in which we can exercise freedom and confront the limits of our existence: physiological, environmental, cognitive, psychosexual, interpersonal, and experiential.

The healthy person is able to balance the limits of freedom and integration in accord with the demands of each situation and is not overwhelmed by feeling of panic and helplessness. Thus, a criterion for healthy functioning (as with person-centered and gestalt theory) is flexibility. People who function optimally acknowledge the ultimate limits and freedom of the human condition but are able to defuse and minimize them so as not be consumed or overwhelmed by them. Schneider and May (1995) suggest that a healthy individual would be able to be "both bold and tender, creative and disciplined, and exploratory and committed in key life areas" (p. 6).

Healthy functioning is represented by sensitivity, flexibility, and choice. In contrast, dysfunction is caused by a dread of the two polarities of freedom and limitation, which leads to the possibility of either extreme oppressiveness or impulsivity. Existentialist theorists see people as operating along a continuum with expansiveness and constriction at opposite ends. Dysfunction occurs when people are chronically attached to one or the other. The ideal mode of operating is in the center.

Fear of total expansion or constriction may be rooted in acute, chronic, or implicit trauma. Acute trauma occurs as the result of a shocking event, like an illness or a death in the family, that produces extreme fear. The greater the discrepancy between a person's condition subsequent to the trauma and her or his original state, the greater will be the need to deny or distort her or his awareness of vulnerability and smallness. If as a child a person is unsuccessful at denying the trauma, this failure may set in motion a cycle of chronic trauma as that person repeatedly focuses on trying to counteract the dread. This focus may result in the person's emphasizing his or her smallness and trying to constrict functioning to avoid harm. Implicit trauma results from intergenerational learning, as children witness parents' or significant others' confrontations and difficulties with traumatic events.

People deploy defenses in an attempt to assuage the anxiety that attends an awareness of the ultimate concerns of existence (May & Yalom, 1989). According to May and Yalom (1989), we not only use the defenses so adequately described and documented by Freud and his followers, but also employ two others in trying to avoid or deal with the conflict induced by the givens of existence: (a) we develop a sense that we are special and somehow above and beyond mortal concerns, as reflected in strivings for omnipotence, power and perfection; (b) we believe in an ultimate rescuer, an omnipotent guardian who is constantly on the lookout for our welfare and who will protect us from harm. Individuals who develop this second defense usually try to seek out dominant others and live out their lives trying to appease them in return for protection and care.

EXPERIENTIAL THEORY

Experiential theorists propose a dialectical-constructivist view of personality that integrates emotion theory and cognitive psychology. From this perspective, meaning arises from an integration of emotion and cognition. This process is guided by biology and culture and is a result of a complex synthesis of information from a variety of levels of information processing (Gendlin, 1981; Greenberg, Rice & Elliott, 193; Greenberg & Safran, 1987; Watson, 1992; Watson & Greenberg, 1996). This view attempts to reconcile and integrate the head and the heart. Experiential theorists emphasize the importance of the growth tendency and subjective experiencing or the role of emotion in personality development and functioning.

Emotions are seen as having two functions in experiential theory: (a) they organize the self, and (b) serve as a communication system. Emotions help people to adapt so that they act in accord with the demands and constraints of their environments and alert them to their needs and goals (Greenberg et al., 1993; Watson & Greenberg, 1996). Thus, the growth tendency is seen as being reliant on emotional experience in order to operate effectively. Emotional experience results from the appraisal of situations relevant to people's needs. Greenberg et al. (1993) suggested that people's emotional reactions to situations are registered more quickly than their rational cognitive appraisals and are usually the result of an appraisal of the specific situation as compared with past situations, and their needs, goals, or concerns and their coping ability. Emotions reveal the impact of the environment on individuals, and thus can be used to guide adaptive choice and action (Greenberg et al., 1993; Greenberg & Safran, 1987; Watson & Greenberg, 1996; Watson & Rennie, 1994).

While emotions provide people with information relevant to their well-being that enhances orientation and problem solving, reflection and integration of this information with other aspects of experience is necessary before it can be translated into action (Greenberg et al., 1993; Watson & Greenberg, 1996). Thus, in therapy an important task is to bring emotions and actions into awareness to help people regulate themselves and their experiences. Awareness of feelings and emotions helps people to identify what they need to change. Like the existentialists, experiential theorists emphasize development of self in the world schemes that guide people's understanding of their world and themselves and act as guides to future action. In experiential theory, people are perceived as being in the process of becoming as they attend to the emotional significance of events and symbolize their experiences.

EPISTEMOLOGICAL ASSUMPTIONS

Experiential theorists see people as actively organizing their views of reality based on experiential referents (Gendlin, 1981). Infants are seen as being born with innate cognitive capacities, including attentional resources, the capacity for self-awareness, symbolic capacities, memory, and an adaptive emotion system. Attention is seen as a limited resource available to individuals. Consequently, there is a need to expend it efficiently in order to maximize its capacity. Thus, several activities are performed automatically and out of awareness to leave the organism free to attend to important and novel information in the environment so as to enhance its survival and growth.

The capacity for self-awareness is seen as a uniquely human attribute that enables people to experience themselves both as subjects and objects (Aboulafia, 1986; Watson & Greenberg, 1996; James, 1983; Rennie, 1992; Taylor, 1990). As the subjects of their experiences, individuals are conceived of as active agents immersed in the process of being and doing. However, such absorption in the process of being is altered when individuals stand back and view themselves from the outside or become self-conscious and see themselves as they might appear to others. Part of the ability to develop self-awareness is a function of our symbolic capacities, most ubiquitously the use of language and other cognitive skills. Greenberg et al. (1993) suggested that self-awareness and self-reflection allow for meaning creation that enhances people's survival and growth.

Experiential theorists, like their existential counterparts, see children representing their experiences of themselves and their world in internal models. As a result of repeated experiences with their environment, children develop self-in-the-world schemes (Greenberg et al., 1993). These schemes are conceived of as active organizations of past reactions or past experiences that operate in any well-adapted organismic response. Experiential theorists emphasize the action tendencies implicit in the notion of schemes. This meaning is closer to the Piagetian view, which highlights the functional aspects of schemes. According to this view, schemes are plans for action and have an intentional goal directed quality. In experiential theory, emotion schemes are learned patterns of action related to certain emotional states. Emotion schemes develop as a result of people's varying capacities to feel, act, develop beliefs about themselves and world, and evaluate consequences of their actions in terms of other criteria (e.g., effectiveness of their actions). Emotion schemes influence people's experience and are in turn changed by these experiences.

ONTOLOGICAL ASSUMPTIONS: THE DEVELOPMENT OF SELF

Individuals are oriented toward interaction with their environments to foster survival and growth. The formative developmental tendency is the growth tendency. It is this that maintains the system's coherence and organismic balance. This definition goes a little beyond that posited by Rogers and incorporates some of Perls's notion of organismic regulation and balance. According to the experiential view, growth is defined as the differentiation of internal structures and their integration and reorganization at higher and higher levels of complexity. More simply, growth can be seen as the potential to change and adapt in order to survive. Experiential theorists see the growth tendency as including a number of other motivations, including the need to be attached, curiosity, mastery of the physical environment, and the satisfaction of basic needs.

Two motives are explicitly identified as necessary to adaptation and growth: (a) relatedness and attachment and (b) mastery. Like the gestalt theorists, experiential theorists see affect as primarily relational. It is assumed that infants are born with innate attachment response systems that facilitate responsiveness to their environment and enhance the environment's responsiveness to them. Thus, infants are thought to have innate expressive motor programs for primary affect (e.g., when distressed, they cry; when frightened, they attempt to look or move away; when happy, they smile or attempt to approach). The ability of infants to regulate and influence their environments is vital to their developing a competent sense of themselves in relationship to others.

According to experiential theorists, infants are born with an adaptive emotion-motivation system that facilitates their orientation to their environment. Attention to emotions provides people with information about their well-being and is relevant to problem solving, making informed choices, making decisions, and taking action. As infants develops and mature, they develop a store of knowledge and skills from interactions with their environments that contributes to the ability to survive and grow. This information is stored in memory, enabling people to recall similar situations, their actions, and their outcomes. This faculty is an important aspect of the self-structure; it assists people in developing a sense of themselves in the world.

PERSONALITY FUNCTIONING

Greenberg *et al.* (1993) saw emotion schemes as complex cognitive, affective, motivational, and relational action structures that are fundamental to people's psychological functioning. According to experiential theorists, emotion schemes are complex self-organizing, information-processing structures that are activated in response to various environmental situations to create people's sense of being in the world. If development proceeds normally, people develop an integrated sense of self characterized by an ability to control actions, own affective responses, and develop a sense of continuity over time. Moreover, these people are motivated to maintain adaptive, functional affect regulation. In the experiential model, healthy functioning individuals are able to be self-supportive and to obtain support from the environment. Healthy functioning requires that individuals be able to trust their organismic needs and tendencies, counterbalance their values with organismic experience, and be empathically attuned to others. Self-acceptance and the ability to connect with others are at the core of healthy functioning in experiential theory.

While emotion schemes adaptively guide experience in healthy functioning, Greenberg *et al.* (1993) suggested that dysfunction can occur in three ways: (a) when inadequate attention is paid to emotion (as posited by Perls and Rogers), (b) when dysfunctional or maladaptive emotion schemes are activated, and (c) when the individuals are unable to assimilate conflicting emotion schemes. If insufficient attention is paid to emotional experiences, if emotional experience are ignored, or if emotion schemes are maladaptive, then people encounter difficulties creating meaning out of their experiences. Thus, dysfunction results when a primary emotional response has not been acknowledged. Healthy functioning can only resume once the primary emotion response has been searched for and incorporated into the organism's emotion schemes. Lack of awareness is posited as the primary source of maladaptive behavior as it is in other humanistic theories.

Greenberg *et al.* (1993) distinguished between primary, secondary, and instrumental emotions. Primary emotions occur directly in response to a stimulus; secondary emotions occur in response to primary emotions. Instrumental emotions are those emotions that are used to produce some response in the environment but are not necessarily reflective of the person's inner affective state. Dysfunctional behavior may occur as a result of the activation of either maladaptive primary or secondary emotions. While primary emotions are seen as fundamentally adaptive, schematic emotional memory may produce primary emotional responses that are not appropriate to the current situation, and these responses can influence behavior and override more adaptive responses (Greenberg & Safran, 1987, 1989). Activation of maladaptive secondary emotions requires people to get in touch with their primary adaptive emotions in order to understand and facilitate the satisfaction of their current needs and goals.

Greenberg *et al.* (1993) proposed several reasons why dysfunctional emotion schemes do not change of their own accord or in the interaction with experience. First, because emotion schemes selectively direct attention, information that may be pertinent and useful to challenge the scheme is screened from awareness; second, emotion schemes distort information; third, certain emotion schemes may make people avoid experiences that would lead them to challenge certain emotion schemes and views of themselves; fourth, people's emotional responses to situations can interfere with their processing their experiences fully and accurately.

CONCLUSION

Within the humanistic and experiential framework, personality is seen as continually developing. People simultaneously reveal and create themselves in the moment. It is in their actions that they reveal themselves and their values. The four systems that we have examined in this chapter emphasize the role of emotion in the development and well-being of the person. However, each system requires further elaboration.

All four systems of thought that we have reviewed refer to the process of evaluation and the role of values in the development and functioning of each individual's personality. Rogers posited that the organismic valuing process is innate and that satisfaction and enhancement of the organism are the criteria by which experiences are evaluated. However, the criteria the organism uses to determine whether experiences are enhancing or not are unclear. At one level, there seems to be a biological criterion of survival, but there also seems to be a more psychological criterion of enhancement that contributes to growth.

Rogers assumed that the organism knows what is in its best interest. However, as observed by numerous theorists (Luria, 1976; Vygotsky, 1978), this knowledge may only come with experience. It is reasonable to expect that additional criteria for evaluating experiences are learned from interaction with the environment and as the infant grows and develops his or her own unique capacities and potential. Rogers discussed incorporation of values from significant others in the construction of an ideal self and the self-concept.

While it is clear that the well-functioning individual is open to information from a variety of sources, it is not obvious how the individual balances multiple sources of information or makes choices among them. It seems likely that there will be moments of conflict between owned values, needs, and desires; yet how people manage these conflicts and balance competing needs and desires is not articulated by Rogers. Similarly, the way in which people integrate and balance their individual and social needs requires further elaboration. Organismic valuing appears to be the primary and ultimate source of evaluation within the individual. However, to the extent that certain values, standards, and expectations are incorporated as part of the self-structure, it seems likely that the self plays a role in the evaluation of experience. It is clear from Rogers's writings that integration is necessary, but he does not discuss how the process occurs.

This process has not been described or explicated by Rogers. Thus, the way the individual incorporates and chooses those social and individual values that best express himself or herself is unclear. While Rogers addressed the possibility of conflict between organismic values and those values incorporated from others that form part of the self-concept, he did not address the possibility that conflict might occur between organismic valuing and higher order social, personal, moral, and esthetic values that the person has owned and endorsed as self-enhancing.

Perls's criterion for what is owned and assimilated by the organism was whether it is nourishing or not. Like the notion of enhancing, the concept of nourishing is rudimentary to the extent that it fails to provide an adequate criterion for choosing between organismic needs, desires, goals, and higher order values. Moreover, attainment of healthy functioning often seems to be synonymous with rejecting certain values and trusting the self. This observation does not seem to be a complete and accurate account of the psychotherapeutic process during which people may endorse certain values at the expense of organismic needs (Taylor, 1975; Watson & Greenberg, 1986; Watson & Rennie, 1994).

The existentialists saw development of value frameworks as important primarily to give life meaning and purpose. Yet, another important reason is to inform our choices and regulate our social interactions, especially as social systems become more complex and

differentiated. Experiential theorists' use and definition of emotion schemes tends to con-
found action and emotion. To the extend that action is seen to emerge from emotion, the
role of values and self-reflection in informing people's actions, along with their organismic needs, desires, and goals is blurred.

In defining that which is distinctively human, humanistic philosopher recognized that
people are not only agents capable of symbolic thought and action, but that they are also
moral agents capable of devising moral frameworks to guide their actions and social transactions. If we are to accurately reflect the complexity of human functioning, then it seems
necessary to posit two different value systems that inform people's decisions and actions. According to this view, organismic valuing would be seen as an intrinsic process necessary to
growth and survival, but it would be counterbalanced by a higher order framework of values
derived from experience and people's knowledge and understanding of their social systems
(Goffman, 1959; Harre, 1984; Taylor, 1990; Watson, 1992; Watson & Greenberg, 1996).

The humanistic and experiential theories we have reviewed imply a cognitive–affective
model of personality. According to cognitive–affective models of human functioning, we
have two different but parallel modes of processing information from our environment: an
experiential system and a rational system (Bucci, 1984; Buck, 1984; Epstein, 1994; Greenberg et al., 1993; Paivio, 1987). The experiential system is tied to our emotions. It processes
information rapidly, is oriented toward immediate action, and is crudely differentiated and
integrated. The experiential system has a long evolutionary history and operates in humans
as well as animals. At lower levels of operation, it processes information automatically,
swiftly, and efficiently; while at higher levels when integrated with higher cognitive capacities, it can represent experience concretely, imagistically, metaphorically, and in myth and
narrative. In interaction with higher order cognitive faculties, Epstein (1994) saw it as being the source of wisdom and creativity.

In contrast, the rational system is slower, abstract, effortful and deliberate, and operates primarily by means of symbols—predominantly language. This system of processing
information has had a shorter evolutionary history and is capable of high levels of abstraction and postponement of gratification. It is a less efficient system than the experiential and
less capable of responding promptly to situations (see Chapter 9).

Humanistic and experiential writers have proposed limited definitions and explanations of pathology or dysfunction, with most of these theorists focusing on anxiety.
Rogers posited a clearly cognitive-affective model of human functioning. However, his
theory of maladjusment is restricted to defensive functioning and a model of incongruence between organismic experience and the self-structure. Perls spoke of individuals
experiencing difficulty at their contact boundaries or in their interactions with their environments in so far as they are either totally absorbed by them or walled off and separate. As with Rogerian theory, Gestalt theory does not clearly explicate the development
of the self. Proponents of both theories were more concerned with explicating the change
process and a theory of therapy.

Perls identified and described a number of dysfunctional processes that were not identified in person-centered theory. Moreover, to the extent that his theory focused on the dynamic relationship between self and environment and emphasized the role of contact
boundaries, it added an extra dimension to the Rogerian view of personality functioning.
Existentialist writers saw pathology as occurring because of people's inability to confront
their ultimate concerns and fears, and because of this inability they distort experience and

live inauthentically. Experiential theorists like Perls and Rogers saw dysfunction as occurring as a result of the denial or distortion of the awareness of emotional processing and the activation of maladaptive schemes.

Each of these systems addresses some aspects of pathology yet do not address the full gamut of dysfunctional behaviors. For a more extensive theory of personality dysfunction it is necessary to more clearly formulate our view of the person and its implications for personality functioning. If personality functioning is conceived as operating in terms of an interaction between an experiential and a rational system as well as a higher order value framework rooted in our rational system (consisting of moral, ethical and aesthetic principles that regulate our social interactions), then several additional sources of pathology become evident.

According to experiential theory in well-adjusted, healthy functioning individuals, the experiential system and its valuing process act like an alarm system that is responsive to various environmental contingencies to help organize the person for action. The organism has a baseline or zero-point level of functioning that allows it to note fluctuations and use them as a guide to allocate attentional resources. While the individual can act on the basis of information and the valuing processes of either his or her rational or experiential systems, at times it may be necessary to integrate the information from both systems to determine the best course of action in certain situations and to solve problems in interpersonal and intrapersonal functioning.

Impaired functioning might result from dysfunction in either the emotional system or the rational system, or in the process of valuing in terms of the organism or the higher order system of values. To elaborate, there may be physiological difficulties in the rational or emotional systems (e.g., a person who is developmentally challenged may have difficulty reasoning about the consequences of her or his actions or be unable to label feelings). Alternatively, some individuals may have physiological difficulties in their emotional systems or they may lack certain skills such that they may be unable to process their reactions, as in alexythymia (Kennedy-Moore & Watson, in preparation).

Alternatively, there may be sociopsychological difficulties in adaptation to the extent that people may suffer from deficits or dysfunction in either their emotional or rational systems, in their organismic valuing processes, or their higher order value systems. For example, an individual may distort or deny emotional experiencing, as proposed by Rogers, because it is at odds with the self-structure. Another person may lack awareness of emotional processing as a result of not being taught to attend to feelings. Yet another may as a result of neglect and abuse be in touch with the emotions but may have a dysfunctional organismic valuing process so that he or she is unable to discriminate and evaluate experiences.

Other people may develop maladaptive action strategies either as a result of previous learning or as a result of an inadequate appraisal of the current situation. The latter may occur as a result of the crude differentiation and integration of emotional experience. Or it may occur because certain features of a situation are overgeneralized as a result of narrow and rigid ways of construing the environment, resulting in action strategies that are inappropriate or hinder people from achieving their goals. Alternatively, the experiential system's homeostatic balance may be disrupted so that it loses its responsiveness and stops acting like an alarm system that organizes the individual to respond to various environmental contingencies. Thus, it may register a chronic response to environmental contingencies, as when a person is suffering from generalized anxiety.

Some people may develop impaired value systems that do not enhance their individual or social functioning. People who have developed higher order value systems that enhance their individual and social functioning may experience conflict between the organismic valuing process and higher order values or between different values. Alternatively, conflict between competing organismic needs and desires may cause the individual distress. Finally, as suggested by existential theorists, people may have concerns about larger existential issues, such as the meaning of life and having to come to terms with their mortality.

In conclusion, humanistic and experiential theorists have emphasized that it is people's growth tendencies (i.e., their capacities for emotional responding and consciousness) that facilitate adaptation to and survival in more and more complex environments. However, people's capacity for self-reflection, their ability to evaluate the significance of things, and their capacity to evaluate the possible consequences of actions also facilitate problem solving and adaptive responding to environments (Taylor, 1975; Watson & Greenberg, 1996; Watson & Rennie, 1994). If they are to do justice to the complexity of human functioning and dysfunction and evolve improved treatment strategies, humanistic and experiential theorists need to articulate the role of these latter processes more fully and completely.

REFERENCES

Aboulafia, R. (1986). *The mediating self: Mead, Sartre, and self-determination.* New Haven, CT: Yale University Press.

Bohart, A. (1995). The person-centered psychotherapies. In A. Gurman & S. Messer (Eds.), *Essential psychotherapies: Theory and practice* (pp. 85–127). New York: Guilford Press.

Bowlby, J. (1982). *Attachment and loss.* New York: Basic Books.

Bucci, W. (1984). Linking words and things: Basic processes and individual variation. *Cognition, 17,* 137–153.

Buck, R. (1984). *Human motivation and emotion.* New York: Wiley.

Bugental, J., & McBeath, B. (1973). Depth existential therapy: Evolution since World War II. In B. Bongar & L. Beutler (Eds.), *Comprehensive textbook of psychotherapy* (pp. 111–122). New York: Oxford University Press.

Bugental, J. F. T., & Sterling, M. M. (1993). New perspectives for existential–humanistic psychotherapy. In S. Webber & A. Gurman (Eds.) *Modern Psychotherapies: Theory and Practice* (pp. 000–000). New York: Guilford Press.

Carmer, J. C., & Rouzer, D. L. (1974). Healthy functioning from the Gestalt perspective. *The Counseling Psychologist, 4,* 20–23.

Deslisle, G. (1991). A Gestalt perspective of personality disorders. *The British Gestalt Journal, 1,* 42–50.

Elliott, R., & Greenberg, L. S. (1993). Experiential therapy in practice: The process-experiential approach. In B. Bongar & L. Beutler (Eds.), *Comprehensive textbook of psychotherapy* (pp. 123–139). New York: Oxford University Press.

Epstein, S. (1994). Integration of the cognitive and psychodynamic unconscious. *American Psychologist, 49,* 709–724.

Fagan, J. (1974). Personality theory and psychotherapy. *The Counseling Psychologist, 4,* 4–7.

Field, T., Schanberg, S. M., Scafidi, F., Bauer, C. R., Vega-Lahr, N., Garcia, R., Nystrom, J., & Kuhn, C. M. (1986). Effects of tactile/kinesthetic stimulation on preterm neonates. *Pediatrics, 77,* 654–658.

Gendlin, E. (1981). *Focusing.* New York: Bantam Books.

Goffman, E. (1959). *The presentation of self in everyday life.* New York: Doubleday.

Greenberg, L. S., Rice, L., & Elliott, R. (1993). *Facilitating emotional change: The moment-by-moment process.* New York: Guilford Press.

Greenberg, L. S., & Safran, J. (1987). *Emotion in psychotherapy: Affect, cognition and the process of change.* New York: Guilford Press.

Harlow, H. F. (1959, June). Love in the infant monkey. *Scientific American,* 68–74.

Harre, R. (1984). *Personal being.* Cambridge, MA: Harvard University Press.

Heidegger, M. (1962). *Being and Time* (J. Macquane & E. S. Robinson, Trans.) New York: Harper & Row. (Originally published 1949)

James, W. (1981). *The principles of psychology.* Cambridge, MA: Harvard University Press.

Jaspers, K. (1963). *General Psychopathology.* Chicago: University of Chicago Press.

Latner, J. (1992). The theory of Gestalt therapy. In E. C. Nevis (Ed.), *Gestalt therapy* (pp. 13–56). New York: Gardner Press.

Lietaer, G. (1991, July). *The authenticity of the therapist: Congruence and transparency.* Paper presented at the 2nd International Conference and Experiential Psychotherapy, Stirling, Scotland, UK.

Luria, A. (1976). *Cognitive development: Its cultural and social foundations.* Cambridge, MA: Harvard University Press.

May, R. (1969). *Love and will.* New York: Norton.

May, R., & Yalom, I. (1989). Existential psychotherapy. In R. Corsini & D. Wedding (Eds.), *Current psychotherapies* (pp. 363–402). Itasca, IL: F. E. Peacock Publishers.

Meador, B., & Rogers, C. (1979). Person-centered therapy. In R. Corsini (Ed.), *Current psychotherapies.* (pp. 131–184). Itasca, IL: F. E. Peacock Publishers.

Melnick, J., & Nevis, S. (1992). Diagnosis: The struggle for a meaningful paradigm. In E. C. Nevis (Ed.), *Gestalt therapy* (pp. 57–78). New York: Gardner Press.

Mermin, D. (1974). Gestalt theory of emotion. *The counseling psychologist, 4,* 15–20.

Paivio, A. (1987). A dual coding approach to perception and cognition. In H. Pick & E. Saltzman, (Eds.), *Modes of perceiving and processing information.* Hillsdale, NJ: Laurence Erlbaum.

Perls, F. (1969). *Ego, hunger and aggression.* New York: Random House.

Perls, F. (1973). *The gestalt approach and eyewitness to therapy.* Palo Alto, CA: Science and Behavior Books.

Perls, F., Hefferline, R., & Goodman, P. (1951). *Gestalt therapy: Excitement and growth in the human personality.* New York: Julian Press.

Polster, E., & Polster, M. (1973). *Gestalt therapy integrated.* New York: Random House.

Raskin, N., & Rogers, C. (1989). Person-centered therapy. In R. Corsini & D. Wedding (Eds.), *Current psychotherapies* (pp. 155–194). Itasca, IL: F. E. Peacock Publishers.

Rennie, D. L. (1992). Qualitative analysis of the client's experience of psychotherapy: The unfolding of reflexivity. In S. Toukmanian & D. Rennie (Eds.), *Psychotherapy process research: Paradigmatic and narrative approaches* (pp. 211–233). Newbury Park, CA: Sage.

Rice, L. N. (1974). The evocative function of the therapist. In D. Wexler & L. N. Rice (Eds.), *Innovations in client-centered therapy* (pp. 282–302). New York: Wiley.

Rice, L. N., & Greenberg, L. S. (1992). Humanistic approaches to psychotherapy. In D. K. Freeheim (Ed.), *History of psychotherapy: A century of change* (pp. 197–224). Washington, DC: American Psychological Association.

Rogers, C. (1959). A theory of therapy, personality, and interpersonal relationships, as developed in the client-centered framework. In S. Koch (Ed.), *Psychology a study of science; Formulations of the person and the social context* (pp. 184–256). New York: McGraw-Hill.

Rogers, C. (1961). *On becoming a person.* Boston, MA: Houghton Mifflin.

Rogers, C. (1965). *Client-centered therapy: Its current practice, implications, and theory.* Boston, MA: Houghton Mifflin.

Schneider, K. J., & May, R. (1995). *The psychology of existence: An integrative clinical perspective.* New York: McGraw-Hill.

Simkin, J. (1979). Gestalt therapy. In R. Corsini (Ed.), *Current psychotherapies* (pp. 272–301). Itasca, IL: F. E. Peacock Publishers.

Stewart, R. D. (1974). The philosophical background of gestalt therapy. *The Counseling Psychologist, 4,* 13–14.

Taylor, C. (1990). *Human agency and language.* New York: Cambridge University Press.

Tiryakian, E. (1962). *Sociologism and existentialism.* Englewood Cliffs, NJ: Prentice-Hall.

Toukmanian, S. (1990). A schema-based information processing perspective on client change in experiential therapy. In G. Lietaer, J. Rombauts, & R. Van Balen. (Eds.), *Client-centered and experiential psychotherapy in the nineties* (309–326). Leuven, Belgium: Leuven University Press.

Vygotsky, L. (1978). *Mind in society: The development of higher psychological processes.* Cambridge, MA: Harvard University Press.

Ward, P., & Rouzer, D. L. (1974). The nature of pathological functioning from a Gestalt perspective. *The Counseling Psychologist, 4,* 24–27.

Watson, J. C. (1992). The process of change when exploring problematic reactions. Unpublished doctoral dissertation, York University, North York, Ontario, Canada.

Watson, J. C., & Greenberg, L. S. (1996). Emotion and cognition in experiential therapy: A dialectical–constructivst perspective. In H. Rosen & K. Kuelwein (Eds.), *Constructing realities: Meaning making perspectives for psychotherapists* (pp. 253–276). San Francisco, CA: Jossey-Bass.

Watson, J. C., & Rennie, D. L. (1994). A qualitative analysis of clients' reports of their subjective experience while exploring problematic reactions. *Journal of Counseling Psychology, 41,* 500–509.

Yontef, G. M. (1995). Gestalt therapy. In A. S. Gurman & S. B. Messer (Eds.), *Essential psychotherapies: Theory and practice* (pp. 261–303). New York: Guilford Press.

Yontef, G. M. (1991). *Awareness, dialogue and process: Essays on gestalt therapy.* New York: Gestalt Journal Press.

Yontef, G. M., & Simkin, J. S. (1989). Gestalt therapy. In R. Corsini & D. Wedding (Eds.), *Current psychotherapies* (pp. 323–361). Itasca, IL: F. E. Peacock Publishers.

Zinker, J. (1977). *Creative process in gestalt therapy.* New York: Bruner/Mazel.

Chapter 5

TRAIT THEORIES
OF PERSONALITY

Paul T. Costa Jr. and Robert R. McCrae

INTRODUCTION

For anyone who truly wishes to understand human personality, trait psychology is not an option.

For decades, most personality psychologists opted for one or another of the major schools of psychology and attempted to understand human beings from its perspective. Psychoanalysts pondered free associations, behaviorists recorded behaviors, and self psychologists inventoried the self-concept. Although eclectic integrations were sometimes advanced (e.g., Murphy, 1947), most personality psychologists regarded perspectives other than their own with scorn and hostility. Dissension was the rule even within schools: Jungians and Freudians disputed the nature of the unconscious; Cattellians and Eysenckians argued about the true number of personality trait dimensions.

To a considerable extent, division is still seen in the field of personality psychology. The *Journal of Personality Assessment* routinely publishes studies using the Rorschach, an instrument that has all but disappeared from the pages of the *Journal of Personality and Social Psychology*. In recent articles, Westen (1995) has lamented the split between clinical and academic approaches to personality, and Cervone (1991) has noted the difficulties of

---

Paul T. Costa Jr. and Robert R. McCrae • Gerontology Research Center, National Institute on Aging, National Institutes of Health, Baltimore, Maryland 21224.

Advanced Personality, edited by David F. Barone, Michel Hersen, and Vincent B. Van Hasselt. Plenum Press, New York, 1998.

integrating the two major schools within contemporary academic personality psychology, the trait/dispositional and the social cognitive. McAdams (1996) has argued that personal concerns and life narratives form distinct levels of analysis of the person that require their own "indigenous theoretical framework" (p. 305).

Yet, something momentous has happened in the past 20 years that has begun to re-shape the field along the lines of more mature sciences, such as medicine. There are, after all, many specialties within medicine, and the methods and interests of the neurosurgeon are far removed from those of the epidemiologist or the renal physiologist. But every medical student, without exception, is expected to understand the basics of anatomy and physiology, of immunology and genetics. There is a core of common knowledge that is not merely a shared cultural heritage (like acquaintance with the classics), but an essential stepping off place for all medical research and practice: One simply cannot do neurosurgery without understanding the brain's susceptibility to infection and its supply of blood. Similarly, over the past two decades, an established body of knowledge has emerged that no personality psychologist can afford to ignore, and much of this knowledge concerns personality traits. For anyone who truly wishes to understand human personality, trait psychology is a requirement.

This chapter will not provide a historical review of trait theories of personality—a review that would typically include a discussion of Allport (1937), Cattell (1950), and Eysenck (1960). Not surprisingly, the details of their systems have often been superseded by later research findings. But much of their thinking about the nature of traits and the methods of trait psychology is still current; as Caspi (1998) put it, "by and large, Allport had it right" (p. 312). A survey of contemporary trait psychology inevitably, if implicitly, addressed the contributions of these giants of the field.

CONCEPTUAL AND EMPIRICAL BASES OF TRAIT PSYCHOLOGY

CROSS-SITUATIONAL CONSISTENCY AND THE EXISTENCE OF TRAITS

Traits are scientific constructs, but they are closely rooted in lay conceptions of human nature. Students need a glossary to understand *conditioned reflex* or *oral fixation;* however, every competent English speaker knows the meaning of *nervous, enthusiastic,* and *open-minded.* Trait psychologists build on these familiar notions, giving precise definitions, devising quantitative measures, and documenting the impact of traits on people's lives. Briefly, traits can be defined as "dimensions of individual differences in tendencies to show consistent patterns of thoughts, feelings, and actions" (McCrae & Costa, 1990, p. 23).

The most problematic part of that definition has been the phrase "consistent patterns." We would not call someone *generous* on the basis of a single act of charity, nor would we attribute neatness to someone who kept a tidy desk but strewed the floor with litter. On the other hand, we could still call people *melancholy* even if they occasionally laughed or smiled. How much consistency is needed to make the notion of a trait meaningful?

This problem is complicated by the fact that traits are continuously and normally distributed. In place of the convenient but misleading dichotomy of introverts versus extraverts or open versus closed individuals, we have found it useful to think of traits in terms of five levels that correspond to 1-standard-deviation-wide bands. About 38% of the population will lie within the *average* range; another 24% each will be in the *high* and *low* ranges, and about 7% will be in the *very high* and the *very low* ranges.

Combined with the fact that traits are probabilistically related to behavior—they are by definition *tendencies*—the continuous distribution of traits has important implications for understanding consistency in behavior. Consider an example. Suppose we conducted an experiment in which we assessed participants' levels of interpersonal warmth and then observed them as they interacted with a stranger to see if they smiled. The results of this hypothetical experiment are presented in Table 5.1: People in the very high range of warmth smiled at strangers fully 90% of the time, those in the high range smiled 70% of the time; low scorers smiled 30% and very low scorers only 10% of the time. This strong and linear association of trait level with probability of behavior would be powerful evidence of the operation of the trait. However, the point-biserial correlation between trait level and smiling behavior is only .41. Furthermore, Table 1 shows that average scorers, the largest of the five groups, would have a 50-50 chance of smiling at a stranger on any given occasion—their behavior would appear to be completely random when in fact it was exactly consistent with their trait standing.

Since the 1920s, when Hartshorn and May (1928) began to document the behavior of schoolchildren, we have known that behavior in one situation is only weakly predictable from behavior in another. It is instructive to examine the magnitude of the predictability. As part of the Riverside Accuracy Project (Funder, Kolar, & Blackman, 1995), David Funder and his colleagues videotaped 83 pairs of research participants interacting for 2 five-minute sessions, and then asked coders to view the tapes and rate the participants on each of 64 specific behaviors (e.g., *laughs frequently, offers advice*) (Sneed, McCrae, & Funder, 1998). Both sessions involved the same individuals on the same day; the first was a get-acquainted period; the second, a cooperative task. Correlations for the 64 behaviors across the two sessions ranged from −.11 to +.47; 53 correlations were positive, but only 30 reached conventional levels of significance (D. C. Funder, personal communication, March 15, 1996). Although there is a pattern of consistency in the data, the magnitude of prediction of specific behaviors across the two sessions is generally quite modest. Even that might be due in part to the similarity of the situations or the effects of transient moods: observed with different partners or on different days, even less consistency might have been seen.

Such findings were once widely interpreted to mean that traits were fictions, or at best such vanishingly weak influences on behavior that they were hardly worth studying (Mischel, 1968). However, over the course of a long debate, it has become clear we should never have expected strong predictions across situations (Ahadi & Diener, 1989; Howard, 1990;

TABLE 5.1. Hypothetical Distribution of Smiling Behavior at Different Levels of Trait Warmth

Level of warmth	T-Score	n	Smiles at stranger		% Smiling
			Yes	No	
Very high	>65	70	63	7	90
High	56–65	240	168	72	70
Average	45–55	380	190	190	50
Low	35–44	240	72	168	30
Very low	<35	70	7	63	10

Note: T-scores have a mean of 50 and a standard deviation of 10.

Kenrick & Funder, 1988). In our hypothetical experiment on warmth and smiling behaviors, on purely statistical grounds the expected correlation between smiling at strangers on two separate occasions is only $.41^2 = .17$. Substantively, this small correlation reflects the fact that many other features of the person and situation besides the trait of warmth help determine behavior in each instance. It is only when aggregated across many instances that these other features average out and the underlying pattern begins to emerge.

For example, in the Riverside Accuracy Project study described earlier, when behavior was averaged across three sessions, significant correlations were found with personality trait measures. People who described themselves or were described by acquaintances as being extroverts were more likely to show high enthusiasm, be talkative, exhibit social skills, behave in a cheerful manner, and enjoy the interaction (Sneed *et al.,* 1998). These correlations ranged in magnitude from .16 to .34—modest in an absolute sense, but rather high in comparison to appropriate expectations. Taken together, they illustrate the consistent pattern that identifies personality traits.

One of the most impressive demonstrations of cross-situational consistency at a molar level was provided by Funder, Kolar, and Blackman (1995). They asked parents, hometown friends, and college friends of a sample of college students to rate the student's personality. The highest agreement was seen between pairs of raters who had observed the student in the same context (two college friends, say, or father and mother); however, there was also substantial and significant agreement between pairs from different contexts (e.g., father and college friend) for all the major trait dimensions. The fact that different raters independently came to similar conclusions about how to describe students' personalities provides crucial evidence that traits are not simply cognitive fictions, but objective realities (McCrae, 1982) that do in fact influence thoughts, feelings, and actions across a range of situations.

A UNIVERSAL STRUCTURE OF TRAITS

Proving that traits really exist does not seem like something that should have revolutionary consequences for the whole of psychology. It was not, after all, Leeuwenhoek's discovery of the existence of microorganisms that transformed medicine, but the much later demonstration that they caused disease. Nevertheless, empirical evidence of the scientific legitimacy of traits (Block, 1981; Epstein, 1979; Eysenck & Eysenck, 1980) was a crucial turning point in the field, stimulating intensified research on the nature and operation of personality traits. And within a few years, one of the perennial problems in trait psychology—the structure of personality—was solved.

The scientific foundations of modern medicine are often traced to the work of the Renaissance anatomist Vesalius, whose painstaking dissections revealed the structure of the human body. By enumerating the organs of the body and documenting their spatial interrelationships, Vesalius laid the groundwork for later discoveries about their dynamic functioning. The structure of personality traits was revealed (later still) by a kind of statistical dissection called *factor analysis.*

For most of the 20th century, psychologists had been cataloging individual differences that seemed important in understanding human nature: instincts, temperaments, motives, character traits, attitudes, cognitive styles, personality disorders. Instruments, such as the Minnesota Multiphasic Personality Inventory (MMPI; Hathaway & McKinley, 1943), the

Guilford-Zimmerman Temperament Survey (GZTS; Guilford, Zimmerman, & Guilford, 1976), and the California Psychological Inventory (Gough, 1957), offered assessments of a wide range of personality characteristics. Adjective check lists drew on the thousands of trait terms available in the English language (Allport & Obert, 1936). The problem for trait psychology was not a lack of concepts but some reasonable system for organizing them.

It was obvious that there was considerable redundancy among trait measures. *Kind, considerate,* and *thoughtful* are near synonyms, as are *brave, courageous,* and *bold.* If we rated a group of people on their bravery and on their courage, we would expect strong positive correlations between the two sets of ratings, whereas correlations with ratings of kindness would presumably be much smaller. Beginning in the 1930s, factor analysis began to be used as a tool for summarizing the correlations among sets of personality variables. In effect, factor analysis identifies groups of variables that go together and that are distinct from other groups of variables. Each group of variables defines a dimension or factor, and each factor summarizes the variables. The hope of factor analysts was that they could identify a small set of factors that would describe economically basic features of personality.

Unfortunately, the results of a factor analysis depend critically on what variables are measured and on a series of more or less arbitrary decisions about how the technique is applied. As a result, it took half a century of work by psychologists and their computers before a convincing set of basic factors was found (not everyone is yet convinced; see Block, 1995; Eysenck, 1991; Waller, in press). The history of the discovery of the Five-Factor Model (FFM) of personality has now been told repeatedly (Digman, 1990; Goldberg, 1993). Suffice it to say here that the five factors were first identified in analyses of the lay terminology of trait adjectives and then extended to the psychological constructs that had been developed by personality theorists. The factors are generally labeled Neuroticism (N) versus Emotional Stability, Extraversion (E) or Surgency, Openness to Experience (O) or Intellect or Imagination, Agreeableness (A) versus Antagonism, and Conscientiousness (C) or Will to Achieve.

It is a remarkable fact that almost every aspect of individual differences in personality is related to one (or sometimes more) of these five factors. Agreeableness, for example, is seen in such lay terms as *kind, generous,* and *forgiving;* in nurturant versus aggressive motives; in preference for feeling over thinking in cognitive style; in unassuming and ingenuous interpersonal behavior; in humanitarian values and tender-minded attitudes; in dependent versus paranoid personality psychopathology. All five factors cut across the traditional distinctions between normal and abnormal personality and between cognitive, affective, and motivational traits and reveal pervasive influences on the psychological functioning of the individual as a whole.

The structure of personality traits is hierarchical. Each of the five broad factors is defined by many more specific traits. People who are competent, orderly, and dutiful are also likely to be high in achievement striving, self-discipline, and deliberation; this configuration of traits defines Conscientiousness. But being dutiful is not the same as being deliberate, and some individuals are one without being the other. Depending on the situation, it is sometimes best to study personality at the level of specific traits, sometimes at the level of broad factors. The FFM simplifies trait psychology, but it does not replace it with a simplistic set of five personality scores.

The organization of specific traits into broad factors is traditionally called the *structure of personality,* although it refers to the structure of traits in a population, not in an individual. To what populations could the FFM be generalized? Would different structures be found in children and adults, in men and women, in African Americans and Hispanic Americans? A series of studies, many of them using the NEO Personality Inventory (NEO-PI; Costa & McCrae, 1985, 1992b), a questionnaire designed specifically to operationalize the FFM, quickly showed that the FFM structure was replicable across all these groups (Costa, McCrae, & Dye, 1991; John, Caspi, Robins, Moffitt, & Stouthamer-Loeber, 1994).

Even more remarkably, studies showed that the same structure could also be found in very different cultures. There had long been evidence that two of the factors, E and N, were cross-culturally invariant (Eysenck, S. B., 1983), and some early studies suggested that all five might be universal (Amelang & Borkenau, 1982; Bond, 1979). Translations of the Revised NEO-PI into German (Ostendorf & Angleitner, 1994), Hebrew (Montag & Levin, 1994), Chinese (McCrae, Costa, & Yik, 1996), and Korean (Piedmont & Chae, 1997) confirmed this hypothesis. In spite of the fact that the FFM originated in English-language trait adjectives, the model itself works quite well among Israeli job applicants and Hong Kong undergraduates.

Of course, not all cultures have been studied; most notably, no one has yet looked for evidence of the FFM in a preliterate culture. It is likely that there will be subtle but real differences in some aspects of trait structure, and it remains possible that there will be additional factors beyond the FFM that are indigenous to particular cultures. However, the replications seen to date are sufficient to demonstrate that the FFM approximates a universal structure of personality.

Universality is not simply good news for advocates of the FFM and for cross-cultural psychologists, who now have a common basis on which to compare cultures; it is a crucial fact about human nature that all personality psychologists must take into account. Despite differences in child-rearing patterns, in social structures, in religion, political systems, and language itself, people everywhere differ from each other along the same basic dimensions. There are always loners and joiners, progressives and traditionalists, bullies and pushovers. Which aspects of personality are encouraged and how they are expressed varies from culture to culture, but the raw material is much the same. The discovery of a universal personality structure begins to shift personality psychology from the social sciences to the biological sciences.

THE BIOLOGICAL BASIS OF TRAITS

In principle, most psychologists have always agreed that there must be some biological basis of personality; as Henry Murray is said to have put it, "no brain, no personality." Personality theorists, however, have generally assumed that the major determinates of personality must be sought in the experiences recorded by the brain, not its intrinsic structure (Janis, Mahl, Kagan, & Holt, 1969).

An important exception to this generalization was the study of temperament. At birth, infants have recognizable patterns of behavior and emotional response (Thomas, Chess, & Birch, 1968). These patterns of temperament seemed to precede experience but to lead to later personality dispositions. Traits related to two of the factors, N and E, were often regarded as temperament variables, especially because they are intimately tied to positive and negative affect (Costa & McCrae, 1980).

Temperament was often contrasted with character, because character traits, such as authoritarianism, altruism, and need for achievement, were thought to be the result of socialization experiences rather than biological dispositions. But this appealing dichotomy has broken down under the weight of recent evidence. Both character and temperament variables fit within the FFM, and all five factors—not just N and E—are related to temperament variables (Angleitner & Ostendorf, 1994). Traits such as liberal thinking and aesthetic sensitivity seem far removed from biology. Yet, the broader dimension of Openness to Experience that they define is familiar to ethologists who study exploratory behavior in animals.

The biological reality of personality traits is documented perhaps most impressively in studies of behavior genetics. Identical twins reared in vastly different families come to resemble each other (Tellegen et al., 1988), sometimes uncannily. There have now been a large number of family, adoption, and twin studies conducted by many different investigators around the world, and the evidence for substantial heritability for all five dimensions is compelling (Jang, McCrae, Angleitner, Riemann, & Livesley, in press; Loehlin, 1992). Typically, genetic influences account for 40% to 50% of the variance in measured personality traits; most of the remainder of the variance is unaccounted for. To almost everyone's surprise, behavior genetics studies have almost uniformly failed to detect the influence of aspects of the environment on adult personality (e.g., social class and child-rearing practices) shared by family members (Plomin & Daniels, 1987).

It would be a serious mistake to conclude from these studies that personality traits are purely biological phenomena, impervious to cultural and interpersonal effects. In fact, every trait is expressed in a culturally conditioned way. The old temperament-character dichotomy erred not only in denying a biological basis to character but also in ignoring cultural influences on temperament. Just as every child is born with an innate capacity for language but must learn French or Bengali or Tagalog in order to speak, so every extravert must learn the culturally dictated forms of emotional response and social interaction in order to express his or her innate enthusiasm and sociability.

Behavior genetics tells us that there must be a biological basis for traits, but it says little about actual biological mechanisms. Psychiatrists and personality psychologists (e.g., Cloninger, 1988; Gray, 1991) have studied psychophysiology and neuropharmacology for many years in an effort to understand that prodigiously complex issue. Most recently, molecular geneticists (e.g., Benjamin et al., 1996) have offered evidence of links between specific genes and normal personality traits—although these results have not yet been successfully replicated (Malhotra et al., 1996). Part of the difficulty in identifying personality-related genes stems from the fact that many genes are probably involved in the regulation of each trait, and thus any one gene is likely to have only a small effect. The complete system by which hundreds or thousands of genes interact to yield an integrated personality is likely to be extraordinarily complex.

Even if the entire genetic architecture of personality were known, it would not mean the reduction of personality psychology to biology. Personality traits are psychological phenomena, even if they have a biological basis, and they must ultimately be understood in terms that make sense of human action and experience (McCrae & Costa, 1995)

Temporal Stability of Traits: New Data from the BLSA

Personality traits are supposed to be enduring dispositions. This means that they are distinguishable from transient moods or states. However, it does not necessarily imply that they cannot change over relatively long periods of time as the result of universal maturational processes, life experiences, or therapeutic interventions. It is possible that one could be an introvert in adolescence, an extravert at midlife, and an introvert again in old age.

Until the 1970s, no one had a very good idea what happened with age. There were theories about life-span development (Erikson, 1950; Levinson, Darrow, Klein, Levinson, & McKee, 1978), and there were many cross-sectional studies comparing young and old, but there were very few longitudinal studies in which the actual course of development could be observed over long periods of adulthood. Since then, however, many longitudinal studies have been reported, all pointing to the conclusion that personality traits are remarkably stable in adults (McCrae & Costa, 1990).

It is somewhat unusual to present new data in a textbook chapter on personality theory; yet, from one perspective it is completely appropriate. Trait psychology is the most data-driven school of personality—indeed, it is often derided as mere "dustbowl empiricism." But most trait psychologists are not atheoretical (Wiggins, 1996); they simply insist that theory should account for the known empirical facts. Many of the most important facts about traits have come from longitudinal studies (Costa & McCrae, 1992a).

The Baltimore Longitudinal Study of Aging (BLSA; Shock *et al.,* 1984) is a multidisciplinary study of normal aging processes. Men, initially ages 20 to 90, have been studied since 1958; women were added to the panel in 1978. Participants visit the Gerontology Research Center in Baltimore every two years; mailed questionnaires are also administered periodically. Participants are generally healthy, well-educated, community dwelling volunteers; they are predominantly White. Participants are enrolled on an on-going basis.

Beginning in 1960, the GZTS (Guilford *et al.,* 1976) has been administered to all participants on their first or second visit, and subsequently approximately 6 and 12 years later. The GZTS is a classic personality inventory, developed before the advent of the FFM. However, most of its scales are easily interpreted in terms of the FFM dimensions: Emotional Stability, Sociability, Thoughtfulness, Friendliness, and Restraint are definers of low N and high E, O, A, and C factors, respectively (McCrae, 1989). Earlier publications have reported longitudinal analyses of the GZTS in men (Costa, McCrae, & Arenberg, 1980) and in women after six years (Costa & McCrae, 1992a); here, we examine data from the second retest in women.

The primary sample—Sample A—consists of 114 women initially ages 23 to 73 who completed a paper-and-pencil version of the GZTS between 1978 and 1982. Six to ten years later they completed the GZTS again, and they were administered their third GZTS by computer after another six to nine years. The interval from first to third administration ranged from 12 to 16 years, with a mean of 13.4 years. According to standard scoring instructions, a GZTS scale is not considered valid if more than three items are missing; for that reason, the number of cases differs from scale to scale. As a partial replication sample, we also examined data from 211 women who did not have valid data on three occasions, but did have one retest after at least six years. Sample B women were initially ages 17 to 82 and were retested on average after 7.8 years.

Longitudinal data are usually used to address two primary questions: Are individual differences preserved? Does the group as a whole increase or decline on the trait? The stability of individual differences is usually calculated as a test-retest correlation. Over a short interval (e.g., a week or month), retest correlations reflect one form of test reliability; personality scales typically show retest reliability coefficients of .70 to .90. When a period of years separate test from retest, the resulting value is influenced both by retest unreliability and by actual changes in personality over the interval; it is thus a very conservative estimate of stability per se.

Table 5.2 reports retest correlations for Sample A from Time 1 to Time 2, Time 2 to Time 3, and Time 1 to Time 3. During that period, many of the women will have experienced stressful life events, health problems, or changes in occupation or residence, and all will have felt the physiological effects of aging. Yet, most of the correlations in Table 5.2 would be respectable as two-week retest reliabilities; given the retest interval, they demonstrate that there is remarkably little change in self-reported personality over six years, and only slightly more over 13 years. Values this high were astounding when they were first reported (Costa & McCrae, 1978; Costa et al., 1980), but they have been repeatedly replicated. Table 5.2 itself shows a partial replication in the data from Sample B.

It is still possible that life experience or intrinsic maturation may have important effects on personality—effects that are common to everyone in the sample. If everyone is becoming more restrained, objective, and thoughtful at the same rate, individual differences will be preserved despite changes in the group as a whole. Such changes might be seen in cross-sectional comparisons of younger and older women as well as in longitudinal changes across time. Table 5.3 summarizes results of repeated measures analyses of variance in which younger (23–49) and older (50–73) women from Sample A were tested three times. The first column shows that older women scored slightly higher on Emotional Stability and Friendliness; the second shows that over the period of the study women increased slightly in Restraint and Ascendance. Note that the cross-sectional findings are not replicated by longitudinal changes—that is, neither Emotional Stability nor Friendliness increased over time. There is very little evidence here of maturational change in any of the traits measured by the GZTS.

Results from Sample B are also given in Table 5.3. Perhaps because the larger sample size gives greater statistical power, these analyses show more numerous effects. But real maturational changes should be seen in both samples, and the only replicated effects in Table 5.3 are a generational difference in Friendliness (older women are friendlier in both samples) and interaction effects suggesting that younger women become more assertive and older women become less active over time. These effects are generally small; however, the

TABLE 5.2. Longitudinal Analysis of GZTS Scales in Women: Stability Coefficients

GZTS Scale	Sample A				Sample B	
	N	r_{12}	r_{23}	r_{13}	n	r_{12}
General activity	104	.81	.84	.72	181	.76
Restraint	95	.63	.78	.62	173	.72
Ascendance	96	.82	.87	.75	174	.81
Sociability	96	.81	.86	.77	174	.83
Emotional stability	99	.72	.69	.64	184	.75
Objectivity	93	.74	.76	.57	179	.73
Friendliness	95	.71	.76	.61	188	.68
Thoughtfulness	95	.71	.72	.63	186	.71
Personal relations	77	.68	.69	.60	151	.68
Masculinity	99	.75	.79	.75	186	.76
Median		.73	.77	.64		.74

Note: For Sample A, mean Time 1/Time 3 retest interval = 13.4 years; for Sample B, mean retest interval = 7.8 years. All correlations significant at $p < .001$.

TABLE 5.3. Longitudinal Analyses of GZTS Scales in Women: Age Differences and Changes

GZTS Scale	Sample A			Sample B		
	Age group	Time	Group X time	Age group	Time	Group X time
General activity			O – – –	– – –	–	O –
Restraint		+		+++		
Ascendance		+	Y +	– – –		Y +
Sociability				–		Y +
Emotional stability	+				+	
Objectivity					+++	
Friendliness	+			+++		
Thoughtfulness						
Personal relations			Y +++			
Masculinity				– – –	+	

Note: Pluses indicate increase with age or time, minuses indicate decreases. +p < .05; +++p < .001; –p < .05,– – –p < .001. For interaction effects, O = older, Y = younger group shows indicated effect.

last one at least is noteworthy because it exactly replicates earlier reports on men: Douglas and Arenberg (1978) found that in BLSA men, "beginning at age 50, preference for rapidly paced activity declined" (p. 744). Men and women tend to slow down after age 50—that truism is one of the few reliable findings of maturational change in personality after age 30.

Personality does show changes between adolescence and full adulthood (Costa & McCrae, 1994); it can change dramatically as a result of dementing disorders (Siegler et al., 1991); and it sometimes changes in response to psychotherapy (Trull, Useda, Costa, & McCrae, 1995). But for most of adult life, personality traits remain relatively constant. One implication is that personality is not a plastic system easily shaped and reshaped by environmental influences; a second is that much of an individual's behavior and experience is predictable years in advance from a knowledge of his or her standing on the dimensions of the FFM. These are two of the major reasons why no personality psychologist can afford to ignore trait psychology.

PERSONALITY THEORY AND TRAIT PSYCHOLOGY

The Pervasive Influence Of Traits

As we have seen, the influence of traits on single behaviors is usually very subtle. A corollary of this fact is that if, despite the subtlety, we rather easily recognize traits in ourselves and the people around us, it must be because traits are very pervasive. Our personality traits permeate virtually every aspect of our lives. In consequence, almost every branch of psychology can benefit from a consideration of traits in the FFM.

Consider vocational behavior, the province of industrial/organizational psychology. Vocational interests are strongly related to E and O: Extraverts are attracted to jobs like sales manager, whereas open people aspire to be artists (Costa, McCrae, & Holland, 1984). Effective job performance across a wide range of occupations is predicted by C (Barrick &

Mount, 1991). Job satisfaction (like satisfaction with most aspects of life) is inversely related to N (Holland, 1996). Managerial styles (Kirton, 1976) and mid-career shifts (McCrae & Costa, 1985) are associated with O.

Personality traits are equally relevant to clinical psychology (Miller, 1991) and psychiatry (Costa & Widiger, 1994), to stress and coping research (Watson & Hubbard, 1996) and health psychology (Marshall, Wortman, Vickers, Kusulas, & Hervig, 1994), to educational psychology (Goff & Ackerman, 1992) and the psychology of religion (Piedmont, 1996). To be sure, the FFM must be adapted for each of these applications and supplemented by constructs more specific to the target problem. But researchers and theorists in each of these subdisciplines need not (and should not) start from scratch in describing individual differences. General personality traits form the first level of description of human activity in almost every sphere.

CLASSIC THEORIES IN PERSPECTIVE

More than any other branch of psychology, personality is steeped in tradition. The grand theories of Freud, Murray, and Lewin are taught today much as they were 40 years ago (Hall & Lindzey, 1957)—as if they stated timeless truths about human nature immune to empirical test. Twenty years ago, when personality psychology was in a period of crisis, and the very existence of personality traits was in doubt, clinging to familiar stories may have been understandable. However, we think the time has come to relegate the first generation of personality theories to history courses (Mendelsohn, 1993) and move on to build a new generation based on our growing knowledge of personality traits and processes (McCrae & Costa, 1996).

It would be a grotesque oversimplification to say that the classic theories are *wrong*. Each is an intricate intellectual construction with multiple premises and conclusions and with its own definition of what personality is and what phenomena are to be explained. It would be a worthwhile exercise to take any one of the classic theories and subject it to rigorous scrutiny in the light of current empirical knowledge, but it would probably require a book-length treatment.

Our impression, however, is that such an exercise would show numerous and significant deficiencies. Although Allport may have "had it right" by and large, we suspect that a careful assessment of most theorists would come to a different conclusion. Certainly, the effect of most classic theories has been *misleading* to the field of personality. They direct our attention to the wrong sets of problems and the wrong candidates for solutions (Scarr, 1987).

Nowhere is this clearer than in the case of personality development. Rogers's emphasis on parental love, Fromm's concern for cultural influences, Mead's attention to social appraisals, Skinner's principles of reinforcement, and Bandura's work on modeling all suggest that personality is shaped by the environment. But if by personality we mean traits—and recall that traits are characteristic emotional, interpersonal, experiential, attitudinal, and motivational styles—then all these theories miss the mark. The evidence suggests that personality traits are endogenous dispositions that unfold under almost any set of circumstances, just as acorns, regardless of soil or sunlight or water, grow (if they grow at all) into oaks.

Psychodynamic theories from Freud's on have had a tremendous influence on 20th-century conceptions of human nature, portraying human beings as irrational, acting on the basis of forces and desires they do not understand. This view was recently seconded on different grounds by cognitive social psychologists (see Funder, 1993, for the argument and rebuttal). No one would dispute that there is more than a little truth to the assertion that people are not wholly rational, but the effect of these theories has been to foster a completely unwarranted distrust of people's self-knowledge. Many clinicians have come to prefer inkblots to interviews, and psychometricians have been obsessed with creating scales to detect socially desirable responding and defensiveness—scales that generally do not work and usually are not needed (McCrae et al., 1989). In fact, evidence on self/other agreement on personality traits (McCrae & Costa, 1989) shows that, in general, people do understand themselves.

In many other ways, classic theories have been poor guides. The most striking feature of personality in adulthood is its stability—not something one would have guessed from Erikson's stages of psychosocial development. The major determinants of happiness are dispositional, not environmental (Costa, McCrae, & Zonderman, 1987)—a surprise, surely, to need-reduction theorists (see chap. 13). The ultimate fact that trait psychology points to is variation. Therefore, the classic debates about whether human beings are basically altruistic or egocentric, creative or conforming, are simplistic from this perspective: Altruism and creativity are normally distributed traits.

We do not mean to disparage the thinkers who gave us the classic theories of personality. Many of them were extraordinarily acute observers, careful scholars, and profound thinkers—truly grand theorists. But their theories, articulated in the infancy of the science of personality psychology, have been outgrown, and it is time to move on.

THE ROLE OF TRAIT PSYCHOLOGY IN PERSONALITY THEORY

Are classic theories then merely to be replaced by trait psychology and the FFM? No. To return to our anatomical metaphor, the circulatory system is absolutely vital to the functioning not only of the organism as a whole but also to each of the organs in it. But although every branch of medicine assumes an understanding of circulation, even the most perfect knowledge of that system would not suffice to understand the human body. In the same way, a knowledge of trait theory is necessary but not sufficient for the science of personality psychology.

Traits are individual difference concepts; they are useful only for contrasting different people. A complete theory of personality must also explain universal aspects of human nature—features that make all people alike (Tooby & Cosmides, 1990). Traits describe recurrent patterns of thought and behavior, but they say nothing about the moment-to-moment flow of behavior. Traits provide one level of scientific explanation of behavior (McCrae & Costa, 1995); however, they do not specify the mechanisms by which enduring dispositions are concretely manifested in specific situations—mechanisms that must be understood in order to modify behavior. Many of the same traits—modesty, dutifulness, liberal thinking—are found in every cultural group, but the FFM does not explain how to act with modesty in Korea, what one's duties are in Iran, or which political positions are liberal in post-Soviet Russia.

What is required of new personality theories is that they integrate what is known about traits into a model that explains more broadly the psychological functioning of the individual. Eventually, perhaps, a single theory will emerge; for the foreseeable future, many alternative theories, focusing on different aspects of the person or postulating different mechanism of development or operation, will be plausible.

It is a sign of new self-confidence among personality psychologists that theory building on a large scale is now beginning to reappear. Mayer (1995) combed the glossaries of personality textbooks to identify 400 personality components that might be taken as the raw material of a comprehensive personality theory. McAdams and Emmons (1995) edited a special issue of the *Journal of Personality* devoted to new insights into the organization of personality as a whole. Wiggins (1996) invited researchers associated with the FFM to offer their own theoretical perspectives on that model.

Our attempt to locate traits within a model of the person as a whole is represented in Figure 5.1. In our Five-Factor Theory of personality, traits are seen as *basic tendencies* of the individual that, over the course of development, influence the establishment of *characteristic adaptations*. It is through these developmental processes that biologically based dispositions come to be expressed in culturally conditioned forms. Specific behaviors are best understood as an indirect consequence of traits; more directly, they are products of the interaction of characteristic adaptations (skills, plans, habits) with external influences (see McCrae & Costa, 1996; McCrae *et al.*, 1996 for extended discussions of the figure).

The Five-Factor Theory is new and has only begun to be used as a guide to research questions (Jang *et al.*, in press). But it should be possible to construe earlier research within its framework, and that exercise can illustrate how the model works. It is also useful in showing the dynamic operation of personality traits as they unfold over time in concrete situations. Consider as an example a social psychological construct called *need for closure* (Kruglanski & Webster, 1996). Defined as "a desire for definite knowledge on some issue" (p. 263), a strong need for closure leads people to "seize" on the first credible answer and then "freeze" on it so that alternatives need not be considered.

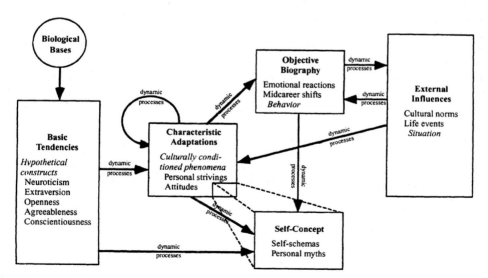

FIGURE 5.1. A model of the person. *Note.* From "Trait Explanations in Personality Psychology," by R. R. McCrae and P. T. Costa Jr., 1995, *European Journal of Personality, 9,* pp. 231–252.

Need for closure was originally viewed as a motivational state of the individual elicited by a situation. In a series of experiments, time pressure, task unattractiveness, and even the distraction of a noisy computer printer were sufficient to induce a need for closure, which had important consequences for forming first impressions, using stereotypes, and rejecting deviant group members. So pervasive are the effects of need for closure that Kruglanski (1996) has argued that it forms the basis for "a new general paradigm for the study of social psychology" (p. 493).

Where within Figure 5.1 would one located the need for closure? Perhaps it is easiest to work backward. The observable behaviors (the hastily formed first impression or the decisions biased by stereotypes) and the accompanying affects (a sense of urgency and frustration) are microevents in the individual's *objective biography.* The situational stimuli (time pressure, noise) are of course *external influences,* and the processes by which the need is induced and expressed are found in the arrows connecting external influences, characteristic adaptations, and objective biography.

Characteristic adaptations are involved because every action of the person is mediated by the network of skills, beliefs, habits, and goals that constitute this aspect of the person. At the most basic level, the experimental subject must perceive the experimenter, understand the language in which instructions are given, activate preexisting stereotypes about different groups, and employ motor skills in writing down responses to questions. The psychological operating system by which human beings function is a necessary part of each individual's characteristic adaptations.

As described so far, need for closure is a universal human response to unanswered questions that can be intensified by certain kinds of task demands. It becomes of interest to trait psychologists when we consider that there may be individual differences in the need. Some people may be more able than others to tolerate uncertainty—they may even enjoy it; some people may have stronger stereotypical beliefs. Webster and Kruglanski (1994) created a Need for Closure Scale (NFCS) to measure such individual differences, reasoning that people who as a general rule preferred order and predictability, were decisive and closed minded, and were uncomfortable with ambiguity would have a chronically high need for closure. They showed that in laboratory settings people scoring high on the NFCS were more likely to base judgments of a job candidate on the first information presented and to attribute views to a speaker even when informed that the speaker had been told what to say.

Completing the NFCS required respondents to respond to such statements as "I hate to change my plans at the last minute" and "I always see many possible solutions to the problems I face" [reverse scored]. The fact that they could do so reliably argues that aspects of the dispositional need for closure must be encoded in the *self-concept:* People have observed their own behavior and reactions enough to have a rather clear opinions about these matters. The fact that the scale successfully predicted laboratory behaviors implies that the self-concept was reasonably accurate.

Where, then, does dispositional need for closure fit in Figure 5.1? In some respects, we can construe it as a part of characteristic adaptations. People have an acquired set of preferences, habits, skills, and attitudes that lead them in varying degrees to choose certainty and closure over uncertainty and ambiguity. In principle, these acquired characteristics might have any number of origins, including early parental modeling, cultural influences, or a history of reinforcements. Indeed, some such set of external influences must have been involved; characteristic adaptations do not emerge from an environmental vacuum.

Five-Factor Theory, however, asserts that many characteristic adaptations can be traced in part to basic tendencies, including personality traits. Table 5.4 provides some data on that hypothesis. In 1996 and 1997, 30 men and 54 women in the BLSA completed the NFCS. Sometime between 1989 and 1997, they had also completed the Revised NEO-PI. The NFCS was scored for five subscales as well as the total; correlations with NEO-PI-R factors are shown in the table. Despite the fact that an average of four years separates the administration of these two instruments, substantial correlations are seen between NFCS measures and NEO-PI-R factors, especially Openness (O) and Conscientiousness (C).

These associations—especially the negative correlation between Need for Closure and Openness (O)—make conceptual sense (McCrae, 1996). People who are closed to experience have a decidedly limited capacity to appreciate experience for its own sake; variety, novelty, and the challenge of thinking things through have no appeal. In contrast, open people relish ambiguity and inconsistency because they make life more interesting. Five-Factor Theory holds that personality traits can affect dynamic processes; thus, the degree of need for closure at any given moment can be seen as being in part a direct expression of basic tendencies toward openness or closedness.

Additionally, there is an indirect effect through the development of characteristic adaptations. Lacking a need for change and uncertainty, closed people come to prefer a simple, structured, familiar world. Through experience they discover that tradition, conventionality, and stereotypes offer tried-and-true answers that they can adopt without much thought. They begin to think of themselves as conservative, down-to-earth people, and they seek out like-minded friends and spouses who will not challenge their beliefs. Thus, basic tendencies of closedness develop into preferences, ideologies, self-construals, and social roles; these characteristic adaptations habitualize, legitimatize, and socially support a way of thinking that expresses a high need for closure.

Readers with a high need for closure will be distressed to hear that the NFCS has recently been criticized on psychometric grounds by Neuberg, Judice, and West (1997). They argue that it is a multidimensional construct because the Decisiveness subscale is unrelated to the other subscales (a finding replicated in the present data). Table 5.4 shows that NFCS is multidimensional in another sense: It seems to measure both low Openness (O) and high Conscientiousness (C). Perhaps, as Neuberg and his colleagues argue, Decisiveness is related to the "seizing" effects and Preference for Order and Predictability to the "freezing"

TABLE 5.4. Correlations between Need for Closure Scales and Revised NEO Personality Inventory (NEO-PI-R) Factors

Need for Closure Scale	NEO-PI-R Factor				
	N	E	O	A	C
Preference for order	−.02	−.04	−.40***	.02	.48***
Preference for predictability	.07	−.13	−.45***	−.08	.26*
Decisiveness	−.29**	.15	−.01	−.08	.41***
Discomfort with ambiguity	.26*	.13	−.16	−.04	.20
Closed-mindedness	.13	.01	−.40***	−.11	.00
Total need for closure	.04	.06	−.42***	−.08	.42***

Note: $N = 84$. *$p < .05$, **$p < .01$, ***$p < .001$.

effects. Perhaps it is only the presence of Openness in the NFCS that accounts for the laboratory findings; Conscientiousness may prove irrelevant. In short, as in most areas of active research, there are many questions left. The Five-Factor Theory of personality provides one framework within which they can be addressed.

Need for closure is only one of a myriad of psychological processes and mechanisms that are needed to account fully for human behavior and experience. Understanding them—using principles from human development, information processing, social cognition, motivation and emotions, coping and defense, and many other aspects of psychology—is one of the great challenges of contemporary personality theory. The heritability, universality, stability, and pervasiveness of traits in the FFM provide essential facts around which new and dynamic theories must be built.

Although medicine has had a scientific foundation since the time of Vesalius, it made slow progress until this century, when advance followed advance: antibiotics, x rays, and vitamins were soon followed by heart transplants, magnetic resonance imaging, and gene therapy. Psychology today may be as scientifically primitive as medicine was in 1900–but how far we may go in the next 100 years!

REFERENCES

Ahadi, S., & Diener, E. (1989). Multiple determinants and effect size. *Journal of Personality and Social Psychology, 56,* 398–406.

Allport, G. W. (1937). *Personality: A psychological interpretation.* New York: Holt.

Allport, G. W., & Odbert, H. S. (1936). Trait names: A psycho-lexical study. *Psychological Monographs, 47* (1, Whole No. 211).

Amelang, M., & Borkenau, P. (1982). Über die faktorielle Struktur und externe Validität einiger Fragebogen-Skalen zur Erfassung von Dimensionen der Extraversion und emotionalen Labilität [On the factor structure and external validity of some questionnaire scales measuring dimensions of extraversion and neuroticism]. *Zeitschrift für Differentielle und Diagnostische Psychologie, 3,* 119–146.

Angleitner, A., & Ostendorf, F. (1994). Temperament and the Big Five factors of personality. In C. F. Halverson, G. A. Kohnstamm, & R. P. Martin (Eds.), *The developing structure of temperament and personality from infancy to adulthood* (pp. 69–90). Hillsdale, NJ: Erlbaum.

Barrick, M. R., & Mount, M. K. (1991). The Big Five personality dimensions and job performance: A meta-analysis. *Personnel Psychology, 44,* 1–26.

Benjamin, J., Li, L., Patterson, C., Greenberg, B. D., Murphy, D. L., & Hamer, D. H. (1996). Population and familial association between the D4 dopamine receptor gene and measures of novelty seeking. *Nature Genetics, 12,* 81–84.

Block, J. (1981). Some enduring and consequential structures of personality. In A. I. Rabin, J. Aronoff, A. M. Barclay, & R. A. Zucker (Eds.), *Further explorations in personality* (pp. 27–43). New York: Wiley-Interscience.

Block, J. (1995). A contrarian view of the five-factor approach to personality description. *Psychological Bulletin, 117,* 187–215.

Bond, M. H. (1979). Dimensions of personality used in perceiving peers: Cross-cultural comparisons of Hong Kong, Japanese, American, and Filipino university students. *International Journal of Psychology, 14,* 47–56.

Caspi, A. (1998). Personality development across the life course. In N. Eisenberg (Ed.), *Handbook of child psychology: Vol. 3: Social, emotional, and personality development* (pp. 311–388). New York: Wiley.

Cattell, R. B. (1950). *Personality: A systematic theoretical and factual study.* New York: McGraw-Hill.

Cervone, D. (1991). The two disciplines of personality psychology. *Psychological Science, 2,* 371–377.

Cloninger, C. R. (1988). A unified biosocial theory of personality and its role in the development of anxiety states: A reply to commentaries. *Psychiatric Development, 2,* 83–120.

Costa, P. T., Jr., & McCrae, R. R. (1978). Objective personality assessment. In M. Storandt, I. C. Siegler, & M. F. Elias (Eds.), *The clinical psychology of aging* (pp. 119–143). New York: Plenum Press.

Costa, P. T., Jr., & McCrae, R. R. (1980). Influence of extraversion and neuroticism on subjective well-being: Happy and unhappy people. *Journal of Personality and Social Psychology, 38,* 668–678.

Costa, P. T., Jr., & McCrae, R. R. (1985). *The NEO Personality Inventory manual.* Odessa, FL: Psychological Assessment Resources.

Costa, P. T., Jr., & McCrae, R. R. (1992a). Multiple uses for longitudinal personality data. *European Journal of Personality, 6,* 85–102.

Costa, P. T., Jr., & McCrae, R. R. (1992b). *The Revised NEO Personality Inventory (NEO-PI-R) and NEO Five-Factor Inventory (NEO-FFI) professional manual.* Odessa, FL: Psychological Assessment Resources.

Costa, P. T., Jr., & McCrae, R. R. (1994). Stability and change in personality from adolescence through adulthood. In C. F. Halverson, G. A. Kohnstamm, & R. R. Martin (Eds.), *The developing structure of temperament and personality from infancy to adulthood* (pp. 139–150). Hillsdale, NJ: Erlbaum.

Costa, P. T., Jr., McCrae, R. R., & Arenberg, D. (1980). Enduring dispositions in adult males. *Journal of Personality and Social Psychology, 38,* 793–800.

Costa, P. T., Jr., McCrae, R. R., & Dye, D. A. (1991). Facet scales for Agreeableness and Conscientiousness: A revision of the NEO Personality Inventory. *Personality and Individual Differences, 12,* 887–898.

Costa, P. T., Jr., McCrae, R. R., & Holland, J. L. (1984). Personality and vocational interests in an adult sample. *Journal of Applied Psychology, 69,* 390–400.

Costa, P. T., Jr., McCrae, R. R., & Zonderman, A. B. (1987). Environmental and dispositional influences on well-being: Longitudinal followup of an American national sample. *British Journal of Psychology, 78,* 299–306.

Costa, P. T., Jr., & Widiger, T. A. (Eds.). (1994). *Personality disorders and the Five-Factor Model of personality.* Washington, DC: American Psychological Association.

Digman, J. M. (1990). Personality structure: Emergence of the Five-Factor Model. *Annual Review of Psychology, 41,* 417–440.

Douglas, K., & Arenberg, D. (1978). Age changes, cohort differences, and cultural change on the Guilford-Zimmerman Temperament Survey. *Journal of Gerontology, 33,* 737–747.

Epstein, S. (1979). The stability of behavior: I. On predicting most of the people much of the time. *Journal of Personality and Social Psychology, 37,* 1097–1126.

Erikson, E. H. (1950). *Childhood and society.* New York: Norton.

Eysenck, H. J. (1960). *The structure of human personality.* London: Methuen.

Eysenck, H. J. (1991). Dimensions of personality: 16, 5, or 3?—Criteria for a taxonomic paradigm. *Personality and Individual Differences, 12,* 773–790.

Eysenck, M. W., & Eysenck, H. J. (1980). Mischel and the concept of personality. *British Journal of Psychology, 71,* 191–204.

Eysenck, S. B. (1983). One approach to cross-cultural studies of personality. *Australian Journal of Psychology, 35,* 381–391.

Funder, D. C. (1993). Judgments as data for personality and developmental psychology: Error versus accuracy. In D. C. Funder, R. Parke, C. Tomlinson-Keasey, & Widamen, K. (Eds.), *Studying lives through time: Personality and development* (pp. 121–146). Washington, DC: American Psychological Association.

Funder, D. C., Kolar, D. C., & Blackman, M. C. (1995). Agreement among judges of personality: Interpersonal relations, similarity, and acquaintanceship. *Journal of Personality and Social Psychology, 69,* 656–672.

Goff, M., & Ackerman, P. L. (1992). Personality-intelligence relations: Assessment of typical intellectual engagement. *Journal of Educational Psychology, 84,* 537–552.

Goldberg, L. R. (1993). The structure of phenotypic personality traits. *American Psychologist, 48,* 26–34.

Gough, H. G. (1957). *California Psychological Inventory manual.* Palo Alto, CA: Consulting Psychologists Press.

Gray, J. A. (1991). The neuropsychology of temperament. In J. Strelau & A. Angleitner (Eds.), *Explorations in temperament: International perspectives on theory and measurement* (pp. 105–128). New York: Plenum Press.

Guilford, J. S. Zimmerman, W. S., & Guilford, J. P. (1976). *The Guilford-Zimmerman Temperament Survey Handbook: Twenty-five years of research and application.* San Diego, CA: EdITS Publishers.

Hall, C. S., & Lindzey, G. (1957). *Theories of personality.* New York: Wiley.

Hartshorn, H., & May, M. A. (1928). *Studies in deceit.* New York: Macmillan.

Hathaway, S. R., & McKinley, J. C. (1943). *The Minnesota Multiphasic Personality Inventory* (Rev. ed.). Minneapolis: University of Minnesota Press.

Holland, J. L. (1996). Exploring careers with a typology: What we have learned and some new directions. *American Psychologist, 51,* 397–406.

Howard, G. S. (1990). On the construct validity of self-reports: What do the data say? *American Psychologist, 45,* 292–294.

Jang, K. L., McCrae, R. R., Angleitner, A., Riemann, R., & Livesley, W. J. (in press). Heritability of facet-level traits in a cross-cultural twin sample: Support for a hierarchical model of personality. *Journal of Personality and Social Psychology,*

Janis, I. L., Mahl, G. F., Kagan, J., & Holt, R. R. (1969). *Personality: Dynamics, development, and assessment.* New York: Harcourt, Brace & World.

John, O. P., Caspi, A., Robins, R. W., Moffitt, T. E., & Stouthamer-Loeber, M. (1994). The "little five": Exploring the Five-Factor Model of personality in adolescent boys. *Child Development, 65,* 160–178.

Kenrick, D. T., & Funder, D. C. (1988). Profiting from controversy: Lessons from the person-situation debate. *American Psychologist, 43,* 23–34.

Kirton, M. (1976). Adaptors and innovators: A description and measure. *Journal of Applied Psychology, 61,* 622–629.

Kruglanski, A. W. (1966). A motivated gatekeeper of our minds: Need for closure effects on social cognition and interaction. In R. M. Sorrentino & E. T. Higgins (Eds.), *Handbook of motivation and cognition: Foundations of social behavior* (pp. 465–497). New York: Guilford Press.

Kruglanski, A. W., & Webster, D. M. (1966). Motivated closing of the mind: "Seizing" and "Freezing." *Psychological Review, 103,* 263–283.

Levinson, D. J., Darrow, C. N., Klein, E. B., Levinson, M. L., & McKee, B. (1987). *The seasons of a man's life.* New York: Knopf.

Loehlin, J. C. (1992). *Genes and environment in personality development.* Newbury Park, CA: Sage.

Malhotra, A. K., Virkkunen, M., Rooney, W., Eggert, M.;, Linnoila, M., & Goldman, D. (1996). The association between dopamine D4 receptor (D4DR) 16 amino acid repeat polymorphism and Novelty Seeking. *Molecular Psychiatry, 1,* 388–391.

Marshall, G. N., Wortman, C. B., Vickers, R. R., Jr., Kusulas, J. W., Hervig, L. K. (1994). The Five-Factor Model of personality as a framework for personality-health research. *Journal of Personality and Social Psychology, 67,* 278–286.

Mayer, J. D. (1995). A framework for the classification of personality components. *Journal of Personality, 63,* 819–878.

McAdams, D. P. (1996). Personality, modernity, and the storied self: A contemporary framework for studying persons. *Psychological Inquiry, 7,* 295–321.

McAdams, D. P., & Emmons, R. A. (Eds.). (1995). Levels and domains in personality [Special issue]. *Journal of Personality, 63*(3).

McCrae, R. R. (1982). Consensual validation of personality traits: Evidence from self-reports and ratings. *Journal of Personality and Social Psychology, 43,* 293–303.

McCrae, R. R. (1989). Why I advocate the Five-Factor Model: Joint analyses of the NEO-PI and other instruments. In D. M. Buss & N. Cantor (Eds.), *Personality psychology: Recent trends and emerging directions* (pp. 237–245). New York: Springer-Verlag.

McCrae, R. R. (1996). Social consequences of experiential Openness. *Psychological Bulletin, 120,* 323–337.

McCrae, R. R., & Costa, P. T., Jr. (1985). Openness to experience. In R. Hogan & W. H. Jones (Eds.), *Perspectives in personality* (pp. 145–172). Greenwich, CT: JAI Press.

McCrae, R. R., & Costa, P. T., Jr. (1989). Different points of view: Self-reports and ratings in the assessment of personality. In J. P. Forgas & M. J. Innes (Eds.), *Recent advances in social psychology: An international perspective* (pp. 429–439). Amsterdam: Elsevier Science Publisher.

McCrae, R. R., & Costa, P. T., Jr. (1990). *Personality in adulthood.* New York: Guilford Press.

McCrae, R. R., & Costa, P. T., Jr. (1995). Trait explanations in personality psychology. *European Journal of Personality, 9,* 231–252.

McCrae, R. R., & Costa, P. T., Jr. (1996). Toward a new generation of personality theories: Theoretical contexts for the Five-Factor Model. In J. S. Wiggins (Eds.), *The Five-Factor Model of personality: Theoretical perspectives* (pp. 51–87). New York: Guilford Press.

McCrae, R. R., Costa, P. T., Jr., Dahlstrom, W. G., Barefoot, J. C., Siegler, I. C., & Williams, R. B., Jr. (1989). A caution on the use of the MMPI K-correction in research on psychosomatic medicine. *Psychosomatic Medicine, 51,* 58–65.

McCrae, R. R., Costa, P. T., Jr., & Yik, M. S. M. (1996). Universal aspects of Chinese personality structure. In M. H. Bond (Ed.), *The handbook of Chinese psychology* (pp. 189–207). Hong Kong: Oxford University Press.

Mendelsohn, G. A. (1993). It's time to put theories of personality in their place, or, Allport and Stragner got it right, why can't we? In K. H. Craik, R. Hogan, & R. N. Wolfe (Eds.), *Fifty years of personality psychology* (pp. 103–115). New York: Plenum Press.

Miller, T. (1991). The psychotherapeutic utility of the Five-Factor Model of personality: A clinician's experience. *Journal of Personality Assessment, 57*, 415–433.

Mischel, W. (1968). *Personality and assessment.* New York: Wiley.

Montag, I., & Levin, J. (1994). The five-factor personality model in applied settings. *European Journal of Personality, 8*, 1–11.

Murphy, G. (1947). *Personality: A biosocial approach to origins and structure.* New York: Harper.

Neuberg, S. L., Judice, T. N., & West, S. G. (1997). What the Need for Closure Scale measures and what it does not: Toward differentiating among related epistemic motives. *Journal of Personality and Social Psychology, 72*, 1396–1412.

Ostendorf, F., & Angleitner, A. (1994, July). *Psychometric properties of the German translation of the NEO Personality Inventory (NEO-PI-R).* Poster session presented at the Seventh Conference of the European Association for Personality Psychology, Madrid, Spain.

Piedmont, R. L. (1996, August). *The Five-Factor Model and its value for religious research.* Symposium presented at the American Psychological Association Convention, Toronto, Canada.

Piedmont, R. L., & Chae, J. H. (1997). Cross-cultural generalizability of the Five-Factor Model of personality: Development and validation of the NEO-PI-R for Koreans. *Journal of Cross-Cultural Psychology, 28*, 131–155.

Plomin, R., & Daniels, D. (1987). Why are children in the same family so different from one another? *Behavioral and Brain Sciences, 10*, 1–16.

Scarr, S. (1987). Distinctive environments depend on genotypes. *Behavioral and Brain Sciences, 10*, 38–39.

Shock, N. W., Greulich, R. C., Andres, R., Arenberg, D., Costa, P. T., Jr., Lakatta, E. G., & Tobin, J. D. (1984). *Normal human aging: The Baltimore Longitudinal Study of Aging* (NIH Publication No. 84-2450). Bethesda, MD: National Institutes of Health.

Siegler, I. C., Welsh, K. A., Dawson, D. V., Fillenbaum, G. G., Earl, N. L., Kaplan, E. B., & Clark, C. M. (1991). Ratings of personality change in patients being evaluated for memory disorders. *Alzheimer Disease and Associated Disorders, 5*, 240–250.

Sneed, C. D., McCrae, R. R., & Funder, D. C. (1998). Lay conceptions of the Five-Factor Model and its indicators. *Personality and Social Psychology Bulletin, 24*, 115–126.

Tellegen, A., Lykken, D. T., Bouchard, T. J., Jr., Wilcox, K. J., Segal, N. L., & Rich, S. (1988). Personality similarity in twins reared apart and together. *Journal of Personality and Social Psychology, 54*, 1031–1039.

Thomas, A., Chess, S., & Birch, H. G. (1968). *Temperament and behavior disorders in children.* New York: New York University Press.

Tooby, J., & Cosmides, L. (1990). On the universality of human nature and the uniqueness of the individual: The role of genetics and adaptation. *Journal of Personality, 58*, 17–68.

Trull, T. J., Useda, J. D., Costa, P. T., Jr., & McCrae, R. R. (1995). Comparison of the MMPI-2 Personality Psychopathology Five (PSY-5), the NEO-PI, and the NEO-PI-R. *Psychological Assessment, 7*, 508–516.

Waller, N. G. (in press). Evaluating the structure of personality. In C. R. Cloninger (Eds.), *Personality and psychopathology.* Washington, DC: American Psychiatric Press.

Watson, D., & Hubbard, B. (1996). Adaptational style and dispositional structure: Coping in the context of the five-factor mode. *Journal of Personality, 64*, 737–774.

Webster, D. M., & Kruglanski, A. W. (1994). Individual differences in need for cognitive closure. *Journal of Personality and Social Psychology, 67*, 1049–1062.

Westen, D. (1995). A clinical-empirical model of personality: Life after the Mischellian Ice Age and the NEO-Lithic Era. *Journal of Personality, 63*, 495–524.

Wiggins, J. S. (Ed.). (1996). *The Five-Factor Model of personality: Theoretical perspectives.* New York: Guilford Press.

CHAPTER 6

PSYCHOBIOLOGICAL THEORIES OF PERSONALITY

MARVIN ZUCKERMAN

HISTORICAL SOURCES

Most modern psychobiological theories of personality have their roots in much older theories of temperament. Table 6.1 outlines some of these origins and their modern areas of application. Most of the theories of origin were prescientific in that they had no methods for assessing and testing the biological aspects of the psychobiological model. Some, such as the ancient Greek humoral theory and the phrenological theory, were totally erroneous because they were based on flawed assumptions about the relationships between observable biological variables—for example, the shape of the skull—and personality traits. Although our methods have become more precise, we can expect that unforeseen developments in methodology will drastically revise our current models.

HUMORS AND NEUROTRANSMITTERS

The oldest model of temperament postulated bodily "humors" (phlegm, blood, black bile, and yellow bile) as the bases for temperaments (phlegmatic, sanguine, melancholic, and

MARVIN ZUCKERMAN • Department of Psychology, University of Delaware, Newark, Delaware 19716-2577.

Advanced Personality, edited by David F. Barone, Michel Hersen, and Vincent B. Van Hasselt. Plenum Press, New York, 1998.

TABLE 6.1. Historical Sources of Modern Psychobiological Theories of Personality

Ancient times–20th century	Mid-20th century	Latter-20th century
"Humor" = temperament theory: Hippocrates (5th cent. B.C., Galen (A.D. 2nd cent.)	Hormones as mediators of stress reactions: Seyle (1956). General Adaptation Syndrome	Neurotransmitters and hormones as the basis of personality dimensions: Cloninger (1987); Gray (1971, 1982); Zuckerman (1979, 1984, 1991).
Brain localization theories of personality traits: Gall (1835). Phrenology	Clinical and comparative neuropsychology: Olds (1954). Reward and punishment systems in the brain.	Clinical and comparative neuropsychology. Brain imaging techniques: MRI and PET. Brain circuits for approach, inhibition, and fight/flight: Gray (1971, 1982, 1987).
Brain physiological traits (as basis of temperaments). Coritical excitation and inhibition and their balance: Pavlov (1927).	Reactive inhibition vs. excitation as basis of extraversion and conditionability: Eysenck (1957). Endurance and sensitivity of nerve cells as the basis for temperament: Teplov (1956); Nebylitsyn (1969).	Pavlov's types translated into behavioral terms and assessed by questionnaire and ratings: Strelau (1983). Reactivity: high reactives have high stimulus sensitivity, low tolerance of intense stimulation.
Optimal levels of stimulation and arousal (OLS & OLA): Wundt (1893). OLS for sensation: Constancy Principle (cortical OLA): Breuer and Freud (1895).	OLA based on sensitivity of reticulocortical system: Hebb (1955). OLS, OLA as basis for extraversion: Eysenck (1963, 1967). Strength of excitation = OLA: Gray (1964). OLS, OLA as basis for sensation seeking: Zuckerman (1964, 1969).	Augmenting-Reducing of cortical EP as basis of sensation seeking. EP augmenting=strong nervous system: Zuckerman (1974). OLA of Catecholamine System Activity (CSA) as basis of sensation seeking: Zuckerman (1984).
Personality as genetically produced variations in temperaments and behavioral mechanisms. Ancient Greeks: four basic temperaments: sanguine, phlegmatic, choleric, and melancholic. Specific instincts: McDougall (1923). General drives: Tolman (1922).	Genetic influence in three major traits: E, N, and P: Eysenck (1967). Approach (A) and withdrawal (W) mechanisms or seeking and avoidance as function of S intensity: Schneirla (1959). Sensation seeking trait as function of S novelty: Zuckerman (1964).	Comparative approach, behavior systems: approach, inhibition, fight-flight: Gray (1971, 1982, 1987). Comparative approach to sensation seeking: Zuckerman (1984). Five basic traits: sociability, anxiety, impulsive SS, aggression, activity: 3 mechanisms: approach, inhibition, arousal: Zuckerman (1991, 1994). Three Temperamental traits: novelty seeking, harm-avoidance, reward-dependence; 3 mechanisms: activation, inhibition, maintenance: Cloninger (1987).

choleric). This theory was first formulated by Greek physicians in the fifth century B.C. and persisted in one form or another for 2,000 years. The theory provided explanations for mental disorders as well as variations in normal temperament. The modern version of this approach is the relatively young science of psychopharmacology based on current knowledge about neurotransmitters, hormones, and enzymes, which regulate mood, motivation, and behavior. This science has emerged from studies of the effects of drugs in the treatment of mental disorders and experimental studies of other species. More recently, several investigators have suggested that individual variations in neurotransmitter systems in the brain are the sources of basic temperament or personality traits (Cloninger, 1987; Cloninger, Svrahahioc, & Przybeck, 1993; Gray, 1971, 1982, 1987; Zuckerman, 1979, 1984, 1991, 1995). The only humor that Hippocrates believed to have its origin in the brain was phlegm. Modern theorists may be wrong in their assessment of the role of specific neurotransmitters in personality and behavioral traits, but at least they are focused on the brain as the site of action.

PHRENOLOGY AND NEUROPSYCHOLOGY

By the 19th century, it was generally agreed that the brain was the source of individual differences, but its inaccessibility prevented real scientific development in psychobiology. Not to be stymied by this impediment, Gall (1835) suggested that different personality traits had specific locations in the brain, and the size of these brain areas was directly related to the size of the parts of the skull directly overlying them. The pseudoscience of phrenology was born, and bump readers became popular in the salons and lecture halls of the time. The real science of neuropsychology developed from studies of the effects of localized brain injuries in humans and experimentally produced brain lesions in other species. Specific nuclei within brain structures, like the amygdala or hypothalamus, have been found to be critical in the development of certain emotional and motivated behavioral traits relevant to personality. Gross structural differences in neuroanatomy do not have to wait on autopsy to be described. The development of magnetic resonance imaging (MRI) methods allow clear images of brain structure in living persons. But static images of brain structures are not likely to be related to personality differences. The most promising brain studies are of specific neuronal tracts served by particular neurotransmitters. Those interested in psychopharmacological bases of personality must also delve into the neuropsychology of personality in order to understand the functional significance of the neurotransmitter. The methods of positron emission tomography (PET) and functional MRI produce pictures of brain activity and its loci. These imaging methods have great potentialities for studying personality, but so far most studies have been of psychiatric disorders. As these methods become less expensive, personality psychologists may use them to test psychobiological theories of personality.

CORTICAL EXCITATION AND INHIBITION

When we encounter Ivan Pavlov in introductory psychology textbooks, it is usually in reference to his discovery of the conditioned reflex. These texts do not mention his extensive work classifying temperaments in terms of the hypothetical characteristics of nervous systems. Pavlov (1927/1960) regarded individual differences in conditioning and inhibition of the conditioned reflex as signs of the physiological characteristics of the cerebral cortex. Little differentiation was made as to parts of the cortex, and the role of subcortical structures was not dealt with at all. Based on their reactions to conditioning procedures, individual dogs were classified as having strong, weak, excitatory or inhibitory types of nervous systems. Basic types of temperament represented different combinations of weak or strong excitation and inhibition as well as "mobility" of nervous processes. Interestingly, Pavlov named his four basic temperaments in the terms derived from the ancient humoral theory. Apparently, he was convinced that the behavioral characteristics described by these types were valid. However, his theory did not deal at all with "humors" or biochemistry, even at a conceptual level.

Strelau (1983, 1996) has developed a modern theory of temperament originally based on Pavlovian and neo-Pavlovian theories. In is early studies, the measurements of temperament, which were based on hypothetical characteristics of the nervous system, used conditioning, psychophysical, and psychophysiological laboratory methods. But then in an attempt to build a bridge to Western concepts of temperament and personality, he devised a self-report questionnaire based on behavioral extrapolations from his concepts of temperament. Most of his recent work has used the questionnaire scales rather than laboratory measures to define the types. His earlier temperament scales used Pavlovian constructs based on hypothetical characteristics of the nervous system, such as strength of excitation, strength of inhibition, and mobility. His newer scales are defined in more behavioral terms, including *briskness, perseverance, sensory sensitivity, emotional reactivity, endurance,* and *activity* (seeking of high levels of stimulation) (Strelau, 1996). His emphasis is now on temperamental traits as regulating the relationship between individuals and their environments, particularly in stressful or demanding situations. Temperamental traits are described in terms of the energetic and temporal characteristics of behavior rather than the direction of behavior or its goals.

OPTIMAL LEVEL OF AROUSAL

Pavlov's temperamental types, based on hypothetical characteristics of the nervous system, were a prominent feature of the early efforts of Western psychobiological theorists, like Eysenck (1957) and Zuckerman (1964). But developments in neuropsychology, particularly the discovery that cortical excitation or arousal was partly mediated by a subcortical reticular activating system, shifted the theories of balance in the central nervous system (excitation vs. inhibition) to ones of regulation of arousal in cortical and limbic brain systems (Eysenck, 1967; Zuckerman, 1969). Strangely enough, the origin of this idea that a basic temperament dimension represented differences in *optimal level of arousal,* can be found in an earlier notion of Freud.

Just as Pavlov's theory emerged from his specialty in physiology, Freud's ideas came from his practice as a neurologist. The first experimental psychologist, Wilhelm Wundt (1893), suggested that there was an optimal level of intensity of sensation for maximal pleasure; below or above this level stimulation became first less pleasurable and finally aversive. Wundt formulated this as a restricted principle that was applicable only to the senses of pressure, temperature, taste, and olfaction and he did not speculate about individual differences. Freud (Breuer & Freud, 1895/1937) suggested a *constancy principle* based on reaction to cerebral excitation: "There is a tendency to preserve at a constant level the intracerebral excitement. An excess of it becomes burdensome and annoying and there arises a need to consume it. . . . I believe we can also assume a level of intracerebral excitement, namely it has an optimum. On this level [the optimal] the brain is accessible to all external stimuli" (Breuer & Freud, 1895/1937, p. 142). Freud also speculated that individual differences in this optimal level of arousal might be the basis of the contrast between "vivacious" and "torpid" temperaments [extravert vs. introvert]. Freud later abandoned this optimal level theory for a simple stimulus or arousal reduction theory and generally lost interest in this kind of physiological theory in favor of more psychological theories, although in his mechanistic "metapsychology," he remained a "biologist of the mind" (Sulloway, 1979).

The optimal level theory was revived by Hebb (1949, 1955). The discovery of the ascending reticular activating system as a regulator of arousal in the cortex (Moruzzi & Magoun, 1949) with the descending system from the cortex acting as a kind of "homeostat" (Lindsley, 1961) to regulate the level of cortical arousal played a central role in Hebb's optimal level of arousal model. Hebb suggested that learning, performance, and emotional tone depended on current levels of cortical arousal relative to an optimal level, but Hebb did not extend the theory to explain individual differences. The *optimal level of arousal* became a central postulate in Eysenck's (1967) theory of introversion-extraversion and Zuckerman's (1964, 1974) early theory of sensation-seeking trait. Another major trait, neuroticism, was supposedly based on subcortical centers that regulated emotional response in the limbic brain and stimulated arousal in the peripheral autonomic nervous system (Eysenck, 1967). The centrality of arousal to these theories of personality led to an increased use of psychophysiological methods to assess cortical and autonomic arousal. For the first time experimental validation of psychobiological theory seemed possible, but as we will see this large body of literature has proven inconclusive for the theories it was used to test. Still, the arousal construct remains as a centerpiece of several psychobiological theories (Strelau & Eysenck, 1987).

BEHAVIORAL MECHANISMS

McDougall (1923) believed that the same instinctual biological forces that regulated mating, nest building, protection of the young, aggression, and other characteristic behaviors in lower organisms also operated in humans. But Tolman (1926) and Hull (1943) preferred to substitute the concept of drive, a generalized need influencing motives. Primary drives, like hunger, thirst, and sex, originated in recurring physiological tensions, but the organism had to learn the means of reducing these tensions. The idea of instinct as behavioral mechanisms evolved over long periods in the history of a species has been revived in the theories of sociobiology (Wilson, 1975, 1978) and evolutionary psychology (Buss, 1994).

Schneirla (1959) described two basic types of behavioral mechanisms involved in animal behavior: approach (A) and withdrawal (W). In lower organisms and in higher organisms in their early stages of their early developmental stages, A and W mechanisms are a function of the intensity of stimulation. Low intensities of stimulation tend to evoke approach reactions, whereas high intensities tend to elicit withdrawal. Intensity of stimulation included the increasing size of the retinal image of a stimulus approaching the organism as contrasted with the decreasing size as the stimulus recedes. Thus, many mammals (like cats) will pursue a retreating object but flee from a rapidly approaching one. In human infants, a soft tone elicits smiling and approach, whereas a loud tone elicits distress and withdrawal. In higher organisms at more mature stages of development, reactions are less automatic and depend more on learned associations to stimuli. At this stage, the A reaction is called *seeking* and the W reaction is termed *avoidance*.

Psychologists interested in individual differences, who believe that comparative psychology (animal behavior) is an important foundation for understanding human behavioral traits, have adopted the idea of broad, biologically based behavioral mechanisms, for instance *sensation seeking* (Zuckerman, 1964, 1979, 1994). Gray (1971, 1982, 1987) described three basic behavioral mechanisms: *behavioral approach, behavioral inhibition,* and the *fight-flight* system. Approach underlies the human trait of impulsivity, inhibition is the basis for the trait of anxiety, and fight-flight corresponds to human aggressiveness. Gray makes a distinction between passive-avoidance, related to the inhibition mechanism, and active-avoidance, characteristic of the fight-flight system. Unlike most other psychobiological theorists, Gray is an active neuropsychological experimenter and practices a "bottom-up" rather than a "top-down" approach to personality. A top-down approach starts with designated human traits and attempts to find correspondence in biologically based behavioral traits in lower organisms. A bottom-up approach starts with the behavioral mechanisms and their biological basis established in nonhuman species and tries to identify them with human traits. Therefore, most of Gray's work consisted of neurophysiological studies of rats; the extension of these results to humans has been largely conceptual. He accepted Eysenck's three-factor system for human personality, but he suggested that the traits corresponding to basic behavioral mechanisms (anxiety, impulsivity, and aggression) may not have a direct one-to-one relationship with Eysenck's basic three factors (extraversion, neuroticism, psychoticism), but may represent dimensions within Eysenck's or different combinations of Eysenck's three factors.

TRAITS AND BEHAVIOR GENETICS

A basic assumption of evolutionary approaches is that behavioral mechanisms, or the biological systems on which they are based, are genetically encoded in the species. Individual differences in the strength of the behavioral mechanisms are presumably due to the genetic variation within the species as well as environmental influences.

Galton (1874), in his book on *English Men of Science: Their Nature and Nurture,* was primarily interested in the heredity of ability, but he also suggested familial transmission of personality characteristics. Early studies of personality traits cited correlations between parents and children on personality scales as evidence of a genetic relatedness. But such studies could not separate the genetic and shared environmental factors, and they used the crude personality measures available at the time. Biometric analysis of twin studies offered a way to control the shared environment while varying the genetic component, comparing identical and fraternal twins in degrees of correlation on a trait. Early twin studies of personality traits (Carter, 1933; Newman, Freeman, & Holzinger, 1937) using objective questionnaires showed the greater resemblance of identical than fraternal twins in a magnitude of about the same as we see today. However, presently we have larger studies using better test and statistical analytic methods. The Newman *et al.* study used separated identical twins and those raised together and found no difference in the substantial correlations (.56 and .58) within both groups on a test probably measuring neuroticism. Since the correlation between separated identical twins is a direct measure of the genetic variance, the estimate of heritability for neuroticism was 58%. Despite this finding, the authors of the study minimized the effect of heredity in personality!

Behavioral genetics now plays a central role in nearly all psychobiological theories of personality (Plomin, 1986). The methods of this science can be experimental in other species, where traits may be selectively bred, crossbred, and cross-fostered. Animal behavior genetics has simply brought into the laboratory what animal and plant breeders were doing long before there was a science of genetics. Until recently, genetic studies in the human have depended on "natural experiments," such as comparing similarities and differences in identical twins and fraternal twins. Identical twins have all their genes in common, but fraternal twins have only an average of half of their genes in common. Identicals are usually compared to fraternal twins in an effort to hold constant the factor of shared environment (i.e., born at the same time into the same family and sharing much of the same environment). In recent years, a refinement of the method is to compare identical and fraternal twins who were adopted into different families in order to answer the criticism that identical twins are treated more alike than fraternals. Adoption studies of nontwins are also used to contrast the effects of the family of biological origin, who share only genes with the adopted away child, with the family of rearing, who provide the social environment for the adoptee. Personality traits have been extensively studied using these methods. Some startling generalizations have emerged from these studies, which will be described in the next section.

PSYCHOBIOLOGY OF PERSONALITY TODAY

GENETICS AND ENVIRONMENT

Many studies of twins raised together in their families of origin have been published. Zuckerman (1991) summarized the data from nine large studies involving a total of 9,470 pairs of identical and 14,183 pairs of fraternal twins. Correlations were grouped by scales of Extraversion (E), Neuroticism (N), and P-ImpUSS (P). The last named factor is derived from factor analytic studies in which Eysenck's P (Psychoticism) scale was found to be the best marker for a factor containing scales measuring impulsivity (Imp), lack of socialization (U), and sensation seeking (SS) (Zuckerman, Kuhlman, & Camac, 1988; Zuckerman, Kuhlman, Thornquist, & Kiers, 1991). Evidence also suggested that a five-factor model was just as robust and replicable as a three-factor one, with the additional factors consisting of aggression and activity. In a three-factor model, the Aggression scales move to the P factor and the Activity scales to the Extraversion factor. Because most of the research on twins was carried out using the three-factor model, this one was used to sort the results from genetic studies of personality.

Summarizing the studies, median correlations for identical twins were .54 for E, .46 for N, and .56 for P-ImpUSS. For fraternal twins median correlations were .19 for E, .22 for N, and .27 for P-ImpUSS. Assuming the operation of additive genetic mechanisms for these complex traits, the correlations for fraternal twins should be half the value of those for identical twins because identical twins have all genes in common, whereas fraternal twins have half of their genes in common. However, if other genetic mechanisms are operative, such as dominance or epistasis (the trait as the result of specific combinations of genes rather than the total number of a set of genes), correlations for fraternal twins would be less than half of the value for identical twins, and in the case of epistasis, they would be close to zero. Correlations for N and P suggest the ratio of 2 to 1, indicating just additive genetic mechanisms. However, the .19 correlation of fraternal twins on E is less than half of the .54 correlation of identical twins, which might indicate the operation of some non-additive genetic mechanisms.

The Falconer (1981) index of heritability (2 × the correlation for identicals—the correlation for fraternals) would give heritabilities of 70% for E, 48% for N, and 59% for P-ImpUSS. But the estimate for E is produced by the low value of the fraternal twin correlation, and an estimate of heritability should not far exceed the correlation for identical twins so that the estimate for E must be modified to 54% (maximum). Estimates of heritabilities using more sophisticated methods of statistical analysis (e.g., Eaves & Young, 1981) yield heritabilities of 49% for E and 41% for N. Eaves and Eysenck (1977), using the same methods, obtained a heritability of 46% for Eysenck's P scale.

A major criticism of estimates of heritability from twins reared together is that they really do not control for shared environment because identical twins are treated more similarly than fraternal twins. Loehlin and Nichols (1976) found that identical twins shared an environment inside and outside of the home, having more friends in common and spending more time together, more similar than that of fraternal twins. In some cases, they were dressed alike by their parents. Direct measures of the degree of shared environment and amount of personality similarity among twins of both types were not correlated, suggesting little effect of shared environment for either identical or fraternal twins. However, this criticism has been put to rest by studies that combined the twin comparison and adoption methods. In these studies, twins who were separated early in life and grew up in adopted families having no genetic relationships were compared. To the extent that shared environment is an important factor in twin similarity, the correlations between adopted twins raised in different families should be considerably lower than correlations between twins raised in the same family. In fact, the correlation between identical twins raised in different adopted families with no contact until their formative years and no selective placement is a direct measure of heritability. Only their shared genes could account for any similarities in personality.

Figure 6.1 shows the mean correlations of identical twins raised apart on specific types of measures (Bouchard, Lykken, McGue, Segal, & Tellegen, 1990). As we might expect, a physical characteristic like height has the highest heritability; but a physiological brain trait, the proportion of alpha wave activity in the resting EEG, has an almost equally high heritability. Blood pressure has a high heritability but not as high as EEG. Intelligence has a higher heritability than personality traits, which in turn have higher heritabilities than measures of vocational interests and social attitudes.

Table 6.2 shows the results for the three primary factors of E, N, and P-ImpUSS in studies of separated identical and fraternal twins and identical and fraternal twins raised in their biological families. Most of the data comes from the Minnesota study (Bouchard, 1993; Bouchard, Lykken, McGue, Segal, & Tellegen, 1990) and a Swedish study (Pederson, Plomin, McClearn, & Friberg, 1988). The Swedish study was larger, but the Minnesota study used twins separated very early in life, more reliable measures of personality, and more precise methods of determining zygosity. Bouchard (1993) suggested that such differences in methodology could account for differences in findings in the two studies. There is also the possibility that the Scandinavian population is different from the American and British ones. Heritability is a population statistic, and populations may differ depending on the variation in environments and genes within the specific population.

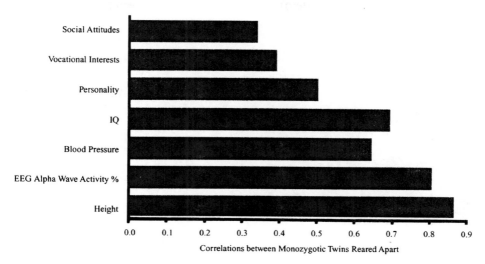

FIGURE 6.1. Mean correlations of identical twins raised apart on different types of measures (based on data from Bouchard *et al.*, 1990).

Looking at the three studies of extraversion, estimates of heritability from the separated identicals alone would range from 30% to 61%. Using more sophisticated methods of analysis, heredity accounts for about 40% of the variance in both the Bouchard (1993) and Pederson *et al.* (1988) studies. In both studies, correlations for identicals raised together are somewhat higher than those raised apart, and in the Bouchard study, there is also some difference between fraternals reared together and apart. Shields (1962) actually found higher correlations in separated identicals than in those raised together, an anomalous finding that has not been replicated. Note that some correlations among the fraternal twins are negative, but these must be attributed to chance variation. The data suggested some contribution of shared environment although it is smaller than the effects of nonshared or specific environment. The much lower correlations of fraternal twins also could be due to nonadditive genetic factors affecting the identical twin correlations.

Neuroticism yields heritabilities of between 25% and 58%, but three of the four studies are in the close range of from 53% to 58%. The lower estimate is closer to the previous estimation of 48% for large samples of twins raised together. With the exception of the Pederson *et al.* (1988) study, correlations for identicals raised apart and together are not very different (except for the Shields study where they are again higher for twins raised apart!).

Heritabilities for the scales within the P-ImpUSS factor range from 20% for Monotony Avoidance to 61% for the Constraint factor (containing 3 subscales) in the Bouchard study. The Monotony Avoidance scale is a short five-item version of a scale, like general Sensation Seeking. Fulker, Eysenck, and Zuckerman (1980) and Lykken (1982) used the total score on the standard Sensation Seeking scale, consisting of 40 items and 4 subscales, and found a high heritability of about 60%, whether estimated from twins raised apart or together. Estimates from the more reliable and comprehensive factors of Constraint and Sensation Seeking have high heritabilities; at the limits of the range for most personality

TABLE 6.2. Correlations of Identical and Fraternal Twins Raised Apart and Together

	I Apart	I Tog	F Apart	F Tog
Extraversion (E)				
Shields (1962)[a]	.61	.42	—	−.17
Pederson et al. (1988)[b]	.30	.54	.04	.06
Bouchard (1993)[c]	.40	.53	−.07	.18
Neuroticism (N)				
Newman et al. (1937)[d]	.58	.56	—	.37
Shields (1962)	.53	.38	—	.11
Pederson et al. (1988)	.25	.41	.28	.24
Bouchard (1993)	.53	.46	.41	.17
P-Impuss				
Pederson: Impulsivity	.40	.45	.15	.09
Monotony Avoidance	.20	.26	.14	.16
Bouchard (1993) Constraint	.61	.59	−.04	.38
Lykken (1992)/Fulker et al.	.54	.60	.32	.21
(1980) Sensation Seeking				

Note: Twins raised apart from Minnesota twin study: separated identicals 46, fraternals 41; twins raised together from Fulker et al. (1980) study: together identicals 233, fraternals 189.
[a]identicals: separated 42, tog 43 pairs; fraternals: together 25 pairs; 71% of identicals separated at birth or during first year of life.
[b]identicals: separated 99, together 160 pairs; fraternals: separated 229, together 212 pairs; 48% of total sample separated before age of 1, 64% by 2, 82% by 5.
[c]identicals: separated 52, together 553 pairs; fraternals: separated 33, together 459 pairs; 97% of identicals separated in first year of life, 83% before 6 months.
[d]identicals: separated 19, together 50 pairs; fraternals: 50 together

measures, no evidence of shared environmental factors (note that correlations for separated and identical twins are nearly identical) or any influence of nonadditive genetic mechanisms.

Nontwin adoption studies show that there is practically no correlation between personality traits of adopted children and their genetically unrelated parents and siblings (Loehlin, 1992; Zuckerman, 1991). Since these parents and siblings represent the pure shared environment factor, this is added evidence of a lack of influence of a shared family environment. However, adopting parents are usually carefully screened and may represent a limited range of environment, which would reduce the potential variation in this source of influence. But curiously, there is also less correlation than one might expect from twin studies between parents and their biological children in intact families. If genetic variation is additive, then the correlation between the average scores of both parents on a trait and the scores of their children should be equivalent to the correlations between identical twins. But identical twins' personality traits correlate typically at .50, whereas the midparent median and child traits correlate between .20 and .30, about half of the expected correlation based on twin studies (Loehlin, Willerman, & Horn, 1985; Scarr, Webber, Winberg, & Wittig, 1981). The discrepancy between the broad, inclusive heritability measure based on identical twins and the additive heredity measure based on parents and siblings may be due to the partial influence of specific or necessary major genes as well as a number of potentiating genes that are more equivalent and contribute to the additive genetic effect. Is it possible to actually identify some of the major genes involved in a personality trait? This question brings us to a new frontier in behavior genetics.

MOLECULAR GENETICS

For the first half of this 20th century, the gene remained a hypothetical construct devised to explain the variation in phenotypes. In 1953, Watson and Crick published their paper describing a model for the molecular structure of deoxyribonucleic acid (DNA) in the journal *Nature,* beginning the study of the gene as a chemical template controlling production and regulation of proteins that form the structure of cells. Of the estimated 100,000 genes in human DNA, about 30,000 are expressed primarily in the brain (Hyman & Nestler, 1993). Techniques evolved over the later part of the 20th century have made it possible to splice and identify specific genes and variation in the forms of genes that could be related to variations in personality. Using these methods, investigators have found specific genes involved in medical disorders like Alzheimer's Disease. Attempts have been made to find specific genes associated with psychiatric disorders like bipolar mood disorder and schizophrenia, but have thus far not produced replicable results.

The problem in applying these methods is the probability that such disorders as well as personality traits involve many genes. The perspective of geneticists has been "one gene, one disorder," or as Plomin (1995) described it in an acronym—the OGOD hypothesis. The conventional polygenic hypothesis assumes that disorders or traits involve many genes, each contributing a minute part of the total additive effect producing the trait. In contrast, Plomin proposes the quantitative trait loci (QTL) hypothesis: "multiple genes that have varying effect sizes, the largest of which may be identifiable" (p. 116). To paraphrase Orwell: All genes are equal, but some genes are more equal than others. This new polygenic model opened the possibility of finding major genes associated with personality traits.

In looking for a major gene associated with a personality trait, it is helpful, if not necessary, to have a hypothesis regarding that gene in terms of what it does in the neurophysiology of the body, otherwise one would have to unscroll the entire DNA with countless comparisons capitalizing on the role of chance. A trait that shows a strong influence of genetics using the biometric twin study methods described earlier would be a major candidate for study.

The sensation seeking trait has shown a strong degree of genetic determination as estimated from both separated twin and twins raised together studies. Furthermore, sensation seeking has shown a variety of biological correlates (Zuckerman, 1979, 1994; Zuckerman & Buchsbaum, 1983) and congruence between these biological markers and models for sensation-seeking behavior in other species (Zuckerman, 1984). Cloninger's system involves a similar major temperament trait called *novelty seeking.* Zuckerman and Cloninger (1996) found that scales of novelty seeking and impulsive sensation seeking correlate about .7, indicating near identity in traits. Zuckerman (1984, 1991, 1995) and Cloninger (1987) suggested that the neurotransmitter dopamine is involved in sensation seeking because of its involvement in approach behaviors and adaptation to novel environments in other species.

Quite recently, two landmark studies have replicated a relationship between measures of novelty seeking and a particular variant form of the dopamine receptor gene, D4DR, located on the short arm of Chromosome 11 (Benjamin et al., 1996; Ebstein et al., 1996). Subjects with a longer form of this allele had significantly higher scores on novelty seeking than subjects with the shorter form, but the two groups did not differ on Cloninger's other scales of temperament (Ebstein et al., 1996). Benjamin et al. (1996) also found differences in subscales of the NEO measuring warmth, excitement seeking, positive emotions, and impulsivity (low deliberation), and subscales of the Novelty-Seeking scale assessing exploratory excitability, extravagance, and disorderliness. Their data suggest that D4DR may also be associated with extraversion.

The D4DR gene accounts for only 10% of the genetic variation in the sensation-seeking trait, and other major genes are certainly involved. Findings on sensation seeking to be discussed suggest other gene candidates, such as gene(s) involved in producing the enzyme monoamine oxidase (MAO) type B, which in primate brain is primarily dedicated to the regulation of dopamine. An as yet unreplicated study shows an association between the monoamine oxidase type A with impulsive aggression (Bruner, Nelson, Breakefield, Rogers, & van Oost, 1993). Before long, we may be able to identify major genes involved in all of the major personality traits. Understanding the functions of these genes will lead to a better understanding of the biological mechanisms underlying the traits.

LEVELS OF ANALYSIS

Figure 6.2 shows an analysis of personality in terms of levels. At the top, we have the "Supertraits." At the time this chart was made, four supertraits were postulated. Factor analyses of scales used in the study of the psychobiology of the personality revealed three robust factors: Extraversion/Sociability, Neuroticism/Anxiety, and Impulsive Unsocialized Sensation Seeking (Zuckerman, Kuhlman, & Camac, 1988). The first two factors corresponded to factors found in all models for personality trait structure, including the Five-Factor Model (FFM) described by Costa and McCrae (Chapter 4). Although Eysenck's P

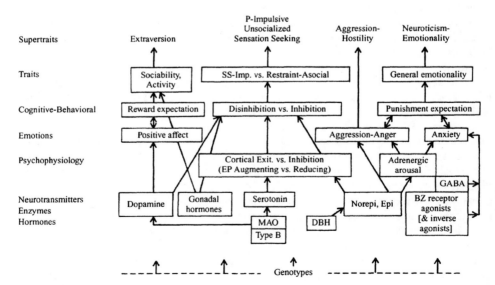

FIGURE 6.2. A psychobiological model for personality. *Source: Psychobiology of Personality* (p. 407), by M. Zuckerman, 1991, Cambridge, UK: Cambridge University Press. Copyright 1991 by Cambridge University Press. Reprinted by permission.

scale was an excellent marker for this third dimension, the factor consisted of scales measuring impulsivity, sensation seeking, aggression, and socialization. It has been suggested that a clinical description of the high end of the factor should be *psychopathy* rather than *psychoticism* (Zuckerman, 1989). A second factor-analytic study, using the best factor markers from the previous study, found a robust five-factor solution, which separated the Aggression-Hostility factor from the ImpUSS and Neuroticism factors and the Activity factor from Extraversion (Zuckerman, Kuhlman, Thornquist, & Kiers, 1991). Figure 6.2 still includes activity under "Extraversion," although it anticipates the Aggression–Hostility factor. Four of these five factors have moderate to strong correlations with the Five-Factor Model described by Costa and McCrae (Chapter 4), but the fifth factor of Activity in our "alternative five" and Openness to Experience in their Big Five do not correspond at all (Zuckerman, Kuhlman, Joireman, Teta, & Kraft, 1993).

COGNITIVE–BEHAVIORAL MECHANISMS AND EMOTIONS

At the level below "Traits" are "Cognitive–Behavioral" mechanisms and "Emotions," which are the most direct expression of underlying differences in physiological and biochemical traits. Gray (1971, 1991) formulated three basic systems: behavioral inhibition (BIS), behavioral approach (BAS), and fight–flight (FF). The behavioral inhibition system is associated with the trait of anxiety, which is suggested to form a dimension between Eysenck's Introversion–Extraversion and Neuroticism dimensions (but closer to Neuroticism). The behavioral approach system corresponds to the trait of impulsivity at the human level, and the dimension lies between Eysenck's Neuroticism and Extraversion dimensions (but closer to Extraversion). The fight–flight system is closely identified with the trait of aggression and Eysenck's third dimension, Psychoticism.

The BIS scans the environment for stimuli associated with punishment or novel stimuli and interrupts ongoing behavior in the presence of such signals, focuses attention on the threatening stimulus, and increases physiological arousal. The BIS is especially sensitive to punishment signals. The BAS performs a similar function for signals of reward and is especially sensitive to such signals.

We have proposed similar mechanisms as shown in Figure 6.2. Instead of sensitivities to conditioned stimuli, generalized expectancies of reward or punishment are associated with major personality traits, particularly Extraversion-Sociability, and Neuroticism-Anxiety or -Emotionality. A Generalized Reward Expectancy is associated with Extraversion and a Generalized Punishment Expectancy with Neuroticism. Emotional traits are suggested at the next level: Negative Affect, particularly anxiety, associated with Neuroticism and Positive Affect associated with Extraversion. Aggression–Anger is associated with both Neuroticism and the major trait of Aggression–Hostility. The factor of Impulsive Sensation Seeking is more closely associated with a weak inhibitory mechanism rather than expectancy or mood traits.

A study of Gray's and Zuckerman's models was done using questionnaires designed to measure expectancies of reward and punishment and sensitivities to reward and punishment and pure mood traits (Zuckerman, Joireman, Kraft, & Kuhlman, 1996). Although the initial three-factor models did not fit the factors well, the fit was improved by modifications in the initial model that were based on the obtained results of the exploratory factor analysis. These results are shown in Table 6.3. The Neuroticism factor, defined by both Eysenck's and Zuckerman and Kuhlman's trait measures, is strongly associated with sensitivity to signals of punishment, generalized punishment expectancies, and the affective traits of anxiety and depression. The Extraversion factor is similarly associated with sensitivity to signals of reward, generalized reward expectancy, and positive affect and sensation-seeking affect (a type of surgency positive affect). The Psychoticism factor is defined by Eysenck's P scale and Zuckerman and Kuhlman's Impulsive Sensation-Seeking and Aggression scales, and the Hostility affect scale. Not predicted by the models were the secondary loadings of depression and positive affect (negative loading) on this factor. Apparently the broad P-ImpUSS dimension has a negative emotional basis beyond the primary mood trait of anger and hostility.

PSYCHOPHYSIOLOGICAL APPROACHES

Part of the attraction of the construct of "arousal" was the possibility of direct measurement using psychophysiological methods. Eysenck's theory (1967) proposed differences in tonic arousal and optimal levels of arousal between introverts and extraverts. His "arousal" construct referred to cortical arousal as regulated by the reticulocortical activating system. Introverts are more sensitive to low levels of stimulation and therefore more aroused than extraverts. Extraverts are less sensitive to low levels of stimulation, but more able to process high levels of stimulation without triggering a "reactive inhibition" mechanism, which reduces intensity of stimulation and arousal. As a consequence of these differences in arousal, extraverts have a higher optimal level of arousal, and feel and perform better at higher intensities of stimulation than introverts.

TABLE 6.3. Factor Analysis of Personality Trait, Affect, and Sensitivities to and Expectancies of Reward and Punishment Measures

	Factor I: N-Anx	Factor II: E-Sy	Factor III: P-ImpUSS
EPQ: Neuroticism	.86	−.09	.15
ZKPQ: Anxiety	.81	−.12	.06
Sensitivity to punishment	.77	−.31	−.06
MAACL: Anxiety	.73	−.22	.31
Gen. punishment expectancy	.69	.07	−.09
MAACL: Depression	.57	−.37	.47
EPQ: Extraversion	−.12	.84	.09
MAACL: SS (Surgency)	−.24	.79	.10
ZKPQ: Sociability	−.05	.66	.01
Sensitivity to reward	.25	.60	.34
Gen. reward expectancy	−.39	.52	.05
MAACL: Positive affect	−.31	.50	−.43
ZKPQ: Activity	−.05	.33	−.04
EPQ: Psychoticism	−.15	.00	.81
MAACL: Hostility	.46	−.16	.63
ZKPQ: Impulsive SS	−.19	.37	.61
ZKPQ: Aggression	.26	.20	.57

Note: N-Anx = Neuroticism-Anxiety; E-Sy = Extraversion-Sociability; P-ImpUSS = Psychoticism–Impulsive Sensation Seeking; EPQ = Eysenck Personality Questionnaire; MAACL = Multiple Affect Adjective Check List-Revised; Gen. = Generalized; SS = Sensation Seeking; ZKPQ = Zuckerman–Kuhlman Personality Questionnaire.

Arousal of subcortical centers in the limbic brain, which control the peripheral autonomic nervous system (ANS), are said to be the basis of the trait of neuroticism, since arousal of the sympathetic branch of the ANS is a major component in anxiety and other emotional responses.

General cortical arousal is measurable by the EEG and more recently by the positron emission tomography (PET) brain-imaging method. Autonomic arousal is measurable by a variety of psychophysiological measures, such as heart rate, blood pressure, skin temperature, and skin conductance. The possibility of direct measurement of physiological constructs led to a vast amount of research correlating personality with physiological response, but the findings have been inconclusive because of the methodological and theoretical problems acknowledged by Eysenck (1991).

Alpha wave activity has been used as a measure of cortical arousal in many studies. Given the high heritability of this measure (Lykken, 1982), one would expect it to be a good marker for personality differences. In reviews of the relationship between EEG measures and introversion-extraversion by Gale and Edwards (1986) and O'Gorman (1984), about half of the studies lent some support to Eysenck's hypothesis, and the other half showed no differences between introverts and extraverts, or differences in a direction opposite to that of the hypothesis. Zuckerman (1991) examined eight studies about which previous reviewers agreed that the methodology was sound for examining Eysenck's hypothesis. Only three of these were unambiguously supportive of the hypothesis of underarousal in extraverts.

Two PET-scan studies have also yielded mixed results. Haier, Sokolski, Katz, and Buchsbaum (1987) found little correlation between cortical glucose uptake and extraversion in a resting condition, but in a stressful condition extraversion correlated *positively* with the glucose measure of activity in frontal and temporal cortex as well as in some limbic brain areas, indicating overarousability instead of the underarousability, which might be predicted from Eysenck's theory. Mathew, Weinman, and Barr (1984) used a different PET technique (xenon inhalation) and found significant *negative* correlations between extraversion and the measure of cerebral blood flow in all cortical areas, a result supportive of Eysenck's underarousal hypothesis for extraversion.

Stelmack's (1990) review of the psychophysiological evidence for Eysenck's theory of extraversion concluded that there is "little compelling evidence" that extraverts and introverts differ in tonic or basal levels of arousal, but a "good deal of evidence" that introverts are more physiologically reactive to sensory stimulation than extraverts. In other words, extraverts are not characteristically less aroused than introverts, but under conditions of low to moderate stimulation, they are less *arousable* than introverts. But other work by Stelmack suggested that the underarousability of extraverts rested on fundamental differences in neuronal reactivity rather than reticulocortical arousal per se. Introverts showed faster response latencies in brain-stem evoked potentials (BERs) than introverts (Stelmack & Wilson, 1982), and BERs are independent of reticular system influences. Going even further down in the nervous system, Pivik, Stelmack, and Blysma (1988) found that reflex recovery time in a spinal motoneuronal circuit in the leg was faster in introverts than in extraverts. An interesting corollary of this finding was that the kind of decreased motoneuronal activity seen in extraverts is associated with increased dopaminergic activity, an association consistent with the psychopharmacological data that will presented later.

The assumption of a connection between autonomic system reactivity and neuroticism (N) is based in part on the evidence that persons with anxiety disorders show increased arousal on many psychophysiological measures. Assuming that these disorders lie at the extreme of a dimension of neuroticism or anxiety trait extending into the normal range, one would expect correlations of N with either tonic arousal or arousability under stress. Actually, anxiety disorders, such as panic disorder, agoraphobia, and obsessive–compulsive disorder, show elevated heart rates and blood pressures in a resting tonic state, but under standard laboratory stresses show less reactivity (stress minus baseline) than normal controls (Kelly, 1980). Persons with specific phobias show no more physiological arousal than normals for baseline measures, but respond much more when confronted with their specific phobic stimulus. The generalized anxiety disorders are characterized by high levels of muscle tension, but are normal in tonic and reactive measures of autonomic arousal.

Studies of the relationship between anxiety or neuroticism and psychophysiological measures have yielded almost universally negative results. Studies by Fahrenberg (1987) and Myrtek (1984) used large samples of subjects, various kinds of stressors, and different physiological and mood measures. Overall, there were no significant links between neuroticism or trait anxiety and either baseline or stress-reactive physiological measures. However, Kagan, Reznik, and Snidman (1988) have found higher heart rates in children described as inhibited and shy than in uninhibited and socially spontaneous children. Heart rates at 21 months of age predicted inhibited behavior at 48 months. Vaillant and Schurr (1988) reported that basal heart rates of young college men predicted adult adjustment 15 years later. Although the correlation was low ($r=-.25$), significant prediction from a physiological to a behavioral measure across such a long time span is remarkable. Other than these two studies of tonic heart rate, there is little to confirm a relationship between autonomic system arousal or arousability and the trait of neuroticism. It may be that high arousal levels in some anxiety disorders represent a state accompanying the disorder, but not a physiological trait prior to the development of the disorder. Another possibility is that only a subgroup of persons high on neuroticism trait manifest anxiety in physiological form. As Lang (1985) has pointed out, anxiety may take many forms, including the behavioral, cognitive, and physiological. It may be that physiological arousal only becomes salient when a person high in a neuroticism trait becomes dysfunctional. Personality disorders in Kelly's (1980) study had higher scores on trait anxiety and neuroticism measures than normal controls, but unlike chronic anxiety cases did not have higher basal heart rates, blood flow, or blood pressure than the controls.

The sensation seeking trait has shown a number of replicable relationships with psychophysiological paradigms (Zuckerman, 1990). Eysenck's model for extraversion stressed the differential response to varying intensities of stimulation. Zuckerman's model (1979) was initially focused on the reaction to novelty, variety, and complexity of stimulation, although a recent change of the definition includes intensity as well (Zuckerman, 1994). High sensation seekers have shown strong orienting reflexes to novel stimuli, as measured by phasic skin conductance increases and heart rate decelerations in response to first presentations of stimuli (Zuckerman 1990). When stimuli are repeatedly presented, the difference in magnitude of response between high and low sensation seekers disappears. The enhanced response of high sensation seekers seems to reflect a strong interest in novel stimuli and a disinterest in repetitive stimulation. These kinds of reactions are reflected in the items and subscales of the Sensation-Seeking Scale (SSS), indicating a desire for unusual kinds of experiences and a susceptibility to boredom when stimuli (or people) are predictable or constant.

However, another psychophysiological paradigm reflects a difference in reactions to stimuli depending on their intensities. *Augmenting–reducing* of the cortical evoked potential (EP) is defined by the relationship between cortical reactivity and intensity of briefly presented stimuli, like flashing lights or repeated tones. An *augmenter* shows increasing amplitude of the averaged EP in proportion to increases of stimulus intensity. A *reducer* shows little increase in cortical EPs and sometimes a decrease in responsiveness at the higher intensities. The mean responses of high and low sensation seekers (as defined by the Disinhibition subscale of the SSS) to increasing brightness intensities of visual stimuli is shown in Figure 6.3, and to auditory stimulation in Figure 6.4. High disinhibiters (impulsive unsocialized sensation seekers) tend to be augmenters and low disinhibiters (constrained) tend to be reducers. These results, usually linking the disinhibitory type of sensation seeking to visual or auditory EP augmenting, have been replicated many times, although a few failures of replication have been reported (Zuckerman, 1990).

Visual EP augmenting-reducing has provided a marker for animal models of sensation seeking. A basic human personality trait should have analogues in individual differences in behavior found in other species (Zuckerman, 1984). Cats who are augmenters differ from cats who are reducers in exploratory behavior, approach to novel stimuli, and social approach behavior, all analogues of human sensation-seeking trait (Hall, Rappaport, Hopkins, Griffin, and Silverman, 1970; Lukas & Siegel, 1977; Saxton, Siegel, & Lukas, 1987a; 1987b). In an

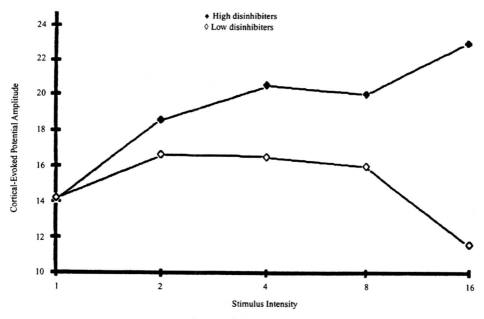

FIGURE 6.3. Mean visual evoked potential amplitudes (P1-N1) at five levels of light intensity for low and high scorers on the Disinhibition subscale of the Sensation Seeking Scale. *Source:* "Sensation seeking and cortical augmenting-reducing," by M. Zuckerman, T. T. Murtaugh, & J. Siegel, 1974, *Psychophysiology, 11,* p. 250. Copyright 1974 by the Society for Psychophysiological Research. Reprinted by permission.

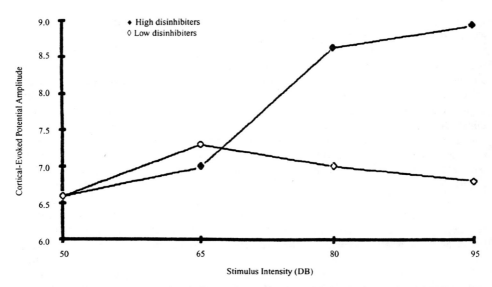

FIGURE 6.4. Mean auditory evoked potential amplitudes (P1-N1) at four levels of sound intensity (50–95db) for low and high scorers on the Disinhibition subscale of the Sensation Seeking Scale. *Source:* "Sensation seeking and stimulus intensity as modulators of cortical, cardiovascular, and electrodermal response: A cross-modality study," by M. Zuckerman, R. F. Simons, & G. Como, 1988, *Personality and Individual Differences, 9,* p. 368. Copyright 1988 by Pergamon Press. Reprinted by permission.

experimentally controlled study by Saxton *et al.* (1987b), augmenter cats performed better on a fixed interval reward schedule because they adapted quickly to the experimental chamber and responded vigorously for reward. However, reducer cats were more effective in a differential reinforcement for low rate of response because they were better able to modulate their reward-driven behavior, whereas augmenter cats responded impulsively at high rates, which resulted in loss of reward on this schedule.

Siegel, Sisson, and Driscoll (1993) also compared two selectively bred pure strains of rats: a behaviorally active strain called Roman High Avoidance (RHA) and a behaviorally inhibited type called Roman Low Avoidance (RLA). Nearly all of RHA rats were visual EP augmenters, and nearly all of RLA rats were reducers or very weak augmenters. Since all members of an inbred strain are like identical twins, generalizations can be made from the EP differentiation to behavioral differences found in other members of the strain. RHA rats are more exploratory, aggressive, and less emotional than RLA rats. RHA augmenters also are more likely to develop a taste for alcohol, and the females are less nurturing toward their pups than RLA rats. RHA rats are more responsive to strong-intensity brain stimulation that is self-delivered to reward centers in the lateral hypothalamus. They are also less stress responsive than the RLAs. In many respects, RHA rats resemble human antisocial personality types who are higher on sensation seeking than prosocial and less antisocial criminals, particularly sensation seeking of the disinhibitory type, the one most closely linked with human augmenting-reducing.

THE MONOAMINE SYSTEMS

Variations in personality traits are assumed by many to correspond in some way with variations in neurotransmitters, the enzymes and hormones that regulate them, and the variety of receptors that respond to them in different parts of the brain. My own interest in the psychopharmacology of personality began on hearing of two studies reporting the discovery of a negative relationship between the general trait of sensation seeking and the enzyme monoamine oxidase (MAO) type B assayed from blood platelets (Murphy *et al.*, 1977; Schooler, Zahn, Murphy, & Buchsbaum, 1978). Subsequent studies more often than not have replicated the significant negative relationship between sensation seeking and MAO, although the typical correlation is not very high (Zuckerman, 1994). Low MAO in humans has also been associated with the trait of extraversion. But this latter relationship gains strength from inverse associations of MAO with social behavior in both humans and monkeys as well as with social dominance, aggression, and sexual and play activity in monkeys. Low MAO in humans has been associated with histories of criminality; drug, alcohol, and tobacco use and abuse; antisocial and borderline personality disorders; and bipolar disorders. Low MAO is associated with greater general motor activity and autonomic lability in newborn babies in the first 72 hours of life. The breadth of the MAO association with personality, behavioral traits, and psychopathology, and its parallel associations with comparable behavior in other species suggest that the enzyme is a marker for a general disinhibitory or impulsive approach tendency. But what is the physiological connection?

In the primate brain, MAO regulates the monoamine neurotransmitters: dopamine, norepinephrine, and serotonin. The former two are referred to as catecholamines, whereas serotonin is an indoleamine. MAO is found in the neurons of the monoamine systems, where it regulates the levels of the neurotransmitters stored in the neurons by breaking them down (catabolism) after reuptake and before storage. The type B MAO is found to have a particular affinity for dopamine, whereas the type A MAO has a stronger affinity for serotonin. Low levels of MAO might mean less catabolism of dopamine and more storage in the neurons which might produce a more reactive system. In humans, type B MAO has a very high heritability, high reliability over time (although showing gradual increases in level with age), and higher levels in women than in men at all ages. Age and sex differences on MAO are consistent with higher levels of sensation seeking in males than in females and the tendency of sensation seeking to drop with age after a peak in late adolescence (Zuckerman, 1994).

The Monoamine Systems and Behavior

Given the imprecise relationship of peripherally measured enzymes like MAO and indicators of neurotransmitter activity in the brain through metabolites assayed from cerebrospinal fluid, blood, and urine, correlations between these measures and personality or behavior in humans are problematic. Fortunately, there is a large body of experimental literature using other species that can provide some insights into the basic behavior mechanisms mediated by particular brain systems. The comparative approach to the psychobiology of personality depends on the assumption of a relationship between animal behavior traits and human personality traits (Zuckerman, 1984). Common physiological and neurochemical correlates can provide some linkage between animal and human models, as has been shown with the cross-species studies of cortical EP augmenting-reducing and MAO-behavioral relationships. The relationship of monoamine systems to behavior and personality has been suggested by a number of investigators (Cloninger, 1987; Dellu, Mayo, Piazza, Le Moal, Simon, 1993; Depue & Iacono, 1989; Gray, 1971, 1987; Panksepp, 1982; Zuckerman, 1979, 1983, 1991; Zuckerman, Ballenger, & Post, 1984). Generally, these theorists claimed that the mesolimbic dopamine system beginning in the ventral tegmental area (A10) (Figure 6.5) is essential in the tendency to search for reward, explore new environments, and approach novel stimuli in animals; and it is especially reactive in human extraverts, impulsives, and sensation seekers. In this respect, it is interesting that sensation seekers tend to abuse drugs which release dopamine from nuclei of the dopamine systems in the brain. Some of these nuclei also mediate intrinsic reward or pleasure from appetitive activities, such as eating and sex.

Stimulant drugs like cocaine and amphetamine also produce a sense of energy and arousal in humans, and up to some optimal dosage they increase general activity in rats. These arousal effects are mediated by the dorsal ascending norepinephrine (noradrenergic)

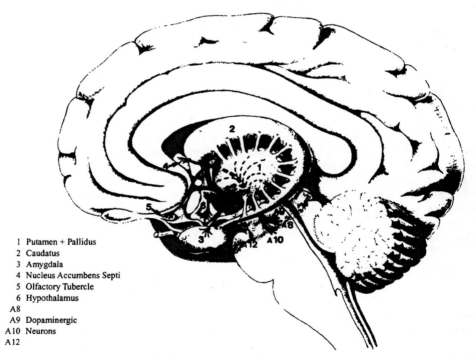

1 Putamen + Pallidus
2 Caudatus
3 Amygdala
4 Nucleus Accumbens Septi
5 Olfactory Tubercle
6 Hypothalamus
A8
A9   Dopaminergic
A10 Neurons
A12

FIGURE 6.5. Dopaminergic system of the human brain, lateral view. *Note:* From *Psychobiology of aggression and violence* (p. 47), by L. Valzelli, 1981, New York: Raven Press. Copyright 1981 by Raven Press. Reprinted by permission.

system (Figure 6.6) originating in the locus coeruleus (A6). This system, which ascends to innervate all parts of the cortex, has been characterized as an arousal system by some. But others describe it as an alarm system at lower levels of activity and a panic system at higher levels (Gray, 1982; Redmond, 1987). The latter interpretation would associate a highly reactive system with the human trait of anxiety or neuroticism and the anxiety disorders.

Cloninger (1987) and Gray (1987) believe that activity of the serotonergic system (Figure 6.7) is also involved in anxiety trait. I have suggested that the behavioral inhibition associated with high serotonergic activity mediates behavioral inhibition, which is strong in the presence of anxiety but characteristically weak in impulsive sensation seekers. Like psychopaths, impulsive sensation seekers are relatively insensitive to signals of punishment in an approach-avoidance situation. Low levels of serotonergic activity are found in persons who attempt or commit impulsive suicides and homicides. Lowered levels of serotonin are associated with disinhibited aggressive and sexual behavior in animals. For these reasons—and because the relationship of serotonin to anxiety is not clear—I believe that a weak or unreactive serotonergic system is more closely associated with the trait of impulsive unsocialized sensation seeking, of which the antisocial personality is an extreme example.

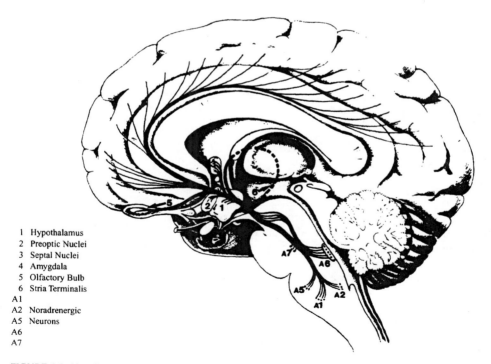

1 Hypothalamus
2 Preoptic Nuclei
3 Septal Nuclei
4 Amygdala
5 Olfactory Bulb
6 Stria Terminalis
A1
A2 Noradrenergic
A5 Neurons
A6
A7

FIGURE 6.6. Noradrenergic system of the human brain, lateral views; A6 = locus coeruleus. *Source: Psychobiology of aggression and violence* (p. 46), by L. Valzelli, 1981, New York: Raven Press. Copyright 1981 by Raven Press. Reprinted by permission.

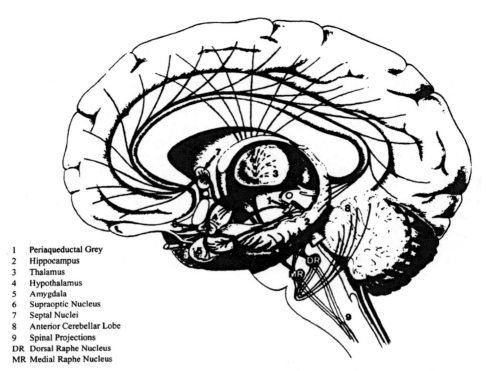

1   Periaqueductal Grey
2   Hippocampus
3   Thalamus
4   Hypothalamus
5   Amygdala
6   Supraoptic Nucleus
7   Septal Nuclei
8   Anterior Cerebellar Lobe
9   Spinal Projections
DR Dorsal Raphe Nucleus
MR Medial Raphe Nucleus

FIGURE 6.7. Serotonergic system of the human brain, lateral view; DR = dorsal raphe, MR = medial raphe nuclei. *Source: Psychobiology of aggression and violence* (p. 45), by L. Valzelli, 1981, New York: Raven Press. Copyright 1981 by Raven Press. Reprinted by permission.

HORMONES

Neurotransmitters affect only adjacent neurons, whereas hormones are biochemicals that affect receptors in distant cells, usually traveling through the blood stream to reach them. The brain influences hormone secretion through a chain of chemical events, beginning with the secretion of releasing hormones, such as gonadotropin and corticotropin releasing hormones, from the hypothalamus (Figure 6.8). These hormones release other tropic hormones, such as gonadotropic (GTH) and adrenocorticoptropic (ACTH) hormones, from the pituitary gland at the base of the brain. These hormones travel through the blood stream to reach their target glands: the gonads in the case of GTH and the adrenal cortex for ACTH. Stimulated by the tropic hormones, these glands release their hormones, testosterone in the case of the male gonads and cortisol from the adrenal cortex.

Hormones may affect personality at many stages of development. Genetic control of the development of the gonads determines whether they take the form of testes or ovaries producing testosterone in males and estrogen in females. However, exposure to exogenous sources of androgens or estrogens in the fetal period of development may also affect the developing brain and have long-term effects on personality. Prenatal exposure to androgens

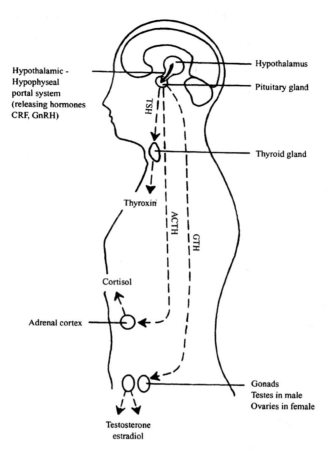

FIGURE 6.8. Hypothalamic-pituitary-hormone systems. *Source: Psychobiology of Personality* (p. 182), by M. Zuckerman, 1991, Cambridge, UK: Cambridge University Press. Copyright 1991 by Cambridge University Press. Reprinted by permission.

affects girl's later play interests, resulting in more "rough-and-tumble" play characteristic of boys, and less interest in "dolls" and "house" play more characteristic of girls (Ehrhart, Epstein, & Money, 1968). These play differences are with their own siblings as well as the general population, thus controlling for possible parental influences. Despite claims that gender differences in play interests are entirely a function of socialization, these findings indicate that genetically influenced hormonal factors may play an important role. Parents trying to change the gender-stereotyped toys and play of their children may find some truth in this conclusion.

An intriguing study of fraternal opposite sex and same sex twins on sensation-seeking trait found higher Sensation Seeking Scale scores in female co-twins of male dizygotic twins than in females who shared the womb with another female twin (Reznick, Gottesman, & McGue, 1993). Male co-twins did not show the effect. Although the result could be attributed in some part to the postnatal social influences of the male twins on their female co-twins, the comparative literature shows direct influences of prenatal hormones from litter mates on subsequent testosterone levels, aggressiveness, and other traits associated with testosterone in rodents.

Whatever the source of the association, plasma testosterone in human males is positively correlated with sensation seeking, particularly with the Disinhibition subscale of the SSS (Daitzman, Zuckerman, Sammelwitz, & Ganjam, 1978; Daitzman & Zuckerman, 1980). However, testosterone was also correlated *positively* with scales measuring extraversion, dominance, and activity, and *negatively* with scales of socialization (conformity to rules), self-control, and MMPI scales of neuroticism and anxiety, introversion, and femininity (Daitzman & Zuckerman, 1980). Testosterone was also correlated with the extent of heterosexual experience in these young single males. Thus, testosterone in males seems to influence almost all of the major personality factors and sexual experience. The comparative literature suggests that the relation between experience and testosterone is a two-way one. Sexual stimulation and winning fights may elevate testosterone. The same might occur in humans; stress may lower testosterone and increase anxiety, and sexual experience might increase testosterone levels. O'Carroll (1984) compared two groups of men complaining about loss of sexual arousal or interest. One group had abnormally low testosterone levels (hypogonadal), whereas the other group had normal levels. The hypogonadal group had lower SSS General and Disinhibiton scores than the normal testosterone group. Both groups received testosterone injections over a nine-months period. Sensation-seeking scores did not change in either group; the difference between them remained even though testosterone levels were raised to normal in the hypogonadal group, and their sexual behavior increased. This result suggests that testosterone influences behavioral and personality traits, but the converse may not be true. However, alterations of hormone level may certainly have some immediate effects on behavior. Anabolic-androgenic steroids used by athletes to enhance muscular groups frequently produce aggressive and violent behavior in those taking the steroids (Pope & Katz, 1994). Chronic use of drugs like cocaine can also produce some marked changes in personality, particularly in aggressiveness and neurotic anxiety; some of these changes may be due to direct drug effects on the brain. However, in most cases the effects are reversible on discontinuance of use of the drug; therefore, one cannot claim that the chemical change has altered the basic personality.

Cortisol is a hormone that is elevated by stress, anticipatory anxiety, and depression, although when injected into humans it does not produce those feelings. (Born, Hitzler, Pietrowsky, Pairschinger, & Fehm, 1988). However, high levels of cortisol are found in timid infants and children who are vulnerable to later social phobias (Kagan, Reznik, & Snidman, 1988). Cortisol is negatively related to the sensation-seeking trait of Disinhibition, reinforcing the idea that a cortisol-reactive person may be overinhibited, particularly in human interations (Ballenger *et al.,* 1983). Kagan's inhibited type seems to represent a combination of high anxiety, low impulsive sensation seeking and low sociability. As with testosterone and MAO, biological markers for personality are not associated with specific traits but seem to underlie broad dispositions or behavioral mechanisms—such as approach, inhibition, and arousal—which may play a role in more than one personality type.

A PSYCHOBIOLOGICAL MODEL FOR PERSONALITY

Figure 6.2 portrayed a model of personality showing all levels from the genetic to the trait. Figure 6.9 is limited to three of the five major factors that are represented in some form in all personality trait models, the major behavioral mechanisms that underlie these traits, and the biochemical factors hypothesized to play a major role in the development of behavioral and personality traits. (Some of the biochemical factors, such as dopamine-beta-hydroxylase—DBH, the enzyme involved in the production of catecholamine neuro-transmitters—endorphins, and gamma-aminobutyric acid—GABA, a neuroregulator with inhibitory effects throughout the brain—have not been previously discussed in this chapter because of space limitations.)

In phrenology, there was the assumption that each personality trait was contained in a specific area of the brain. This view now seems naive because behavioral reactions always involve structures and neuronal tracts that extend across large parts of the brain. Although there may be important centers, like the amygdala and hypothalamus for emotions, we cannot say that emotions—or even specific emotions like fear—are localized in any one brain structure. For an appreciation of the complexity of the neuroanatomy of fear, one should read Gray (1987). However, this kind of simple isomorphism has been characteristic of some of the hypotheses relating brain biochemistry to personality. Cloninger (1987), for instance, sees Novelty Seeking (sensation seeking) as a primary function of dopamine, Harm Avoidance (neuroticism or fear-produced inhibition) as a function of serotonin, and Reward Dependence (a dependent type of sociability) as a function of norepinephrine. It would be

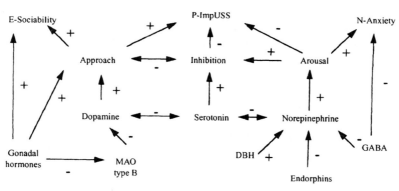

+ Agonistic interactions between factors
− Antagonistic interactions between factors
MAO   Monamine oxidase
DBH   Dopamine-beta-hydroxylase
GABA   Gamma-aminobutyric acid

FIGURE 6.9. A psychobiological model for extraversion-sociability (E-Sociability), impulsive unsocialized sensation seeking (P-ImpUSS), and neuroticism-anxiety (N-Anxiety), showing underlying behavioral mechanisms (approach, inhibition, and arousal) and neurotransmitters, enzymes, and hormones involved. *Source:* Modified from Figure 14.2 in *Behavioral Expressions and Biosocial Bases of Sensation Seeking* (p. 38), by M. Zuckerman, 1994, New York: Cambridge University Press. Copyright 1994 by Cambridge University Press. Reprinted by permission.

convenient if nature had built the neurochemical nervous systems in parallel with human personality traits, and behavioral mechanisms in a one-to-one relationship with personality traits. Basic personality traits are usually assumed to be independent descriptors, but we know that behavior mechanisms and neurochemical actions are not independent and, in fact, interact at all levels. My model suggests that personality traits represent combinations of mechanisms and neurochemical actions that underlie the behavioral dispositions.

Let us take the Impulsive Unsocialized Sensation-Seeking (ImpUSS) trait as an example (see Figure 6.9). Behaviorally, the trait is represented by the strong tendency to approach novel stimuli or situations. Novel stimuli are classified as provokers of fear and are grouped with signals of punishment or nonreward in Gray's (1982) theory. But the reaction to novel stimuli is a major distinction between high and low sensation seekers or between exploratory and nonexploratory strains of rodents. To the high sensation seeker, most novel stimuli are seen as potentially rewarding, but to the low sensation seeker, they are seen as potentially dangerous. The high sensation seeker is highly attentive (orienting reflex) to such stimuli and prone to investigate the stimuli without much attention to signals or thoughts of potential punishment. Thus, the behavioral outcome (approach-avoidance) is a function of the relative balance between anticipations of reward or punishment. When this relative balance is toward the reward end, and there is a general weakness of inhibition (constraint) mechanisms, the impulsive sensation seeker tries many more experiences, such as drugs and sexual partners, than the low sensation seeker (Zuckerman, 1994). The low sensation seekers become overaroused in the presence of signals of punishment, contributing to their inhibition in the situation.

Dopaminergic reactivity, particularly in the mesolimbic dopaminergic system and the left prefrontal lobe, is a biological trait associated with the general approach mechanism. Strength of the approach mechanism is common to both extraversion or sociability and impulsive unsocialized sensation seeking. What differentiates them is the weak inhibitory and arousability mechanisms associated with ImpUSS but not extraversion. Both of these mechanisms have historically been associated with extraversion in Eysenck's model, but most of the evidence supporting this claim applied more strongly to the impulsivity component of extraversion as it was then defined. The realignment of factors here in our trait model differentiates impulsivity from sociability. Sociability now constitutes the core of the extraversion definition and impulsivity is closely linked with sensation seeking in the new ImpUSS dimension. As a matter of fact, Eysenck and Eysenck (1985) also described impulsivity as a subfactor of psychoticism (P) rather than extraversion (E). Of course, even if the factors share only one of three behavioral mechanisms, there should be some residual relationships. Most recent factor analyses place ImpUSS primarily along the P dimension but with some loadings on E, particularly in a three factor solution. Gray (1987) has a point when he suggests that biologically significant dimensions of personality may not lie precisely along the axes defined by Eysenck's three factors. ImpUSS defines a factor in the P-E quadrant with a stronger leaning toward P. But most of the significant correlations with biological factors are along this impulsive sensation-seeking dimension or P rather than the pure E-sociability one.

Serotonin is involved in behavioral inhibition. This is what has led Gray (1982) to associate it with the trait of anxiety and Cloninger (1987) to link it to harm avoidance. But unless one regards impulsivity as the opposite of anxiety, it is clear that the capacity to inhibit approach behavior is not solely a function of fear but is also a special mechanism that may serve approach, as well. The predator stalking its prey must inhibit the tendency to leap before it is close enough to catch the prey. It is not fear that creates the constrained, cautious approach, it is an ability to moderate the approach drive. The overeager, impulsive predator goes hungry, and the impulsive psychopathic criminal goes to prison. Serotonergic reactivity in a pathway originating in the medial raphe nucleus is weak in the impulsive sensation seeker, resulting in a disinhibited approach tendency.

Norepinephrine in the dorsal noradrenergic ascending system originating in the locus coeruleus is postulated to mediate an arousal mechanism. This is not the reticulocortical arousal system suggested by Eysenck as the basis for extraversion, but one more intimately related to appetitive and emotional signals, signals of punishment, *and* signals of potent reward and increased vigilance, in general. Although it is not entirely devoted to conditioned fear signals, it constitutes a major pathway along which the central nucleus of the amygdala sends signals that arouse the cortex to deal with an external danger. Descending noradrenergic pathways increase peripheral cardiovascular arousal, which is so prominent in anxiety conditions like panic disorder. Autonomic arousability is certainly a major component of anxiety trait, or neuroticism, but it is not the entire story. Norepinephrine production is regulated by DBH, and this enzyme, which converts dopamine to norepinephrine, may potentiate arousal and anxiety proneness. At low levels, it may attenuate arousal and thus contribute to the low levels of norepinephrine found in high sensation seekers (Ballenger *et al.*, 1983). Endorphins, or endogenous opiate-like peptides, act on receptors in norepinephrine neurons and dampen NE activity. A deficit in endorphins may account for emotional arousability and anxiety. The benzodiazepine receptors are influenced by an as yet undiscovered endogenous tranquilizer agonist and react on the GABAnergic neurons to inhibit NE activity. Thus, low levels of GABA or reduced numbers of benzodiazepine receptors may play a role in the trait of anxiety, perhaps through arousal or more directly through an enhanced processing bias for signals of punishment.

This model allows for interactions at all levels and across levels, including the production of neurotransmitters, their uptake mechanisms, and inhibition or facilitation of activity by other transmitters or hormones. But the picture is even more complex. The relation of personality to neurotransmission may be a function of the "lock" rather than the "key"— that is, the receptor characteristics rather than neurotransmitter production or disposal traits. The recent discovery of the link between the D4 receptor gene and the trait of sensation (novelty) seeking suggests the possibility that different forms of the gene (polymorphic variants) may result in different actions of the neurotransmitter in different pathways, mediated by the particular forms of the transmitter. The dopamine D4 receptor, for instance, has at least eight polymorphic variants in the human (Seeman, 1995). High sensation-seeking (novelty) scores are associated with one variant, the seven-repeat allele or the longer forms of the gene. Low scores are associated with shorter forms of D4 (2–5 repeats). Many serotonergic receptors have been found, and many have a number of variants. At least several receptors exist in the noradrenergic system. The discovery of the connection between the D4 receptor variants and sensation seeking may be the prelude to the search for other connections between receptors and personality traits.

Quantitative differences in the densities of specific receptors may also play a role in personality differences. The density of benzodiazepine receptors is reduced in anxious humans (Weizman *et al.*, 1987) and anxious strains of rats (Robertson, Martin, & Candy, 1978). Future collaboration between molecular geneticists, psychopharmacologists, and personality psychologists could produce undreamed of breakthroughs in the biological bases of personality.

CONCLUSION

A psychobiological approach to personality is often accused of reductionism. This charge is usually baseless. All types of phenomena may be studied at different levels, from the most molecular to the most molar. Each level has its own methods, constructs, and limitations. An analysis at one level may be perfectly compatible with one at another level. The cognitive, behavioral, and biological are complementary and not conflicting modes of explanation. Great discoveries will occur at the borders of the different levels.

Biological and social psychologies have both made their claims on the field of personality, but until recently most American personality psychologists have approached personality from the social psychology viewpoint. But strictly social-environmental theories have never been satisfactory to those interested in individual differences and their sources. The idea of inborn differences in temperament became less fashionable but persisted, and now they are quite popular again (Bates & Wachs, 1994; Hettema & Deary, 1992; Strelau & Angleiter, 1991). Psychiatry led the way in a shift from the psychoanalytic paradigm to the psychobiological. Breathtaking advances in the neurosciences provided the opportunities to develop drugs for treating mental disorders and understand how these drugs work in the brain. In psychology, behavior genetics has been a major influence in reviving the biosocial approach to personality. Given the results of biometric twin and adoption studies, it is difficult to deny the role of genetic factors in personality traits and most forms of psychopathology. It will be even more difficult as new genes are linked with personality traits.

The trick is to find the biological factors that are inherited and predispose the behavioral outcomes. It is a long way between genes and traits. But the new science of molecular genetics provides a way of testing hypotheses about these intervening mechanisms by finding primary genes and determining what biological and behavioral mechanisms they control.

Making these connections will not be easy, and few theorists will risk venturing out of their familiar scientific territories to new lands, where the inhabitants speak strange languages and practice unfamiliar customs and rites. But the penalty of parochialism is stagnation and the reward of openness is discovery.

REFERENCES

Ballenger, J. C., Post, R. M., Jimerson, D. C., Lake, C. R., Murphy, D. L., Zuckerman, M., & Cronin, C. (1983). Biochemical correlates of personality traits in normals: An exploratory study. *Personality and Individual Differences, 4,* 615–625.

Benjamin, J., Li, L., Patterson, C., Greenberg, B. D., Murphy, D. L., & Hamer, D. H. (1966). Population and familial association between the D4 dopamine receptor gene and measures of sensation seeking. *Nature Genetics, 12,* 81–84.

Born, J., Hitzler, V., Pietrowsky, R., Pairschinger, P., & Fehm, H. L. (1988) Influences of cortisol on auditory evoked potentials and mood in humans. *Neuropsychobiology, 20,* 145–151.

Bouchard, T. J., Jr. (1993). Genetic and environmental influences on adult personality: Evaluating the evidence. In J. Hettema & I. J. Deary (Eds.), *Foundations of personality* (pp. 15–44). Dordrecht, Netherlands: Kluwer Academic Publishers.

Bouchard, T. J., Jr., Lykken, D. T., McGue, M., Segal, N. L., & Tellegen, A. (1990). Sources of human psychological differences: The Minnesota study of twins reared apart. *Science, 250,* 223–228.

Breuer, J., & Freud, S. (1937). *Studies in hysteria* (A. A. Brill, Trans.). New York: Nervous and Mental Disease Publishing (Original work published 1895)

Bruner, H. G., Nelen, M., Breakenfeld, X. O., Rogers, H. H., & van Oost, B. A. (1993). Abnormal behavior associated with a point mutation in the structural gene for monoamine oxidase A. *Science, 262,* 578–580.

Buss, D. M. (1994). *The evolution of desire: Strategies of human mating.* New York: Basic Books.

Carter, H. D. (1933). Twin similarities in personality traits. *Journal of Genetic Psychology, 43,* 312–321.

Cloninger, C. R. (1987). A systematic method for clinical description and classification of personality. *Archives of General Psychiatry, 44,* 573–588.

Cloninger, C. R., Svrahahioc, D. M., & Przybeck, T. R. (1993). A psychobiological model of temperament and character. *Archives of General Psychiatry, 50,* 975–990.

Daitzman, R. J., & Zuckerman, M. (1980). Disinhibitory sensation seeking, personality, and gonadal hormones. *Personality and Individual Differences, 1,* 103–110.

Daitzman, R. J., Zuckerman, M., Sammelwitz, P. H., & Ganjam, V. (1978). Sensation seeking and gonadal hormones. *Journal of Biosocial Science, 10,* 401–408.

Dellu, F., Mayo, W., Piazza, P. V., Le Moal, M., Simon, H. (1993). Individual differences in behavioral responses to novelty in rats: Possible relationship with the sensation-seeking trait in man. *Personality and Individual Differences, 4,* 411–418.

Depue, R. A., & Iacono, W. G. (1989). Neurobehavioral aspects of affective disorders. *Annual Review of Psychology, 40,* 457–492.

Eaves, L. J., & Eysenck, H. J. (1977). A genotype-environmental model for psychoticism. *Advances in Behaviour Research and Therapy, 1,* 5–26.

Eaves, L. J., & Young, P. A. (1981). Genetical theory and personality differences. In R. Lynn (Ed.), *Dimensions of personality* (pp. 129–179). Oxford, UK: Pergamon.

Ebstein, R. P., Novick, O., Umansky, R., Priel, B., Osher, Y., Blaine, D., Bennett, E. R., Nemanov, L., Katz, M., & Belmaker, R. H. (1966). Dopamine D4 receptor (D4DR) exon III polymorphism associated with the human personality trait of novelty seeking. *Nature Genetics, 12,* 78–80.

Ehrhardt, A., Epstein, R., & Money, J. (1968). Fetal androgens and female gender identity in the early treated adrenogenital symptom. *Johns Hopkins Medical Journal, 122,* 160–167.

Eysenck, H. J. (1957). *The dynamics of anxiety and hysteria.* New York: Praeger.

Eysenck, H. J. (1963). *Experiments with drugs.* New York: Pergamon Press.

Eysenck, H. J. (1967). *The biological basis of personality.* Springfield, IL: Charles C. Thomas.

Eysenck, H. J. (1991). *Dimensions of personality: The biosocial approach to personality.* In J. Strelau & A. Angleitner (Eds.), *Explorations in temperament: International perspectives in theory and measurement.* London: Plenum Press.

Eysenck, H. J., & Eysenck, M. W. (1985). *Personality and individual differences: A natural science approach.* New York: Plenum Press.

Fahrenberg, J. (1987). Concepts of activation and arousal in the theory of emotionality (neuroticism): A multivariate conceptualization. In J. Strelau & H. J. Eysenck (Eds.). *Personality dimensions and arousal* (pps. 99–120). New York: Plenum Press.

Falconer, D. S. (1981). *Introduction to quantitative genetics* (2nd ed.). London: Longman.

Fulker, D. W., Eysenck, S. B. G., & Zuckerman, M. (1980). The genetics of sensation seeking. *Journal of Personality Research, 14,* 261–281.

Gale, A., & Edwards, J. A. (1986). Individual differences. In M. G. H. Coles, E. Donchin, & S. W. Porges (Eds.), *Psychophysiology: Systems, processes and applications* (pp. 431–507). New York: Guilford Press.

Gall, F. J. (1835). *On the origins of the moral qualities and intellectual faculties of man.* Carlsruhe, Germany: C. L. Muller.

Galton, F. (1874). *English men of science: Their nature and nurture.* London: Macmillan.

Gray, J. A. (1971). *The psychology of fear and stress.* New York: McGraw-Hill.

Gray, J. A. (1982). *The neuropsychology of anxiety: An enquiry into the functions of the septo-hippocampal system.* New York: Oxford University Press.

Gray, J. A. (1964). Strength of the nervous system and levels of arousal: A reinterpretation. In J. A. Gray (Ed.), *Pavlov's typology* (pp. 289–364). Oxford, UK: Pergamon Press.

Gray, J. A. (1987). The neuropsychology of emotion and personality. In S. M. Stalh, S. D. Iverson, & E. C. Goodman (Eds.), *Cognitive neurochemistry* (pp. 171–190). Oxford, UK: Oxford University Press.

Gray, J. A. (1991). The neurophysiology of temperament. In J. Strelau & A. Angleitner (Eds.), *Explorations in temperament: International perspectives on theory and measurement* (pp. 105–128). London: Plenum Press.

Haier, R. J., Sokolski, K., Katz, M., & Buchsbaum, M. S. (1987). The study of personality with positron emission tomography. In J. Strelau & H. H. Eysenck (Eds.), *Personality dimensions and arousal* (pp. 251–267). New York: Plenum Press.

Hall, R. A., Rappaport, M., Hopkins, H. K., Griffin, R. B., & Silverman, J. (1970). Evoked response and behavior in cats. *Science, 170,* 998–1000.

Hebb, D. O. (1949). *The organization of behavior.* New York: Wiley.

Hull, C. L. (1943). *Principles of behavior.* New York: Appleton.

Kagan, J., Reznik, J. S., & Snidman, N. (1988). Biological bases of childhood shyness. *Science, 240,* 167–171.

Kelly, D. (1980). *Anxiety and emotions.* Springfield, IL: Charles C Thomas.

Lang, P. J. (1985). The cognitive psychophysiology of emotion: Fear and anxiety. In A. H. Tuma & J. D. Maser (Eds.), *Anxiety and the anxiety disorders* (pps. 131–170). Hillsdale, NJ: Erlbaum.

Lindsley, D. B. (1961). Common factors in sensory deprivation, sensory distortion, and sensory overload. In P. Solomon, P. E. Kubansky, P. H. Leiderman, J. H. Mendelsohn, R. Trumbull, & D. Wexler (Eds.), *Sensory deprivation.* Cambridge, MA: Harvard University Press.

Loehlin, J. C., Nichols, R. C. (1976). *Heredity, environment, and personality.* Austin, TX: University of Texas Press.

Loehlin, J. C. (1992). *Genes and environment in personality development.* Newbury Park, CA: Sage.

Loehlin, J. C., Willerman, L., & Horn, J. M. (1985). Personality resemblances in adoptive families when the children are late-adolescent or adult. *Journal of Personality and Social Psychology, 48,* 376–392.

Lukas, J. H., & Siegel, J. (1997). Cortical mechanisms that augment or reduce evoked potentials in cats. *Science, 196,* 73–75.

Lykken, D. T. (1982). Research with twins: The concept of emergenesis. *Psychophysiology 19,* 361–373.

Mathew, R. J., Weinman, M. L., & Barr, D. L. (1984). Personality and regional cerebral blood flow. *British Journal of Psychiatry, 144,* 529–532.

McDougall, W. (1923). *Outline of psychology.* New York: Charles Scribner's Sons.

Moruzzi, G., & Magoun, H. W. (1949) Brain stem reticular formation and activation of the EEG. *EEG Clinical Neurophysiology, 1,* 455–473.

Murphy, D. L., Belmaker, R. H., Buchsbaum, M. S., Martin, N. F., Ciaranello, R., & Wyatt, R. J. (1977). Biogenic amine-related enzymes and personality variations in normals. *Psychological Medicine, 7,* 149–157.

Myrtek, M. (1984). *Constitutional psychophysiology.* London: Academic Press.

Nebylitsyn, V. D. (1972). *Fundamental properties of the nervous system:* New York: Plenum Press.

Newman, H. H., Freeman, F. N., & Holzinger, K. J. (1937). *Twins: A Study of heredity and environment.* Chicago: University of Chicago Press.

O'Gorman, J. G. (1984). Extraversion and the EEG, Part I: An evaluation of Gale's hypothesis. *Biological Psychiatry, 19,* 95–112.

Olds, J., & Milner, P. (1954). Positive reinforcement produced by electrical stimulation of septal area and other regions of rat brain. *Journal of Comparative and Physiological Psychology, 47,* 419–427.

Panksepp, J. (1982). Toward a general psychobiological theory of emotions. *The Behavioral and Brain Sciences, 5,* 407–422.

Pavlov, I. P. (1960). *Conditioned reflexes: An investigation of the physiological activity of the cerebral cortex* (G. V. Anrep, Ed. and Trans.). New York: Dover. (Original was published 1927)

Pederson, N. L., Plomin, R., McClearn, G. E., & Friberg, L. (1988). Neuroticism, extraversion and related traits in adult twins reared apart and reared together. *Journal of Personality and Social Psychology, 55,* 950–957.

Pivik, R. T., Stelmack, R. M., & Blysma, F. W. (1988). Personality and individual differences in spinal motoneuronal excitability. *Psychophysiology, 25,* 16–24.

Plomin, R. (1986). *Development, genetics, and psychology.* Hillsdale, NJ: Erlbaum.

Plomin, R. (1995). Molecular genetics and psychology. *Current Directions in Psychological Science, 4,* 114–117.

Pope, H. G., & Katz, D. L. (1994). Psychiatric and medical effects of anabolic-androgen steroid use: A controlled study of 160 athletes. *Archives of General Psychiatry, 51,* 375–382.

Resnick, S. M., Gottesman, I. I., & McGue, M. (1933). Sensation seeking in opposite-sex twins: An effect of prenatal hormones. *Behavior Genetics, 23,* 323–329.

Robertson, H. A., Martin, I. L., & Candy, J. M. (1978). Differences in benzodiazepine receptor binding in Maudsley reactive and Maudsley nonreactive rats. *European Journal of Pharmacology, 50,* 455–457.

Saxton, P. M., Siegel, J., & Lukas, J. H. (1987). Visual evoked potential augmenting/reducing slopes in cats: Part 2. Correlations with behavior. *Personality and Individual Differences, 8,* 511–519.

Scarr, S., Webber, P. L., Weinberg, A., & Wittig, M. A., (1981). Personality resemblance among adolescents and their parents in biologically related and adoptive families. *Journal of Personality and Social Psychology, 40,* 885–898.

Schalling, D. Asberg, M., & Edman, G. (1984). Personality and CSF monoamine metabolites. Unpublished manuscript, Department of Psychiatry and Psychology, Karolinska Hospital, Stockholm.

Schneirla, T. C. (1959). An evolutionary and development theory of biphasic processes underlying approach and withdrawal. In M. R. Jones (Ed.), *Nebraska Symposium on Motivation: Vol. 7.* (pp. 1–42). Lincoln: University of Nebraska Press.

Schooler, C., Zahn, T. P., Murphy, D. L., & Buchsbaum, M. S. (1978). Psychological correlates of monoamine oxidase in normals. *Journal of Nervous and Mental Diseases, 166,* 177–186.

Seyle, H. (1956). *The stress of life.* New York: McGraw-Hill.

Shields, J. (1962). *Monozygotic twins brought up apart and together.* London: Oxford University Press.

Siegel, J., Sisson, D. F., & Driscoll, P. (1993). Augmenting and reducing of visual evoked potentials in Roman high- and low-avoidance rats. *Physiology and Behavior, 54,* 707–711.

Stelmack, R. M. (1990). Biological bases of extraversion: Psychophysiological evidence. *The Journal of Personality, 58,* 293–311.

Stelmack, R. M., & Wilson, K. G. (1982). Extraversion and the effects of frequency and intensity of the auditory brainstem evoked response. *Personality and Individual Differences, 3,* 373–380.

Strelau, J. (1983). *Temperament, personality, activity.* London: Academic Press.

Strelau, J. (1996). The regulative theory of temperament: Current status. *Personality and Individual Differences, 20,* 131–142.

Strelau, J., & Eysenck, H. J. (1987). (Eds.). *Personality dimensions and arousal.* New York: Plenum Press.

Sulloway, F. J. (1979). *Freud: Biologist of the mind.* New York: Basic Books.

Teplov, B. M. (1964). Problems in the study of general types of higher nervous activity in man and animals. In J. A. Gray (Ed.), *Pavlov's typology* (pp. 3–153). Oxford, UK: Pergamon Press.

Tolman, E. C. (1926). The nature of the fundamental drives. *Journal of Abnormal Psychology, 20,* 349–358.

Vaillant, G. E., & Schnurr, P. (1988). What is a case? *Archives of General Psychiatry, 45,* 313–319.

Valzelli, L. (1981). *Psychobiology of aggression and violence.* New York: Raven Press.

Watson, J. D., & Crick, F. H. C. (1953). Genetical implications of the structure of deoxyribonucleic acid. *Nature, 171,* 964–967.

Weizman, R., Tanne, Z., Granek, M., Karp, L., Golomb, M., Tyano, S., & Gavish, M. (1987). Peripheral benzodiazephine binding sites on platelet membranes are increased during diazepam treatment of anxious patients. *European Journal of Pharmacology, 138,* 289–292.

Wilson, E. O. (1978). *On human nature.* Cambridge, MA: Harvard University Press.

Wilson, E. O. (1975). *Sociobiology: The new synthesis.* Cambridge, MA: Harvard University Press.

Zuckerman, M. (1969). Theoretical formulations: I. In J. P. Zubek (Ed.), *Sensory deprivation: Fifteen years of research* (pp. 407–432). New York: Appleton Century.

Zuckerman, M. (1979). *Sensation seeking: Beyond the optimal level of arousal.* Hillsdale, NJ: Erlbaum.

Zuckerman, M. (1984). Sensation seeking: A comparative approach to a human trait. *Behavioral and Brain Sciences, 7,* 413–471.

Zuckerman, M. (1989). Personality in the third dimension: A psychobiological approach. *Personality and Individual Differences, 10,* 391–418.

Zuckerman, M. (1990). The psychophysiology of sensation seeking. *Journal of Personality, 58,* 313–345.

Zuckerman, M. (1991). *Psychobiology of personality.* Cambridge, UK: Cambridge University Press.

Zuckerman, M. (1994). *Behavioral expressions and biosocial bases of sensation seeking.* New York: Cambridge University Press.

Zuckerman, M. (1995). Good and bad humors: Biochemical bases of personality and its disorders. *Psychological Science, 6,* 325–332.

Zuckerman, M., Ballenger, J. C., & Post, R. M. (1984). The neurobiology of some dimensions of personality. In J. R. Smythies & R. J. Bradley (Eds.), *International review of neurobiology: Vol. 25* (pp. 392–436). New York: Academic Press.

Zuckerman, M., Buchsbaum, M. S., & Murphy, D. L. (1980). Sensation seeking and its biological correlates. *Psychological Bulletin, 88,* 187–214.

Zuckerman, M., & Cloninger, C. R. (1996). Relationships between Cloninger's, Zuckerman's, and Eysenck's dimension of personality. *Personality and Individual Differences, 21,* 283–285.

Zuckerman, M. Kolin, E. A., Price, L., & Zoob, I. (1964). Development of a sensation seeking scale. *Journal of Consulting Psychology, 28,* 477–482.

Zuckerman, M., Kuhlman, D. M., & Camac, C. (1988). What lies beyond E and N? Factor analyses of scales believed to measure basic dimensions of personality. *Journal of Personality and Social Psychology, 54,* 96–107.

Zuckerman, M., Kuhlman, D. M., Joreman, J., Teta, P., & Kraft, M. (1993). A comparison of three structural models for personality: The big three, the big five, and the alternative five. *Journal of Personality and Social Psychology, 65,* 757–768.

Zuckerman, M., Kuhlman, D. M., Thornquist, M., & Kiers, H. (1991). Five (or three) robust questionnaire scale factors of personality without culture. *Personality and Individual Differences, 12,* 929–941.

Zuckerman, M., Murtaugh, T. T., and Siegel, J. (1974). Sensation seeking and cortical augmenting-reducing. *Psychophysiology, 11,* 535–542.

Zuckerman, M., Simons, R. F., and Como, P. G. (1988). Sensation seeking and stimulus intensity as modulators of cortical, cardiovascular, and electrodermal response." *Personality and Individual Differences, 9,* 361–372.

CHAPTER 7

OPERANT THEORY OF
PERSONALITY

CHAUNCEY R. PARKER, MADELON Y. BOLLING,
AND ROBERT J. KOHLENBERG

THE OPERANT PERSPECTIVE OF PERSONALITY:
AND NOW FOR SOMETHING REALLY DIFFERENT

The term *personality* has considerable meaning as used in our everyday lives and in psychological theory. However, the operant approach leads us to reject the concept of personality as "a thing" while providing an understanding of personality in its deepest sense. We believe this analysis has many practical implications and avoids some of the pitfalls that often occur in nonoperant approaches.

Because the operant perspective is counterintuitive to many people, we hope the reader will keep an open mind as we present its ideas. You may come to agree that there actually are a number of valid ways to explain what we experience and observe around us.

WHAT IS MEANT BY *PERSONALITY*

We have chosen two definitions of *personality:* one from a textbook on personality and the other from an encyclopedia. These definitions are representative of how people use

CHAUNCEY R. PARKER, MADELON Y. BOLLING, AND ROBERT J. KOHLENBERG • Department of Psychology, University of Washington, Seattle, Washington 98195-1525.

Advanced Personality, edited by David F. Barone, Michel Hersen, and Vincent B. Van Hasselt. Plenum Press, New York, 1998.

the term both in scholarly contexts and in daily life. The same general approach we use to analyze the definitions given would apply to other definitions as well. First, here is a textbook definition: "We define personality as consistent behavior patterns originating within the individual" (Burger, 1993, p. 3); next, the encyclopedia definition:

> [By personality, we mean] deeply ingrained and relatively enduring patterns of thought, feeling, and behavior. Personality usually refers to that which is unique about a person, the characteristics that distinguish him or her from other people. Thought, emotion, and behavior as such do not constitute a personality, which is, rather, the dispositions that underlie these elements. Personality implies predictability about how a person will act or react under different circumstances. (*Encarta*, 1994)

Certain features are common to both of these definitions. First, there is the notion of "consistency" referred to in the textbook. A similar quality is conveyed by the encyclopedia's reference to "enduring." Both definitions refer to "patterns" of behavior. Patterns can only be construed when behavior is consistent or perceived to recur. Patterns then would be a function of consistency in behavior at various times and under various conditions. Consistency in behavior has everything to do with predictability, which is why we are interested in the study of persons in the first place.

Next, the textbook definition specifies that patterns of behavior originate from "within." The encyclopedia definition references this quality by using the descriptors "deeply ingrained" and "dispositions that underlie." And finally, although the textbook definition does not directly refer to individual differences, the notion of "uniqueness" given in the encyclopedia is included later in the textbook's discussion.

We will examine each of these—*consistency,* the *quality within,* and *uniqueness*—from an operant viewpoint to throw some light on the causes of predictability in behavior. As part of the process, we will explain how an individual might come to have or not have one or more of these features. Our interest in the absence of one or more of these features is relevant to understanding what is meant by "not having any personality" or having a "disturbed personality." But before turning to our analysis of these factors, we will cover the basics of operant conditioning. In a brief discussion, we hope to clear up some common misunderstandings. We will explain what is meant by contingencies of reinforcement, explanations, and behavior.

OPERANT THEORY

The operant approach is the centerpiece of the theory and philosophy known as radical behaviorism, originated by B. F. Skinner (1945, 1953, 1957, 1976). *Radical* comes from the Latin word for "root": *radix*. Radical behaviorism analyzes the roots of behavior. In a nutshell, operant theory is the following: people (you, I, our family and friends) act or behave the way we do because of the consequences (contingencies of reinforcement) of our experiences in past relationships with the inanimate and the animate environments. We believe this deceptively simple theory has profound and far reaching implications for understanding personality. It should be noted that according to radical behavioral theory, a complete account of our acts also involves two other types of contingencies—those of survival (genetic predispositions) and of culture or social evolution (Skinner, 1953, 1957, 1976). In our discussion, we will focus on operants (acts resulting from contingencies of reinforcement) although, for the sake of completeness, we may also refer to the two other types of contingencies.

CONTINGENCIES OF REINFORCEMENT

Unfortunately, typical images that come to mind when the term *reinforcement* is mentioned involve saying "Good!" or offering a reward to a child, client, or friend for doing what we want. These images are not only technically erroneous, but they focus inappropriately on superficial aspects of reinforcement and incorrectly portray operant theory as Machiavellian and chauvinistic. We use the term *contingencies of reinforcement* in its technical, generic sense, referring to all consequences that affect (increase or decrease) the strength (or likelihood) of behavior, including positive reinforcement, negative reinforcement, and punishment. Even though a conscious experience of pleasure often accompanies positive reinforcement and displeasure accompanies punishment, the presence of these feelings is not a necessary part of the process and should not be confused with it.

Reinforcement is omnipresent in our daily lives—it almost always occurs naturally and is rarely the result of someone "trying" to reinforce another's behavior. The strengthening or weakening of behavior (e.g., increasing or decreasing the tendency to do it again) occurs at an unconscious level; that is, awareness—either of what you are "supposed to do" or of particular feelings—is not required. In operant theory, such strengthening or weakening of the likelihood of behavior constitutes our reinforcement history, the ultimate cause of our actions.

Notice how neatly the notion of the probability of a behavior recurring or the "tendency to do it again" fits with the encyclopedia's specification that personality consists of "dispositions that underlie" behavior. *Disposition* is sometimes defined as "a tendency or inclination, especially when habitual" (*American Heritage Dictionary,* 1978). These dispositions or tendencies refer to the likelihood of behavior, which, as we said, is changed by the consequences of that behavior.

It is important to note the operant distinction between near-at-hand influences on behavior (your present environment, feelings, and/or thinking) and the ultimate fundamental cause—reinforcement. It may be useful or even sufficient at times to view our behavior as resulting from more proximal (near at hand) influences, such as the current environment, thoughts, and emotions. However, radical behaviorists maintain that complete explanations require one to go back into the past and take reinforcement history into account. For example, you might say that you yelled at your friend because you were angry. That is, you explain your yelling as being *caused* by your anger. This might be a sufficient explanation in a social situation. As a behavioral explanation, however, it is incomplete because it does not contain information about past contingencies that account for (a) your getting angry and (b) your yelling. That is, not everyone would necessarily have gotten angry under the circumstances you did, nor does everyone yell when they are angry. A complete or causal explanation addresses these issues in addition to internal states and current situations.

EXPLANATIONS

People have learned to attribute varying reactions in situations to a "personality" that we are said to bear within us. But from the operant perspective, personality means the tendency to behave in a certain way. The way operant theorists see it, this merely says that things are as they are, much as T. S. Eliot said of his tomcat: "For he will do/As he do do/And there's no doing anything about it" (*The Rum Tum Tugger*, 1940, p. 19). This is hardly a satisfactory analysis for psychologists, who are often faced with the task of "doing something about" behavior.

So operant explanations always give accounts of the behavior of interest in terms of the history of the individual's interactions with others (and/or the physical environment) as well as her or his current situation and internal state. Explanations that refer to mental structures as causes of behavior are not as satisfactory to the behaviorist. For example, Jeremy puts a coin into a candy vending machine. His behavior could be explained in different ways: (a) he has a desire for a candy bar; (b) he has regressed to an oral needs stage; (c) he is under the influence of a specific expectancy of success; or (d) he is driven by hunger.

These are all explanations of Jeremy's actions. Still, behaviorists will ask, where did the desire come from? What does it mean to be driven by hunger? How did the specific expectancy come to be? How is it that, having regressed to an oral stage, Jeremy finds and operates a candy machine?

In each of these cases, operant theory inquires after the same three things: history, the current situation, and the internal state. That is, desire, expectancy, or hunger for a candy bar would be seen as a function of (a) a history of having watched others put coins in such a machine and receive food, plus a history of having eaten a candy bar and finding that it relieves the discomfort of not having eaten (reinforcement); (b) being in the vicinity of a vending machine with sufficient coins in hand (current situation), given this history; and (c) the number of hours without eating (history accounting for the internal state). These are all (at least potentially) publicly observable events (or "events in the environment") that account for Jeremy's behavior. They also account for the inferred nonbehavioral entities such as drive, desire, expectancy, and the manifestation of a breakdown in ego function.

Now we may inquire into your reinforcement history by asking: Which of these explanations seems most satisfactory to you?

Similarly, if a woman takes off in a small boat to circumnavigate the world singlehandedly, the operant explanation would focus on her past experiences, such as past results (contingencies) of taking risks, sailing alone, and being "adventurous." Nonoperant explanations might explain her behavior as being the result of "inner strength," or having a risktaker's personality. Radical behaviorists call this mentalism: inner, nonbehavioral processes, such as willpower, and fear of failure, are given the power to cause other more observable events to come about, just as though a little person named *willpower* or *adventurousness* resided within the individual and caused the individual to do or not do certain things.

Such explanations are part of what is known as the homuncular problem: attributing agency to some unseen entity (literally like a *homunculus*—"little man") within the individual. The homunculus originally referred to a 17th-century explanation of the way in which an ovum eventually became a full-sized animal. It was postulated that a microscopic miniature human is encased within the sperm and grows into the full-sized organism during gestation. The problem with this explanation is that we now are left with a puzzle to solve that is very much like the one with which we started. Rather than explaining where the full-sized animal came from, we are instead left with trying to explain the origins of the microscopic one.

To review: we consider explanations of behavior to be incomplete if they do not involve tracing the observable antecedents of behavior back as far as possible in the environment. These observable antecedents are the "controlling variables" for the behavior in question. Many current psychological explanations do little more than specify some inner process as the cause of a particular aspect of behavior. We feel that it is only reasonable to ask, in turn, what makes that inner process work as it does.

Context and Function

The search for controlling variables amounts to a deep concern for the *context* within which behavior takes place. Context is not only a matter of the local surrounds and events (the current situation) wherein the behavior takes place, but also necessarily includes the historical surrounds, or the past experiences of the person or persons involved. For example, if my friend says, "Wow, it's roasting out today!" and I am puzzled by her remark, it helps to know the current context—an outside temperature of 73° F; and the historical context—she just arrived in Southern California after spending most of the winter in the Aleutian Islands. An incomplete explanation would simply point to her "sensitivity to heat." Furthermore, I may consider it "pleasantly cool," since I have just returned from two weeks of fighting forest fires in Arizona. An incomplete explanation might simply point to my "heat tolerance."

Notice here that the stimulus "73° F" is not "the same stimulus" to my friend as it is to me. That is, there is not an inherent quality of the "experience of 73°-ness" independent of the context within which the behaviors of response occur. Context is all that is outside of behavior and surrounds it, so to speak. It is of central importance to operant theory because what we know about a behavior changes when the context of that behavior changes. Context determines the function of a behavior. That is why radical behaviorists' central approach to human behavior is *functional analysis.*

A functional analysis, according to Skinner, yields "the external variables of which behavior is a function" (1953, p. 35). The analysis consists of three parts: (a) the context or environmental setting, including the person's history, physiological and behavioral state; (b) the response of the individual; and (c) the consequences brought about due to acting on the environment.

The importance of context to the analysis of behavior is illustrated in the following example: Four students are studying late at night for a physics exam. You might say that they are all engaged in the same behavior. You could compare the percentage of students studying with the grade point outcome of the exam or with career expectancies and outcomes. There would be a certain truth in these observations and correlations. But let us do something really different (yet familiar to our everyday thinking) and examine context. (Notice that context is much more than the library location and time of day.) Adam is studying because he wants his dad to keep paying for school and living expenses. Beth, on the other hand, is working for a 4.0 GPA so she will qualify for a physics honor society. Carl is studying so that Beth will want to go for a walk with him. And Denise finds studying preferable to the chaos at home. In each case, that is, in each context, a different function is served by the same behavior. Knowing what we know now, are we still watching four people engaged in the same behavior? It does look the same on a certain level, but this apparent similarity is due to very different outcomes and so serves very different functions.

Most accounts of personality deal with describing and predicting behavior. To reiterate, there are two general ways to do this. One approach, the formal or topographical analysis, tells us what behavior looks like: studying late for a physics exam. A different approach, functional analysis, tells us the effect or function of behavior: earning living expenses, seeking accolades, pursuing a relationship, avoiding an aversive situation. Which kind of analysis is more likely to help us predict behavior?

The formal or topographical approach is close to the everyday usages in the realm of "personality." That is, we ordinarily say such things as "he is gentle" or "she's the embodiment of politeness, but make no mistake, she's vicious." Notice that this kind of description, or those using many other more professional psychological terms—aggressive, passive, delusional, obsessive, compulsive, sociopathic, inattentive, manic, hyperactive, apathetic, depressed—consist of abstract modifiers of a sort that we naturally tend to turn into nouns: aggression, gentleness, obsessions, mania, depression, and the like. This process, as we will mention later, is reification. We believe such a grammatical turn confuses more than it clarifies.

If we remember that a certain person is not, for instance, "an obsessive" but a person "behaving obsessively," we are more likely to look for the causes of such behavior. What effect does behaving obsessively have in this person's life? What are the consequences of this way of being? What function does it serve in her life?

In seeking explanations of behavior, then, operant theorists view themselves as engaged in a search for controlling variables in the environment. Events are considered controlling variables when they are perceived to contribute to the behavioral result or process being observed, and when changing such events would change the behavior or process.

BEHAVIOR

Operant theory explains (gives the causes of) acts or behavior. Since most people incorrectly envisage behavior in a narrow, restricted fashion, the operant approach also is usually seen as narrow, restricted theory. For example, introductory psychology books often wrongly describe operant theory as dealing only with overt behavior, not thoughts or feelings.

It is important to note that the operant approach eschews things that are mentalistic, not things that are private. Private behaviors, however, are not given any unique status other than their privacy (they are available only to the individual, not subject to public observation). Private behaviors are cut from the same cloth as is public behavior, and are subject to the same discriminative and reinforcing stimuli that affect all behavior. Thus, private behaviors, such as thinking, planning, and feeling, can have as much or as little causal effect on subsequent behavior as do public responses.

With an understanding of how Skinner defined behavior (1945, 1957), it is possible to see that the behavioral approach deals with the same phenomena of interest that are considered to be nonbehavior by many personality theorists. Specifically, acts are anything a person does. This covers not only public behaviors, such as walking, talking, driving, and pushing levers; but also private, beneath the skin acts, such as thinking, feeling, seeing, hearing, experiencing, and knowing. Every aspect of being human is included in the definition of *behavior*, as long as it is expressed as a verb. This position was stated by Woodworth (cited in Catania, 1984): "Instead of 'memory' we should say 'remembering'; instead of 'thought' we should say 'thinking'. . . . But, like other learned branches, psychology is prone to transform its verbs into nouns." Woodworth goes on to say: "Then what happens? We forget that our nouns are merely substitutes for verbs, and go hunting for the things denoted by the nouns; but there are no such things, there are only the activities that we started with" (Catania, 1984, p. 303).

Woodworth described what we feel is the major problem with the notion of personality. In our opinion, too many psychologists have forgotten about the problem that occurs when we transform verbs into nouns. Technically, this is known as *reification,* from the Latin *res,* "thing," so to reify is to treat an abstraction as though it were concrete, having a material existence. Thus we end up engaging in a futile hunt for a thing called personality that, in reality, does not exist. Instead, we suggest that using processes or verbs to account for the phenomena referred to as personality will keep the researcher closer to the actual phenomena under investigation.

Verbal Behavior

Because language—talking or verbal behavior—seems to take a privileged position as a uniquely human and uniquely comprehensive phenomenon between private and public behaviors, it is the source of much confusion. Talking and other verbal activity, however, is just behavior; as such it is under the control of the environment every bit as much as is any other behavior.

All verbal behavior, no matter how private its subject matter may appear to be, has its origins in the environment. Although phenomena related to human verbal functioning vary from the most intimately personal to the most publicly social, all meaningful language is shaped into effective form by the action of an environmental verbal community. Thus, when a speaker says she sees an image in her mind's eye, what is said has been taught to her in childhood by others who could not see into her mind's eye. These "teachers" have used directly observed events in the teaching process.

What factors are involved in leading the speaker to say what he or she does? To know thoroughly what has caused a person to say something is to understand the significance of what has been said in its very deepest sense (Day, 1969). That is, "to know thoroughly" is to have identified the controlling variables, an analysis just as relevant to verbal behavior as it is to any other. For example, to understand what a man means when he says he just had an out-of-body experience, we would search for its causes. First, we would want to know about the stimulation in the body that was just experienced (the proximal cause). Then, we would want to know why a particular bodily state is experienced as being "out-of-body." Thus, we would look for environmental causes going back into the man's history, including the circumstances he encountered as he was growing up that resulted in his saying "body," "out of," "just had," and "I." As soon as we knew all of these, then we would understand thoroughly the significance of what was said.

This process, of course, is the reason we started with commonly held verbal definitions of *personality.* When we have found the controlling variables (just what it is we see in each other that causes us to speak of *consistent* behavior, originating from *within* the person, manifesting *uniquely*) for the verbalization "personality," then we will have understood it thoroughly.

Assumptions

The relevant philosophical principles that underlie radical behavioral thought are that knowledge is contextual; behavior is to be viewed nonmentalistically; private events such as thinking, feeling, seeing, hearing, and so on are behaviors, and even the most private verbal behavior has its origins in the environment. Furthermore, the likelihood of behavior is changed by its consequences. These assumptions provide a language and concept of human nature that clarify the interaction between an individual's behavior and the natural (which includes the social) environment.

OPERANT ACCOUNT OF PERSONALITY

So in operant terms, what is *personality?* Personality refers to behaving consistently over time and across situations. It has the quality of coming from within the individual and is the uniqueness that distinguishes one individual from another. The operant approach explains these features in terms of past and current functional relationships between context and the consequences of behaviors.

CONSISTENCY AND PREDICTABILITY

Behaving consistently results from a consistent environment with consistent contingencies over time. As we explained earlier, if a behavior results in consequences that reduce deprivation or remove aversive stimuli, then the probability is increased that we will behave that some way again in those circumstances in the future. "Those circumstances" would be the context of deprivation of reinforcers (needs) and a setting in which those reinforcers are available. As long as these conditions occur and reinforcement is reliable, the behavior will be maintained over time.

Generally speaking, most of us have experienced a relatively consistent environment. Many factors come together to make this the case. Parents do not usually change drastically from day to day, much less from hour to hour, in the way that they treat their children. Social contingencies also select for consistent behavior: It is important to the culture, to us as individuals, and to physical survival that we behave consistently. Systems such as traffic lights only work so long as people behave consistently with respect to them. We tend to reject or avoid people who on a regular basis say one thing and do another, or behave in wildly different ways from day to day or moment to moment. If we can predict another's behavior, our life is made easier. We can make plans, count on others, avoid unpleasant or dangerous social situations, feel safer, and lead more productive lives. For the most part, then, we have relatively consistent experiences.

But not everyone is so lucky. In fact, if a person is not predictable they may be considered to have a disordered personality. An extreme example of this is Borderline Personality Disorder. People exhibiting this style of behavior are notorious for their unpredictability. Their behaviors can swing dramatically from ingratiating to furious, from frightened to confident. These individuals "frequently vacillate between avoidance of conflict and intense confrontation" (Linehan, 1993, p. 152). In relationships, someone with borderline symptoms will suddenly switch from idealizing the other person to devaluing them. These people show a great need for intimate relationships and attention, but on the other hand, they reject intimacy after a short time and often terminate relationships prematurely. They often show abrupt and dramatic shifts in self-image with concomitant changes in values, opinions, goals, and so on. The history of people with this behavioral style usually includes a very troubled or traumatic childhood. The family environment in some way invalidated the individual's needs and/or feelings, was typically quite inconsistent, and often contained contradictory communications, negligence, and abuse.

With this, we need to clarify use of the term *consistency*, as it is quite clear that we have been describing people who consistently—even predictably—vacillate among extreme behaviors. Even though a person may be "predictably unpredictable," the norm for acceptable consistency seems to be more restrictive. People like to be able to pinpoint probable behavior at least within a relatively narrow range of the possible spectrum of behaviors. We would fire a weather forecaster who always predicted "heavy snow tomorrow, or possibly a mild day with high overcast—and yes, it might be another gorgeous hot summer day!"

The point here is that even "unpredictable" behavior actually has causal antecedents in the environment. People who carry the rather stigmatizing label of Borderline Personality Disorder do not "lack personality" because they are seen as inconsistent in their responses. It is just that the logic (or inferred causality) of their responses baffles most people, and the variability in their behavior precludes accuracy in prediction. Because most of their extremely variable responses are apparently in the interpersonal realm, they are experienced as being compellingly painful to relate to, which in turn causes even more trouble and pain to the individuals in question.

If, however, you or I had parents who were on occasion very attentive, but mostly not at home; were often distracted by the stress of work and impatient with us; who held impossibly high standards for our behavior and only listened to grievances from us if they were life threatening; who protested that they loved us dearly, yet would from time to time beat us severely—we might have similar expectations from other people as we grew up.

Children naturally pick up on incidental cues in the environment, in this case while trying to find some reliable way to predict the parents' irritability or accessibility. Because the child could not know the actual antecedents of the parents' behavior, these cues might be irrelevant—a certain quality of light, a certain time of day, or the color of the clothing the parents wore. Nonetheless, these cues might become part of the setting for puzzling behaviors on a child's part in the presence of intimate others, even after she or he grows up. Such an antecedent experience could account for an "unaccountable" behavior of frantic avoidance in a friend you meant to meet for coffee. She wanted to meet you, arranged for everything, but when you showed up, she slammed the door, ran, and hid, and would not come back. You might be wearing a sweater the same color as the one that your friend's mom wore the day she blamed your friend for breaking the dishwasher, beat her with the lamp cord, and locked her in a closet. Remember that such conditioning does not require awareness on the part of the one being conditioned: Your friend would probably not be able to explain her actions. Again, even inconsistent or incomprehensible behavior has environmental antecedents.

Cross-Situational Consistency

We have just been talking about consistency (or lack of it) over time. Consistency across different situations is another important feature of personality. Some theories of personality claim that cross-situational consistency indicates that personality traits are at work controlling behavior. Others argue that behavior changes depending on what the situational factors are; therefore, the situation is more important than traits. Operant theory takes a different stance and provides an explanation of cross-situational consistency and cross-situational inconsistency, through functional analysis.

To the behaviorist, similar behavior across differing situations does not indicate that a drive or a trait is causing that particular style of behavior, no matter what the situation. Nor do we agree that the situation is most important. Rather, it is the current situation *in combination with* an individual's history that dictates the probability (but not the necessity) of behavior. A functional analysis of the different situations based on the individual's reinforcement history relative to those stimulus conditions will reveal contextual similarities that evoke the behavior. In other words, people are sensitive to different situations (contexts) based on their past experience with similar settings.

For example, Bill tends to act in outgoing or extroverted ways, such as speaking more loudly than others, dominating social interactions with frequent witty remarks and humor, and dressing more stylishly than most of his acquaintances. But there are other situations in which he does not act that way. It turns out that for most of his life, Bill was able to get attention, approval, or "just one more cookie" from his mother and his friends when he was loud and witty and well dressed, so he is quite likely to act that way now and in the future under similar circumstances.

On the other hand, Bill's father avoided him and criticized him for "having a loud mouth" while he was growing up. And neither his seventh-grade teacher nor the scout leaders appreciated his brand of humor. Hence, Bill tended to be more restrained when there were men in charge of a situation.

So we may see Bill acting in his loud and funny manner when he is hanging out with friends at a pub, when he is trying to make a new acquaintance into a sweetheart, when he is attending Professor Linda Gromwell's anthropology class, and when he is spending a Sunday afternoon with the college Bible study group. At one glance, these seem to be rather different situations. But they all share stimulus properties with Bill's experiences in situations involving his mother and his friends.

If we were to see Bill interacting during a meeting at work (where the supervisor bears a distinct resemblance to Mr. Folger of the seventh grade) or discussing his driving speed with a local police officer, Bob Greenspan, we would see "a different Bill." These situations have stimulus qualities similar to those he ran into with his father, so he is likely to behave in a more restrained fashion under these circumstances.

Andy, on the other hand, was always able to get what he wanted and to get out of uncomfortable predicaments with his parents when he used wit and humor. His teachers and recreation leaders all seemed to appreciate his humor. For him, this behavior is likely even when dealing with Officer Greenspan. Andy did not have Mr. Folger in seventh grade; he pretty reliably contributes the humor even during meetings at work.

Consistency of behavior (personality), rather than being determined exclusively by the situation or exclusively by biological dispositions or by traits, largely reflects the combined effects of reinforcement history and the functional qualities of a situation.

WITHIN

Both actors and observers sense that the tendency to behave a certain way comes from within, whether they call it personality or not. How has this come to be?

From the observer's point of view, seeing two people in the same situation react differently, we naturally ask where do these reactions come from? The stimuli in the environment were the same. The only observable difference was that the stimuli affected two different bodies, or reached two different people, who then reacted quite differently. The observer's logical conclusion is that the reactions must have come from within the bodies.

In contrast, not all behavior is usually accounted for by personality or said to come from within. If you were watching a troop of soldiers drilling on the parade grounds, it would be highly unlikely that you'd say their lockstep precision was due to their personalities or that the behavior came from within.

A little more difficult to account for is the actor's own experience of his or her reactions. What are the stimuli that are experienced when a person speaks of his or her behavior as coming from within? Sensations interior to the body (or as behaviorists say, private or "within the skin") always accompany one's actions, both public and nonpublic. From there, it is a perfectly logical move to assume that those actions came from within simply because they are inevitably preceded and accompanied by sensations not observable by anyone else.

Though there is a certain simple truth to the statement, to say that the behaviors came from within is itself an incomplete explanation, similar to saying you yelled at your friend because you were angry (as pointed out earlier). Though one's behavior may be perceived as coming from within largely due to normal development of language and usages of the verbal community (as we'll explain shortly), there is no accounting for the particular form of the behavior without tracing it back into its antecedent causes, which are always in the environment.

There are instances, however, when a person does not perceive her or his own behavior as coming from within. Cases like these help us to ask how anyone comes to say "it just welled up from inside." If your behavior does not come from within, does it mean you do not have a personality? That you are nobody? These are statements that people who say their behavior is not their own or does not come from within are apt to make.

Let us now look at how we learn to attribute behaviors to ourselves, how we learn to say they "come from inside" or not, as the case may be.

Development of the Sense of Self

We learn to say "I" when we first learn to talk. Not only do we learn to make the sound, but we also learn the acceptable referents for the sound from other people who teach us to talk, primarily our parents. Radical behaviorists refer to these people as the *verbal community*. Linguists and developmental psychologists call the period of life from about six months to two years of age the "single-word speech period." Toward the second year of life, many of these single words actually are two or three-word phrases, such as "Mommy hit," "juice all gone," "beep-beep trucks," but they serve as single functional units (Kohlenberg & Tsai, 1991, p. 132).

A functional unit is the behavior that occurs between the cue (technically, the discriminative stimulus) and the reinforcer. In language acquisition, the actual size of the functional unit changes with experience and the coaching of the verbal community. That is, most parents will reinforce any approximation of speech with a natural, delighted response. Whatever is reinforced is likely to recur, in such instances, as the "single functional unit" of early speech. Single functional units are phrases, such as "memorejuice," "babyicecream" or "meseemama," that serve as self-referent phrases.

Now, there is evidence that children learn abstractions, such as "big" or "red," or self-referent pronouns gradually, after they have learned them as larger functional units, such as "bigtruck," "bigdoll," "bigGregor," "redball," "redshirt," "rednose," "memorejuice," "mebearbear," or "Billypiano." This will not seem so strange if you recall (as I do) thinking that "ellemenopee" was a single unit within the thing called "alphabet" or that the song phrase "My country tizovthee" ended with "of the icing." Remember also, that it took some years to straighten them all out.

Kohlenberg and Tsai (1991) propose that "I" (also "me," "my," "mine," one's name, etc.) emerges as a separate functional unit gradually, from the larger functional units that include it. Thus, "I am hot," "I am hungry," "I am here," all have "I am" in common; "I feel sad," "I feel icky," "I feel happy," have "I feel" in common; "I want ice cream," "I want juice," "I want mommy," have "I want" in common; and so forth for all the "I x" type statements a person may ever make. (Keep in mind, of course, that in real life the actual statements from this first stage may be more like "me see mama" or "baby ice cream." The function is the same, so we'll just use "I" here as the generic form of self-reference.)

In the second stage of the emergence of "I," the smaller functional units such as "I want," "I see," "I have," emerge as separate. The child can then combine them with new objects, making statements she or he has never said or heard before. "I want Yellowstone," "I see fireman," "I am very unhappy" may be heard at this stage.

In turn, "I am," "I feel," "I want," "I see," all have "I" in common. In the third stage—not only "I" as a functional verbal unit, but "I" as referent—the experience of "I" emerges. The *experience* of "I" is acquired just as the experience of a football, ice cream, Mommy, or heat was acquired with the learning of the word for each. These experiences differ from "I," however, in that they are under the control of specific public stimuli and can be learned separately. "I," on the other hand, is under the control of a complex private stimulus. What is common to all, in addition to the vocable "I" or its equivalents, is perspective, the child's location in space in relation to others. It is where she or he is—right here—as opposed to where she or he is not—over there—and perspective is the only element that is present across all responses containing "I."

Remember, however, that the real-life processes are much more complex and not as linear as these outlined here, which amounts to the merest sketch of a very rich continuum of phenomena. (For a more detailed description of this process, see Kohlenberg & Tsai, 1991, 1995.)

Perspective is the stimulus that remains constant for all the "I want x," and "I see x," types of statements, since the "x" or object and the activity (wanting, seeing, etc.) vary from time to time. The public aspects of the stimulus vary considerably with the particular situation. Sometimes the child may be 5 feet to the left of the parent; at other times he or she may be 50 feet away. Given the wide variation in where "here" versus "there" may be, a private aspect seems likely to gain control. Thus, the response "I" as a unit is under the stimulus control of a locus.

During normal development, this perspective is the physical location of such private activities as seeing, wanting, and having; "the self" is experienced as relatively unchanging, centrally located, and continuous. Here is where the sense of "within" develops. The locus of awareness is where the body is, but it also observes the body. "I hurt my finger," "I have a tummy ache," and the like teach us that the "I" possesses the body, but the "I" *is not* the body. This is consistent with the continuity of self-experience; that is, the experience that it was you at your birthday party (an early one you remember) even though your body is now completely different. Although it is not the body, the "I" observes things that happen inside the body as well as outside. Since such observing has the perspective from behind the eyes, as it were, the "I" is experienced as within. Activities under private control then—activities attributed to the "I"—are experienced as coming from within.

Although normal development leads to a large degree of control of the "I" response by private (within the skin) stimuli, maladaptive development involves the opposite—a small degree of control of "I" by private stimuli. That is, several "I x" responses have come under public control. Now what does this mean in real-people terms? It means that some parents (or other early caretakers) inadvertently teach their children to get their cues from people or situations outside themselves (public stimuli) rather than from the private events and responses that only the child can access.

For example, little Tammy is in the grocery store with her mom. She says, "I want a candy bar." Mom, in a hurry to finish shopping, says, "No you don't. We've got to get home." This teaches Tammy that her private experience is not valid when her mom is in a hurry. Furthermore, it is likely that on other occasions when her mother is in a hurry, Tammy will tend to ignore her private experience again. That is, the public stimulus of Mom-in-a-hurry is more important than whatever private stimulus may have led to Tammy's statement. If this happens regularly or under punishing circumstances, "I want" may come to be under public control under other circumstances as well, even when Tammy is with other people. That is, she may come to scan the environment for any important person who looks anxious or hurried as the discriminative stimulus for whether she really wants something or not. Behaviorists call this *generalization,* and that is exactly what is going on here.

If similar invalidations of Tammy's other "I x" statements occur, she may eventually come to have a more or less severe psychological problem.

"I feel sick today."
"Nonsense, you're perfectly fine."

"Look, I'm taking giant steps!"
"You call those 'giant steps'?! Quit exaggerating."

"OK, I'm gonna do the shopping for you today."
"You wouldn't know how to do the shopping if your life depended on it."

"He hurt me!"
"Ah baloney, act like a grown-up."

These kinds of exchanges may pervade the history of people who eventually say their actions do not come from within or that they are not doing what they appear to be doing. This assertion may still sound a little far-fetched, but how many times have you heard disclaimers like these?

"Are you writing that paper?"
"No, not really."
"I mean, are you or aren't you?"
"Well, I can't really write, so I'm just sort of fakin' it."

"Do you want to go out tonight?"
"I don't know, do you?"

"Is that your poem on the wall, there?"

"Well, sort of."

"Didn't you write it?"

"Well, not exactly. The words came to me. I just kind of heard 'em and wrote 'em down. It's not, like, my words or anything."

Although these statements are relatively nonpathological, they show self-referent behaviors that are being spoken of ("tacted," radical behaviorists say) as under public control. There is a continuum of possible severity of problems with self, depending on the degree of private control of the functional unit "I." Keep in mind that we are not referring to someone suppressing a verbal report of feelings or needs. Rather, we are discussing the development antecedents of being aware of one's feelings (private stimuli) and needs (reinforcers) and how one comes to notice and define them in the first place.

Thus, you can see that if a person's tendency to behave a certain way is always (consistently) checked by a punishing or invalidating environment so that he or she comes to restrain himself or herself to avoid punishment or the humiliation of invalidating responses, that person may readily perceive that his or her own behavior does not come from within. Indeed, in a sense it does not if it is always (or nearly always) determined by what is going on outside, in other people—that is, if the tendency to behave is under public control. We are not just referring to unassertive people who may know what they prefer, but are reluctant to speak of it. People whose "I" is under public control really do not know what they want, what they can do, what they feel, see and so on, until and unless they find out what significant others want or will allow.

It is a short step from this situation to "I have no personality," if most of what a person does is actually subject to the modifications of others. The statement, "You have no personality," on the other hand, is more in the nature of a put-down than a diagnosis. It means "your behavior does not interest me" or "you are uninteresting." Curiously enough, a person who always defers to the wishes of others may be exactly the one who will receive such a put-down. However, this person still behaves consistently and uniquely (or identifiably). Whether such a person feels that his/her behavior comes from within or not, other people will still attribute behaviors to him or her as though it did. In this sense, there is no such thing as "having no personality."

Although in normal development, we do experience our behavior as originating within ourselves, the root of behavior still lies in the environment. Access to private stimuli, the sense of private control, and even the experience of "within" itself are learned.

Uniqueness

The third factor in the concept of personality is uniqueness, a quality observed by actors and observers alike. What is it that distinguishes one person from another? From the observer's point of view, we notice that in any given situation (under the same stimulus conditions, in behavioral terms), no two people will act exactly the same way.

For example, Ron and DJ, both in their middle twenties, are groundskeepers in an industrial park. The supervisor has assigned a project for the day: trimming all the hedges and clipping the ivy back off the curbs of all the parking lots. So Ron starts the hedger and begins squaring up the hedges. DJ, on the other hand, starts pruning dead twigs out of the maple trees. Then he cuts some old flowers out of the geranium beds. He pulls Johnson grass out of one ivy planting and rakes up some of the hedge trimmings that Ron is still steadily producing. After drinking a can of cola he brought from home, DJ finally picks up his pruners and starts cutting the ivy back from a parking-lot curb.

We could perhaps account for these differences by referring to biological factors (what we usually refer to as "biological endowment"), such as Ron's higher energy level, or we might say that DJ is "a little slow on the uptake." While it is true that biological factors provide the foundation on which behavior is built, and this foundation can determine certain limits of behavior (you can not build a high-rise on four-inch timber post supports), biological factors are not the whole story. In fact, there is plenty of evidence that experience alters physiology (Kalb, 1994; Salm, Modney, & Hatton, 1988; Weiler, Hawrylak & Greenough, 1995).

There are any number of ways of behaving given the same biological foundation (e.g., there's no biological necessity that Ron should have expressed his high energy by starting the work assignment right away—he might equally have done a few handsprings, or decided today was the day to take the machete to the thorn bushes behind the dumpster). What we want to do is account for the behavioral differences over and above the biological foundations.

So what accounts for Ron and DJ's differing behaviors? If the situation or stimulus conditions are exactly the same, and if the actors in question perceive them as the same, must there be an internal structure or personality difference to account for different behavior? Is it that Ron is a diligent, disciplined, no-nonsense worker, while DJ is headstrong, somewhat unreliable, a procrastinator? By now you know that these are descriptions of behavior but not causal structures.

A different way to look at this is that the situation is actually *not the same* to the two men. How could this be?

At three years of age, Ron's dad praised him for picking up the hairbrush right away when asked. His parents continued to notice and appreciate it whenever Ron responded promptly to requests and carried tasks to completion. Such a history of positive reinforcement (barring complications, of course) leads to a lasting tendency to behave the same way. To Ron the situation at the industrial park was yet another opportunity to receive positive consequences for a job done quickly and well.

To DJ, on the other hand, the situation at work is entirely different. When he was very small, his mom once asked him to hold her coffee cup while she looked at the map in the car, checking the route to the hospital. The mug was heavier than he expected and he did not get a good grip, so it slipped and fell, spilling coffee on him and all over the car. Mom was frightened lest he burn himself, DJ was naturally shocked, and to top it all off, his dad who was in the back seat holding his badly cut arm, yelled, "That's the last time we'll ask you to do anything, you useless bastard!" And that was not an isolated incident. They did ask him to do other things, of course. But each time, his dad found something wrong with what he did: he was too slow, too hasty, reckless, careless, not accurate enough. Not once did either parent tell him what was right with what he did. He was raised under a regime of punishment.

Although he had other experiences with playmates and at school, situations like the one at work, where the supervisor lays out tasks to be done, seem to be threatening, promising only negative consequences no matter what he does. No creature on earth will readily approach a punishing situation.

DJ is not at all aware of this state of affairs. To him it just naturally seems that a dark cloud always hangs over the work situation—that is the way it is with work, he figures, and a person has to overcome it the best he can. So he tends to do little tasks that were not assigned first, things he knows need taking care of but that nobody has asked him to do. If he does enough of these, he feels that at least he has accomplished something, so he can face the main awful task and get on with it.

Operant theory acknowledges biological endowment as a factor, and also accounts for the uniqueness of behavior through the individual's reinforcement history. This history will actually change the experience of the environment: no situation is exactly the same to any two people. Hence, their responses will be unique.

There is also an internal or subjective aspect to uniqueness: many people "feel unique." In the discussion of the quality within, we mentioned that the sense of self is normally a *perspective* or the location from which a person sees, hears, speaks, feels, and so on. Because no two bodies can occupy the same space at the same time, this locus of experience is indeed unique. The subjective feeling of uniqueness is not merely a private experience, then, but is based on physical laws as well as the unique history of which each of us is a product.

Uniqueness, then, from the point of view of the observer is a product of the reinforcement history of the individual. From the point of view of the actor, the sense of uniqueness is based on private stimuli that are available to no other, and on the truly unique perspective—or locus of experience—that each of us has learned to call "I."

CONCLUSION

Though its assumptions differ considerably from those in common use, operant theory can be turned toward explaining the phenomenon known as personality. Reinforcement history has been shown to account for consistency in behavior, the sense that behavior comes from within, and for the uniqueness of behavior from objective and from subjective points of view.

One of the most difficult areas to approach through behavior theory is the interiority of the sense of self. We have demonstrated in an abbreviated fashion that radical behaviorist thought can deal with issues of the self and private experience, though it is reputed not to be able to do so.

Since it is a theory of change, operant theory helps us not only to perceive the sources of current behavior, but also to find the function of that behavior in context and to discern ways to change it. Hence, one of the strengths of this approach is in helping people with difficulties in living.

REFERENCES

Burger, J. M. (1933). *Personality: Theory and research.* Pacific Grove, CA: Brooks/Cole.

Catania, A. C. (1984). *Learning.* Englewood Cliffs, NJ: Prentice-Hall.

Day, W. F. (1969). Radical behaviorism in reconciliation with phenomenology. *Journal of the Experimental Analysis of Behavior, 12,* 315–328.

Eliot, T. S. (1940). *Old Possum's book of practical cats.* London, UK: Faber and Faber.

Encarta: The Complete Multimedia Encyclopedia [CD-ROM]. 1994. Seattle, WA: Microsoft.

Kalb, R. G. (1994). Regulation of motor neuron dendrite growth by NMDA receptor activation. *Development, 120,* 3063–3071.

Kohlenberg, R. J., & Tsai, M. (1991). *Functional analytic psychotherapy: Creating intense and curative therapeutic relationships.* New York: Plenum Press.

Kohlenberg, R. J., & Tsai, M. (1995). I speak, therefore I am: A behavioral approach to understanding problems of the self. *The Behavior Therapist, 18* (6), 113–116.

Linehan, M. (1993). *Cognitive-behavioral treatment of borderline personality disorder.* New York: Guilford Press.

Morris, W. (Ed.). (1978). *The American heritage dictionary of the English language* (New College Edition). Boston: Houghton Mifflin.

Salm, A. K., Modney, B. K., & Hatton, G. I. (1988). Alterations in supraoptic nucleus ultrastructure of maternally behaving virgin rats. *Brain Research Bulletin, 21,* 685–691.

Skinner, B. F. (1945). The operational analysis of psychological terms. *Psychological Review, 52* (5), 270–277.

Skinner, B. F. (1953). *Science and human behavior.* New York: Macmillan.

Skinner, B. F. (1957). *Verbal behavior.* New York: Appleton-Century-Crofts.

Skinner, B. F. (1976). *About behaviorism.* New York: Vintage.

Weiler, I. J., Hawrylak, N., & Greenough, W. T. (1995). Morphogenesis in memory formation: Synaptic and cellular mechanisms. 69th Titisee Conference: The neurobiology of memory formation in vertebrates: Neuronal plasticity and brain function (1994, Titisee, Germany). *Behavioural Brain Research, 66* (1–2), 1–6.

CHAPTER 8

SOCIAL COGNITIVE THEORIES
OF PERSONALITY

S. Lloyd Williams and Daniel Cervone

INTRODUCTION

Social cognitive theory is based upon two key principles: (a) that the psychological person, the environment, and behavior reciprocally influence one another; and (b) that people are best understood in terms of conscious cognitive capabilities that enable them to symbolically represent events, to reflect upon themselves, and to act as agents of their own development (Bandura, 1986, 1997; Cervone & Williams, 1992). Social cognitive theory evolved from efforts to understand complex psychosocial functioning and adaptation according to basic principles of learning, with special emphasis on how people learn from one another

S. Lloyd Williams • Department of Psychology, Lehigh University, Bethlehem, Pennsylvania 18015-3068. Daniel L. Cervone • Department of Psychology, University of Illinois at Chicago, Chicago, Illinois 60607-7128.

Advanced Personality, edited by David F. Barone, Michel Hersen, and Vincent B. Van Hasselt. Plenum Press, New York, 1998.

(Bandura, 1969; Bandura & Walters, 1963). Originally called *social learning theory,* it drew much of its early inspiration from behavioral approaches (e.g., Skinner, 1953). Social cognitive theory retains an admiration of behaviorism's empirical and technical rigor, its focus on overt coping behavior as a primary phenomenon to be explained by psychological theories, its documentation of strong environmental influences on behavior, and its numerous benefits to society in ameliorating otherwise intractable human problems. But long before social learning theory came to be called social *cognitive* theory, it departed sharply from behaviorism. By the late 1960s, it had become outspokenly cognitive in orientation (Bandura, 1969). Subsequent elaborations on the theory (Bandura, 1977b, 1986, 1988, 1997) and developments in closely related social-cognitive conceptions (Mischel & Shoda, 1995; see Cervone & Shoda, in press) have moved it farther still from its early origins in behaviorism.

RECIPROCAL DETERMINISM

The broad framework within which the other social cognitive principles operate is the principle of reciprocal determinism, which holds that personal factors, behavior, and the environment mutually influence one another (Bandura, 1978a). Personal factors are the various cognitive, affective, and biological processes that constitute the psychological individual. The environment includes such factors as prevailing incentives and opportunities, social modeling influences, physical attributes, and the broader cultural context. Behavior refers primarily to action in the world, although social cognitive theory holds that people can exercise agency in the realm of consciousness as well as in overt action. In social cognitive theory, the three aspects of psychological functioning must be understood in dynamic interaction with one another.

Over the years, various approaches to psychological functioning have tended to emphasize only one of the pathways of mutual causality among persons, behaviors, and environments. Traditional psychodynamic, trait, and humanistic theories of personality have tended to emphasize personal causes of behavior, such as various cognitive structures, dynamisms, dispositions, and motives. The view was that such inner causes drive action, with environment playing a secondary role. Behavioristic theories took the opposite position, arguing against internal personal causes altogether in favor of the stimulus environment as the main driver of behavior.

Departing from the strong opposing positions, other theorists proposed that personal and environmental factors interact with each other to determine behavior (e.g., Bowers, 1973; Magnusson & Endler, 1977). Although this approach partly corrected for the earlier one-sided determinism of traditional personality theories and of behaviorism, it still was an incomplete account of behavior. For one, the interaction of persons and situations occurs dynamically, not merely in a predictive, statistical sense. Personal factors, such as values and self-appraisals, partly determine the environments in which people put themselves (Betz & Hackett, 1981; Snyder, 1981). Environments in turn influence personality processes, not only affecting the accessibility of personal beliefs (Higgins, 1996, in press) and the activation of self-regulatory processes (Bandura & Cervone, 1983, 1986; Cervone, Jiwani, & Wood, 1991), but also transmitting to people personal values, beliefs, expectations, competencies, and self-perceptions that can profoundly affect their behavior (e.g., Betz & Hackett, 1981; Rosenthal & Bandura, 1978). Second, behavior is not only caused by personal and situational factors, but it also causes those factors. For example, people's views of themselves are partly based on observations of their own behavior (Bandura, 1977b; Bem, 1972). Actions create physical and social environments, in part because they evoke reactions in others (Buss, 1991; Ickes, W., Snyder, M., & Garcia, S., 1977; Patterson, 1976). And actions that people undertake to master serious personal problems can produce large and enduring changes in their thoughts and feelings (Bandura, 1997; Williams, 1996).

Reciprocal influence does not necessarily mean that there is uniformity or invariant symmetry of strength of influence in the six causal pathways of the triadic reciprocal system. Under some circumstances, environmental influences overpower individual personal differences, such as among drivers responding to a police officer directing traffic; whereas in less compelling circumstances, as when people are selecting a videotape to rent, personal tastes may well be more accurate than environmental stimuli in predicting choice behavior. Influences can exert their effects variably over time, enabling the investigation of sequential triadic reciprocal relations (e.g., Cervone et al., 1991; Wood & Bandura, 1989).

Reciprocal determinism does not mean that research must always look at complex six-way causal interactions. Indeed, few investigations have examined simultaneously the reciprocal interactions among personal, behavioral, and situational factors (Kihlstrom & Harackiewicz, 1990; Lerner, 1990). Although methodologies have been specifically designed to analyze dynamic reciprocal processes (e.g., Thomas & Malone, 1979), such processes can be surpassingly complex. Fortunately, there is much of value to be learned by isolating and investigating separate causal pathways in the reciprocal system.

THE PSYCHOLOGICAL PERSON

THE SOCIAL COGNITIVE MODEL

Central to the social cognitive person are the conscious, reasoning, reflective, and especially self-reflective faculties (Bandura, 1986, 1997; Cervone & Williams, 1992). People are not just driven along by inner promptings or by external stimuli. They also reflect on themselves and their circumstances, they ponder the meaning and value of things, they reason and appraise evidence, and they actively guide their own lives. Moreover, they orchestrate their actions to try to attain a positive, stable sense of self and to have their lives make sense. People expend a lot of time and energy attending to what Baumeister (1989) called "needs for meaning"; that is, for finding purpose to their lives, for valuing and justifying their actions, for maintaining a sense of esteem and self-worth, and for developing feelings of personal efficacy and accomplishment.

The social cognitive person consists of a set of basic capabilities that enable such activities. These include capacities for symbolizing, forethought, learning from direct and vicarious experiences, self-regulation, appraising one's capabilities, and related psychological contents, such as goals, subjective values, competencies, self-perceptions, and expectations (Bandura, 1986; Mischel, 1973). Most of the remainder of this chapter will be devoted to considering these various personal factors in light of social cognitive theory. First, we will briefly contrast the broad fundamental assumptions of the social cognitive approach with those of alternative conceptions of people (see Caprara, Cervone, & Hampson, in press).

PSYCHODYNAMIC MODELS

In the psychodynamic approach, behavior is motivated by inner drives and impulses, which may have a life of their own outside of awareness. Given their inherent inaccessibility, these unconscious contents and their mechanisms of influence over behavior are difficult to verify or manipulate. Indeed, the existence of these hidden drives and motives often must be inferred from the very behavior they supposedly cause, thereby rendering them of little value scientifically. The record of psychodynamic theories in empirically predicting, explaining, and modifying behavior has been weak (Bandura, 1969; Bower & Hilgard, 1981; Rachman & Wilson, 1980). In contrast, conscious cognitive causes, which are readily observable and demonstrably changeable, powerfully affect emotional reactions and behavior, as shown by evidence to be reviewed in subsequent sections.

TRAIT OR DISPOSITIONAL MODELS

In the trait or dispositional approach, personality consists of broad response dispositions, tendencies to behave in certain general ways in diverse circumstances. The trait approach generally seeks to identify basic traits and to sort traits into basic categories for describing individual differences in the population (John, 1990; McCrae & Costa, 1996). Although people do differ in their average tendencies to respond in particular ways, the social cognitive view is that psychological constructs such as "traits" that characterize these average tendencies are an inadequate basis for a theory of personality (Cervone, 1991, 1997). Much behavior is highly attuned to specific situations and is idiosyncratically organized, creating cross-situational variability in responding (Mischel, 1968; Mischel & Peake, 1982). People with the same average tendencies display characteristic patterns of both high and low response rates that are important "signatures" of personality (Mischel & Shoda, 1995). Dispositional approaches, such as the five-factor model (McCrae & Costa, 1996), provide little insight into the specific psychological processes underlying either variability or consistency in behavior (Cervone, in press). Rather than response tendencies (cf. Buss & Craik, 1983), social cognitive theory explores the cognitive and affective mechanisms that underlie the individual patterns of action and experience that distinguish people from one another (Cervone & Shoda, in press). Knowing the particular psychological mechanisms underlying coping behavior enables more powerful prediction of individual behavior in particular circumstances than is afforded by broad response dispositions. We will discuss the issue of cross-situational generality and specificity of behavior at greater length in a later section.

BEHAVIORAL MODELS

In behavioral approaches, behavior is determined, within the limits of biological constraints, solely by external events, namely, antecedent paired stimuli in classical conditioning, and reinforcing and discriminative stimuli in operant conditioning. Because presumably any internal cognitive or emotional processes can be traced directly to earlier stimulus events, there is no need for an inner person in psychological causation (Skinner, 1953). Later, we will review evidence showing that "conditioning" stimuli influence behavior mainly through their intervening influence on thought processes (e.g., Dulany, 1968; Grings, 1973; Kaufman, Baron, & Kopp, 1966). We will also review evidence that predicting future behavior from people's history of past stimuli or past behavior can be less accurate than predicting future behavior from their current cognitive self-appraisals (e.g., Bandura, Adams, & Beyer, 1977; Williams, Dooseman, & Kleifield, 1984; Williams, Kinney, & Falbo, 1989). People's mental transformations and interpretations of stimulus events, rather than the events themselves, determine their subsequent behavior (Mischel, Cantor, & Feldman, 1996).

COMPUTATIONAL MODELS

Some people liken human cognition to mechanical computation. The brain certainly does gather, modify, store, retrieve, and process information in a most powerful way, and thus "is (at least) a physical symbol system" (Simon, 1990, p. 3). Social cognitive theory is concordant with information-processing principles, but the analogy of person to computing machine fails to focus attention on the aspects of cognition that are among the most central to social cognition: the subjective frame of reference and the conscious cognitive self-determinants of action in the world. Through conscious reflection on themselves and the environment, people gain not only knowledge, but also the power to affect their own motivation, achievements, and development (Bandura, 1989). Self-reference cognitions intervene between knowledge and action, and they figure heavily in adaptive coping behavior (Bandura, 1997). Computational models of cognition, in contrast, have led cognitive scientists to devote limited attention to subjectively experienced mental states and to the link between cognition and action (Bruner 1990), in short, to the processes of conscious human agency.

BIOLOGICAL MODELS

Humans are biological organisms, but social cognitive theory rejects biodeterministic analyses in which behavior is seen as driven solely by neuromolecular processes. Behavior must be consistent with the neural and chemical mechanisms subserving it, but it cannot be reduced to such mechanisms. Indeed, predicting most classes of psychosocial behaviors (e.g., people's career paths or their future vacation activities) can be done far more accurately from people's conscious thoughts than from any known measures of neurophysiology. And psychological processes reciprocally influence biological processes (e.g., Bandura, Taylor, Williams, Mefford, & Barchas, 1985); recalling an insult can make one's heart pound in anger.

Psychological principles must be understood in their own right. For example, we know a great deal about how to teach people many things, but this knowledge of teaching methods could not be derived, even in principle, from knowledge of genetics or biochemisty. As Bandura (1997) put it, "Were one to embark on the road to reductionism, the journey would traverse biology and chemistry and would eventually end in subatomic particles, with neither the intermediate locales nor the final stop supplying the psychological laws of human behavior" (p. 4).

HUMANISTIC MODELS

The humanistic or phenomenological approach to personality has several points in common with the social cognitive view. Both emphasize the central importance of a subjective frame of reference and of self-reflective thought, the self-directed course of human potentialities, and the emergent creative quality of mental life. However, the theories diverge in fundamental ways. Social cognitive theory places more emphasis on environmental factors and their influence on people and behavior. Social cognitive treatment approaches also contrast with those in the humanistic tradition by emphasizing therapist directiveness to guide and assist people in their attempts at mastery. In place of generalized tendencies such as self-actualization, social cognitive theory examines human nature in terms of specific cognitive processes and basic human capabilities, to which we now turn.

BASIC HUMAN CAPABILITIES

The key personality-related question in reciprocal determinism is, what are the basic units of personality, the elements that comprise the "person" aspect of the triadic model? Social cognitive theory examines the psychological processes through which people learn about themselves and the world and orchestrate courses of action. The basic units of study in this analysis are the cognitive and affective processes that interact with the environment to determine behavior. These units include the motivational processes that mediate social behavior and the cognitive structures underlying human competencies, values, and rules of conduct.

SYMBOLIZING CAPABILITY

The most basic of human mental capabilities is the ability to use symbols. People can mentally represent a tremendous variety of things, including past events and possible or impossible future events. Moreover, they can manipulate these symbolic representations in rich and varied ways that allow them to accommodate to environmental demands. They remember past errors and adjust what they do accordingly. They can envision possible future environments and mentally represent possible alternative courses of action and their likely outcomes to guide themselves in acting effectively in ever-changing circumstances. Symbols also serve an important motivational function in representing future goals and possibilities for oneself, which can function as cognitive incentives for current behavior (Markus & Nurius, 1986).

Human language is one of the most complex and most pervasive example of people's ability to use symbols. Much of our cognitive activity involves linguistic symbols through which we assign meaning to events, and with which we communicate with one another. Largely through language, we learn how our beliefs and our interpretation of events are congruent with those of others. Language is also a major medium by which social information and social influences are transmitted. By words, people convey not only factual information, but also values, tastes, emotional reactions, moral standards of conduct, and so on. Much of our reasoning about important decisions take place on a linguistic level; a kind of verbal "inner monologue" occupies people's consciousness much of the time.

Mental representations are essential to help people exercise the self-control needed to delay gratification, a capacity that is a major dimension of mature functioning. When children are faced with a choice between a less attractive food item that they can consume immediately, and a more attractive item for which they must wait, their success at delaying gratification is determined in part by how they represent the food to themselves mentally. If they think about its tasty properties, they are unable to delay gratification, and they settle for the less attractive immediate reward. But if they mentally transform the savory treat into an inedible object, or they think of its barren physical dimensions, they can delay much longer (Mischel, Cantor, & Feldman, 1996; Mischel, Shoda, & Rodriguez, 1989).

Symbolic self-representations of effective copying behavior can help people to master challenging situations and overcome severe stress reactions, as in various imagery-based treatments for maladaptive fears and inhibitions. In systematic desensitization (Wolpe, 1958), phobic people imagine themselves attempting a graduated sequence of progressively more scary activities while keeping their anxiety low. In implosion therapy (Stamfl & Levis, 1967), people imagine themselves rapidly and massively confronting their most terrifying fears. In covert modeling (Kazdin, 1984), they imagine someone else dealing with the phobic stressor. A vast body of research reveals that anxious people lastingly benefit from such imagery, showing reduced fear and increased ability to manage the once-scary activities (Bandura, 1969; Kazdin, 1984). Symbolic self-representations of action thus can modify personality processes and enduringly reduce behavioral disabilities and vulnerability to distress.

FORETHOUGHT

One of our most important symbolizing capabilities is that of representing the future. Much human behavior is regulated by future considerations. People are skilled at anticipating situations that will likely confront them, how they will react to those situations, and the likely consequences that will follow from possible alternative actions. This forethought faculty derives from people's ability to store information about past experiences, to reason about that information, and to project it into the future. Indeed, classical and operant learning phenomena are best understood as reflecting changes in expectations.

The ability to predict future events accurately, which is of great adaptive value, rests in large part on the ability to detect covariations among events. People actively search for covariations, and they are good covariation detectors in many circumstances. Even rats can be remarkably sophisticated covariation detectors (Hernnstein, 1966). However, people are also subject to certain systematic biases and errors (Nisbett & Ross, 1980). Their search for covariation is partly guided by prior expectations. Strongly held erroneous beliefs about what ought to covary often override the actual objective stimulus information and lead people to see "illusory correlations" or fail to detect real correlations (Alloy & Tabachnik, 1984; Chapman & Chapman, 1963; Nisbett & Ross, 1980). If they do not have strong expectations, people can detect objective associations more accurately.

People often must predict future events and behavior under complex and uncertain circumstances with little time available for extensive analysis. Predictions, therefore, rely partly on simple judgmental heuristic shortcuts, such as judging the likelihood of an outcome by the subjective ease with which information suggesting that outcome comes to mind (Schwarz, Bless, Strack, Klumpp, Rittenauer-Schatka, & Simons, 1991; Tversky & Kahneman, 1973, 1974). These simple strategies efficiently produce adequate judgments in many instances, but they leave ample room for systematic errors that can lead to serious negative consequences (Nisbett & Ross, 1980). Predictive accuracy can be improved by instruction in statistical reasoning (Nisbett, Fong, Lehman, & Cheng, 1987).

DIRECT LEARNING

People are quite good at learning from their firsthand experiences with co-occurring stimuli and from the outcomes of their own responses, that is, from classical and operant learning procedures. In social cognitive theory, although some responses can be evoked, learned, or carried out automatically and with little awareness, most learning of complex behaviors requires the heavy contribution of conscious cognitive processes. "Conditioning" in actuality reflects the operation of cognitive processes and is increasingly viewed from an information-processing perspective (Brewin, 1988, 1989). The very term *conditioning* is no longer viable because of its misleading implication of an automatic nonconscious stamping-in of responses by stimulus events.

Classical Learning

Classical learning procedures teach organisms to expect that one stimulus signals the likely occurrence of another stimulus, and the organism responds accordingly. In other words, Pavlov's dog salivates because the bell leads it to think that food is on the way. Well-learned Pavlovian autonomic responses to signaling stimuli can be almost instantaneously eliminated or transferred to other stimuli by mere verbal information that indicates the changed stimulus arrangement (Grings, 1973).

Avoidance Learning

Avoidance learning is often cast in terms of the mechanical conditioning of anxiety arousal, which then functions to reinforce avoidance behavior (Mowrer, 1960). However, avoidance learning cannot be easily explained except by organisms' mentally representing future events. In response to a signaling stimulus, such as a light, animals quickly learn how to avoid electric shock. Thereafter, they resolutely avoid in response to the light signal for countless trials, despite never again experiencing the shock and, indeed, long after the shock apparatus has been disabled. In other words, even after a large number of classical extinction trials (the light without the shock), avoidance continues undiminished. Learning theorists chary of cognition strove to account for this and related troublesome phenomena in terms of a classically conditioned fear drive that connected the present avoidance behavior to the long-absent conditioning stimuli; organisms were not avoiding the long-absent shock stimulus, but escaping from the presently activated fear drive whose reduction reinforced the avoidance (Mowrer, 1960). However, a vast body of evidence shows that fear and anxiety, however defined, have only a weak and variable relationship with avoidance behavior (Bandura, 1969; Bolles, 1975; Carr, 1979; Mineka, 1979; Rachman, 1976; Schwartz, 1984; Williams, 1987, 1988). A more powerful and parsimonious (i.e., conceptually straightforward) way to explain the persistence of avoidance is that the animal *thinks* that the light signals the imminent arrival of shock and *expects* that avoidant action will prevent the shock (Schwartz, 1984; Seligman & Johnston, 1973). In humans, the cognitive interpretation of phobic behavior receives strong empirical support (Williams, 1996a, 1996b), as we will consider in some detail in the section on perceived self-efficacy below.

Operant Learning

Similar considerations apply to operant conditioning. There can be no doubt that environmental consequences profoundly affect social behavior, but those effects are largely mediated by forethought. Rewards and punishments serve an informative and motivational function. They inform organisms of the contingent relationship between actions and outcomes and motivate them to act in ways likely to secure rewarding outcomes and avoid punishing ones (Bandura, 1986). Indeed, people's beliefs about behavior-outcome relations, even if erroneous, easily override the actual contingencies. People perform in markedly different ways depending on which of several different schedules they were told governed their rewards, when, in fact, all subjects were on the same fixed-interval schedule (Kaufman *et al.*, 1966; cf. Dulaney, 1968). It was once assumed that operant learning occurred outside of awareness, but that assumption was challenged by findings that learning accelerates greatly when people become aware of the contingencies (Dulany, 1968; Spielberger & DeNike, 1966).

VICARIOUS LEARNING

Much of what we know comes from observing the world around us. Observing the behavior of other people, in particular, is perhaps the single most important mode of learning social functioning (Bandura, 1986, 1977; Rosenthal & Bandura, 1978). We mentally represent not only others' behavior per se, but also the circumstances and outcomes of their behavior, thereby learning about how to deal with situations without having to experience them firsthand. We vicariously learn from others' writing or speech as well as from seeing them act, and what we learn extends well beyond overt actions to include beliefs, emotional reactions, values, goals, and diverse other psychological contents. Vicarious learning stands in sharp contrast to learning by successive differentially reinforced, trial-and-error approximations. The latter would be dreadfully tedious and inefficient, not to mention hazardous to physical or psychosocial health, for complex human activities (Bandura, 1986). Fledgling pilots and surgeons spend considerable time in observing more experienced counterparts; thereby, they have already learned a great deal about requisite responses long before being rewarded for attempts to fly or operate.

Observational learning goes far beyond the mere mimicry of others' actions. Rather, observers abstract forms of grammar (Brown, 1979), strategies for dealing with problems (Rosenthal & Zimmerman, 1978), styles of expression and aesthetics, generalized aggressive strategies (Bandura, 1973; Eron, 1987), and diverse other capabilities that can then be used generatively—beyond simply duplicating the literal behavioral sequences that have been observed.

Subprocesses of Vicarious Learning

Social cognitive theory conceives of observational learning in terms of several distinct informational subprocesses, centering on mechanisms of attention to information, retention of it, behavioral reproduction, and motivation. Observers must first attend to the modeling display. The extent to which they do so depends on many considerations. For example, they attend more to similar than dissimilar models, to models who control valued outcomes, to modeling displays that are clear and vivid, to modeling of behaviors they know to be of functional value, and to modeled behaviors that are punished or rewarded (Bandura, 1986; Cervone & Williams, 1992; Rosenthal & Bandura, 1978; Rosenthal & Zimmerman, 1978).

Next, observers must retain a mental representation of the attended-to action if they are to later reproduce it. Various memory-enhancing strategies, such as generating verbal labels and descriptions that summarize the response and rehearsing vivid mental images of the modeled sequence (Gerst, 1971), work well for retaining those sequences. Verbal coding enhances reproduction accuracy by increasing the accuracy of the cognitive representations (Carroll & Bandura, 1990). With practice, the verbal codes drop away as the cognitive conception becomes well integrated, and the performance becomes routine and automatized.

Having observed and acquired a representation of the modeled behavior, the next stage concerns the ability to reproduce the observed behavior. This ability centers on the adequacy of the acquired mental representation as a guide for action. As anyone who has attended an event featuring accomplished musicians, dancers, or athletes, can attest, rapt attention to a performance will not necessarily enable one to reproduce it. Achieving proficiency in all but rudimentary tasks requires practice in addition to observation. Refining skills is a "conception-matching" process (Carroll & Bandura, 1982, 1985) in which people compare their reenactments with their mental conception of adequate performance, progressively adjusting what they do to match the ideal. This process can be assisted by media aids, which enable people to view aspects of their reenactments that they would not otherwise be able to observe (Carroll & Bandura, 1982).

Having acquired an adequate representation, people still may not enact modeled responses if they have no reason to do so. Social cognitive theory accepts the distinction between competence and performance, between what people are capable of doing, and what they actually do. People use their capabilities mainly in response to perceived incentives. Incentive motivators also enter into the acquisition of responses because people will attend to and retain modeled information better if they believe it will benefit them. However, perceived incentives are by no means necessary for acquiring modeled response. For example, when children observe a model engage in novel behavior that is unrewarded or even punished, they nevertheless acquire a mental representation of the action, and they can readily reproduce the behavior when offered rewards for doing so (Bandura, 1965).

Vicarious Motivators

People's motivational processes generally are very much affected by what they observe. They judge the likely consequences of behavior partly by the consequences that befall models who have displayed the behavior. They are more likely to emulate behavior that they have seen rewarded and less likely to reproduce behavior for which the model was punished (Bandura, 1965). Modeling also alters other powerful motivators of behavior, such as people's self-perceptions of their abilities and their standards of self-evaluation (Bandura, Adams, & Beyer, 1977; Bandura & Kupers, 1964; Brown & Inouye, 1978; Lepper, Sagotsky, & Mailer, 1975).

Vicarious Emotional Learning

Vicarious processes heavily influence the acquisition of emotional responses. Neutral stimuli can become enduringly arousing when an observer sees other people aroused by them (Berger, 1962). This process is illustrated particularly well by the vicarious acquisition of phobic responses, in which strong, persistent, dysfunctional emotional and behavioral reactions can be acquired almost entirely vicariously. For example, snake phobias appear often to have been acquired from observing frightened models (Murray & Foote, 1979; cf. Merckelbach, Arntz, & DeJong, 1991).

Phobias are acquired by diverse means, including direct and vicarious experiences, verbal information, and genetic inheritance (Rachman, 1977). The independent contribution of vicarious processes is not easy to separate out in retrospective studies with people who have already developed a phobia. However, strong prospective experimental evidence shows that modeling alone can produce severe persistent phobic reactions in primates. Laboratory-reared rhesus monkeys were initially fearless in the presence of snakes, but they became intensely afraid immediately on observing wild-reared monkeys behaving fearfully toward the reptiles. Their strong fear reactions were undiminished even three months later (Cook, Mineka, Wolkenstein, & Laitsch, 1985; Mineka, Davidson, Cook, & Keir, 1984). Modeling transmits not only fear but also fearlessness; it can be a potent treatment for phobia (Rosenthal & Bandura, 1978).

SELF-REGULATION

People guide their own behavior. They plan courses of action directed toward distant aims, judge whether they are succeeding, and make adjustments in response to discrepancies between their attainments and their standards and goals (Bandura, 1986; Carver & Scheier, 1990; Pervin, 1989). The outstanding achievements of some solitary artists and writers verify this capacity for self-direction. Self-regulation means much more than just having willpower. Several subprocesses are involved in effective self-regulation, including setting personal standards and goals, observing one's performances, and rewarding oneself for successes (Kanfer, 1980). Many researchers have held that personality is best characterized by the aims, aspirations, and goals toward which individuals are working at various points in their lives (see Buss & Cantor, 1989; Pervin, 1989). Personal goals and aims often explain why people adopt particular courses of action, and how they orchestrate daily activities toward serving a larger purpose.

Locke (1968; Locke & Latham, 1990) has extensively analyzed how goals regulate action. Under some circumstances, variations in goals are highly predictive of differences in performance (Bandura & Cervone, 1986). The effect of goals is by no means uniform, just as goals themselves can differ in level, difficulty, specificity, and temporal proximity, among other dimensions. Specific goals are clearly more effective than general goals because they specify what needs to be done (Locke, Shaw, Saari, & Latham, 1981). Similarly, proximal goals are superior to distal goals because they more clearly mark progress, better constrain what needs to be done in the here-and-now, and boost motivation more by providing frequent occasions for self-satisfaction on attaining subgoals (Bandura & Schunk, 1981; Stock & Cervone, 1990). As long as individuals accept and remain committed to their goals, more difficult goals foster superior achievement (Mento, Steel, & Karren, 1987; Tubbs, 1986).

Self-referent thinking processes central to the regulation of goal-directed action include self-evaluative reactions to one's performance and judgments of self-efficacy. People motivate their own behavior by making self-satisfaction contingent on achieving desired outcomes, thereby accomplishing pursuits even in the relative absence of external constraints or rewards for behavior. They are unhappy and self-reproving when their performances fall short (Ahrens, 1987; Higgins, 1987; Rehm, 1977) and pleased and satisfied when their performances meet their goals. Various social and personal factors influence the standards that people adopt (Locke & Latham, 1990). People adopt stringent standards for themselves if they observe models displaying high performance standards (Bandura, Grusec, & Menlove, 1967; Bandura & Kupers, 1964; Lepper et al., 1975). Those with a stronger sense of self-efficacy set higher personal goals (Bandura & Cervone, 1986; Wood, Bandura, & Bailey, 1990). When attainment falls markedly short of the goal, higher perceptions of efficacy and greater dissatisfaction with one's performance spur individuals to greater effort (Bandura & Cervone, 1986).

In the absence of relatively specific performance feedback or clear performance standards, one cannot compare goals to ongoing efforts, outcomes are unlikely to elicit strong self-reactions, and performance, in turn, should be only weakly affected by self-referent thinking. Varying goal and feedback conditions moderates the impact of self-regulatory processes (Bandura & Cervone, 1983, 1986; Cervone et al. 1991; Cervone & Wood, 1995). The combination of challenging goals and clear performance feedback substantially boosts performance, whereas neither goals without feedback nor feedback without goals increases motivation by the end of an effortful task (Bandura & Cervone, 1983). Cervone et al. (1991) found that higher attainments predicted greater self-satisfaction, increased self-efficacy, and more challenging personal goal levels. These self-processes, in turn, significantly predicted subsequent performance.

PERCEIVED SELF-EFFICACY

Few, if any, aspects of self-referent thought are more important to personal functioning than people's judgments of their capabilities to do the various tasks needed to meet life's demands. People are often faced with deciding what courses of action to follow, and how long to keep to those they have adopted. Perceptions of self-efficacy, people's judgments of how effectively they can act in a given context, and of how effectively they can marshal and deploy their cognitive resources, play a critical role in such decisions (Bandura, 1977b, 1986, 1997; Cervone & Williams, 1992). Relatively accurate appraisal of one's mental and physical capabilities is required for adaptive functioning. Overestimating one's ability to manage tasks fosters action that is futile or even dangerous. Underestimating one's ability to perform potentially rewarding activities leads one to needlessly restrict opportunities for personal development.

Although it is not adaptive to greatly misjudge one's self-efficacy, it can be adaptive to slightly overestimate it. Slight overoptimism can motivate efforts toward enriching self-development that more realistic efficacy judgments would prevent. Overestimating self-efficacy may actually promote mental health by insulating people from being discouraged and depressed by their own limitations (Bandura, 1990; Bjorklund & Green, 1992; Taylor & Brown, 1988).

In social cognitive theory, self-efficacy judgments influence what people choose to do, how much effort they expend, and how strongly they persist in the face of difficulties, setbacks, and aversive experiences (Bandura & Cervone, 1983, 1986; Schunk, 1984; Weinberg, Gould, & Jackson, 1979). People who have higher self-efficacy display greater effort and persistence in facing challenges (Brown & Inouye, 1978; Cervone, 1989; Cervone & Peake, 1986; Peake & Cervone, 1989) and in tolerating physically or emotionally aversive stimulation (Bandura, O'Leary, Taylor, Gossard, & Gauthier, 1987; Manning & Wright, 1983; Williams, 1996a; Williams & Kinney, 1991). They more readily enter into challenging environments (Betz & Hackett, 1986).

Self-efficacy beliefs affect thinking and emotional arousal. Doubts about coping in the face of potential dangers gives rise to anticipated disasters, feelings of fear, and visceral distress (Bandura et al., 1977; Bandura, Cioffi, Taylor, & Brouillard, 1988; Bandura, Reese, & Adams, 1982; Bandura, Taylor, Williams, Mefford, & Barchas, 1985; Williams et al., 1984; Williams, Turner, & Peer, 1985; Williams & Watson, 1985). Threat is not a fixed property of stimuli or circumstances, but arises from weighing the relation between potential dangers in the environment and one's ability to manage them (Beck, Emery, & Greenberg, 1985). A view down a steep snowy slope can be terrifying or delightful, depending upon one's self-perceived skiing capabilities.

Anxiety results not only from inefficacy for coping with perceived threats behaviorally, but also cognitively, that is, from inefficacy for controlling scary trains of thought (Bandura, 1988). It is not the sheer frequency of distressing thoughts, but the perceived ability to turn them off, that bears more directly on fear arousal (Kent, 1987; Kent & Gibbons, 1987; Salkovskis & Harrison, 1984). Depression and despondency, on the other hand, are partly the result of doubts about being able to do what is necessary to achieve valued personal goals. Such inefficacy leads people to be preoccupied with their deficiencies, feel down on themselves, and become depressed (Beck, Rush, Shaw, & Emery, 1979; Cutrona & Troutman, 1986; Holahan & Holahan, 1987; Kanfer & Zeiss, 1983; Seligman, 1975; Stanley & Maddux, 1986).

SELF-EFFICACY JUDGMENTS AND OUTCOME EXPECTATIONS

Many theories of motivation and personality emphasize the role of outcome expectations, that is, people's thoughts regarding the consequences or outcomes that are likely to follow a given action (Atkinson, 1964; Bolles, 1975; Rotter, 1966; Seligman, 1975; Tolman, 1932). Self-efficacy judgments are distinct from outcome expectations, both conceptually and, as we will discuss in detail later, empirically. Self-efficacy judgments concern whether one can carry out a particular course of action, in contrast to outcome expectations about what outcomes might follow if an action were to be carried out. One can believe oneself able to do something that would produce undesirable outcomes (e.g., park illegally in Manhattan), and believe oneself quite unable to do something that would produce desirable outcomes (e.g., compose lovely music).

Outcome expectations differ clearly from self-efficacy judgments, and they are a powerful source of motivation. Consequences influence behavior largely by creating and altering expectations about action-outcomes relationships, as discussed earlier when considering operant learning. Outcome expectations can affect behavior independently of self-efficacy judgments. People are certainly more likely to do what they expect to be rewarding than what they expect to be aversive or harmful, other things being equal. But self-efficacy judgments comprise an independent source of motivation. However marvelous the outcomes of an action might appear, people will not attempt or persist at that action if they profoundly disbelieve they can execute it. Students might be sure that earning a degree in engineering or medicine will result in a prosperous career, but if they are also sure that they cannot manage the mathematics and physical science requirements, they will not major in engineering or medicine. In short, resolute effective action requires both positive self-efficacy judgments and positive outcome expectations.

Although self-efficacy judgments and outcome expectations are distinct concepts, empirically they can be strongly related. In many if not most circumstances, outcomes are largely a function of how well one executes prior actions. For example, inept social approach fosters rejection, whereas adept approach fosters acceptance. In many fields, people with good track records of previous effective behavior command better positions and higher pay than do those with poor track records. When actions and outcomes are thus strongly linked, the outcomes one expects must reflect the self-efficacy one has. Efficacy judgments and outcome expectations may be unrelated, for example, when victims of social prejudices learn that no matter how well they perform, they cannot gain professional advancements or pay raises. In such cases, efficacy beliefs and outcomes expectations might be not only distinct but uncorrelated altogether.

GENERALITY AND SPECIFICITY OF SELF-EFFICACY PERCEPTIONS

A self-efficacy belief is not a generalized disposition to respond, but rather a judgment of one's ability to manage a set of activities within a specific domain. People usually have high self-efficacy for some activities but low self-efficacy for others. It is difficult to be competent—or incompetent—in every realm of human endeavor. Even within a domain, self-efficacy judgments can vary markedly as a function of subtle situational differences. A university lecturer may expound confidently before an undergraduate class but be filled with dread at lecturing on the same topic before professional colleagues. But neither are efficacy perceptions entirely bound to specific activities. People can have a generalized sense of efficacy across a range of activities they perceive as functionally related, and successes can produce relatively generalized gains in self-efficacy (Williams et al., 1989). Indeed, self-efficacy theory arose from the observation that phobic people who master their dread of snakes often report gaining confidence to tackle other quite distinct inhibitions (Bandura et al., 1977).

Research on therapeutic change in agoraphobia reveals the generality and specificity of self-efficacy judgments (Williams et al., 1989). People with agoraphobia (multiple phobias of activities away from home, such as driving, shopping, crossing bridges, and ascending heights) each received performance mastery treatment for some phobic areas, while other phobic areas were left untreated. In the treated areas, subjects displayed large gains in self-efficacy and coping behavior. In their transfer phobias, subjects showed highly variable and idiosyncratically patterned degrees of change, and, moreover, the degree of generalization did not follow any obvious gradient of physical, topographical, or stimulus similarity to the treated phobic area. For example, in two individuals treated successfully for height phobia, one might show a large gain in self-efficacy for shopping but not for driving, whereas the other might show large gains for driving but not for shopping (Williams *et al.,* 1989). The findings reveal specificity not only in the variability of transfer within subjects, but also in that the transfer phobias improved on the average only about half as much as the treated phobias. On the other hand, the findings reveal generality in that the transfer phobias improved much more than did the phobias of people who received no treatment for any phobias (Williams *et al.,* 1989).

SOURCES OF SELF-EFFICACY INFORMATION

If self-efficacy theory is to be useful for developing better educational and treatment programs, it must identify not only the effects of self-efficacy but also its causes. Social cognitive theory addresses the personal, behavioral, and environmental influences that create feelings of self-efficacy or inefficacy. Self-efficacy perceptions are products of cognitive processing in which individuals select, interpret, and integrate information from diverse sources, of which there are six principal ones: performance accomplishments, vicarious experiences, imaginal experiences, verbal persuasion, physiological arousal, and subjective emotional states. Bandura (1997) cited only four of these sources; later, we will discuss the basis for separating out imaginal performance and subjective emotional responses as distinct sources of self-efficacy.

Performance Accomplishments

Performance successes comprise the most powerful single source of information about one's capabilities because they convey vivid and self-relevant information based on first-hand experiences of success or failure. Self-efficacy and performance achievements are linked reciprocally. Successes tend to raise and strengthen self-efficacy judgments, which in turn promote further successes. However, performance successes do not automatically instate a corresponding increase in self-efficacy. Sometimes people will judge themselves unable to do again what they have just performed, and, at other times, they will believe they can do what they have not yet performed (Bandura, Reese, & Adams, 1982). Because there are discrepancies between past performance and current self-efficacy, self-efficacy can be more accurate than past behavior in predicting future behavior (e.g., Bandura *et al.* 1977; Williams *et al.,* 1984, 1989). People may judge themselves relatively inefficacious without a corresponding poor performance if they attend mainly to a task's difficult aspects (Cervone, 1989); attribute their success to external, unstable factors (Weiner, 1985); or are in a sad mood state that biases information processing (Kavanagh & Bower, 1985; Salovey & Birnbaum, 1989). Thus, similar achievements can have different effects on the efficacy perceptions of different people (Bandura *et al.,* 1982) and can lead to marked differences in the generality and specificity of treatment gains (Williams *et al.,* 1989).

Vicarious Experiences

People partly base self-efficacy judgments on vicarious experiences in which they observe, in one mode or another, the actions of others. Vicarious information will be especially powerful when people have little firsthand experience from which to judge, or when those experiences contain mixed or ambiguous information about their capabilities. Because the personal relevance of vicarious sources is more uncertain than that of direct personal experiences, they are less trustworthy. As a result vicarious success is generally less potent than direct firsthand success at increasing people's self-efficacy (Bandura & Adams, 1977; Bandura et al., 1977, 1982; Bandura, Adams, Hardy, & Howells, 1980).

A number of factors influence the potency of modeling displays on perceptions of self-efficacy (Bandura, 1997). One of the most generally important factors is people's appraisal of the similarity of the model to themselves along dimensions relevant to the performance in question. People judge that if a similar other can do it, they can do it too (Bandura et al., 1977, 1980, 1982; Schunk, Hanson, & Cox, 1987), whereas performance successes by dissimilar others are easily dismissed as irrelevant to oneself. One clever way of maximizing the similarity of the model is to use people as their own models of superior performance. People can gain greatly in self-efficacy and performance capabilities after watching videotapes of their own best aided performances, edited to further enhance the effect by splicing together sequences of successful behaviors that exceed what the person has ever actually achieved and by removing awkward moments, mistakes, and signs of outside assistance (Dowrick, in press, 1983, 1989; Dowrick & Hood, 1981).

Imaginal Experiences

In imagery-based treatments for anxiety, such as systematic desensitization therapy (Wolpe, 1958), implosion (Stamfl & Levis, 1967), and covert modeling (Kazdin, 1984), clients imagine themselves or others succeeding in coping actions. Considerable research reveals that imagined success experiences clearly benefit many anxious individuals (Bandura, 1969; Kazdin, 1984; Leitenberg, 1976). Such treatments appear to operate by increasing perceptions of self-efficacy (Bandura et al., 1977, 1980). Nevertheless, imaginal treatments are less effective than performance-based treatments because imagining oneself doing something is just not as convincing as actually doing it (Bandura, Blanchard, & Ritter, 1969; Emmelkamp & Wessels, 1975; Leitenberg, 1976).

In his original self-efficacy analysis, Bandura (1977b) included systematic desensitization as a physiologically mediated self-efficacy source, but his more recent analysis (Bandura, 1997) referred to it and other imaginal learning experiences as "imaginal self-modeling" and thus placed them in the vicarious mode of efficacy learning. Although such a designation might be workable, it seems clearer and more straightforward to distinguish between vicarious experiences, in which one gathers information about the target response through the sense organs, and imaginal experiences, in which one can generate information in imagination without immediate sensory involvement.

Verbal Persuasion

People sometimes come to believe in their coping capabilities by persuasory dialogue aimed at altering their beliefs. Because talking about coping effectively is an indirect experience, it should be less potent than direct coping successes in improving self-efficacy. Indeed, verbal-cognitive therapies for phobia have been found to be weak compared with performance-based treatments for improving self-efficacy and behavior (e.g., Emmelkamp, Kuipers, & Eggeraat, 1978; Emmelkamp & Mersch, 1982; Ladouceur, 1983;

Williams & Rappoport, 1983). If combined with more potent sources of information, persuasion can, however, have some value. For example, encouragement to try tasks, given with assurance that the person might well do better than he or she expects, can facilitate attempts at mastery (Williams, 1990). The most enduring changes in self-efficacy result from performance itself.

Physiological Arousal

Physiological responses are another source of efficacy information. People may judge perceived autonomic arousal to signify impending inability to cope or tranquil viscera as a sign that they can handle a situation. Athletes might judge their efficacy partly by how tired, winded, or sore they feel. Although autonomic arousal figures prominently in some theories of phobia, it is a relatively weak source of efficacy information because people know from long experience that their viscera tell them relatively little about what they can manage. Autonomic responses can be a treacherous guide because people are poor at perceiving their autonomic arousal accurately (e.g., Mandler, 1962; Reed, Harver, & Katkin, 1990). Various autonomic responses, such as sweating and heart rate, bear no clear or consistent relationship with one another, and often change in opposite directions in a single individual, thus yielding contradictory guides for action (Lacey, 1967; Lang, 1971, 1985).

Even if people accurately perceived their viscera, and even if those visceral responses were consistent with one another, people would still be misled by following visceral cues because of the well-documented poor empirical relationship between physiological arousal and coping effectiveness (Lang, 1985; Leitenberg, Agras, Butz, & Wincze, 1971; Mineka, 1979; Rachman & Hodgson, 1974; Williams, 1987). The psychological importance of physiological arousal has more to do with the interpretations people give to whatever they think they feel than with the arousal itself. A perceived pounding heart can be "fired up" "exhilarated" or "passionate" for one person but "terrified" or "angry" for another. The interpretation is what is important not the perceived or actual physical sensation per se (Cioffi, 1991).

Subjective Emotional States

People partly judge their self-efficacy by their subjective states of feeling and mood, which are not simply a function of physiological arousal. Bandura (1997) included subjective moods and subjective emotions within the physiological mode. But doing so risks obscuring the fact that there is no clear correspondence between particular physiological arousal indices and particular subjective emotional and mood states—indeed, very far from it. Although people tend to be generally aroused physiologically while subjectively feeling strong emotions, they are not always so, and the correlations between physiological arousal indices and subjective emotional states are typically very low (e.g., Morrow & Labrum, 1978). Although there are some consistent autonomic differences between emotions (Levenson, 1992), especially between positive emotions (e.g., happiness) and negative emotions (e.g., fear), average differences are small compared with the overriding similarities (Frankenhauser, 1975; Lacey, 1967; Schwartz, Weinberger, & Singer, 1981).

For many years it was thought that anxious feelings were the direct cause of phobic behavior, but a sizable body of evidence indicating a poor relationship between anxiety and behavior challenged that assumption (Bandura, 1969; Mineka, 1979; Rachman, 1976; Seligman & Johnston, 1973; Williams, 1987). The evidence indicates that any effects of subjective fear on avoidant behavior are mediated by perceptions of self-efficacy: Anxiety consistently fails to correlate with avoidant behavior with self-efficacy held constant, whereas self-efficacy consistently predicts avoidant behavior with anxiety held constant (Williams *et al.*, 1984, 1985, 1989). High subjective anxiety and sad mood might sometimes dampen people's self-efficacy and thereby undermine their coping effectiveness (Kavanaugh & Bower, 1981). But people know that they sometimes do well despite feeling scared, as terrified stage performers, dissertation defenders, and agoraphobics often display (Bandura, 1988; Williams, 1987). Conversely, they know that they can be fearless but incompetent. Therefore, they will often give greater weight to other, more reliable sources of information about what they can manage.

SELF-EFFICACY AND PERCEIVED CONTROL

Personality psychologists increasingly recognize that feeling able to exercise personal control has major implications for psychological and physical well-being (Abramson, Seligman, & Teasdale, 1978; Heckhausen & Schultz, 1996; Lazarus & Folkman, 1984; Miller, 1979; Mineka & Kelly, 1989; O'Leary, 1985; Skinner, 1996). Perceived self-efficacy is intimately related to perceived control because having control means being able to effectively exercise it. Without the self-efficacy belief that one can enact a controlling response, the perception of control does not exist.

One benefits from control beyond merely predicting the events. People who can influence the number, intensity, or pattern of aversive events will be less vulnerable to depression or fear than others who do not exercise influence, even when the aversive events they experience are identical (Miller, 1979; Seligman, 1975). Perceived control also lowers anxiety even when one does not make any controlling responses. It is enough to believe that one can potentially do so (Miller, 1979; Mineka, 1985; Mineka & Kelly, 1989; Sanderson, Rapee, & Barlow, 1989). Control also has implications for physiological responses. The causal link between low self-efficacy and physiological stress reactions has been established in research in phobic individuals, who show high levels of autonomic arousal and plasma catecholamine release when confronting phobic stressors. When their self-efficacy is raised to high levels by guided performance mastery experiences, their physiological stress reactions toward the phobic object decline (Bandura *et al.*, 1982, 1985).

CAUSAL ANALYSIS OF SELF-EFFICACY

Do conscious thoughts cause behavior? Although laypeople take it as self-evident that thinking causes action, many psychologists have viewed such "mentalistic" explanations as fundamentally flawed. The behaviorist would argue that cognitions are not causes of action but are themselves responses that may accompany an overt action of interest; both overt actions and inner "behaviors," such as thinking and feeling, must be explained in terms of previous environmental stimuli that have acted upon the person (Skinner, 1953, 1974).

Even if one accepts the general principle of cognitive causation, it is a problem for any cognitive theory to demonstrate scientifically that its particular favored cognition is the primary determinant of behavior. Correlational data are necessary, but not sufficient, to sustain a claim of causality. In addition, it is desirable to experimentally influence cognitive processes and observe the effects on behavior. Experimenters generally cannot simply set the extent of a person's self-efficacy beliefs (or other cognitive determinants) in quite the way they can set the intensity of an external stimulus. Nevertheless, they can experimentally instate and alter judgments of self-efficacy and relate those changes to subsequent coping behavior under circumstances in which noncausal explanations can be ruled out.

In social cognitive theory, the issue has been explored most extensively in two domains: the effect of self-efficacy judgments on phobic behavior change, and the effects on task performance of self-efficacy judgments that have been biased by subtle situational cues. Results from both lines of research converge in the conclusion that self-efficacy judgments cause behavior (Cervone & Williams, 1992). The following discussion will consider some of the issues related to causal self-efficacy; more detailed and extensive discussions of these issues can be found elsewhere (e.g., Bandura, 1978a, 1982, 1984, 1997; Cervone & Scott, 1996; Rachman, 1978; Williams, 1995, 1996a,b).

SELF-EFFICACY AND PHOBIC BEHAVIOR

Much research has explored the causal association between changes in self-efficacy and in phobic behavior (Bandura, 1997; Williams, 1995, 1996a). The most basic question is whether self-efficacy correlates strongly with phobic disability since causation requires correlation. Research measuring perceptions of self-efficacy and behavioral disability in relation to diverse phobic activities and stimuli, and before and after diverse vicarious, imaginal, and performance-based treatments reveals a close correspondence between the level to which self-efficacy is raised by treatment and the level of actual functional capabilities instated (e.g., Bandura et al., 1977, 1980, 1982, 1985; Emmelkamp & Felten, 1985; Ladouceur, 1983; Williams et al., 1984, 1985, 1989).

Such correlations have not gone unchallenged. Some have concluded that self-efficacy merely "reflects," not causes, behavioral change (Borkovec, 1978). There are several grounds for rejecting this conclusion. Changes in self-efficacy judgments following treatments with vicarious or imaginal methods that involve no actual coping with phobic activities or objects strongly predict changes in coping behavior (Bandura & Adams, 1977; Bandura et al., 1977, 1980, 1982). Similarly, when individuals with multiple disabling phobias are treated for one phobia (e.g., driving) while another phobia (e.g., grocery shopping) is left untreated, generalized improvement in the untreated phobias is accurately predicted by the self-efficacy changes for those phobias, despite subjects having no behavioral experience during treatment with those activities (Williams et al., 1989). In other words, the self-efficacy changes precede the behavioral changes. Both in phobia-related behaviors and in dynamic decision-making performance, when subjects perform the target behaviors during learning procedures, self-efficacy predicts changes in subsequent behavior more accurately than does the level of performance achieved during learning (Bandura et al., 1977, 1980; Cervone et al., 1991; Williams et al., 1984; 1989; Wood & Bandura, 1989).

Another common criticism is that correlations between self-efficacy and coping behavior are due to the operation of a third variable. One such variable is conditioned autonomic anxiety. But autonomic arousal and avoidance behavior are weakly correlated (Bandura, 1969, 1988; Lang, 1971; Leitenberg et al., 1971; Mineka, 1979; Rachman, 1976;

Schwartz, 1984; Seligman & Johnston, 1973; Williams, 1987, 1988), which logically eliminates a strong causal role for arousal.

Other, more cognitive, "third variable" candidates are anticipated negative outcomes, such as personal or psychosocial harm, and anticipated high distress (e.g., Beck, 1976; Beck et al., 1985; Chambless & Gracely, 1989). The most direct test of these competing possible cognitive causes is to see which independently contributes the most to predicting behavior. A series of studies with severely phobic subjects (Arnow et al., 1985; Telch et al., 1985; Williams & Rappoport, 1983; Williams & Watson, 1985; Williams et al., 1984, 1985, 1989) measured perceived self-efficacy and one or more kinds of anticipated negative consequence prior to assessing subjects' actual coping behavior. The measures were gathered before and after treatment. Partial correlation analyses showed that self-efficacy consistently remained a strong predictor of behavior when the anticipated outcomes were held constant, whereas the outcomes consistently failed to predict behavior when self-efficacy was held constant (summarized in Bandura, 1997; Williams, 1996a). These data support the view that perceptions of self-efficacy influence behavior independently, and that one must demonstrate, not simply assume, the primacy of another cognitive process.

Some have proposed that the correspondence between self-efficacy judgments and behavior simply reflects social pressure subjects might feel to match their performances to their previous self-ratings. Although such pressures are possible under some circumstances, it is highly doubtful that they influence results in phobia research. The research methods minimize such social pressure by having subjects complete the self-efficacy scales in relative or complete privacy, and their saliency is further reduced because the scales are embedded among other rating forms. Moreover, the wording of self-efficacy scales does not imply that subjects are committing to what they "will" do, but to indicate what they think they *can* do, with many scale values representing uncertainty. When experimenter surveillance of the ratings is made salient, the correspondence between self-efficacy ratings and behavior is *lowered* because subjects report conservative underestimates of their capabilities (Telch, Bandura, Vinciguerra, Agras, & Stout, 1982).

The psychological context of behavioral tests with phobic subjects also renders the efficacy-matching hypothesis implausible. People come for treatment of a serious personal problem, and they feel a correspondingly strong stake in performing as well as they can. The behavioral test confronts them with authentic, and distressing, phobic threats. In this context, social pressures for congruence between behavior and questionnaire responses made many minutes, hours, or sometimes days earlier are trivial. Studies corroborate that the mere act of rating self-efficacy has no bearing on subsequent coping behavior unless the experimenter deliberately introduces distorting factors (Bandura, 1997; Gauthier & Ladouceur, 1981).

Analyses of discrepancies that do occur between efficacy judgments and coping behavior also call into question the claim that subjects are motivated to match their behavior to their self-ratings. If that were so, then the distribution of discrepancies between self-efficacy judgments and actual performance would be asymmetric because subjects would infrequently do more than they judged. Once their behavior reached the level of their judgment, they would simply quit so as to produce an exact match. In fact, analyses from many hundreds of behavioral tests with diverse phobias reveals that coping behavior tends to slightly *surpass* the previous efficacy judgment (Williams & Bauchiess, 1992).

Last, it has been suggested that when subjects rate self-efficacy scales, they are indicating their "willingness," not their perceived ability (Kirsch, 1982). What keeps them from walking across the bridge or picking up the snake is lack of incentives to function, or too powerful disincentives in the form of anticipated anxiety reactions. First, people with phobias and compulsions pay frightfully high costs for their disabilities, not only in major financial reversals, but also in lost social and recreational functioning and in lowered self-esteem and humiliation. People who have abandoned fulfilling and lucrative careers or have endured other heartbreaking personal hardships because of a phobia or compulsion do not lack incentives to behave normally even if it means enduring anxiety. Second, the considerable body of research reviewed in the preceding paragraphs indicates that perceptions of self-efficacy override both anticipations of anxiety and actual experiences of anxiety in predicting phobic behavior (Williams, 1996a).

Phobic disability is a genuine disability. It also sometimes involves routine avoidance of activities that people could do if they tried (Williams, 1985; Zane & Williams, 1993). Approach behavior, and "willingness," thus derive from the combination of positive self-efficacy judgments and positive incentives. Kirsch (1982) argued that raters of self-efficacy scales are "invoking a linguistic habit" (p. 133) of confusing their confidence in what they can do for their willingness to do it. It would be a dysfunctional habit indeed to confuse ability and willingness. Most of us are quite unwilling to do many things that we know we could do, so we had better keep the distinction straight. As mentioned earlier, the self-efficacy scales are clearly written to indicate perceived ability, including intermediate values of uncertainty more befitting a confidence judgment about one's ability than a willingness decision.

Self-Efficacy and Judgment under Uncertainty

An arguably even stronger case supporting the causal potency of self-efficacy judgments involves not just statistical controls but the experimental manipulation of self-efficacy (Cervone & Williams, 1992). Self-efficacy judgments typically require people to weigh a variety of personal factors and the demands of the performance situation under uncertain circumstances. People commonly use a simplifying judgmental strategy known as "anchoring and adjustment" (Tversky & Kahneman, 1974), in which they consider an initial value and then adjust this value to yield a final estimate, which is often biased in the direction of the initially considered "anchor" value even when people know that the anchor value was random (Tversky & Kahneman, 1974).

Cervone and Peake (1986) manipulated perceived self-efficacy using anchoring cues to create groups of people with different levels of self-efficacy, but with equivalent experience of, and information about, a challenging cognitive task. Subjects first considered whether they could successfully complete more or fewer than a designated high or low number of tasks where the number appeared random. They then indicated the exact number of items they judged they could complete and then worked on the task. Subjects exposed to a high anchor judged they could solve approximately 50% more items than did low anchor subjects and showed a corresponding difference in actual task persistence. This effect has been replicated and extended across a variety of factual judgments (Cervone & Palmer, 1990; Peake & Cervone, 1989). That the effects of the initial self-efficacy judgments persist despite subjects receiving a considerable amount of subsequent authentic performance feedback is striking.

SOCIAL COGNITIVE PERSON VARIABLES
CONTRASTED WITH TRAITS

Traditional approaches to personality conceived it as consisting of broad response tendencies known as traits or dispositions. Whether the source of these tendencies was inherited temperaments, unconscious dynamisms, or some other factor, their effect was to make behavior broadly consistent across dissimilar situations. Personality traits are not defined contextually, but simply as a tendency to act in a certain way irrespective of context. The Big Five personality factors (Norman, 1963; McCrae & Costa, 1996) are prototypical of such personality units. Each factor is a context-free personality dimension. For example, "conscientiousness" refers to a disposition to achieve and to act in a "directed" manner (McCrae & Costa, 1987), defined independently of the settings where or the reasons why one acts conscientiously. Of course, there are many other possible context-free units of personality, such as generalized expectations, overall social IQ, anxiety sensitivity, attributional styles, and so on. In some analyses, traits are not merely statistical summaries of tendencies to act (Buss & Craik, 1983), but internal psychological entities that cause behavior in their own right (Funder, 1991).

In contrast, most social cognitive units of personality are person-in-context variables (Cervone, 1991; Cervone & Williams, 1992). People's appraisals of themselves and their behavior, their goals and performance standards, motivations, and expectations are assessed in relation to the contexts and life tasks toward which people must bring their knowledge to bear (Cantor & Kihlstrom, 1987). Social cognitivists reject context-free units for a number of reasons. People's knowledge, skills, and strategies for coping necessarily have developed within specific life contexts and are deployed toward challenges that arise in specific life contexts. Adopting context-free units sacrifices much important information and obscures the processes by which people flexibly and idiosyncratically adapt their behavior to meet varying situational requirements.

A large body of evidence supports the social cognitive view that behavior often is far more variable across situations than broad context-free personality units would imply (Chaplin & Goldberg, 1984; Mischel, 1968; Mischel & Peake, 1982; Mischel & Shoda, 1995). Considerable evidence reveals clearly that one cannot predict specific behaviors accurately without attending to context. The accuracy of disposition-based predictions can increase when one narrows down either the environmental conditions under which a disposition is most relevant (Wright & Mischel, 1987) or the specific cluster of behaviors that comprise the trait to those that empirically intercorrelate (Jackson & Paunonen, 1985; Mischel, 1983). Otherwise, cross-situational predictions are weak (Mischel & Peake, 1982; Mischel & Shoda, 1995).

From the social cognitive perspective, the degree of consistency in social behavior across situations is an empirical question (Cantor & Kihlstrom, 1989) whose answer is likely to depend on the particular persons, situations, and behaviors under consideration. People may show stronger cross-situational consistencies under some circumstances, such as when they perceive situations as similar (Champagne & Pervin, 1987; Lord, 1982), when they acquire coping skills that can be applied in diverse contexts (Smith, 1989), or when they suffer from certain psychological problems that impair the discriminative faculties (Mischel, 1973). The social cognitivist does not deny all consistency, but adopts units of analysis and assessment strategies that allow for idiosyncratically patterned discriminations between seemingly similar situations.

Trait approaches may begin by observing patterns of behavior (e.g., "generous" acts), then infer traits ("generosity") as personality units that both summarize and explain the behavior (Funder, 1991). Or, they may begin with the set of personality adjectives from the dictionary, then use sophisticated correlational techniques to reduce the lengthy list into a simple framework (Cattell, 1943; Goldberg, 1981). In contrast, social cognitive approaches start from the analysis of cognition, affect, and social learning in relation to adaptive functioning (Bandura, 1986; Cervone, 1991; Cervone & Williams, 1992; Mischel, 1973). The units of analysis are psychological processes and structures by which people learn about the world and themselves and guide their behavior. Personality is then described in terms of these same variables. The manner in which these variables influence specific categories or patterns of social behavior under different circumstances is then an empirical question.

Mischel (1973; Mischel & Shoda, 1996) suggested social cognitive personality variables, such as competencies and knowledge, encoding strategies, expectancies, values, and self-regulatory plans. Bandura (1986, 1997) emphasized additional dimensions, such as self-perceptions of efficacy, which are current self-judgments not just future expectations. In the social cognitive view, there is not one best, all-purpose system of classifying personal attributes and determinants, nor is there a set of such determinants that is invariably optional or even relevant to every situation and purpose (Cervone, 1997).

The social cognitive strategy is well illustrated by Dweck and colleague's (Dweck & Leggett, 1988) analysis of different achievement patterns in terms of goal structures and self-perceptions. Variations in self-perceived capability affect achievement behavior when individuals have the goal of documenting their level of competence. Individual differences in achievement are cast in terms of the explanatory theory: Some people with low perceptions of competence have implicit beliefs about intelligence that lead them to systematically interpret situations as involving the documentation of competence, fostering goal orientations that generate maladaptive patterns of behavior (Dweck & Leggett, 1988; Elliot & Dweck, 1988). Once one understands the processes that underlie different patterns of achievement and the enduring knowledge structures that generate individual differences in this behavior, global disposition terms are not necessary for explaining behavior or describing the individual in this achievement context (Cervone & Williams, 1992). An observer may conclude that some children appear to be "helpless" in achievement contexts. The psychologist, however, need not explain their behavior by postulating a trait of "helplessness."

Another related class of person variables that the social cognitive approach rejects is personality types. Most types share with traits the property of being indwelling, context-free determinants of behavior and as such are generally regarded as dubious in the social cognitive approach. Moreover, typologies typically encounter numerous ill-fitting cases. One of the most influential typological systems is that of mental illnesses or "mental disorders," as devised by the American Psychiatric Association (1994). Social cognitive theory does not consider problems of psychosocial suffering and maladaptation to be mental "illnesses." There is neither need for nor advantage in such misleading medicalization of human experience (Bandura, 1969, 1978a; Szasz, 1960). In the social cognitive view, abnormal personality functioning must be conceived, measured, studied, and ameliorated, using the same kinds of reciprocally interacting personal (including biological), environmental, and behavioral determinants that are involved in normal personality functioning, which excludes any role for mental diseases.

Nor does social cognitive theory accept that psychological problems can be neatly and exhaustively arrayed in a catalogue that dictates the one way that psychological problems shall be characterized for every scientific and therapeutic purpose. Such catalogues contain a large element of arbitrariness in which kinds of psychological phenomena are included and excluded, and in how these phenomena are combined into putative mental illnesses (e.g., Boyd, Burke, Gruenberg et al., 1984; Carson, 1991; Detre, 1985). Problems of diverse kinds tend to be at least moderately intercorrelated (Clark, Watson, & Reynolds, 1995), and people are highly idiosyncratic in the particular constellations of problems they experience. Psychological problems must be analyzed and studied in different ways to suit different purposes. For example, an investigator might wish to examine people who have both sad mood and panic attacks, irrespective of their psychiatric diagnoses, and without regard to whether a committee has designated such a combination an official "mental disorder."

The bases for the categories in the various DSMs over the decades are a variegated collection of historical traditions, passing diagnostic fashions, and often disputable but unstated theoretical assumptions (Carson, 1991). Although DSM avows an atheoretical stance, it amounts to a set of nontheories that potently affects how psychological problems are conceived, studied, and treated—and not necessarily for the better (e.g., Carson, 1991; Detre, 1985; Persons, 1986; Williams, 1985). For example, the 1987 revision (DSM-III-R) that subsumed "agoraphobia" under "panic disorder" was not only bad psychological theory given the empirical lack of correlation between agoraphobic severity and panic severity (Craske & Barlow, 1988), but it resulted in a sudden precipitous decline in research measuring and treating agoraphobic behavior. The latter was replaced largely by research on panic attacks. Clearly panic and agoraphobia are two separate and substantially independent psychological dimensions, neither of which deserves special status as somehow superior to, or inclusive of, the other, and both of which merit therapeutic and scientific attention (Williams, 1985).

Persons (1986) has argued persuasively, using examples drawn from formal thought disorder and "schizophrenia," that it makes more sense scientifically to study problematic psychological phenomena directly, according to a particular scientific or therapeutic purpose, than to study the rather arbitrary combinations of problem phenomena enshrined as official psychiatric diagnoses. Dictionaries of terminology and lists of phenomena related to psychological dysfunctions are useful, but a rigid all-purpose catalogue of mental diseases, which, as Detre (1985) warned, sometimes seems in danger of going from research catalyst to catechism, can hamper more than help our ability to understand and alleviate psychological suffering.

MEASUREMENT OF PERSONALITY

Although the scope of the present chapter does not permit a detailed analysis of measurement issues, a few comments on measurement are in order. The social cognitive approach to personality measurement begins with the principle of reciprocal determinism, that is, that persons, their behavior, and the environment mutually influence one another, as discussed earlier. Personality cannot be understood or measured separately from behavior and the environment.

The reciprocal model places a special emphasis on measuring behavior as one of the three interacting determinants. Although overt behavior is by no means the only class of psychological responses worth considering, for many purposes behavior is the "bottom line" of human affairs, the first moment of psychological functioning and adaptation (Williams, 1985). Our paths through life, and our fulfillments and sufferings in it, have much to do with what we do, and fail to do, outwardly. Overt behavior often vividly reveals the inner person; actions often "speak louder than words" about people. Moreover, the validity of proposed internal personality processes is tested in part by whether they actually link strongly to behavior. Therefore, measuring personality well often means measuring not just inner personal factors but also overt action in the world.

A second implication is that persons and their behavior must be understood in relation to specific contexts, as discussed at length earlier. Behavioral, cognitive, and emotional reactions vary markedly as a function of circumstances (Mischel, 1968; e.g., Williams, 1985). Therefore, the social cognitive assessor does not seek to broadly characterize personality-as-a-whole, but to characterize the person's responses of interest in contexts of interest.

A third related implication is that whereas traditional personality assessment procedures view test responses as indirect "signs" of underlying personality attributes, in which the assessment responses per se are of little interest, social cognitive measures seek to gather direct "samples" of responses of interest in context (Mischel, 1968, 1973). This method of information gathering leads to a strong emphasis on behavioral assessment in the natural environment and on emotional and cognitive measures that constrain the context of responding (Williams, 1985). Self-efficacy measures illustrate the latter. People indicate the strength of their belief that they can perform a series of clearly specified actions—cognitive or behavioral—in specified contexts.

SELF-EFFICACY-BASED TREATMENT
OF PERSONALITY PROBLEMS

Theories of personality must be judged in part by their capacity to generate effective means of helping people change. This has long been a major focus of social cognitive theory (Bandura, 1969, 1977, 1997; Cervone & Scott, 1996; Cervone & Williams, 1992). Self-efficacy theory prescribes performance-based mastery experiences as central elements in treatment programs because such experiences are the most potent source of information for building a strong sense of efficacy (Bandura, 1997).

The social cognitive approach to helping people change is well exemplified by the treatment of phobic dysfunctions. Phobias are common, debilitating, distressing, and representative of the self-defeating patterns of behavior that bedevil many people. Moreover, phobias have long been a major focus of theorizing in personality and psychopathology. It is clear that people with phobias benefit most from performing avoided activities directly. Interpretations of such performance-based treatment often emphasize the noncognitive concept of "exposure" to phobic stimuli (Marks, 1978). This likens treatment to a classical extinction procedure in which performance serves to put people near scary stimuli until deconditioning of anxiety occurs. A similar but somewhat more elaborate version of this analysis specifies a complex, largely unconscious underlying "fear structure" that is aroused and activated by stimulus exposure and eventually deactivated by it in a sort of emotional extinction or deconditioning process (e.g., Foa & McNally, 1996).

The exposure and anxiety-extinction principles have serious empirical and conceptual limitations because they fail to specify a way to measure stimulus exposure as required to test exposure theory, and because anxiety correlates poorly with therapeutic changes in phobic behavior (Rosenthal & Bandura, 1978; Williams, 1987, 1988, 1996a, 1996b). The exposure view also gives therapists little guidance as to the specific procedures to follow beyond the broad suggestion to somehow bring clients into some sort of prolonged contact with phobic stimuli.

In treatment based on self-efficacy theory, or guided mastery therapy (Williams, 1990), treatment is seen as a behaviorally and cognitively active coping process in which the important thing is the quality and amount of information people gain about what they can manage. The therapist's aim is to guide and assist people to succeed at tasks that otherwise would be too difficult and thereby to increase their self-efficacy, which in turn should enable them to tackle yet more challenging tasks, continuing in an ascending spiral of therapeutic change. The mastery therapist also helps clients do treatment tasks more proficiently, free of embedded defensiveness and self-restrictions that limit their sense of accomplishment (Williams & Zane, 1988; Zane & Williams, 1993). Once the person is progressing and performing proficiently, the therapist withdraws the assistance and arranges for people to have varied and independent success experiences so their sense of mastery will be unconditional. In the exposure view, in contrast, such active therapist assistance could be construed as reducing exposure because it might reduce anxiety and the threat value of the stimuli.

Guided mastery treatment has been applied successfully to a wide range of phobias, including agoraphobia and mixed multiphobic conditions (Williams & Zane, 1989; Williams et al., 1984; Zane & Williams, 1993), social phobias (Mattick & Peters, 1988), and specific phobias (e.g., Bandura et al., 1969, 1974, 1977, 1985; Ost, Salkovskis, & Hellstrom, 1991; Williams et al., 1985). A number of studies have found that providing people with a varied repertoire of guided mastery aids during therapeutic performance produces better results than simply giving them strong encouragement to remain fully exposed to scary stimuli with few specific mastery aids (Bandura et al., 1974; O'Brien & Kelley, 1980; Ost et al., 1991; Williams & Zane, 1989; Williams et al., 1984, 1985). These findings illustrate that self-efficacy theory can help structure treatments to achieve maximal therapeutic impact.

Self-efficacy theory has been successfully applied in diverse domains, such as health behavior (O'Leary, 1985), pain (Bandura et al., 1987; Williams & Kinney, 1991), sports performance (Weinberg, Gould, & Jackson, 1979), organizational management (Wood & Bandura, 1989), addictive behavior (DiClemente, 1986), career development (Betz & Hackett, 1986), and others. This diversity of domains of applicability provide eloquent testimony to the explanatory breadth and generality of self-efficacy theory.

CONCLUSION

Although this chapter has emphasized the particular approach to social cognition and personality functioning embodied in Bandura's (1986, 1997) work, that theory is but one member of a family of theories concerned with conscious thinking and adaptation (Cervone, 1991; Cervone & Shoda, in press; Cervone & Williams, 1992). Although differing in specifics, three overriding shared themes characterize this general social cognitive perspective: (a) a focus on the social foundations of cognition, especially cognitions about the self; (b) the effects of contexts in activating these self-related cognitions; and (c) the reciprocal interactions among persons, their behavior, and environments (Cervone, 1991). Various investigators work in this tradition, although not all of them explicitly label their work "social-cognitive" (Cantor & Kihlstrom, 1987, 1989; Dweck & Leggett, 1988; Higgins, 1990; Markus & Wurf, 1987; Mischel, 1990; Wright & Mischel, 1987).

Social cognitive theory has become a predominant perspective in personality psychology. Pervin and John (1997) stated, "Within the academic community, social cognitive theory is probably the most popular theory, and it is gaining increasing numbers of adherents in the clinical community as well" (p. 444). It is a broadly unifying approach rooted in a strong theoretical and empirical tradition. It promises to further our understanding of how people, their behavior, and their environments interact.

REFERENCES

Abramson, L. Y., Seligman, M. E. P., & Teasdale, J. D. (1978). Learned helplessness in humans: Critique and reformulation. *Journal of Abnormal Psychology, 87*, 49–74.

Ahrens, A. H. (1987). Theories of depression: The role of goals and the self-evaluation process. *Cognitive Therapy and Research, 11*, 665–680.

Alloy, L. B., & Tabachnik, N. (1984). Assessment of covariation by humans and animals: The joint influence of prior expectations and current situational information. *Psychological Review, 91*, 112–149.

American Psychiatric Association (1994). *Diagnostic and statistical manual of mental disorders*, (4th ed.). Washington, DC: Author.

Arnow, B. A., Taylor, C. B., Agras, W. S., & Telch, M. J. (1985). Enhancing agoraphobia treatment outcome by changing couple communication patterns. *Behavior Therapy, 16*, 452–467.

Atkinson, J. W. (1964). *An introduction to motivation*. Princeton, NJ: Van Nostrand.

Bandura, A. (1965). Influence of models' reinforcement contingencies on the acquisition of imitative responses. *Journal of Personality and Social Psychology, 1*, 589–595.

Bandura, A. (1969). *Principles of behavior modification*. New York: Holt, Rinehart & Winston.

Bandura, A. (1973). *Aggression: A social learning analysis*. Englewood Cliffs, NJ: Prentice-Hall.

Bandura, A. (1977a). *Social learning theory*. Englewood Cliffs, NJ: Prentice-Hall.

Bandura, A. (1977b). Self-efficacy: Toward a unifying theory of behavioral change. *Psychological Review, 84*, 191–215.

Bandura, A. (1978a). The self system in reciprocal determinism. *American Psychologist, 33*, 344–358.

Bandura, A. (1978b). Reflections on self-efficacy. *Advances in Behaviour Research and Therapy, 1*, 237–269.

Bandura, A. (1982). The assessment and predictive generality of self-percepts of efficacy. *Journal of Behavior Therapy and Experimental Psychiatry, 13*, 195–199.

Bandura, A. (1984). Recycling misconceptions of perceived self-efficacy. *Cognitive Therapy and Research, 8*, 231–255.

Bandura, A. (1986). *Social foundations of thought and action: A social cognitive theory*. Englewood Cliffs, NJ: Prentice-Hall.

Bandura, A. (1988). Self-efficacy conception of anxiety. *Anxiety Research, 1*, 77–98.

Bandura, A. (1989). Self-regulation of motivation and action through internal standards and goal systems. In L. A. Pervin (Ed.), *Goal concepts in personality and social psychology* (pp. 19–85). Hillsdale, NJ: Erlbaum.

Bandura, A. (1990). Reflections on nonability determinants of competence. In J. Kolligan & R. J. Sternberg (Eds.), *Competence considered: Perceptions of competence and incompetence across the lifespan*. New Haven, CT: Yale University Press.

Bandura, A. (1997). *Self-efficacy: The exercise of control*. New York: Freeman.

Bandura, A., & Adams, N. E. (1977). Analysis of self-efficacy theory of behavioral change. *Cognitive Therapy and Research, 1,* 287–308.

Bandura, A., Adams, N. E., & Beyer, J. (1977). Cognitive processes mediating behavior change. *Journal of Personality and Social Psychology, 35,* 125–139.

Bandura, A., Adams, N. E. Hardy, A., & Howells, G. (1980). Tests of the generality of self-efficacy theory. *Cognitive Therapy and Research, 4,* 39–66.

Bandura, A., Blanchard, E. B., & Ritter, B. (1969). Relative efficacy of desensitization and modeling approaches for inducing behavioral, affective, and attitudinal changes. *Journal of Personality of Social Psychology, 13,* 173–199.

Bandura, A., & Cervone, D. (1983). Self-evaluative and self-efficacy mechanisms governing the motivational effects of goal systems. *Journal of Personality and Social Psychology, 45,* 1017–1028.

Bandura, A., & Cervone, D. (1986). Differential engagement of self-reactive influences in cognitive motivation. *Organizational Behavior and Human Decision Processes, 38,* 92–113.

Bandura, A., Cioffi, D., Taylor, C. B., & Brouillard, M. E. (1988). Perceived self-efficacy in coping with cognitive stressors and opioid activation. *Journal of Personality and Social Psychology, 55,* 479–488.

Bandura, A. Grusec, J. E., & Menlove, F. L. (1967). Some social determinants of self-monitoring reinforcement systems. *Journal of Personality and Social Psychology, 5,* 449–455.

Bandura, A., Jeffrey, R. W., & Wright, C. L. (1974). Efficacy of participant modeling as a function of response induction aids. *Journal of Abnormal Psychology, 83,* 35–64.

Bandura, A., & Kupers, C. J. (1964). The transmission of patterns of self-reinforcement through modeling. *Journal of Abnormal and Social Psychology, 69,* 1–9.

Bandura, A., O'Leary, A., Taylor, C. B., Gossard, D., & Gauthier, J. (1987). Perceived self-efficacy and pain control: Opioid and nonopioid mechanisms. *Journal of Personality and Social Psychology, 55,* 479–488.

Bandura, A., Reese, L., & Adams, N. E. (1982). Microanalysis of action and fear arousal as a function of differential levels of perceived self-efficacy. *Journal of Personality and Social Psychology, 43,* 5–21.

Bandura, A., & Schunk, D. H. (1981). Cultivating competence, self-efficacy and intrinsic interest through proximal self-motivation. *Journal of Personality and Social Psychology, 41,* 586–598.

Bandura, A., Taylor, C. B., Williams, S. L., & Mefford, I. N., & Barchas, J. D. (1985). Catecholamine secretion as a function of perceived coping self-efficacy. *Journal of Consulting and Clinical Psychology, 53,* 406–414.

Bandura, A., & Walters, R. H. (1963). *Social learning and personality development.* New York: Holt, Rinehart & Winston.

Bandura, A., & Wood, R. (1989). Effect of perceived controllability and performance standards on self-regulation of complex decision making. *Journal of Personality and Social Psychology, 56,* 805–814.

Baumeister, R. (1984). The problem of life's meaning. In D. M. Buss & N. Cantor (Eds.), *Personality psychology: Recent trends and emerging directions.* New York: Springer-Verlag.

Beck, A. T. (1976). *Cognitive therapy and the emotional disorders.* NY: International Universities Press.

Beck, A. T., Emery, G., & Greenberg, R. L. (1985). *Anxiety disorders and phobias: A cognitive perspective.* New York: Basic Books.

Beck, A. T., Rush, A. J., Shaw, B. F., & Emery, G. (1979). *Cognitive therapy of depression.* NY: Guilford Press.

Bem, D. J. (1972). Self-perception theory. *Advances in Experimental Social Psychology, 6,* 1–62.

Berger, S. M. (1962). Conditioning through vicarious instigation. *Psychological Review, 69,* 450–466.

Betz, N. E., & Hackett, G. (1981). The relationship of career-related self-efficacy expectations to perceived career options in college men and women. *Journal of Counseling Psychology, 28,* 399–410.

Betz, N. E., & Hackett, G. (1986). *Applications of self-efficacy theory to understanding career choice behavior.* Journal of Social and Clinical Psychology, 4, 279–289.

Bjorklund, D. F., & Green, B. L. (1992). The adaptive nature of cognitive immaturity. *American Psychologist, 47,* 46–54.

Bolles, R. C. (1975). *Learning theory.* New York: Holt, Rinehart & Winston.

Borkovec, T. D. (1978). Self-efficacy: Cause or reflection of behavioral change? *Advances in Behaviour Research and Therapy, 1,* 163–170.

Bower, G. H., & Hilgard, E. R. (1981). *Theories of learning* (5th ed.). Englewood Cliffs, NJ: Prentice-Hall.

Bowers, K. S. (1973). Situationism in psychology: An analysis and critique. *Psychological Review, 80,* 307–336.

Boyd, J. H., Burke, J. D., Gruenberg, E., Holzer, C. E., Rae, D. S., George, L. K., Karno, M. Stoltzman, R., McEvoy, L., & Nestadt, G. (1984). Exclusion criteria of DSM-III: A study of co-occurrence of hierarchy-free syndromes. *Archives of General Psychiatry, 41,* 983–989.

Brewin, C. R. (1988). *Cognitive foundations of clinical psychology.* Hillsdale, NJ: Erlbaum.

Brewin, C. R. (1989). Cognitive change processes in psychotherapy. *Psychological Review, 96,* 379–394.

Brown, I., Jr. (1979). Language acquisition: Linguistic structure and rule-governed behavior. In G. J. Whitehurst & B. J. Zimmerman (Eds.), *The functions of language and cognition* (pp. 141–173). New York: Academic Press.

Brown, I., Jr., & Inouye, D. K. (1978). Learned helplessness through modeling: The role of perceived similarity in competence. *Journal of Personality and Social Psychology, 36,* 900–908.

Bruner, J. (1990). *Acts of meaning.* Cambridge, MA: Harvard University Press.

Buss, D. M. (1991). Evolutionary personality psychology. *Annual Review of Psychology, 42,* 459–491.

Buss, D. M., & Cantor, N. (Eds.). (1989). *Personality psychology: Recent trends and emerging directions.* New York: Springer-Verlag.

Buss, D. M., & Craik, K. H. (1983). The act frequency approach to personality. *Psychological Review, 90,* 105–126.

Cantor, N., & Kihlstrom, J. F. (1987). *Personality and social intelligence.* Englewood Cliffs, NJ: Prentice-Hall.

Cantor, N., & Kihlstrom, J. F. (1989). Social intelligence and personality: There's room for growth. *Advances in Social Cognition, 2,* 197–214.

Caprara, G. V., Cervone, D., & Hampson, S. (in press). *Personality psychology: An advanced text.* New York: Cambridge University Press.

Carr, A. T. (1979). The psychopathology of fear. In W. Sluckin (Ed.), *Fear in animals and man* (pp. 199–235). New York: Van Nostrand Reinhold.

Carroll, W. R., & Bandura, A. (1982). The role of visual monitoring in observational learning of action patterns: Making the unobservable observable. *Journal of Motor Behavior, 14,* 153–167.

Carroll, W. R., & Bandura, A. (1985). Role of timing of visual monitoring and motor rehearsal in observational learning of action patterns. *Journal of Motor Behavior, 17,* 269–281.

Carroll, W. R., & Bandura, A. (1990). Representational guidance of action production in observational learning: A causal analysis. *Journal of Motor Behavior, 22,* 85–97.

Carson, R. C. (1991). Dilemmas in the pathway of *DSM-IV. Journal of Abnormal Psychology, 100,* 302–307.

Carver, C. S., & Scheier, M. F. (1990). Principles of self-regulation: Action and emotion. In E. T. Higgins & R. M. Sorrentino (Eds.), *Motivation and cognition: Foundations of social behavior* (Vol. 2, pp. 527–561). New York: Guilford Press.

Cattell, R. B. (1943). The description of personality: Basic traits resolved into clusters. *Journal of Abnormal and Social Psychology, 38,* 476–506.

Cervone, D. (1989). Effects of envisioning future activities on self-efficacy judgments and motivation: An availability heuristic interpretation. *Cognitive Therapy and Research, 13,* 247–261.

Cervone, D. (1991). The two disciplines of personality psychology. *Psychological Science, 2,* 371–377.

Cervone, D. (1997). Social-cognitive mechanisms and personality coherence: Self-knowledge, situational beliefs, and cross-situational coherence in perceived self-efficacy. *Psychological Science, 8,* 43–50.

Cervone, D. (in press). Bottom-up explanation in personality psychology: The case of cross-situational coherence. In D. Cervone & Y. Shoda (Eds.), *The coherence of personality: Social-cognitive bases of consistency, variability, and organization.* NY: Guilford Press.

Cervone, D., Jiwani, N., & Wood, R. (1991). Goal-setting and the differential influence of self-regulatory processes on complex decision-making performance. *Journal of Personality and Social Psychology, 61,* 257–266.

Cervone, D., & Palmer, B. W. (1990). Anchoring biases and the perseverance of self-efficacy beliefs. *Cognitive Therapy and Research, 14,* 401–416.

Cervone, D., & Peake, P. K. (1986). Anchoring, efficacy, and action: The influence of judgmental heuristics on self-efficacy judgments and behavior. *Journal of Personality and Social Psychology, 50,* 492–501.

Cervone, D., & Scott, W. D. (1996). Self-efficacy theory of behavioral change: Foundations, conceptual issues, and therapeutic implications. In W. O'Donohue & L. Krasner (Eds.), *Theories of behavior therapy: Exploring behavior change* (pp. 349–383). Washington, DC: American Psychological Association.

Cervone, D., & Shoda, Y. (in press). *The coherence of personality: Social-cognitive bases of consistency, variability, and organization.* NY: Guilford Press.

Cervone, D., & Williams, S. L. (1992). Social cognitive theory and personality. In G.-V. Caprara & G. L. Van Heck (Eds.), *Modern personality psychology: Critical reviews and new directions* (pp. 200–252). New York: Harvester-Wheatsheaf.

Cervone, D., & Wood, R. (1995). Goals, feedback, and the differential influence of self-regulatory processes on cognitively complex performance. *Cognitive Therapy and Research, 19,* 519–545.

Chambless, D. L., & Gracely, E. J. (1989). Fear of fear and the anxiety disorders. *Cognitive Therapy and Research, 13,* 9–20.

Champagne, B., & Pervin, L. A. (1987). The relation of perceived situation similarity to perceived behavior similarity: Implications for social learning theory. *European Journal of Personality, 1,* 79–92.

Chaplin, W. F., & Goldberg, L. R. (1984). A failure to replicate the Bem and Allen study of individual differences in cross-situational consistency. *Journal of Personality and Social Psychology, 47,* 1074–1090.

Cioffi, D. (1991). Beyond attentional strategies: A cognitive-perceptual model of somatic interpretation. *Psychological Bulletin, 109,* 25–41.

Clark, L. A., Watson, D., & Reynolds, S. (1995). Diagnosis and classification of psychopathology: Challenges to the current system and future directions. *Annual Review of Psychology, 46,* 121–153.

Cook, M., Mineka, S., Wolkenstein, B., & Laitsch, K. (1985). Observational conditioning of snake fear in unrelated rhesus monkeys. *Journal of Abnormal Psychology, 94,* 591–610.

Craske, M. G., & Barlow, D. H. (1988). A review of the relationship between panic and avoidance. *Clinical Psychology Review, 8,* 667–685.

Cutrona, C. E., & Troutman, B. R. (1986). Social support, infant temperament, and parenting self-efficacy: A mediational model of postpartum depression. *Child Development, 57,* 1507–1518.

Detre, T. (1985). Is the grouping of anxiety disorders in *DSM-III* based on shared beliefs or data? In A. H. Tuma & J. Maser (Eds.), *Anxiety and the anxiety disorders* (pp. 783–786). Hillsdale, NJ: Erlbaum.

DiClemente, C. C. (1986). Self-efficacy and the addictive behaviors. *Journal of Social and Clinical Psychology, 4,* 302–315.

Dowrick, P. W. (1983). Self-modeling. In P. W. Dowrick & S. J. Biggs (Eds.), *Using Video: Psychological and social applications* (pp. 105–124). New York: Wiley.

Dowrick, P. W. (in press). A review of self modeling and related interventions. *Applied and Preventive Psychology.*

Dowrick, P. W. (1989). Videotraining strategies for beginners, champions, and injured athletes. In A. A. Turner (Ed.), *Arctic Sports Medicine: Proceedings of the first Alaska regional chapter of the American College of Sports Medicine* (pp. 1–9). Anchorage: American College of Sports Medicine.

Dowrick, P. W., & Hood, M. (1981). Comparison of self-modeling and small cash incentives in a sheltered workshop. *Journal of Applied Psychology, 66,* 394–397.

Dulany, D. E. (1968). Awareness, rules, and propositional control: A confrontation with S-R behavior theory. In T. R. Dixon & D. L. Horton, (Eds.), *Verbal behavior and general behavior theory* (pp. 340–387). Englewood Cliffs, NJ: Erlbaum.

Dweck, C. S., & Leggett, E. L. (1988). A social-cognitive approach to motivation and personality. *Psychological Review, 95,* 256–273.

Elliott, E. S., & Dweck, C. S. (1988). Goals: An approach to motivation and achievement. *Journal of Personality and Social Psychology, 54,* 5–12.

Emmelkamp, P. M. G., & Felten, M. (1985). The process of exposure in vivo: Cognitive and physiological changes during treatment of acrophobia. *Behaviour Research and Therapy, 23,* 219–223.

Emmelkamp, P. M. G., Kuipers, C. M., & Eggeraat, J. B. (1978). Cognitive modification versus prolonged exposure in vivo, *Behaviour Research and Therapy, 16,* 33–41.

Emmelkamp, P. M. G., & Mersch, P. P. (1982). Cognition and exposure in vivo in the treatment of agoraphobia: Short-term and delayed effects. *Cognitive Therapy and Research, 6,* 77–88.

Emmelkamp, P. M. G., & Wessels, H. (1975). Flooding in imagination vs. flooding in vivo: A comparison with agoraphobics. *Behavior Research and Therapy, 13,* 7–16.

Eron, L. D. (1987). The development of aggressive behavior from the perspective of a developing behaviorism. *American Psychologist, 42,* 435–442.

Foa, E. B., & McNally, R. J. (1996). Mechanisms of change in exposure therapy. In R. Rapee (Ed.), *Current controversies in the anxiety disorders* (pp. 329–343). New York: Guilford Press.

Frankenhauser, M. (1975). Experimental approaches to the study of catecholamines and emotion. In L. Levi (Ed.), *Emotions: Their parameters and measurement* (pp. 209–234). New York: Raven Press.

Funder, D. C. (1991). Global traits: A neo-Allportian approach to personality. *Psychological Science, 2,* 31–39.

Gauthier, J., & Ladouceur, R. (1981). The influence of self-efficacy reports on performance. *Behavior Therapy, 12,* 436–439.

Gerst, M. S. (1971). Symbolic coding processes in observational learning. *Journal of Personality and Social Psychology, 19*, 7–17.

Goldberg, L. (1981). Language and individual differences: The search for universals in personality lexicons. *Review of Personality and Social Psychology, 2*, 141–165.

Grings, W. W. (1973). The role of consciousness and cognition in autonomic behavior change. In F. J. McGuigan & R. Schoonover (Eds.), *The psychophysiology of thinking*. New York: Academic Press.

Heckhausen, J., & Schultz, R. (1996). A life-span theory of control. *Psychological Review, 102*, 284–304.

Hernnstein, R. J. (1966). Method and theory in the study of avoidance. *Psychological Review, 76*, 49–69.

Higgins, E. T. (1987). Self-discrepancy: A theory relating self and affect. *Psychological Review, 94*, 319–340.

Higgins, E. T. (1990). Personality, social psychology, and person-situation relations: Standards and knowledge activation as a common language. In L. A. Pervin (Ed.), *Handbook of personality: Theory and research*. New York: Guilford Press.

Higgins, E. T. (1996). Knowledge activation: Accessibility, applicability, and salience. In E. T. Higgins & A. W. Kruglanski (Eds.), *Social psychology: Handbook of basic principles* (pp. 133–168). NY: Guilford Press.

Higgins, E. T. (in press). Persons and situations: Separate variables or variability in general principles? In D. Cervone & Y. Shoda (Eds.), *The coherence of personality: Social-cognitive bases of consistency, variability, and organization*. NY: Guilford Press.

Holahan, C. K., & Holahan, C. J. (1987). Life stress, hassles, and self-efficacy in aging: A replication and extension. *Journal of Applied Social Psychology, 17*, 574–592.

Ickes, W., Snyder, M., & Garcia, S. (1997). Personality influences on the choices of situations. In R. Hogan, J. Johnson, & S. Briggs (Eds.), *Handbook of personality psychology* (pp. 165–195), San Diego, CA: Academic Press.

Jackson, D. N., & Paunonen, S. V. (1985). Construct validity and the predictability of behavior. *Journal of Personality and Social Psychology, 49*, 554–570.

John, O. P. (1989). Towards a taxonomy of personality descriptors. In D. M. Buss & N. Cantor (Eds.), *Personality psychology: Recent trends and emerging directions*. New York: Springer-Verlag.

John, O. P. (1990). The "Big Five" factor taxonomy: Dimensions of personality in the natural language and in questionnaires. In L. A. Pervin (Ed.), *Handbook of personality: Theory and Research* (pp. 66–100). New York: Guilford Press.

Kanfer, F. H. (1980). Self-management methods. In F. H. Kanfer & A. P. Goldstein (Eds.), *Helping people change* (2nd ed., pp. 334–389). New York: Pergamon Press.

Kanfer, R., & Zeiss, A. M. (1983). Depression, interpersonal standard-setting, and judgments of self-efficacy. *Journal of Abnormal Psychology, 92*, 319–329.

Kaufmann, A., Baron, A., & Kopp, R. E. (1966). Some effects of instructions on human operant behavior. *Psychonomic Monograph Supplements, 1*, 243–250.

Kavanagh, D. J., & Bower, G. H. (1985). Mood and self-efficacy: Impact of joy and sadness on perceived capabilities. *Cognitive Therapy and Research, 9*, 507–525.

Kazdin, A. E. (1984). Covert modeling. *Advances in Cognitive-Behavioral Research and Therapy, 3*, 103–129.

Kent, G. (1987). Self-efficacious control over reported physiological, cognitive and behavioral symptoms of dental anxiety. *Behaviour Research and Therapy, 25*, 341–347.

Kent, G., & Gibbons (1987). Self-efficacy and the control of anxious cognitions. *Journal of Behavior Therapy and Experimental Psychiatry, 18*, 33–40.

Kihlstrom, J. F., & Harackiewicz, J. M. (1990). An evolutionary milestone in the psychology of personality: Book review essay on Bandura's Social foundations of thought and action. *Psychological Inquiry, 1*, 86–92.

Kirsch, I. (1982). Efficacy expectations or response predictions: The meaning of efficacy ratings as a function of task characteristics. *Journal of Personality and Social Psychology, 42*, 132–136.

Lacey, J. I. (1967). Somatic response patterning and stress: Some revisions of activation theory. In M. H. Appley & R. Trumbull (Eds.), *Psychological stress: Issues in research* (pp. 14–42). New York: Appleton-Century-Crofts.

Ladouceur, R. (1983). Participant modeling with or without cognitive treatment of phobias. *Journal of Consulting and Clinical Psychology, 51*, 942–944.

Lang, P. J. (1971). The application of psychophysiological methods to the study of psychotherapy and behavior modification. In A. E. Bergin & S. L. Garfield (Eds.), *Handbook of psychotherapy and behavior change* (pp. 75–125). New York: Wiley.

Lang, P. J. (1985). The cognitive psychophysiology of emotion: Fear and anxiety. In A. H. Tuma & J. D. Maser (Eds.), *Anxiety and the anxiety disorders* (pp. 131–170). Hillsdale, NJ: Erlbaum.

Lazarus, R. S., & Folkman, S. (1984). *Stress, appraisal, and coping.* NY: Springer Verlag.

Leitenberg, H. (1976). Behavioral approaches to treatment of neuroses. In H. Leitenberg (Ed.), *Handbook of behavior modification and behavior therapy* (pp. 124–167). Englewood Cliffs, NJ: Prentice-Hall.

Leitenberg, H., Agras, S., Butz, R., & Wincze, J. (1971). Relationship between heart rate and behavioral change during the treatment of phobias. *Journal of Abnormal Psychology, 78,* 59–68.

Lepper, M. R., Sagotsky, J., & Mailer, J. (1975). Generalization and persistence of effects of exposure to self-reinforcement models. *Child Development, 46,* 618–630.

Lerner, R. M. (1990). Weaving development into the fabric of personality and social psychology—On the significance of Bandura's Social foundations of thought and action. *Psychological Inquiry, 1,* 92–96.

Locke, E. A. (1968). Toward a theory of task motivation and incentives. *Organizational Behavior and Human Performance, 3,* 157–189.

Locke, E. A., & Latham, G. P. (1990). *A theory of goal setting and task performance.* Englewood Cliffs, NJ: Prentice-Hall.

Locke, E. A., Shaw, K. N., Saari, L. M., & Latham, G. P. (1981). Goal setting and task performance: 1969–1980. *Psychological Bulletin, 90,* 125–152.

Lord, C. G. (1982). Predicting behavioral consistency from an individual's perception of situational similarities. *Journal of Personality and Social Psychology, 42,* 1076–1088.

Magnusson, D., & Endler, N. S. (Eds.). (1977). *Personality at the crossroads: Current issues in interactional psychology.* Hillsdale, NJ: Erlbaum.

Mandler, G. (1962). Emotion. In R. Brown, E. Galanter, E. Hess, & G. Mandler (Eds.), *New directions in psychology* Vol. I (pp. 269–343). New York: Holt, Rinehart & Winston.

Manning, M. M., & Wright, T. L. (1983). Self-efficacy expectancies, outcome expectancies, and the persistence of pain control in childbirth. *Journal of Personality and Social Psychology, 45,* 421–431.

Marks, I. M. (1978). Behavioral psychotherapy of adult neurosis. In S. L. Garfield & A. E. Bergin (Eds.), *Handbook of psychotherapy and behavior change* (pp. 493–547). New York: Wiley.

Markus, H., & Nurius, P. (1986). Possible selves. *American Psychologist, 41,* 954–969.

Markus, H., & Wurf, E. (1987). The dynamic self-concept: A social psychological perspective. *Annual Review of Psychology, 38,* 299–337.

Mattick, R. P., & Peters, L. (1988). Treatment of severe social phobia: Effects of guided exposure with and without cognitive restructuring. *Journal of Consulting and Clinical Psychology, 56,* 251–260.

McCrae, R. R., & Costa, P. T., Jr. (1987). Validation of the five-factor model of personality across instruments and observers. *Journal of Personality and Social Psychology, 52,* 81–90.

McCrae, R. R., & Costa, P. T., Jr. (1996). Toward a new generation of personality theories: Theoretical contexts for the five-factor model. In J. Wiggins (Ed.), *The five-factor model of personality: Theoretical perspectives.* New York: Guilford Press.

Mento, A. J., Steel, R. P., & Karren, R. J. (1987). A meta-analytic study of the effects of goal setting on task performance: 1966–1984. *Organizational Behavior and Human Decision Processes, 39,* 52–83.

Merckelbach, H., Arntz, A., & DeJong, P. (1991). Conditioning experiences in spider phobics. *Behaviour Research and Therapy, 29,* 333–335.

Miller, S. M. (1979). Controllability and human stress: Method, evidence, and theory. *Behaviour Research and Therapy, 17,* 187–304.

Mineka, S. (1979). The role of fear in theories of avoidance learning, flooding, and extinction. *Psychological Bulletin, 86,* 985–1010.

Mineka, S. (1985). The frightful complexity of the origins of fears. In F. Brush & J. Overmier (Eds.), *Affect, conditioning, and cognition: Essays on the determinants of behavior* (pp. 55–73). Hillsdale, NJ: Erlbaum.

Mineka, S., Davidson, M., Cook, M., & Keir, R. (1984). Observational conditioning of snake fear in rhesus monkeys. *Journal of Abnormal Psychology, 93,* 355–372.

Mineka, S., & Kelly, K. A. (1989). The relationship between anxiety, lack of control, and loss of control. In A. Steptoe & A. Appels (Eds.), *Stress, personal control and health* (pp. 163–191). New York: Wiley.

Mischel, W. (1968). *Personality and assessment.* New York: Wiley.

Mischel, W. (1973). Toward a cognitive social learning reconceptualization of personality. *Psychological Review, 80,* 252–283.

Mischel, W. (1983). Alternatives in the pursuit of the predictability and consistency of persons: Stable data that yield unstable interpretations. *Journal of Personality, 51,* 578–604.

Mischel, W. (1990). Personality dispositions revisited and revised: A view after three decades. In L. A. Pervin (Ed.), *Handbook of personality: Theory and research* (pp. 111–164). New York: Guilford Press.

Mischel, W., Cantor, N., & Feldman, S. (1996). Goal-directed self-regulation. In E. T. Higgins & A. W. Kruglanski (Eds.), *Social psychology: Handbook of basic principles* (pp. 329–360). NY: Guilford Press.

Mischel, W., & Peake, P. K. (1982). Beyond deja-vu in the search for cross-situational consistency. *Psychological Review, 89,* 730–755.

Mischel, W., Shoda, Y., & Rodriguez, M. (1989). Delay of gratification in children. *Science, 244,* 933–938.

Mischel, W., & Shoda, Y. (1995). A cognitive-affective system theory of personality: Reconceptualizing situations, dispositions, dynamics, and invariance in personality structure. *Psychological Review, 102,* 246–268.

Morrow, G. R., & Labrum, A. H. (1978). The relationship between psychological and physiological measures of anxiety. *Psychological Medicine, 8,* 95–101.

Mowrer, O. H. (1960). *Learning theory and behavior.* New York: Wiley.

Murray, E. J., & Foote, F. (1979). The origins of fear of snakes. *Behaviour Research and Therapy, 17,* 489–493.

Nisbett, R. E., Fong, G. T., Lehman, D. R., & Cheng, P. W. (1987). Teaching reasoning. *Science, 238,* 625–631.

Nisbett, R., & Ross, L. (1980). *Human inference: Strategies and shortcomings of social judgment.* Englewood Cliffs, NJ: Prentice-Hall.

Norman, W. T. (1963). Toward an adequate taxonomy of personality attributes: Replicated factor structure in peer nomination personality ratings. *Journal of Abnormal and Social Psychology, 66,* 574–583.

O'Brien, T., & Kelley, J. (1980). A comparison of self-directed and therapist-directed practice for fear reduction. *Behaviour Research and Therapy, 18,* 573–579.

O'Leary, A. (1985). Self-efficacy and health. *Behaviour Research and Therapy, 23,* 437–451.

Ost, L., Salkovskis, P. M., & Hellstrom, K. (1991). One-session therapist-directed exposure versus self-exposure in the treatment of spider phobia. *Behavior Therapy, 22,* 407–422.

Patterson, G. R. (1976). The aggressive child: Victim and architect of a coercive system. In E. J. Mash, L. A., Hamerlynck, & L. C. Handy (Eds.), *Behavior modification and families* (pp. 267–316). New York: Brunner/Mazel.

Peake, P. K., & Cervone, D. (1989). Sequence anchoring and self-efficacy: Primacy effects in the consideration of possibilities. *Social Cognition, 7,* 31–50.

Persons, J. (1986). The advantages of studying psychological phenomena rather than psychiatric diagnoses. *American Psychologist, 11,* 1251–1260.

Pervin, L. A. (Ed.). (1989). *Goal concepts in personality and social psychology.* Hillsdale, NJ: Erlbaum.

Pervin, L. A. (1993). *Personality: Theory and research* (6th ed.). New York: Wiley.

Pervin, L. A., & John, O. P. (1997). *Personality: Theory and research* (7th ed.). New York: Wiley.

Rachman, S. (1976). The passing of the two-stage theory of fear and avoidance: Fresh possibilities. *Behaviour Research and Therapy, 14,* 125–131.

Rachman, S. (1977). The conditioning theory of fear-acquisition: A critical reexamination. *Behaviour Research and Therapy, 15,* 375–387.

Rachman, S. (Ed.). (1978). Perceived self-efficacy: Analyses of Bandura's theory of behavioral change [Special issue]. *Advances in Behaviour Research and Therapy, 1* (2).

Rachman, S., & Hodgson, R. (1974). I. Synchrony and desynchrony in fear and avoidance. *Behaviour Research and Therapy, 12,* 311–318.

Rachman, S. J., & Wilson, G. T. (1980). *The effects of psychological therapy* (2nd ed.). Oxford: Pergamon.

Reed, S. D., Harver, A., & Katkin, E. S. (1990). Interoception. In J. T. Cacioppo & L. G. Tassinary (Eds.), *Principles of psychophysiology: Physical, social, and inferential elements* (pp. 253–294). New York: Cambridge University Press.

Rehm, L. P. (1977). A self-control model of depression. *Behavior Therapy, 8,* 787–804.

Rosenthal, T. L., & Bandura, A. (1978). Psychological modeling: Theory and practice. In S. L. Garfield & A. E. Bergin (Eds.), *Handbook of psychotherapy and behavior change* (2nd ed., pp. 621–658). New York: Wiley.

Rosenthal, T. L., & Zimmerman, B. J. (1978). *Social learning and cognition.* New York: Academic Press.

Rotter, J. B. (1966). Generalized expectancies for internal versus external control of reinforcement. *Psychological Monographs, 80* (1, Whole No. 609).

Salkovskis, P. M., & Harrison, J. (1984). Abnormal and normal obsessions—a replication. *Behaviour Research and Therapy, 22,* 549–552.

Salovey, P., & Birnbaum, D. (1989). Influence of mood on health-relevant cognitions. *Journal of Personality and Social Psychology, 57,* 539–551.

Sanderson, W. C., Rapee, R. M., & Barlow, D. H. (1989). The influence of an illusion of control on panic attacks induced via inhalation of 5.5% carbon-dioxide enriched air. *Archives of General Psychiatry, 46,* 157–162.

Schunk, D. H. (1984). Self-efficacy perspective on achievement behavior. *Educational Psychologist, 19,* 48–58.

Schunk, D. H., Hanson, A. R., & Cox, P. D. (1987). Peer-model attributes and children's achievement behaviors. *Journal of Educational Psychology, 79,* 54–61.

Schwartz, B. (1984). *Psychology of learning and behavior.* New York: W. W. Norton.

Schwartz, G. E., Weinberger, D. A., & Singer, J. A. (1981). Cardiovascular differentiation of happiness, sadness, anger, and fear following imagery and exercise. *Psychosomatic Medicine, 43,* 343–364.

Schwarz, N., Bless, H., Strack, F., Klumpp, G., Rittenauer-Schatka, H., & Simons, A. (1991). Ease of retrieval as information: Another look at the availability heuristic. *Journal of Personality and Social Psychology, 61,* 195–202.

Seligman, M. E. P. (1975). *Helplessness: On depression, development, and death.* San Francisco, CA: Freeman.

Seligman, M. E. P., & Johnston, J. C. (1973). A cognitive theory of avoidance learning. In F. J. McGuigan & D. B. Lumsden (Eds.), *Contemporary approaches to conditioning and learning* (pp. 69–110). Washington, DC: Winston & Sons.

Simon, H. A. (1990). Invariants of human behavior. *Annual Review of Psychology, 41,* 1–19.

Skinner, B. F. (1953). *Science and human behavior.* New York: Macmillan.

Skinner, B. F. (1974). *About behaviorism.* New York: Random House.

Skinner, E. (1996). A guide to constructs of control. *Journal of Personality and Social Psychology, 71,* 549–570.

Smith, R. E. (1989). Effects of coping skills training on generalized self-efficacy and locus of control. *Journal of Personality and Social Psychology, 56,* 228–233.

Snyder, M. (1981). On the influence of individuals on situations. In N. Cantor & J. F. Kihlstrom (Eds.), *personality, cognition, and social interaction.* Hillsdale, NJ: Erlbaum.

Snyder, M., & Ickes, W. (1985). Personality and social behavior. In G. Lindzey & E. Aronson (Eds.), *Handbook of social psychology* (pp. 883–947). New York: Random House.

Spielberger, C. D., & DeNike, L. D. (1966). Descriptive behaviorism versus cognitive theory in verbal operant conditioning. *Psychological Review, 73,* 306–326.

Stamfl, T. G., & Levis, D. J. (1967). Essentials of implosive therapy. *Journal of Abnormal Psychology, 72,* 270–276.

Stanley, M. A., & Maddux, J. E. (1986). Self-efficacy theory: Potential contributions to understanding cognitions in depression. *Journal of Social and Clinical Psychology, 4,* 268–278.

Steptoe, A., & Vogele, C. (1992). Individual differences in the perception of bodily sensations: The role of trait anxiety and coping style. *Behaviour Research and Therapy, 30,* 597–607.

Stock, J., & Cervone, D. (1990). Proximal goal-setting and self-regulatory processes. *Cognitive Therapy and Research, 14,* 483–489.

Szasz, T. (1960). The myth of mental illness. *American Psychologist, 15,* 113–118.

Taylor, S. E., & Brown, J. D. (1988). Illusion and well-being: A social psychological perspective on mental health. *Psychological Bulletin, 103,* 193–210.

Taylor, S. E., & Fiske, S. T. (1978). Salience, attention, and attribution: Top of the head phenomena. In L. Berkowitz (Ed.), *Advances in experimental social psychology* (Vol. 11, pp. 249–288). New York: Academic Press.

Telch, M. J., Agras, W. S., Taylor, C. B., Roth, W. T., & Gallen, C. C. (1985). Combined pharmacological and behavioral treatment for agoraphobia. *Behaviour Research and Therapy, 23,* 325–335.

Telch, M. J., Bandura, A., Vinciguerra, P., Agras, A., & Stout, A. L. (1982). Social demand for consistency and congruence between self-efficacy and performance. *Behavior Therapy, 13,* 694–701.

Thomas, E. A. C., & Malone, T. W. (1979). On the dynamics of two-person interactions. *Psychological Review, 86,* 331–360.

Tolman, E. C. (1932). *Purposive behavior in animals and men.* New York: Century.

Tubbs, M. E. (1986). Goal setting: A meta-analytic examination of the empirical evidence. *Journal of Applied Psychology, 71,* 474–483.

Tversky, A., & Kahneman, D. (1973). Availability: A heuristic for judging frequency and probability. *Cognitive Psychology, 5,* 207–232.

Tversky, A., & Kahneman, D. (1974). Judgment under uncertainty: Heuristics and biases. *Science, 185,* 1123–1131.

Weinberg, R. S., Gould, D., & Jackson, A. (1979). Expectations and performance: An empirical test of Bandura's self-efficacy theory. *Journal of Sport Psychology, 1,* 320–331.

Weiner, B. (1985). An attributional theory of achievement motivation and emotion. *Psychological Review, 92,* 548–573.

Williams, S. L. (1985). On the nature and measurement of agoraphobia. *Progress in Behavior Modification, 19,* 109–144.

Williams, S. L. (1987). On anxiety and phobia. *Journal of Anxiety Disorders, 1,* 161–180.

Williams, S. L. (1988). Addressing misconceptions about phobia, anxiety, and self-efficacy: A reply to Marks. *Journal of Anxiety Disorders, 2,* 277–289.

Williams, S. L. (1990). Guided mastery treatment of agoraphobia: Beyond stimulus exposure. *Progress in Behavior Modification, 26,* 89–121.

Williams, S. L. (1992). Perceived self-efficacy and phobic disability. In R. Schwarzer (Ed.), *Self-efficacy: Thought control of action.* New York: Hemisphere.

Williams, S. L. (1995). Self-efficacy, anxiety, and phobic disorders. In J. Maddux (Ed.), *Self-efficacy, adaptation, and adjustment: Theory, research, and application* (pp. 69–107). New York: Plenum Press.

Williams, S. L. (1996a). Therapeutic changes in phobic behavior are mediated by changes in perceived self-efficacy. In R. Rapee (Ed.), *Current controversies in the anxiety disorders* (pp. 344–368). New York: Guilford Press.

Williams, S. L. (1996b). Overcoming phobia: Unconscious bioinformational deconditioning or conscious cognitive reappraisal? In R. Rapee (Ed.), *Current controversies in the anxiety disorders* (pp. 373–376). New York: Guilford Press.

Williams, S. L., & Bauchiess, R. (1992). *Cognitive factors influencing the persistence of agoraphobic avoidance and the rapidity of change during treatment.* Unpublished manuscript, Lehigh University.

Williams, S. L., Dooseman, G., & Kleifield, E. (1984). Comparative effectiveness of guided mastery and exposure treatments for intractable phobias. *Journal of Consulting and Clinical Psychology, 52,* 505–518.

Williams, S. L., & Kinney, P. J. (1991). Performance and nonperformance strategies for coping with acute pain: The role of perceived self-efficacy, expected outcomes, and attention. *Cognitive Therapy and Research, 15,* 1–19.

Williams, S. L., Kinney, P. J., & Falbo, J. (1989). Generalization of therapeutic changes in agoraphobia: The role of perceived self-efficacy. *Journal of Consulting and Clinical Psychology, 57,* 436–442.

Williams, S. L., & Rappoport, A. (1983). Cognitive treatment in the natural environment for agoraphobics. *Behavior Therapy, 14,* 299–313.

Williams, S. L., Turner, S. M., & Peer, D. F. (1985). Guided mastery and performance desensitization treatments for severe acrophobia. *Journal of Consulting and Clinical Psychology, 53,* 237–247.

Williams, S. L., & Watson, N. (1985). Perceived danger and perceived self-efficacy as cognitive determinants of acrophobic behavior. *Behavior Therapy, 16,* 237–247.

Williams, S. L., & Zane, G. (1988). Guided mastery and stimulus exposure treatments for severe performance anxiety in agoraphobics. *Behaviour Research and Therapy, 27,* 237–247.

Wolpe, J. (1958). *Psychotherapy by reciprocal inhibition.* Stanford, CA: Stanford University Press.

Wood, R., & Bandura, A. (1989). Impact of conceptions of ability on self-regulatory mechanisms and complex decision making. *Journal of Personality and Social Psychology, 56,* 407–415.

Wood, R., Bandura, A., & Bailey, T. (1990). Mechanisms governing organizational productivity in complex decision-making environments. *Organizational Behavior and Human Decision Processes*

Wright, J. C., & Mischel, W. (1987). A conditional analysis of dispositional constructs: The local predictability of social behavior. *Journal of Personality and Social Psychology, 53,* 1159–1177.

Zane, G., & Williams, S. L. (1993). Performance-related anxiety in agoraphobia: Treatment procedures and cognitive mechanisms of change. *Behavior Therapy, 24,* 625–643.

PART III

SPECIAL TOPIC: CONSCIOUS AND UNCONSCIOUS FUNCTIONING

As is apparent from the diverse theories presented in Part II, there are numerous controversies in personality theory. In their simplest version, they are formulated dialectically: intrapsychic versus interpersonal, person versus situation, nature versus nurture, stability versus change, and so on. These controversies are about enduring issues; better understanding grows out of reformulation.

In the last 20 years there has been renewed interest in the issue of conscious and unconscious processing. While some contemporary theorists reject a causal role for conscious thought (Skinner) or for unconscious processing (Bandura), other personality theorists and cognitive psychologists have found the need to include both processes to account for observed human functioning and have invented methods of researching them. In recent reformulations, these processes are construed as complementary, each serving an essential function.

Cognitive approaches to personality, including self-theory, are beset with the problem of how to account for the automatic, involuntary, and affective aspects of human functioning. Seymour Epstein presents his integrative theory, which combines cognitive and experiential ways of knowing (Chapter 9). Epstein also presents research, especially that of his own research group, to support his theory. Included is research on the way personalities differ in relying on rational and experiential information processing.

Just as Freud went beyond cultural understandings of consciousness, so too have philosophers of mind and contemporary psychologists. Howard Shevrin presents his answer to Freud's question about the function of consciousness in Chapter 10. Consciousness enables the discrimination between internal and external information (i.e., between biased knowledge structures and data inconsistent with them). Shevrin finds support for his answer in the theorizing of others, in and out of psychology, and in research conducted by cognitive psychologists and by himself. Like Epstein, he discusses personality differences and their degrees of openness to conscious functioning and unconscious knowledge.

(For social cognitive treatments of different modes of knowing and schema-data transactions, see Barone, Maddux, and Snyder, 1997; Johnson, Hashtroudi, and Lindsay, 1983; Johnson and Raye, 1981; and Wegner, 1989, 1994.)

REFERENCES

Barone, D. F., Maddux, J. E., & Snyder, C. R. (1997). *Social cognitive psychology: History and current domains.* New York: Plenum Press.

Johnson, M. K., Hashtroudi, S., & Lindsay, D. S. (1993). Source monitoring. *Psychological Bulletin, 114,* 3–28.
Johnson, M. K., & Rayne, C. L. (1981). Reality monitoring. *Psychological Review, 88,* 67–85.
Wegner, D. M. (1989). *White bears and other unwanted thoughts.* New York: Viking.
Wegner, D. M. (1994). Ironic processes of mental control. *Psychological Review, 101,* 34–52.

CHAPTER 9

COGNITIVE-EXPERIENTIAL SELF-THEORY

SEYMOUR EPSTEIN

SEYMOUR EPSTEIN • Department of Psychology, University of Massachusetts, Amherst, Massachusetts 01003.

Advanced Personality, edited by David F. Barone, Michel Hersen, and Vincent B. Van Hasselt. Plenum Press, New York, 1998.

INTRODUCTION

The book, *Letters from Jenny*, by Gordon Allport (1965) presented a series of letters written over an extended period by a woman named Jenny to her son, Ross. Jenny was a poor, hard-working woman who sacrificed almost everything she had for Ross. She supported him in an affluent lifestyle at an Ivy League college, while she barely had enough to eat. All that mattered to her was his well-being. Yet, she failed miserably in bringing fulfillment and happiness to him as well as to herself. When Ross began to form relationships with other women, Jenny disowned him, very likely contributing to his early death. She then derived more happiness from his memory than she had from his presence.

Allport (1965) raised the interesting question, "Why does an intelligent lady behave so persistently in a self-defeating manner?" (p. viii). He sought an answer by viewing the case from the vantage point of several major personality theories; he concluded that no one theory was able to provide a satisfactory answer. Rather, each had something to offer, and each had serious limitations. The solution, he believed, was to develop an eclectic theory that contained the best of the current theories: "Yet the challenge remains: if there is truth in all, to what extent and in what direction, is each approach most valid? Eclecticism in personality theory is no doubt necessary, but it is a task for the future to blend the approaches so that a *systematic* eclecticism, a true synthesis of theories will emerge" (p. 211).

THE DEVELOPMENT OF COGNITIVE-EXPERIENTIAL SELF-THEORY

Cognitive-experiential self-theory (CEST) goes a considerable way, I believe, toward fulfilling Allport's vision. I do not mean to imply that I deliberately set out to construct an integrative, eclectic personality theory along the lines advocated by Allport. Rather, it occurred fortuitously because of the confluence of two circumstances. First, as with Allport, although I was impressed favorably with certain aspects of several theories, I was never sufficiently enamored with any to adopt it as my own. Second, I had a sudden insight that caused the various disconnected aspects of the theories I favored to fall into place within a single framework.

The insight occurred as I was wondering how Carl Rogers's conceptualization of the self-concept, to which he ascribed agentic and growth properties, could be reconceptualized scientifically in a more meaningful way. William James (1910) and Gordon Allport (1961) had independently considered and then dismissed the notion of an agentic self. They decided that, although the self as an object of knowledge was a scientifically viable construct—as people can have views about themselves just as they can about others—the self as an agent of behavior should be relegated to the realm of philosophy. As for the growth principle, Rogers asserted its presence but provided no evidence or logic to support it.

The insight I had was that a person's self-concept is more accurately described as a person's implicit self-theory (Epstein, 1973). People do not simply have independent views about what they are like; rather, their views are organized into an adaptive, hierarchical conceptual system that organizes experience, directs behavior, and grows through its interaction with the data of experience, much as does a scientific theory. A person's self-theory is assumed to be part of a broader theory of reality that includes a self-theory, a world theory, and connections between the two. Furthermore, it is assumed that everyone, like it or not, automatically constructs a personal theory of reality because it is in the nature of the human brain to make sense of experience, and there are emotional rewards for doing so. Thus, a personal theory of reality, although cognitive, is assumed to be emotionally driven.

When I first presented CEST to professional audiences, I was surprised by the number of people with different theoretical orientations who said that CEST had much in common with their own views. Their reactions suggested to me that, although I had not set out to construct an eclectic theory of personality, I had somehow managed to do so. I hasten to add that, despite sharing common features with several other theories, CEST differs from all in important ways. In common with psychoanalytic theories, it assumes unconscious and psychodynamic processes but differs in its emphasis on the preconscious, as contrasted with deeply repressed, unconscious processes. Like classical psychoanalytic theory, it recognizes the importance of the pleasure principle as a fundamental motive but adds three other motives that it considers equally important. Like Kohutian theory, it assigns a central role to the need to enhance self-esteem but differs in regarding it as only one of four basic motives. Like ego psychology, it assumes that autonomous ego-functions that are not simply derivatives of more primitive id functions exist, but differs in that it further assumes that there are experiential and rational modes of information processing that operate by different rules.

Like object-relations theory, CEST assumes that many of the most important schemas in an individual's implicit theory of reality are derived from relationships with significant others, but it differs in regarding the need for relatedness as only one of four basic needs. Like Adler's theory, it is a constructionist theory, but assumes that behavior is less driven by conscious intentions than is assumed by Adler, and that the need to enhance self-esteem, or overcome inferiority, is but one of four basic motives. Like Jung, it assumes that unconscious processes have important implications for mental and physical well-being, and that there exist emotional complexes (referred to as *sensitivities* in CEST) that selectively influence perception and operate as strong motivaters, often producing maladaptive thoughts, feelings, and behavior. Unlike Jung, however, it rejects the view that the tendency to experience "archetypal" images is inherited, and that mystical constructs are required to explain esoteric behavior. Like Rogers's and other phenomenological and existential theories, it is a constructionist theory that assumes that everyone constructs an implicit theory of reality, and that maintaining the integrity of this theory is a fundamental motive. It differs in assuming that there are three other equally important motives, and that the self can be studied with objective, normative procedures. Like learning theory, it assumes that the schemas in a personal theory of reality are primarily learned from emotionally significant past experiences, but, unlike learning theory, it emphasizes a personal theory of reality, two modes of information processing, and four basic needs. Like Kelly's theory of constructive alternativism, as well as modern cognitive theories, it assigns a central role to human cognition, but differs in assuming that the cognitions are emotionally driven.

THE NEED FOR A NEW THEORY OF THE UNCONSCIOUS

One of the most influential events in the history of psychology was Freud's introduction of his concept of the unconscious. Up to that time, irrational behavior, including self-destructive behavior such as that exhibited by Jenny, had been attributed to either physical disorders or evil spirits. Freud placed the study of maladaptive behavior squarely in the domain of the natural sciences, and, more particularly, in the field of psychology. Deviant, out-of-character behavior could thereafter be explained by the same scientific principles as any other behavior. He taught us that we are not as rational as we would like to believe, that our conscious rational thinking is often subverted by unconscious, irrational processes.

From the perspective of CEST, there is only one thing wrong with Freud's theory of the unconscious: He had the wrong unconscious. As Freud's theory of the unconscious was derived from the study of dreams, the unconscious that he described operates by the principles of wish fulfillment, association, condensation, displacement, and symbolic representation. As such, it is a maladaptive unconscious that, if acted on in real life, would correspond to psychosis. People and nonhuman animals operating solely on the basis of the principles of the Freudian unconscious, referred to by Freud as the "primary process," would starve to death amidst wish fulfillment fantasies of unlimited gratification.

To deal with this problem, Freud introduced a conscious, logical, reality-oriented "secondary process" that operated through language. The trouble with this solution is that it has no counterpart in nonhuman animals. Thus, Freud's concept of the primary process made little sense from an evolutionary perspective. As the presumed foundation of the mind, it is difficult to imagine how the maladaptive primary process could have ever evolved. What is required is an unconscious that works by principles that are adaptive for both nonhuman and human animals. This is accomplished in CEST by the introduction of an experiential system. Freud's principles of the primary process can be understood from the perspective of CEST as a degradation of the experiential system, which occurs in the altered state of consciousness produced by sleep. This is not to deny that important information can become available in such a state.

The principles of the unconscious, as proposed by CEST, have many of the advantages of the Freudian unconscious without its disadvantages. CEST shares with psychoanalysis an emphasis on the importance of unconscious processing in maladjustment, on the influence of unconscious on conscious thought, and on the importance of psychodynamic processes. It can account for almost everything that traditional psychoanalysis can in a more scientifically acceptable and parsimonious manner, and it can account for other phenomena that are either problematic for psychoanalysis, such as the importance of maintaining the coherence of one's conceptual system, or about which psychoanalysis has had little to say, such as the ubiquity of prejudice and ethnic strife.

Before providing a more detailed description of CEST, it will be instructive to consider some real-life evidence for the existence of two systems of information processing that correspond to the experiential and rational systems proposed by CEST, but not to the division between the primary and secondary process proposed by Freud.

EVIDENCE IN EVERYDAY LIFE OF TWO FUNDAMENTAL WAYS OF KNOWING

There is no dearth of evidence in everyday life that people apprehend reality by two fundamentally different cognitive systems.

THE INFLUENCE OF EMOTIONS ON THINKING

The transformation that occurs in people's thinking when they are emotionally aroused is a dramatically different way of thinking from the way people think when they are unemotional. People, when they are highly emotional, characteristically think in a manner that is categorical, personal, concretive, unreflective, and action oriented; and, the stronger the emotion, the more they think that way and the more their thinking appears to them to be self-evidently valid. As will be seen later, all of these responses identify fundamental attributes of the experiential system.

That most people are intuitively aware of two modes of information processing, which correspond to the experiential and rational systems, is indicated by the advice they typically give others who are emotionally overwrought, such as, "Get a grip on yourself. You're too emotional to think straight. Once you calm down, you will see things differently."

THE INFLUENCE OF THINKING ON EMOTIONS

Emotions in everyday life are almost invariably produced by the preconscious interpretation of events. People are angry, sad, or frightened not as a direct result of what objectively occurs, but because of how they interpret what occurs. If a person interprets an action directed at him or her as unwarranted and deserving of punishment, the person will most likely feel angry, whereas if the same action is interpreted as a serious threat to life or limb from which escape is the desired response, the person will more likely feel frightened (e.g., Averill, 1980; Beck, 1976; Ellis, 1973; Epstein, 1984; Lazarus, 1982; also see Epstein, 1983a, for a study of the characteristic interpretations that precede emotions in everyday life). The preconscious construals that are the effective instigators of such emotions occur so automatically and rapidly as to preclude the deliberative, linear, analytical thinking that is characteristic of the rational system. Such automatic, preconscious thinking, therefore, suggests a mode of information processing that operates by different principles from a more deliberative, analytical type of thinking.

CONFLICTS BETWEEN THE HEART AND THE HEAD

Usually the two systems of knowing operate in seamless harmony with each other, which is why people are not normally aware of their simultaneous operation in everyday decisions. However, sometimes they are in direct conflict with each other. For instance, a young woman may have difficulty deciding between two suitors, one who is more trustworthy and the other who is a greater source of pleasure. She identifies her conflict as between the head and the heart. The heart, of course, is a metaphor for emotions. But emotions have no more capacity than the heart for making judgments. Because assessments are judgments, they are necessarily the product of cognitions. It follows that conflicts between the heart and the head must be between two cognitive processes, one associated with emotions and the other not. From the perspective of CEST, the former corresponds to processing in the mode of the experiential system, which is intimately associated with affect; the latter corresponds to processing in the mode of the rational system, which is relatively affect-free.

THE DIFFERENCE BETWEEN INSIGHT AND INTELLECTUAL KNOWLEDGE

It is widely recognized that there are important differences between intellectual knowledge and insight. Information obtained from textbooks and lectures is of a different quality from information acquired directly from experience. Experientially derived knowledge is often more compelling and more likely to influence behavior than abstract knowledge (e.g., Brewin, 1989; Fazio & Zanna, 1981; Shiffrin & Schneider, 1977). Psychotherapists have long recognized the importance of this distinction. They widely regard information gained through personally meaningful experience as more effective in changing feelings and behavior than impersonal information acquired from textbooks and lectures. The observation that there are two fundamentally different kinds of knowledge, intellectual and insightful, is consistent with the view that there are two kinds of information processing: analytic-rational and intuitive-experiential.

THE APPEAL AND INFLUENCE OF NARRATIVES

Narratives are assumed in CEST to appeal to the experiential system because they are emotionally engaging and represent events in a manner similar to the way in which they are experienced in real life, involving location in place and time, goal-directed characters, and a sequential progression of events (Bruner, 1986). The result is that narratives are intrinsically appealing in a way that lectures on abstract subjects and technical documents are not. Such appeal may explain why including anecdotes increases the persuasiveness of messages (Kahneman & Tversky, 1973). It is no accident that the Bible, the most influential Western book of all time, teaches through parables and stories and not through philosophical discourse (see Vitz, 1990, for a discussion of teaching morality through stories). Relatedly, good literature is valued beyond its entertainment function because it is a vicarious source of significant experience.

IRRATIONAL FEARS

Irrational fears provide evidence of an automatic, nonrational way of processing information. People often maintain distressing irrational beliefs at great personal cost, despite recognizing that these beliefs are irrational. Those who are afraid of flying in aircraft but not of traveling in automobiles know full well that on an objective basis, their fear is unrealistic. Nevertheless, many are willing to drive great distances in order to avoid air travel. Paradoxically, they feel safer in a situation they know intellectually to be more dangerous.

An interesting example of an irrational fear was reported in a newscast in the fall of 1991. A commercial airliner had to turn back because women ran screaming into the aisles, endangering the aircraft, when a mouse appeared on board. The degree of objective danger produced by their behavior as calculated by their rational system was apparently no match for the threat posed by the mouse as assessed by their experiential system.

THE APPEAL OF PICTURES

Advertisers have learned through trial and error, focus groups, and intuition that people's behavior and attitudes are governed by a cognitive system that is more responsive to pictures than to words. (For experimental evidence, see Paivio, 1986.) The tobacco industry is willing to bet millions of dollars in advertising costs that the *visual* appeal of its messages to the experiential system will prevail over the *verbal* message of the surgeon general that smoking can endanger one's life, an appeal directed at the rational system. One wonders if the ads would be continued if the playing field were leveled, presenting the surgeon general's message in vivid, pictorial form.

Superstitious Thinking

The widespread prevalence of superstitious thinking provides compelling evidence that the human mind does not process information by reason alone. In a recent Gallup poll (cited in *Science News,* 1991), 1,236 U.S. adults were interviewed about their superstitions. One in four reported that they believe in ghosts, one in six that they have communicated with someone deceased, one in four that they have telepathically communicated with someone, one in ten that they have been in the presence of a ghost, one in seven that they have seen a UFO, one in four that they believe in astrology, and about one in two said they believe in extrasensory perception. It is evident from such data that even extreme forms of nonrational thinking are common.

The Ubiquity of Religion

Religion provides perhaps the most impressive evidence of all that there are two fundamentally different modes of processing information. There have been few societies, if any, throughout recorded history that have not developed some form of religion. For many individuals, rational, scientific thinking fails to provide as satisfactory a way of understanding the world and of directing their behavior in it as does religious teaching. Why is this so? The answer, I believe, is that religious practices are better suited for communicating with the experiential system.

Conclusion

It is evident from this discussion that there is a fundamental way of thinking that is different from rational reasoning, that is very common in everyday life, and that does not correspond to the dream logic of Freud's primary process; but, as will shortly be demonstrated, corresponds very well to the principles of operation of the experiential system as described in CEST.

THE BASIC THEORY

In the discussion that follows, basic assumptions in CEST previously suggested are developed further, and new aspects of the theory are introduced. First, we present a comparison of the operating principles of the experiential and rational systems. Second, we discuss psychodynamics from the perspective of CEST, emphasizing what CEST can contribute beyond psychoanalysis. Third, we discuss the importance of four basic belief-dimensions that arise from four basic needs and are among the most important schemas in an individual's implicit theory of reality. Last, we consider some key concepts associated with maladjustment, namely, incongruence, sensitivities and compulsions, and the frustration of basic needs.

COMPARISON OF THE EXPERIENTIAL AND RATIONAL SYSTEMS

Table 9.1 presents a comparison of the operating principles of the experiential and rational systems. The *experiential system* has a very long evolutionary history and operates in a similar way in nonhuman and human animals. However, because of humans' more highly developed brains, it is assumed to operate in them in more complex ways. At its lower levels of operation, it is a crude system that automatically, rapidly, effortlessly, and efficiently processes information. At its higher reaches, particularly in interaction with the rational system, it is a source of intuitive wisdom and creativity. Although it represents events primarily concretely and imagistically, it is capable of generalization and abstraction through the use of prototypes, metaphors, and narratives.

In contrast, the *rational system* is a deliberative, effortful, abstract system that operates primarily in the medium of language and has a very brief evolutionary history. It is capable of very high levels of abstraction and long-term delay of gratification. However, it is a very inefficient system for responding to everyday events, and its adaptability over the long haul of evolutionary history remains to be tested. (It may yet lead to the destruction of all life on earth.)

PSYCHODYNAMICS

All behavior is assumed in CEST to be the product of the joint operation of the experiential and rational systems. Their relative influence is determined by various parameters, including individual differences in styles of thinking, degree of emotional involvement, and particular

TABLE 9.1. Comparison of the Experiential and Rational Systems

Experiential	Rational
1. Holistic	1. Analytic
2. Automatic, effortless	2. Intentional, effortful
3. Affective: pleasure-pain oriented (what feels good)	3. Logical: Reason oriented (what is sensible)
4. Associationistic connections	4. Logical connections
5. Behavior mediated by "vibes" from past events	5. Behavior mediated by conscious appraisal of events
6. Encodes reality in concrete images, metaphors, and narratives	6. Encodes reality in abstract symbols, words, and numbers
7. More rapid processing: oriented toward immediate action	7. Slower processing: capacity for long-delayed action
8. Slower and more resistant to change: changes with repetitive or intense experience	8. Changes more rapidly and easily: changes with strength of argument and new evidence
9. More crudely differentiated: broad generalization gradient, stereotypical thinking	9. More highly differentiated
10. More crudely integrated—dissociative, emotional complexes; context-specific processing	10. More highly integrated: context-general principles
11. Experienced passively and preconsciously: we believe we are seized by our emotions	11. Experienced actively and consciously: we believe we are in control of our conscious thoughts
12. Self-evidently valid: "experiencing is believing"	12. Requires justification via logic and evidence

Source: From *The relational self: Theoretical convergences in psychoanalysis and social psychology* (pp. 111–137, at 123), R. C. Curtis (Ed.), 1992. New York: Guilford Press. Copyright 1992 by Guilford Press. Adapted with permission.

situational variables, such as the degree to which a situation is identified as one that requires formal analysis. For example, mathematics problems primarily engage the rational system and interpersonal relationships the experiential system. Emotional involvement and relevant past experience shift the balance of influence in the direction of the experiential system.

According to CEST, there are two basic kinds of schemas: descriptive and motivational. Descriptive schemas refer to people's implicit beliefs about what they and the world are like; for example, "Authority figures are cruel and not to be trusted (or kind and to be trusted)." Motivational schemas refer to people's implicit beliefs about means-ends relations; for example, "I can protect myself from authority figures by defying (or placating) them."

Most theories of personality posit a single fundamental need. For Freud (1900/1953), it was the pleasure principle—the need to maximize pleasure and minimize pain; for Rogers (1959), Lecky (1961), and other phenomenologists, it was the need to maintain a relatively stable, coherent conceptual system; for Bowlby (1988), Fairbairn (1954), and other object-relations theorists, it was the need for relatedness; and for Adler (1954), Allport (1961), and Kohut (1971), it was the need to overcome feelings of inferiority or enhance self-esteem. According to CEST, these four motives are equally important, and behavior is determined by their joint influence.

Like psychoanalysis, CEST is a psychodynamic theory that posits two levels of information processing: conscious and unconscious (or, more precisely, preconscious in CEST). Each level functions according to its own principles. Also, like psychoanalysis, CEST assumes that the unaware (preconscious) level continuously influences processing at the conscious level. This is well illustrated in priming studies (e.g., Bargh, 1989; Epstein, Lipson, Holstein, & Huh, 1992; Higgins, 1989), in which priming the automatic level of information processing influences people's conscious thinking without their awareness. Like psychoanalysis, there is an emphasis in CEST on the interaction of needs within and across levels of processing. However, unlike psychoanalysis, which emphasizes the pleasure principle, CEST considers the needs for coherence, relatedness, and self-esteem as no less important than the pleasure principle.

There are several interesting principles that involve the interaction of the four basic needs. One, as already noted, is that behavior can be viewed as a compromise among them. A second not unrelated principle is that the needs serve as checks and balances against each other. When one need is fulfilled at the expense of the others, the need to fulfill the others increases, which normally moderates the fulfillment of the first need, thereby keeping it in most circumstances within normal limits. An important source of maladaptive behavior occurs when a particular need becomes so important that fulfillment of the other needs is sacrificed. An extreme example is provided by a delusion of grandeur, in which the need for self-esteem is fulfilled at the expense of the needs for realistically assimilating the data of reality, maintaining relationships with others, and maximizing pleasure and minimizing pain (it is not very enjoyable to be confined to a mental institution).

A third principle is that good adjustment is fostered by fulfillment of the four basic needs in a synergistic, harmonious manner and poor adjustment by fulfilling the needs in a conflictual manner, in which satisfying one need interferes with fulfilling the others (e.g., the delusion of grandeur). A fourth principle is that well-being is associated with a fulfillment orientation (i.e., satisfying the basic needs); disturbance, with a defensive orientation (e.g., avoiding pain, maintaining a constricted model of the world, limiting the depth and extent of one's relationships, and protecting the self against devaluation).

Consideration of the ways in which the basic needs interact can clarify some otherwise anomalous observations. For example, it has recently been concluded by some that the widespread view that realistic thinking is an important criterion of adjustment has been overstated. Research has demonstrated that well-adjusted individuals characteristically maintain positive illusions (see review in Taylor & Brown, 1988). According to CEST, this paradox is readily resolved once it is recognized that self-evaluation is influenced by the need to maintain a realistic, coherent conceptual system and the need for self-enhancement. The interaction of these two needs results in a compromise between them, as manifested by a preference for a modest degree of self-enhancement. Thus, the observation that well-adjusted people have moderate positive illusions does not indicate that reality-awareness is an inadequate criterion of adjustment, but only that it is not the only criterion.

The experiential system is assumed to be intimately associated with the experience of affect, including "vibes," subtle feelings of which people are often unaware. When a person responds to an emotionally significant event, the sequence of reactions is assumed to be as follows: The experiential system automatically searches its memory banks for related events, including their emotional accompaniments. The recalled feelings influence the course of further processing and reactions, which are actions in nonhuman animals and conscious and unconscious thoughts as well as actions in humans. If the recalled feelings are pleasant, they motivate actions and thoughts anticipated to reproduce the feelings. If the feelings are unpleasant, they motivate actions and thoughts anticipated to avoid reproducing the feelings.

As in psychoanalysis, CEST assumes there is a ubiquitous influence of automatic thinking outside of awareness on conscious thinking and behavior. In most situations, the automatic processing of the experiential system is dominant over the rational system because it is less effortful and more efficient and, accordingly, is the default option. Moreover, because it is generally associated with affect, it is apt to be experienced as more compelling than dispassionate, logical thinking. Finally, since the influence is usually outside of awareness, the rational system fails to control it because the person does not know there is anything to control. The advantage of insight in such situations is that it permits control, at least within limits. Thus, CEST does not diminish the importance of the unconscious in human behavior, but emphasizes a different kind of unconscious than does psychoanalysis.

BASIC BELIEFS

Associated with the four basic needs are four basic beliefs. Because people particularly attend to and are reinforced by the events associated with fulfillment or frustration of their basic needs, they develop a network of descriptive and motivational schemas relevant to their basic needs. For example, given the need to enhance self-esteem, people automatically tend to dwell on events related to success and failure and to events associated with love and rejection. The result is that they develop descriptive, implicit beliefs about their abilities and "loveworthiness." They also develop beliefs about how the world reacts to their attempts to enhance their self-esteem, and, relatedly, beliefs about what they have to do to succeed in enhancing their self-esteem and protecting it from being diminished.

Let us now consider the relationship between basic needs and basic belief dimensions:

1. The corresponding basic belief dimension for the need to maximize the favorability of a person's pleasure-pain balance is that the world is benevolent versus malevolent.

2. The corresponding basic belief dimension for the need to maintain a coherent, stable conceptual system is that the world is meaningful (including predictable, controllable, and just) versus unpredictable and chaotic.
3. The corresponding basic belief dimension for the need to maintain relatedness is that people are trustworthy and supportive versus untrustworthy and dangerous.
4. The corresponding basic belief dimension for the need to enhance self-esteem is that the self is worthy (including competent, lovable, and good) versus unworthy (including incompetent, unlovable, and bad).

A person's positions on the four basic belief dimensions are among the most important schemas in his or her implicit theory of reality. Thus, should the validity of any of these beliefs be seriously invalidated, the organization of the person's personality structure would be destabilized; destabilization would be accompanied by overwhelming anxiety. This can explain why people are automatically driven to maintain their basic beliefs, even unfavorable ones that they consciously recognize are the source of misery. It also suggests that understanding a person's basic beliefs is one of the most important steps one can take in understanding a person's personality structure. An instrument for measuring the four basic beliefs, the Basic Beliefs Inventory (BBI; Catlin & Epstein, 1992) was developed for this purpose.

REPRESSION AND DISSOCIATION

According to the psychoanalytic view, *repression* occurs when a person has unconscious thoughts, images, or impulses that are so guilt arousing that if they were consciously recognized they would evoke intense anxiety. The result is that relevant material is kept in a state of inaccessibility by the expenditure of psychic energy. The repressed material presumably strives for expression, thereby generating conflict with the forces of repression. The person experiences heightened tension and manifestations of displacement in different forms: symptoms, dreams, slips of the tongue. The task of psychoanalysis is to eliminate the more troublesome repressions. By making the unconscious conscious, the person is able to bring his or her intelligence to bear on solving problems in living. Thus, psychoanalysis places great faith in rational thinking.

In CEST, the concept of *dissociation* is used in preference to repression. According to CEST, material is dissociated when it cannot be assimilated. There are two kinds of dissociation: dissociation between the experiential and rational systems, which corresponds to repression in psychoanalysis; and dissociation within the experiential system itself. If dissociated material within the experiential system is activated to the extent that the dissociation cannot be maintained, the unassimilable material can threaten the stability of the entire experiential system. The appearance of the striving to express the dissociated material does not occur because it has an energy of its own that seeks expression as proposed by Freud, but because there is a fundamental motive to assimilate emotionally significant material into a unified, coherent conceptual system. Material that can neither be ignored nor assimilated keeps reemerging into consciousness in an abortive attempt at assimilation. This process continues until assimilation is accomplished. The process is essentially adaptive, as it promotes assimilation and therefore the construction of a coherent model of the world that is consistent with experience.

The main sources of serious maladjustment from the perspective of CEST are sensitivities and compulsions (shortly to be discussed), disharmony (including dissociation) within the experiential system, and a failure in need fulfillment. Discrepancies between conscious and unconscious beliefs are not in themselves a fundamental source of maladjustment according to CEST. This is not to deny that making the unconscious conscious can be useful in making the higher mental processes available to correct problems within the experiential system, but to note that it is corrections in the experiential system that are of primary importance.

From this perspective, insight is not necessary for therapeutic results, although it can be useful in identifying problems in the experiential system that have to be solved. The task of therapy is to change the maladaptive schemas in the experiential system, including those that are a source of sensitivities and compulsions, disharmony, and the frustration of basic needs. To the extent that insight helps in this endeavor, it is therapeutic. If it does not, it may simply succeed in making a neurotic without insight into one with insight.

SENSITIVITIES AND COMPULSIONS AS A MAJOR SOURCE OF MALADJUSTMENT

In a personal theory of reality, central beliefs are relatively stable, whereas peripheral beliefs can change readily with experience. This arrangement is highly adaptive; it preserves the organization of the conceptual system while, at the same time, permitting flexibility. However, there are certain isolated belief complexes—namely, sensitivities and compulsions—that are rigid to the point that they are a serious source of problems in living.

Sensitivities in CEST refer to unrealistic, inflexible, descriptive schemas that certain kinds of situations or events are dangerous. A person reacting to a mouse as if it were a life-threatening beast is an example of a sensitivity. Compulsions refer to inflexible motivational schemas that certain kinds of behavior are effective in reducing the threat associated with sensitivities. A common compulsion associated with a fear of mice is to be on the alert continuously for their presence, enabling one to avoid being surprised. Compulsions and sensitivities are resistant to modification and extinction because they were learned under conditions of high emotional arousal.

It should be noted that the word *compulsion* as used in CEST differs from its traditional use in one important respect. In its traditional use, it refers to a narrowly defined abnormal class of ritualistic behavior. For example, an individual may have a hand-washing compulsion, in which case he or she may feel compelled to wash his or her hands hundreds of times a day. In CEST, the meaning of the term is expanded to include more general patterns of driven behavior that are relatively common and often include a person's most salient behavioral characteristics.

Sensitivities can be identified from situations that "get to people," that make them unreasonably upset, that their friends know they must avoid if they wish to maintain peace. The hallmarks of compulsions are as follows: (a) the person acts in a rigid way, such as always having to be dominant or always having to be ingratiating; (b) the person experiences distress whenever he or she is unable to behave in the manner fostered by the compulsion; (c) the compulsion is exacerbated to the extent that a relevant sensitivity has been activated.

According to CEST, sensitivities and compulsions, not repression, are among the most fundamental sources of maladaptive behavior. Repression introduces an important complication that makes the source and sometimes the nature of the sensitivities and compulsions unavailable to awareness. Accordingly, in many cases, removing repressions, that is, making the unconscious conscious, can be helpful in identifying the problem in the experiential system that has to be solved, but is rarely sufficient for correcting maladaptive behavior because the initial sensitivities and compulsions remain intact.

A good example of the limitations of insight is provided by the case of a fighter pilot in World War II who nearly had his left wing shot off (Bond, 1952). He became so sensitized to attacks from the left that he compulsively scanned the sky for enemy aircraft approaching from that direction, while neglecting the possibility of an attack from the right. He also developed a compulsion to fire at objects on the left, including weather balloons and birds. Despite his awareness that such reactions could cost him his life, he felt powerless to control them. The insight he had into his problem obviously did not make it go away.

FRUSTRATION OF BASIC NEEDS AS A SECOND MAJOR SOURCE OF MALADJUSTMENT

As previously noted, implicit theories of reality are not developed for their own sake, but for the purpose of achieving an emotionally satisfying life, which means satisfying one's basic needs. To the extent that basic needs are unfulfilled, the entire conceptual system is placed under stress, and, if the stress continues to mount, the end-state is disorganization of the conceptual system, corresponding to an acute schizophrenic reaction. This phenomenon presumably evolved because of its adaptive significance. Disorganization of the elements in a system can provide the opportunity for a new, more effective organization to be constructed (for further discussion of this issue, see Epstein, 1979).

One important reason basic needs in the experiential system are frustrated is because they conflict with motives in the rational system. As people may not even know what their frustrated basic needs are, they are often not in a position to take active steps to fulfill them. Rather, they are likely to view the problem as a failure to fulfill consciously identifiable motives in the rational system. This is particularly apt to be the case in people who are so highly invested in their rational systems that they are out of touch with their experiential systems. Horney (1950) views such people as having a "false self," which she considers to be the central problem in neurosis. In the language of CEST, such people, being overly invested in their rational self, are alienated from their experiential self. An important aspect of therapy, according to CEST, is to find adaptive ways of fulfilling the frustrated needs in the experiential self.

INCOHERENCE AS A THIRD MAJOR SOURCE OF MALADJUSTMENT

It will be recalled that establishing and maintaining a coherent conceptual system for organizing the data of experience and directing behavior is one of the four basic needs in the experiential system. Accordingly, a discussion of the consequences of a failure to fulfill this need could have been included in the preceding section. However, a failure to establish or maintain coherence, harmony, or congruence is sufficiently unique and complicated to warrant discussion in its own right.

According to CEST, there are three possible kinds of incoherence: (1) incoherence within the experiential system, (2) incoherence within the rational system, and (3) incoherence between the two systems. Incoherence between the two systems has already been discussed in the form of alienation from the experiential self, or as the disparity between true and false selves. It should be noted that one of the important consequences of alienation from the experiential self is that it prevents fulfillment of the person's basic needs in the experiential self. This illustrates that the three major sources of maladjustment are not completely independent but interact with each other.

Not all conflicts between the two systems are as encompassing as an overall incoherence between the two self-systems. Most, such as everyday conflicts between the heart and the head, are much more limited in scope and therefore in their maladaptive consequences. An example is a person who has to decide between purchasing a car that he or she finds very attractive but knows has a poor service record and one that has the opposite characteristics. Admittedly, similar conflicts can be more serious if they encompass more significant life issues, such as in having to decide between marrying a person who is more fun to be with or one who is likely to be a better provider and parent to one's children.

Turning to incoherence within the rational system, it normally is associated with only minor problems in adjustment. To be sure, people are expected to be logically consistent, and when they are not, the contradictions in their logic are often criticized. Nevertheless, most people appear to live contentedly with many such contradictions. When they are called to their attention, they can either deny or rationalize their inconsistencies or acknowledge them and either correct them or shrug them off.

It is another matter when the incoherence is completely within the experiential system, for if such a state is sufficiently encompassing, it can render the system incapable of effectively functioning, which would be accompanied by overwhelming anxiety. An example of this is the occurrence of posttraumatic stress disorder (PTSD) following an experience that is so emotionally intense that it cannot be ignored and so discrepant with a person's previous view of the world that it cannot be assimilated. The result is a conflict between two basic world views. How such a conflict is ultimately resolved, as previously noted, is critically important with respect to the person's adjustment (Epstein, 1991a). The treatment of such a disorder, according to CEST, is to help the person establish a broader conceptual system that can assimilate both world views by recognizing that, although the world is potentially far more dangerous than initially imagined, it still offers the possibility for leading a happy and fulfilling life. The challenge with respect to this solution, of course, is in having the message reach the experiential system and not just the rational system.

A less encompassing kind of incoherence within the experiential system that can produce serious problems in living is a conflict between broad motivational systems, such as between the desire for autonomy and relatedness. Such conflicts are more or less debilitating depending on the intensity and breadth of the motives that are involved and their degree of perceived incompatibility. Therapy, according to CEST, consists of finding an integrative solution, such as having the person learn at the experiential level that it is possible to have a love relationship in which one's autonomy is supported rather than stifled.

ADDITIONAL INFORMATION ABOUT CEST

It is beyond the scope of this chapter to describe CEST in greater detail. More complete information can be found elsewhere. (For reviews of the overall theory, see Epstein 1973, 1980, 1991c, 1993c, 1994; for in-depth discussions of particular aspects of the theory, see Epstein, 1976, 1983b, 1984, 1985, 1987, 1990, 1991a, 1991b, 1993a, 1993b; Epstein & Erskine, 1983; Epstein & Katz, 1992; Epstein, Lipson, Holstein, & Huh, 1992; Epstein & Meier, 1989.)

RESEARCH SUPPORT

Research from a wide variety of dual-mode processing theories other than CEST has produced findings that are consistent with formulations in CEST (Epstein, 1994). Rather than attempt to review this vast literature, the review presented here will emphasize research specifically designed to test hypotheses derived from CEST.

RESEARCH ON HEURISTIC PROCESSING

Heuristic processing refers to the use of cognitive shortcuts for arriving at decisions under conditions of uncertainty. Much of our research on heuristic processing is modeled after an influential series of studies conducted by Tversky and Kahneman (1974, 1983) and their associates (Kahneman, Slovic, & Tversky, 1982) that demonstrated that people typically think in heuristic ways that are automatic, rapid, and efficient but are error prone when judged against logical standards. Of particular interest to us was the observation that the principles of heuristic processing inductively derived by cognitive psychologists such as Tversky and Kahneman could be explained by the principles of operation of the experiential system as described in CEST (Epstein, 1994; Epstein et al., 1992). We were so impressed by this correspondence of principles that my associates and I embarked on an extensive research program to more thoroughly test the validity of the principles of the experiential system by employing modifications of the vignettes used by Tversky, Kahneman, and other cognitive psychologists. We provide a brief, selective review of the research we conducted on heuristic processing with the use of vignettes in the following section.

Arbitrary Outcome-Oriented Processing

People in everyday life often irrationally judge a person by outcomes that are only arbitrarily associated with the person's behavior. For example, a messenger who brings good news is treated with special favor, whereas one who delivers an unfavorable message is treated less kindly—and at one time might have paid for it with his head. That people react in such a manner makes no sense, of course, for the messenger is simply doing his or her job. Yet, the behavior toward the messenger is perfectly understandable from the associationistic principle of the experiential system.

To examine reactions to arbitrary outcomes more systematically with a particular interest in the role of a nonrational, experiential processing mode as contrasted with a rational, analytical processing mode, we conducted a study (Epstein et al., 1992) in which participants were requested to respond in three ways to vignettes with arbitrary outcomes: how they believed most people would react in everyday life; how they, themselves, would react; and how a completely logical person would react. An example of a vignette we adapted from Tversky and Kahneman was one that described two protagonists who arrived at an airport a half-hour late for their scheduled flights. One of them learned that her flight had left on time and the other that her flight was delayed and had just left. Participants are asked to judge which protagonist, if either, was more upset. Since the outcome was beyond the control of the protagonists, and since the consequences were identical, a completely logical person would be equally upset in the two conditions. Of course, the point of the study is to demonstrate that most people know that they and others would not react that way, but rather would react according to the principles of the experiential system.

According to CEST, although all behavior is determined by a combination of both processing modes, in everyday life most behavior, particularly where interpersonal relations are involved, is determined primarily by the automatic operation of the experiential system. Under appropriate circumstances, such as doing arithmetic problems and discussing philosophy, however, people can and do switch to operating almost exclusively in the rational mode. Responses from the self- and others-perspective in our experiment were assumed to be primarily under the jurisdiction of the experiential system, and responses from the logical perspective were assumed to be primarily under the jurisdiction of the rational system. In order to test the hypothesis that the two modes of processing are interactive, we presented the logical mode first in half of the cases and last in the other half. This allowed us to determine whether the first mode of processing would influence the second.

We tested the following hypotheses: There exist two different modes of information processing, experiential and rational, that operate by different rules; the experiential system is an associationistic system that connects events by similarity and proximity rather than by an understanding of causality; the systems are interactive, so that processing in one system can influence subsequent processing in the other.

All of the hypotheses were supported. Because they were derived from CEST, the results contributed to the construct validity of CEST. Support for the last hypothesis is of particular interest because it suggests that automatic processing in the experiential system can bias conscious processing in the rational system. To the extent this is true, it follows that try as one might, one cannot be rational unless one is aware of and can compensate for one's automatic experiential processing.

The Ratio-Bias Phenomenon

Imagine that on every trial in which you blindly pick a red jelly bean from a bowl containing red and white jelly beans you receive two dollars. To make matters interesting, you have a choice between drawing from two bowls, each of which contains 10% red beans. The smaller bowl has a total of 10 jelly beans, one of which is red; the larger one has a total of 100 jelly beans, 10 of which are red. Which tray would you choose to draw from? How much would you pay for the privilege of drawing from the tray of your choice, rather than having the decision made by the flip of a coin?

This situation provides an interesting paradigm for testing fundamental assumptions in CEST because it pits the experiential system against the rational system. It does so because the experiential system is a concretive system that is responsive to numerosity (the frequency of items) but is less able to comprehend ratios; whereas the rational system, as an abstract system, can understand ratios. It follows that people should be attracted (in their experiential system) to the large bowl because it has more winning beans, but should recognize (in their rational system) that it makes no difference from which bowl they draw.

When participants in a study by Kirkpatrick and Epstein (1992) were given the above problem in the form of a vignette, most said they would have no preference between the two trays and would not pay a cent for the privilege of choosing between them. However, when participants were presented with the real situation, which was expected to be more compelling to the experiential system, most chose from the large bowl and readily parted with dimes for the privilege of doing so. Many sheepishly commented that they knew their behavior was irrational, but somehow they felt they had a better chance of getting a red jelly bean when there were more of them.

We refer to the phenomenon of assigning a greater subjective probability for an event represented by a ratio of two smaller numbers than the same ratio represented by two larger numbers as the *ratio-bias phenomenon*. In studies of the ratio-bias phenomenon in which uneven ratios were presented in the two bowls (e.g., Denes-Raj & Epstein, 1994), most participants preferred to draw from a bowl that contained more red jelly beans but offered only an 8% chance of winning (e.g., 8 in 100) than from one that had fewer red jelly beans but offered a 10% chance of winning (e.g., 1 in 10).

In a study of elementary school children by Pacini, Epstein, & Barrows (1998), they found that children who did not understand ratios made their choices almost exclusively on the basis of the numerosity of the target beans, preferring, for example, a 2% chance of winning that offered them more red jelly beans to choose (e.g., 2 in 100) than a 10% chance that offered fewer red jelly beans (e.g., 1 in 10). The children who understood ratios behaved in between the children who did not know ratios and the adults, many of whom selected a 9% probability (9 in 100) over a 10% probability (1 in 10). Unlike the children who did not understand ratios, none of the children who understood ratios selected 2% over 10% probabilities, but most selected 5% over 10% probabilities so long as there was a greater number of red jelly beans in the 5% condition. Thus, like the adults, the children who understood ratios exhibited a compromise between their experiential and rational modes of information processing. They differed from the adults by compromising between the two modes in a manner that favored the experiential system to a greater extent. Therefore, the results on compromises suggest that rational dominance tends to increase with maturity, but that it is less than complete even in adults' responses to a task as simple as the jelly bean experiment.

Other research (Pacini *et al.*, 1996) has demonstrated that vividly imagining the jelly beans when responding to vignettes produces results similar to those obtained in real situations but different from findings with vignettes in the absence of imagination.

A finding that has generated considerable interest is that depressed people are often more accurate in laboratory experiments than nondepressed controls. The finding that depressives are more realistic than nondepressives is in direct contradiction to CEST and cognitive theories of depression that assume that the emotions of depressives are the result of unrealistic negative cognitions (e.g., Abramson, Metalsky, & Alloy, 1989; Abramson, Seligman, & Teasdale, 1978; Beck, 1967). Support for the cognitive position has been provided recently by research that is more realistic and emotionally engaging than the initial research (see reviews in Ackerman & DuRubeis, 1991; Colvin & Block, 1994; Dobson & Franche, 1989). This research raises the question of why depressives are more realistic than others in laboratory situations that are relatively uninvolving and remote from everyday experience. The answer according to CEST is that depressives in such situations compensate in their rational system for the unrealistic information processing in their experiential system. When they are more emotionally engaged, their rational control is not sufficient to suppress their unrealistic experiential processing. For nondepressives, the situation is reversed: They rely on their automatic processing in unimportant situations but behave more rationally in situations that are important to them.

Support for this interpretation was provided in a study by Pacini, Muir, and Epstein (in press) that compared the responses of depressives and controls to the jelly bean task under two incentive conditions, $.10 versus $2.00, on each trial in which a red jelly bean was drawn. In support of hypothesis, depressives were more realistic (i.e., made more optimal choices) than controls only in the low-incentive condition. In the high-incentive condition, the depressives became less realistic and the controls became more realistic, so the groups converged, as predicted.

A postexperiment questionnaire revealed that the depressives were more unrealistic than the nondepressives in many ways, including basing their predictions of future outcomes in the jelly bean task less on their actual experience and more on a personal agenda. The depressives also obtained scores in a self-report inventory that indicated that they were more experiential and less rational than the controls. Of particular interest was the relatively strong positive correlation for the depressives between their experiential scores and nonoptimal responses in the jelly bean task, suggesting that reliance on experiential processing was more maladaptive for the depressives than for the controls.

In summary, the findings from these and other jelly bean experiments (Denes-Raj & Epstein, 1994; Epstein, 1994; Kirkpatrick & Epstein, 1992; Pacini et al., 1996; Pacini et al., in press) provide support for the following hypotheses derived from CEST: There are two different modes of information processing, rational and experiential, which can conflict with each other; each system can override the other; experiential processing can be experienced as more compelling even when people "know better" in their rational system; the experiential system is more responsive to concrete than to abstract representations; the experiential system is primarily an imagistic system; the experiential system is more responsive to affirmative than to negative representations; there are important individual differences in the extent to which people rely on experiential relative to rational processing and in the adequacy of their experiential processing.

The Sequential Relation of Experiential and Rational Processing

As already noted, a basic assumption in CEST is that the two modes of information processing are interactive. For example, processing in one mode influences subsequent processing in the other mode. Processing in the experiential mode usually occurs first and is often followed by more deliberative responses in the rational mode, which often serve corrective functions. In one of our studies (reported in Epstein, 1993c, 1994), subjects were asked to respond to vignettes that described arbitrary unfavorable outcomes by listing the first three thoughts that came to mind. The first thought was usually consistent with the principles of the experiential system, whereas the third was consistent more often with the principles of the rational system. As an example, when subjects put themselves in the place of a protagonist who had an accident while backing an automobile from a space that a friend suggested he park in, many subjects reported their first thought to be that the accident was their friend's fault, and their emotion was one of anger: "It's his fault. Except for him, I wouldn't have had the accident." By the third thought, their thinking was more rational; they accepted the responsibility as their own. They then reported a corresponding change in their emotion from anger to guilt. Similar results were obtained with a wide variety of other vignettes. This study supports CEST assumptions that the experiential system is a rapid, nonrational, associationistic system, in contrast to the rational system, which is a more reflective logical system.

The Good-versus-Bad-Person Heuristic

A study by Sloat (1992) provided evidence of a very high priority "good-versus-bad-person" heuristic that can be attributed to the holistic, categorical nature of information processing in the experiential system. No one in real life is completely good or completely bad; everyone has some redeeming features and some limitations. Although most people know this, they are nevertheless quick to judge people as "good" or "bad," depending on how the person has personally affected them. Relatedly, as the following experiment demonstrates, people are quick to judge others as winners or losers based on the most arbitrary outcomes. Although the good-versus-bad-person heuristic can be derived from more fundamental heuristics in CEST, it warrants a designation in its own right because of its significance.

Participants in the study by Sloat responded to a vignette adapted from Miller and Gunasegaram (1990) that described a situation in which three protagonists are told by a rich benefactor that if each of them throws a coin that comes up heads, he will give each $100. The first two throw a heads, but Smith, the third, throws a tails. The rich benefactor gives them another chance only to have the situation repeat itself. Participants rated the emotions of the three protagonists and judged whether the first two would invite Smith to join them on a gambling vacation in Las Vegas in which they would pool their resources. Most said that Smith would feel guilty, that the others would be angry, and that they definitely would not invite him because "he is a loser." They reported that although they knew such behavior is irrational, this is the way they believed most people, themselves included, behaved in real life. Sophistication about probability statistics had no effect on reported reactions. Moreover, even those who believed in the gambler's fallacy (as determined by endorsement of the statement that following three heads the next throw will probably be a tails) reacted in the same way as the others. To be logically consistent, they should have invited Smith because it was about time he started winning. Apparently, the good-versus-bad person heuristic is a high-priority heuristic that takes precedence over other heuristics, such as the gambler's fallacy.

The study was run in two conditions, one in which subjects were told the prize was $100, and the other in which they were told it was $1.00. The $1.00 condition produced similar results to a reduced degree.

The results of the study on the good-versus-bad-person heuristic support the hypotheses that there are two independent systems for processing information, and that experiential relative to rational processing increases as emotional consequences increase. The results further indicate that the experiential system is not constrained by considerations of internal consistency in the same way that the rational system is. The findings also suggest that the good-versus-bad person heuristic is a particularly high-priority heuristic.

Conjunction Problems

Linda is described as a 31-year-old woman who is single, outspoken, and very bright. In college, she was a philosophy major who participated in antinuclear demonstrations and was concerned with issues of social justice. How would you rank the likelihoods of the following possibilities: Linda is a feminist, Linda is a bank teller, and Linda is both? If you respond like most people, you will rank the probability that Linda is a feminist and a bank teller as greater than that Linda is a bank teller (Tversky & Kahneman, 1983). If you do, you will commit a conjunction error (CE) because the occurrence of two events cannot be more likely than the occurrence of one of them.

Some social cognitive psychologists have expressed their concern that CEs can have dire consequences in real life in situations involving financial matters (Gavanski & Roskos-Ewoldsen, 1989) and medical diagnosis (Tversky & Kahneman, 1983). The interpretation of the phenomenon from the perspective of CEST is more reassuring. According to CEST, the experiential system is generally adaptive in situations that arise in everyday life, and therefore people are unlikely to make CEs in practical situations.

The explanation provided by CEST for the high rate of CEs in response to problems like the "Linda problem" follows from the attributes of the experiential system. Because the experiential system is a natural, concretive system that interprets events in terms of past experience, it fosters appropriate responses in situations that require natural responses and inappropriate responses in situations that require unnatural responses. *Natural* is defined in this context as the customary way in which a particular kind of situation is interpreted, which can be established independently from the occurrence of CEs. In a situation such as in the Linda problem, when information is provided on personality characteristics and behavior, it is natural to interpret the problem as one that requires matching behaviors to personality; the unnatural interpretation is to interpret it as a statistical problem. In situations in which probabilistic responses are natural, such as judging the likelihood of winning two lotteries compared with winning one, virtually everyone, including those without explicit knowledge of the conjunction rule (in their rational system), avoid CEs, thereby demonstrating that their intuitive understanding (in the experiential system) of the conjunction rule is greater than their rational understanding.

Our research on conjunction problems (Epstein, Denes-Raj, & Pacini, 1995) provided evidence consistent with assumptions in CEST that the experiential system is a concretive, natural system; that although it is generally adaptive, it can easily be misled by presenting it with situations that require unnatural responses; and that in natural situations it can be smarter than the rational system.

RESEARCH ON BASIC BELIEFS

The Influence of Life-Events on Basic Beliefs

In a study by Catlin and Epstein (1992), college students filled out a Major Life Events Schedule, in which they reported whether they had experienced a number of very favorable and unfavorable events. They also took the Basic Beliefs Inventory (BBI), which provides scores on the four basic beliefs, and the Mother-Father-Peer (MFP) questionnaire, which provides scores on whether one's parents were accepting versus rejecting and independence encouraging versus over protecting when one was a child. As expected, current basic beliefs were coherently associated with past life events, such as loss of a loved one, and with early relationships with parents. These findings are consistent with the assumption in CEST that basic beliefs are acquired through emotionally significant experiences, including repetitive early experiences with parents.

Changes in Basic Beliefs Following Trauma

In a study of veterans of the Vietnam War, Kenneth Fletcher (1988) compared the basic beliefs of combat veterans suffering from post-traumatic stress disorder (PTSD) with matched combat and noncombat veterans without PTSD. Traumatic experiences were associated with negative changes in all basic beliefs, but some beliefs changed more than others, depending on the nature of the trauma. These findings are consistent with the CEST assumption that basic beliefs are influenced by emotionally significant experiences. Although childhood is a particularly propitious time for the acquisition of basic beliefs, and although the amount of repetitive experience is also important, single events of traumatic intensity can be an important influence on basic beliefs.

Of particular interest was a "negative spiral" observed only in veterans with PTSD. Noncombat veterans and combat veterans without PTSD reported a temporary decline in their positive basic beliefs during their tour of duty in Vietnam and up to six months following return to the United States, after which the positive nature of their basic beliefs rebounded to only slightly below prewar levels. These observations indicate that negative beliefs were gradually relinquished as the veterans experienced a more benign world.

In contrast, the veterans with PTSD reported a continuous decline up to the current period, 20 years after the trauma. How is their continuing negativity to be explained despite their living in a benign environment? Why did the veterans with PTSD not learn from their more recent experiences? According to CEST, an answer is that they had consolidated a view of themselves and the world based on the trauma they had experienced. Once this occurred, they had a vested interest (in their experiential system) in maintaining the stability of this new identity, no matter how much misery it produced. Accordingly, they created and assimilated new experiences in a manner that maintained and enhanced this identity. Although a negative identity is distressing, it has the adaptive advantage of protecting the individual from being surprised and overwhelmed again in the manner of the previous trauma.

Compromises among Basic Beliefs

To test for the existence of compromises between basic beliefs, as proposed in CEST, Morling and Epstein (1997) investigated the interaction of the motives for self-verification and self-enhancement, corresponding in CEST, to basic needs for maintaining a stable conceptual system and enhancing self-esteem, respectively. They conducted three studies in which college students responded to a series of vignettes in which they were told to imagine they had received different levels of favorable and unfavorable feedback from people they had just met. In all studies, enhancement and verification were measured by the degree to which the feedback was more or less favorable than a person's self-assessment. As predicted, participants favored feedback that was slightly more favorable than their own self-assessments, thereby providing evidence of a compromise between self-enhancement and self-verification. More favorable assessments were undesirable because they threatened a person's desire for verification; less favorable assessments were undesirable because they threatened a person's desire for enhancement.

INDIVIDUAL DIFFERENCES IN EXPERIENTIAL PROCESSING

In CEST, it is assumed that there are important individual differences in the degree to which individuals employ the two modes of information processing and in their effectiveness in doing so. Two self-report instruments have been constructed to investigate these assumptions: the Rational-Experiential Inventory (REI), which assesses intuitive-experiential and analytical-rational thinking styles (Epstein *et al.*, 1996), and the Constructive Thinking Inventory (CTI), which assesses *constructive thinking,* defined as the ability to solve problems in everyday living at a minimum cost in stress. Constructive thinking, as measured by the CTI, is primarily a measure of the adaptiveness of experiential processing (Epstein & Meier, 1989).

Individual Differences in Degree and Coherence of Experiential and Rational Information Processing

In addition to the assumption in CEST that there are individual differences in the degree to which people rely on their experiential and rational modes of information processing, it is assumed that responses across different situations with the same underlying theme are more consistent when people respond from a rational perspective than when they respond from an experiential one. This follows from the more situation-specific operation of the experiential system and the more context-free operation of the rational system. To test these hypotheses, a study in which participants responded to a varied sample of vignettes from experiential (how people actually behave) and rational (how a completely logical person would behave) perspectives was conducted. In support of the hypothesis, broad, reliable individual differences were found for both kinds of responses, and the responses from a rational perspective had a higher degree of coherence, indicated by a much higher coefficient of internal consistency than responses from an experiential perspective. Furthermore, individual differences in responses to the vignettes were reliably and coherently associated with scores on the REI self-report scales of experiential and rational processing, to which we turn next.

The REI contains two self-report scales, a modified Need for Cognition (NFC) scale (Cacioppo & Petty, 1982) and a newly constructed Faith in Intuition (FI) scale (Epstein *et al.*, in press). The NFC scale provides a measure of rational processing; the FI, of experiential processing. Typical items in the NFC scale are, "I prefer complex to simple problems," and "I don't like to have to do a lot of thinking" (reverse scored). Typical items in the FI include, "I believe in trusting my hunches," and "I can usually feel when a person is right or wrong, even if I can't explain how I know." It might be expected that the scales are inversely related. However, they are virtually independent and, accordingly, establish significant correlations with different variables rather than opposite correlations with the same variables. The FI scale is more strongly directly associated with heuristic responses to vignettes with arbitrary outcomes, with establishing secure relationships with partners, with unusual beliefs, and with a belief in superstitions than the NFC scale. The NFC scale is more strongly directly associated with self-esteem, dominance, SAT verbal and quantitative scores, emotional and behavioral coping ability, and dismissive relationships with romantic partners. It is also more strongly inversely associated with racist attitudes, depression, anxiety, stress in college life, and self-reported alcohol consumption than the FI scale. These relations indicate that each style of information processing has its advantages and disadvantages. They further suggest that insofar as good adjustment is concerned people cannot afford to reason irrationally, but they have considerable latitude in the degree to which they reason experientially.

Because the two styles of information processing are independent, four types of people can readily be selected: those who are high on both variables, those who are low on both, those who are high on one and low on the other, and those who exhibit the reverse combination. Current research is exploring the differences among these types.

Individual Differences in the "Intelligence" of the System

Just as there is an intelligence of the rational system, there is an intelligence of the experiential system. Remember that constructive thinking is defined as the ability to solve problems in living at a minimum cost in stress, and that it is considered to be determined primarily by information processing in the experiential system, which can be measured by the Constructive Thinking Inventory (CTI). The CTI contains mainly items that describe the ways that people automatically think in everyday life. For example, "I tend to classify people as either for me or against me," and, "If I said something foolish when I spoke up in a group, I would chalk it up to experience and not worry about it." The CTI provides a global scale of constructive thinking and six main scales, most of which contain several facets, or subscales. The main scales are Emotional Coping, Behavioral Coping, Categorical Thinking, Naive Optimism, Personal Superstitious Thinking, and Esoteric Thinking. Emotional Coping includes subscales of Self-Acceptance, Absence of Negative Overgeneralization, Nonsensitivity, and Absence of Dwelling on Past Events, for example. Facets of Behavioral Coping include Positive Thinking, Action Orientation, and Conscientiousness.

In support of hypotheses, scores on the CTI have been found to be unrelated to IQ and to be positively associated with a wide variety of measures of success in living, including success in the workplace, success in human relations, and emotional and physical well-being (e.g., Epstein, 1992, 1993a, 1993b, 1993c; Epstein & Brodsky, 1993; Epstein & Katz, 1992; Epstein & Meier, 1989; Katz & Epstein, 1991).

SUMMARY OF THE RESEARCH FINDINGS

The research on nonrational thinking provides support for the CEST assumption that there are two independent modes of information processing that operate by different principles. Many of our findings support the principles of operation of the experiential system outlined in Table 9.1. Of particular interest are the number of the investigations that revealed conflict between the two systems, with subjects often finding the outcome of processing in the experiential mode more compelling than processing in the rational mode. In other words, they favored the heuristic choice despite "knowing better," even when winning and losing money was at stake. There was also support for reliable individual differences in the efficacy of and the degree of engagement in rational and experiential reasoning, which were found, as hypothesized, to be broadly associated with a wide variety of variables, including mental and physical well-being.

BROADER IMPLICATIONS OF COGNITIVE-EXPERIENTIAL SELF-THEORY

According to CEST, the experiential system processes information over a wide range of complexity. In its lower and moderate reaches, its operation is manifested in conditioning and in the rapid and automatic processing identified as heuristics. It is important to recognize that the experiential system is sometimes more effective in solving problems than the rational system (e.g., Epstein & Denes-Raj, 1993; Lewicki, Hill, & Czyzewska, 1992). Relatedly, it has been demonstrated that people often have intuitive knowledge that they can effectively apply without being aware of the principles that are involved (e.g., Epstein & Denes-Raj, 1993; Nisbett & Ross, 1980). Moreover, rational analysis in some circumstances can interfere with the efficient functioning of the experiential system, resulting in people making poorer judgments than when they respond according to unanalyzed, intuitive impressions (Wilson & Schooler, 1991).

The experiential system also has the capacity to operate at higher levels of complexity (e.g., Fisk & Schneider, 1983; Lewicki, Hill, & Czyzewska, 1992) and to contribute to intuitive wisdom (e.g., Bucci, 1985). This assumption identifies an important area for research. Relatively little is currently known about it, very likely because there has been an absence of theory for encouraging such research. Hopefully, recent developments in theory (e.g., Bucci, 1985, 1997; Curtis & Zaslow, 1991; Epstein 1991c, 1993c, 1994; Labouvie-Vief, 1989, 1990; Singer & Singer, 1990) and research techniques (Lewicki et al., 1992) will remedy this situation. In sum, the experiential system has important implications for understanding the nature of creativity and intuition.

Another important implication follows from the intimate association of the experiential system with emotions. As a result of this relationship, the content and organization of the schemas in the experiential system are associated with physical well-being as well as with mental well-being. Such a relationship has been demonstrated in a series of studies on emotional and minor physical disorders (e.g., Epstein 1987, 1990, 1991a, 1992a, 1992b, 1993a; Epstein & Katz, 1992; Epstein & Meier, 1989; Katz & Epstein, 1991). That the processing in the experiential system has the potential for influencing the course of more serious diseases is suggested by unusual cures that have been attributed to faith healing, shamanism, and placebo effects. An important challenge for future research is to learn how to harness the power of the experiential system for alleviating illness and promoting well-being. Integration within and between the two systems will very likely be found to be important, in this respect. A remarkable case history (A. Epstein, 1989) revealed the potential of such an approach in the treatment of a case of terminal cancer from which the likelihood of remission was negligible. Following the use of fantasy procedures designed to communicate with the experiential system, there was a surprisingly rapid reorganization of the personality, followed by complete recovery from the disease.

As already noted, CEST, through its assumption of an experiential system, can account for important behavioral phenomena, such as the ubiquity of superstitions and religion and the nature of appeals in politics and in advertising, about which other personality theories have had little to say.

The experiential system also has important implications for psychotherapy (Epstein, 1983b, 1984, 1985, 1987, 1991a, 1991c, 1993a, 1993c; Epstein & Brodsky, 1993). According to CEST, the objective of therapy is to produce changes in the experiential system.

There are three basic procedures for accomplishing this: (a) the use of the rational system to correct the experiential system (e.g., disputing irrational thoughts, as in cognitive therapy); (b) learning directly from emotionally significant experiences (e.g., by "working through" in real life, and through constructive relationships with significant others, including therapists); and (c) communicating with the experiential system in its own medium, namely fantasy. This last approach is particularly promising because, not only can the rational system use directed fantasy to influence the experiential system, but it also can learn from the experiential system by understanding how that system operates. These three fundamental approaches provide a unifying framework for integrating the various approaches in psychotherapy, including insight approaches, cognitive-behavioral approaches, and experiential approaches, such as Gestalt therapy and psychosynthesis (Epstein, 1993c, 1994; Epstein & Brodsky, 1993).

A FINAL COMMENT

Having begun the chapter with a quotation from Allport, it is fitting to close with one. The following statement by Allport illustrates the pervasive influence of heuristic on rational reasoning, even in highly sophisticated psychologists: "It required years of effort and billions of dollars to gain the secret of the atom. It will take a still greater investment to gain the secret of man's irrational nature" (Allport, 1954, p. xvii). From a heuristic way of thinking, it may seem apparent that the solution to important problems on which the very fate of humankind may depend will require a prodigious effort and investment of resources. Yet, there is no law of logic that states that the more important the problem, the more complicated the solution. Would it not be ironic if the very elusiveness of the solution is itself a consequence of the quest for complexity? After all, the laws of gravity and of the relationship between mass and energy, which describe fundamental properties of the universe, are summarized in equations that require no more space than a single small word. The point is that the simplicity, clarity, and parsimony of a theory should be regarded as virtues, not as an absence of profundity or significance.

Acknowledgments: Preparation of this manuscript and the research reported in it were supported by NIMH research grant MH 01293 and NIMH Research Scientist Award 5 KO5 MH00363 to Epstein.
I wish to express my appreciation to Alice Epstein for her constructive criticisms and to the many students and associates without whose help the research reported here could not have been conducted.

REFERENCES

Abramson, L. Y., Metalsky, G. I., & Alloy, L. B. (1989). Hopelessness depression: A theory-based subtype of depression. *Psychological Review, 96,* 358–372.
Abramson, L. Y., Seligman, M. E. P., & Teasdale, J. (1978). Learned helplessness in humans: Critique and reformulation. *Journal of Abnormal Psychology, 87,* 49–74.
Ackerman, R., & DeRubeis, R. J. (1991). Is depressive realism real? *Clinical Psychology Review, 11,* 565–584.
Adler, A. (1954). *Understanding human nature.* New York: Fawcett.
Allport, G. W. (1954). *The nature of prejudice.* Reading, MA: Addison-Wesley.

Allport, G. W. (1961). *Pattern and growth in personality.* New York: Holt, Rinehart & Winston.

Allport, G. W. (1965). *Letters from Jenny.* New York: Harcourt, Brace & World.

Averill, J. R. (1980). A constructionist view of emotion. In R. Plutchik & H. Kellerman (Eds.), *Emotion, theory, research, and experience: Vol. 1. Theories of emotion* (pp. 305–339). San Diego, CA: Academic Press.

Bargh, J. A. (1989). Conditional automaticity: Varieties of automatic influence in social perception and cognition. In J. S. Uleman & J. A. Bargh (Eds.), *Unintended thought* (pp. 3–51). New York: Guilford Press.

Beck, A. T. (1967). *Depression: Clinical, experimental, and theoretical aspects.* New York: Harper & Row.

Beck, A. T. (1976). *Cognitive therapy and the emotional disorders.* New York: International Universities Press.

Bond, D. D. (1952). *The love and fear of flying.* New York: International Universities Press.

Bowlby, J. (1988). *A secure base.* New York: Basic Books.

Brewin, C. R. (1989). Cognitive change processes in psychotherapy. *Psychological Review, 96,* 379–394.

Bruner, J. (1986). *Actual minds, possible worlds.* Cambridge, MA: Harvard University Press.

Bucci, W. (1985). Dual coding: A cognitive model for psychoanalytic research. *Journal of the American Psychoanalytic Association, 33,* 571–607.

Bucci, W. (1997). *Psychoanalysis and cognitive science: A multiple code theory.* New York: Guilford Press.

Cacioppo, J. T., & Petty, R. E. (1982). The need for cognition. *Journal of Personality and Social Psychology, 42,* 116–131.

Catlin, G., & Epstein, S. (1992). Unforgettable experiences: The relation of life-events to basic beliefs about self and world. *Social Cognition, 10,* 189–209.

Colvin, C. R., & Block, J. (1994). Do positive illusions foster mental health? An examination of the Taylor and Brown formulation. *Psychological Bulletin, 116,* 3–20.

Curtis, R. C., ,& Zaslow, G. (1991). Seeing with the third eye: Cognitive-affective regulation and the acquisition of self-knowledge. In R. Curtis (Ed.), *The relational self: Convergences in psychoanalysis and social psychology* (pp. 140–159). New York: Guilford Press.

Denes-Raj, V., & Epstein, S. (1994). Conflict between experiential and rational processing: When people behave against their better judgment. *Journal of Personality and Social Psychology, 66,* 819–829.

Dobson, K. S., & Franche, R. L. (1989). A conceptual and empirical review of the depressive realism hypothesis. *Canadian Journal of Behavioural Science, 21,* 419–433.

Ellis, A. (1973). *Humanistic psychotherapy.* New York: Macmillan.

Epstein, A. (1989). *Mind, fantasy, and healing.* New York: Delacorte. (Out of print copies can be obtained by writing to Balderwood Books, 37 Bay Road, Amherst, MA 01002 and enclosing a check for $18.00, which includes postage and handling.)

Epstein, S. (1973). The self-concept revisited, or a theory of a theory. *American Psychologist, 28,* 404–416.

Epstein, S. (1976). Anxiety, arousal and the self-concept. In I. G. Sarason & C. D. Spielberger (Eds.), *Stress and anxiety* (pp. 183–224). Washington, DC: Hemisphere Publishing.

Epstein, S. (1980). The self-concept: A review and the proposal of an integrated theory of personality. In E. Staub (Ed.), *Personality: Basic issues and current research* (pp. 82–132). Englewood Cliffs, NJ: Prentice Hall.

Epstein, S. (1983a). A research paradigm for the study of personality and emotions. In M. M. Page (Ed.), *Personality—Current Theory and Research: 1982 Nebraska Symposium on Motivation* (pp. 91–154). Lincoln: University of Nebraska Press.

Epstein, S. (1983b). The unconscious, the preconscious and the self-concept. In J. Suls & A. Greenwald (Eds.), *Psychological perspectives on the self* (Vol. 2, pp. 219–247). Hillsdale, NJ: Erlbaum.

Epstein, S. (1984). Controversial issues in emotion theory. In P. Shavaer (Ed.), *Annual review of research in personality and social psychology* (pp. 64–87). Beverly Hills, CA: Sage.

Epstein, S. (1985). The implications of cognitive-experiential self-theory for research in social psychology and personality. *Journal for the Theory of Social Behaviour, 15,* 283–310.

Epstein, S. (1987). Implications of cognitive self-theory for psychopathology and psychotherapy. In N. Cheshire & H. Thomae (Eds.), *Self, symptoms and psychotherapy* (pp. 43–58). New York: Wiley.

Epstein, S. (1990). Cognitive-experiential self-theory. In L. Pervin (Ed.), *Handbook of personality theory and research: Theory and research* (pp. 165–192). New York: Guilford Press.

Epstein, S. (1991a). The self-concept, the traumatic neurosis, and the structure of personality. In D. Ozer, J. M. Healy Jr., & A. J. Stewart (Eds.), *Perspectives in personality* (Vol. 3A, pp. 63–98). London: Jessica Kingsley Publishers.

Epstein, S. (1991b). Cognitive-experiential self-theory: Implications for developmental psychology. In M. Gunnar & L. A. Sroufe (Eds.), *Self-processes and development, Vol. 23. Minnesota Symposia on Child Psychology* (pp. 79–123). Hillsdale, NJ: Erlbaum.

Epstein, S. (1991c). Cognitive-experiential self-theory: An integrative theory of personality. In R. Curtis (Ed.), *The relational self: Convergences in psychoanalysis and social psychology* (pp. 111–137). New York: Guilford Press.

Epstein, S. (1992a). Constructive thinking and mental and physical well-being. In L. Montada, S. H. Filipp, & M. J. Lerner (Eds.), *Life crises and experiences of loss in adulthood* (pp. 385–409). Hillsdale, NJ: Erlbaum.

Epstein, S. (1992b). Coping ability, negative self-evaluation, and overgeneralization: Experiment and theory. *Journal of Personality and Social Psychology, 62,* 826–836.

Epstein, S. (1993a). Bereavement from the perspective of Cognitive-experiential self-theory. In M. S. Stroebe, W. Stroebe, & R. O. Hansson (Eds.), *Handbook of bereavement: Theory, research, and intervention* (pp. 112–125). New York: Cambridge University Press.

Epstein, S. (1993b). Emotion and self-theory. In M. Lewis & J. Haviland (Eds.), *Handbook of emotions* (pp. 313–326). New York: Guilford Press.

Epstein, S. (1993c). Implications of cognitive-experiential self-theory for personality and developmental psychology. In D. Funder, R. Parke, C. Tomlinson-Keasey, & K. Widamen (Eds.), *Studying lives through time: Personality and development* (pp. 399–438). Washington, DC: American Psychological Association.

Epstein, S. (1994). Integration of the cognitive and the psychodynamic unconscious. *American Psychologist, 49,* 709–724.

Epstein, S., & Brodsky, A. (1993). *You're smarter than you think.* New York: Simon & Schuster.

Epstein, S., & Denes-Raj, V. (1993). Conjoint probability: The influence of context and cueing effects on solutions to the Linda problem. In review.

Epstein, S. (1992). Constructive thinking and mental and physical well-being. In L. Montada, S. H. Filipp, & M. J. Lerner (Eds.), *Life crises and experiences of loss in adulthood* (pp. 385–409). Hillsdale, NJ: Erlbaum.

Epstein, S., Denes-Raj, V., & Pacini, R. (1995). The Linda problem revisited from the perspective of cognitive-experiential self-theory. *Personality and Social Psychology Bulletin, 11,* 1124–1138.

Epstein, S., & Erskine, N. (1983). The development of personal theories of reality. In D. Magnusson & V. Allen (Eds.), *Human development: An interactional perspective* (pp. 133–147). New York: Academic Press.

Epstein, S., & Katz, L. (1992). Coping ability, stress, productive load, and symptoms. *Journal of Personality and Social Psychology, 62,* 813–825.

Epstein, S., Lipson, A., Holstein, C., & Huh, E. (1992). Irrational reactions to negative outcomes: Evidence for two conceptual systems. *Journal of Personality and Social Psychology, 62,* 328–339.

Epstein, S., & Meier, P. (1989). Constructive thinking: A broad coping variable with specific components. *Journal of Personality and Social Psychology, 57,* 332–350.

Epstein, S., Pacini, R., Denes-Raj, V., & Heier, H. (1996). Individual differences in intuitive-experiential and analytical-rational thinking style. *Journal of Personality and Social Psychology, 71,* 390–405.

Fairbairn, W. R. D. (1954). *An object relations theory of the personality.* New York: Basic Books.

Fazio, R. H., & Zanna, M. P. (1981). Direct experience and attitude-behavior consistency. In L. Berkowitz (Ed.), *Advances in experimental social psychology* (Vol. 14, pp. 162–203). New York: Academic Press.

Fisk, A. D., & Schneider, W. (1983). Category and word search: Generalizing search principles to complex processing. *Journal of Experimental Psychology: Learning, Memory, and Cognition, 9,* 177–195.

Fletcher, K. E. (1988). *Belief systems, exposure to stress, and posttraumatic stress disorder in Vietnam veterans.* Unpublished doctoral dissertation, University of Massachusetts-Amherst.

Freud, S. (1953). The interpretation of dreams. In J. Strachey (Ed. and Trans.), *The standard edition of the complete psychological works of Sigmund Freud* (Vols. 4–5). London: Hogarth Press. (Original published in 1900)

Freud, S. (1959). *Beyond the pleasure principle.* New York: W. W. Norton. (Original work published 1920)

Gavanski, I., & Roskos-Ewoldsen, D. R. (1989). Representativeness and conjoint probability. *Journal of Personality and Social Psychology, 61,* 181–194.

Higgins, E. T. (1989). Knowledge accessibility and activation: Subjectivity and suffering from unconscious sources. In J. S. Uleman & J. A. Bargh (Eds.), *Unintended thought* (pp. 75–123). New York: Guilford Press.

Horney, K. (1950). *Neurosis and human growth.* New York: Norton.

James, W. (1910). *Psychology: The briefer course.* New York: Holt.

Kahneman, D., Slovic, P., & Tversky, A. (1982). *Judgment under uncertainty: Heuristics and biases.* New York: Cambridge University Press.

Kahneman, D., & Tversky, A. (1973). On the psychology of prediction. *Psychology Review, 80,* 237–251.

Katz, L., & Epstein, S. (1991). Constructive thinking and coping with laboratory-induced stress. *Journal of Personality and Social Psychology, 61,* 789–800.

Kirkpatrick, L. A., & Epstein, S. (1992). Cognitive-experiential self-theory and subjective probability: Further evidence for two conceptual systems. *Journal of Personality and Social Psychology, 63,* 534–544.

Kohut, H. (1971). *The analysis of the self.* New York: International Universities Press.

Labouvie-Vief, G. (1989). Modes of knowledge and the organization of development. In M. L. Commons, J. D. Sinnott, F. A. Richards, & C. Armon (Eds.), *Adult development* (Vol. 2, pp. 43–62). New York: Praeger.

Labouvie-Vief, G. (1990). Wisdom as integrated thought: Historical and developmental perspectives. In R. J. Sternberg (Ed.), *Wisdom: Its nature, origins, and development* (pp. 52–83). New York: Cambridge University Press.

Lazarus, R. S. (1982). Thoughts on the relations between emotion and cognition. *American Psychologist, 37,* 1019–1024.

Lecky, P. (1961). *Self-consistency: A theory of personality.* Hamden, CT: Shoe String Press.

Lewicki, P., Hill, T., ,& Czyzewska, M. (1992). Nonconscious acquisition of information. *American Psychologist, 47,* 796–801.

Miller, D. T., & Gunasegaram, S. (1990). Temporal order and the perceived mutability of events: Implications for blame assignment. *Journal of Personality and Social Psychology, 59,* 1111–1118.

Morling, B., & Epstein, S. (1997). Compromises produced by the dialectic between self-verification and self-enhancement. *Journal of Personality and Social Psychology, 73,* 1268–1283.

Nisbett, R., & Ross, L. (1980). *Human inference: Strategies and shortcomings of social judgment.* Englewood Cliffs, NJ: Prentice-Hall.

Pacini, R., Epstein, S., & Barrows, P. (1996). *Lessons in intuitive reasoning from the ratio-bias phenomenon: The concretive, experiential, associationistic, imagistic, and affirmative representation principles.* Manuscript submitted for publication.

Pacini, R., Muir, F., & Epstein, S. (1996). Depressive realism from the perspective of cognitive-experiential self-theory. *Journal of Personality and Social Psychology.*

Paivio, A. (1986). *Mental representations: A dual-coding approach.* New York: Oxford University Press.

Rogers, C. R. (1959). A theory of therapy, personality, and interpersonal relationships, as developed in the client-centered framework. In S. Koch (Ed.), *Psychology: A study of a science* (Vol. 3, pp. 184–256). New York: McGraw-Hill.

Science News, 1991.

Shiffrin, R. M., & Schneider, W. (1977). Controlled and automatic human information processing: II. Perceptual learning, automatic attending and a general theory. *Psychological Review, 84,* 127–190.

Singer, D. G., & Singer, J. L. (1990). *The house of make-believe: Play and the developing imagination.* Cambridge, MA: Harvard University Press.

Sloat, R. A., Jr. (1992). *The influence of arbitrary outcomes on emotions and decisions.* Unpublished honor's thesis. University of Massachusetts-Amherst.

Taylor, S. E., & Brown, J. D. (1988). Illusion and well-being: A social psychological perspective on mental health. *Psychological Bulletin, 103,* 193–210.

Tversky, A., & Kahneman, D. (1974). Judgment under uncertainty: Heuristics and biases. *Science, 185,* 1124–1131.

Tversky, A., & Kahneman, D. (1983). Extensional versus intuitive reasoning: The conjunction fallacy in probability judgment. *Psychological Review, 90,* 293–315.

Vitz, P. S. (1990). The use of stories in moral development: New psychological reasons for an old education method. *American Psychologist, 45,* 709–720.

Wilson, T. D., & Schooler, J. W. (1991). Thinking too much: Introspection can reduce the quality of preferences and decisions. *Journal of Personality and Social Psychology, 60,* 181–192.

CHAPTER 10

WHY DO WE NEED TO BE CONSCIOUS?

A Psychoanalytic Answer

HOWARD SHEVRIN

> But what part is then left to be played in our scheme by consciousness which was once so omnipotent and hid all else from view?
>
> Sigmund Freud, *The Interpretation of Dreams*

INTRODUCTION

It is an odd quirk of history that two such opposite approaches to psychology as behaviorism and psychoanalysis should each have looked with skepticism at the role of consciousness. For the behaviorist, consciousness was suspect on methodological grounds—it was

HOWARD SHEVRIN • Department of Psychiatry, University of Michigan Medical Center, Ann Arbor, Michigan 48105.

Advanced Personality, edited by David F. Barone, Michel Hersen, and Vincent B. Van Hasselt. Plenum Press, New York, 1998.

untrustworthy and not a suitable subject for scientific investigation. For the psychoanalyst, consciousness was suspect on empirical grounds—it did not tell the whole story and had to be seen through in order to arrive at the underlying unconscious causes. It has only been fairly recently that consciousness has emerged as a subject in its own right worthy of both philosophical examination and scientific investigation. In the sentence following the epigraph quoted above, Freud (1900/1953) continued on to say, "Only that of a sense organ for the perception of psychical qualities," (p. 615) an attempt at an answer to the question posed in the title of this paper. But, as we shall also see, Freud gave a number of different answers at various points in his theorizing.

Before launching into an account of Freud's answers, their strengths and weaknesses, it will be useful to set forth the different ways in which the role of consciousness has been conceptualized, first in the philosophical literature and then in the contemporary psychological literature. Following that, I shall give a brief historical account of Freud's theories, including a detailed consideration of the "sense organ" model. The chapter will then turn to an examination of the relationship between perception and memory as a testing ground for any theory of consciousness, first presenting the views of Freud on this subject, then comparing a contemporary, up-dated version of Freud's views by Opatow with the neural Darwinian theory of the biologist Gerald Edelman. Finally, I shall propose a function of consciousness based on these theories that will attempt to answer the question posed in the title and cite evidence in support of this function.

HOW PHILOSOPHERS VIEW THE PROBLEM OF CONSCIOUSNESS

In a recent article in *The New York Review of Books,* the philosopher of mind, John Searle (1997), surveyed various traditional philosophical approaches to consciousness and its relationship to the mind. A brief paragraph from this review will succinctly summarize these positions:

> Traditionally in philosophy of mind there is supposed to be a basic distinction between dualists, who think there are two fundamentally different kinds of phenomena in the world, minds and bodies, and monists, who think that the world is made of only one kind of stuff. Dualists divide into "substance dualists," who think that "mind" and "body" name two kinds of substances, and "property dualists," who think "mental" and "physical" name different kinds of properties or features in a way that enables the same substance—a human being, for example—to have both kinds of properties at once. Monists in turn divide into idealists, who think everything is ultimately mental, and materialists, who think everything is ultimately physical or material. (p. 43)

As Searle went on to point out, each position has its problems. Although there are few "substance dualists" nowadays among philosophers, there are a number of well-known "property dualists" such as Thomas Nagel and Colin McGinn. The problem for "property dualists" is how to account for two such different properties emerging from a common underlying substance. According to Searle, the most widely accepted position among philosophers and scientists is one of two versions of the materialist solution: reductionism or functionalism. Reductionists believe that consciousness and mental life are entirely reducible to the material substance of the brain, its molecules, neurons, synapses, and so on, which cause behavior of various kinds. Mental states can simply be ignored as epiphenomenal. Our beliefs and desires do not cause our behavior, but the true causes reside in the physical reality of our brains. Functionalists, on the other hand, account for consciousness and the mental as caused by brain *processes,* or the cause-and-effect relationships among the parts of the brain. These cause-and-effect functional relationships need not be instantiated in a nervous system, but could, for example, also be found in a computer. Consciousness is nothing but these functional relationships, just like the computer readout is nothing but a hard copy of what has already been instantiated in the programmed operation of the computer hardware. According to Searle, the functionalists explain consciousness away by equating it with patterns of organization, while the reductionists deny consciousness any ontological status.

The problem, according to Searle, is how to account for consciousness as an *emergent* property of the brain, which in turn can play a causative role in behavior. This emergent property is not a different substance (substance dualists), a property coordinate with the physical (property dualists), or nothing but the molecules and neurons making up the brain (reductionists), nor does it reside in the cause-and-effect activity of the brain (functionalists), but is a physical property of the brain that achieves a causative status in its own right. Searle likened the nature of this emergent property to the quality of wetness that a certain combination of hydrogen and oxygen we call water possesses. Insofar as consciousness is a physical property of the brain, it is not so clear that it can emerge as a property of any other system, such as a computer. In order to be conscious, you have to have a brain, and perhaps only a mammalian brain or only a human brain. And this is Searle's problem: how and under what circumstances does this property emerge? For Searle, this is a purely empirical issue, and he called on neuroscientists to solve this problem.

Where can we place Freud with respect to these different positions? In a certain special sense, Freud appears to be among those who explain away consciousness or appear to deny consciousness a causal status. The true causes, if not in the material substance of the brain, are to be found in other, but unconscious, mental processes. In the epigraph, Freud suddenly seems to realize that he has left consciousness without a role, which he then tries to make up for by assigning it the role of a "sense organ" for mental qualities. But, as we shall explore later, what does this mean, and what is the status of this "sense organ" metaphor with respect to the different philosophical positions, and—equally if not more importantly—what role, if any, does consciousness play in psychoanalytic treatment? Ironically, in one important respect consciousness has had an honored role in psychoanalytic treatment; it was by making the unconscious conscious that cure was supposed to happen. But as psychoanalysts discovered that mere explanation, no matter how correct, did not appear to work, that simply informing the patient of what was in his unconscious had no mutative effect, interest shifted to the importance of the transference experience, which then could constitute the shared experiential basis for a more effective interpretation. Yet, bringing the transference experience into consciousness in the form of interpretations relating past and present remained important. It makes it possible for the patient to become conscious of the relationship between current perceptions of the analyst and memories enacted in the transference. This continued importance of consciousness in treatment strongly implies that being conscious is more than simply a "sense organ" but plays some significant functional role.

A BRIEF HISTORY OF FREUD'S VIEWS ON CONSCIOUSNESS

We can identify at least three different stages in Freud's thinking about consciousness. The first stage was best set forth in his collaborative work with Josef Breuer, *Studies on Hysteria* (1895/1955a); the second in *The Interpretation of Dreams* (1900/1953); and the third in *The Ego and the Id* (1923/1961). Freud was not a systematic theoretician so that hints of later theories can be found in earlier formulations and allusions to earlier formulations in later theories. The summaries to follow should thus be understood as Freud's modal or predominant views at a given time. But more important than historical precision is an appreciation of the different ideas Freud entertained on consciousness, making an assessment of them in their own right, identifying wherever possible their strengths and weaknesses.

Freud's earliest ideas on consciousness were closely wedded to the 19th-century psychological concept of idea. An idea in its broadest reference meant any psychological content or representation. Keeping this in mind, Freud considered that an idea can be conscious, preconscious, or unconscious. So, for example, an idea could be a memory that was repressed, it could be a name that could be easily recalled, or it could be a perception immediately in awareness. The repressed memory is unconscious, the easily recalled name is preconscious, and the perception in immediate awareness is conscious. At this point in his thinking, consciousness was simply the experience of subjective awareness; it had no other qualities or attributes. A given idea, in this sense, could be unconscious (repressed), easily recalled (preconscious), or present in subjective awareness (conscious). This so-called topographic theory (see Chapter 2) had several virtues. For one, the criteria for discriminating the status of an idea were clear and unambiguous. It also made clinical sense—if a patient found it hard to recall the material from a previous session it likely involved repression, if material was easily recovered it was preconscious. Another strength was the emphasis on consciousness as subjective awareness that could occur in any state—dream, psychotic, fugue, intoxication, and so on. As we shall see later, this important characteristic of consciousness is often forgotten. But this topographic theory also had weaknesses, chief among which was any consideration as to what consciousness did, what it was for; it was simply a quality of an idea. Yet clinical experience appeared to suggest that it made a difference once an idea became conscious; certainly, this was the experience with the many hysterics treated in the *Studies on Hysteria*. For a previously repressed idea to become conscious made a difference, but why?

The second, or systems theory, attempted to correct this weakness, but also lost some of the strength of the topographic theory. Consciousness was now elevated from being a mere quality or attribute of an idea to being a mental system or agency. This difference was signified by referring to this consciousness system with a capital *Cs,* whereas in the earlier theory consciousness was simply referred to by a lower case *c.* Analogously, the preconscious became the *Pcs* and the unconscious became *Ucs.* Moreover, the system Cs was closely linked to perception, so that the new system was often named the *Pcpt-Cs* system. This close alliance between consciousness and perception caused mischief because it became impossible to conceive theoretically of an unconscious perception. Subliminal perception, for which there is much experimental support, was thus an impossibility according to this theory.

But the systems theory also had some strengths. Consciousness was now associated with the alert, waking state in which self-reflection (i.e., being aware of being aware) occurred, and in which reality testing and secondary process rational thought generally prevailed. It was indeed consciousness with a capital C. By becoming conscious, an idea was now more than simply conscious; it was tested for its fit with reality and judged accordingly. Consciousness was now the arbiter of reality and the gatekeeper of action. But problems remained; one in particular that made the next theoretical step necessary.

With increasing clinical experience and the further development of the theory of defense, Freud recognized that defenses were instituted unconsciously but from the direction of the system Cs. Anomalously, a system identified with consciousness was performing an unconscious function. Freud corrected this anomaly by replacing the system Cs with the ego and the system Unc with the id. Consciousness was now a function of the ego along with the ego's capacity to institute defenses. But consciousness was still very much identified with one particular state, the normal, waking, self-reflective state. In this model, the ego had taken over functions, such as reality testing, previously assigned to the system Cs (see discussion of the structural model in chap. 2). What was then left for consciousness, the question posed by Freud in our epigraph? His answer, as already quoted, was that of a sense organ "for the perception of psychical qualities."

FREUD'S SENSE ORGAN MODEL OF CONSCIOUSNESS

In hypothesizing a sense organ model for consciousness, Freud was attempting to confront a truly staggering theoretical problem: how to differentiate the unconscious from consciousness by designating a unique function to consciousness. Once Freud embarked on this undertaking, there lurked in the background, whether acknowledged or not, the philosophical issues summarized earlier. Certainly, Freud identified himself as a materialist, and he often affirmed the materialist belief that fundamentally everything was matter in motion in one form or another. For Freud, there was no spirit or soul; he was not a substance dualist or idealist. Judging from his many writings on consciousness and mental life in general, he comes close to being a property dualist insofar as he believed that psychological phenomena can have entirely psychological explanations that in principle would prove to be consistent with whatever is discovered about the brain; but one need not wait until the instantiating brain processes are discovered to arrive at satisfactory explanations in purely psychological terms. The sense organ hypothesis is an example of this kind of thinking.

Interestingly, Freud believed that processes in the unconscious were basically quantitative in nature; qualities as such did not exist unconsciously. What could this mean? In one important respect, it is similar to the contemporary cognitive science belief that all mental life is computational in nature, that numerical, or quantitative, relationships describe the fundamental nature of psychological events. For cognitive scientists, this assumption would also apply to consciousness; for them the so-called qualia of conscious experience are reducible and explained by yet to be discovered computational processes that might be instantiated in a computer as easily as in a brain. For this reason, Searle believed that most if not all cognitive scientists subscribe to a functionalist position. But as we shall see, Freud's sense organ model does not appear to fit in this mold.

Just as our physical sense organs are capable of transducing a particular form of physical energy into a specific quality of experience, Freud reasoned that consciousness transduces the quantitative processes in the unconscious into qualitative conscious experiences.

Light energy impinges on the retina, and, following a complex set of neurophysiological events, we experience a visual perception that is qualitatively different from an auditory perception. Note that the experienced difference between vision and hearing cannot be accounted for by anything quantitative; it is not that vision is somehow less than or greater than hearing—it is simply different. We would never experience a whisper as somehow less than a sunlit visual scene or a loud drum sound as more than a twilight scene because of apparent differences in intensity. Yet, it is of interest that in synesthesias we do experience a confounding of sensory qualities, but this is rare and its rarity underscores the customary stable qualitative differences between sensory modalities.

Freud hypothesized that the unique quality that consciousness introduced in "perceiving" the quantitative unconscious processes had to do with the experience of pleasure and unpleasure. Just as our eyes make possible visual experience and the ears auditory experience, consciousness makes possible the experience of pleasure and unpleasure. Presumably, without consciousness we would lack the experience of pleasure and unpleasure, just as we would be blind without eyes. Clearly, consciousness serves an important function. According to this view, our readiness to act on our thoughts, beliefs, and desires is in large part determined by how they are experienced along the dimension of pleasure-unpleasure. Without consciousness our actions would not be guided by this important principle; we would presumably "act out" our impulses solely on the basis of their strength (i.e., quantity), the strongest impulse at any time gaining access to action over any weaker impulse, no matter how pleasant or unpleasant the consequences. So, if we were more hungry than thirsty, or more sexually desirous than either, we would immediately seek to gratify our sexual impulse by the most immediate means possible, no matter how unhappy the consequences. Indeed, we would not experience the unpleasantness created by our actions; in fact, we would not experience anything in any conscious sense. We would be, in effect, unconscious automatons.

And it is at this point that this sense organ model begins to run into problems. A closer examination of how pleasure and unpleasure is determined in any one instance raises questions about how parallel the analogy with a true sense organ really is. The eye simply transduces light energy into visual percepts; no thought or judgment is involved in the process, although at some later processing stage so-called top-down processes, such as thought, memory, and judgment, may influence the subsequent course of the percept. When consciousness transforms quantitative unconscious processes into pleasant-unpleasant qualities, more than a simple transducing process has to take place. Complex judgments, memories of previous pertinent experience, and thinking through consequences are all involved and determine whether a given unconscious process will prove pleasurable or unpleasurable. It would be as if the light transducing function of the eye were biochemically affected by the personal significance of the object, although these influences may be at work much later in visual processing. In cases of hysterical blindness or functional amblyopia, the evidence points to an intact visual receiving system, but an inhibition or repression operative after the visual percept has formed. The hysterical blind person can act on the visual information while remaining unconscious of it.

But sense organ consciousness cannot simply, automatically, and immediately register pleasure and unpleasure and leave it to some later stages to figure out why it is pleasurable or unpleasurable. These assessments have logically to be made *before* the experience of pleasure or unpleasure. But if these assessments are made prior to consciousness, then they must be unconscious. Yet, ordinary experience tells us that we are conscious all the time of making judgments, recalling memories, and thinking through possibilities; they are not necessarily prior to consciousness but concomitant with it. And if this is the case, then we can be conscious of far more than the qualities of pleasure and unpleasure. It would be as if the eye went well beyond transducing light into vision, but also made us aware of thoughts, judgments, memories, and so on.

Freud was aware of this problem with his sense organ model and attempted to correct it by hypothesizing that for thoughts to become conscious the auditory traces of the words associated with the thoughts had to be activated. These auditory traces could then be "heard" by consciousness. It is hard to see how this deals with problem. For one thing, it extends the function of consciousness beyond that of transforming quantitative unconscious processes into the qualities of pleasure and unpleasure to include what appears to be the "perception" of activated auditory traces. And why stop there? Why not the "perception" of images, feelings, memories, desires? These too can have their associated traces activated and "perceived" by consciousness. But once we have opened the door this wide, we are then saying that the function of consciousness is to make us aware of everything going on in the mind. In effect, we have arrived at a tautology: consciousness makes us conscious. Moreover, if consciousness is simply to make us aware of processes that are already going on unconsciously, why do we need consciousness? We are back to Freud's lament: "But what part is to be played in our scheme by consciousness . . ." How better do current cognitive science views of consciousness succeed?

RECENT COGNITIVE SCIENCE VIEWS OF THE NATURE OF CONSCIOUSNESS

Searle placed most cognitive psychologists in the functionalist school. According to Searle, they believe that consciousness is a function of the cause-and-effect processes of the brain, much as the programmed operation of a computer instantiates its computational function. The computer analogy can be pressed further: the program, or computational algorithm, controls how the computer hardware will operate. The computer hardware has certain built-in, or "hard-wired" characteristics, its "architecture." Thus, there can be serial or parallel computers that differ in their hardware. Similarly, cognition has been divided into controlled and automatic processes (Shiffrin & Schneider, 1977). The controlled processes are like the computer program that organizes and guides the way in which the architecture is used. The automatic processes are like the more "hard-wired" architecture of the computer. This analogy cannot be pressed too far because the automatic processes are not in the literal sense hardware but other functional organizations. Nevertheless, there is a kinship between the controlled-automatic distinction and the program-hardware relationship in computer science. There is in fact much in cognitive science that is modeled after computers, most particularly the assumption that cognitive processes are computational in nature.

The distinction between controlled and automatic processes has largely captured the imagination of most cognitive psychologists, with a few notable exceptions (see Allport, 1989). Of immediate importance to our current inquiry is the role assigned to consciousness in this model. As one might expect, only controlled processes are conscious; they are also voluntary, dispense attention from a limited reservoir, and are effortful. Automatic processes, on the other hand, are unconscious, unintentional, require no attention, and are effortless. It is reasonably clear that the controlled-automatic pair is the modern inheritor of the earlier classic distinction in psychology between voluntary action and habit. A perusal of William James's chapter on habit in his *Principles of Psychology* (1890) will convince the reader that the modern distinction offers very little new theoretically, but it can draw upon a growing body of empirical evidence not available in James' time that appears to support the distinction.

The link between consciousness and controlled processes is theoretically very similar to Freud's later systems and structural theories in which consciousness is tied to a particular psychological state—the normal, alert, waking, adult state. It is different from his first topographic theory in which consciousness is simply a condition of subjective awareness that can occur in any state. By linking consciousness to one state, it becomes impossible to explain the role of consciousness in all the other states in which it occurs. And more importantly, the opportunity is missed thereby to identify a common function of consciousness across all states. To his credit, Freud did attempt to specify a unique function to consciousness in his structural theory—that of a sense organ for pleasure-unpleasure. We saw, however, how this effort at specification ran into trouble, in part, because consciousness was linked to one state with its own special characteristics, such as self-reflection, thought, reasoning, and so on.

The same problem is encountered by cognitive psychologists who rely on the controlled-automatic distinction. Posner and Boies (1971) and Mandler (1982) talked about consciousness as being characterized by a single channel, while automatic processes are multichanneled or operate in parallel. This single-channel property is consistent with serial, logical thought and stands in contrast to the paralogical, condensed thought, characterizing dreams and psychosis; yet dreamers and psychotics are conscious in their respective states. There are, in fact, many subtle gradations of states occurring in normal adults during the course of any 24 hours: waking-alert, day-dreaming, distraction, falling asleep, dreaming sleep, to identify the most obvious state shifts. Consciousness is present in all of them, and only in one is it associated with logical, single-channel processing. We can say that cognitive psychology has not provided an answer to our question: Why do we need to be conscious? They seem to have provided an answer similar to Freud's in some respects and subject to the same limitations.

PERCEPTION AND MEMORY: A CRUCIAL TESTING GROUND FOR ANY THEORY OF CONSCIOUSNESS

In a paper, "Formulations on the Two Principles of Mental Functioning," Freud (1911/1958) addressed one of the most interesting considerations his thinking and clinical experience had brought him to: qualitative differences in the nature of cognition as a function of psychopathology and individual development. The distinctions he drew, and the hypotheses he formulated, have important implications for answering our question.

Freud had long observed that neurotic symptoms are based on different kinds of thinking from rational thought. In his classic study of an obsessional neurotic, the invidiously but accurately named Rat Man, Freud (1909/1955b) reported how his obsessions traded prolifically on the multiple meanings of *rat* in German. Similar mechanisms of displacement and condensation could be identified in dream formation, psychotic thinking, and in jokes. Freud hypothesized that there were, in fact, two different principles of mental functioning: the rational, secondary process and the seemingly irrational primary process. In his "Two Principles" paper, Freud offered a highly imaginative and eminently challengeable thesis as to the developmental origins of these different principles, which are echoed in at least two current theories of the origin of consciousness, one quite deliberately (Opatow, 1997), and the other quite independently (Edelman, 1989). Freud speculated that at the start of life, following the first experiences of satisfaction (presumably in feeding), memory traces of these first gratifying experiences were laid down. When the infant next became hungry, Freud hypothesized that the memory traces laid down by these previous gratifications were activated. One might think that the infant would remember these good experiences and anticipate more of them in the offing. Not so, said Freud, something quite different takes place: the infant experiences the reawakened memories not as *memories* but as current and immediate *experiences*. The infant, argued Freud, does not as yet possess the means for distinguishing between a memory and an immediate experience; rather, it *hallucinates* a former gratification as a present and immediate one. The desire for gratification takes the shortest possible route—the arousal of the memory of previous gratifications experienced as current gratifications. This, he described, was the quintessential operation of the primary process.

How long, one might wonder, can such a state of affairs go on? Surely any organism gratified by hallucinations could not long survive. Fortunately, the infant is not left to its own devices; there is a caretaker about. But more importantly, something is going on in the experience of the infant. No matter how intensely it might experience the hallucinatory wish fulfillment the fact remains that its hunger persists. The hallucination cannot produce true gratifications; the inner reality of continuing hunger disrupts the inner peace transiently provided by the hallucination, and the infant begins to wail and thrash, behavior that attracts the concerned caregiver who then finally provides real gratification.

If this theory has some merit, it might permit us to explain a sequence of observable behaviors that any intent infant-watcher can note: The infant is asleep, fleetingly little smiles often no more than twitches at the corners of the lips but smilelike in nature appear, sleep continues, more such smiles, but now followed by incipient frowns, marked by little creases in the currogator muscles of the forehead, accompanied by large head and arm movements. The baby is becoming, as we say, *restless,* an apt word because in fact the infant *is* becoming rest-less. Finally, the sequence shifts more and more in the direction of frowning and restlessness, and, at some point, the infant is wide awake and crying. It is time for feeding. This observable sequence might be placed in Freud's framework: As hunger intensifies in the sleeping infant, the little smiles betoken the experience of hallucinated wish fulfillment, which for a brief time permits sleep to continue (the later presumed function of dreaming) but does nothing to abate hunger. Gradually, the balance shifts away from hallucination of wish fulfillment toward a demand for it.[1]

---

[1] It is also possible to view this same sequence entirely differently: In paradoxical sleep, the forerunner of true rapid-eye-movement dreaming sleep, there is a "warming up" of various expressive mechanisms, which appear from our adult perspective to be smiles and frowns, but which are simply motor actions without affective significance. As an infant gets hungrier, it eventually wakes up, with no intervening hallucinatory wish fulfillment. There is no more conclusive evidence in favor of this explanation than there is for Freud's; both are tenable. However, the *sequence* of observed behaviors—smile, sleep, frown, restlessness, awakening—seems more in accord w th Freud's explanation. Also, it seems arbitrary to deny affect status to smiles and frowns during sleep but not to crying and responsiveness during waking.

According to Freud, a momentous change in a principle of mental life is underway, from the primary process under the sway of the pleasure principle to the secondary process under the sway of the reality principle. This change will not happen overnight; in fact, it will take much of childhood to swing the balance in favor of the reality principle. Along the way, repression will cut off segments of inner life in which the primary process will continue to hold sway. Neurotic symptoms, such as those experienced by the Rat Man, will be conscious expressions of this repressed, primary-process mental life. Dreams will allow them expression during sleep, as they did for the infant, whom we know spends up to 40% of sleep in rapid-eye-movement dream sleep—not the complex, narrative dreams of later life but brief snatches of wish-fulfillments.

Where does consciousness enter this picture? For Freud, the function of consciousness present from the beginning was, as we have seen to transform the quantitative processes of the unconscious into conscious experiences of pleasure and unpleasure. As we have also seen, there are problems with this formulation. With the gradual advent of the reality principle, Freud posited that consciousness now extended its domain to the external world, making us aware of surrounding stimuli; it did so not in terms of immediate pleasure and unpleasure but in terms of reality relevance. Presumably, at some point, the infant became capable of distinguishing what it was conscious of in the actual world from what it was conscious of in its inner life. The wish for immediate gratification, with its tendency toward hallucinated wish fulfillment, is then held in abeyance until the surrounding world provides true gratification, or until the individual develops the means to seek it out. Because this often proves to be a hard road and does not always end successfully, there remain a part of all of us that continues to hanker after immediate wish fulfillment—that land of milk and honey, as the Bible portrays the promised land, whose actual history was a succession of trials and tribulations.

Basic to understanding this momentous shifts from the pleasure principle to the reality principle—from the primary process to the secondary process—and the role that consciousness plays in it is a closer consideration of two fundamental processes—memory and perception: the former, cognitively available inside us; the latter, available from outside us. Freud hypothesized that the infant confounded memory and perception; more accurately, that re-aroused *memories* of gratification were responded to as if they were *experiences* of gratification. Or still another useful way of describing the infant's situation—the re-aroused memory traces are not experienced as referring to past events as in a true memory, but to a current experience based on treating the *content* of the memory as a present perception. Assuming that the infant's earliest cognitive modalities are sensory motor (following Jean Piaget), then the content of the re-aroused memory trace would contain prominent sensory and motor elements, much as after an active day at a fair filled with exciting rides on Ferris wheels and roller coasters, we feel ourselves remembering through our bodies by hallucinating the same exciting movements (and, perhaps, for the same reason—to recapture the gratifying excitement of the day). The infant treats a memory of a past event as a current enactment (just as we do after a fair). For the infant, wanting makes it so, at least for a time. But the actual current reality contains no true cause of the enactment of satisfaction; any perception of that reality would register that fact. Thus, what the infant is actually perceiving of the external world and what it is experiencing in its inner world are starkly at variance. And to this gross disparity must then be added the other salient reality—the enactment of the past, in which the infant is caught up, cannot appease growing hunger. According to two theories that we will next explore, it is out of this tension that consciousness is born.

TWO THEORIES OF CONSCIOUSNESS

On the face of it, no two theories are as different as the ones proposed by Opatow (1997) and Edelman (1989). Opatow bases his theory squarely on Freud; in particular, his speculative ideas about consciousness that were summarized in the preceding section. Opatow, a psychoanalyst, firmly believes that these ideas are at the heart of what is important and unique in what psychoanalysis can contribute to an understanding of consciousness. Edelman, who won a Nobel Prize in genetics, has formulated a comprehensive theory of brain organization and development based on applying Darwinian principles of natural selection to the organization of the brain. The organism's interaction with the environment from the start works to select some rather than other neuronal systems to guide the subsequent activities of the organism. These neuronal systems are not representations of the environment (as they are in much of cognitive psychology), but are, in effect, adaptive guidance systems that are constantly in flux as a function of the changing environment and the internal state of the organism. On the foundation of this conceptualization of brain functioning, Edelman proposes a theory of primary consciousness that is comparable to Freud's consciousness with a lower case *c* and can simply be defined as the experience of subjective awareness in any state.

OPATOW'S NEGATION THEORY OF CONSCIOUSNESS

Opatow started with the model of hallucinated wish fulfillment, which operates on the basis of the pleasure principle, and then tried to account for the means through which the infant achieves a realistic fulfillment of its wishes, operating on the reality principle. In the course of this transformation, argued Opatow, consciousness and the unconscious emerge as necessary counterparts of each other. When one considers carefully what the state of the infant must be like during the experience of hallucinated wish fulfillment, there are two aspects of the experience, one the projected shadow of the other. While the infant is experiencing hallucinated satisfaction, the object that can truly gratify is absent. Thus, as the hallucinated gratification wanes in its power, as it must in the face of ungratified need, the perception of absence grows. At some point, Opatow hypothesized, a momentous developmental step is taken: a negation of the *entire* mental mode of hallucinated wish fulfillment not simply of individual instances. At this juncture, consciousness and the unconscious are born. The negated mode of hallucinated wish fulfillment under the aegis of the pleasure principle now constitutes the unconscious; at the same time, and inextricably bound up with the act of negation, consciousness is constituted under the aegis of the reality principle. But there is no hard and fast boundary between the two, quite otherwise. Each conscious act is permeated to a greater or lesser degree with partial forms of hallucinated wish fulfillment. Every human relationship is a combination of what is new and realistic and what harks back to earlier hallucinated wish fulfillment. The psychoanalytic method helps the patient become aware of those experiences transferred from the past to be enjoyed in the present that are at such variance with reality so that his or her ability to obtain current, appropriate satisfaction is impaired.

It seems reasonably clear from Opatow's account that the enacted but not remembered encounters from the past, the hallucinated wish fulfillments, have to give rise to a perception of the absence of gratification insofar as no true gratification can occur. Yet, for Opatow, it is critically important that the hallucinated wish fulfillment provide a sense of gratification that for some crucial time cannot be differentiated from a true gratification. Otherwise, the power of the modality of hallucinated wish fulfillment, the foundation of the unconscious, could not be explained. It is not a fake that must be disavowed, but a sweet pleasure that does not last—although one wishes it would—and one keeps trying to make that happen despite what reality has in store.

What kind of consciousness is Opatow talking about, however? Is the infant conscious in the state of hallucinated wish fulfillment? If so, then what is the consciousness that Opatow posited as coming into existence when the mental mode of hallucinated wish fulfillment is negated? It would seem that for Opatow there are two consciousness: the consciousness of hallucinated wish fulfillment, which is then superseded by the consciousness associated with the reality principle. But what purpose does consciousness in any state serve, our original question? Although Opatow provided an intriguing theory for the emergence of a later state of consciousness, this later consciousness would appear to have certain systematic properties similar to Freud's account and that of other cognitive psychologists, such as Michael Posner and George Mandler. As a result, he can say nothing about a common underlying function for consciousness itself, whether it be associated with hallucinated wish fulfillment or the later consciousness constituted by the negation of wish fulfillment.

EDELMAN'S PERCEPTION-MEMORY THEORY OF PRIMARY CONSCIOUSNESS

Edelman's theory of primary consciousness is an integral part of a comprehensive conceptualization of the brain as a whole in which hypotheses are formulated to account for the evolution of the brain and its individual development. (Although the model is closely articulated with particular parts of the brain and their individual and integrated functioning, for our present purposes I will not go into these relationships.) The fundamental engine of the brain's evolution in species-wide terms and its development in individual terms is neuronal group selection on the basis of interaction with the environment. Populations of neurons, like populations of individuals, are formed by interactions with the surround, limited only by the inherent capacities of the particular neuronal populations. It follows from this position insofar as the environment differs from individual to individual, and these differences are present from the womb on, that there are many degrees of freedom in the formation of brain organization. Individual brains will vary greatly from individual to individual; even the brains of identical twins will demonstrate significant differences despite their genetic identity. And this is exactly the point: It is the interaction of genetic givens with unique environments that determines how different the phenotypes will be from each other.

For Edelman, the story of primary consciousness—what we have called immediate subjective awareness—begins very early in the evolution of the brain, at a time when the capacity to distinguish self from nonself appears. Self is not meant here in any psychological sense, but closer to its meaning in immunology, in which it refers to the ability biochemical in nature for antibodies to distinguish between cells that belong to the host (self) and those that are foreign (nonself). Yet it is fundamental. All else that follows is built on this basic distinction. The self neuronal system is primarily concerned with maintaining and protecting the inner homeostatic balance that is concerned with the brute survival of the organism—its needs and physiological requirements. It is the origin of what Edelman calls the *value dimension*. The nonself neuronal system is the system in close touch with the external world. These two systems are supported by different and independent neuronal populations, although it is vitally important that the information from both be correlated. All this can take place without benefit of consciousness of any kind. According to Edelman, the next step in brain evolution was momentous: the appearance of a memory system that could maintain a record of past coordinations of the values of the self-system with the exteroceptive, perceptual inputs of the nonself system. This coordination was achieved on the basis of a new conceptual capacity to distinguish objects from events, that is, space- versus time-based stimuli. According to Edelman, no primary consciousness was required for this evolutionary achievement. Imagine an organism capable of maneuvering through a complex environment filled with different objects and a succession of events affecting these objects on the basis of established memory systems. It would not need consciousness to adapt itself to such a world as long as that world remained uniform and predictable.

The second important evolutionary event was the appearance of the capacity to relate the self-value–perceptual-category memory system to current sampling of the environment by the nonself system. The operative term here is *current* because the older memory system was not easily modifiable by fresh input and was mainly formed by the values of the self-system. Imagine an organism mainly guided by past experience, a workable arrangement in a relatively unchanging environment, now faced with problems in a rapidly changing environment. The new capacity made it possible to coordinate new information, not previously encountered and remembered, with the nonself-value system. It is at this important juncture that primary consciousness makes its appearance. To have a clear idea of what Edelman (1989) had in mind we will quote him on this critical point:

> Past correlations of category with value are now themselves interactive in real time with current perceptual categorizations *before* they are altered by the value-dependent portions of the nervous system. A kind of bootstrapping occurs in which current value-free perceptual categorization interacts with value-dominated memory before further contributing to alterations of that memory. (p. 97)

At the heart of this conceptualization is the proviso that current perceptual categorizations be value-free, uninfluenced by the value-based parts of the brain. Only in this way can new experience, objectively evaluated (unbiased by current values), be adaptively incorporated into new memory systems. In Edelman's terms, the memory is recategorized on the basis of value-free environmental input. Present and past, inner state and outer reality interact to form more adaptive memories and guides for action in a changing world. It is precisely at this juncture that primary consciousness appears. A few sentences after the previous quote Edelman (1989) states explicitly what the function of primary consciousness is in his theory: "It constitutes a *discrimination* of the acquired self-nonself memory from current ongoing perceptual categorizations. This discrimination occurs in parallel across all perceptual modalities. It can alter the relative salience to the animal of particular events in the stimulus domain and help it choose goals and actions" (pp. 97–98).

One thread runs through Freud's, Opatow's, and Edelman's accounts of consciousness despite the differences among them: Somehow something that is purely an internal organismic event is *discriminated* from an event external to the organism. For Freud, it is embodied in the shift from the pleasure principle to the reality principle; for Opatow, it is the negation of the entire mode of hallucinatory wish fulfillment that creates and constitutes the difference between consciousness and the unconscious; for Edelman, the value-dominated memory system can be recategorized in the light of new input unaffected by value. Or to put it more simply, if schematically, consciousness emerges as the means through which memory and perception are discriminated as different. Note that this new capacity has nothing to do with the specific contents of a memory or perception; such contents have been registered before on an unconscious level, but no distinction could be made as to their significantly different sources. Rather, it has to do with discriminating the *qualitative* difference between *any* memory and *any* perception. In Edelman's terms, the earlier brute distinction between self and nonself now can begin to be based on a more advanced and flexible integration of internal state and external circumstance. But it is still a far cry from the later capacity to form higher level concepts of the self and nonself, which require a particular reflexive state of consciousness in which there can be an awareness of being aware. But since our interest, at this point, is in consciousness in the most general sense, we will leave this issue for a later discussion.

There is one apparent difference in emphasis between Freud and Opatow, on the one hand, and Edelman on the other. Both Freud and Opatow emphasized the importance of the internal state of affairs: for Freud, the psyche under the dominance of the pleasure principle and indifferent to external input; for Opatow, an entire mode of being, the state of hallucinated wish fulfillment. Also, for Freud and Opatow, this internal state does not disappear once consciousness makes its appearance, rather it remains as a continuing influence and imposes demands and limitations on conscious states. Edelman (1989) appeared to emphasize more the qualitatively improved coordination with external reality. Primary consciousness allows the animal to "direct attention to particular events in a selective fashion that serves its own adaptive needs" (p. 98). It is also compatible with Edelman's position that structures antecedent to consciousness remain functional on an unconscious basis. Although he does not elaborate on their continuing role, it can be assumed that if they are primarily concerned with homeostatic regulation, they must remain operative.

Despite this difference in emphasis, however, the core resemblance among the theories is paramount: In each theory, consciousness frees the animal from complete dominance by its needs or drives, from a psychoanalytic standpoint, and from the dominance of its values, linked closely with its homeostatic requirements, from Edelman's standpoint. Consciousness does so by making possible a need-free, drive-autonomous, value-independent perception of the environment. In the language of ego psychology advanced by Heinz Hartmann and David Rapaport, consciousness makes possible conflict-free adaptive behavior, and it does so by providing a discrimination between memory and perception. This is why we need consciousness. But the consciousness story does not end there.

A GENERALIZED FUNCTION OF CONSCIOUSNESS

When we consider the range of mental activities, especially in a human being, we realize that more than memory and perception are involved. Human beings think, judge, fantasize, dream, daydream, feel, desire, and imagine—in addition to remembering and perceiving—to name a few of the mental activities that transiently appear and disappear during the course of any 24 hours. Moreover, most of time we have little trouble in knowing that we are in the midst of one or another of these activities. We are usually not fooled even if a thought, fantasy, dream, memory, or perception has the very same content. We instantly seem to know whether it is a thought or dream about the same person or event. Moreover, it is vitally important to our adaptation in the real world that we be able to appreciate these differences. Elsewhere (Shevrin, 1986a, 1992), I have proposed that consciousness provides a "tagging" function that allows these discriminations to be made. I cited evidence, which I shall elaborate on later, that in subliminal perception experiments, for example, the fact that the subliminal stimulus has never been in consciousness means that it can never be remembered as a perception. It is confounded with other on-going mental activity and identified with whatever actual conscious activity it becomes part of. I shall try to show that the same can be said of the fate of what is repressed, and of what cognitive psychologists call implicit memories.

What I have proposed is a generalization of the function of consciousness beyond the discrimination of memory and perception. As I have stated elsewhere, *"The function of consciousness as subjective awareness in any state is to distinguish the actual source of a mental content and to reveal the source as a quality or category of experience"* (italics added) (Shevrin, 1992, p. 137). Categories of experience refer, not to particular contents but to mental activities, such as perception, memory, thought, desire, and so on. Perhaps a more apt term would be mental *vehicle* insofar as a mental vehicle can be said to contain particular mental contents; the dream vehicle contains hallucinated perceptual contents, memories contain past contents, fantasies contain wished-for contents, perceptions contain current contents, and so on. It is also possible for different mental vehicles to contain the same content.

In an interesting and informative critique of this proposed generalized function of consciousness, Brakel (1989) has suggested that more than consciousness as subjective awareness is required for the proposed discriminations to occur. Her critique, as all useful critiques do, forces a further clarification of the proposed function (which I will offer later after a fuller presentation of Brakel's critique and alternate hypothesis). While she agreed that consciousness as subjective awareness—Edelman's primary consciousness—does provide the proposed tagging function, it in itself cannot be sufficient. She argued, for example, that a dream is simply experienced at the time as something really happening; it is only on awakening in a self-reflexive state of consciousness that we identify it as a dream. In fact, it happens occasionally that in the first few minutes of awakening we may still be in the grips of the dream and still believe it to be real, creating momentary confusion. Only when we are fully awake and *reflect* on the remembered dream experience in the context of waking reality, do we identify the hallucinated experience as a dream. This point is reminiscent of a similar point made by Opatow (for other reasons): A transparently wish-fulfilling sexual dream, for example, is experienced as a real gratification, no different from actual gratification. Only on awakening do we become aware that it was "just a dream."

Yet, on closer examination, higher level, reflexive consciousness may not be necessary. In fact, from a strictly theoretical vantage point by giving reflexive consciousness a role in these discriminations, we bring back the problems mentioned previously in linking the need for consciousness to a particular state—the normal, alert waking state. It would also be more parsimonious if one function were to prove sufficient. But beyond these purely theoretical predilections, there is a more crucial consideration intrinsic to the conception of consciousness so far developed. The unique function of consciousness is to discriminate between an internal and external state, and thus provide the basis for coordinating the two in real time, as Edelman proposed. When a value loaded, need-dominated memory is activated and primary consciousness is doing its job, a concurrent perception unaffected by the memory is related to that memory and a difference between the two "tagged." In other words, whenever consciousness is functioning, this "tagging" discrimination is being made.

With these considerations in mind, let us now turn to the case of the dream. The dream itself is an entirely internal event. It shares a number of characteristics with Edelman's homeostatic self-system insofar as it is capable of assimilating some but not all current perceptions into its narrative, depending on their suitability and fit. But, at the same time, there are other current perceptions, having mainly to do with the sleep state itself—all the distinctive proprioceptive inputs; nighttime external stimuli, such as bed-clothes pressure and feel; and other more adventitious stimuli that are at variance with the dream hallucinations. Consciousness is enabled to "tag" the dream *as a dream* because it provides the discriminations between the surrounding perceptual context and the dream experience *at the time of dreaming*. It is further proposed that there is likely a continually shifting balance between the dominance of the hallucinatory experience as perception and the hallucinatory experience as dream. In other words, there may be dreams for which the tagging function of consciousness has failed, in which case it might be better to talk of a dream delusion; in this respect, it allies itself with fully psychotic experiences. But most of the time the tagging function works reasonably well; when we recall the dream in the morning, we are immediately aware of it as a dream. Reflexive consciousness, as proposed by Brakel, may only be necessary when the tagging function has failed and may not constitute an additional required condition. A clinical illustration might further clarify the point at issue: A psychoanalytic patient experiencing the transference with the analyst, in which earlier patterns of behavior are being reenacted, can experience it as a transference because simultaneously primary consciousness is performing its function, making available in a transference-free manner other perceptions, memories, and judgments having to do with the analyst as a person different from the transference figure. These transference-free mental activities, operating on the fringes of consciousness, can readily be brought into focal consciousness and serve to keep a neurotic transference from becoming a psychotic transference, in which primary consciousness has failed in its function. Reflexive consciousness enters the picture when either patient or analyst focuses attention on the transference itself as an object of scrutiny and understanding; prior to that point, the transference is still tagged and thus experienced as different from the analytic reality.

When we turn to examine other mental vehicles, such as thinking, fantasizing, feeling, or desiring, we should not be misled by their occurrence in the alert, waking state in which consciousness is associated with higher level functions of reflexive awareness, in addition to its property of subjective awareness. Just as with dreams, but much more certainly, as we think or fantasize, consciousness as subjective awareness links on-going perceptions and the co-occurrence of other mental vehicles with our thoughts or fantasies, thus providing and sustaining the necessary tagging—so that we do not altogether lose ourselves in thought or fantasy and lose track of where we are. When this happens, we are momentarily deluded. Normally, however, this tagging goes on without the need for reflexive consciousness.

The proposed generalized function of consciousness as subjective awareness can help us to explain findings from subliminal perception and implicit memory research, as well as throw new light on what repression does to mental vehicles and their contents. We now turn to these considerations.

SUBLIMINAL PERCEPTION

Subliminal perception research has been one of the growth fields in psychological research. Since the early and influential work of Fisher (1957) at Mt. Sinai Hospital in New York, the number of subliminal perception studies has increased exponentially. Following an extended period of controversy as a consequence of which many important methodological problems were addressed and solved, emphasis in the field has shifted to understanding the differences between conscious and unconscious perception. (The interested reader is referred to several comprehensive reviews: Dixon, 1971, 1981; Shevrin, 1986b, 1990.)

One main finding of subliminal perception research will concern us for our present purposes: from the earliest work by Fisher, it has been observed that no matter how accurately the subliminal content is recovered or reflected in any of a number of different response modalities (dreams, images, free associations, priming) the subject remains unaware of its true source in the subliminal stimulus. Fisher (1957) demonstrated that even when the subject was confronted with the pictorial stimulus and could see that the dream, image or free association contained accurate information from the stimulus, there was no "Ah, yes, I remember now!" reaction. Instead, the subject reacted with surprise and amazement as to how the information somehow got into his or her responses.

Let us now apply the proposed generalized function of consciousness to this phenomenon. Because the subliminal perception was never in consciousness to begin with, it could not be tagged as a perception, even though all of its content registered, formed a memory trace, and influenced subsequent responses. However, when the stimulus content emerged in consciousness as part of a dream, image, free association, or some priming bias, it was tagged by consciousness as belonging to that mental vehicle and could no longer be experienced as being derived from another source. When confronted with the true source, the subject could reflect on the relationship but not experience it.

It is also the case, as some of our recent research has shown, that for some people to operate against the dictates of what their consciousness has made known to them results in inhibitions akin to defensive activity. In a series of subliminal experiments, we have shown that different instructions (essentially these are performance strategies) interact with subject preferences to determine the subliminal effects obtained (Snodgrass, Shevrin, & Kopka, 1993). In these experiments, subjects were instructed to guess which of four words had been flashed for 1 msec. One set of instructions invited the subject to look carefully at the visual field, try to see what might be there, and use that information to guess the correct word. We call this the *look strategy*. The other set of instructions invited the subject to relax and to let one of the four words just "pop" into mind. We call this the *pop strategy*. Subjects were also asked to state which of the two strategies they preferred.

The result of interest is that subjects who preferred the look strategy but asked to follow the pop strategy did significantly *worse* than chance in guessing at the correct subliminally presented word. We have replicated this finding four times, and it has also been replicated in another laboratory. The phenomenon appears to be reasonably well established. But what do we make of it in the light of our discussion of the function of consciousness?

Let us first try to imagine what a subject experiences during the course of this experiment. Because of the extreme brevity of the exposure, the subject can see nothing but the fixation point, which is replaced for 1 msec. at the exact same luminance (10 ft/lambert) by the stimulus field. The subject is unaware of any such millisecond replacement; as far as the subject's conscious experience is concerned nothing has happened. But the subject is asked to determine which of four words has been presented. In the pop strategy, the subject is instructed to let one of the four words pop into mind. For those subjects who prefer the look strategy, an interesting paradox is created: Their consciousness tells them that nothing has been presented, but they are nevertheless asked to let a word pop into mind. The pop strategy flies in the face of their preferred mode of dealing with conscious experience. The explanation developed so far would lead us to expect that these subjects should perform at chance. They simply are averse to playing this strange game of guessing at something that is not really there. Indeed, in one of the early pattern-masking subliminal studies done by Marcel (1983), he reported that there were a number of subjects who simply refused to believe anything had been presented and refused to guess.

But our *below*-chance results suggest that these subjects *did know* the flashed word *unconsciously*, or else they could not have performed significantly below-chance. The correct word did register subliminally, was activated by the instructions to guess the word, but was *rejected* before it could become conscious. Only in this way could one account for below-chance performance. Subjects had to know which word not to say without being consciously aware of doing so.

Now it is important to know that the four words were essentially ordinary words: *pleasure, fighting, rose, pain*. We could find no consistent differences in effect related to word meaning. For example, the negative words (*fighting* and *pain*) did not result in greater below-chance performance than the positive words (*pleasure* and *rose*). Thus, it could not be claimed that subjects were avoiding unpleasant affect or connotations. This point is important because it is this fact that returns us to a consideration of the role of consciousness, as such.

For those subjects who preferred the look strategy, a conflict was created between their commitment to their conscious experience and the instruction to let an unconsciously activated word pop into mind. The latter word had never been in consciousness, nor could it be in any way accounted for by their conscious experience. It is this experience of not allowing something unbidden and unconscious to emerge consciously without any apparent justification in immediate conscious experience that is akin to a defensive operation. Furthermore, supporting the defense hypothesis is the finding that subjects scoring high on a measure of hysterical (versus obsessional) personality style score high on the below-chance effect. Those with a more hysterical style are most likely repressors who are uneasy about any prompting from the side of the unconscious.

It is of further interest that when these same subjects who preferred the look strategy were asked to follow it, rather than the pop strategy, their performance was elevated *above* chance. When the strategy provided them with a means to account for their guesses by reference to a conscious experience, no matter how insubstantial, they could now allow the correct subliminally activated word to become conscious. There was no longer any conflict between conscious experience and unbidden unconscious activations.

Again, we can see how the relationship between perception and memory, the juncture at which consciousness enters the picture and plays a critical role in understanding the results just described. When perception is experienced as being at variance with memory, the memory is rejected, in particular for those subjects for whom a perceptual justification is essential. To put it quite concretely, when those subjects who prefer to look are asked to let the correct subliminal word "pop" into mind, the absence of any conscious perception results in the *recategorization* (to use Edelman's term) of the activated subliminal memory as wrong. When on the other hand, some "peg" on which to hang a conscious perception is provided, as in the look instructions, the activated subliminal memory is recategorized as correct.

The results could also be construed in Opatow's and Freud's terms: In the pop condition for the look-preferring subjects, the correct subliminally activated word carries with it the mark of the hallucinatory wish-fulfillment mode, according to which things are as you wish them to be rather than as they really are. As with any cooperative subject, the look-preferring subject would like to respond with the correct word, but when the correct word threatens to "pop" into mind, it is at variance with perceptual reality and must be rejected. When some conscious justification is provided, the correct word can be more readily accepted because it is no longer simply wished for but has some relationship to reality. This explanation helps us to understand further the role of defense in the finding, and why in particular repressors are more subject to the effect.

It should be noted that when combined the Edelman and Freud-Opatow theories account for the cognitive and emotional-motivational factors involved in the below-chance finding. Edelman's theory accounts for what happens to the activated subliminal memory, while the Freud-Opatow theory accounts for the reason it happens.

IMPLICIT MEMORY

Another growth field in recent psychological research is implicit memory. Whereas subliminal perception research deals with perception, implicit memory research extends the phenomenon of unconscious mentation to memory. The key experiments were done with organic amnesiacs with extremely faulty immediate memory. The typical experiment involved presenting amnesiacs with a word list and having them learn it according to a certain criterion (Squire, 1992; Warrington & Weiskrantz, 1970). They were later asked to recall the list or recognize words from a new list containing previously seen and new words. The amnesiacs failed both tasks. However, when they were asked to complete a word stem like *win _ _ _* with the first word that came to mind, they would more often than chance complete it with a word from the list although other options were possible. Thus they would complete *win _ _ _* with the letters *d o w* forming the word *window* that was on the list, but which they could not explicitly recall or recognize when given the opportunity. It is also important to note that if the amnesiacs were asked directly to complete the same word stems with a word from the list, they were unable to comply. Only free association worked. These findings led to the conclusion that even though the amnesiacs could not recall or recognize words from the list, a memory trace nevertheless formed and could influence subsequent responses as long as no effort to explicitly link the response to the list were required.

Immediately, one can see parallels to the research on subliminal perception: instead of a perception, a memory forms; instead of indirect influences of a perception that remain unconscious, there are indirect influences of a memory that remain unconscious. The most important parallel is that in both cases the true source of the information cannot be retrieved or experienced. When the amnesiac completes the word stem correctly, he or she is unaware of having done so, or that he or she has done so because of a previous experience. Like the subject in a subliminal perception experiment, the amnesiac experiences the retrieved content as belonging to the mental vehicle currently experienced and tagged.

Yet, there is one important difference between the implicit memory and subliminal perception research. For the amnesiac, the word list was once fully in consciousness and, in fact, rehearsed enough times to be immediately remembered; in the subliminal perception research, the stimulus was never in consciousness. If we were to apply the proposed generalized function of consciousness to the amnesiacs difficulty, we would need to posit that there was an *impairment* of the function of consciousness so that tagging did not take hold despite transient consciousness. The all important link between the inner state involved in remembering and the perception of the environmental context proves fragile, and instead of being maintained it is lost as the elements of the environmental context become assimilated to the inner state—much as happens in a dream with respect to certain concurrent stimuli. Once having lost its perceptual and memory tag, the contents cannot be retrieved as such, but can indirectly influence other on-going mental activities as is true for subliminal perception.

REPRESSION

But what of repression? Certainly, in the case of most repressions based on the subsequent expulsion of a content that was clearly in consciousness, we cannot speak either of subliminal perception or of an organic impairment of consciousness. According to our proposed generalized function of consciousness, most mental contents that are subsequently repressed should have had ample opportunity to be tagged for whatever mental vehicle with which the content was associated. And yet, it is a commonplace clinical observation that repressed contents generally make themselves known indirectly through derivatives or screen memories without the patient's awareness and seem to be acting like a subliminal perception or an implicit memory. A good example is provided by an analytic patient who, in the midst of an intensely erotic transference, spoke with much feeling of her abhorrence of childbirth and what it would do to her body. The very next session, less than 24 hours later, she attempted to recall what she had expressed in the previous hour because she knew it was important but could not remember any of it. At some later point in the session, she found herself free associating to the novel, *The Good Earth,* and a particular scene in which the heroine gives birth in a field. Remarkably enough, the association did not trigger the memory; instead, it functioned as an implicit memory.

If we hypothesize that the act of repression *undoes* the proposed generalized function of consciousness, we can begin to make sense of what happened to the patient, and what happens in repression generally. Once a perception, memory, thought, desire, or fantasy is repressed, the mental content loses its mental vehicle, and it can begin to act like a subliminal perception or an implicit memory. It can be "carried" into consciousness on other mental vehicles without any awareness of its true source.

If, as hypothesized, repressed contents lose their mental vehicle or true source, then we might also account for some of the characteristics of the unconscious: the equivalence of thought and action, perception and memory. In particular, if the distinction between perception and memory is lost, then there can be no ordering of events in time, and the unconscious becomes, in Freud's term, *timeless*. Treatment undertakes undoing the work of repression by restoring a knowledge of source, that is, the original mental vehicle in which the content originally appeared, and equally important, an ordering of events in time. But we also know that it is not easy to undo the work of repression. When the contents of fantasy and memory, freed of their mental vehicle as a result of repression, fuse and intermingle and then indirectly influence consciousness, it is often hard to undo the untagging function of repression.

With this examination of the effects of repression on perception and memory, we have come full circle in our analysis. It is the supreme function of consciousness as subjective awareness to distinguish between perception and memory and to make possible adaptive changes in memory (*recategorization* in Edelman's term) in the light of current perceptions of reality. This is also fundamentally what Freud believed when he posited a momentous shift in development from the pleasure principle to the reality principle, in which consciousness played a vital role. And this is also what Opatow had in mind when he posited that consciousness arose in the act of negation of the mode of hallucinated wish fulfillment. On the basis of these formulations, I have posited a generalized function of consciousness that works to distinguish all categories, or vehicles, of mental life. I have then drawn on evidence from subliminal perception and implicit memory research to support this proposal, and I have also demonstrated how an understanding of repression can be advanced by showing how it undoes the function of consciousness.

CONCLUSION

Why do we need to be conscious? The psychoanalytic answer we propose is that without it we would be entirely at the mercy of our internal states (hallucinated wish fulfillments for Opatow, values for Edelman, drives for Freud) and bound to recapitulate the past without modifying it in the light of present experience.

In the course of this chapter, we have provided a philosophical frame of reference for considering different ways of thinking about consciousness: dualism, property dualism, reductionism, and functionalism, as well as those, like Searle, who view consciousness as an emergent property of the brain. We next considered three stages in Freud's thinking about consciousness, ending with his "sense organ" model for consciousness, in which consciousness makes us aware of the qualitative dimensions of pleasure and unpleasure.

After demonstrating that this sense organ model runs into difficulties in trying to account for the full range of conscious experiences, we considered current cognitive views of consciousness and found them wanting. These theories appeared to link consciousness to a particular state—the normal waking state—and thus failed to account for subjective awareness in other states.

We then compared the theories of Opatow and Edelman. Although they start from vastly different points, the two theories converge on the view that consciousness emerges when current perceptions become capable of modifying past experience or memory.

Based in part on these theories, we proposed a general function of consciousness, according to which consciousness served to mark or tag different vehicles of mental life: perception, memory, fantasy, thought, dreams, and so on. Without this function of consciousness, we would not be able to discriminate these different vehicles of mental life.

Finally, we cited findings from subliminal research, the implicit memory literature, and the operation of repression to support this formulation of the function of consciousness.

REFERENCES

Allport, G. (1989). Visual attention. In M. I. Rosner (Ed.), *Foundation of cognitive science* (pp. 631–682). Cambridge, MA: MIT Press.

Brakel, I. A. W. (1989). Negative hallucinations, other irretrievable experiences, and two functions of consciousness. *International Journal of Psychoanalysis, 70*(3), pp. 461–479.

Dixon, N. F. (1971). *Subliminal perception: The nature of a controversy.* London: McGraw-Hill.

Dixon, N. F. (1981). *Preconscious processing.* London: Wiley.

Edelman, G. M. (1989). *The remembered present.* New York: Basic Books.

Fisher, C. (1957). A study of the preliminary stages of the construction of dreams and images. *Journal of the American Psychoanalytic Association, 5,* 60–97.

Freud, S. (1953). The interpretation of dreams. In J. Strachey (Ed. and Trans.), *The standard edition of the complete psychological works of Sigmund Freud* (Vol. 4, pp. 1–630). London: Hogarth Press. (Original work published in 1900)

Freud, S. (1955a). The studies on hysteria. In J. Strachey (Ed. and Trans.), *The standard edition of the complete psychological works of Sigmund Freud* (Vol. 2, pp. 1–310). London: Hogarth Press. (Original work published in 1895)

Freud, S. (1955b). Notes upon a case of obsessional neurosis. In J. Strachey (Ed. and Trans.), *The standard edition of the complete psychological works of Sigmund Freud* (Vol. 10, pp. 151–251). London: Hogarth Press. (Original work published in 1909)

Freud, S. (1958). Formulations on the two principles of mental functioning. In J. Strachey (Ed. and Trans.), *The standard edition of the complete psychological works of Sigmund Freud* (Vol. 12, pp. 213–226). London: Hogarth Press. (Original work published in 1911)

Freud, S. (1961). The ego and the id. In J. Strachey (Ed. and Trans.), *The standard edition of the complete psychological works of Sigmund Freud* (Vol. 19, pp. 1–182). London: Hogarth Press. (Original work published 1923)

James, W. (1890). *Principles of psychology.* New York: Holt.

Mandler, G. (1992). Toward a theory of consciousness. In H.-G. Geissler, S. W. Link, and J. T. Townsend (Eds.), *Cognition, information processing, and psychophysics: Basic issues* (pp. 43–65). Hillsdale, NJ: Erlbaum.

Marcel, A. (1983). Conscious and unconscious perception: Experiments in visual masking and word recognition. *Cognitive Psychology, 15,* 197–257.

Opatow, B. (1997). The distinctiveness of the psychoanalytic unconscious. *Journal of the American Psychoanalytic Association, 54*(3), 865–890.

Posner, M., & Boies, S. W. (1971). Components of attention. *Psychological Review, 78,* 391–408.

Searle, J. (1997). Consciousness and the philosophers. *The New York Review of Books, 44*(4), 43–50.

Shevrin, H. (1986a, August 22). *A proposed function of consciousness relevant to theory and practice.* Paper presented at the American Psychological Association Convention, Washington, DC.

Shevrin, H. (1986b, Spring/Summer). Subliminal perception and dreaming. *Journal of Mind and Behavior, 7* (2 & 3), 379–395.

Shevrin, H. (1990). Subliminal perception and repression. In J. P. Singer (Ed.), *Repression and dissociation: Implications for personality theory, psychopathology, and health* (pp. 103–119). Chicago: University of Chicago Press.

Shevrin, H. (1992). Subliminal perception, memory, and consciousness: Cognitive and dynamic perspectives. In R. F. Bornstein & T. S. Pitman (Eds.), *Perception without Awareness: Cognitive, clinical, and social perspectives.* New York: Guilford Press.

Shiffrin, R. M., & Schneider, W. (1977). Controlled and automatic information processing: II. Perceptual learning, automatic attending, and a general theory. *Psychological Review, 84,* 127–190.

Snodgrass, M., Shevrin, H., & Kopka, M. (1993). The mediation of intentional judgments by unconscious perceptions: The influences of task strategy, task preference, word meaning, and motivation. *Consciousness and Cognition, 2,* 169–193.

Squire, L. R. (1992). Declarative and non-declarative memory: Multiple brain systems supporting learning and memory [Special issue]. *Memory Systems: Journal of Cognitive Neuroscience, 4*(3), 232–243.

Warrington, E. K., & Weiskrantz, C. (1970). Amnesic syndromes: Consolidation or retrieval? *Nature, 228,* 628–630.

PART IV

CURRENT RESEARCH TOPICS
IN PERSONALITY

Current research in personality is based on one or more of the theories in Part II, as discussed in Chapter 1 and presented in Table 1.3. Research derivative of particular theories is included in the chapters in Part II, especially Chapters 5–8; and research related to the conscious and unconscious processing is included in Chapters 9 and 10 of Part III. The chapters in Part IV show how illustrative personality phenomena are conceptualized and assessed. They address basic issues, such as a personality variable's consistency across situations, its stability over time of personality, and genetic and experiential influences on it.

Chapter 11 on aggression is instructive in that it addresses many of the basic issues involved in researching any topic in personality. It deals with how to define and assess the topic of aggression, the subtyping of aggression, and the definition of it as a disorder. In addition, it addresses the issues of consistency and stability as they apply to aggressive behavior. Leonard Berkowitz has contributed particularly to the discussion of hostile and affective aggression and the ways in which they are distinct from instrumental aggression. This chapter is a good example of how contemporary personality researchers approach topics that have been of concern to personality theorists as far back as Freud.

Chapter 12 on learned helplessness briefly presents the original laboratory work on how dogs are rendered apathetic and then focuses on the study of how people explain aversive events. It presents evidence that there is a traitlike explanatory style consistent across situations and methods of measurement. More recent research addresses the heritability and sociocultural context of explanatory styles. Christopher Peterson and Curie Park also discuss how this work connects with previous theorists and the larger social cognitive school. This topic is a good example of how smaller scale contemporary theories based on a particular phenomenon in one school of thought are developed by comprehensive research cutting across many schools.

The chapter on subjective well-being, Chapter 13, focuses on the study of positive and negative affect, in keeping with the interest of humanistic and experiential theories. These theories have been found to be separate dimensions rather than poles of a single one, a finding consistent with other research that has suggested two fundamental behavioral-motivational systems of approach and avoidance (Carver, 1996). Like the previous two chapters, it presents evidence for subjective well-being's (SWB) being a stable, consistent traitlike tendency, associated with extraversion and neuroticism. Consistent with the argument presented in Chapter 5 on trait theories, it supplements findings about the structure of personality with research on the processes through which SWB is involved in personality functioning. As in the previous two chapters, Ed Diener shows that understanding of this topic has been advanced by research drawing on personality processes of importance across many schools of personality study.

Chapter 14 goes beyond particular aspects of personality to characterizations of entire personalities as disordered. It connects the study of personality traits to clinical diagnosis. It highlights the limited range of subjects studied in most personality research, and it raises the issue of the social construction of abnormality by clinicians. It shows how we can understand maladaptive functioning as an extreme variant of normal functioning. In so doing, Thomas Widiger provides a contemporary answer to a question posed by clinicians, beginning with Freud.

Chapter 15 on self-with-other representations (SWORs) presents a contemporary reformulation of a topic of long-standing interest, especially to object relations and interpersonal schools of thought. A dynamic self-concept, particular components of which are activated by relationships and other situational factors, is central to social cognitive formulations (Baldwin, 1992; Barone, 1997; Barone, Maddux, & Snyder, 1997). Daniel Ogilvie and Christopher Fleming show how the assessment of SWORs with the aid of computer technology and multivariate statistics provides a mapping of a person's interpersonal constellations. They demonstrate, in a case study, the value of such feedback to a person trying to gain insight and make changes.

The final chapter, Chapter 16, on sex/gender covers not only cognitive constructions of the individual based on personal experiences, as in Chapter 15, but also cultural constructions about gender. Initially, research on this topic was from the perspective that personality differences would follow biological sex differences. More recent research has emphasized the social construction of gender, which can produce highly polarized masculine and feminine schemas or androgynous ones, combining characteristics from each of these. Another recent perspective focuses on sociocultural arrangements, such as division of labor by sex, which can produce personality differences. In this chapter, Richard Ashmore and Andrea Sewell show that understanding increases as phenomena are construed differently—the lesson about personality study that this book has sought to convey.

REFERENCES

Baldwin, M. W. (1992). Relational schemas and the processing of social information. *Psychological Bulletin, 112,* 461–484.
Barone, D. F. (1997). Introduction to Symposium on constructing self with others. *Review of General Psychology,*
Barone, D. F., Maddux, J. E., & Snyder, C. R. (1997). *Social cognitive psychology: History and current domains.* New York: Plenum Press.
Carver, C. S. (1996). Emergent integration in contemporary personality psychology. *Journal of Research in Personality, 30,* 319–334.

CHAPTER 11

AGGRESSIVE PERSONALITIES

LEONARD BERKOWITZ

INTRODUCTION

Everyone is not equal, at least in the proclivity to violence. We are all capable of becoming aggressive, and undoubtedly, all of us have at one time or another attacked someone who offended us—in our thoughts or verbally if not in an open assault. Nevertheless, some people seem to be particularly prone to violence. They attack others relatively frequently, insulting them, criticizing them, or even at times attacking them physically. Because of their apparently strong predisposition to aggression, we can say they have aggressive personalities.

Hans Toch, a psychologist long known for his pioneering analyses of violent criminals, identified one such aggressive person in the sample of men he interviewed in California jails:

> Jimmy was 23 years old, with a work record consisting of a successful career as a minor league pimp. Jimmy's "rap sheet" included many and diverse offenses, such as forcible rape . . . kidnapping, intoxication, grand theft, and disturbing the peace. Most revealing, there were several instances of battery and assaults with deadly weapons, and two attacks on police officers. (Toch, 1969, pp. 68–69)

LEONARD BERKOWITZ • Department of Psychology, University of Wisconsin–Madison, Wisconsin 53706.

Advanced Personality, edited by David F. Barone, Michel Hersen, and Vincent B. Van Hasselt. Plenum Press, New York, 1998.

Jimmy, of course, differed from other violence-prone men in the details of his life story, but some of his characteristics are not atypical at all. For one thing, Jimmy had a history of repeated violence. Many other violent offenders seem to have the same kind of consistency. As just one example, in a large sample of men convicted of serious violent crimes studied by Miller, Dinitz, and Conrad (1982), only 30% had ended their criminal careers after committing just one violent offense. Most of these men had developed a continuing pattern of aggressive behavior that often lasted into their middle age.

Basically, this chapter asks, how common is this? Are there other people, who are less extremely violent and not imprisoned for serious offenses, who are also apt to be consistently prone to aggression? Then too, Jimmy's law-breaking was not confined to violent assaults. He had pimped, raped, become intoxicated, and robbed as well. Here again, this chapter seeks to determine whether this conduct is a general phenomenon. Are strong aggressive inclinations just one component of a broad pattern of antisocial conduct?

In trying to answer these questions, this author will be fairly selective in the review of the pertinent literature. Rather than providing an exhaustive survey, I will look at only some of the major investigations in this field. And moreover, the focus largely will be on self-report, paper-and-pencil tests of predispositions to anger and aggression, neglecting other ways of assessing aggressive proclivities, because these tests are commonly employed and have given rise to a substantial body of findings. I should also acknowledge that nothing will be said about the relationship between Attention Deficit Disorder (ADD) and aggressiveness, even though mounting evidence indicates that ADD can be implicated in many cases of antisocial conduct (see Moffitt, 1990). Nonetheless, our discussion will highlight many of the issues in the study of aggressive personalities and summarize much of what researchers have learned about them.

ANALYZING BEHAVIORAL CONSISTENCY

SOME DEFINITIONS

Before proceeding further, however, we should define some terms. The words *anger,* *hostility,* and *aggression* are often used interchangeably in psychology as in everyday speech. I believe this terminological looseness makes for confusion and may well be an impediment to an adequate scientific understanding of anger and aggression (see Berkowitz, 1993a, Chap. 1). I will employ these words in a fairly narrow manner in this chapter. Consistent with other writers' usage (e.g., Buss, 1961; Spielberger, Reheiser, & Sydeman, 1995), *aggression* is here regarded as any kind of behavior that is intended to hurt or destroy others, while *aggressiveness* refers to a fairly consistent pattern of this kind of conduct. I think of *violence* only as a relatively extreme form of aggression. *Anger,* on the other hand, has more to do with the feelings and expressive-motor reactions that are activated by a provocative condition. Consequently, insulted persons may become angry, they may have the particular feelings and facial and bodily reactions that are usually associated with this emotional state, but they may or may not aggress against someone openly. Along with several other researchers, I view *hostility* as an attitude, a dislike of a particular person, object, or issue, accompanied by a desire to see this target injured or even destroyed. Aggression, anger, and hostility are often seen together, of course, and it is useful to regard them as components of a general syndrome. For me, as for other writers (e.g., Anderson, Deuser, & DeNeve, 1995), these are the components of affective aggression, whereas Spielberger and his associates (e.g., Spielberger, Krasner, & Solomon, 1988) speak of them as belonging to an "AHA! Syndrome," a constellation of anger, hostility, and aggression. Nevertheless, although anger, hostility, and aggression are often correlated, any of these syndrome components can arise without the others, and they should be thought of as essentially separate but somewhat linked reactions.

My mentioning affective aggression, the aggression instigated by an aversive state of affairs, brings up another distinction that should be made. Most researchers, following Feshbach (1964), believe there are important differences between *instrumental aggression* and *hostile aggression*. In the former case, the attackers attempt to injure their target, but do this primarily in pursuit of some other goal, such as money, social approval, or to regain self-esteem in their own eyes. Hostile aggression, on the other hand, is mainly directed at the injury (or sometimes, destruction) of the target. This latter type of behavior can be reinforced by rewards other than the target's suffering, but still, the target's injury is the primary goal (see Berkowitz, 1993a). Hostile aggression is, of course, often *affective aggression* in that it is most likely to arise when the person is angry or otherwise emotionally aroused. It is this type of aggression that is frequently termed *expressive aggression*. We have to recognize, however, that some people take delight in hurting others, by insults, for example, even when they are not especially upset or angry; their attacks on others can also be regarded as hostile aggression. By and large, the personality measures discussed in this chapter typically will be more concerned with an individual's predisposition to engage in hostile (or affective) aggression rather than instrumental aggression, although many highly aggressive persons exhibit both.

Whatever the kind of aggression that is carried out, saying people differ in their probability of becoming aggressive means that they show considerable consistency in their display of this behavior. But how is this regularity revealed? Looked at broadly, there are two kinds of consistency: one involving a *response generalization* in that these persons might display any of a wide variety of aggressive responses, depending on the situation they are in; and the other, involving a *stimulus generalization* in that the aggression, whatever its form, might occur in many different situations. This chapter will inquire into both types of consistency. It will seek to determine whether aggressive personalities are either assaultive in different ways (that is, whether they exhibit a high degree of response generalization) or if they tend to specialize in the form of their attacks. Also, with regard to stimulus generalization, the chapter reviews evidence indicating whether these persons are either assaultive over a broad range of conditions or if their aggression is a reaction only to a particular type of situation.

THE PROBLEM OF CONSISTENCY

The contention that some people can appropriately be labeled as being violence-prone personalities certainly does not imply that they are aggressive all the time. They obviously do not always attack other persons around them and sometimes may even be kind and considerate to others. Their behavior will vary from one situation to another. Indeed, this situational variation may well be far more substantial than most of us realize.

Walter Mischel (1968) was one of the first psychologists to draw his colleagues' attention to the significance of this variability in the study of individual personalities. Summarizing the findings from a good many investigations, Mischel pointed out that when researchers looked at the relationships between measures of a particular personality trait (such as honesty or dependency) and behavioral indices of that characteristic, they typically obtained correlations no higher than .20 or .30. The personality scores evidently could not be used to predict with any real degree of success how an individual would act in a given situation. For Mischel, the weak correlations were probably due to the great variability in behavior from one situation to another. In the case of honesty, as an example, an individual might be morally proper on one occasion but yield to temptation and steal at another time. Given this variability in conduct, the question then is, why do we believe people are consistent in their behavioral styles? Why do we so confidently characterize someone as honest, extraverted, impulsive, or, for that matter, aggressive, if her or his actions are so changeable? Mischel suggested that the answer could be found in our thought processes: We want to form stable conceptions of those around us because we realize it would be helpful to have a firm impression of those with whom we are dealing. We could then believe we understand them and can cope with them adequately. Desiring those clear conceptions, we then "see" more consistency in people's behavior than actually exists.

Some researchers sought to counter Mischel's argument by insisting that we will find more behavioral consistency than he had proposed if we look for this consistency in the proper way. Two of the answers to Mischel are especially pertinent to our present concern with aggressive personalities.

Epstein's (1979) reply to Mischel relied mainly on statistical reasoning. He noted that in many studies investigators tried to relate their test scores to a single behavioral observation only, that is, to how the research participants acted at one time in one situation. This single observation was likely to be fairly unreliable because the subjects' reactions when tested could have been influenced by all kinds of unknown chance factors. Epstein pointed out it would be far better to try to cancel out these random errors by employing aggregated observations. In other words, we should look for relationships between personality test scores (and these scores should be based on multiple responses) and an outcome measure dealing with the participants' reactions over a number of situations. This multiple-observation index would give us the most reliable indicator of how strong the participants' inclination to aggression was.

Bem and Allen (1974) took a different tack in their answer to Mischel. They maintained that we should expect consistency in a particular type of behavior only from those persons for whom this kind of behavior is important. Extending the Bem and Allen argument to the assessment of honesty, it is certainly possible that quite a few people do not place much value on honesty, and these individuals would not always seek to keep to "the straight and narrow" when faced with temptation. On the other hand, those who regard being honest as central to their self-conceptions are more apt to be consistently honest from one occasion to another. Now, apply this reasoning to aggressiveness: Some persons, such as Jimmy (mentioned earlier) and others prone to violence, could believe that it is very important for them to show they are tough and ready to fight. Valuing their aggressiveness, they are the kind of people whom Bem and Allen would expect to be fairly consistent in their use of violence.

CONSISTENCY IN AGGRESSIVE BEHAVIOR

RESPONSE GENERALIZATION IN AGGRESSIVE PERSONALITIES

I will begin this inquiry into the consistency of aggressive reactions with an examination of several popular self-report inventories that attempt to assess an individual's likelihood of becoming aggressive and/or angry. Over the years psychologists have devised a great many such instruments (see Miller, Jenkins, Kaplan, & Salonen, 1995; Spielberger *et al.*, 1995). This discussion will not provide a comprehensive survey of these measures and will not analyze the psychometric properties of the scales we do consider. Instead, we will first look for evidence of a general consistency across different kinds of anger/aggression-related reactions and then will delve more deeply into some of the more differentiated patterns of anger/aggression reactions. The first part of this review essentially asks whether those who have one kind of anger/aggression-related characteristic, such as a proclivity to strong anger, will also have other anger/aggression-related qualities, such as a hostile attitude toward the social world. In the second part of the chapter, we will consider each of these patterns in more detail.

The Buss Questionnaires

The Hostility Inventory devised by Buss and Durkee (1957), the BDHI, is among the most popular of anger/aggression-measuring tools. Consisting of 75 true-false items, this self-report inventory was intended to assess seven somewhat different traits, all supposedly related to the propensity to act aggressively: assault, indirect aggression, irritability, negativism, resentment, suspicion, and verbal aggression. Evidence indicates, however, that these characteristics are not necessarily as independent as Buss and Durkee had initially thought. According to a statistical review of several factor-analytic investigations of the BDHI (Bushman, Cooper, & Lemke, 1991), when people rate themselves on the seven scales in this instrument, their ratings typically tend to fall along two underlying dimensions. One of these dimensions has to do with the tendency to display aggression openly and consists primarily of the assault and verbal aggression scales. The second factor is more covert in nature and seems to be best represented by the resentment and suspicion scales. This factor appears to reflect the attitude of hostility.

Whatever the response dimensions tapped by the BDHI are, it is worth noting that the total score on inventory does seem to assess a general aggressiveness. Thus, men imprisoned for violent crimes have a higher score on the total inventory than do men incarcerated for nonviolent offenses. In another study, the participants' total scores were positively correlated with the intensity of the electric shocks they administered to peers as punishment for their mistakes on a learning task (see Buss & Perry, 1992, p. 452).

More recently, Buss and Perry (1992) sought to improve on the BDHI by developing a 29-item Aggression Questionnaire (AQ). Unlike the BDHI's true-or-false items, each of the self-report items in this instrument is rated on a five-step scale having to do with how characteristic the description is of the person. Using factor analyses, the data gathered in two fairly large samples of men and women revealed the four factors the investigators had intended. These factors—and an item representing each one—are *physical aggression* (e.g., "Given enough provocation, I may hit another person"), *verbal aggression* (e.g., "When people annoy me, I may tell them what I think of them"), *anger* (e.g., "I have trouble controlling my temper"), and *hostility* (e.g., "Other people always seem to get the breaks").

Here too, the components are not unrelated. The physical aggression, verbal aggression, and anger scales all seem to tap an inclination to be highly reactive to provocations. Not unexpectedly, these scales were moderately intercorrelated in the two samples studied by Buss and Perry: the correlation coefficients varied from .45 to .48. The hostility scale had lower but still significant correlations with the other scales, ranging from .25 to .45 (the latter r with anger). When Buss and Perry asked fraternity members to rate each others' aggressiveness the results pointed to the interrelationships among the subscales. They found that the participants' total AQ scores correlated about .31 with their peers' impressions of their general aggressiveness.

Siegel's MAI

Taking a somewhat different approach, Judith Siegel (1986) devised a 38-item, self-report trait questionnaire, the Multidimensional Anger Inventory (MAI), intended to measure aspects of angry feelings: a person's characteristic frequency, duration, and magnitude of anger; the range of situations provoking this feeling; and his or her typical way of expressing anger. Siegel then carried out factor analyses of the responses made to the MAI by two samples of participants, one consisting of male and female college students and the other of male factory employees, to determine what dimensions were tapped by these responses. All in all, the analyses indicated that the frequency, duration, and magnitude aspects of anger clustered together to form a single dimension dealing with the proclivity to anger arousal. (The item with the highest loading on this factor was "I tend to get angry more frequently than most people.") In addition, there also were separate factors involving (a) the range of anger-eliciting situations, (b) a hostile outlook (e.g., "People can bother me just by being around"), (c) anger-out tendencies (e.g., "When I am angry with someone, I let that person know"), and (d) a tendency toward anger-in and brooding (e.g., "Even after I have expressed my anger, I have trouble forgetting about it").

According to Siegel, the significant correlations between her measures and conceptually similar scales developed by other researchers support the construct validity of her factors. Nevertheless, the pattern of these relationships indicates that her anger/aggression-related dimensions are far from completely independent. With the exception of the anger-out scale, they were all correlated at roughly the same level with these other scales. Indeed, research findings obtained by Miller et al. (1995) in Finland also show that the components of the MAI often go together. The intercorrelations among the components of the MAI ranged from .43 to .68 in one Finnish sample and from .43 to .69 in another sample.

The Spielberger Inventories

All of the instruments described so far are trait measures in that they attempt to assess characteristic (or habitual) response patterns. Charles Spielberger and his associates (cf. Spielberger et al., 1985; Spielberger et al., 1988; Spielberger et al., 1995) believed that it was advisable to have indices of people's current angry feelings (anger state) as well as of their habitual anger reactions (anger-related traits) and developed the State-

Trait Anger Scale (STAS) to do this. The anger state measure (S-Anger scale) requires the participants to rate the degree to which items, such as "I am furious," and "I feel irritated," characterize their present feelings, whereas for the anger trait measure (T-Anger scale), they have to indicate how often they have the reactions described by such items as "I have a fiery temper."

As is now standard in the development of personality scales, factor analyses have been carried out to determine what are the dimensions along which the individual items in the STAS are grouped together. One such analysis (see Spielberger *et al.,* 1995) indicated that the anger state items constituted a single dimension having to do with the intensity of the person's present angry feelings. The anger trait items, on the other hand, seemed to be clustered into two correlated factors, one having to do with an angry temperament but without specifying any provoking situation (a representative item is "I am a hotheaded person"), and the other involving the inclination to become angry when frustrated or evaluated negatively (e.g., "It makes me furious when I am criticized in front of others"). Although related, these seem to be psychologically different dispositions. One study (Crane, 1981, cited in Spielberger *et al.,* 1995) found, for example, that medical patients with very high blood pressure tended to have higher scores on the reactive anger trait than did their counterparts with normal blood pressure, though there was no difference between these two groups on the angry temperament scale.

The Spielberger team did not stop there. Realizing that some people have a tendency to hide their feelings, Spielberger and his colleagues constructed the Anger Expression (AX) Scale, consisting of such items as "I boil inside, but I don't show it," and "I say nasty things." This measure was intended to assess a continuum of reaction patterns, ranging from a persistent inclination to suppress one's anger (at one end of the postulated dimension) to a characteristic tendency to express anger openly (at the other extreme). However, research soon indicated that the AX items tapped two independent dimensions that could be labeled *anger-in* and *anger-out* (see, for example, Spielberger *et al.,* 1988, pp. 95–97; Spielberger *et al.,* 1995, p. 58). For our purposes, it is important to recognize that people who become angry often are also apt to be high on the anger-out dimension. Those "who experience anger more frequently are more likely to express anger toward other persons or objects in the environment than to suppress it" (Spielberger *et al.,* 1988, p. 97).

Further research with the AX Scale led to the development of yet another scale, this one measuring the person's ability to control the expression of anger (see Spielberger *et al.,* 1988). One item, for example, asks how characteristic of the person is the statement, "I calm down faster than most other people." The individual scoring high on this scale evidently invests "a great deal of energy in monitoring and preventing the expression of anger" (Spielberger *et al.,* 1995, p. 60).

Spielberger and his associates have recently combined all of their measures to form a 44-item, State-Trait Anger Expression Inventory (STAXI) (Spielberger *et al.,* 1995). Again, however, I believe it is worth noting that the various scales in the STAXI are not entirely independent. Thus, supporting the results obtained in other investigations, the Finnish research by Miller *et al.* (1995) showed that a factor composed of the anger control items had a substantial negative relationship with the factor based on the anger-out items. Just as we would expect, in other words, people who are concerned about regulating the expression of their anger typically do not show their anger openly.

INDICATIONS OF RESPONSE–STIMULUS GENERALIZATION

Interrelationships among Anger/Aggression Scales and Inventories

There seem to be some common threads running through the research findings obtained with these different anger/aggression inventories. For one thing, even though the investigations reviewed here identified different types of anger/aggression-related traits (and more will be said about this shortly), these characteristics are often found together. Therefore, for each of the instruments just examined, the component factors underlying the responses to these scales tend to be moderately intercorrelated. There is *some* chance, in other words, that a person who has one of the qualities making for a predisposition to aggression will also have other aggression-facilitating characteristics. In this respect, then, the findings indicate that the high scorers on these scales exhibit a small to moderate degree of response generalization.

The response generalization involved in this measurement can also be seen in the way scores on one anger/aggression/hostility inventory are typically correlated with scores on the other instruments. As an illustration of this, I mentioned earlier that scores on Siegel's (1986) Multidimensional Anger Inventory have moderate relationships with scores on other, similar scales. Yet another example can be found in the significant correlations between a very brief anger/aggression questionnaire (the BAAQ) and the total score on the 75-item BDHI (Maiuro, Vitaliano, & Cah, 1987). Each of the six items in the BAAQ was intended to represent one of the six subscales from the original BDHI (e.g., assault, indirect aggression, irritability). Nevertheless, each item was significantly related to the total BDHI score as well as to each of the component subscales. Still, these six items did form somewhat different clusters. The four dealing with the tendency to display open aggression (corresponding to the overt aggression factor found in factor-analytic investigations of the BDHI) were more strongly interrelated than were the other two.

Relationships with Other Indicators of Aggressiveness

Going beyond the interrelationships among the various self-report inventories, there are studies showing that scores on these instruments often are correlated with other, quite different indications of aggressiveness. (These findings thus point to a moderate degree of stimulus generalization and response generalization because there is a consistency over different situations.) One such investigation was cited by Buss and Perry (1992). British men incarcerated for violent offenses had higher totals on the BDHI than did nonviolent prisoners. And similarly, when Maiuro *et al.* (1987) used their six-item BAAQ to compare a sample of nonviolent U.S. men with men who had documented histories of assaultiveness, they showed that the latter had reliably higher total scores than did the former.

Anger/aggression scales have also been correlated with the anger experiences of less extremely violent persons. In an investigation by Deffenbacher, Demm, and Brandon (1986), the male and female university students scoring highest on the Spielberger STAS-Temperament scale reported having the most frequent and most intense anger experiences in the week covered by the study. Their characterization of themselves on the paper-and-pencil instrument predicted, on the average, how often and how strongly they were angered during the test week. More importantly, the self-report measures have at times also predicted actual aggressive behavior. Buss and Perry (1992, p. 452) provided an example. In one experiment they cited, scores on the BDHI were correlated with the intensity of the electric shocks the research participants gave peers as punishment for mistakes on assigned tasks. (Restraints against open aggression probably were quite weak in this experimental setting.) Similarly, in another study (Wilkins, Scharff, & Schlottmann, 1974), the Aggression scale from the MMPI was related to the intensity of the shocks the male subjects delivered.

Aggressiveness as One Part of a Pattern of Antisocial Conduct

Jimmy, the violent offender interviewed by Toch (1969), illustrated yet another kind of response-stimulus generalization. As was noted earlier, this violence-prone man had engaged in a wide variety of socially disapproved actions. Jimmy was not at all atypical in this regard. West and Farrington (1977) saw the same broad pattern of antisocial conduct in their longitudinal study of a sample of English working-class youths. The most aggressive boys in their investigation were apt to have violated a number of different social norms by engaging in gambling, drug use, reckless driving, and vandalism. The researchers concluded that extreme aggressiveness is to a considerable degree merely one component of a more general antisocial tendency. Loeber and Dishion (1984) have reported comparable findings. In their sample of 9- to 16-year-old boys, those youngsters who were regarded as highly aggressive by their mothers and their teachers (who tended to be aggressive at home and at school) were the ones who were most likely to have gotten into trouble with the law. Personality measures of aggressiveness have also been found to relate to indicators of antisocial conduct. As an example, Caspi et al. (1994) employed an aggression scale (from a multidimensional personality inventory) that was very similar to the anger/aggression factors in the inventories discussed earlier. In their sample of over 800 18-year-olds in New Zealand, scores on this scale had a significant correlation of approximately .2 with the number of contacts the young men and women had with the police as well as with their convictions for law-breaking. The relationships were about the same for the males and females.

CHILDHOOD CONDUCT DISORDER AND ADULT ANTISOCIAL PERSONALITY

This proclivity to engage in a wide variety of antisocial actions was recognized in two diagnostic categories within the American Psychiatric Association's diagnostic manual, DSM-III-R (American Psychiatric Association, 1987). According to this manual, a child can be regarded as having a conduct disorder if he or she displayed at least three of the following characteristics for at least six months:

- has stolen . . . on more than one occasion
- has run away from home overnight at least twice
- often lies (other than to avoid physical or sexual abuse)
- has deliberately engaged in fire-setting
- is often truant from school
- has broken into someone else's house, building, or car
- has deliberately destroyed other's property
- has been physically cruel to animals

- has forced someone into sexual activity with him or her
- has used a weapon in more than one fight
- often initiates physical fights

The second category, *antisocial personality disorder*, is diagnosed, according to DSM-III-R, when a person over 18 years old has exhibited, for at least six months, several characteristics, such as the following:

- showed conduct disorder before 15
- has repeatedly been involved in physical fights
- fails to plan ahead or is impulsive
- repeatedly lies
- drives recklessly

DSM-III-R estimates that about 3% of U.S. adult males have an antisocial personality disorder.

Following this classification system, many of the youthful aggressive persons of concern to us here would be viewed as having an aggressive conduct disorder if they also exhibited a broad pattern of antisocial behaviors. An earlier version of this diagnostic manual, DSM-III, did focus more closely on aggression by speaking explicitly of "aggressive conduct disorder." At any rate, DSM-III-R established several types of conduct disorder within this broad category, including a *group type*, in which the antisocial behavior occurs as a group activity with peers; and a *solitary type*, in which aggressive physical behavior is initiated by an individual and not as a group activity.

This latter subtyping, it should be noted, has not met with universal approval. Herbert Quay (e.g., 1993), for one, preferred the terminology that had been employed earlier in *DSM-III*, referring to *socialized* and *undersocialized* aggressive conduct disorders. Although the socialized aggressor engages in fighting and illegal activities, many of these behaviors are group oriented (as the later term *group type* indicates), and there are close relations with peers also involved in this form of conduct. By contrast, the label *undersocialized* better indicates that the undersocialized aggressor has disturbed relations with peers and adults and is ready to assault, bully, and exploit others regardless of their age. Quay also cited evidence that socialized aggressors are generally "less impaired" cognitively and socially than their undersocialized counterparts (p. 166).

LONGITUDINAL STABILITY

The consistency in angry and aggressive reactions discussed up until now has been over a relatively brief period. Other research indicates that, in a good number of cases, a predisposition to aggression can also persist over a considerable span of time. For persons so predisposed, a high level of youthful aggressiveness predicts a tendency toward antisocial conduct later in life.

Dan Olweus (1979) of the University of Bergen in Norway highlighted this consistency in his influential review of American, English, and Swedish research. In these longitudinal investigations, the male participants were first assessed when they were fairly young, usually from between 2 to 18 years of age; and then were evaluated again at intervals ranging from 6 months to 21 years later. A variety of procedures was employed in these behavioral assessments, including direct observations, teachers' ratings, and even reports from the participants' peers.

According to Olweus, the findings obtained from the 16 different samples of men involved in these studies were remarkably similar. Generally speaking, there was a moderately high relationship between initial and follow-up aggressiveness scores, although the magnitude of the correlation tended to decline as the time between the two measurements became longer. The average correlation was over .7 when the follow-up was only a year or less after the first assessment, and then decreased regularly to about .4 when there was a 21-year gap between the two evaluations. Interestingly, the aggression scores based on observations of the participants' actual behavior were just as consistent as the scores derived from teacher ratings, at least for the time periods involved in these particular studies.

Other longitudinal studies have also demonstrated this stability in aggressiveness over the years. One of these studies followed over 400 working class boys from a densely populated section of London, England (e.g., Farrington, 1989; West & Farrington, 1977), while another looked at a wide sample of over 800 boys and girls from a county in upstate New York (e.g., Eron, 1987; Huesmann, Eron, Lefkowitz, & Walder, 1984). Despite the differences in country, community size, degree of urbanization, and methodology, both investigations found that youthful aggressiveness was a fairly good predictor of aggressiveness and antisocial conduct later in life (see also Berkowitz, 1993a).

I will mention only a few of the results to illustrate this stability. In one part of the London study, Farrington and his associates found that of those youths who were in the highest quartile of the aggressiveness distribution at 9 years of age, fully 40% were still in the upper quarter of this distribution eight years later. In comparison, only 27% of the less aggressive boys at 9 years of age (who were in the bottom three-quarters of the aggressiveness distribution at this time) were in the highly aggressive group when they were 17 years old. According to this fairly crude indicator, then, most of the boys evidently had changed to some extent, but there was still a good chance that those who were highly aggressive before puberty would also be highly aggressive in late adolescence. And pointing to the response–stimulus generalization noted in the previous section, the very aggressive 9-year-olds were more apt to have gotten into trouble with the law by the time they reached adulthood than were their less aggressive counterparts: Fourteen percent of the former were convicted of a violent offense by 21 years of age, in comparison to only 4% of the less aggressive 9-year-olds (see Berkowitz, 1993a, pp. 136–137).

As I noted before, very comparable results were obtained by Leonard Eron and his colleagues in their study of schoolchildren residing in a semirural area of New York state. The boys and girls who were regarded by their classmates as being highly aggressive at 8 years of age were also likely to be viewed by their peers as highly aggressive ten years later. And as with the English youths, the children's violent tendencies were apt to continue into adulthood. For example, those people who had been most aggressive as 8-year-olds were three times more likely to have been convicted of a crime by the time they reached 19 than were their less aggressive counterparts. The former also tended to have the greatest number of criminal convictions by the time they were 30 years of age (see Berkowitz, 1993a, p. 139).

Consistency of Antisocial Conduct

Just as it is true that, as the old saying goes, "a leopard cannot change his spots," we have to be impressed by the degree to which some individuals do not change their mode of behavior and continue their antisocial conduct from childhood into adulthood. Only some of the relevant evidence can be cited here.

Adding to the results from the longitudinal studies mentioned so far, Farrington (1991) later made use of the DSM-III-R diagnostic system to identify the youths in his London sample who could be regarded as having a conduct disorder. The participants' scores on this new index in any one year were significantly related to their scores in the later periods, showing some consistency even from prepuberty to adulthood. More interestingly, about one third of the 98 10-year-old boys in the "worst" quarter of the distribution on this index, but only one fifth of their less disturbed counterparts, were among the 92 highly antisocial adults at 32 years of age. In agreement with other researchers, Farrington concluded that there apparently was a broad syndrome of antisocial behaviors that arose in childhood and had some likelihood of continuing into adulthood.

Lee Robins's (e.g., 1991) research has been exceedingly important in drawing attention to this continuity in patterns of antisocial conduct. According to a large-scale study he conducted, for example, more than one quarter of the U.S. men who showed three or more symptoms of childhood conduct disorder had four or more characteristics of adult antisocial personality disorder later in life. If we raise the childhood conduct disorder requirement to six or more childhood symptoms, we find that about one half of the men could be classified as having an adult antisocial personality. The stability over time looks even more impressive if, retrospectively, we go backward and see what qualities adult antisocials had as youngsters. In Robins's research, fully three quarters of the adult males with four or more antisocial characteristics could be classified as having a childhood conduct disorder (i.e., as having three or more childhood signs).

Research conducted in New Zealand testified to the generality of this phenomenon. As part of their ongoing study of a large birth cohort in New Zealand, White, Moffitt, Earls, Robins, and Silva (1990) reported that behavioral problems before starting school were a significant predictor of delinquent behavior in adolescence.

DIFFERENTIATING AMONG THE VIOLENCE PRONE

The discussion up to this point has directed little attention to the different characteristics that appear to be involved in the high scores on the various self-report measures of anger/aggression tendencies. Nevertheless, it is important to look at these special qualities and consider their implications for the behavior of aggressive personalities.

Whatever else the factor analyses reviewed earlier might have identified, over all they point to at least four different aggression-related characteristics: (a) an inclination to be highly reactive to perceived threats and provocations, (b) a somewhat more general hostile outlook or attitude, (c) a propensity to experience intense anger, and (d) a disposition to commit open aggression. We will look more deeply into each of these qualities from a variety of perspectives.

AFFECTIVE AGGRESSORS VERSUS INSTRUMENTAL AGGRESSORS

Before we look more closely at aggression-related characteristics, however, it should be clear that most of these traits are conducive to intense emotional (that is, affective) aggression. Those persons who possess these qualities—particularly but perhaps not only (a) an inclination to be highly reactive to perceived threats, and (c) a propensity for intense anger—are easily aroused and especially likely to become assaultive when they see themselves provoked. Getting back to the distinction between affective and instrumental aggression (mentioned near the start of this chapter), we can say they are affective aggressors whose attacks on others are more apt to be impelled by rage and an urge to do injury rather than by the more calculated pursuit of such goals as money, social approval, or selfenhancement. They may be gratified by the attainment of these noninjurious goals and may also desire them to some degree; however, their primary motive is to hurt or perhaps even to destroy.

Instrumentally inclined aggressors may be quite different. These are persons who have learned that aggression often pays, that they have a good chance of achieving their aims by attacking others. "Contract killers" display instrumental aggression in that they murder for money rather than in an outburst of rage. According to Millon, one of the mental health authorities who helped construct the American Psychiatric Association's *DSM-III*, many aggressive antisocial personalities assault others instrumentally in an attempt to enhance their image of themselves.

> [T]hey intentionally provoke others into conflict. They carry "a chip on their shoulder," often seem to be spoiling for a fight, and appear to enjoy tangling with others to prove their strength and test their competencies and powers. (Millon, quoted in Berkowitz, 1993a, p. 144)

School-age bullies also exhibit this kind of instrumental aggression. Their attacks frequently are more of an attempt to dominate others than an effort to injure or destroy their targets. Olweus's (1978, 1991) ambitious investigation in Swedish schools points to the bullies' use of aggression to coerce and dominate. Studying 12- to 16-year-old boys who had been identified by their teachers as frequently oppressing or harassing their classmates, Olweus concluded that these youngsters' aggression was largely self-initiated rather than a response to specific, unpleasant conditions. Rather than attacking in a fit of temper, they typically acted coolly and deliberately, selecting and creating their aggressive encounters, apparently because of their intense need to dominate others. Olweus's findings also indicated that these bullies generally approved of the use of violence in social relationships and had little empathy for their victims. And furthermore, he believed, they were not compensating for underlying feelings of insecurity. In agreement with other investigators, Olweus also found there was a high degree of response-stimulus generalization and longitudinal consistency in his sample. About two thirds of those who were identified as bullies when they were young were convicted of a crime by the time they were in their midtwenties.

Farrington's (1992) more recent review of quantitative studies of bullying supported Olweus's characterizations. Summarizing the results obtained in many of these studies, Farrington concluded that, "Generally, bullies are aggressive, tough, strong, confident . . . derive pleasure from bullying and have a strong need to dominate" (p. 3). They evidently intimidate and assault others more in an effort to enhance their sense of power and control over others rather than because they want to harm these people.

An interesting experiment by Dodge and Coie (1987; also see Berkowitz, 1993a, pp. 149–150) substantiates the difference between affective and instrumentally oriented aggressors that I have been positing here. Their study also throws light on the psychology of those who are easily angered. Working with young schoolboys, the researchers used teacher ratings on such items as "When this child has been teased or threatened, he . . . gets angry easily and strikes back" to identify those youngsters who were very "emotionally reactive" (i.e., affective) aggressors. By contrast, those said to be more "proactive" (i.e., instrumentally oriented) aggressors were likely to be described by their teachers as bullying others and/or as using physical force in order to dominate other kids. All of the boys were then shown a series of videotaped vignettes, each depicting a child knocking over another youngster's building blocks. In some instances, it was unclear why this had happened; in other cases, the viewers saw that the child had intentionally disrupted the other's play; and in still other vignettes, the event was obviously an accident.

The two kinds of aggressive youngsters differed primarily in their interpretations of the *ambiguous* scenes and not those in which the child's behavior was clearly either intentional or inadvertent. When the boys were asked to explain these unclear incidents, those who had been identified as highly emotional (affective) aggressors were particularly apt to attribute hostility to the child knocking the blocks down. And presumably because of this attribution, when the children indicated how they themselves would react to the occurrence, the affective aggressors were most likely to say they would carry out some form of aggression. The instrumentally oriented aggressors, on the other hand, did not formulate these hostile interpretations to any marked degree. Some youngsters, of course, had a mixture of affective- and instrumental-aggression tendencies. The chances that these "affective and instrumental" boys would make hostile attributions and say they would react aggressively to the event were between those of the "pure" affective aggressors and the "pure" instrumentally oriented aggressors.

PERCEIVING THREATS AND PROVOCATIONS

From a number of the items in the anger/aggression inventories, it would appear that many highly aggressive personalities, and especially the affective aggressors, tend to see many threats and bothersome annoyances in the world around them. This disposition is particularly reflected in the hostility component identified in the factor analyses of the item responses. For example, in the Buss-Perry (1992) AQ, one statement loading on the hostility factor reads, "I am suspicious of overly friendly strangers"; the similar factor in Siegel's (1986) MAI includes items such as, "Some of my friends have habits that annoy me very much."

Hostile Information Processing

In contemporary psychological terminology, *hostile information processing* refers to a way of processing information about social interactions. Modifying the argument made by Dodge and Coie (1987) to a slight extent, it could be argued that affective aggressors often interpret other people's actions (i.e., process the information they obtain about the others' behavior) in such a way that they think the others have deliberately affronted them or are in some way a threat to them.

Although he had not always explicitly differentiated between affective and instrumental aggression, Dodge (1982) had emphasized the way the actions of highly aggressive personalities are often governed by the way they pick up and then interpret information from the situations they are in. In his social information-processing model, when people are in an ambiguous encounter with others, they (a) search for relevant cues that can tell them what these others are doing and why; (b) interpret these cues, that is, make inferences and attributions as to why these persons are acting as they are; and then (c) consider the possible responses they might make, decide on an action, and carry it out. Those who are prone to violence, especially if they are the affective aggressors, theoretically exhibit their aggressive inclinations throughout this sequence:

Step 1. In many different situations they tend to look for and detect signs (cues) that may be indicative of potential threats or hostility. The second factor identified in Siegel's MAI, indicating that aggressively inclined persons can be provoked by a wide range of occurrences, might reflect this propensity to see aggression-related cues everywhere. The anger temperament (T-Anger) subscale within Spielberger's STAXI also seems to tap this inclination. According to Spielberger and Sydeman (1994), this subscale deals with "the tendency to perceive a wide range of situations as annoying or frustrating" (p. 310).

Step 2. They are apt to assign a hostile meaning to ambiguous cues. We saw this tendency in the Dodge and Coie affective aggressors, but it also might be characteristic of many highly aggressive individuals whether they are "pure" affective aggressors or not. According to Zelli, Huesmann, and Cervone (1995), the assaultive individuals' propensity to think of other people's actions as hostile might reflect their disposition to regard other persons as generally highly aggressive in nature. In their experiment, male and female university students who reported displaying physical aggression relatively often were more likely than their less aggressive counterparts to spontaneously think of other persons' aggressive actions as arising from their hostile personalities.

Step 3. And then, according to Dodge, violence-prone persons are likely to consider very few alternative, nonaggressive ways of responding to the situation before them.

All three of these steps are important in Dodge's analysis, but most of the studies bearing on this model have focused on the first two to the neglect of the last phase, the part concerned with the performance of the aggressive behavior. As I will soon note, Dodge's conception also did not give sufficient attention to anger intensity and other factors influencing the display of aggression.

GENERAL HOSTILE ATTITUDES

Rowell Huesmann and his colleagues have now extended Dodge's information-processing approach. Zelli and Huesmann (1995), for example, proposed that the propensity to make hostile inferences about others' actions might well grow out of a fairly general set of hostile beliefs.

The first part of this research looked closely at the components of these hostile beliefs. On the basis of their factor analyses, Zelli and Huesmann concluded that individuals with an extremely hostile outlook typically tended to (a) regard themselves as being persecuted by others (and so, they would tend to agree that "People want to be mean to [them]"), (b) believe that their social world is a mean one (e.g., they are apt to think that "People like doing things that bother others just for the sake of doing it"), and (c) view themselves as tougher and more aggressive than most others (e.g., they agree that "I am a better fighter than most people"). Interestingly, the "persecution" and "mean world" belief components were more strongly related to each other than to the "toughness" component, which tended to be fairly independent of the other hostile beliefs.

The next phase of the Zelli-Huesmann research tested the relationship between each of these sets of hostile beliefs and attributional tendencies. Modifying the Dodge-Coie paradigm summarized earlier, the investigators showed their university student subjects a series of videotaped incidents and asked them to rate the likelihood that the actors in these scenes had been deliberately hostile, had sought to be helpful, or had not intended the action depicted. Over all of the vignettes, both the persecution and mean world beliefs were significantly related to hostile attributions: The more the participants saw themselves as persecuted, and the more they regarded the world as nasty, the greater was the hostile intent they attributed to the actors. The toughness belief had a weaker, not quite statistically significant, relationship with this attribution. All in all, a disposition to interpret other people's ambiguous actions as being hostile in nature and then to attribute this hostility to the actors' aggressive personalities may well reflect a generally hostile outlook on life.

ANGER INTENSITY

According to many of the anger/aggression inventories, when highly aggressive people are provoked, they tend to react with intense anger. We can see this, for example, in the anger factor identified in the Buss-Perry AQ, with items such as, "Some of my friends think I'm a hothead." Similarly, Siegel's MAI assessed this strong anger with items such as, "I often feel angrier than I think I should," and "I get so angry, I feel like I might lose control." And then too, Spielberger's STAXI tapped this characteristic with items such as, "I lose my temper."

Let us consider, briefly, what role anger might have in aggressive behavior.

The Problem of Impulsive (Expressive) Aggression

In my view, most cognitive analyses of aggressive personalities, such as Dodge's social information-processing model, do not give sufficient attention to anger intensity. These formulations typically hold that emotionally aroused aggressors *decide,* consciously or unconsciously, to carry out an aggressive action. The anger state presumably shapes this decision. By contrast, my own "cognitive-neoassociationistic" approach (e.g., Berkowitz, 1974, 1990, 1993a) maintains that affective aggression is often, in part at least, impulsive (or expressive) in nature. Somewhat like the commonsense notion of how anger affects aggression, this conception basically envisions affective aggression as substantially "driven out" by an internal mechanism.

Put simply, I suggest that a decidedly unpleasant state of affairs activates motor reactions inside the person that make for an urge to assault an available target, particularly a target that is associated with the aversive occurrence. Angry feelings only accompany these activated, aggression-related motor reactions and do not, of themselves, cause the aggression. In other words, it is the unpleasant stimulation rather than the felt anger alone that produces the affective aggression. However, the intensity of the anger is presumably in direct ratio to the strength of the activated motor reactions as well as the degree of aggression-related thoughts and memories that also come to mind.

A growing number of research findings are consistent with this argument, at least in showing that angry feelings are typically accompanied by an urge to aggressive action. I can cite two examples here: In one of these cases, Spielberger (1996, personal communication) has recently extended the development of his angry state questionnaire by factor analyzing items assessing this emotional experience. Three factors were uncovered. One has to do with angry feelings (e.g., "I am furious," "I feel irritated"). The other two factors, however, have to do with felt urges. One of these involves an experienced pressure to express anger verbally (e.g., "I feel like screaming," "I feel like cursing out loud"), whereas the other factor reflects an urge to physical aggression (e.g., "I feel like kicking somebody," "I feel like pounding somebody"). These latter two factors, of course, point to the activated aggression-related motor reactions and hostile thoughts that typically accompany the felt anger experience.

Roseman, Wiest, and Swartz (1994) also found indications of this urge to aggressive action when they asked their subjects to recall and describe how they felt, and what they wanted to do when they had a negative experience. The participants reporting anger arousal were also likely to say that they "felt like yelling and like hitting someone . . . and wanted to hurt and get back at someone" (p. 213).

Associative Networks in Aggressive Personalities

The cognitive-neoassociationistic approach does not believe that aggressive urges arise only as a result of a perceived threat or affront. As this formulation's name implies, it proposes that external stimuli can also activate aggression-related motor reactions and hostile ideas because of their previously acquired associations (see Berkowitz, 1993, pp. 70–79). Two kinds of associations can have this effect: one is based on linkages with decidedly unpleasant occurrences, and the other has to do with connections with aggression per se, particularly with rewarded aggression.

In the first case, a person might see something in the surrounding situation that reminds her of a painful event she had experienced earlier. Since pain often prompts aggression-related reactions (Berkowitz, 1993b), even environmental features that have become associated with pain can promote aggression (see Berkowitz, 1993a, p. 76). And so, this individual might then display more aggression than she otherwise would exhibit.

The second kind of association has to do with the external stimulus's aggressive meaning. In this case, a person might encounter some object, such as a weapon, that makes him think of aggression. The sight of this aggression-connected object can then activate hostile thoughts and even aggressive inclinations (see Berkowitz, 1993a, pp. 70–74).

Because it is entirely consistent with the cognitive-neoassociationistic analysis, we would expect violence-prone personalities to have developed strong associations that link stimuli having an aggressive meaning with aggression-related motor reactions and ideas. These people should exhibit relatively strong aggressive reactions when they encounter aggression-related stimuli. One recent demonstration of this assumption employed filmed violence as the aggressive stimulus. Bushman (1996) showed in three separate experiments that high scorers on the Buss-Perry AQ, in comparison with low scorers, were not only more interested in watching violent films but also reported stronger anger feelings after seeing a violent videotape. Also they were the only participants who became more punitive toward peers after exposure to the violent video.

Intense Negative Feelings as the Source of Affective Aggression

As was indicated earlier, the most distinctive feature of the cognitive-neoassociationistic approach is its contention that decidedly unpleasant feelings are the basic spur to affective aggression. Based on this view, I have proposed (see Berkowitz, 1990, 1993), for example, that frustrations instigate an aggressive urge only to the extent that people are aversive, and that people undergoing highly stressful experiences—and who therefore are apt to feel very bad—are also likely to become aggressively inclined.

Caspi *et al.* (1994) have interpreted some of their personality test results in terms that are consistent with my analysis. Investigating adolescents in New Zealand and in Pittsburgh, they found that the delinquents in both samples were characterized by "high negative emotionality" as well as by weak self-restraints. The researchers concluded that when "the tendency to experience aversive affective states" is accompanied by poor "impulse control," "negative emotions may be translated more readily into antisocial acts" (p. 163).

EXHIBITING AGGRESSION OVERTLY

The final characteristic considered here is also prominent in several anger/aggression inventories. I mentioned earlier that factor analyses of the responses to a number of testing instruments, such as Siegel's MAI and Spielberger's STAXI, have differentiated between "anger-in" and "anger-out" tendencies. According to Spielberger, those persons having high scores on his anger-in subscale (AX/In) are apt to experience intense anger "but tend to suppress these feelings rather than express them in either physical or verbal behavior," whereas people having strong anger-out inclinations (high on AX/Out) are much more likely to display aggression openly in either physical or verbal form (Spielberger & Sydeman, 1994, p. 312).

Anger-In and Heart Disease

Psychologists have been interested in these two personality dimensions—anger in and anger out—not only because they might affect how someone deals with aversive events but also because they might influence physical health, especially the chances of developing heart disease (see Geen, 1990, pp. 170–177). Spielberger, for one, has written extensively about the possibility that persons with strong inclinations to suppress their felt anger are particularly at risk to develop elevated blood pressure and hypertension (e.g., Spielberger *et al.*, 1988; Spielberger & Sydeman, 1994). The studies he cited appear to support the widespread contention that it is unhealthy to keep one's angry feelings hidden.

However, the evidence actually is unclear. Consider a finding summarized by Geen (1990, pp. 171–172). In one study, hypertensives were more likely than people with normal blood pressure to characterize themselves (on an item in Siegel's MAI) as harboring grudges that they do not reveal to others. While this self-description indicates that these people tend to suppress their resentment, it also indicates that they "harbor grudges," that is, brood about the wrongs they believe they have suffered, and thus keep themselves stirred up. We can also see this connection between anger suppressive tendencies and brooding in the factor analysis of Siegel's MAI discussed earlier. Her anger-in factor was linked to a strong disposition to ruminate about past affronts. An item in the MAI shows this combination clearly: "When I hide my anger from others, I think about it for a long time."

In summary, we really do not know if those who are disposed to suppress their intense anger are apt to develop hypertension because they do not show their anger openly or because they brood about the "wrongs" done to them, thus experiencing frequent and prolonged periods of anger.

Normative Beliefs Opposing Aggression

Whatever the consequences of suppressed aggressive urges, to date, psychologists have not devoted much attention to the reasons why people might habitually attempt to hide the anger they feel. One possibility, of course, is that they hold attitudes that frown on the open display of aggression. Guerra, Huesmann, and Hanish (1996) have referred to these views as "normative beliefs," people's beliefs regarding the acceptability of their own aggressive behavior. Guerra and her colleagues think of these beliefs as relatively stable guides to behavior that do not have to be backed by external sanctions to restrain attacks on others.

The researchers first developed a 20-item scale that assessed the extent to which children hold such beliefs (using such questions as, "How often do you think it is okay for a boy, Tom, to hit a girl, Julie, if Julie says something bad to Tom first?") They then administered the scale to over 2,000 boys and girls in the first through fifth grades from economically disadvantaged elementary schools in the Chicago area and looked to see how the responses to this instrument related to the youngsters' aggressiveness (as determined by their peers' judgments of them).

Over the entire sample, those children having the strongest beliefs that aggression was unacceptable to them were generally viewed as relatively unaggressive by their classmates. Other results suggested that these normative beliefs tended to exert a greater influence over the youngsters' assaultiveness as they grew older; the strength of any one child's beliefs in a given year predicted how aggressive he or she was a year later (according to the peers' judgments).

SOME INFLUENCES PROMOTING INCONSISTENCY

Having reported all of these demonstrations of a consistency in anger and aggressive reactions across a wide variety of situations and in many different forms, I must remind the reader that this consistency is far from perfect. There is only a *probability*, and not a certainty, that people who respond aggressively on one occasion (such as on an anger/aggression inventory or after being threatened) will feel angry and/or act aggressively in other situations. Our behavior can be greatly affected by the momentary conditions existing in the situations around us, as Mischel (1968) and a number of social psychologists (e.g., Ross & Nisbett, 1991) have emphasized. This chapter is not complete without at least a brief reference to this matter.

INCONSISTENCY WITHIN A RELATIVELY NARROW TIME SPAN

Contrary to a widely shared but oversimplified psychodynamic conception of aggressive personalities, such people do not have a storehouse of violent energy bubbling within them, driving them to assault others. It is far better to say they have a latent disposition to anger and aggressiveness that has to be activated by an appropriate cue before they will attack an available, and suitable, target. Some of these cues can activate inclinations to affective aggression: a perceived threat or an unpleasant frustration or some affront or, as the cognitive-neoassociationistic analysis proposes, an external stimulus associated with either aggression or decidedly aversive occurrences. Other cues can create an urge to instrumental aggression by pointing to the rewards that might be obtained by attacking an appropriate target. In any case, however, aggressive actions do not arise all by themselves in the absence of instigating cues (see Berkowitz, 1993).

In addition, of course, even if people's aggressive inclinations are activated, they refrain from assaulting someone either because they fear punishment for the action and/or because this behavior would violate their personal standards of conduct. However, these inhibitory influences are also not constant and can vary from one occasion to another.

Threat of Punishment

The history of humankind amply demonstrates the frequent ineffectiveness of punitive policies in controlling undesirable conduct (see Berkowitz, 1993). The threat of punishment sometimes does deter such behavior, but, not infrequently, it does not work at all.

Most obviously, especially in the case of affective aggression, the threat may not be apparent in a given situation. Would-be aggressors at times are so strongly aroused emotionally that they do not think of the possibility of being punished for assaulting their victims. This is one of the reasons why the threat of capital punishment is often ineffective in reducing homicide rates (see Berkowitz, 1993, pp. 320–323). Most murders are committed in anger (Berkowitz, 1993, p. 329; Block & Christakos, 1995). In such cases, the killers could well have been so narrowly focused on the wrongs they believed they suffered and the perpetrators of the affronts that they were, at that time, psychologically unaware of any negative consequences they might experience. In general, it is not the severity of the punishment that serves as an effective deterrent but the certainty of being caught and penalized.

Aggression-Opposing Beliefs

Where the threat of punishment is an external influence, personal beliefs opposing a particular kind of behavior come from within the individual. As an example, I mentioned earlier how children's beliefs about the acceptability of their own aggression tended to regulate how aggressive they were in their dealing with their peers (Guerra et al., 1996). But even internally located beliefs are not necessarily constantly operative and do not always control action. People may be so focused on surrounding situations and the goals they seek to attain in these situations that they do not consider how their beliefs and values are relevant to the present circumstances. Even those persons who frequently believe aggression is wrong sometimes forget themselves and strike out in rage at tormentors.

This general phenomenon can be readily understood in terms of the self-awareness theory initiated by Duval and Wicklund (1972). According to this formulation, when people are highly conscious of themselves for one reason or another, they are likely to become highly aware of their personal normative beliefs and the gap between these beliefs and what they may be tempted to do in an immediate situation that has presented itself to them. Presumably uncomfortable at the thought of deviating from their now conscious beliefs, they try to act in conformity with their ideals (see also Berkowitz, 1993a, pp. 111–112). And so, as Carver (1975) demonstrated experimentally, even people who ordinarily disapprove of the use of electric shocks in psychology experiments can be induced to give shocks to peers when their attention is temporarily diverted from their shock-opposing views. The Chicago schoolchildren studied by Guerra *et al.* (1996) probably used their aggression-related beliefs to guide their behavior only when they thought of these ideals.

INFLUENCES PROMOTING INCONSISTENCY IN AGGRESSIVENESS OVER TIME

Situational influences can also lead to inconsistency in aggressiveness over the years. Although this chapter has emphasized the existence of a significant degree of longitudinal consistency, it also noted (more or less in passing) that there are a fair number of exceptions. Some highly aggressive children do "change their spots," so to speak, and cease their antisocial conduct, at least to a substantial extent, as they grow older.

This kind of inconsistency can readily be seen in Farrington's London sample. Thus, 40% of those who were in the most aggressive quartile of the sample at age 9 were still in this highly aggressive quartile at 17 years of age. This observation means that a good proportion of the other youths had apparently declined in their relative aggressiveness during adolescence (see Berkowitz, 1993, pp. 137). And then too, Farrington (1991) had also reported that a number of his youths seemed to have decreased in their relative antisocial conduct even during the period in which there was the greatest overall longitudinal consistency, from late adolescence to 32 years of age. When he scored the research participants in terms of their antisocial characteristics at various ages, he found that about 40% of those classified as highly antisocial (in the worst quarter of the distribution on these scores) when they were 18 years old were no longer in the highly antisocial group at age 32, again suggesting that a fraction of them were no longer engaged in extremely antisocial conduct.

All in all, a number of investigators have accepted a rough rule of thumb as descriptive of these changes in antisocial behavior from childhood to adulthood. As Farrington (1991) put it on the basis of his data and the results of other research, only about "half of antisocial children become antisocial adults" (p. 394). Given the fact that a substantial number of children do become somewhat less aggressive and less antisocial as they grow older, it is strange to observe that, at the time of this writing, there is next to no research seeking to discover the reasons why these changes come about (Moffitt, 1996, personal communication). Still, we can conclude on a relatively positive note. To quote Farrington (1991):

> [W]hile the costs of antisocial personality are high (in terms of crime, broken families, unemployment, substance abuse, and so on), and the bad news is that it tends to persist from childhood to adulthood, the good news is that a great deal of change is occurring and that persistence is by no means inevitable. (p. 394)

REFERENCES

American Psychiatric Association. (1987). *Diagnostic and statistical manual of mental disorders* (3rd ed., rev.). Washington, DC: Author.

Anderson, C. A., Deuser, W. E., & DeNeve, K. M. (1995). Hot temperatures, hostile affect, hostile cognition, and arousal: Tests of a general model of affective aggression. *Personality and Social Psychological Bulletin, 21*, 434–448.

Bem, D. J., & Allen, A. (1974). On predicting some of the people some of the time: The search for cross-situational consistencies in behavior. *Psychological Review, 81*, 506–520.

Berkowitz, L. (1974). Some determinants of impulsive aggression: Role of mediated associations with reinforcements for aggression. *Psychological Review, 81*, 165–176.

Berkowitz, L. (1990). On the formation and regulation of anger and aggression: A cognitive neo-associationistic analysis. *American Psychologist, 45*, 494–503.

Berkowitz, L. (1993a). *Aggression: Its causes, consequences, and control.* New York: McGraw-Hill.

Berkowitz, L. (1993b). Pain and aggression: Some findings and implications. *Motivation and Emotion, 17*, 277–295.

Block, C. R., & Christakos, A. (1995). Chicago homicide from the sixties to the nineties. In C. Block & R. Block (Eds.), *Trends, risks, and interventions in lethal violence: National Institute of Justice Research Report* (pp. 17–50). Washington, DC: National Institute of Justice.

Bushman, B. J. (1996). Individual differences in media-related aggression. *Personality and Social Psychology Bulletin, 22*, 811–819.

Bushman, B. J., Cooper, H. M., & Lemke, K. M. (1991). Meta-analysis of factor analyses: An illustration using the Buss-Durkee Hostility Inventory. *Personality and Social Psychology Bulletin, 17*, 344–349.

Buss, A. H. (1961). *The psychology of aggression.* New York: Wiley.

Buss, A. H., & Durkee, A. (1957). An inventory for assessing different kinds of hostility. *Journal of Consulting Psychology, 21*, 343–349.

Buss, A. H., & Perry, M. (1992). The aggression questionnaire. *Journal of Personality and Social Psychology, 63*, 452–459.

Carver, C. S. (1975). The facilitation of aggression as a function of objective self-awareness and attitudes toward punishment. *Journal of Experimental Social Psychology, 11*, 510–519.

Caspi, A., Moffitt, T. E., Silva, P. A., Stouthamer-Loeber, M., Krueger, R. F., & Schmutte, P. S. (1994). Are some people crime-prone? Replications of the personality-crime relationship across countries, genders, races, and methods. *Criminology, 32*, 163–195.

Deffenbacher, J. L., Demm, P. M., & Brandon, A. D. (1986). High general anger: Correlates and treatment. *Behaviour Research and Therapy, 24*, 481–489.

Dodge, K. A. (1982). Social information-processing variables in the development of aggression and altruism in children. In C. Zahn-Waxler, M. Cummings, & M. Radke-Yarrow (Eds.), *The development of altruism and aggression: Social and sociobiological origins* (pp. 280–302). New York: Cambridge University Press.

Dodge, K. A., & Coie, J. D. (1987). Social information-processing factors in reactive and proactive aggression in children's peer groups. *Journal of Personality and Social Psychology, 53*, 1146–1158.

Duval, S., & Wiscklund, R. A. (1972). *A theory of objective self-awareness.* New York: Academic Press.

Epstein, S. (1979). The stability of behavior: I. On predicting most of the people much of the time. *Journal of Personality and Social Psychology, 37*, 1097–1126.

Eron, L. D. (1987). The development of aggressive behavior from the perspective of a developing behaviorism. *American Psychologist, 42*, 197–211.

Farrington, D. P. (1989). Early predictors of adolescent aggression and adult violence. *Violence and Victims, 4*, 79–100.

Farrington, D. P. (1991). Antisocial personality from childhood to adulthood. *The Psychologist, 4*, 489–394.

Farrington, D. P. (1992). *Understanding and preventing bullying* (Executive Summary). Unpublished report to the Home Office, United Kingdom. Cambridge, UK: Institute of Criminology.

Feshbach, S. (1964). The function of aggression and the regulation of aggressive drive. *Psychological Review, 71*, 257–272.

Geen, R. G. (1990). *Human aggression.* Milton Keynes, UK: Open University Press.

Guerra, N. G., Huesmann, L. R., & Hanish, L. (1996). The role of normative beliefs in children's social behavior. In N. Eisenberg (Ed.), *Review of personality and social psychology, development and social psychology: The interface.* Newbury Park, CA: Sage.

Huesmann, L. R., Eron, L. D., Lefkowitz, M. M., & Walder, L. O. (1984). The stability of aggression over time and generations. *Developmental Psychology, 20*, 1120–1134.

Loeber, R., & Dishion, T. (1984). Boys who fight at home and school: Family conditions influencing cross-setting consistency. *Journal of Consulting and Clinical Psychology, 52*, 759–768.

Maiuro, R. D., Vitaliano, P. P., & Cahn, T. S. (1987). A brief measure for the assessment of anger and aggression. *Journal of Interpersonal Violence, 2*, 166–178.

Miller, S. J., Dinitz, S., & Conrad, J. P. (1982). *Careers of the violent.* Lexington, MA: Lexington Books.

Miller, T. Q., Jenkins, C. D., Kaplan, G., & Salonen, J. (1995). Are all hostility scales alike? Factor structure and covariation among measures of hostility. *Journal of Applied Social Psychology, 25*, 1142–1168.

Mischel, W. (1968). *Personality and assessment.* New York: Wiley.

Olweus, D. (1978). *Aggression in the schools: Bullies and whipping boys*. Washington, DC: Hemisphere.

Olweus, D. (1979). Stability of aggressive reaction patterns in males: A review. *Psychological Review, 86,* 852–875.

Olweus, D. (1991). Bully/victim problems among schoolchildren: Basic facts and effects of a school based intervention program. In D. J. Pepler, & K. H. Rubin (Eds.), *The development and treatment of childhood aggression* (pp. 411–448). Hillsdale, NJ: Erlbaum.

Quay, H. C. (1993). The psychobiology of undersocialized aggressive conduct disorder: A theoretical perspective. *Development and Psychopathology, 5,* 165–180.

Robins, L. N. (1991). Antisocial personality. In L. N. Robins & D. Regier (Eds.), *Psychiatric disorder in America* (pp. 259–290). New York: MacMillan/Free Press.

Roseman, I. J., Wiest, C., & Swartz, T. S. (1994). Phenomenology, behaviors, and goals differentiate discrete emotions. *Journal of Personality and Social Psychology, 67,* 206–221.

Ross, L., & Nisbett, R. E. (1991). *The person and the situation*. New York: McGraw-Hill.

Siegel, J. M. (1986). The multidimensional anger inventory. *Journal of Personality and Social Psychology, 51,* 191–200.

Spielberger, C. D., Johnson, E. H., Russell, S. F., Crane, R. J., Jacobs, G. A., & Worden, T. J. (1985). The experience and expression of anger: Construction and validation of an anger expression scale. In M. A. Chesney & R. H. Rosenman (Eds.), *Anger and hostility in cardiovascular and behavioral disorders* (pp. 5–30). New York: Hemisphere.

Spielberger, C. D., Krasner, S. S., & Solomon, E. P. (1988). The experience, expression, and control of anger. In M. P. Janisse (Ed.), *Health psychology: Individual differences and stress* (pp. 89–108). New York: Springer-Verlag.

Spielberger, C. D., Reheiser, E. C., & Sydeman, S. J. (1995). Measuring the experience, expression, and control of anger. In H. Kassinove (Ed.), *Anger disorders* (pp. 49–67). Washington, DC/London: Taylor & Francis.

Spielberger, C. D., & Sydeman, S. J. (1994). State-trait anxiety inventory and state-trait anger expression inventory. In M. E. Maruish (Ed.), *The use of psychological tests for treatment planning and outcome assessment* (pp. 292–321). Hillsdale, NJ: Erlbaum.

Toch, H. (1969). *Violent men*. Chicago: Aldine.

West, D. J., & Farrington, D. P. (1977). *The delinquent way of life*. London: Heinemann.

White, J. L., Moffitt, T. E., Earls, F., Robins, L., & Silva, P. A. (1990). How early can we tell?: Predictors of childhood conduct disorder and adolescent delinquency. *Criminology, 28,* 507–533.

Wilkins, J. L., Scharff, W. H., & Schlottmann, R. S. (1974). Personality type, reports of violence, and aggressive behavior. *Journal of Personality and Social Psychology, 30,* 243–247.

Zelli, A., & Huesmann, L. R. (1995). *Accuracy of social information processing by those who are aggressive: The role of beliefs about a hostile world*. Unpublished manuscript, University of Illinois at Chicago.

Zelli, A., Huesmann, L. R., & Cervone, D. (1995). Social inferences and individual differences in aggression: Evidence for spontaneous judgments of hostility. *Aggressive Behavior, 21,* 405–417.

CHAPTER 12

LEARNED HELPLESSNESS AND EXPLANATORY STYLE

CHRISTOPHER PETERSON AND CURIE PARK

The purpose of this chapter is to describe theory and research in learned helplessness and explanatory style, particularly as this work pertains to personality psychology. The chapter begins by providing basic background about these topics and ends by discussing some current areas of investigation.[1]

---

[1]The interested reader may wish to consult several general sources on learned helplessness and explanatory style. Seligman (1975) presented an overview of the early work on learned helplessness in animals and people; Peterson, Maier, and Seligman (1993) provided a more recent overview. The volume edited by Buchanan and Seligman (1995) focused on current investigations of explanatory style. Mikulincer (1994) described learned helplessness research with people and proposed his own account of the findings, which differs somewhat from that presented here. Seligman's (1991) *Learned Optimism* was an accessible account of research into helplessness and explanatory style, with a focus on applications. Peterson and Bossio's (1991) *Health and Optimism* discussed the relationship between explanatory style and physical well-being.

CHRISTOPHER PETERSON AND CURIE PARK • Department of Psychology, University of Michigan, Ann Arbor, Michigan 48109-1109.

Advanced Personality, edited by David F. Barone, Michel Hersen, and Vincent B. Van Hasselt. Plenum Press, New York, 1998.

LEARNED HELPLESSNESS

Learned helplessness was first described by psychologists studying animal learning. Researchers immobilized a dog and exposed it to a series of electric shocks—painful but not damaging—that could be neither avoided nor escaped. Twenty-four hours later, the dog was placed in a situation in which electric shock could be terminated by a simple response. However, the dog did not make this response, instead sitting there and passively enduring the shock. This behavior was in marked contrast to dogs in a control group that reacted vigorously to the shock and learned readily how to turn it off (Overmier & Seligman, 1967; Seligman & Maier, 1967).

These investigators proposed that the dog had learned to be helpless. In other words, when originally exposed to uncontrollable shock, it learned that nothing it did mattered. The shocks came and went independently of the dog's behaviors. They hypothesized that this learning of response-outcome independence was represented cognitively as an expectation of future helplessness that was generalized to new situations, producing a variety of deficits: motivational, cognitive, and emotional.

The deficits that follow in the wake of uncontrollability have come to be known as the *learned helplessness phenomenon,* and their cognitive explanation as the *learned helplessness model* (Maier & Seligman, 1976). Learned helplessness in animals continues to interest experimental psychologists, in large part because it provides an opportunity to investigate the interaction between mind and body (e.g., Peterson, Maier, & Seligman, 1993). Current investigations of learned helplessness among animals focuses on the neurochemical basis of the phenomenon and its relationships to immunity, analgesia, and the like.

Psychologists interested in humans and human problems, in particular, were quick to see the parallels between learned helplessness as produced by uncontrollable events in the laboratory and maladaptive passivity as it exists in the real world. Thus began several lines of research looking at learned helplessness in people. In one line of work, helplessness in people was produced in the laboratory, much as it was in dogs, by exposing subjects to uncontrollable events and seeing the effects on motivation, cognition, and emotion (e.g., Hiroto & Seligman, 1975). Unsolvable problems were usually substituted for uncontrollable electric shocks, but the critical aspect of the phenomenon remained: Following uncontrollability, people showed a variety of deficits.

In another line of work, researchers proposed various failures of adaptation as analogous to learned helplessness and investigated the similarity between those failures and learned helplessness. Especially popular was Seligman's (1974) proposal that reactive depression and learned helplessness shared critical features: causes, symptoms, consequences, treatments, and preventions.

As these lines of work were pursued, it became clear, in both cases, that the original learned helplessness explanation was an oversimplification when applied to people. Most generally, it failed to account for the range of reactions that people displayed in response to uncontrollable events (see reviews by Miller & Norman, 1979; Roth, 1980; Wortman & Brehm, 1975). Some people showed pervasive deficits, as the model hypothesized, that were general across time and situation, whereas others did not. Furthermore, failures of adaptation that the learned helplessness model was supposed to explain, such as depression, were sometimes characterized by a striking loss of self-esteem, about which the model was silent.

EXPLANATORY STYLE

In an attempt to resolve these discrepancies, Abramson, Seligman, and Teasdale (1978) reformulated the helplessness model as it applied to people. The contrary findings could all be explained by proposing that when people encounter an uncontrollable event, they ask themselves why it happened. The nature of their answer—the *causal attribution* they entertain—sets the parameters for the helplessness that follows.

If their causal attribution is stable ("it's going to last forever"), then induced helplessness is long lasting; if unstable, then it is transient. If their causal attribution is global ("it's going to undermine everything"), then subsequent helplessness is manifest across a variety of situations; if specific, then it is correspondingly circumscribed. Finally, if the causal attribution is internal ("it's all my fault"), the individual's self-esteem drops following uncontrollability; if external, self-esteem is left intact.

ATTRIBUTIONAL REFORMULATION

The hypotheses just presented comprise the *attributional reformulation* of helplessness theory. This new theory left the original model in place; uncontrollable events were still hypothesized to produce deficits when they gave rise to an expectation of future response—outcome independence. However, the nature of these deficits was now said to be influenced by the causal attribution offered by the individual.

In some cases, the situation itself provides the explanation made by the person, and the extensive social psychology literature on attributions documents many situational influences on the process (e.g., Harvey, Ickes, & Kidd, 1976–1981). In other cases, the person relies on his or her habitual way of making sense of events that occur, which is called one's *explanatory style* (Peterson & Seligman, 1984). All things being equal, people tend to offer similar sorts of explanations for disparate bad (or good) events. Explanatory style is a distal influence on helplessness and the failures of adaptation that involve helplessness.

According to the attributional reformulation, explanatory style in and of itself is not a direct cause of problems but rather a risk factor (Peterson & Seligman, 1984). Given uncontrollable events and the lack of a clear situational demand on the proffered attribution for uncontrollability, explanatory style should influence how the person responds. Helplessness will be long lasting or transient, widespread or circumscribed, damaging to self-esteem or not, all in accordance with the individual's explanatory style.

Explanatory style as studied by learned helplessness researchers has a specific meaning: the way that people habitually explain the causes of bad events involving themselves along the dimensions of internality, stability, and globality. Explanatory style can only be identified by looking across different explanations; to the degree that individuals are consistent, we can sensibly speak of them as showing a style of explanation. Helplessness theorists expect a degree of consistency across the explanations for different events offered by individuals, that is, these explanations should correlate at above-chance levels. But perfect agreement is not expected, in part, because explanatory style is but one of several influences on the actual causal explanations that people offer; in part, because the consistency of one's explanatory style appears to be an individual difference in its own right.

We have gone into this definition in some detail because explanatory style has become popular enough that other psychologists are questioning whether this particular definition is the best for all purposes. It is clear that it may not be. Researchers are beginning to look at explanations that do not entail causes; consider explanations about other people; study actual explanations rather than their abstract properties; ascertain the simplicity or complexity of causal schemas; study dimensions other than or in addition to internality, stability, and globality; and study not the consistency of explanations but instead their waxing and waning.

People no doubt have a variety of explanatory styles. Cataloging these styles, their origins and their consequences, would be a step toward depicting human nature as seen from the vantage of explanatory style. At the present time, however, explanatory style usually has the specific meaning we have offered.

HOPELESSNESS THEORY

The attributional reformulation itself has been reformulated by Abramson, Metalsky, and Alloy (1989), who made several modifications to the theory to improve its specific applicability to depression. These theorists hypothesized that there is a particular subtype of depression, which they identify as *hopelessness depression,* that is immediately caused by the belief that rewards will not occur and/or that punishments will. Other types of depression presumably exist as well and have different etiologies, such as disordered biochemistry or ruptured social relationships.

According to Abramson *et al.*'s (1989) *hopelessness theory* of depression, belief in a hopeless future is increased by stable and global explanations for actual bad life events that occur, and a high degree of importance is attached to these events. These cognitions are influenced in turn by an individual's explanatory style, specifically, the habitual tendency to offer stable and global explanations for bad events.

As applied to depression, hopelessness theory differs from the attributional reformulation in several ways. The immediate cause of depression is hopelessness ("the future will be unpleasant") as opposed to helplessness ("nothing I do matters"). In contrast to the attributional reformulation, the importance of bad life events is given an explicit role in hopelessness theory. This emphasis strengthens the link between hopelessness theory and the original learned helplessness model, which was based on the finding that uncontrollable *trauma* (i.e., electric shocks) was debilitating. The attributional reformulations treats all uncontrollable events as equally likely to produce helplessness, so long as they are explained in the same way. But this position is unreasonable: Traffic lights are uncontrollable and presumably regarded by many commuters as stable and global, yet few would argue that they are depressing. Finally, neither internal causal attributions nor internality of explanatory style is accorded central importance in this new theory, which is consistent with findings showing that low self-esteem is not specifically linked to internality (Peterson, 1991).

A major contribution of hopelessness theory is its ability to explain why people may show increased perseverance and good moods in the wake of life events: They entertain a belief in a *hopeful* future, presumably because of the operation of mechanisms analogous—yet opposite—to those implicated in the maintenance of a hopeless belief (cf. Needles & Abramson, 1990). The original helplessness model and the attributional reformulation do not distinguish among types of nonhelpless responses, yet these do exist and require an explanation.

Hopelessness theory has not yet been extensively tested (Abramson, Alloy, & Metalsky, 1995), and it is therefore too early to say how different in practice the theory will be from its immediate ancestors. For example, hopelessness and helplessness are conceptually distinct, but these cognitions may be so entwined with one another in actual thought that they prove impossible to tease apart. These three accounts of learned helplessness—the original model, the attributional reformulation, and hopelessness theory—do not compete with each other across the board, but rather they differ in terms of their emphases on the particular cognitive mechanisms linking uncontrollability and deficits.

EXPLANATORY STYLE AND PERSONALITY PSYCHOLOGY

As explained, the notion of explanatory style originated in the animal learning tradition, making a strong case for the importance of expectations in accounting for learning and performance. The original learned helplessness theory was therefore at odds with strict behaviorism but compatible with other learning theories that acknowledged the role of cognition in mediating the transaction between the organism and the environment (e.g., Tolman, 1948).

These concepts can be placed within a broad personality tradition that is concerned with *personal control:* how people's thoughts and beliefs influence their attempts to control important outcomes in their lives (Peterson & Stunkard, 1989). In Cronbach's (1957) terms, the personal control tradition differs from strict behavioral approaches, which emphasize situational causes of behavior. The personal control tradition instead looks at individual differences and internal determinants. People differ in how they make sense of the world, and these differences channel their behavior in some directions rather than others. In this way, beliefs are accorded motivational and emotional significance.

One of the important figures here is Alfred Adler (1910/1964, 1927), who introduced the notion of *striving for superiority* to explain why people pursued the goals they did. To be sure, striving for superiority was considered a drive, but it was a drive that made sense only in light of the beliefs that one entertains about one's self and one's abilities. Adler was influenced by Vaihingers's (1911) "as-if" philosophy, which proposed that people act according to how they take the world to be. Said in more modern psychological language, people's goals and motives are shaped by their beliefs about the causal texture of the world—by their explanatory styles, as it were.

Adler inspired a whole generation of subsequent personality theorists, individuals like Karen Horney, Erich Fromm, and Harry Stack Sullivan, who are called neo-Freudians but should probably be identified as neo-Adlerians (Peterson, 1992). These theorists deemphasized biological drives and instincts and instead suggested that people's behavior is better explained by attending to the social situations in which they find themselves (Brown, 1964). Furthermore, people do more than respond blindly to their conflicts. They also seek active solutions. Their egos are creative, and defense mechanisms are seen not simply as responses but as coping strategies. Again, these ideas can be recast in the language of causal explanations. Indeed, most if not all of the classic defense mechanisms are explicitly attributional, so here is another precedent for looking at how individual differences in causal explanations affect subsequent behavior: mood, motivation, and thought.

At the time that the neo-Freudian approach was coalescing, social psychologist Kurt Lewin (1935, 1951) was proposing his highly influential topological psychology. His central construct was the *lifespace,* defined as all the forces acting on an individual at a given time. The lifespace was defined by Lewin as a psychological reality, not a physical one, which drew the attention of psychologists to the ways in which people interpreted themselves, their worlds, and the relationships between the two. Modern attributional theorizing like the learned helplessness reformulation owes a direct debt to Lewin (Weiner, 1990).

Another important figure in the personal control tradition was Robert White (1959), who argued that people are driven to interact in a competent way with the environment. He called this drive *effectance motivation,* and the feeling that accompanied it he called *efficacy.* Importantly, effectance motivation could not be reduced to tissue needs. It legitimized, once again, a view of people as motivated to master their world and to control its outcomes.

Still other contributors to the personal control tradition were David McClelland (1961) and John Atkinson (1957), who studied *achievement motivation.* They were interested in individual differences: Why were some people driven to achieve—to accomplish something difficult against a standard of excellence—and other people not? Because a standard of excellence is part of the definition of achievement motivation, one's beliefs are put front and center. The person must believe that an outcome is worth pursuing, and he or she must constantly monitor progress toward that goal.

At about the same time, *attribution theory* began in earnest with Fritz Heider's (1958) seminal discussion of naive psychology. He addressed how people made sense of their own actions and those of others, and he explicitly drew psychology's attention to how people answered "why" questions. Some of the contrasts he introduced—such as that between internal and external explanations—still dominate the field, as do such issues as whether causal attributions are accurate.

Heider's naive psychology was elaborated by several different theorists, notably Jones and Davis (1965), Kelley (1973), and Weiner (1986), who made it into contemporary attribution theory. The purely cognitive aspects of attributions were increasingly emphasized. Motives and emotions were no longer seen as part of how the person makes sense of the world but rather as a consequence of given causal beliefs. Indeed, Kelley (1973) likened the everyday person to an experimental psychologist, "accounting for variance" via analysis of variance (ANOVA)-like designs, trying to decide what caused what.

As attribution theory evolved, it took too forms, one asked about the causes of attributions; the other, about their consequences. The former line of inquiry investigated such issues as whether people were "rational" or not in how they used information to arrive at their causal beliefs. The consensus that emerged was that people are somewhat sensitive to the actual events in the world, but that they are not normatively so; that is, they do not use information in a perfectly logical way (Nisbett & Ross, 1980).

The other line of inquiry examined how people's attributional beliefs influenced their motives and emotions (Weiner, 1986). It was shown repeatedly that certain attributions undercut one's motivation, whereas others enhanced it. And certain attributions were linked to given feelings, whereas others were related to different feelings.

Both these lines of investigation were carried out largely within social psychology, which means attribution researchers usually did not look at individual differences in their own right. There is an irony here, of course, given where the tradition started and that many of those doing attribution research were personality psychologists. But, in this case, it was a personality psychology devoid of individual differences, as was common in the 1970s. The yield of these lines of investigation was a rich vocabulary and set of research procedures tapped by learned helplessness investigators. Interestingly, the notion of individual differences in causal attributions came not from attribution theorists whose feet were clearly in personality psychology, but rather from experimental psychologists, working in animal learning laboratories.

Yet another important influence along the way was the theorizing of Julian Rotter (1954), whose social learning theory acknowledged the existence and importance of broad interpretive tendencies. Specifically, Rotter (1966) suggested that performance was under the sway of one's generalized expectancies. One did not do something unless it was expected to turn out in a given way. Several generalized expectancies exist, but perhaps the *locus of control* concept—whether someone generally expects rewards to emanate from his or her own actions (internal) or from outside, through chance, fate, or the machinations of powerful others (external)—is most germane to explanatory style.

Locus of control is obviously related to explanatory style, particularly to the internality dimension (cf. Peterson & Stunkard, 1992). Both concern themselves with the source of outcomes, inside or outside the person. Locus of control is an expectancy about the future, whereas internality refers to a cause in the past. However, this cause in turn sets the expectancy. In practice, because these concepts are measured in different ways, they often diverge. Locus of control, at least as conceptualized by Rotter, collapses across good and bad events. In contrast, explanatory style assumes that one must look separately at responses to bad events and good events. As it turns out, attributions for bad and good events often are independent, so this decision is a good one.

Another version of social learning theory was proposed by Albert Bandura (1969, 1973; Bandura & Walters, 1963). In recent years, it has become increasingly cognitive, stressing the importance of an individual's *self-efficacy*, defined as his or her belief that a given response leading to a specific outcome can be performed (Bandura, 1977, 1986). Like locus of control, self-efficacy is obviously related to explanatory style (cf. Peterson & Stunkard, 1992).

So, learned helplessness and explanatory style fit within the contemporary tradition of theorizing about personality usually identified as *social learning* or *social cognitive* (see chap. 8). Indeed, expectations of helplessness and causal explanations are examples of what social learning theorist Walter Mischel (1990) identified as *person variables*. Person variables are distinguished from invariant traits because they are tied not only to the individual but also to particular events in the person's world. However, learned helplessness theorists usually regard expectations and causal explanations as more general than did Mischel in his vision of person variables, as being traitlike (Peterson & Seligman, 1984). The research evidence seems to support the former conceptualization.

MEASURING EXPLANATORY STYLE

Explanatory style took off as its own line of research when measures of this individual difference began to be developed. Several such measures now exist, and they are described here briefly (see Reivich, 1995, for a more extensive discussion of measures).

A caveat is in order: The relationships of these measures to one another have not been extensively investigated. They presumably measure the same characteristic and hence should converge impressively. However, studies to date show a range of convergence, and, in some cases, alternative measures are almost independent of one another (e.g., Peterson,

Bettes, & Seligman, 1985). At the same time, the different measures of explanatory style invariably are correlated in theoretically predicted ways with such "external" variables as depression and poor health.

Taken together, these results are paradoxical, implying that measures of explanatory style have better validity than reliability. A possible resolution may lie in recognizing that each measure taps explanatory style at a somewhat different level of abstraction and distance from the actual causal attributions that people offer for events that occur. Future research needs to use all of the available measures of explanatory style in the same investigation so that this speculation can be tested.

THE ATTRIBUTIONAL STYLE QUESTIONNAIRE

The first measure of explanatory style to be developed was the Attributional Style Questionnaire (ASQ) (Peterson et al., 1982), used in a study by Seligman, Abramson, Semmel, and von Baeyer (1979), investigating predictions of the attributional reformulation—specifically, that people differed with respect to their habitual explanatory tendencies, and that those who favored internal, stable, and global explanations for bad events would be more likely to report symptoms of depression than those who favored external, unstable, and specific explanations.

The ASQ presents subjects with hypothetical good and bad events. Subjects are asked to imagine the event happening to themselves and then to write down the event's "one major cause," if it were to happen to them. Then, they use seven-point rating scales to indicate the degree to which the cause is internal, stable, and global (see Table 12.1).

These ratings are combined in various ways: scores for the three dimensions of internality, stability, and globality may be formed separately for bad events and for good events

TABLE 12.1. Example of Attributional Style Questionnaire

In the Attributional Style Questionnaire, respondents are presented with a series of items such as the following:

Please try to vividly imagine that a friend tells you that you cannot be trusted. If this situation were to happen to you, what would be the one major cause? Write this cause in the space below.

1. Is this cause due to something about you or something about other people or circumstances? (circle one number)

totally due to other people or circumstances	1 2 3 4 5 6 7	totally due to me

2. In the future when interacting with friends, will this cause again be present? (circle one number)

will never again be present	1 2 3 4 5 6 7	will always be present

3. Is this cause something that just influences interacting with friends, or does it also influence other areas of your life? (circle one number)

influences just this particular area	1 2 3 4 5 6 7	influences all areas of my life

by averaging the appropriate ratings; a composite explanatory style for bad events may be formed by averaging across the three dimensions for bad events; and so on.

Because the earliest version of the ASQ had modest reliability at best, researchers fell into the practice of using composites as just described (Peterson *et al.*, 1982). The effect was twofold. On the one hand, reliabilities were typically increased because that many more items were used to estimate someone's explanatory style. But on the other hand, researchers were not able to investigate the roles assigned to the specific attributional dimensions by the helplessness reformulation (Carver, 1989).

Once available, the ASQ was used mainly in investigations of depression, following the lead of the attributional reformulation. Literally hundreds of studies were conducted that correlated ASQ responses with various indices of depression (Sweeney, Anderson, & Bailey, 1986). The following points can be made about this work.

First, because of the format of the ASQ, many helplessness researchers stopped being interested in the uncontrollability of events and contented themselves with studying attributions about bad events. Bad events and uncontrollable events overlap, perhaps considerably, but a moment's reflection shows that they are not identical. What was lost—at least in this research—was the original helplessness model's concern with uncontrollability. This neglect makes the helplessness literature less coherent than it should be. It also introduces possible error into research that uses the ASQ because several studies suggest that it may be advantageous for a person to view controllable bad events as internally, stably, and globally caused (e.g., Brown & Siegel, 1988; Sellers & Peterson, 1993).

Second, researchers took to calling explanatory style for bad events *pessimistic* when it was relatively internal, stable, and global; and *optimistic* when it was relatively external, unstable, and specific (Seligman, 1991). The motive for this was largely to make the construct's meaning more accessible to the psychological community and the general public. Explanatory style does not necessarily mean anything to most people, but an optimistic view of the causes of events certainly does. The danger in this switch in terminology is that psychologists and everyday people are tempted to adopt a shorthand way of describing people as optimists or pessimists.

However, people do not exist in two discrete clumps. By the way explanatory style is actually measured, most people find themselves in the middle, neither optimists nor pessimists. It is only those at the extremes who can be accurately described as either one or the other. A cautious use of the terms *optimistic* and *pessimistic* as adjectives to describe explanatory style, not as labels for a personality typology, is demanded (Peterson, 1991).

Third, the majority of studies did not test the full helplessness reformulation but only aspects of it. The reformulation and the related hopelessness theory specify a detailed account of the process by which people become depressed. Explanatory style, as already noted, is regarded as a risk factor not an inevitable cause of problems. Presumably, explanatory style is catalyzed by actual bad events, and it is only when explanatory style induces someone to offer a given explanation that helplessness follows. Most studies have not investigated these subtleties. To do so would require at the very least a longitudinal design and an independent assessment of the occurrence of stressful life events.

Instead, studies have usually calculated the synchronous correlation between explanatory style and presumed outcomes, usually finding the predicted correlations. But as Peterson and Seligman (1984) noted, these are the least compelling studies vis-à-vis the helplessness reformulation because they are compatible with other possibilities (e.g., that the outcome influences attributions and/or that some third variable is responsible for the outcome and pessimistic attributional style).

Fourth, other researchers began to examine explanatory style in its own right, extending it to questions and topics not explicitly part of the original helplessness model or its revisions. Some of this work was simply exploratory, made possible by the existence of a questionnaire that—despite problems with reliability—seemed to offer valid results. Researchers correlated explanatory style with a variety of outcomes, from binge eating to compulsive gambling (see Peterson *et al.*, 1993). The conclusion suggested by these far-flung studies is that explanatory style is a basic individual difference, tapping something very important about people.

Other extensions were more deliberate, reflecting a conscious decision to see if explanatory style applied to topics to which by the logic of its meaning it should apply. Some of these applications—to achievement, to physical health, and of course to depression—will be discussed later in the chapter.

CONTENT ANALYSIS OF VERBATIM EXPLANATIONS

A number of these extensions followed the development of a new way to measure explanatory style, using a flexible content analysis method. This technique, Content Analysis of Verbatim Explanations (CAVE), stemmed from the observation that causal explanations, identical to those given by respondents to the ASQ, were abundant in spontaneous writing or speaking. Was it possible to identify these explanations in verbatim material, extract them, and then rate them along the dimensions of internality, stability, and globality, having researchers do what subjects do on the ASQ? The answer proved to be yes. Explanatory style so assessed proved reliable, consistent, and valid (Peterson, Schulman, Castellon, & Seligman, 1992). Table 12.2 shows how the CAVE technique is used.

The CAVE technique made a new chapter in explanatory style research possible. Potential research subjects neither able nor willing to participate in typical research could be studied as long as they had left behind suitable material containing causal explanations about themselves. To date, the CAVE technique has been used with psychotherapy transcripts, inter-

TABLE 12.2. Example of Content Analysis of Verbatim Explanations

---

Researchers scrutinize written or spoken material for mention of bad events that are accompanied by causal explanations. These are identified, removed, and presented to judges for ratings of each cause along seven-point scales, according to its internality, stability, and globality (as the following example illustrates).

Here is a sad story. **My dog died** several years ago. She was fifteen years old and had been my first and only pet. She tried to jump up on my bed, and **she missed and broke her back.** I think it was my fault because **my room is always such a mess,** and she probably slipped on something left on the floor. She had to be put to sleep, and I still miss her.

bad event: **my dog died . . . she missed** (my bed) **and broke her back**
cause: **my room is always such a mess**
ratings
   internality: 6
   stability: 6
   globality: 2

views, open-ended questionnaires, political speeches, sports stories, religious texts, and song lyrics (e.g., Oettingen & Seligman, 1990; Peterson, Luborsky, & Seligman, 1983; Satterfield & Seligman, 1994; Sethi & Seligman, 1993; Zullow, 1991; Zullow & Seligman, 1990).

Perhaps the greatest methodological virtue of this approach to the study of explanatory style is that it allows longitudinal research to be conducted retrospectively. If suitable verbal material can be located from early in the lives of individuals whose long-term fate is known, then the CAVE technique allows studies that span decades to be done very quickly. For example, Peterson, Seligman, and Vaillant (1988) used the technique to predict successfully the health outcomes of men who had completed CAVEable questionnaires more than 30 years earlier.

FORCED-CHOICE MEASURES OF EXPLANATORY STYLE

Because children have trouble following the directions of the ASQ, a forced-choice questionnaire called the Children's Attributional Style Questionnaire (CASQ; Seligman *et al.*, 1984) was devised. This questionnaire presents children with bad or good events involving themselves and then asks them to choose from two possible explanations. These options hold constant two of the attributional dimensions of theoretical interest, while systematically varying the third dimensions. Consider this item:

You go on a vacation with a group of people, and you have a good time.
  A. I was in a good mood.
  B. The people I was with were in good moods.

The event is a good one, and the available options allow either an internal (Choice A) or external (Choice B) explanation; the options are presumably of equal stability and globality.

Children are given scores for internality, stability, and globality, separately for bad events and good events, according to how many of the appropriate options they choose. CASQ scores are moderately reliable, consistent over time, and relate as expected to measures of depression and poor achievement (e.g., Kaslow, Rehm, Pollak, & Siegel, 1988; Nolen-Hokesema, Girgus, & Seligman, 1986, 1992).

More recently, a forced-choice measure of explanatory style suitable for adult respondents has been devised by Reivich and Seligman (1991). Its format is similar to that of the CASQ. The psychometric properties of this Forced-Choice ASQ are still being explored, but the questionnaire appears to correlate with the extent of depressive symptoms and to converge with corresponding scores from the original ASQ (Reivich, 1995).

AN MMPI MEASURE

Colligan, Offord, Malinchoc, Schulman, and Seligman (1994) described a way to score answers to the Minnesota Multiphasic Personality Inventory (MMPI; Hathaway & McKinley, 1943) for explanatory style. The MMPI sees wide use as an aid in the diagnosis of psychological problems. Respondents are presented with hundreds of pairs of items and asked to endorse the one that is more appliable to themselves. Colligan *et al.* (1994) chose items—about half of those in the original MMPI—that referred unambiguously to bad or good events. Then they used the CAVE technique to rate each item on seven-point scales in terms of its internality, stability, and globality.

For example, the MMPI item "I am afraid when I look down from a high place" refers to a bad event of moderate internality (= 4), moderate stability (= 4), and low globality (= 1). The item "I cannot do anything well" is a bad event with the highest scores (= 7) on all three dimensions. An MMPI respondent is given an explanatory style score by summing the items chosen—separately for bad events and good events—after weighting them by the appropriate CAVE ratings. As might be expected, explanatory style for bad events is highly correlated with the Depression subscale of the MMPI.

The MMPI measure of explanatory style, if it proves useful, will allow learned helplessness researchers to rescore MMPIs already completed in previous studies. Over the years, hundreds of thousands of individuals have completed the MMPI, along with a vast array of other measures. Like the CAVE technique, the MMPI approach might allow explanatory style to be piggy-backed onto previous research, much of it longitudinal in nature.

FANTASY-BASED MEASURES

In a projective test, an individual is presented with an ambiguous stimulus and asked to respond to it. Sometimes the response requested is in the form of a story; in the resulting narrative, causal explanations frequently appear. For example, with the Thematic Apperception Test (TAT; Morgan & Murray, 1935), subjects are shown a series of grainy black-and-white pictures, usually depicting one or more people, and asked to tell a story—with a beginning, middle, and end—about each picture.

Can such responses be scored with the CAVE technique for explanatory style? One problem with fantasy-based measures vis-à-vis the typical meaning of explanatory style is that one cannot tell in most cases if the respondent is identifying with the characters in the pictures. Explanatory style pertains to events that occur to the individual, so it is conceivable that a TAT story is irrelevant if it is told about someone else.

Several studies have nonetheless scored fantasy-based stories for stability and globality of explanatory style (e.g., Peterson & Park, 1995; Peterson, Schulman, Castellon, & Seligman, 1992; Peterson & Ulrey, 1994). As just explained, internality ratings are not meaningful, and so these were not undertaken. Evidence to date suggests that explanatory style can be reliably assessed from narratives told in response to TAT and TAT-like pictures. Furthermore, individuals are consistent in terms of the stability and globality of the causal explanations they offer.

The most intriguing result from these preliminary studies is Peterson and Park's (1995) finding that stability plus globality for bad events in TAT stories told by college women was *positively* correlated with their emotional and physical well-being as measured several decades later. These researchers concluded that this finding, which reverses the correlation found with all other measures of explanatory style, makes sense in terms of the special nature of fantasy.

Perhaps in a fantasy, we explore frightening possibilities (cf. Bettelheim, 1976). The more we explore these possibilities in a safe context, the better we come to grips with them, and, hence, the better we can lead our lives. Stable and global explanations for bad events *in a fantasy* may reflect this process of trying out what frightens us. Indeed, in Peterson and Park's (1995) research, subjects who used stable and global explanations in their fantasies but unstable and specific explanations in describing actual events fared particularly well. Further research is obviously demanded, and the previous speculation that different measures of explanatory style get at different aspects of how people make sense of events in their lives should be underscored.

REPRESENTATIVE APPLICATIONS

Learned helplessness has become a popular line of investigation because the phenomenon seems analogous to various humans ills involving passivity. Helplessness theory the attributional reformulation, and hopelessness theory suggest an explanation of such instances of passivity as well as interventions to prevent or remedy them (e.g., Peterson, 1982; Seligman, 1981). At the same time, some applications have been promiscuous, overstating the similarity between learned helplessness, on the one hand, and some failure of adaptation, on the other (Peterson et al., 1993).

The best applications of learned helplessness ideas are to phenomena with the following three critical features:

1. *Contingency.* The applied researcher must take into account the objective contingency between a person's actions and the outcomes that he or she then experiences. Learned helplessness is present when there is no contingency between actions and outcomes. Learned helplessness must therefore be distinguished from extinction (where active responses once producing reinforcement no longer do so) as well as from instrumental passivity (where active responses have been contingently punished and/or passive responses have been contingently reinforced). Only some types of helplessness are of the "learned" variety.
2. *Cognition.* Learned helplessness also involves a characteristic way of perceiving, explaining, and extrapolating contingencies. Both the attributional reformulation and hopelessness theory specify cognitive processes that make helplessness more (versus less) likely following uncontrollable events. If measures of these processes are not sensibly related to passivity, then learned helplessness is not present.
3. *Behavior.* Finally, learned helplessness is shown by passivity in a situation different from the one in which uncontrollability was first encountered. Does the individual give up and fail to initiate actions that might allow him or her to control the situation? It is impossible to argue that learned helplessness is present without the demonstration of passivity in new situations. Other consequences may accompany the behavioral deficits that define learned helplessness: cognitive retardation, low self-esteem, sadness, reduced aggression, immunosuppression, and physical illness.

With these ideas in mind, consider three lines of work that represent the best applications to date of helplessness ideas to complex failures of human adaptation (Peterson et al., 1993): depression, poor achievement, and physical illness. In each case, researchers have attempted to demonstrate the critical features of learned helplessness, contingency, cognition, and behavior.

So, uncontrollable events are a risk factor for depression (e.g., Lloyd, 1980), illness (e.g., Visintainer, Volpicelli, & Seligman, 1982), and poor achievement (e.g., Kennelly & Mount, 1985). A pessimistic explanatory style has been linked to all three phenomena as well, often in longitudinal studies (e.g., Peterson & Barrett, 1987; Peterson et al., 1988; Schulman & Seligman, 1986). And finally, cross-situational passivity is a defining characteristic of all three. In the case of depression and poor achievement, passivity is obvious. In the case of illness, passivity is evident metaphorically in a sluggish response of the immune system to a foreign challenge (e.g., Kamen-Siegel, Rodin, Seligman, & Dwyer, 1991) and literally in the failure to engage in health-promoting or illness-combating behaviors (e.g., Lin & Peterson, 1990; Peterson, 1988; Peterson, Colvin, & Lin, 1992).

Helplessness researchers do not claim that these various problems involve only the constructs deemed important by helplessness theory. Depression, achievement, and physical health are obviously overdetermined, and as Abramson *et al.* (1989) implied, there are instances of each not being explained at all from the perspective of helplessness and hopelessness. Nonetheless, the case has been made for at least some involvement of the three critical features of learned helplessness in many instances of these phenomena.

A remaining puzzle is why learned helplessness appears so widely applicable. What determines whether a given individual who has experienced uncontrollable events and thinks about them in pessimistic ways becomes depressed, fails at school, or becomes ill? It might be that all these outcomes occur to the same individuals, in which case their problems probably exacerbate one another. Or it might be that other considerations—biological, psychological, and/or social—on which helplessness theory is silent lead an individual in one disastrous direction or another once a state of helplessness is present.

SOME CONTEMPORARY LINES OF INVESTIGATION

Learned helplessness research continues on many fronts, addressing loose ends and contradictions from previous studies and extending the theory into new areas. In this section, we briefly sketch some of these current extensions, starting with a basic question: How does explanatory style originate?

ORIGINS OF EXPLANATORY STYLE

It is easy to explain why a person maintains his or her given explanatory style. Belief systems by nature resist contradictory evidence, assimilating new experiences into what is already believed, even if these beliefs have negative consequences (Quine & Ullian, 1978). The more intriguing question is, why would someone arrive at damaging beliefs in the first place?

The origins of explanatory style have not been extensively investigated, although more recently, its origins have attracted growing interest. One general answer to the earlier question is that a negative explanatory style arises from actual events. Trauma, illness, and failure experienced early in life foreshadow a pessimistic explanatory style later in life (e.g., Bunce, Larsen, & Peterson, 1995; Burn, 1992; Cerezo-Jimenez & Frias, 1994; Henry, Martinko, & Pierce, 1993; Kaufman, 1991; Orsillo, McCaffrey, & Fisher, 1993). For example, Gold (1986) found that women who had been sexually victimized as children or adolescents were more likely to have a pessimistic style, explaining bad events as having internal, stable, and global causes. Most of the studies in this area have relied on retrospective reports of bad events in childhood by adults. Although these reports often correlate with explanatory style (and depression), the question of causality remains unanswered.

More recent attempts to investigate the impact of bad life events on the development of explanatory style have looked at children currently experiencing trauma or neglect.

Perez-Bouchard, Johnson, and Ahrens (1993) found that children of substance abusers had a more pessimistic explanatory style than children without such a family history. However, they also found a multiplicative effect of family intactness for the children of substance abusers, such that the children of nonintact, substance-abusing families had the most pessimistic explanatory style.

As research into the origins of explanatory style becomes more sophisticated, investigators have begun to formulate developmentally sensitive models of the process by which explanatory style originates in childhood. So, Rose and Abramson (1992) argued that when children experience a bad event (such as maltreatment), they try to understand the event: its causes, meanings, and consequences. Children generate possible hypotheses about the causes of the event in order to guide future behaviors to prevent its recurrence. The process of generating and then evaluating these hypotheses is developmentally constrained. Children at different developmental stages and in different settings may arrive at different answers and end up with different explanatory styles.

What follows is one example of such a cascade: For very young and isolated children living in abusive situations, other people and circumstances may seem unchangeable, and so they focus on changing their own behaviors in an attempt to change their situations. They end up placing the blame for abuse on themselves, concluding that they did something wrong that deserves punishment. The child eventually regards herself or himself as bad, and a pessimistic explanatory style becomes a sensible way to interpret subsequent events.

Nolen-Hoeksema et al.'s (1992) five-year, longitudinal study of children's life events in childhood, explanatory style, and depression sheds some light on the matter. In early childhood, negative life events—but not explanatory style—predicted depressive symptoms. Later in childhood, pessimistic explanatory style became a strong predictor of depressive symptoms.

Cole and Turner (1993) similarly proposed that a pessimistic explanatory style develops from aversive feedback from the environment. Early in life, negative life events themselves have a direct impact on depressive symptoms, but as children grow older and their explanatory styles become more stable, the impact of life events is mediated by them (Turner & Cole, 1994).

Other researchers have investigated more proximal influences on explanatory style, in particular how children's parents explain events. Findings in this area have not been consistent (Holloway, Kashiwagi, Hess, & Azuma, 1986; Parsons, Meece, Adler, & Kaczala, 1982; Yamauchi, 1989). For example, Seligman et al. (1984) found that the explanatory style for bad events of 8- to 13-year-old children correlated significantly with the explanatory style of their mothers but not their fathers. Turk and Bry (1992) found just the opposite pattern in a study of adolescents and their parents. Perhaps parental feedback about the child's behavior may be a more critical determinant of the child's explanatory style than is parental explanatory style.

Along these lines, Radke-Yarrow, Belmont, Nottelman, and Bottomly (1990) studied the natural discourse between mothers and their young children, finding a strong association between the number of disapproving comments made by the mother and the number of negative self-referent comments made by the child. Furthermore, a study by Heyman, Dweck, and Cain (1992) demonstrated that teacher feedback can also affect the process by which children come to think poorly of themselves. In this investigation, kindergarten students created classroom projects that were criticized by their teachers. Although 60% of the children were unswayed by what the teachers said, the remaining students gave up their own positive evaluations of their work and adopted their teachers' negative evaluations. Future research should investigate the joint effects of parent and teacher criticism to see if these explain individual differences in children's explanatory styles.

A final bit of information about the origins of explanatory style is the finding that explanatory style is heritable (Schulman, Keith, & Seligman, 1993); that is, identical twins resemble each other more than do fraternal twins with respect to their explanatory styles. It is unlikely that there is a specific gene for explanatory style, which has a direct and invariant effect on an individual's causal explanations. Rather, if explanatory style results from life experiences, such as successes and failures, researchers need to turn their attention to the heritability of factors—such as temperament—that might influence these. Success in life is influenced by heritable characteristics, physical prowess, attractiveness, and intelligence, and failures by their absence, which means that explanatory style shows a genetic influence because some of its basic determinants do.

In sum, explanatory style seems to have no single origin. It appears to result from a confluence of biological, psychological, and social processes, but the details are far from having been explicated.

CHANGING EXPLANATORY STYLE

Explanatory style is not immutable, and some researchers have investigated how it might be deliberately changed from pessimistic to optimistic. There are two approaches being used. The first focused on how cognitive characteristics—including explanatory style—change as a result of interventions deployed against depression. The second line of research looked at how direct attribution retraining affects explanatory style. Let us give you a sample of each type of work.

The Cognitive Pharmacotherapy Project compared the effects on depression of cognitive therapy, pharmacotherapy, and a combination of the two (DeRubeis et al., 1990; DeRubeis & Hollon, 1995; Hollon et al., 1992). Cognitive therapy and pharmacotherapy alleviated depressive symptoms to a similar extent, but only cognitive therapy changed explanatory style (from pessimistic to optimistic). For individuals who received cognitive therapy but not pharmacotherapy, changes in explanatory style mediated changes in depression. Individuals receiving cognitive therapy were less likely to relapse (18%) than patients who had stopped receiving pharmacotherapy (50%) during the two-year follow-up. When posttreatment levels of depression were controlled, explanatory style at termination of treatment was the only predictor of relapse two years later.

Can cognitive therapy similarly change the explanatory styles of children? Jaycox, Reivich, Gillham, and Seligman (1994) developed a 12-week program to prevent depression in high-risk, school-age children. The program included cognitive-behavioral interventions as well as training in social problem solving. Specifically, the program helped the children identify causal attributions and change them from pessimistic to optimistic. Interestingly, only the stability of explanatory style was changed by this intervention, but changes in stability predicted decreased depressive symptoms at posttest and follow-up.

The programs just described attempted to change explanatory style in the context of a more general intervention. A second approach to changing explanatory style focused only on causal attributions. So, when students are encouraged to attribute failure at academic tasks to a lack of effort (an unstable and specific cause), they increase their persistence at these tasks (e.g., Andrews & Debus, 1978; Dweck, 1975; Fowler & Peterson, 1981).

A further study suggested that direct attribution retraining is more effective in changing explanatory style than providing individuals with successes. Aydin (1988) selected a group of unpopular schoolchildren who evidenced a pessimistic explanatory style. They were assigned to an attribution retraining condition, a success condition, or a control condition. The children in the reattribution training condition were read a story that attributed social failure to lack of effort rather than lack of ability and then asked to role-play the story. They were read a different story—albeit with the same message—each week for 10 weeks. In the success training condition, the experimenter manipulated feedback from bogus tests so that the children were receiving 90% success feedback by the end of the 10 weeks. Attribution retraining but not success changed explanatory style. Attribution retraining also improved the peer relationship of these unpopular children, although it should be noted that the children remained relatively unpopular.

The sensible implication of this study is not that successes can be ignored in changing explanatory style. Instead, direct attribution retraining is more efficient in the short term. We suspect that if successes do not eventually accompany a newly acquired optimistic style, the individual will soon revert to a pessimistic—that is, realistic—way of explaining events.

CULTURAL AND HISTORICAL LIMITS OF EXPLANATORY STYLE

The helplessness phenomenon—that is, deficits following experience with uncontrollability—has considerable universality across human groups and indeed a variety of species. However, people's tendencies to offer causal attributions may show historical or cultural boundaries, which means that explanatory style needs to be located in its sociocultural context. It is doubtful that a time or place has ever existed in which individuals did not engage in making sense of what they saw, particularly their own behaviors and the behaviors of others. But causal explanations—those pointing to antecedent events that covary with phenomena of interest—are obviously but one way to make sense of the world (cf. Pepper, 1942).

For example, Duda and Allison (1989) observed that not all cultures juxtapose internal and external causes. If someone attributes an event to his or her group and defines the self only in terms of the group, the attribution is somehow both internal and external. Cultures also differ in how they interpret what seem to be the same attributions. According to Betancourt and Weiner (1982), students in Chile regard given "stable" causes as more stable than do their United States counterparts, and given "external" causes as more external.

Some cultures have a profoundly different concept of causality than those in the Western world (Ladd, 1957, Little, 1987). Causes may have effects over decades, work backward in time, or be circular. Explanatory style as we have conceived it does not do justice to any of these causal worldviews.

So, causal attributions like those studied by helplessness researchers may be a special concern of residents in Western societies during the late 20th century (Peterson et al., 1993). In other words, causal attributions for behavior may be offered only by people who possess a highly articulated sense of self as distinct from the world, who exalt individuality, and who try to "predict and control" the events that befall them (Baumeister, 1986; van den Berg, 1983; Weisz, Rothbaum, & Blackburn, 1984). Perhaps the popularity of explanatory style as a research topic reflects its good fit with the collective psychology of the United States in the late 20th century.

Cultural and historical differences with respect to the given causal attributions that people offer have been documented. For instance, Miller (1984) compared the causal attributions for behaviors made in India and the United States and found that Indians favored contextual explanations (e.g., roles, norms), whereas Americans favored dispositional explanations (e.g., traits, attitudes). Her subjects were of different ages, and she found that this cultural difference became more pronounced with increasing age. Socialization into a particular culture apparently entails learning characteristic explanations for behavior.

Guimond and Palmer (1990) provided another example of how causal explanations are socialized. They studied the causal explanations that students from different disciplines—for example, social science, commerce, and engineering—offered for poverty and unemployment at the beginning of the academic year and again at the end of the academic year. Instruction in the social sciences led students of this field to make more systems-blaming attributions.

If people in a given time or place do not offer causal explanations, then explanatory style is a meaningless construct with which to characterize these people. If people offer causal explanations that differ from those usually made by research subjects in the here and now, then we have several interesting empirical questions in need of answers. Can these explanations be sensibly described along dimensions of internality, stability, and globality? Do these individuals show a characteristic style? Does this style relate to outcomes as predicted by the reformulation and/or hopelessness theory?

Much of the cross-cultural research to date has been descriptive, documenting cultural differences in the internality, stability, or globality of causal explanations. Particularly popular have been cross-cultural comparisons of explanations for academic success and failure (e.g., Chandler, Shama, Wolf, & Planchard, 1981; Fry & Ghosh, 1980; Salili, Maehr, & Gillmore, 1976).

For example, Hess, Chang, and McDevitt (1987) compared the attributions that parents made about their children's math performances and found that Chinese mothers living in China tended to attribute their children's failures to lack of effort, whereas Chinese mothers in the United States viewed effort as important but also held other factors responsible. In this study, European-American mothers assigned the least importance to effort. Stevenson and Stigler (1992) reported similar results: Asian parents attributed their children's math performances—good or bad—to effort, whereas in the United States parents attributed their children's performances to ability. However, Stipeck, Weiner, and Li (1989) suggested that these results may hold only for older Asian parents.

Americans are more likely than individuals from many other nations to attribute success to internal, stable, and/or global factors, while attributing failure to external, unstable, and/or specific factors. This phenomenon has been dubbed a self-serving or positivity bias, and it has been the focus of many cross-national studies (e.g., Chandler et al., 1981; Fry & Ghosh, 1980; Kashima & Triandis, 1986; Nurmi, 1992).

These descriptive studies become more informative when we try to explain why culture has the effects that it does on explanatory style. Theorizing often involves attention to whether the culture in question is individualist or collectivist (Lee, Hallahan, & Herzog, 1996). In an individualist culture—like the mainstream United States—people are expected to cope on their own; they need to protect themselves from the psychological implications of bad events; thus, they adapt a self-serving bias. In a collectivist culture, there is less need for such a bias because people are expected to cope as a group.

It does not follow, therefore, that a collectivist explanatory style—despite its appearance—is necessarily pessimistic or depressogenic. It may better be described as modest (Crittenden, 1991). Future cross-cultural research must move beyond mere description of explanatory styles in different nations to look at their supposed consequences.

CONCLUSION

Since their focused beginning in the tradition of animal learning, studies of learned helplessness have steadily grown to touch on many issues of general concern within psychology. The addition of explanatory style and the development of ways to measure this individual difference have made learned helplessness an important topic within contemporary personality psychology.

Explanations of learned helplessness have always been cast in cognitive terms, and the focus of research has long been on the link between learned helplessness and adaptation (Peterson et al., 1993). However, we see a steady progression in the complexity that researchers "allow" the helplessness phenomenon. So, early studies of explanatory style approached this characteristic as a fixed trait with invariant consequences. As work continued, researchers began to approach explanatory style in a contextualized manner. We expect that the most interesting work in this tradition is yet to be conducted.

REFERENCES

Abramson, L. Y., Alloy, L. B., & Metalsky, G. I. (1995). Hopelessness depression. In G. M. Buchanan & M. E. P. Seligman (Eds.), *Explanatory style*. Hillsdale, NJ: Erlbaum.

Abramson, L. Y., Metalsky, G. I., & Alloy, L. B. (1989). Hopelessness depression: A theory-based subtype of depression. *Psychological Review, 96*, 358–372.

Abramson, L. Y., Seligman, M. E. P., & Teasdale, J. D. (1978). Learned helplessness in humans: Critique and reformulation. *Journal of Abnormal Psychology, 87*, 49–74.

Adler, A. (1927). *The theory and practice of individual psychology*. New York: Harcourt, Brace & World.

Adler, A. (1964). Inferiority feelings and defiance and obedience. In H. L. Ansbacher & R. R. Ansbacher (Eds.), *The individual psychology of Alfred Adler*. New York: Harper. (Original work published 1910)

Andrews, G. R., & Debus, L. R. (1978). Persistence and the causal perception of failure: Modifying cognitive attributions. *Journal of Educational Psychology, 70*, 154–166.

Atkinson, J. W. (1957). Motivational determinants of risk-taking behavior. *Psychological Review, 64*, 359–372.

Aydin, G. (1988). The remediation of children's helpless explanatory style and related unpopularity. *Cognitive Therapy and Research, 12*, 155–165.

Bandura, A. (1969). *Principles of behavior modification*. New York: Holt, Rinehart & Winston.

Bandura, A. (1973). *Aggression: A social learning analysis*. Englewood Cliffs, NJ: Prentice-Hall.

Bandura, A. (1977). Self-efficacy: Toward a unifying theory of behavioral change. *Psychological Review, 84*, 191–215.

Bandura, A. (1986). *Social foundations of thought and action*. Englewood Cliffs, NJ: Prentice-Hall.

Bandura, A., & Walters, R. (1963). *Social learning and personality development*. New York: Holt, Rinehart & Winston.

Baumeister, R. F. (1986). *Identity: Cultural change and the struggle for self*. New York: Oxford University Press.

Betancourt, H., & Weiner, B. (1982). Attributions for achievement-related events, expectancy, and sentiment: A study of success and failure in Chile and the United States. *Journal of Cross-Cultural Psychology, 13*, 362–374.

Bettelheim, B. (1976). *The uses of enchantment: The meaning and importance of fairy tales.* New York: Knopf.

Brown, J. A. C. (1964). *Freud and the post-Freudians.* New York: Penguin.

Brown, J. D., & Siegel, J. M. (1988). Attributions for negative life events and depression: The role of perceived control. *Journal of Personality and Social Psychology, 54,* 316–322.

Buchanan, G. M., & Seligman, M. E. P. (Eds.). (1995). *Explanatory style.* Hillsdale, NJ: Erlbaum.

Bunce, S. C., Larsen, R. J., & Peterson, C. (1995). Life after trauma: Personality and daily life experiences of traumatized people. *Journal of Personality, 63,* 165–188.

Burn, S. M. (1992). Loss of control, attributions, and helplessness in the homeless. *Journal of Applied Social Psychology, 22,* 1161–1174.

Carver, C. S. (1989)/ How should multi-faceted personality constructs be tested? Issues illustrated by self-monitoring, attributional style, and tardiness. *Journal of Personality and Social Psychology, 56,* 577–585.

Cerezo-Jimenez, M. A., & Frias, D. (1994). Emotional and cognitive adjustment in abused children. *Child Abuse and Neglect, 18,* 923–932.

Chandler, T. A., Shama, D. D., Wolf, F. M., & Planchard, S. K. (1981). Multiattributional causality: A five-national samples study. *Journal of Cross-Cultural Psychology, 12,* 207–221.

Cole, D. A., & Turner, J. E. (1993). Models of cognitive mediation and moderation in childhood depression. *Journal of Abnormal Psychology, 102,* 271–281.

Colligan, R. C., Offord, K. P., Malinchoc, M., Schulman, P., & Seligman, M. E. P. (1994). CAVEing the MMPI for an optimism-pessimism scale: Seligman's attributional model and the assessment of explanatory style. *Journal of Clinical Psychology, 50,* 71–95.

Crittenden, K. S. (1991). Asian self-effacement or feminine modesty? Attributional patterns of women university students in Taiwan. *Gender and Society, 5,* 98–117.

Cronbach, L. J. (1957). The two disciplines of scientific psychology. *American Psychologist, 12,* 671–684.

DeRubeis, R. J., Evans, M. D., Hollon, S. D., Garvey, M. J., Grove, W. M., & Tauson, V. B. (1990). How does cognitive therapy work? Cognitive change and symptom change in cognitive therapy and pharmacotherapy for depression. *Journal of Consulting and Clinical Psychology, 58,* 862–869.

DeRubeis, R. J., & Hollon, S. D. (1995). Explanatory style in the treatment of depression. In G. M. Buchanan & M. E. P. Seligman (Eds.), *Explanatory style.* Hillsdale, NJ: Erlbaum.

Duda, J. L., & Allison, M. T. (1989). The attributional theory of achievement motivation: Cross-cultural considerations. *International Journal of Intercultural Relations, 13,* 37–55.

Dweck, C. S. (1975). The role of expectations and attributions in the alleviation of learned helplessness. *Journal of Personality and Social Psychology, 31,* 674–685.

Fowler, W. J., & Peterson, L. P. (1981). Increasing reading persistence and altering attributional style of learned helpless children. *Journal of Educational Psychology, 73,* 251–260.

Fry, P. S., & Ghosh, R. (1980). Attribution of success and failure. *Journal of Cross-Cultural Psychology, 11,* 343–363.

Gold, E. (1986). Long-term effects of sexual victimization in childhood: An attributional approach. *Journal of Consulting and Clinical Psychology, 54,* 471–475.

Guimond, S., & Palmer, D. L. (1990). Type of academic training and causal attributions for social problems. *European Journal of Social Psychology, 20,* 61–75.

Harvey, J. H., Ickes, W., & Kidd, R. F. (Eds.). (1976–1981). *New directions in attribution research* (Vols. 1–3). Hillsdale, NJ: Erlbaum.

Hathaway, S. R., & McKinley, J. C. (1943). *Minnesota Multiphasic Personality Inventory.* Minneapolis: University of Minnesota Press.

Heider, F. (1958). *The psychology of interpersonal relations.* New York: Wiley.

Henry, J. W., Martinko, M. J., & Pierce, M. A. (1993). Attributional style as a predictor of success in a first computer course. *Computers in Human Behavior, 9,* 341–352.

Hess, R. D., Chang, C. M., & McDevitt, T. M. (1987). Cultural variation in family beliefs about children's performance in mathematics: Comparisons among People's Republic of China, Chinese-American, and Caucasian American families. *Journal of Educational Psychology, 79,* 179–188.

Heyman, G. D., Dweck, C. S., & Cain, K. M. (1992). Young children's vulnerability to self-blame and helplessness: Relationship to beliefs about goodness. *Child Development, 63,* 401–415.

Hiroto, D. S., & Seligman, M. E. P. (1975). Generality of learned helplessness in man. *Journal of Personality and Social Psychology, 31,* 311–327.

Hollon, S. D., DeRubeis, R. J., Evans, M. D., Wiemer, M. J., Garvey, M. J., Grove, W. M., & Tuason, V. B. (1992). Cognitive therapy and pharmacotherapy for depression: Singly and in combination. *Archives of General Psychiatry, 49,* 774–781.

Holloway, S. D., Kashiwagi, K., Hess, R. D., & Azuma, H. (1986). Causal attributions by Japanese and American mothers and children about performance in mathematics. *International Journal of Psychology, 21,* 269–286.

Jaycox, L. H., Reivich, K., Gillham, J., & Seligman, M. E. P. (1994). Prevention of depressive symptoms in school children. *Behaviour Research and Therapy, 32,* 801–816.

Jones, E. E., & Davis, K. E. (1965). From acts to dispositions: The attribution process in person perception. In L. Berkowitz (Ed.), *Advances in experimental social psychology* (Vol. 2). New York: Academic Press.

Kamen-Siegel, L., Rodin, J., Seligman, M. E. P., & Dwyer, J. (1991). Explanatory style and cell-mediated immunity in elderly men and women. *Health Psychology, 10,* 229–235.

Kashima, Y., & Triandis, H. C. (1986). The self-serving bias in attributions as a coping strategy: A cross-cultural comparison. *Journal of Cross-Cultural Psychology, 17,* 83–97.

Kaslow, N. J., Rehm, L. P., Pollak, S. L., & Siegel, A. W. (1988). Attributional style and self-control behavior in depressed and nondepressed children and their parents. *Journal of Abnormal Child Psychology, 16,* 163–175.

Kaufman, J. (1991). Depressive disorders in maltreated children. *Journal of the American Academy of Child and Adolescent Psychiatry, 30,* 257–265.

Kelley, H. H. (1973). The process of causal attribution. *American Psychologist, 28,* 107–128.

Kennelly, K. J., & Mount, S. A. (1985). Perceived contingency of reinforcement, helplessness, locus of control, and academic performance. *Psychology in the Schools, 22,* 465–469.

Ladd, J. (1957). *The structure of a moral code.* Boston: Harvard University Press.

Lee, F., Hallahan, M., & Herzog, T. (1996). Explaining real-life events: How culture and domain shape attributions. *Personality and Social Psychology Bulletin, 22,* 732–741.

Lewin, K. (1935). *A dynamic theory of personality.* New York: McGraw-Hill.

Lewin, K. (1951). *Field theory in social science: Selected theoretical papers.* New York: Harper.

Lin, E. H., & Peterson, C. (1990). Pessimistic explanatory style and response to illness. *Behaviour Research and Therapy, 28,* 243–248.

Little, A. (1987). Attributions in a cross-cultural context. *Genetic, Social, and General Psychology Monographs, 113,* 61–79.

Lloyd, C. (1980). Life events and depressive disorder reviewed: I. Events as predisposing factors. II. Events as precipitating factors. *Archives of General Psychiatry, 37,* 529–548.

Maier, S. F., & Seligman, M. E. P. (1976). Learned helplessness: Theory and evidence. *Journal of Experimental Psychology: General, 105,* 3–46.

McClelland, D. C. (1961). *The achieving society.* Princeton, NJ: Van Nostrand.

Mikulincer, M. (1994). *Human learned helplessness: A coping perspective.* New York: Plenum Press.

Miller, I. W., & Norman, W. H. (1979). Learned helplessness in humans: A review and attribution theory model. *Psychological Bulletin, 86,* 93–119.

Miller, J. G. (1984). Culture and the development of everyday social explanation. *Journal of Personality and Social Psychology, 46,* 961–978.

Mischel, W. (1990). Personality dispositions revisited and revised: A view after three decades. In L. A. Pervin (Ed.), *Handbook of personality: Theory and research.* New York: Guilford Press.

Morgan, C. D., & Murray, H. A. (1935). A method for investigating fantasies. *Archives of Neurology and Psychiatry, 34,* 289–306.

Needles, D. J., & Abramson, L. Y. (1990). Positive life events, attributional style, and hopefulness: Testing a model of recovery from depression. *Journal of Abnormal Psychology, 99,* 156–165.

Nisbett, R., & Ross, L. (1980). *Human inference: Strategies and shortcomings of social judgment.* Englewood Cliffs, NJ: Prentice-Hall.

Nolen-Hoeksema, S., Girgus, J. S., & Seligman, M. E. P. (1986). Learned helplessness in children: A longitudinal study of depression, achievement, and explanatory style. *Journal of Personality and Social Psychology, 51,* 435–442.

Nolen-Hoeksema, S., Girgus, J. S., & Seligman, M. E. P. (1992). Predictors and consequences of childhood depressive symptoms: A 5-year longitudinal study. *Journal of Abnormal Psychology, 101,* 405–422.

Nurmi, J. (1992). Cross-cultural differences in self-serving bias: Responses to the Attributional Style Questionnaire by American and Finnish students. *The Journal of Social Psychology, 132,* 69–76.

Oettingen, G., & Seligman, M. E. P. (1990). Pessimism and behavioral signs of depression in East versus West Berlin. *European Journal of Social Psychology, 20,* 207–220.

Orsillo, S. M., McCaffrey, R. J., & Fisher, J. M. (1993). Siblings of head-injured individuals: A population at risk. *Journal of Head Trauma Rehabilitation, 8,* 102–115.

Overmier, J. B., & Seligman, M. E. P. (1967). Effects of inescapable shock upon subsequent escape and avoidance learning. *Journal of Comparative and Physiological Psychology, 63,* 23–33.

Parsons, J. E., Meece, J. L., Adler, T. F., & Kaczala, C. M. (1982). Sex differences in attributional patterns and learned helplessness? *Sex Roles, 8,* 421–432.

Pepper, S. C. (1942). *World hypotheses.* Berkeley: University of California Press.

Perez-Bouchard, L., Johnson, J. L., & Ahrens, A. H. (1993). Attributional style in children of substance abusers. *American Journal of Drug and Alcohol Abuse, 19,* 475–489.

Peterson, C. (1982). Learned helplessness and attributional interventions in depression. In C. Antaki & C. Brewin (Eds.), *Attributions and psychological change: A guide to the use of attribution theory in the clinic and classroom.* London: Academic Press.

Peterson, C. (1988). Explanatory style as a risk factor for illness. *Cognitive Therapy and Research, 12,* 117–130.

Peterson, C. (1991). The meaning and measurement of explanatory style. *Psychological Inquiry, 2,* 1–10.

Peterson, C. (1992). *Personality* (2nd ed.). Fort Worth, TX: Harcourt Brace Jovanovich.

Peterson, C., & Barrett, L. C. (1987). Explanatory style and academic performance among university freshmen. *Journal of Personality and Social Psychology, 53,* 603–607.

Peterson, C., Bettes, B. A., & Seligman, M. E. P. (1985). Depressive symptoms and unprompted causal attributions: Content analysis. *Behaviour Research and Therapy, 23,* 379–382.

Peterson, C., & Bossio, L. M. (1991). *Health and optimism.* New York: Free Press.

Peterson, C., Colvin, D., & Lin, E. H. (1992). Explanatory style and helplessness. *Social Behavior and Personality, 20,* 1–13.

Peterson, C., Luborsky, L., & Seligman, M. E. P. (1983). Attributions and depressive mood shifts: A case study using the symptom-context method. *Journal of Abnormal Psychology, 92,* 96–103.

Peterson, C., Maier, S. F., & Seligman, M. E. P. (1993). *Learned helplessness: A theory for the age of personal control.* New York: Oxford University Press.

Peterson, C., & Park, C. (1995). *Implicit and explicit explanatory styles in the lifecourse of college-educated women.* Unpublished manuscript, University of Michigan.

Peterson, C., Schulman, P., Castellon, C., & Seligman, M. E. P. (1992). The explanatory style scoring manual. In C. P. Smith (Ed.), *Handbook of thematic analysis.* New York: Cambridge University Press.

Peterson, C., & Seligman, M. E. P. (1984). Causal explanations as a risk factor for depression: Theory and evidence. *Psychological Review, 91,* 347–374.

Peterson, C., Seligman, M. E. P., & Vaillant, G. E. (1988). Pessimistic explanatory style is a risk factor for physical illness: A thirty-five year longitudinal study. *Journal of Personality and Social Psychology, 55,* 23–27.

Peterson, C., Semmel, A., von Baeyer, C., Abramson, L. Y., Metalsky, G. I., & Seligman, M. E. P. (1982). The Attributional Style Questionnaire. *Cognitive Therapy and Research, 6,* 287–299.

Peterson, C., & Stunkard, A. J. (1989). Personal control and health promotion. *Social Science and Medicine, 28,* 819–828.

Peterson, C., & Stunkard, A. J. (1992). Cognates of personal control: Locus of control, self-efficacy, and explanatory style. *Applied and Preventive Psychology, 1,* 111–117.

Peterson, C., & Ulrey, L. M. (1994). Can explanatory style be scored from TAT protocols? *Personality and Social Psychology Bulletin, 20,* 101–106.

Quine, W. V., & Ullian, J. S. (1978). *The web of belief* (2nd ed.). New York: Random House.

Radke-Yarrow, M., Belmont, B., Nottelman, E., & Bottomly, L. (1990). Young children's self-conceptions: Origins in the natural discourse of depressed and normal mothers and their children. In D. Cicchetti & M. Beeghly (Eds.), *The self in transition.* Chicago: University of Chicago Press.

Reivich, K. (1995). The measurement of explanatory style. In G. M. Buchanan & M. E. P. Seligman (Eds.), *Explanatory style.* Hillsdale, NJ: Erlbaum.

Reivich, K., & Seligman, M. E. P. (1991). The Forced-Choice Attributional Style Questionnaire. Unpublished manuscript, University of Pennsylvania.

Rose, D. T., & Abramson, L. Y. (1992). Developmental predictors of depressive cognitive style: Research and theory. In D. Cicchetti & S. L. Toth (Eds.), *Rochester Symposium on Developmental Psychopathology: Developmental perspectives on depression.* Rochester, NY: University of Rochester Press.

Roth, S. (1980). A revised model of learned helplessness in humans. *Journal of Personality, 48,* 103–133.

Rotter, J. B. (1954). *Social learning and clinical psychology.* Englewood Cliffs, NJ: Prentice-Hall.

Rotter, J. B. (1966). Generalized expectancies for internal versus external control of reinforcement. *Psychological Monographs, 81* (1, Whole No. 609).

Salili, F., Maehr, M. L., & Gillmore, G. (1976). Achievement and morality: A cross-cultural analysis of causal attribution and evaluation. *Journal of Personality and Social Psychology, 33,* 327–337.

Satterfield, J. M., & Seligman, M. E. P. (1994). Military aggression and risk predicted by explanatory style. *Psychological Science, 5,* 77–82.

Schulman, P., Keith, D., & Seligman, M. E. P. (1993). Is optimism heritable? A study of twins. *Behaviour Research and Therapy, 31,* 569–574.

Schulman, P., & Seligman, M. E. P. (1986). Explanatory style predicts productivity among life insurance agents. *Journal of Personality and Social Psychology, 50,* 832–838.

Seligman, M. E. P. (1974). Depression and learned helplessness. In R. J. Friedman & M. M. Katz (Eds.), *The psychology of depression: Contemporary theory and research.* Washington, DC: Winston.

Seligman, M. E. P. (1975). *Helplessness: On depression, development, and death.* San Francisco: Freeman.

Seligman, M. E. P. (1991). *Learned optimism.* New York: Knopf.

Seligman, M. E. P., Abramson, L. Y., Semmel, A., & von Baeyer, C. (1979). Depressive attributional style. *Journal of Abnormal Psychology, 88,* 242–247.

Seligman, M. E. P., & Maier, S. F. (1967). Failure to escape traumatic shock. *Journal of Experimental Psychology, 74,* 1–9.

Seligman, M. E. P., Peterson, C., Kaslow, N. J., Tanenbaum, R. L., Alloy, L. B., & Abramson, L. Y. (1984). Attributional style and depressive symptoms among children. *Journal of Abnormal Psychology, 93,* 235–238.

Sellers, R. M., & Peterson, C. (1993). Explanatory style and coping with controllable events by student-athletes. *Cognition and Emotion, 7,* 431–441.

Sethi, S., & Seligman, M. E. P. (1993). Optimism and fundamentalism. *Psychological Science, 4,* 256–259.

Stevenson, H. W. J., & Stigler, J. W. (1992). *The learning gap: Why our schools are failing and what we can learn from Japanese and Chinese education.* New York: Summit.

Stipeck, D., Weiner, B., & Li, K. (1989). Testing some attribution-emotion relations in the People's Republic of China. *Journal of Personality and Social Psychology, 56,* 109–110.

Sweeney, P. D., Anderson, K., & Bailey, S. (1986). Attributional style in depression: A meta-analytic review. *Journal of Personality and Social Psychology, 50,* 974–991.

Tolman, E. C. (1948). Cognitive maps in rats and men. *Psychological Review, 55,* 189–208.

Turk, E., & Bry, B. H. (1992). Adolescents' and parents' explanatory styles and parents' causal explanations about their adolescents. *Cognitive Therapy and Research, 16,* 349–357.

Turner, J. E., & Cole, D. A. (1994). Developmental differences in cognitive diatheses for child depression. *Journal of Abnormal Child Psychology, 22,* 15–32.

Vaihinger, H. (1911). *The psychology of "as if": A system of the theoretical, practical, and religious fictions of mankind.* New York: Harcourt, Brace & World.

van den Berg, J. H. (1983). *The changing nature of man.* New York: W. W. Norton.

Visintainer, M., Volpicelli, J. R., & Seligman, M. E. P. (1982). Tumor rejection in rats after inescapable or escapable shock. *Science, 216,* 437–439.

Weiner, B. (1986). *An attributional theory of motivation and emotion.* New York: Springer-Verlag.

Weiner, B. (1990). Searching for the roots of applied attribution theory. In S. Graham & V. S. Folkes (Eds.), *Attribution theory: Applications to achievement, mental health, and interpersonal conflict.* Hillsdale, NJ: Erlbaum.

Weisz, J. R., Rothbaum, F. M., & Blackburn, T. C. (1984). Standing out and standing in: The psychology of control in America and Japan. *American Psychologist, 39,* 955–969.

White, R. W. (1959). Motivation reconsidered: The concept of competence. *Psychological Review, 66,* 297–333.

Wortman, C. B., & Brehm, J. W. (1975). Response to uncontrollable outcomes: An integration of reactance theory and the learned helplessness model. In L. Berkowitz (Ed.), *Advances in experimental social psychology* (Vol. 8). New York: Academic Press.

Yamauchi, H. (1989). Congruence of causal attributions for school performance given by children and mothers. *Psychological Reports, 64*, 359–363.

Zullow, H. M. (1991). Pessimistic rumination in popular songs and newsmagazines predict economic recession via decreased consumer optimism and spending. *Journal of Economic Psychology, 12*, 501–526.

Zullow, H. M., & Seligman, M. E. P. (1990). Pessimistic rumination predicts defeat of presidential candidates, 1900 to 1984. *Psychological Inquiry, 1*, 52–61.

CHAPTER 13

SUBJECTIVE WELL-BEING AND PERSONALITY

ED DIENER

Happiness and misery depend as much on temperament as on fortune.

François de la Rochefoucauld, *Maximes*

INTRODUCTION

La Rochefoucauld argued that personality is an important cause of happiness and of unhappiness. Modern researchers find, however, that he was incorrect in *underestimating* the size of this influence. It appears that happiness, the experience of unpleasant emotions, and life satisfaction often depend *more* on temperament than on one's life circumstances. Indeed, it is now reasonable to hypothesize that personality is a major determinant of long-term, subjective well-being. Walter Mischel (1968) argued in a well-known book, *Personality and Assessment,* that dispositions are weak determinants of behavior, and that situations are much stronger predictors of overt responses. In the realm of subjective well-being, Mischel's argument is turned on its head—it appears that situations are weak predictors, and personality is a strong correlate, of long-term subjective well-being.

Subjective well-being (SWB) is the psychological term for what in popular parlance is referred to as "happiness." *Subjective well-being* is preferred to *happiness* because the latter term has many different meanings. Subjective well-being refers to people's evaluations

ED DIENER • Department of Psychology, University of Illinois, Champaign, Illinois 61820.

Advanced Personality, edited by David F. Barone, Michel Hersen, and Vincent B. Van Hasselt. Plenum Press, New York, 1998.

311

of their lives—including cognitive judgments, such as life satisfaction; and affective evaluations (moods and emotions), such as positive and negative emotional feelings. When a person reports that her life is satisfying, that she is frequently experiencing pleasant affect and infrequently experiencing unpleasant affect, that person is said to have high subjective well-being. Both her cognitive and affective systems react favorably to what is happening in her life. She likes the life she is leading—it is desirable from her point of view.

In the past two decades, as psychology moved beyond the bounds of radical behaviorism, scientists have shown increasing interest in SWB. Their interest is not surprising because happiness and life satisfaction are major goals of most people. It seems desirable, therefore, that psychologists study this ubiquitous concern. Furthermore, as the nations of the world move into an era of postmaterialism in which sheer physical survival is no longer the major care, SWB is likely to become a central goal of societies throughout the world. Thus, policymakers will become increasingly interested in the factors that increase subjective well-being. In studying SWB, scientists hope to further our understanding of the age-old questions of what composes the "good life" and the "good society."

Subjective well-being has several major divisions, including global life satisfaction; contentment with particular life domains, such as one's marriage and work; the presence of frequent positive affect (pleasant moods and emotions); and a relative absence of negative affect (unpleasant moods and emotions). Although there is some tendency for these components to occur within the same individuals to form a broad factor of SWB, they sometimes diverge. Therefore, it is necessary to separately study each of them. A researcher, for example, can examine people's hedonic balance (positive emotions minus negative emotions), but can gain a complete picture of affective well-being only if he or she separately measures positive *and* negative affect. In fact, a major finding in this field is that pleasant and unpleasant emotions form separable factors that have different correlates. There are individuals who are high on positive and negative affect, and there are also people who are low on both of them. Therefore, it does not make sense to think of people who experience lots of pleasant affect as opposites of people who experience frequent unpleasant affect. Figure 13.1 shows the relation between positive and negative affect, which are relatively independent—people's scores on one tell us little about their scores on the other. Figure 13.1 uses names derived from the ancient Greeks for the four personality types that result from combinations of positive and negative affect: melancholic, choleric, phlegmatic and sanguine. A complete understanding of SWB can be obtained only if we understand both emotional dimensions. If we oversimplify and conceive of "happiness" (high positive affect) and "unhappiness" (high negative affect) as exact opposites, we ignore the phlegmatic and choleric types of persons. Although the sanguine and melancholic persons represent individuals in whom positive and negative affect do appear to be opposite, the phlegmatic is a person who has relatively little of each, and the choleric person is one who experiences a good deal of both types of emotion.

The major components of SWB can be broken down into even more specific elements. For example, positive affect can be divided into joy, contentment, affection, and pride; negative affect can be separated into anger, sadness, guilt, shame, anxiety, and so forth. These emotions can in turn be parsed even more finely. The level at which a researcher studies SWB will depend on the particular questions asked. Although some researchers advocate studying only the narrower units, one can further understanding by examining broader units as well, because some factors simultaneously influence many of the specific feelings. For

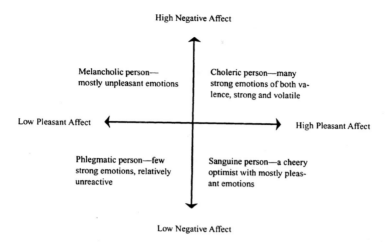

FIGURE 13.1. Personality types arising from combinations of positive and negative affect.

example, a negative life event, such as the death of one's spouse, is likely to induce a number of different negative emotions; therefore, it often makes sense to study these emotions in tandem.

The field of SWB has several cardinal characteristics (Diener, 1984). First, it is concerned with well-being from the respondent's perspective. An onlooker might consider the respondent to be unfortunate, and a psychologist might believe the respondent to be mentally ill. If the respondent thinks, however, that life is going well, he has high subjective well-being. It follows that SWB is not a complete definition of well-being. We can easily enumerate additional characteristics that are necessary for complete well-being: self-efficacy, contact with reality, helping others, and so forth. Although SWB is not sufficient for mental health, it is nevertheless an important aspect of well-being, which grants importance to the respondent's own views of his or her life. Thus, the field of SWB retreats from the "psychologist knows best" approach to well-being and acknowledges that how people evaluate their own lives deserves recognition. The field empowers lay persons rather than leaving judgments about their well-being strictly in the hands of professionals.

A second cardinal characteristic of the field of SWB is that it does not consider only momentary moods and emotions; it also examines people's well-being over longer time periods. Thus, winning $100 million may induce joy when the lottery is announced, but the SWB researcher will want to know whether the windfall permanently increases the winner's moods and life satisfaction. Thus, although the SWB researcher is concerned with momentary moods and emotions, the primary interest is in people's long-term levels of affect and satisfaction.

A third key attribute of SWB is that it ranges from despair to elation to consummate life satisfaction and does not simply focus on negative states, such as depression and stress. Therefore, the field of SWB recognizes that although negative states are worthy of study, most people are determined to rise above negativity and obtain a positive level of well-being. Avoiding misery is not sufficient for complete SWB; people must also experience life satisfaction and pleasant emotions.

Behavioral scientists have studied a range of factors that might influence SWB, including demographic variables, such as age and marriage; life events; personality; and temperament (Diener, 1984; Myers, 1992). Some factors, such as marriage and income, reliably predict SWB; other factors, such as education and intelligence, do not. Nevertheless, the single most important correlate of SWB may be personality.

TEMPERAMENTAL PREDISPOSITIONS TO SWB

Both temperament and personality have a strong relation with subjective well-being. *Temperament* is often defined as a biological predisposition to certain types of responding that appears early in life. Many believe that temperament has a large genetic component. In contrast, *personality* is often defined as characteristic response tendencies in adults, which have biological and learned components.

A number of lines of evidence point to the fact that temperament plays a causal role in predisposing some people to high SWB and others to lower levels of SWB. Perhaps the most convincing evidence for the role of temperament comes from heritability studies that clearly indicate that SWB is influenced by one's genetic makeup. Studies based on twins reared together and apart, on people of differing genetic relations, and on adopted people, all indicate that differences in temperament, personality, and subjective well-being are influenced substantially by genetic differences. For example, Tellegen *et al.* (1988) at the University of Minnesota conducted a study of monozygotic (identical) and dizygotic (fraternal) twins who were separated and reared apart from a very early age. Monozygotic twins have virtually the same genetic makeup, and dizygotic twins share on average half of their genes. By examining how similar the separated monozygotic twins were and then comparing them with identical twins reared together and dizygotic twins reared together and apart, the Minnesota researchers were able to estimate the amount of variability in SWB that was due to heredity and the amount due to environmental differences among the participants. Approximately one half of the variability (defined in terms of variance) in positive affect and negative affect appeared to be due to genetic differences among the participants. In contrast, negative affect on average appeared to be influenced very little by respondents' early shared family environment, and positive affect was influenced only to a modest degree by shared home environment. These conclusions were based on the fact that even when monozygotic twins grew up in separate homes, they were extremely similar in SWB from an early age. In contrast, dizygotic twins who were raised within the same homes were on average far less similar. In terms of the effects of shared family environment, twins reared together were not much more similar than were twins who were reared apart.

Table 13.1 shows the estimates made by Tellegen *et al.* (1988) of the amount of variance in SWB variables that are due to heredity and to the shared home environment of the twins. Other studies have drawn conclusions similar to those of the Tellegen *et al.* (1988) study, although adoption studies often lead to lower heritability estimates than do twin studies. Perhaps more surprising than the fact that SWB is in part heritable is the fact that the shared family environment in which people grew up has so little influence. In the case of positive affect, there appears to be some small environmental influences, but negative affect seems to be influenced very little by the environment that children growing up in the same household shared.

TABLE 13.1. Estimate of Genetic and Environmental Variance
Components Based on Twins Being Reared Together and Apart

	Amounts of variance	
	Heritability	Shared family environment
Positive affect	.40	.22
Negative affect	.55	.02
Well-being	.48	.13

Tellegen *et al.* (1988) also found that the genetic effects are largely additive for negative affect, whereas the genetic effects are largely nonadditive for positive affect. This finding indicates that genetic effects for negative affect depend on the sheer number of genes that two people have in common; whereas the interaction of genes creates the predisposition for positive affect. Thus, identical twins may be very similar for positive affect because they have the exact same sequence of genes, while siblings may not be that similar. Although on average siblings have half of their genes in common, they do not necessarily have the same sequence of genes, which will result in similar levels of positive affect. The different patterns of heritability for positive and negative affect point to the independence of these two systems. Because identical twins reared apart are so similar in SWB, and adopted individuals are not very similar to their adopted siblings, the current conclusion is that feelings of well-being are influenced by genetic factors.

The conclusions of heritability studies that SWB is substantially influenced by one's inherited biology are supported by studies of temperament in early life. Differences in emotional reactions appear early in life and persist over time. For example, Kagan found that fetuses in utero show individual differences in reactivity that persist into childhood. Infants who are more reactive to novel stimuli grow up to be children who have a lower threshold for fear and respond negatively to separation from their mothers. Thus, infants exhibit typical emotional reactions to novel stimuli, and these responses show a degree of stability over time. Kagan (1994; Kagan, Snidman, & Arcus, 1992) reviewed evidence showing that inhibited toddlers are more likely to be inhibited in childhood and early adolescence.

The differences that are apparent in the emotional behavior of toddlers are also seen in markers of emotion in the brain. For example, Davidson and Fox (1982) found that infants tested at about one year of age varied in the amount of fearful behavior they exhibited in the laboratory situation. Interestingly, this fearful behavior was predicted by the relative amounts of left-frontal versus right-frontal cerebral activity that the infants showed before the testing began. Frontal cerebral asymmetry appears to reflect current emotional states and a predisposition to experience these states; the Davidson and Fox (1982) data are thus suggestive of early differences in a biological predisposition to experience certain emotions. Therefore, it is plausible that genetic factors lead to differences in the reactivity of the emotional centers of the brain, which in turn predispose people to experience positive and negative moods and emotions to a greater or lesser degree. These differences possibly represent basic physiological predispositions to experience higher or lower levels of SWB.

If biologically based personality predispositions influence SWB, we would expect there to be considerable stability over time and consistency across situations in personality and SWB. In fact, adult personality shows a surprising level of stability over time. Costa (1994) reviewed evidence showing that even over a period of as long as 30 years, adults are very stable in their personalities. In the realm of SWB, Magnus and Diener (1991) found that life satisfaction measured over four years correlated .58. Even when life satisfaction at Time 1 was self-reported and at other times was reported by the family and friends of the respondent, the correlation over four years was .52. The use of two measurement sources is important in demonstrating that the stability of SWB is not simply an artifact of the stability of such response sets as acquiescence or social desirability. Similarly, Costa and McCrae (1988) found that there were significant stability coefficients between spouse's ratings of one's emotions at Time 1 and the target person's rating six years later. For example, positive emotions showed a stability of .56, and anxiety showed a stability of .53. The six-year stability correlations for hostility and for depression were .55 and .44, respectively. Again, these results are impressive because measurement at the two times was by different methods—by spouse-report versus self-report. Thus, methodological factors such as response biases are not likely to inflate these stability estimates. Furthermore, the underlying true stability of the traits is likely to be greater than the coefficients because the random error of measurement in both methods was not controlled.

Not only is SWB stable across time, but it is also consistent across situations. Diener and Larsen (1984), for example, found that average levels of pleasant mood in work situations correlated .70 with average levels of pleasant mood in recreation situations. Similarly, mean levels of unpleasant affect in work situations correlated .74 with mean levels of negative affect in recreation situations. Thus, the stereotype that there are certain people who enjoy work, but other people who enjoy play, is unfounded. In fact, there is a tendency for the same people to enjoy both work and leisure situations. Levels of consistency for positive and negative affect were similar across social versus alone situations and novel versus typical situations. Mean levels of life satisfaction, however, showed even higher stability coefficients in the .95 range. The consistency across situations and the stability over time of SWB point to the potential long-term influence of stable personality predispositions.

One might argue that the stability in people's SWB over time is due to stability in their environment rather than to stable temperament factors. Doubt was cast on this alternative explanation, however, by findings of Costa, McCrae, and Zonderman (1987). They examined people who had lived under relatively stable circumstances or in more changing conditions over a 10-year period. For example, the high-environmental-change group had retired, gotten divorced or become widowed, and so forth. The low-change groups had not experienced these alterations in their life situations. Costa et al. (1987) found only slightly lower stability estimates for the high-change group than for the low-change groups. Similarly, Diener, Sandvik, Seidlitz, and Diener (1993) found that people whose incomes went up, down, or stayed about the same over a 10-year period remained approximately the same. Thus, the stability in SWB over years seems not to be due to unvarying circumstances, but instead seems to be based on stability within the person.

Other interesting evidence suggesting the importance of temperament is that the environment may not be as crucial to subjective well-being as was once thought. Vaillant and Vaillant (1990) studied a sample of Harvard graduates over a period of 45 years. As time went by, they found that the early traumas of childhood had less effect on the well-being of respondents. By the time respondents were in late midlife, the effects of early traumas, such as a parent's death and the stability of the parental marriage, were gone. In combination with heritability studies that suggest a small role for the early shared home environment on personality, these results suggest that childhood events may not have an overwhelming influence on later SWB.

Other studies point to the fact that many situational variables barely covary with SWB (Myers, 1992). For example, we found that income in the United States correlates only about .13 with SWB. Physical attractiveness was a similarly weak correlate of SWB, even though we computed this correlation using a group of dating college students for whom one might think that attractiveness would be quite important (Diener, Wolsic, & Fujita, 1995). Perhaps even more surprising, Okun and George (1984) found that objective physical health as determined by a physician was barely correlated with SWB in a group of elderly participants. Although subjective health (whether a person feels healthy), covaried moderately with SWB, objectively assessed health correlated almost zero with SWB. It is surprising that three of the most important resources in Western society—health, money, and good looks—barely show any covariation at all with happiness. Based on a national sample of Americans, Campbell, Converse, and Rodgers (1976) concluded that all of the demographic factors they measured (including age, sex, income, race, education, and marital status), taken together accounted for less than 20% of the variance in SWB.

We see that SWB shows substantial levels of stability in adulthood, and that certain environmental factors influence it less than one might think. Can we attribute, however, levels of SWB to personality? The connection between the two was demonstrated by Headey and Wearing (1992). They showed in a longitudinal panel study that extraversion and neuroticism predict levels of SWB several years later. Similarly, Magnus (1991) found over a four-year period that Time 1 personality predicted Time 2 life satisfaction and other measures of subjective well-being beyond the influence of intervening life events. Indeed, personality was a much stronger predictor of Time 2 SWB than were life events. In other words, personality predicts later SWB even when events are held constant, suggesting a possible causal role of personality on SWB. In contrast, people's changes in life events were not related to changes in long-term SWB, indicating a less important long-term role for life events.

In conclusion, a number of different types of evidence point to the fact that there are temperament influences on SWB. Infants show typical emotional reactions that to some degree persist over time. Based on adoption and twin studies, adult subjective well-being appears to be in part inherited and is also fairly stable over time. The strong stability of adult personality and the relative stability of SWB, combined with the correlation between the two, suggest that personality may exert a continuous influence on feelings of well-being. This idea is supported by longitudinal data that indicate that personality can predict SWB over a period of years. Biological markers, such as cerebral asymmetry, correlate with people's typical emotional reactions. Finally, environmental factors often have only small influences on SWB in the long run. Thus, one is led to infer that people's biologically based temperament is influential in determining their SWB, whereas their environment and circumstances may be of less significance than formerly thought. The data are not definitive, and situational factors undoubtedly do have some influence on SWB. Nevertheless, there is increasing evidence that suggests that stable personality has an influence on feelings of well-being.

ADULT PERSONALITY TRAITS

Traits are behavioral response tendencies that show a degree of cross-situational consistency and temporal stability. Which of these consistent response tendencies correlate most strongly with adult SWB?

In recent years, the Five-Factor Model or "Big Five" has become extremely popular. The Five-Factor Model is based on the idea that there are five cardinal traits—extraversion, neuroticism, conscientiousness, agreeableness, and openness to experience—and that other personality characteristics are derived from these. The low pole of each Big-Five trait is anchored by antonymous terms: *introversion, emotional stability, spontaneity, assertiveness,* and low *openness to experience.* Some theorists, such as Gray, hypothesize fewer than five cardinal traits (he posits behavioral activation and behavioral inhibition systems), whereas other theorists, such as Tellegen, postulate the existence of more than five basic traits. Nevertheless, many other traits can be mapped onto the Big Five. (See Chapter 4 for more coverage of trait theory and the Five-Factor Model.)

EXTRAVERSION

Evidence clearly supports a relation between the first of the five factors, extraversion, and positive affect. Extraversion includes such characteristics as sociability, stimulus seeking, dominance, high activity, warmth, and dominance. Surprisingly, extraversion shows substantial correlations with pleasant emotions, such as joy and affection, but little inverse covariation with negative affect. In contrast, the second of the Big Five traits, neuroticism, is strongly related to the experience of negative affect, but shows a very small inverse relation with positive affect.

In an early study, Bradburn (1969) found that social experience was related to positive affect but not to negative affect. Costa and McCrae (1980) extended this finding to personality by showing that positive affect was related to extraversion but not to neuroticism. Figure 13.2 illustrates preliminary correlations between types of affect and extraversion for a sample of 6,311 college students in 40 nations. The affect measures include the frequency and intensity of negative and positive affect. As shown, there was a small (but significant) correlation between the frequency of negative affect and extraversion. The correlations between extraversion and both the frequency and intensity of positive affect were, however, much larger. Based on findings such as these, it has been suggested that extraversion and neuroticism reflect individual differences in the basic approach and avoidance systems in the brain, systems that are likely to be linked but are separate.

The relation between positive affect and extraversion has been replicated in many studies. For example, Diener, Sandvik, Pavot, and Fujita (1992) found that extraversion predicted SWB in a representative sample of Americans. They found that this relation held despite the living circumstances of the respondents. Extraverts were on average happier whether they lived alone or with others, whether they worked in solitary or social occupations, and whether they lived in small towns or large cities. Extraverts were also happier across diverse ethnic, gender, and age groups. The fact that the relation between extraversion and SWB was similar across different environments and samples suggested that it might be based on biological temperament factors rather than simply on situational differences in the lives of extraverts versus introverts. In support of this reasoning, Pavot, Diener,

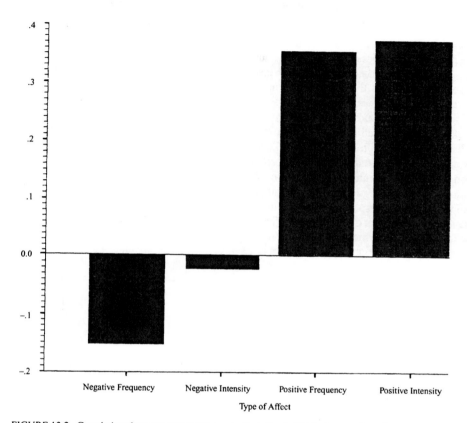

FIGURE 13.2. Correlations between extraversion and affect. $N = 6, 311$ (college students from 40 nations).

and Fujita (1990) found that extraverts reported more positive affect at random moments in an experience sampling study whether they were alone or with others, again suggesting that the relation may be due to a temperament characteristic. However, we also found that both introverts and extraverts report more pleasant emotions when they are in social settings. Therefore, the fact that extraverts experience greater levels of positive affect may be due to a general propensity to experience positive affect and also to the greater amount of time they spend with others.

Experience sampling in which respondents report their emotions when signaled by a pager is an established method of obtaining reports of affect. If each subject is signaled a number of times over a period of weeks, the investigator can obtain a good estimate of her or his average moods and emotions. Such measures based on experience sampling are desirable because they are not as likely as are one-time self-reports of SWB to be biased by memory lapses and global self-labels. When experience sampling is used, extraverts show greater SWB over a period of time. Figure 13.3, a graph derived from Larsen and Kasimatis (1990), shows the positive levels of well-being reported each day by introverts and by extraverts. As can be seen, well-being for introverts and extraverts was lowest on Mondays and increased all week, reaching a climax on Saturdays. It is evident, however, that extraverts experienced more positive well-being than introverts each day. The level of well-being of introverts on Saturday barely surpassed the extraverts' lowest (Sunday and Monday) levels.

The use of alternate methods of measurement when establishing the relation between extraversion and positive affect is an important precaution because it helps rule out an explanation based on response artifacts. For example, it might be that if one obtained extraversion self-ratings and reports of positive emotions from the respondent, social desirability could cause a correlation between the two. Perhaps both positive emotions and extraverted behaviors are desirable in the culture. Therefore, individual differences in social desirability might lead some individuals to report higher levels of both positive affect and extraversion and create a spurious correlation between the two constructs. We have collected alternative measures of extraversion and positive affect that help to disconfirm this explanation in terms of response artifacts. For example, we asked family and friends to rate the extraverted behaviors of the target subjects, and these reports correlated substantially with the levels of positive moods and emotions reported by the participants. Additionally, the extraverted behaviors recorded on a daily basis by respondents correlated with the positive

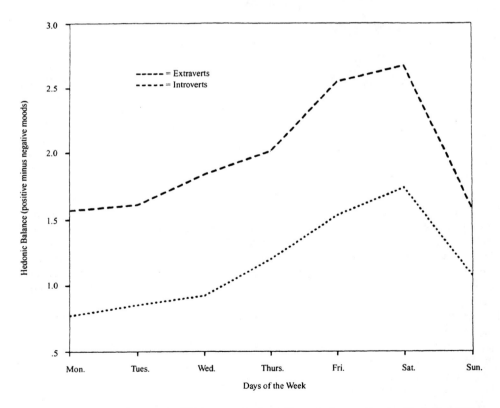

FIGURE 13.3. Moods of introverts and extraverts across days of the week. *Source:* Based on "Individual Differences in Entrainment of Mood to the Weekly Calendar" by R. J. Larsen and M. Kasimatis, 1990, *Journal of Personality and Social Psychology, 58,* p.1680. Copyright 1990 by *American Psychological Association.* Adapted with permission.

emotions for the subjects reported by her or his family and friends. Thus, the correlation between SWB and extraversion is unlikely to be due to measurement difficulties.

In assessing the size of the relation between extraversion and SWB, Fujita (1993) used a latent trait approach in order to correct for random error of measurement. Measurement error is caused by factors other than the phenomenon of interest that influence the measuring instrument. Random measurement error is reduced or eliminated by using multiple measures of extraversion and SWB and examining the relation between the underlying *latent traits* that represent the common core of each set of variables. By using multiple measures, random factors that might influence one scale are unlikely to affect all the measures of that construct. Fujita found that the correlation between the extraversion and positive affect latent factors was in the neighborhood of .80 when measurement error was controlled, indicating an extremely strong relation between the two.

Although the covariation between extraversion and positive affect is well-established in Western nations, the reasons for this relation are not fully understood. One hypothesis alluded to earlier is the temperament idea that extraverts are biologically predisposed to react more strongly to rewards. For example, Larsen and Ketelaar (1991) exposed extraverts and introverts to positive emotional stimuli in the form of guided imagery and found that extraverts were more reactive to the positive stimuli. Another reason that extraverts may experience more positive affect is that they spend time in social situations that tend to generate positive affect. A third possible reason is that extraverts may experience more positive events. In other words, the behavior of extraverts might be more successful in bringing rewarding outcomes to them. Extraverts may have skills that are valued in Western society; therefore, they may experience more positive life events. Headey and Wearing (1992) found in a longitudinal study that extraverts experienced more positive events over a period of years. In our laboratory, Magnus, Diener, Fujita, and Pavot (1993) replicated this finding with a longer list of objective positive events. These findings suggest the possibility that extraverts experience more positive moods and emotions because they are adept at behaviors that are reinforced in Western culture. Earlier work by Kette (1991) serves to support this hypothesis. Kette found that extraverted prisoners were less happy than introverted ones, suggesting the possibility that the relation between extraversion and SWB is due to extraverts' ability to create rewarding social environments for themselves in the everyday world. In prison, however, extraverts may find it harder than introverts to obtain rewards that please them.

Thus, there are a number of viable hypotheses about why extraversion relates to positive affect, and when it will do so. Furthermore, we do not yet know whether the relation between extraversion and pleasant affect replicates across diverse cultures. As we explore the role of extraversion in SWB across cultures and with different measuring instruments, we will come to a greater understanding of when and why extraversion influences SWB. It may be that the relation between extraversion and positive affect is overdetermined, or caused by several different factors.

OTHER BIG FIVE TRAITS

Neuroticism

Included in this trait are characteristics such as anxiety, pessimism, irritability, bodily complaints, and interpersonal sensitivity. In other words, neuroticism includes a wide range of unpleasant thoughts and emotions. Because neuroticism measures are filled with items about the experience of unpleasant emotions, it is not surprising that this trait correlates with negative moods and emotions. Indeed, Fujita found in a latent trait analysis that neuroticism and the experience of negative affect were virtually indistinguishable. It is more noteworthy, however, that both unpleasant affect and negative cognitions are experienced together. Furthermore, there is a tendency for a variety of negative emotions—sadness, hostility, guilt, and anxiety—to be experienced by the same people. Thus, neuroticism represents a broad tendency to experience negative thoughts and emotions. Watson and Clark (1984) postulated that there is a factor, which they labeled "negative affectivity," that predisposes people to experience many forms of unpleasant affect. It is possible that a pervasive response tendency is based on reactivity in a basic brain area, such as the amygdala.

In the case of neuroticism, the causal direction between the negative cognitions and the neurotics' negative moods is an interesting issue for study. Neurotics tend to experience negative thoughts, such as impending failure, pessimism, unworthiness, and helplessness. Do these thoughts cause or result from negative affect? This chicken-and-egg problem is difficult to unravel because negative thoughts can not only cause negative moods but also are likely to result from them. It is possible that neurotics have a system that is very reactive to negative stimuli; therefore, they experience many negative emotions that lead to negative thoughts. Another possibility, however, is that neurotics tend to concentrate on the undesirable aspects of events and experience greater levels of negative emotions as a result. Careful longitudinal and experimental studies are needed to unravel the causal pathways.

Neurotics tend to experience more unpleasant life events. Headey and Wearing (1992) found that highly neurotic people recurrently experience more negative life events than do less neurotic individuals. The Magnus et al. study (1993) replicated this finding with objective negative events. If neurotics react with more unpleasant affect to unfavorable events, why would they continue to bring such events on themselves? One possibility is that negative thoughts and emotions trap neurotics into performing self-defeating behaviors.

Another question regarding neuroticism is, do a number of other traits that relate to negative affect do so because of their relation with neuroticism? In other words, these other personality variables may not in themselves cause negative affect, but they may relate to it because neuroticism causes them and negative emotions. One example is the congruence between one's actual self and one's ideal self, believed by Carl Rogers as well as more recent theorists to be a sign of mental health. Pavot, Fujita, and Diener (1996) found that neurotics have a larger discrepancy between their actual and ideal selves than do nonneurotics; their study raised the possibility that the self-discrepancy score may correlate with SWB because neuroticism leads to both variables. Another example is whether healthy forms of coping, such as directly working on problems or seeking social support, correlate with lack of negative affect because problem-focused coping lowers one's negative affect, or because neurotics are likely to engage in less effective forms of coping, such as denial or blame. Thus, researchers must rule out the role of neuroticism before concluding that other factors influence SWB. In addition, they need to establish the processes through which neuroticism produces its effects.

Conscientiousness and Agreeableness

Conscientiousness and agreeableness appear to be related to SWB but show lower levels of relation to it than do extraversion and neuroticism. Conscientiousness and agreeableness correlate moderately with SWB, although this covariation has not been as intensely studied as have extraversion and neuroticism. It may be that extraversion and neuroticism are based on neural approach-and-avoidance systems and automatically are associated with more positive or negative affect, respectively, whereas the relation of conscientiousness and agreeableness to SWB depends on whether in particular environments individuals with these traits are rewarded. Theoretically, some traits are connected through temperament to SWB, while other traits are associated in an instrumental way with behaviors that produce certain emotions. This model, however, has not yet received probing research analyses.

Openness to Experience

Openness to experience, the fifth trait of the Big Five, usually is not related on the hedonic level to whether people experience more or less positive or negative affect or life satisfaction. For example, Gottfredson (1994) found that openness did not correlate with job satisfaction. Openness, however, may be related to more intense emotional experiences. As we will see later, emotional intensity may be an individual difference that does not influence how happy or unhappy a person is but does influence how the happy and unhappy moments are experienced.

Additional Traits

Self-esteem and optimism. Popular lore as well as clinical experience suggests that people must like themselves before they can enjoy the world and their lives. Indeed, many clinicians believe that self-acceptance is the sine qua non of psychological well-being. Supporting this idea, self-esteem is a trait that strongly predicts SWB in Western cultures. For example, we collected data in the United States that showed that the self-esteem of college women correlated .60 with their life satisfaction. (This correlation is deflated because, unlike some reported earlier, it is not disattenuated for random measurement error.)

Caution must be used in concluding, however, that self-esteem is a universal determinant of SWB. Diener and Diener (1995) found that for women in collectivist societies self-esteem was only a weak correlate of SWB. For example, for women in India the correlation between self-esteem and life satisfaction was only .08. In a collectivist culture that values the family over the individual, it may be that how satisfied a person is with herself is much less important to well-being than how satisfied that person is with family. In other words, the individual self may be of particular concern in westernized societies and, therefore, is a good predictor of life satisfaction in those cultures. An alternative explanation of the cross-cultural findings is that even in collectivist societies people must like themselves in order to experience SWB. However, in these societies it may be inappropriate to say good things about oneself or report that one is satisfied with oneself. Thus, it might be that a deep sense of self-esteem is important to SWB in all cultures, but that the conscious labeling of oneself as a good person has varying meaning in different cultures. In order to fully understand the reasons that self-esteem is highly correlated with SWB in the West, additional cross-cultural research is necessary, including indirect or subtle measures of self-esteem.

A second issue is whether self-esteem is independent of neuroticism and possesses a separate causal influence on SWB. Recall that neurotics are likely to entertain many negative thoughts about themselves and about the world. Neurotics tend to denigrate themselves and blame themselves for failure; therefore, they tend to suffer from low self-esteem. Given the very high relation that Fujita found between neuroticism and negative affect, it is possible that neuroticism is the underlying cause of the relation between self-esteem and SWB. Lucas, Diener, and Suh (1996) found evidence that measures of self-esteem do not converge with each other more strongly than they converge with measures of other concepts, such as life satisfaction. Unless self-esteem can be measured sufficiently well so that it can be clearly discriminated from other constructs, its separate causal influence on SWB cannot be established. Once again, further research is needed to determine whether self-esteem has an independent causal influence on SWB.

An individual difference characteristic that is related to self-esteem, but conceptually distinct from it, is self-efficacy, the feeling that a person has that he can accomplish important goals. Feasel (1995) found that global feelings of self-efficacy predicted life satisfaction and positive emotions. She also found, however, that feeling efficacious in terms of one's most important goals was a stronger predictor of well-being than feeling high self-efficacy regarding one's less important goals. Thus, not only is a general feeling of self-efficacy important to well-being, but one must also believe that one has efficacy in the areas of life that one considers important.

Optimism, a cognitive variable that is highly related to self-mastery (Marshall & Lang, 1990), is also correlated with SWB. Scheier and Carver (1993) reviewed evidence showing that optimists maintain higher levels of SWB when faced with a stressor. In addition, there is evidence that optimism has benefits for physical health. Why are optimists or positive thinkers better off? Scheier, Weintraub, and Carver (1986) found that optimists tend to use problem-focused coping, seek social support, and emphasize positive aspects of the situation when they encounter difficulties. In contrast, pessimists tend toward denial, focus on stressful feelings, and disengage from relevant goals. Thus, people who tend to think in positive ways seem to use more effective forms of coping.

Is optimism really separate from SWB, or is it an inherent part of it? Lucas, Diener, and Suh (1996) found that optimism is related to SWB but distinct from it. What is not yet known is how a variety of personality variables, such as optimism, hardiness, self-mastery, and neuroticism, all interrelate to influence SWB.

Sex-typed behavior and sex differences. In this age of concern for gender equality, much recent research attention has been focused on the traits of masculinity and femininity. Because the traditional sex roles for a masculine person and a feminine person are breaking down, the trait that was formerly called *femininity* is now labeled *"communion,"* and includes characteristics such as warmth, concern for others, and understanding. The trait that was formerly called *masculinity* is now labeled *"agency"* and encompasses such characteristics as independence, self-confidence, and decisiveness. The new terms of *agency* and *communion* are preferred to the old terms because these words recognize that men or women can possess either set of characteristics. Furthermore, the two sets of traits are relatively independent so that people can be characterized by one set of characteristics or by the other but can also possess neither or both sets of attributes.

Although our language for discussing the former gender-typed characteristics has become more enlightened, the results of studies show that the formerly masculine characteristics are still those that most strongly predict SWB in Western nations. That is, agency correlates with SWB in the West, but communion shows weaker correlations with it. The agentic characteristics of competitiveness, independence, and decisiveness correlate substantially with SWB, while androgyny, the interactive combination of agency and community, does not predict SWB beyond the effects of the individual traits (Lubinski, Tellegen, &

Butcher, 1981, 1983). It should be noted that the relation of the former sex-typed traits with SWB might be confounded with more basic temperaments, such as extraversion and neuroticism, and until these relations are also explored and statistically controlled, we cannot be certain that agency has causal effects on SWB.

It is also interesting to note that sex differences in SWB are small or nonexistent in Western nations. The largest data set examining this issue was the World Value Survey (Inglehart, 1990) in which approximately 170,000 representatively sampled respondents from 16 nations were surveyed. In this study, the differences in SWB between men and women were vanishingly small. In a study of over 18,000 college students in over 30 nations from around the globe, Michalos (1991) also found very small sex differences in life satisfaction and happiness. Although men do not report higher SWB than women, people with agentic characteristics report higher SWB, meaning that men and women who are agentic have higher SWB, and men and women who are low in agency have lower SWB.

There is another interesting but seemingly paradoxical finding in the sex and SWB research literature. Men and women report approximately the same levels of global happiness, although women report more negative affect. In addition, women report greater levels of depression and are more likely to seek therapy for this disorder. If women are as happy as men, how can they experience more negative affect? One potential explanation is that women are not as happy as men, but say they are because of social desirability pressures. The problem with this explanation is that it does not help us understand why women would report more negative affect but not less happiness. Another possible explanation is in terms of self-report artifacts. It is possible that women more readily admit to negative feelings, while men deny these feelings. Thus, it might be that both sexes experience the same levels of negative affect and depression, but that women report these feelings and seek help more often for them.

Yet a third explanation for the paradoxical sex differences in SWB is that offered by Fujita, Diener, and Sandvik (1991). They maintained that women are socialized to be more open to emotional experiences, including positive and negative emotions. This socialization for openness to emotion may be based on the fact that traditionally women have the social role of nurturer, which requires being in touch with emotions. Thus, women may experience more positive and more negative affect in Western cultures. Because reports of global SWB depend on the hedonic balance between pleasant and unpleasant emotions, men and women report roughly the same levels of SWB. When negative emotions alone are reported, however, women also report more of these. The prediction of Fujita and Diener that women would also report greater amounts of positive affect was also supported, however. Thus, it may be that women have more feelings of stress and depression, but also have more "highs" and on average have the same general level of hedonic balance between pleasant and unpleasant emotions. (See Chapter 16 for coverage of sex differences.)

THE QUALITY OF SWB

Is it possible that two people might be equally happy but experience their SWB in qualitatively different ways? For example, one person might feel very aroused and euphoric when she is in a good mood, whereas a second individual might be more likely to feel contented and calm when he is in a good mood. Thus, their typical experiences of SWB might be quite different. They may both report high SWB but experience it in different ways.

Larsen and Diener (1987) hypothesized that there may be an individual difference dimension, which they labeled affect intensity, that could account for such differences. Larsen's Affect Intensity Measure was designed to identify people who feel intense emotions of positive and negative types. Such individuals are thought to experience more "lows" and more "highs," whereas people who score low on the scale are believed to more frequently experience contentment when they are in a good mood and mild melancholia when they are in a bad mood. An individual who frequently experiences pleasant moods, whether of the aroused or nonaroused variety, would be said to have high SWB. In contrast, an individual who frequently experienced unpleasant affect, whether of an aroused or nonaroused nature, would be said to have low SWB. However, two individuals might feel equally happy if they experienced frequent positive moods of different arousal levels.

Diener, Sandvik, and Pavot (1991) reviewed evidence that suggested that the frequency of one's pleasant versus unpleasant moods may be more important to happiness than the intensity of these experiences. However, in-depth research has not been conducted on whether people who are euphoric versus those who are contented feel and report equal well-being. Furthermore, research has not been conducted on whether some individuals prefer one positive state, and other individuals prefer another. For example, perhaps low-key individuals actually prefer contentment to euphoria, while intense individuals seek ecstasy and are not attracted to contentment. Thus, all the implications of emotional intensity for subjective well-being have not yet been explored empirically.

DISCRIMINANT VALIDITY

Although we have focused so far on whether various traits correlate sufficiently with SWB to predict it, an opposite concern is that of discriminant validity. The concept of discriminant validity questions whether two constructs are really separable, or whether they are in fact the same thing. SWB would show a lack of discriminant validity from other established personality constructs if in fact the measures were really just "old wine in new bottles"—new labels and measures for the same underlying constructs that have long been measured by personologists.

We noted that measures of neuroticism and negative affect appeared to measure the same thing; Fujita's (1993) latent trait analyses of these constructs confirmed this belief. Thus, neuroticism and the propensity to experience negative affect appear to be the same thing, at least as far as the measures are concerned. Fujita found that extraversion and positive affect were highly correlated, but separable. Lucas, Diener, and Fujita (1996) verified this finding by showing that extraversion and positive affect had different predictors and were separable in a multitrait-multimethod (MTMM) analysis. The MTMM analysis is based on the idea that one can test the convergent and discriminant validity of concepts by using several different methods to measure each of several constructs. For example, self-esteem, positive affect, and life satisfaction might each be measured by three methods, such as self-report, daily experience sampling, and informant report. For convergent validity, it is necessary for different measures of the same construct to correlate highly with each other. If discriminant validity is to be confirmed, correlations of different constructs with each other cannot be as high as the convergent validities. In other words, measures of the same characteristic should correlate more highly with each other than they do with measures of other characteristics. Although there are complexities in interpreting MTMM matrices, the underlying idea is that measures of the same construct should correlate highly even when measured with different methods, and that separate constructs should correlate highly with each other. Thus far, measures of SWB have fared well in MTMM analyses.

Traits such as conscientiousness and agreeableness are conceptually separable from SWB, and the modest correlations between these constructs also suggests that they are discriminably different concepts from SWB. Lucas *et al.* (1996) found that optimism was separable from positive affect, negative affect, and life-satisfaction, although it is clearly a cognitive construct related to SWB.

Self-esteem was more problematical in the MTMM analysis of Lucas *et al.* (1996). The self-esteem measures tended to correlate no more highly with each other than they did with several of the other concepts. Thus, although self-esteem seems to be conceptually distinct from life satisfaction, optimism, and so forth, the measures of it are not clearly distinct from the other variables. Different methods of measuring self-esteem correlate no more highly with each other than they do with measures of other concepts. Therefore, although the SWB concepts tended to show good discriminant validity, self-esteem did not do so. Perhaps self-esteem measures primarily identify individuals who feel positive about the world in general rather than just about themselves.

PROCESS THEORIES

The relations between traits and SWB help us understand the correlates of SWB but do not shed full light on the processes that are responsible for these relations. We must also explore general processes that can connect the descriptive level of traits with SWB. One critique that is often leveled against traits is that they are descriptive but not explanatory. In the case of extraversion, several different potential processes were discussed that might lead to higher SWB. For example, extraverts might have more positive affect because they are more frequently in positive-affect-producing social situations, because their biological temperaments give them greater reactivity to rewarding events, or because they have skills that lead to greater rewards in our culture. A more complete scientific understanding will be gained if we can specify the processes that relate traits to SWB.

DENSITY OF REINFORCEMENTS

One general explanation connecting certain traits to SWB is the idea of behavior-contingent reinforcements. It may be that people with certain traits are able to wrest more rewards from their environments or more often are able to avoid punishments. For example, we mentioned the extravert whose social skills may allow her to have more rewarding social relationships, greater advancement at work, and perhaps even a better chance of talking her way out of difficult situations. Evidence for this explanation comes from the fact that extraverts do report more positive events in their lives. Similarly, conscientiousness might be related to SWB because there are many situations in which the dependable individual is granted more rewards. In some circumstances, however, dependability may not be valued, and a more carefree individual may receive greater reinforcements. In these life circumstances, the conscientious individual might show lower SWB. Thus far, few studies have measured the rewards and punishments received by people who have different traits.

Person–Environment Fit

A related process that might connect personality traits to SWB is person–environment fit. The idea is that a person will experience SWB to the extent that he or she finds the environment rewarding, but with the additional stipulation that environments are most rewarding when the individual's personality "fits" the situation. Individuals with certain personalities might be able to gain more rewards in a certain environment than are other individuals. To follow the example of extraversion again, a person–environment fit model predicts that extraverts would be happy as long as they live in circumstances in which sociability is rewarded. If they lived in a cloistered nunnery with a rule of silence, however, extraverts might be less happy than introverts. Of course, individuals normally select the environments that fit their personalities. For example, Diener, Sandvik, Pavot, and Fujita (1992) found that extraverts less often live alone and more frequently work in social occupations. Nonetheless, individuals may sometimes find themselves in life circumstances that do not fit their personalities, and in these cases the person–environment fit model predicts that they would experience lower levels of SWB.

In support of a person–environment fit model of well-being, Brandstatter (1994) found that extraverts are happier in high-stimulation situations, whereas this is not true of introverts. Nonetheless, the person–environment fit model has received only mixed empirical support (Diener, Larsen, & Emmons, 1984; Furnham, Toop, Lewis, & Fisher, 1995). Extending the person–environment fit logic to the relation of behavior and dispositions, Moskowitz and Coté (1995) found that people experience pleasant affect when they engage in behaviors that are concordant with their traits. For example, hostile, assertive people experienced unpleasant affect when engaging in agreeable behaviors and pleasant affect when quarreling.

Memory Models

A third set of processes that may connect personality to SWB is based on the idea that memory and retrieval may predispose some individuals to higher SWB. For example, some individuals may spontaneously reminisce about positive events, putting them in a good mood, while other individuals may ruminate about negative events, that create an unpleasant mood. When reacting to new events, people must interpret the happenings based on material retrieved from memory. If the person connects the event to many positive associations, her or his mood is likely to be pleasant. People with high SWB may build up a strong associative network of richly interconnected positive events and have only isolated and disconnected associations for infrequent unpleasant events. Therefore, a person who has frequently been happy in the past may be predisposed to continue to be happy in the future because of the rich interconnection of pleasant associations. Such a memory network is likely to predispose the individual to think of more pleasant associations in reaction to new events.

In initial explorations of this model, Seidlitz and Diener (1993) found that happy people initially encode more events as positive. They seem both to interpret events as positive and also to experience more objectively positive events. We did not find, however, that rumination played much part in the fact that happy people can recall more positive events than can unhappy people. In addition, Seidlitz and Diener found that people's memories were more strongly organized by content domains rather than by valence. Thus, happy people seem to be most characterized by their initial reactions to positive events, but strong evidence supporting the idea that the memory structures are very different for happy and unhappy people does not exist.

RETURN TO BASELINE MODELS

The dynamic equilibrium model of Headey and Wearing is yet another interesting process theory. They maintained that person's baseline level of happiness is decided by his or her temperament. Headey and Wearing (1992) suggested that extraversion and neuroticism determine a person's baseline level of happiness because these traits index the reactivity of the basic reward and punishment systems. Events can, however, move people temporarily away from their baselines. For example, winning the lottery will move a person above her normal state for a period of time, but slowly she will adapt and move back to her baseline. Eventually the lottery income will not have an effect on the person's happiness, and she will be at the baseline determined by her temperament. Similarly, according to Headey and Wearing, a bad event such as a spouse's dying will move the person below his baseline. It may require several years for the person to return to his prior baseline, but eventually he will adapt and no longer suffer from the undesirable event.

Headey and Wearing supported their theory with an Australian panel study that showed that people did return to their previous levels of positive and negative affect after good and bad events. Furthermore, Headey and Wearing found that baseline levels of well-being were predicted by extraversion and neuroticism, even across a number of years. Further analyzing the dynamic equilibrium model, Suh, Diener, and Fujita (1996) found that people adapt to most life events in a surprisingly short time. Their respondents seemed to react to major life events that occurred only in the last three months; however, Suh et al. did not examine respondents with severe life events, such as the death of a spouse or a child. Silver (1980) found that quadriplegics and paraplegics adapted to their spinal cord injury in remarkably short periods of time. Supporting the idea of adaptation, Mehnert, Krauss, Nadler, and Boyd (1990) found that individuals who acquired disabilities later in life were less satisfied with life than those who acquired their disabilities at birth or in early life.

The idea of a return of people's affect to baseline is founded on the concept of adaptation. Important questions can be raised, however, about whether people habituate to all events, and whether they adapt completely. People's ability to adapt to conditions seems considerable when one considers that quadriplegics have primarily positive affect within eight weeks of their accidents, and even very disadvantaged groups report predominantly positive SWB. However, there may be limits to adaptation. For example, Vitaliano, Russo, Young, Becker, and Maiuro (1991) found that family caregivers of Alzheimer's patients showed deteriorating SWB over time. Mehnert, Krauss, Nadler, and Boyd (1990) found that a nationally representative sample of people with disabilities were less satisfied with their lives than a national sample of the nondisabled, and this was especially true for individuals with multiple disabilities. Furthermore, long-term and severe poverty in a nation may lead to lower SWB, even over prolonged periods of time. Diener, Diener, and Diener (1995) found that respondents in very poor nations, such as India and Nigeria, on average reported much lower SWB than people in highly industrialized nations, such as northern European countries. Thus, personality may exert a long-term baseline influence on SWB, but some life conditions may also influence this baseline. It also should be noted that we do not yet understand the processes that cause a return to baseline. Is adaptation due to biologically based habituation that is inexorable, does it depend on coping mechanisms, or does it depend on adjusting one's goals and expectations? Certainly, these are among the most vital questions in the field.

LIFE TASK AND GOAL THEORIES

The earlier discussion might leave the impression that personality influences on SWB are limited to traits, but this would be mistaken because other personality variables are crucial to understanding SWB. Central to this understanding are the related concepts of goals, life tasks, and personal constructs. Nancy Cantor, Brian Little, Eric Klinger, and Robert Emmons all have hypothesized that a person's goals are central to understanding her or his behavior. Goals can be examined at a very broad level, such as values; at a somewhat narrower level, such as life tasks; or at an even narrower level, such as one's current concerns. For example, a person might value achievement, have a life task of working toward becoming a famous scientist, and have the current concern of completing a particular research project. Thus, more specific goals are nested within a hierarchical framework of broader, more abstract goals. Which goals a psychologist chooses to study will depend on the phenomena he/she is trying to understand.

Emmons (1986) found that different aspects of goals are related to different components of SWB. He found, for example, that positive affect is related to the degree to which a person accomplishes her goals. However, negative affect tends to be related to the individual's ambivalence about her goals (she sees positive and negative outcomes to accomplishing many of her goals) and conflict between her goals (achieving one goal makes it more difficult to achieve another goal). In contrast, Emmons found that life satisfaction was highest in those who possessed goals that were very important to them. It is interesting that conflict between a person's goals is correlated with negative affect. If a person has many goals in conflict, she cannot possibly achieve her goals without simultaneously sacrificing the achievement of other goals.

Nancy Cantor (1994) focused on life tasks in a way that integrates person and situational factors by examining the problem-solving strategies people use to meet their goals. People enter situations that encourage and allow their particular purposes. People's tasks, in turn, are influenced by what they can accomplish in their life situations. The strategic solutions that people select for achieving their life tasks are thus determined interactively by the needs of individuals and by their circumstances.

We can best understand people and the differences between them if we focus on what they are trying to accomplish. According to Cantor, individual factors, such as the need for power, as well as age-specific life tasks, such as finding a mate, influence a person's tasks. These personal dispositions, however, are channeled by the circumstances of the person's life. In turn, situations can be understood best in terms of what individuals are trying to do in them.

Cantor's life task approach can be understood in terms of the life satisfaction of older people. Harlow and Cantor (1995) found that life satisfaction is higher in older people who are involved in community service, presumably because such work allows them to meet their social and generativity needs. However, if the older person was not retired and was still involved in paid work, community service was not as important to life satisfaction. Thus, according to Harlow and Cantor, subjective well-being derived from being involved in life tasks that are appropriate to one's life circumstances, to the expectations of the culture, and to meeting a person's needs. People can meet their needs in different ways, depending on their circumstances. People with high SWB are those who have developed effective strategies for meeting their needs within the constraints of age-specific cultural expectations and life circumstances.

Other theorists focus on the specific content of goals rather than on their structural or individual characteristics. In other words, they believe the goals that people work for are important to SWB, not simply whether the goals are in conflict or meet cultural expectations. Kasser and Ryan (1993, 1996) maintained that all goals are not created equal, and it is much better to work for some goals than for others. They hypothesized that certain goals are intrinsically rewarding, whereas other goals may be imposed on the individual by the society. Kasser and Ryan found that goals they considered to be extrinsic, such as the desire for material goods, for physical attractiveness, and for social recognition, were associated with lower well-being. They maintained that this is because these goals have no intrinsic value and are sought for the approval of others or for some other end. In contrast, goals related to self-acceptance, helping the community, affiliation, and physical health were positively correlated with SWB. Kasser and Ryan maintained that these intrinsic goals are expressive of inherent self-actualizing and growth tendencies and satisfy the inherent psychological needs of humans.

In a similar argument, Veenhoven (1991) suggested that money may relate to SWB in poor nations because in those nations it is related to the fulfillment of universal and basic needs. Thus, in a nation such as Bangladesh income may be related to happiness because it is used to obtain universal needs, such as food and shelter. Veenhoven found, however, that income was not strongly related to SWB in richer nations where income presumably is not primarily used to obtain intrinsic satisfactions. Instead, in these nations income may be used to compete with others or obtain extrinsic desires that are produced by advertising. Thus, Veenhoven, and Kasser and Ryan believe that true happiness must be based on fulfilling intrinsically rewarding goals.

CONCLUSION

Personality appears to be a major influence on SWB and situations sometimes seem to matter very little. Why might this be? It may be that the internal experience on which SWB is based is less subject to situational social learning contingencies, and, therefore, it is more due to temperament than is external behavior. Also, SWB may be more heavily reliant on personality than is external behavior because it is by definition a long-term phenomenon. Although Diener and Larsen (1984) found that moods and emotions of the moment are quite unstable, they found that long-term average affect is much more consistent. Therefore, the focus in the field of SWB on long-term mood may mean that situational variables take second place to personality influences.

One scientific challenge for personologists is to determine which personality variables are of fundamental importance to SWB. For example, do certain fundamental traits have a pancultural relation to SWB and mediate the effects of other personality variables? Central to this challenge is determining the generalizability across cultures of the relation between personality variables and SWB. Another major task for personality psychologists is to determine why key traits are related to SWB and to pinpoint the processes that are responsible for the relations. Finally, personologists need to determine how personality variables interact with situations in producing SWB. For example, are extraverts happier in virtually any environment, or do they experience higher SWB only when sufficient positive stimuli are present?

Traits and other personality processes appear to be of pivotal importance to SWB. It is now our task to determine why.

REFERENCES

Bradburn, N. M. (1969). *The structure of psychological well-being.* Chicago: Aldine.

Brandstatter, H. (1994). Pleasure of leisure-pleasure of work: Personality makes the difference. *Personality and Individual Differences, 16,* 931–946.

Campbell, A., Converse, P. E., & Rodgers, W. L. (1976). *The quality of American life.* New York: Russell Sage Foundation.

Cantor, N. 91994). Life task problem solving: Situational affordances and personal needs. *Personality and Social Psychology Bulletin, 20,* 235–243.

Costa, P. T. (1994, August 12–16). Traits through time, or the stability of personality: Observations, evaluations, and a model. 102nd Annual Convention of the American Psychological Association, Los Angeles, CA.

Costa, P. T., & McCrae, R. R. (1980). Influence of extraversion and neuroticism on subjective well-being: Happy and unhappy people. *Journal of Personality and Social Psychology, 38,* 668–678.

Costa, P. T., & McCrae, R. R. (1988). Personality in adulthood: A six-year longitudinal study of self-reports and spouse ratings on the NEO Personality Inventory. *Journal of Personality and Social Psychology, 54,* 853–863.

Costa, P. T., McCrae, R., & Zonderman, A. (1987). Environmental and dispositional influences on well-being: Longitudinal follow-up of an American national sample. *British Journal of Psychology, 78,* 299–306.

Davidson, R. J., & Fox, N. A. (1982). Asymmetrical brain activity discriminates between positive versus negative affective stimuli in human infants. *Science, 218,* 1235–1237.

Diener, E. (1984). Subjective well-being. *Psychological Bulletin, 95,* 542–575.

Diener, E., & Diener, M. (1995). Cross-cultural correlates of life satisfaction and self-esteem. *Journal of Personality and Social Psychology, 68,* 653–663.

Diener, E., Diener, M., & Diener, C. (1995). Factors predicting the subjective well-being of nations. *Journal of Personality and Social Psychology, 69,* 851–864.

Diener, E., & Larsen, R. J. (1984). Temporal stability and cross-situational consistency of affective, behavioral, and cognitive responses. *Journal of Personality and Social Psychology, 47,* 871–883.

Diener, E., Larsen, R. J., & Emmons, R. A. (1984). Person X situation interactions: Choice of situations and congruence response models. *Journal of Personality and Social Psychology, 47,* 580–592.

Diener, E., Sandvik, E., & Pavot, W. (1991). Happiness is the frequency, not the intensity, of positive versus negative affect. In F. Strack, M. Argyle, & N. Schwarz (Eds.), *Subjective well-being: An interdisciplinary perspective* (pp. 119–139). New York: Pergamon Press.

Diener, E., Sandvik, E., Pavot, W., & Fujita, F. (1992). Extraversion and subjective well-being in a U.S. national probability sample. *Journal of Research in Personality, 26,* 205–215.

Diener, E., Sandvik, E., Seidlitz, L., & Diener, M. (1993). The relationship between income and subjective well-being: Relative or absolute? *Social Indicators Research, 28,* 195–223.

Diener, E., Wolsic, B., & Fujita, F. (1995). Physical attractiveness and subjective well-being. *Journal of Personality and Social Psychology, 69,* 120–129.

Emmons, R. A. (1986). Personal strivings: An approach to personality and subjective well-being. *Journal of Personality and Social Psychology, 51,* 1058–1068.

Feasel, K. E. (1995). *Mediating the relation between goals and subjective well-being: Global and domain-specific variants of self-efficacy.* Unpublished master's thesis. University of Illinois.

Fujita, F. (1993). *An investigation of the relation between extraversion, neuroticism, positive affect, and negative affect.* Unpublished master's thesis, University of Illinois.

Fujita, F., Diener, E., & Sandvik, E. (1991). Gender differences in negative affect and well-being: The case for emotional intensity. *Journal of Personality and Social Psychology, 61,* 427–434.

Furnham, A., Toop, A., Lewis, C., & Fisher, A. (1995). P-E fit and job satisfaction: A failure to support Hollands's theory in three British samples. *Personality and Individual Differences, 19,* 677–690.

Gottfredson, G. (1994, August 12–16). The person in person-environment interactions. 102nd Annual Convention of the American Psychological Association, Los Angeles, CA.

Harlow, R. E., & Cantor, N. (1995). To whom do people turn when things go poorly? Task orientation or functional social contacts. *Journal of Personality and Social Psychology, 69,* 329–340.

Headey, B., & Wearing, A. (1992). *Understanding happiness: A theory of subjective well-being.* Melbourne, Australia: Longman Cheshire.

Inglehart, R. (1990). *Culture shift in advanced industrial society.* Princeton, NJ: Princeton University Press.

Kagan, J. (1994). *Galen's prophecy: Temperament in human nature.* New York: Basic Books.

Kagan, J., Snidman, N., & Arcus, D. M. (1992). Initial reactions to unfamiliarity. *Current Directions in Psychological Science, 1,* 171–174.

Kasser, T., & Ryan, R. M. (1993). A dark side of the American dream: Correlates of financial success as a central life aspiration. *Journal of Personality and Social Psychology, 65,* 410–422.

Kasser, T., & Ryan, R. M. (1996). Further examining the American dream: Differential correlates of intrinsic and extrinsic goals. *Personality and Social Psychology Bulletin, 22,* 280–287.

Kette, G. (1991). *Haft: Eine socialpsychologische analyse (Prison: A social psychological analysis).* Gottingen, Germany: Hogrefe.

Larsen, R. J., & Diener, E. (1987). Emotional response intensity as an individual difference characteristic. *Journal of Research in Personality, 21,* 1–39.

Larsen, R. J., & Kasimatis, M. (1990). Individual differences in entrainment of mood to the weekly calendar. *Journal of Personality and Social Psychology, 58,* 164–171.

Larsen, R. J., & Ketelaar, T. (1991). Personality and susceptibility to positive and negative emotional states. *Journal of Personality and Social Psychology, 61,* 132–140.

Lubinski, D., Tellegen, A., & Butcher, J. N. (1981). The relationship between androgyny and subjective indicators of emotional well-being. *Journal of Personality and Social Psychology, 40,* 722–730.

Lubinski, D., Tellegen, A., & Butcher, J. N. (1983). Masculinity, femininity, and androgyny viewed and assessed as distinct concepts. *Journal of Personality and Social Psychology, 44,* 428–439.

Lucas, R., Diener, E., & Suh, E. (1996). Discriminant validity of subjective well-being, self-esteem, and optimism. *Journal of Personality and Social Psychology, 71,* 616–628.

Magnus, K. B. (1991). *A longitudinal analysis of personality, life events, and subjective well-being.* Unpublished honors thesis, University of Illinois.

Magnus, K., & Diener, E. (1991, May). *A longitudinal analysis of personality, life events, and subjective well-being.* Paper presented at the 63rd Annual Meeting of the Midwestern Psychological Association, Chicago, IL.

Magnus, K., Diener, E., Fujita, F., & Pavot, W. (1993). Extraversion and neuroticism as predictors of objective life events: A longitudinal analysis. *Personality and Social Psychology, 65,* 1046–1053.

Marshall, G. N., & Lang, E. L. (1990). Optimism, self-mastery, and symptoms of depression in professional women. *Journal of Personality and Social Psychology, 59,* 132–139.

McFatter, R. M. (1994). Interactions in predicting mood from extraversion and neuroticism. *Journal of Personality and Social Psychology, 66,* 570–578.

Mehnert, T., Krauss, H. H., Nadler, R., & Boyd, M. (1990). Correlates of life satisfaction in those with disabling conditions. *Rehabilitation Psychology, 35,* 3–17.

Michalos, A. C. (1991). *Global report on student well-being.* New York: Springer-Verlag.

Mischel, W. (1968). *Personality and assessment.* New York: Wiley.

Moskowitz, D. S., & Coté, S. (1995). Do interpersonal traits predict affect? A comparison of three models. *Journal of Personality and Social Psychology, 69,* 915–925.

Myers, D. G. (1992). *The pursuit of happiness: Who is happy—and why.* New York: Morrow.

Okun, M. A., & George, L. K. (1984). Physician- and self-ratings of health, neuroticism, and subjective well-being among men and women. *Personality and Individual Differences, 5,* 533–539.

Pavot, W., & Diener, E. (1993). Review of the Satisfaction with Life Scale. *Psychological Assessment, 5,* 164–172.

Pavot, W., Diener, E., & Fujita, F. (1990). Extraversion and happiness. *Personality and Individual Differences, 11,* 1299–1306.

Pavot, W., Fujita, F., & Diener, E. (1996). The relation between self-aspect congruence, personality, and subjective well-being. *Personality and Individual Differences, 22,* 183–191.

Scheier, M. F., & Carver, C. S. (1993). On the power of positive thinking: The benefits of being optimistic. *Current Directions in Psychological Science, 2,* 26–30.

Scheier, M. F., Weintraub, J. K., & Carver, C. S. (1986). Coping with stress: Divergent strategies of optimists and pessimists. *Journal of Personality and Social Psychology, 51,* 1257–1264.

Seidlitz, L., & Diener, E. (1993). Memory for positive versus negative life events: Theories for the differences between happy and unhappy persons. *Journal of Personality and Social Psychology, 64,* 654–664.

Silver, R. L. (1980). *Coping with an undesirable life event: A study of early reactions to physical disability.* Unpublished doctoral dissertation, Northwestern University, Evanston, Illinois.

Suh, E., Diener, E., & Fujita, F. (1996). Events and subjective well-being: Only recent events matter. *Journal of Personality and Social Psychology, 70,* 1091–1102.

Tellegen, A., Lykken, D. T., Bouchard, T. J., Wilcox, K. J., Segal, N. L., & Rich, S. (1988). Personality similarity in twins reared apart and together. *Journal of Personality and Social Psychology, 54,* 1031–1039.

Vaillant, G. E., & Vaillant, C. O. (1990). Natural history of male psychological health: XII. A 45-year study of predictors of successful aging at age 65. *American Journal of Psychiatry, 147,* 31–37.

Veenhoven, R. (1991). Is happiness relative? *Social Indicators Research, 24,* 1–34.

Vitaliano, P. P., Russo, J., Young, H. M., Becker, J., & Maiuro, R. D. (1991). The screen for caregiver burden. *The Gerontologist, 31,* 76–83.

Watson, D., & Clark, L. A. (1984). Negative affectivity: The disposition to experience aversive emotional states. *Psychological Bulletin, 96,* 456–490.

Chapter 14

PERSONALITY DISORDERS

Thomas A. Widiger

INTRODUCTION

Personality traits are one's characteristic manner of thinking, feeling, perceiving, and/or relating to others across a wide range of situations that have been evident since late childhood or adolescence. Personality is the way one normally or typically behaves. It is what we mean when we describe our selves and each other. It includes that which is unique about us and that we share with others.

Unfortunately, personality need not always be adaptive, functional, and beneficial. One's characteristic manner of thinking, feeling, perceiving, and/or relating to others can be problematic, harmful, dysfunctional, or even destructive in some, many, or even most situations. The American Psychiatric Association (APA) recognizes the existence of the following 10 personality disorders within the *Diagnostic and Statistical Manual of Mental Disorders* (DSM-IV; APA, 1994): antisocial, avoidant, borderline, dependent, histrionic, narcissistic, obsessive-compulsive, paranoid, schizoid, and schizotypal. This list, however, is hardly exhaustive. Additional diagnoses discussed within the clinical literature include the depressive (Phillips, Gunderson, Hirschfeld, & Smith, 1990), passive-aggressive (APA, 1987), self-defeating (Cooper, 1993), sadistic (Spitzer, Fiester, Gay, & Pfohl, 1991), psychopathic (Hare, 1992), pleonexic or Machiavellian (Nikelly, 1992), malevolent (Hurlbert

---

Thomas A. Widiger • Department of Psychology, University of Kentucky, Lexington, Kentucky 40506-0044.

Advanced Personality, edited by David F. Barone, Michel Hersen, and Vincent B. Van Hasselt. Plenum Press, New York, 1998.

& Apt, 1992), delusional dominating (Pantony & Caplan, 1991), aberrant self-promoting (Gustafson & Ritzer, 1995), abusive (Dutton, 1995), and racist (Hamlin, 1990).

The purpose of this chapter is to discuss personality disorders from the perspective of normal personality theory and research. There is much that can be learned about personality disorders from the study of normal personality functioning, in part because there may be no qualitative distinction between a personality disorder and normal personality functioning. Persons with a personality disorder may not be qualitatively different from those (of us) without an officially recognized or clinically diagnosed personality disorder. The DSM-IV personality disorders might be simply maladaptive or extreme variants of common personality traits.

NORMAL VERSUS ABNORMAL PERSONALITY

"The diagnostic approach used in [DSM-IV] represents the categorical perspective that Personality Disorders represent qualitatively distinct clinical syndromes" (APA, 1994, p. 633). It is acknowledged in DSM-IV that there is "an alternative to the categorical approach [that considers] Personality Disorders [to] represent maladaptive variants of personality traits that merge imperceptibly into normality and into one another" (APA, 1994, p. 633). However, the predominant perspective within psychiatry is that personality disorders are qualitatively distinct from normal functioning (Gunderson, Links, & Reich, 1991). As stated by Benjamin (1994), "normality is not a mild version of pathology, it is qualitatively different" (p. 286).

Yet, there are many reasons to doubt this assumption (Livesley, Schroeder, Jackson, & Jang, 1994; Widiger, 1993; Widiger & Sanderson, 1995). For example, virtually every attempt that has been made to identify a distinct point of demarcation among the personality disorders or between personality disorders and normal personality functioning has failed. Nestadt et al. (1990) obtained ratings of the DSM-III histrionic personality disorder symptomatology from a representative sample of 810 persons within the Baltimore community and concluded that "this personality diagnosis is rather arbitrarily given individuals who extend beyond a cut-off level, yet others less severe but similar in the nature of their dispositional features might have identical symptoms under certain life circumstances" (p. 420). Zimmerman and Coryell (1990) obtained ratings on all of the DSM-III-R personality disorders in 808 presumably normal relatives of psychiatric patients and never-ill controls and concluded that the "scores are continuously distributed without points of rarity to indicate where to make the distinction between normality and pathology" (p. 690). Livesley, Jackson, and Schroeder (1992) assessed 100 aspects of personality dysfunction in 158 psychiatric patients and 274 community subjects. "Discontinuities were not apparent in our data. That continua exist and that a substantial number of persons drawn from the nonclinical population have scores extending into the clinical distribution poses, in our view, great difficulties for the use of a simple class or categorical model" (Livesley et al., 1992, p. 438).

A conceptual distinction between normal personality traits and personality disorders is provided in DSM-IV. "Only when personality traits are inflexible and maladaptive and cause significant functional impairment or subjective distress do they constitute Personality Disorders" (APA, 1994, p. 630). One would certainly expect personality disorders to involve more inflexibility, maladaptivity, and personality distress than normal personality functioning, but the differences may be more quantitative than qualitative. Each of these fundamental distinctions will be considered in turn.

INFLEXIBILITY

Inflexibility is a cardinal, defining feature of a personality disorder (APA, 1994). Persons with a personality disorder lack adequate control of their behavior. For example, persons with a borderline personality disorder are not simply choosing or deciding to engage in substance abuse, reckless driving, binge eating, or wrist slashing. They are compelled by their personality disorder to become angry, dissociative, distraught, and impulsive. If it were a matter of voluntary or free choice, they would not need professional interventions to change their behavior patterns. They would simply behave otherwise.

However, normal personality functioning might be comparably inflexible, or at least there may not be any qualitative distinction between the degree of flexibility of normal personalities and the degree of inflexibility of abnormal personalities. The consistency in normal human behavior that is evident across substantial periods of time and situations may also fail to be simply a matter of choosing to behave in a consistent manner. Normal persons may also be compelled to be characteristically conscientious, introverted, agreeable, or antagonistic (Costa & McCrae, 1994). The difference between the normal and the abnormal personality might be a matter of degree rather than kind. Persons with a DSM-IV personality disorder may only be less flexible than those without a diagnosable disorder.

It is an untested presumption that persons who are extremely or excessively conscientious are less flexible than persons who are only moderately conscientious. Alternatively, persons who are only moderately conscientious may not be any more flexible with respect to conscientiousness than persons who are highly conscientious. They may simply be characteristically less conscientious. They fail to be as perfectionistic, deliberate, or diligent than persons who are more conscientious, but they may be as compelled to be this way as persons who are highly conscientious. It would then be as difficult for them to become highly conscientious, as it is for persons who are highly (or even excessively) conscientious to be less conscientious. Similarly, persons who are highly (or even excessively) introverted may not be any less flexible than persons who are only moderately introverted; they may simply display more extreme variants of introversion. It may then be as difficult for the mildly introverted person to become highly introverted, as it is for the highly introverted person to become only mildly introverted.

It would also be of interest to explore the extent to which the etiological determinants of normal personality differ qualitatively or quantitatively from the determinants of personality disorder. For example, that which contributes to the development of normal criminality (Wilson & Herrnstein, 1985) may overlap substantially with that which contributes to the development of an antisocial personality disorder (Sutker, Bugg, & West, 1993). Similarly, that which contributes to the development of normal introversion may overlap substantially with that which contributes to the development of a schizoid personality disorder. There is substantial research to indicate the heritability of normal introversion (Bouchard, Lykken, McGue, & Tellegen, 1990). It would be of interest to determine whether the heritability of the schizoid or avoidant personality disorders is distinct from the heritability of this normal introversion (Nigg & Goldsmith, 1994). Finally, Benjamin (1993b) suggested that the qualitatively distinct narcissistic personality disorder is the result of parental noncontingent love, adoration, deference, and indulgence, coupled with an ever-present threat of a fall from grace. It would be of interest to determine whether such experiences are indeed unique to persons with this disorder, or whether persons within a normative range of narcissism (e.g., those with only moderate degrees of neuroticism and antagonism) have had comparable, but less severe, childhood experiences.

MALADAPTIVITY

Fundamental to the construct of a personality disorder is maladaptivity, defined in DSM-IV as a "clinically significant impairment" (APA, 1994, p. 7). However, nowhere in DSM-IV is *clinical significance* defined. It is only stated that this "is an inherently difficult clinical judgment" (APA, 1994, p. 7). Spitzer and Williams (1982), the original authors of the DSM-IV definition of mental disorder, defined a clinically significant impairment as that point at which the attention of a clinician is warranted. A level of impairment that does not warrant the attention of a clinician is perhaps too low for a diagnosis of a mental disorder. Some impairments are so inconsequential that it might trivialize the concept of personality disorder to provide them with mental disorder diagnoses. However, many physical disorders fail to warrant the attention of a physician and the absence of this attention does not indicate the absence of a disorder. "A correct definition of disorder must classify every pathological condition as a disorder whether or not the condition is . . . an object of professional attention" (Wakefield, 1992, p. 234). Frances, First, and Pincus (1995), the principal authors of DSM-IV, acknowledge that the criterion of clinical significance "is likely to vary in different cultures and to depend on the availability and interests of clinicians" (p. 15).

In addition, it is apparent that the DSM-IV personality disorder diagnostic thresholds have no relationship to this threshold of a clinically significant impairment. For example, the decision to require five or more of nine narcissistic features for a diagnosis of narcissistic personality disorder was based on a subjective judgment that requiring six narcissistic features appeared to be too restrictive and requiring less than five appeared to be too inclusive. However, the presence of just one or two of the features of a narcissistic personality disorder, such as being preoccupied with fantasies of unlimited success or requiring excessive admiration (APA, 1994), could be associated with a clinically significant impairment. The DSM-IV cutoff points for a personality disorder diagnosis (e.g., four of seven for a diagnosis of avoidant personality disorder) do not attempt to identify that point at which personality traits become a personality disorder.

As a result, many persons below the DSM-IV thresholds may have clinically significant maladaptive personality traits, as evident in studies on dependent (Overholser, 1991), borderline (McGlashan, 1987), histrionic (Nestadt *et al.,* 1990), compulsive (Nestadt *et al.,* 1991), and antisocial (Nestadt *et al.,* 1992) personality disorders. The single most prevalent personality disorder diagnosis is personality disorder, not otherwise specified (PDNOS; Widiger & Costa, 1994). PDNOS is provided by a clinician when the patient fails to meet the DSM-IV threshold for any one of the 10 officially recognized personality disorders but still evidences clinically significant maladaptive personality traits. The popularity of the PDNOS diagnosis is a testament to the inadequacy of DSM-IV personality disorders to adequately cover the full range of clinically significant maladaptivity (Clark, Watson, & Reynolds, 1995).

Widiger and Corbitt (1994) identified four possible interpretations for the warranting of clinical attention: (a) impairment for which treatment by a clinician would be beneficial,

(b) impairment for which treatment by a clinician would be necessary, (c) impairment for which treatment is necessary, and (d) impairment for which treatment is desirable. Each of these interpretations provides a viable threshold for the diagnosis of a personality disorder. However, each could suggest a threshold of impairment that is substantially below an officially recognized DSM-IV personality disorder diagnosis.

For example, it is reasonable to suggest that a level of impairment that warrants clinical attention is one for which treatment would be beneficial. However, it is difficult to imagine a person who would not benefit from some form of psychotherapy (Ellis, 1987; Freud, 1937/1957). Some persons would benefit by becoming more assertive; others by becoming less assertive. Some would benefit by becoming less dependent; others by becoming less aloof. Some would benefit by becoming less emotional; others by becoming less reserved. In other words, most to all persons would meet this threshold. Some persons might consider themselves to have the ideal personality, with no flaws, defects, or impairments for which alteration or change would be beneficial, but this belief may itself be a reflection of a maladaptive personality trait (e.g., psychopathy or narcissism). Community research would be informative in assessing the manner and extent to which ostensibly normal persons fail to experience significant personal, social, or occupational dysfunction secondary to their manner of thinking, feeling, perceiving, and/or relating to others.

Distress

The third and final DSM-IV criterion for when a personality trait constitutes a personality disorder is distress. There is perhaps little doubt that most persons who are receiving DSM-IV personality disorder diagnoses within clinical settings are significantly more distressed than ostensibly normal persons, as the presence within clinical treatment suggests the presence of dissatisfaction or distress. However, personal distress is perhaps better understood as a fallible indicator for a disorder than as a defining feature of disorder (Frances, Widiger, & Sabshin, 1991; Shedler, Mayman, & Manis, 1993; Wakefield, 1992).

Distress is a valid (but fallible) indicator for the presence of a mental disorder. It suggests that a person has a behavior pattern that he or she finds to be maladaptive and is unable to change (Widiger & Trull, 1991). However, distress is also a very fallible indicator; some persons will not be distressed by their disorder and the distress of other persons will be excessive or misdirected. For example, homosexuality was considered to be a mental disorder in DSM-II (APA, 1968) because it involved a sexual interest "directed primarily toward objects other than people of the opposite sex" (APA, 1968, p. 44). However, in DSM-III (APA, 1980), homosexuality became a mental disorder only if it was ego-dystonic. The person had to be distressed by his or her sexual orientation in order for a clinician to consider the homosexuality to be a disorder.

> Homosexuality that is ego-syntonic is not classified as a mental disorder. In addition, the attitude that "I guess life would be easier if I were heterosexual" does not warrant this diagnosis. This category is reserved for homosexuals for whom changing sexual orientations is a persistent concern. (APA, 1980, p. 282)

Distress regarding one's sexual preferences is a valid indicator for the presence of a mental disorder. The person is apparently finding the sexual behavior to be maladaptive and is unable to simply do otherwise (i.e., absence of adequate control of the behavior). However, the distress of many homosexuals is due primarily to the lack of an acceptance of the sexual orientation (and even condemnation) by other members of the society (Spitzer, 1981). It is unclear whether homosexuality is any more maladaptive than an obligate heterosexuality. In any case, the presence of distress in persons with a homosexual orientation would not actually distinguish homosexuality that is a mental disorder from homosexuality that is not. It serves primarily to allow a clinician to provide a mental disorder diagnosis only to those homosexuals who would not disagree with the diagnostic label.

A comparable difficulty occurs in the diagnosis of personality disorders. Distress is a valid, but quite fallible indicator for the presence of a personality disorder. Some personality disorders, such as the dependent disorder, are characterized in part by excessive self-blame and self-denigration. For example, a woman might seek professional assistance because she finds that she is unable to maintain the interest and love of her husband (Walker, 1984). She may be distressed by what she perceives to be her inadequate tolerance, cooperativeness, or agreeableness. However, the clinician may discover that she has in fact been excessively tolerant, and that the discord is as much, if not more, a reflection of the husband's unreasonable demands, domination, and perhaps even abuse. The distress in her case may suggest the presence of a personality disorder, but it would be a disorder of excessive submissiveness rather than excessive intolerance.

On the other hand, some personality disorders will involve an inadequate appreciation of the maladaptivity of the behavior pattern. Psychopathy is defined in part by an impairment in feelings of remorse, guilt, or shame (Hare, 1992). Persons with this disorder are impaired in their ability to feel anxious or distressed (Patrick, 1994), contributing to their engagement in dangerous, foolhardy, and vicious acts. It is difficult for them to feel even realistically concerned about risks, costs, harm, and dangers. The absence of distress in these persons is an indication of the presence of a personality disorder, rather than an indication of its absence.

PERSONALITY DISORDERS FROM THE PERSPECTIVE OF NORMAL PERSONALITY

The individual DSM-IV personality disorders can also be understood from the perspective of models of personality functioning derived from research on normal community subjects. There are a number of dimensional models of personality disorder (Livesley et al., 1994), but one which was explicitly derived from normal personality functioning is the Five-Factor Model (FFM). The operationalization of the FFM by Costa and McCrae (1992) consists of the five domains of neuroticism, introversion versus extraversion, conscientiousness, openness versus closedness to experience, and antagonism versus agreeableness, with each of these broad domains further differentiated into six underlying facets (see Chapter 5). Space limitations prohibit a discussion of all of the DSM-IV personality disorders from the perspective of the FFM. Further illustrations are provided elsewhere (Widiger, Trull, Clarkin, Sanderson, & Costa, 1994). This chapter will be confined to the borderline, schizoid, histrionic, schizotypal, and obsessive-compulsive personality disorders.

Borderline Personality Disorder (BPD)

Borderline personality disorder (BPD) is among the most frequently diagnosed, heavily researched, dysfunctional, and clinically problematic personality disorders. It is characterized by the presence of such features as frantic efforts to avoid abandonment, markedly unstable and intense relationships, self-damaging impulsivity (e.g., binge eating, substance abuse, and indiscriminate sexual relationships), recurrent suicidality, effective instability, feelings of emptiness, inappropriate and intense anger, and severe dissociative symptoms (APA, 1994). Persons with this disorder are so dysfunctional that it has been difficult for some clinicians to consider BPD as simply a maladaptive variant of common (normal) personality traits. "The five-factor [model] does not convey the intensity of [her] turmoil, the threat of suicide, or the ritualistic-like painful carving on her own body" (Benjamin, 1993a, p. 92).

It is indeed the case that a term such as *neuroticism* does not adequately convey the severely dysfunctional behavior of persons with BPD. However, there may be no single term that could adequately describe the entire range of this domain of personality functioning. A term that described well the most extreme variants of excessive neuroticism (e.g., *borderline personality disorder*) would not describe well the more common variants within the average range, nor the most extreme variants of low neuroticism (John, 1990).

However, the facets of neuroticism identified by Costa and McCrae (1992), such as angry hostility, impulsivity, vulnerability, anxiousness, and depression, do appear to describe borderline symptomatology quite well. Persons who are the most highly elevated on neuroticism would be excessively vulnerable to stress, repeatedly angry and hostile, highly anxious, destructively impulsive, and often terribly depressed. These persons would be diagnosed with BPD. Coupled with such facets of antagonism as manipulation, oppositionalism, and argumentativeness, BPD appears to be described well in terms of the Five-Factor Model (FFM).

The close relationship of normal neuroticism and antagonism with the mental disorder of BPD was illustrated clearly in a case study by Bruehl (1994). It was also documented empirically in a study of 62 hospital patients diagnosed with BPD at Cornell University Medical Center by Clarkin, Hull, Cantor, and Sanderson (1993) and in a series of studies that correlated various measures of the FFM domains with various measures of BPD sampled from a variety of populations (e.g., Costa & McCrae, 1990; Soldz, Budman, Demby, & Merry, 1993; Trull, 1992; Wiggins & Pincus, 1989; Yeung, Lyons, Waternaux, Faraone, & Tsuang, 1993). These findings are particularly remarkable when one appreciates that the measures of the FFM (e.g., the revised Neo-Personality Inventory, NEO-PI-R; Costa & McCrae, 1992) were derived from and developed for a normal range of neuroticism rather than for maladaptive, DSM-IV personality disorder symptomatology (Widiger & Costa, 1994).

Conceptualizing BPD as an extreme variant of neuroticism is also helpful in addressing a variety of controversies that have beset the diagnosis, particularly its excessive prevalence and comorbidity (Widiger & Trull, 1992). The FFM domain of neuroticism "contrasts adjustment or emotional stability with maladjustment" (Costa & McCrae, 1992, p. 141). The other domains of the FFM also involve maladaptive behavior patterns, but the general tendency to experience negative affects, such as fear, sadness, anger, embarrassment, and guilt, is the core of the neuroticism domain. Watson and Clark (1984) characterized this domain of the FFM as negative affectivity. It is not surprising, then, to find that neuroticism is an almost ubiquitously elevated trait within clinical populations (Eysenck, 1994), and that most of the DSM-IV personality disorders involve some degree of neuroticism. A personality disorder that is defined in large part as excessive neuroticism would have a substantial prevalence within clinical populations and would often be "comorbid" with other personality disorder diagnoses.

Conceptualizing BPD as extreme neuroticism may also be consistent with Kernberg's (1984) psychoanalytic formulation of borderline personality organization. Borderline personality organization and neuroticism both refer to a level or degree of personality functioning that traverses the DSM-IV personality disorder diagnoses. Persons with an antisocial, histrionic, or obsessive-compulsive personality disorder will be at varying levels of personality organization or, in terms of the FFM, at varying degrees of neuroticism. Kernberg would use a more inferential means with which to assess a person's level of personality organization than is provided by a measure of FFM neuroticism. He would assess for identity diffusion and such primitive defenses as splitting and projective identification, which he hypothesizes to be the underlying pathology for the disorder. However, the nonspecific manifestations of borderline personality organization identified by Kernberg (e.g., low anxiety tolerance, impulse dyscontrol, and vulnerability to stress) resemble closely the facets of neuroticism identified by Costa and McCrae (1992). It would be of interest to determine empirically whether there is indeed a substantial correlation between FFM neuroticism and Kernbergian level of personality organization.

BPD might represent a qualitatively distinct mental disorder if it possessed a unique, specific etiology. For example, there are studies that indicate a history of abandonment, parental separation, and severe sexual and/or physical abuse of persons with BPD during childhood (Gunderson & Zanarini, 1989). However, sexual and physical abuse are not confined to persons with this disorder, and there are certainly varying degrees of abuse that one can experience during childhood. BPD, as an extreme form of neuroticism, may result in part from the most extreme forms of abuse, whereas the more common forms of neuroticism may result from less extreme forms of abuse, including psychological abuse (e.g., devaluation) or neglectful, inconsistent parenting rather than separation and abandonment. It may not be the case that the childhood experiences of ostensibly normal persons lack any significant difficulties, conflicts, or other pathogenic experiences. Rather than consider those with BPD as the only persons who have been so harmed, it may be more realistic and useful from a theoretical and public health perspective to recognize that their experiences are simply the most extreme forms of problematic childhood histories.

SCHIZOID PERSONALITY DISORDER (SZPD)

The schizoid personality disorder (SZPD) includes such features as indifference to close relationships, preference for solitary activities, little interest in sexual relationships, lack of close friends or confidants, emotional coldness, pleasure in few activities, detachment, and flattened affectivity (APA, 1994). SZPD is defined in DSM-IV as a pervasive pattern of social detachment and restricted emotional expression, which is readily understood as an extreme variant of normal introversion, particularly the FFM facets of low warmth (cold, impersonal, and indifferent), low gregariousness (socially withdrawn and isolated), and low positive emotions (anhedonic, constricted, or flat affect). The close association of SZPD with FFM introversion has again been documented in a series of studies correlating various measures of the FFM domains with various measures of SZPD from a variety of populations (e.g., Costa & McCrae, 1990; Soldz *et al.*, 1993; Trull, 1992; Wiggins & Pincus, 1989; Yeung *et al.*, 1993).

SZPD is among the least prevalent of the personality disorders within clinical and epidemiological settings (Weissman, 1993). This is due in part to its overlap with the avoidant and schizotypal personality disorders, both of which were new additions to the 1980 DSM-III (APA, 1980). Many of the persons who had been given the diagnosis of SZPD prior to DSM-III are now given a diagnosis of either avoidant or schizotypal personality disorder (Widiger, Frances, Spitzer, & Williams, 1988). The differentiation of SZPD from avoidant personality disorder has been controversial (Livesley, West, & Tanney, 1985), but their excessive co-occurrence and overlap are readily understood from the perspective of the FFM. Both involve excessive introversion (e.g., social withdrawal and isolation); however, the avoidant personality disorder is also characterized by a greater breadth and degree of neuroticism, particularly the facets of self-consciousness, vulnerability, and anxiousness. To the extent that a person is characterized by excessive neuroticism and introversion, he or she would represent a prototypic case of avoidant personality disorder; to the extent that he or she was characterized by excessive introversion without neuroticism, he or she would represent a prototypic case of schizoid personality disorder. However, in clinical practice one may observe all possible combinations of elevations on neuroticism and introversion. As a result, actual cases will not fall neatly into distinct categories; most will present with various shades of avoidant and schizoid traits. The most precise and informative description of the person's maladaptive personality traits would then be to indicate the respective levels on the relevant facets of introversion (e.g., extent of social withdrawal, passivity, coldness, and anhedonia) and neuroticism (e.g., extent of anxiousness, self-consciousness, and vulnerability) rather than force the person into either diagnostic category, both of which will be inaccurate and misleading.

HISTRIONIC PERSONALITY DISORDER (HPD)

The DSM-IV histrionic personality disorder (HPD) may represent in part excessive, extreme extraversion (Widiger *et al.*, 1994). It is easy to conceptualize maladaptive variants of introversion. It is perhaps not as easy to conceptualize maladaptive variants of extraversion. Extraversion involves the tendency to be outgoing, talkative, and affectionate (the FFM facet of warmth); to actively seek social contacts and friendships (gregariousness); to be assertive and forceful (assertiveness); to be energetic, fast-paced, and vigorous (activity); to seek stimulation, excitement, and risks (excitement seeking); and to be high-spirited, buoyant, optimistic, and joyful (positive emotions). These FFM facets of extraversion describe well the histrionic personality disorder. Being outgoing, optimistic, and gregarious is not inherently maladaptive; however, being extremely, excessively extraverted could indicate a histrionic personality disorder. Features of the histrionic personality disorder include expressing emotions with inappropriate exaggeration (excessive positive emotions), craving excitement and stimulation (excessive excitement seeking), quickly forming many superficial relationships (excessive gregariousness), and feeling or displaying inappropriate affection, intimacy, and seductiveness (excessive warmth). Millon *et al.* (1996) referred to the histrionic personality disorder as the pathologic "gregarious pattern" (p. 357).

A significant controversy for the diagnosis of histrionic personality disorder has been the question of sex bias (Kaplan, 1983; Widiger & Spitzer, 1991). The features of HPD do resemble in part caricatures of stereotypic femininity (Chodoff, 1982), suggesting to some that the diagnostic criteria are biased against women. Kaplan (1983), for example, argued that "via assumptions about sex roles made by clinicians, a healthy woman automatically earns the diagnosis of Histrionic Personality Disorder" (p. 789). It has been suggested, therefore, that the diagnostic criteria for HPD should be revised to provide equal representation of masculine and feminine variants, so that an equal proportion of males and females would receive the diagnosis of HPD (Caplan, 1991; Cooper, 1987; Kaplan, 1983).

However, research within normal populations has indicated differences between men and women with respect to a variety of personality traits (Eagly, 1995; Feingold, 1994). To the extent to which personality disorders represent extreme, maladaptive variants of normal personality traits, one would expect to find more women than men with personality disorders that involve maladaptive variants of traits seen more often in women, and more men than women with personality disorders that involve maladaptive variants of traits that are seen more often in men (Widiger & Spitzer, 1991).

Costa and McCrae (1988) reported that women tend to score higher than men on the extraversion facets of warmth, gregariousness, and positive emotions, which are precisely those facets of extraversion that are heavily apparent in the histrionic personality disorder (Widiger et al., 1994). Men, on the other hand, tend to score higher on the extraversion facets of excitement seeking and assertiveness, which are evident in the antisocial personality disorder that is diagnosed much more frequently in males (APA, 1994).

The statistically significant mean differences between normal men and women on these facets is small. On a scale from 0 to 32, Costa and McCrae (1988, 1992) reported differences of only 1.3 for warmth, 1.0 for gregariousness, and 1.3 for positive emotions. There is clearly more overlap among and similarity between men and women with respect to these facets of extraversion than there are differences. However, Corbitt and Widiger (1995) noted that small differences at the center of a distribution can be associated with substantial differences in the proportion of persons at the most extreme tails of the distribution. Despite the small mean differences noted above, Costa and McCrae (1992) estimated that 67% of the persons who are highly elevated on warmth will be female, 67% of the persons who are highly elevated on gregariousness will be female, and 78% of those highly elevated on positive emotions will be female. The percentage of women will be even greater at the highest levels of these facets of extraversion. It would be of interest for future research to determine whether sex differences in the prevalence rates of the various personality disorders, including the histrionic, can be accounted for by the sex differences in normal personality traits (Corbitt & Widiger, 1995; see Chapter 16).

SCHIZOTYPAL PERSONALITY DISORDER (STPD)

The schizotypal personality disorder (STPD) has been perhaps the most difficult personality disorder to account for in terms of the FFM (Costa & McCrae, 1990; Trull, 1992; Soldz et al., 1993). Some of its features are readily understood in terms of the FFM. For example, STPD lack of close friends or confidants and constricted affect are consistent with introversion; STPD social anxiety is consistent with neuroticism; and STPD suspicious, paranoid ideation is consistent with antagonism (Widiger et al., 1994). However, schizotypal ideas of reference, magical thinking, odd beliefs, eccentric or peculiar behavior, unusual perceptual experiences, and odd thinking are not represented within the FFM, at least as it is described by Costa and McCrae (1992). Costa and McCrae (1990) have acknowledged that "disturbances in thinking would appear to be needed in addition to neurotic, introverted dispositions" (p. 370) to adequately account for STPD.

Persons characterized by extreme neuroticism are "prone to have irrational ideas" (Costa & McCrae, 1992, p. 14), hence, the occurrence of brief dissociative episodes, paranoid ideation, and pseudopsychotic thinking in persons with a borderline personality disorder (Zanarini, Gunderson, & Frankenburg, 1990). However, aberrant thinking and behavior are not included explicitly among the facets of neuroticism and do not appear to be represented well within the trait terms included within this domain of the FFM (Goldberg, 1982, 1990). Costa and McCrae (1990) suggested that "a sixth dimension of aberrant cognitions might be needed" (p. 370) to represent the cognitive-perceptual aberrations of STPD, thus placing this particular personality disorder outside of the realm of the FFM. STPD is also conceptualized by most clinicians as a characterologic variant of the mental disorder of schizophrenia rather than on a continuum with normal personality functioning (Siever, 1992).

An alternative hypothesis is that the odd, peculiar, and aberrant ideation and behavior of STPD are maladaptive variants of FFM openness. FFM openness includes an "active imagination, aesthetic sensitivity, attentiveness to inner feelings, preference for variety, intellectual curiosity, and independence of judgment" (Costa & McCrae, 1992, p. 15). The aberrant beliefs, perceptions, and behaviors of persons with STPD may represent maladaptive variants of an openness to fantasy, ideas, and actions. The relationship of schizotypic thinking to creativity is an open area of research (e.g., Schuldberg, French, Stone, & Heberle, 1988), although a disposition to be creatively open to aberrant beliefs may not be comparable to a disposition to be compelled to have aberrant beliefs. McCrae and Costa (1985) have not considered the NEO-PI-R Openness to Experience scale to assess schizotypal aberrant thinking, as openness was originally conceptualized as an "aspect of mental health, to be contrasted with closedness, defense, and neurosis" (p. 150). "Costa and I borrowed the term [of *openness*] most directly from the work of Coan (1974), whose Experience inventory was the starting point for the development of the Openness scales in the NEO-PI-R" (McCrae, 1994, p. 257). Coan (1974) had included within his Experience scale items that involved aberrant experiences, such as losing the sense of self, entering a trance, and believing in reincarnation. McCrae and Costa (1985), however, "deliberately excluded these types of items" (p. 151) to facilitate the distinction of openness from neuroticism. As a result, the correlation of the NEO-PI-R Openness scale with indicators of schizotypal thinking has been mixed.

Tellegen and Waller (in press), on the other hand, have argued that the exclusion of evaluative terms from the original FFM lexical studies (e.g., Goldberg, 1982) has resulted in a failure to provide adequate recognition of maladaptive variants. Examples of such excluded terms are *unusual, odd, peculiar, weird,* and *strange.* These terms would clearly represent the magical ideation, eccentric behavior, and unusual experiences of persons with STPD. The lexical analyses of Tellegen and Waller (in press) place these terms within the "Openness" domain, which Tellegen and Waller redefine as "unconventionality." The construct of unconventionality would capture creative and schizotypic cognitive-perceptual aberrations.

Nevertheless, it may be difficult to argue that STPD is on a continuum with normal personality functioning if it is indeed a form of schizophrenia (Siever, 1992). However, cognitive-perceptual aberrations will be evident in a wide variety of persons for reasons other than having the mental disorder of schizophrenia. The cognitive-perceptual aberrations of STPD within normal college students have been studied for sometime by Chapman and his colleagues, who conceptualize such aberrant cognitions as existing on a continuum with normal personality functioning (Chapman & Chapman, 1980). A useful analogy is perhaps provided by the disorders of Down's syndrome and mental retardation. Down's syndrome is a qualitatively distinct physical disorder that contributes to the development of mental retardation. Mental retardation, on the other hand, is a mental disorder that is on a continuum with normal intelligence. Mental retardation occurs for many reasons other than Down's syndrome, some of which will involve normal genetic variation, nutrition during infancy, and childhood development. STPD as a form of schizophrenia would be comparable to Down's syndrome, but STPD as a personality disorder characterized by cognitive perceptual aberrations would be comparable to mental retardation, which is on a continuum with normal functioning.

OBSESSIVE–COMPULSIVE PERSONALITY DISORDER (OCPD)

The obsessive–compulsive personality disorder (OCPD) could be a maladaptive variant of the FFM domain of conscientiousness (Widiger et al., 1994). OCPD includes such features as perfectionism, preoccupation with order and organization, workaholism, and, most explicitly, overconscientiousness. FFM conscientiousness includes such facets as dutifulness, self-discipline, deliberation, and order. Adaptively conscientious persons tend to be organized, reliable, hard working, self-disciplined, businesslike, and punctual (Costa & McCrae, 1992). Persons who are excessively conscientious will be devoted to their work to the detriment of social and leisure activities, perfectionistic to the point that tasks fail to be completed, and preoccupied with organization, rules, order, and details.

However, there has been only marginal or inconsistent support for the hypothesized relationship of OCPD with FFM conscientiousness (Costa & McCrae, 1990; Soldz et al., 1993; Trull, 1992; Wiggins & Pincus, 1989; Yeung et al., 1993). Widiger and Costa (1994) suggested that this is due in part to limitations of the current measures of FFM conscientiousness, such as the NEO-PI-R (Costa & McCrae, 1992). The NEO-PI-R was derived from and developed for normal populations, and it may not provide an adequate representation of the maladaptive variants for all of the FFM domains and facets. For example, workaholism is one of the DSM-IV diagnostic criteria for compulsive personality disorder, along with other indicators of excessive deliberation, dutifulness, discipline, and perfectionism. However, only one of the eight NEO-PI-R items to assess the conscientiousness facet of achievement striving concerns excessive, maladaptive conscientiousness (i.e., "I'm something of a 'workaholic,'" Costa & McCrae, 1992, p. 73). The other seven items describe an adaptive functioning (e.g., "I have a clear set of goals and work toward them in an orderly fashion," Costa & McCrae, 1992, p. 73). It is not surprising then for NEO-PI-R Conscientiousness to fail to correlate with measures of the obsessive-compulsive personality disorder (Widiger & Costa, 1994). The one exception has been with the Millon Clinical Multiaxial Inventory assessment of OCPD (Millon et al., 1986), which itself includes a number of indicators of adaptive conscientiousness within its item pool for OCPD (Widiger & Corbitt, 1993), such as "I always make sure that my work is well planned and orga-nized," "I keep very close track of my money so I am prepared if a need comes up," and "If a person wants something done that calls for real patience, they should ask me," (Millon *et al.*, 1986). It would be informative for future studies to assess the relationship of FFM con-scientiousness to OCPD with measures that are at least equally weighted with respect to adaptive and maladaptive variants.

An additional issue for future research will be a consideration of the particular situa-tions or contexts in which OCPD is especially maladaptive. Each of the DSM-IV symptoms of OCPD is considered to be maladaptive (Pfohl & Blum, 1991). However, OCPD is among the least dysfunctional of the personality disorders (Nakao *et al.*, 1992). Some of the fea-tures of OCPD may be only marginally dysfunctional (e.g., unable to discard worn-out or worthless objects), and some may even have adaptive value for work or career (e.g., exces-sive devotion to work and productivity to the exclusion of leisure activities and friendships).

The maladaptivity of personality is unlikely to be black-and-white, such that all of the traits are problematic within all possible circumstances (Leaf *et al.*, 1990). For example, the emotionality, intimacy, and warmth of the histrionic personality disorder can be very useful in developing personal relationships. Tough-minded antagonism that is maladaptive within some contexts (e.g., within a marriage) might be quite useful within another context (e.g., for success as a soldier or police officer). In addition, the traits of persons with a personality disorder are unlikely to be confined to just the symptomatology of that personality disorder. Each person is likely to have adaptive and maladaptive personality traits. Conceptualizing personality disorders from the perspective of a normal model of personality emphasizes that each person will have adaptive and maladaptive traits, that any particular trait can have adaptive as well as maladaptive consequences, and that the maladaptivity of a trait should be assessed within the personal, social, and occupational context in which the person is functioning (Widiger, 1993).

It is then misleading to classify persons as being simply disordered or not disordered. A more informative approach might be to provide a comprehensive description of the per-son's personality and then assess the adaptivity and maladaptivity of these traits relative to the personal and environmental context in which the person must function. Persons below any particular cutoff point along a dimension of personality will likely experience some de-gree of maladaptivity within certain situations (with respect to that or another domain of personality), and persons above any particular cutoff point will likely have some degree of adaptivity (with respect to that or another domain of personality).

CONCLUSION

The suggestion that personality disorders are on a continuum with normal personality functioning is considered by some to be inconsistent with the concept of mental disorder. Many persons, particularly the general public, consider persons with mental disorders to be uniquely different from themselves, as if only a minority of the population is "mentally ill," while they are themselves perfectly "sane." However, this is perhaps an unfair and mislead-ing characterization of mental disorder.

Physical disorders will often involve qualitative alterations from normal functioning, but it is normative to have at least some physical dysfunction, impairment, abnormality, and/or disorder. It is not unusual to state that everybody during his or her lifetime has suffered from many different physical disorders, and that most everybody will have at least one chronic physical dysfunction (e.g., myopia, allergies, herpes, or obesity). Yet, it seems unusual to suggest that everybody will have suffered from at least one mental disorder during his or her lifetime, and that most everybody will have at least one enduring psychosocial impairment.

This inconsistency in how one thinks about mental and physical disorders is due perhaps to the special pejorative nature of a mental disorder diagnosis (Schacht, 1985), as if having a mental disorder is comparable to being severely mentally ill or insane. People are not psychologically threatened by the acknowledgment that they lack complete physical health, but they might be threatened by the suggestion that they are not fully in control of their own behavior and of their own lives. It is as if people equate the presence of a mental disorder with the presence of the most severe variants of mental disorder (e.g., schizophrenia), comparable to equating the presence of a physical disorder with the presence of an incurable cancer. It is not at all unusual (it is in fact normative) to fail to be entirely physically healthy and to suffer from the consequences of a variety of physical disorders. There is little reason to think that it should be any different for psychosocial (mental) disorders.

It is useful in this regard to recognize that persons who are at the normative level of FFM neuroticism are not without neuroticism. Average neuroticism involves a degree of vulnerability, self-consciousness, and dysphoria (Costa & McCrae, 1992). It is only those exceptional persons who are excessively low in neuroticism who "are usually calm, even-tempered, and relaxed, and are able to face stressful situations without becoming upset or rattled" (Costa & McCrae, 1992, p. 15). Normal neuroticism is not normal in the sense of being without maladaptivity, it is normal in the statistical (normative) sense of representing the common or average level of negative affectivity. The normal person does suffer from a characteristic disposition toward negative affectivity.

Just as few (if any) persons have a body that is physically ideal, optimal, or entirely healthy, few (if any) persons will have an ideal, optimal personality. Nobody is entirely flexible. Nobody is able to respond in the ideal, optimal manner to every situation that might arise. Each person may have an Achilles heel, or a situation in which he or she will have significant difficulty responding effectively or adaptively due to his or her characteristic disposition(s).

Most of us try to avoid such situations. We avoid careers, encounters, or relationships in which we are likely to experience substantial frustration, conflict, or failure. We try to find the niche that is most suited to our personality. We try to find the environment in which our personality profile (e.g., extent of agreeableness, antagonism, introversion, or extraversion) is most ideally suited. However, we are rarely entirely successful. At some point, or at many points, we clash with our environment. We then experience our own inability to meet our aspirations, wishes, or needs because of who we are.

The tendency for clinicians to perceive personality disorders as conditions that are qualitatively distinct from normal functioning may reflect the limited and narrow perspective provided by clinical settings. Normal personality researchers can have a comparable limitation. Personality researchers who have never conducted psychotherapy or have rarely interacted with persons with severe personality disorders at times fail to appreciate the severity of distress, suffering, and dysfunction that are involved. Clinical experience is indeed very useful and important in truly understanding personality disorders. However, confining one's observations of personality disorders to the behaviors that are present within mental health settings is comparable to confining one's understanding of height to one's personal experiences with members of the National Basketball Association. If one's experience is limited to this population, then being tall will seem to be qualitatively distinct from being of average height. Basketball players do indeed appear to be very different from us. However, when one observes the entire distribution, the continuum of height (and personality functioning) becomes more apparent. In summary, there is much to be learned about the avoidant, dependent, antisocial, and even borderline personality disorder from the study of normal personality functioning, not least of which is that the persons with these disorders are more like our neighbors down the street than aliens from another planet.

REFERENCES

American Psychiatric Association. (1968). *Diagnostic and statistical manual of mental disorders* (2nd ed.). Washington, DC: Author.

American Psychiatric Association. (1980). *Diagnostic and statistical manual of mental disorders* (3rd ed.). Washington, DC: Author.

American Psychiatric Association. (1987). *Diagnostic and statistical manual of mental disorders* (3rd ed., Rev.). Washington, DC: Author.

American Psychiatric Association. (1994). *Diagnostic and statistical manual of mental disorders*. (4th ed.). Washington, DC: Author.

Benjamin, L. S. (1993a). Dimensional, categorical, or hybrid analysis of personality: A response to Widiger's proposal. *Psychological Inquiry, 4,* 91–95.

Benjamin, L. S. (1993b). *Interpersonal diagnosis and treatment of personality disorders.* New York: Guilford Press.

Benjamin, L. S. (1994). SASB: A bridge between personality theory and clinical psychology. *Psychological Inquiry, 5,* 273–316.

Bouchard, T. J., Lykken, D. T., McGue M., & Tellegen, A. (1990). Sources of human psychological differences: The Minnesota study of twins reared apart. *Science, 250,* 223–228.

Bruehl, S. (1994). A case of borderline personality disorder. In P. T. Costa & T. A. Widiger (Eds.), *Personality disorders and the five-factor model of personality* (pp. 189–198). Washington, DC: American Psychological Association.

Caplan, P. J. (1991). How do they decide who is normal? The bizarre, but true, tale of the DSM process. *Canadian Psychology, 32,* 162–170.

Chapman, L. J., & Chapman, J. P. (1980). Scales for rating psychotic and psychotic-like experiences as continua. *Schizophrenia Bulletin, 6,* 476–489.

Chodoff, P. (1982). Hysteria and women. *American Journal of Psychiatry, 139,* 545–551.

Clark, L. A., Watson, D., & Reynolds, S. (1995). Diagnosis and classification of psychopathology: Challenges to the current system and future directions. *Annual Review of Psychology, 46,* 121–153.

Clarkin, J. F., Hull, J. W., Cantor, J., & Sanderson, C. (1993). Borderline personality disorder and personality traits: A comparison of SCID-II BPD and NEO-PI. *Psychological Assessment, 5,* 472–476.

Coan, R. W. (1974). *The optimal personality.* New York: Columbia University Press.

Cooper, A. M. (1987). Histrionic, narcissistic, and compulsive personality disorders. In G. Tischler (Ed.), *Diagnosis and classification in psychiatry* (pp. 290–299). New York: Cambridge University Press.

Cooper, A. M. (1993). Psychotherapeutic approaches to masochism. *Journal of Psychotherapy Practice and Research, 2,* 51–63.

Corbitt, E. M., & Widiger, T. A. (1995). Sex differences among the personality disorders: An exploration of the data. *Clinical Psychology: Science and Practice, 2,* 225–238.

Costa, P. T., & McCrae, R. R. (1988). Personality in adulthood: A six-year longitudinal study of self-reports and spouse ratings on the NEO Personality Inventory. *Journal of Personality and Social Psychology, 54,* 853–863.

Costa, P. T., & McCrae, R. R. (1990). Personality disorders and the Five-Factor Model of personality. *Journal of Personality Disorders, 4,* 362–371.

Costa, P. T., & McCrae, R. R. (1992). *Revised NEO Personality Inventory (NEO-PI-R) and NEO Five-Factor Inventory (NEO-FFI) professional manual.* Odessa, FL: Psychological Assessment Resources.

Costa, P. T., & McCrae, R. R. (1994). Set like plaster? Evidence for the stability of adult personality. In T. F. Heatherton & J. L. Weinberger (Eds.), *Can personality change?* (pp. 21–40). Washington, DC: American Psychological Association.

Dutton, D. G. (1995). Intimate abusiveness. *Clinical Psychology: Science and Practice, 2,* 207–224.

Eagly, A. H. (1995). The science and politics of comparing women and men. *American Psychologist, 50,* 145–158.

Ellis, A. (1987). The impossibility of achieving consistently good mental health. *American Psychologist, 42,* 364–375.

Eysenck, H. J. (1994). Normality-abnormality and the Three-Factor Model of personality. In S. Strack & M. Lorr (Eds.), *Differentiating normal and abnormal personality* (pp. 3–25). New York: Springer.

Feingold, A. (1994). Gender differences in personality: A meta-analysis. *Psychological Bulletin, 116,* 429–456.

Frances, A. J., First, M. B., & Pincus, H. A. (1995). *DSM-IV guidebook.* Washington, DC: American Psychiatric Press.

Frances, A. J., Widiger, T. A., & Sabshin, M. (1991). Psychiatric diagnosis and normality. In D. Offer & M. Sabshin (Eds.), *The diversity of normal behavior* (pp. 3–38). New York: Basic Books.

Freud, S. (1957). Analysis terminable and interminable. In J. L. Strachey (Ed. and Trans.), *The standard edition of the complete psychological works of Sigmund Freud* (Vol. 23, pp. 209–254). London: Hogarth Press. (Original work published 1937)

Goldberg, L. R. (1982). From ace to zombie: Some explorations in the language of personality. In C. D. Spielberger & J. N. Butcher (Eds.), *Advances in personality assessment* (Vol. 1, pp. 203–234). Hillsdale, NJ: Erlbaum.

Goldberg, L. R. (1990). An alternative "description of personality: The Big Five factor structure. *Journal of Personality and Social Psychology, 59,* 1216–1229.

Gunderson, J. G., Links, P. S., & Reich, J. H. (1991). Competing models of personality. *Journal of Personality Disorders, 5,* 60–68.

Gunderson, J. G., & Zanarini, M. C. (1989). Pathogenesis of borderline personality disorder. In A. Tasman, R. E. Hales, & A. J. Frances (Eds.), *Review of psychiatry* (Vol. 8, pp. 25–48). Washington, DC: American Psychiatric Press.

Gustafson, S. G., & Ritzer, D. R. (1995). The dark side of normal: A psychopathy-linked pattern called aberrant self-promotion. *European Journal of Personality, 9,* 147–183.

Hamlin, W. T. (1990). Racism as a personality disorder. *The chains of psychological slavery: The mental illness of racism* (pp. 107–142). Baltimore, MD: ICFP.

Hare, R. D. (1992). *Hare Psychopathy Checklist—Revised.* Odessa, FL: Psychological Assessment Resources.

Hurlbert, D. F., & Apt, C. (1992). The malevolent personality disorder? *Psychological Reports, 70,* 979–991.

John, O. P. (1990). The "Big Five" factor taxonomy: Dimensions of personality in the natural language and in questionnaires. In L. A. Pervin (Ed.), *Handbook of personality: Theory and research* (pp. 66–100). New York: Guilford Press.

Kaplan, M. (1983). A woman's view of DSM-III. *American Psychologist, 38,* 786–792.

Kernberg, O. F. (1984). *Severe personality disorders.* New Haven, CT: Yale University Press.

Leaf, R. C., DiGiuseppe, R., Ellis, A., Mass, R., Back, W., Wolfe, J., & Alington, D. E. (1990). "Healthy" correlates of MCMI scales 4, 5, 6, and 7. *Journal of Personality Disorders, 4,* 312–328.

Livesley, W. J., Jackson, D. N., & Schroeder, M. L. (1992). Factorial structure of traits delineating personality disorders in clinical and general population samples. *Journal of Abnormal Psychology, 101,* 432–440.

Livesley, W. J., Schroeder, M. L., Jackson, D. N., & Jang, K. L. (1994). Categorical distinctions in the study of personality disorder: Implications for classification. *Journal of Abnormal Psychology, 103,* 6–17.

Livesley, W. J., West, M., & Tanney, A. (1985). Historical comment on DSM-III schizoid and avoidance personality disorders. *American Journal of Psychiatry, 142,* 1344–1347.

McCrae, R. R. (1994). Openness to experience: Expanding the boundaries of Factor V. *European Journal of Personality, 8,* 251–272.

McCrae, R. R., & Costa, P. T. (1985). Openness to experience. In R. Hogan and W. H. Jones (Eds.), *Perspective in personality* (Vol. 1, pp. 145–172). Greenwich, CT: JAI Press.

McGlashan, T. (1987). Borderline personality disorder and unipolar affective disorder: Long-term effects of comorbidity. *Journal of Nervous and Mental Disease, 175,* 467–473.

Millon, T., Davis, R. D., Millon, C. M., Wenger, A., Van Zullen, M. H., Fuchs, M., & Millon, R. B. (1996). *Disorders of personality, DSM-IV and beyond* (2nd ed.), New York: Wiley.

Nakao, K., Gunderson, J. G., Phillips, K., Tanaka, N., Yorifuji, K., Takaishi, J., & Nishimura, T. (1992). Functional impairment of personality disorders. *Journal of Personality Disorders, 6,* 24–33.

Nestadt, G., Romanoski, A. J., Brown, C. H., Chahal, R., Merchant, A., Folstein, M. F., Gruenberg, E. M., & McHugh, P. R. (1991). DSM-III compulsive personality disorder: An epidemiologic survey. *Psychological Medicine, 21,* 461–471.

Nestadt, G., Romanoski, A. J., Chahal, R., Merchant, A., Folstein, M. F., Gruenberg, E. M., & McHugh, P. R. (1990). An epidemiological study of histrionic personality disorder. *Psychological Medicine, 20,* 413–422.

Nestadt, G., Romanoski, A. J., Samuels, J. F., Folstein, M. F., & McHugh, P. R. (1992). The relationship between personality and DSM-III Axis I disorders in the population: Results from an epidemiological survey. *American Journal of Psychiatry, 149,* 1228–1233.

Nigg, J. T., & Goldsmith, H. H. (1994). Genetics of personality disorders: Perspectives from personality and psychopathology research. *Psychological Bulletin, 115,* 346–380.

Nikelly, A. G. (1992). The pleonexic personality: A new provisional personality disorder. *Individual Psychology, 48,* 253–260.

Overholser, J. C. (1991). Categorical assessment of the dependent personality disorder. *Journal of Personality Disorders, 5,* 243–255.

Pantony, K., & Caplan, P. J. (1991). Delusional dominating personality disorder: A modest proposal for identifying some consequences of rigid masculine socialization. *Canadian Psychology, 32,* 120–133.

Patrick, C. J. (1994). Emotion and psychopathy: Startling new insights. *Psychophysiology, 31,* 319–330.

Pfohl, B., & Blum, N. (1991). Obsessive-compulsive personality disorder: A review of available data and recommendations for DSM-IV. *Journal of Personality Disorders, 5,* 363–375.

Phillips, K. A., Gunderson, J. G., Hirschfeld, R. M., & Smith, L. E. (1990). A review of the depressive personality. *American Journal of Psychiatry, 147,* 830–837.

Schacht, T. (1985). DSM-III and the politics of truth. *American Psychologist, 40,* 513–521.

Schuldberg, D., French, C., Stone, B. L., & Heberle, J. (1988). Creativity and schizotypal traits: Creativity test scores and perceptual aberration, magical ideation, and impulsive nonconformity. *Journal of Nervous and Mental Disease, 176,* 648–657.

Shedler, J., Mayman, M., & Manis, M. (1993). The illusion of mental health. *American Psychologist, 48,* 1117–1131.

Siever, L. J. (1992). Schizophrenia spectrum personality disorders. In A. Tasman & M. B. Riba (Eds.), *Review of psychiatry* (Vol. 11, pp. 25–42). Washington, DC: American Psychiatric Press.

Soldz, S., Budman, S., Demby, A., & Merry, J. (1993). Representation of personality disorders in circumplex and Five-Factor space: Explorations with a clinical sample. *Psychological Assessment, 5,* 41–52.

Spitzer, R. (1981). The diagnostic status of homosexuality in DSM-III. *American Journal of Psychiatry, 138,* 210–215.

Spitzer, R. L., Fiester, S. J., Gay, M., & Pfohl, B. (1991). Results of a survey of forensic psychiatrist on the validity of the sadistic personality disorder diagnosis. *American Journal of Psychiatry, 148,* 875–879.

Spitzer, R. L., & Williams, J. B. W. (1982). The definition and diagnosis of mental disorder. In W. Gove (Ed.), *Deviance and mental illness* (pp. 15–31). Beverly Hills, CA: Sage.

Sutker, P. B., Bugg F., & West, J. A. (1993). Antisocial personality disorder. In P. B. Sutker & H. E. Adams (Eds.), *Comprehensive handbook of psychopathology* (2nd ed., pp. 337–369). New York: Plenum Press.

Tellegen, A., & Waller, N. G. (in press). Exploring personality through test construction: Development of the Multidimensional Personality Questionnaire. In S. R. Briggs & J. M. Cheek (Eds.), *Personality measures: Development and evaluation* (Vol. 1). Greenwich, CT: JAI Press.

Trull, T. J. (1992). DSM-III-R personality disorders and the Five-Factor Model of personality: An empirical comparison. *Journal of Abnormal Psychology, 101,* 553–560.

Wakefield, J. C. (1992). Disorder as harmful dysfunction: A conceptual critique of DSM-III-R's definition of mental disorder. *Psychological Review, 99,* 232–247.

Walker, L. E. (1984). *The battered woman syndrome.* New York: Springer.

Watson, D., & Clark, L. A. (1984). Negative affectivity: The disposition to experience aversive emotional states. *Psychological Bulletin, 96,* 465–490.

Widiger, T. A. (1993). The DSM-III-R categorical personality disorder diagnoses: A critique and an alternative. *Psychological Inquiry, 4,* 75–90.

Widiger, T. A., & Corbitt, E. M. (1993). The MCMI-III personality disorder scales and their relationship to DSM-III-R diagnosis. In R. Craig (Ed.), *The Millon Clinical Multiaxial Inventory: A clinical research information synthesis* (pp. 181–201). New York: Erlbaum.

Widiger, T. A., & Corbitt, E. M. (1994). Normal versus abnormal personality form the perspective of the DSM. In S. Strack & M. Lorr (Eds.), *Differentiating normal and abnormal personality* (pp. 158–175). New York: Springer-Verlag.

Widiger, T. A., & Costa, P. T. (1994). Personality and personality disorders. *Journal of Abnormal Psychology, 103,* 78–91.

Widiger, T. A., Frances, A. J., Spitzer, R. L., & Williams, J. B. W. (1988). The DSM-III-R personality disorders: an Overview. *American Journal of Psychiatry, 145,* 786–795.

Widiger, T. A., & Sanderson, C. J. (1995). Toward a dimensional model of personality disorders. In W. J. Livesley (Ed.), *The DSM-IV personality disorders* (pp. 433–458). New York: Guilford Press.

Widiger, T. A., & Spitzer, R. L. (1991). Sex bias in the diagnosis of personality disorders. *Clinical Psychology Review, 11,* 1–22.

Widiger, T. A., & Trull, T. J. (1991). Diagnosis and clinical assessment. *Annual Review of Psychology, 42,* 109–133.

Widiger, T. A., & Trull, T. J. (1992). Personality and psychopathology: An application of the Five-Factor Model. *Journal of Personality, 60,* 363–393.

Widiger, T. A., Trull, T. J., Clarkin, J. F., Sanderson, C. J., & Costa, P. T. (1994). A description of the DSM-III-R and DSM-IV personality disorders with the Five-Factor Model of personality. In P. T. Costa & T. A. Widiger (Eds.), *Personality disorders and the Five-Factor Model of personality* (pp. 41–56). Washington, DC: American Psychological Association.

Wiggins, J. S., & Pincus, A. L. (1980). Conceptions of personality disorders and dimensions of personality. *Psychological Assessment: A Journal of Consulting and Clinical Psychology, 1,* 305–316.

Wilson, J., & Herrnstein, R. (1985). *Crime and human nature.* New York: Simon & Schuster.

Yeung, A. S., Lyons, M. J., Waternaux, C. M., Faraone, S. V., & Tsuang,, M. T. (1993). The relationship between DSM-III personality disorders and the Five-Factor Model of personality. *Comprehensive Psychiatry, 34,* 227–234.

Zanarini, M. C., Gunderson, J. G., & Frankenburg, F. R. (1990). Cognitive features of borderline personality disorder. *American Journal of Psychiatry, 147,* 57–63.

Zimmerman, M., & Coryell, W. H. (1990). DSM-III personality disorder dimensions. *Journal of Nervous and Mental Disease, 178,* 686–692.

CHAPTER 15

SELF-WITH-OTHER REPRESENTATIONS

DANIEL M. OGILVIE, CHRISTOPHER J. FLEMING, AND GRETA E. PENNELL

INTRODUCTION

There are two major divisions in psychology. One is occupied by descendants of 19th-century Leipzig and the other by descendants of 19th-century Vienna. Erdelyi (1985) observed that this division has resulted in not one, but two, psychologies. He labeled one Apollonian and the other Dionysian. Apollonians (intellectual off-spring of Wundt in Leipzig) thrive in the laboratory where variables are fashioned to meet scientific standards. As this division is played out in personality psychology, the principal goal of Apollonians is to establish objective measures of behavior. Only things that can be observed, counted, or otherwise quantified fall within this province. Modern-day trait psychology falls mostly within this tradition. In contrast, Dionysians (intellectual descendants of Freud in Vienna) are "untrammeled by method" (Erdelyi, 1994, p. 670). Personality psychologists who resist being constricted by numbers and standard statistics argue that if one must postulate the operation of unconscious, unobservable, and nonrational mental processes in order to make headway in understanding the subjective worlds of individuals, so be it. Such inferences regarding psychodynamic forces operating behind the curtains of consciousness provide fuel for Apollonian outrage. They are premises for disparaging charges pertaining to illusive,

DANIEL M. OGILVIE, CHRISTOPHER J. FLEMING, AND GRETA E. PENNELL • Department of Psychology, Rutgers, The State University of New Jersey, New Brunswick, New Jersey 08903.

Advanced Personality, edited by David F. Barone, Michel Hersen, and Vincent B. Van Hasselt. Plenum Press, New York, 1998.

chameleonlike sorts of data garnered as evidence for psychoanalytic models of the person. In their turn, Dionysians complain about the sparse, even trivial, content of findings that emanate from the "positivistic" labs of their counterparts.

Our position is that both "camps" have much to contribute to the study of personality. We believe that the strengths of Apollonian rigor and the power of Dionysian theory can be combined in ways that weaken boundaries that seem to characterize and limit progress in the field. Our effort to contribute to a merger of the two psychologies is made in the context of describing a system of data collection and analysis that results in an integrated representation of an individual's subjective perceptions of self in the social world. This endeavor is Dionysian in that we posit unobservable mental processes that record and organize certain elements of important interpersonal relationships. Furthermore, we propose that these records of past experiences are automatically and nonconsciously scanned in order to discern evidence of any self-guiding matches among currently perceived cues and past ways of being in the context of such cues. The Apollonian nature of this work rests on the premise that sophisticated quantitative methods are now available to articulate the structure of nonconscious representations of self in interpersonal affairs.

SETTING THE STAGE

Before introducing self-with-other representations as the primary building-block units of analysis in this work, we provide a brief overview of past developments in self psychology. Our purpose is to highlight the resurgence of an earlier interest in the social nature of the self. (See Barone, Maddux, & Snyder, 1997, Chapter 1, for a more complete discussion of the convergences of past and present ideas regarding the interpersonal roots of self and the centrality of such notions in the relatively new hybrid branch of our discipline, social cognitive psychology.)

Psychological discourse in the late 19th century stressed the critical importance of others in the development of self. For example, Rosenberg (1988) noted that Baldwin (1897/1973) found it impossible to conceive of self as existing independently of interpersonal relationships. Baldwin was so impressed with the social nature of self that he coined the term *socius* to describe the dialectic space containing ego and alter. Rosenberg (1988, p. 57) wrote, "For Baldwin, the socius *is* the self and *is* personality." James's (1890) notion that we have as many selves as people with whom we interact strikes a similar chord.

In the early part of the 20th century and for a considerable period thereafter, psychologists abandoned leads provided by James (1890) and Baldwin (1897/1973) and left theoretical advancements in the hands of sociological social psychologists, particularly Cooley (1902) and Mead (1934), both of whom acknowledged James and Baldwin as trend-setters in the conceptualizations of self as a social outcome. There are several reasons why self lost its currency in psychology. Foremost among them was the fact that the concept of self met none of the criteria for respectable science. "It" could not be brought into the lab for scrutiny. Self was a black-box item. It could not be observed, touched, weighed, experimentally manipulated, or in any way measured. This hiatus gradually ended in the 1950s and 1960s with the appearance of empirical investigations of the self-concept. As Wylie's (1974) comprehensive review made evident, self became a stand-alone unit (that is, "ego" was separated from "alter"), a primary focus for the development of assessment strategies.

In the meantime, Kelly (1955) devoted his attention to the manner in which self construes others. He proposed that people, acting as lay scientists, construct theories about what other people are like and how they are predisposed to behave. The basic elements of these theories are bipolar descriptors (e.g., serious-carefree) that are arranged into larger units called "personal constructs." Personal constructs are internally organized into a hierarchical system for the purpose of structuring perceptions of other people. In contrast with Baldwin's relational construct of personality, for Kelly the individual's construct system is his or her personality. The success of Kelly's model is partly due to the fact that he paved the way for measuring and displaying implicit construct systems. His Repertory Grid method, a clear forerunner of the method described in this chapter, was a welcome contribution to a field struggling to find suitable ways to convert clinically based observations into "hardcopy" displays.

During the era when personality psychologists divided their attention between ego and alter, post-Freudian psychoanalysts, individuals less confined by or even interested in numeric methods, became more social in their theorizing. By the 1950s, it was no longer sufficient to think of the individual as a separate psychodynamic entity, frozen in time since childhood, whose repetitive impulses frequently clashed with external reality. Sullivan (1953) broke ranks with tradition by offering a distinctly *interpersonal* theory of personality and psychiatry (see Chapter 3). In Great Britain, Klein (1948), Fairbairn (1952), Guntrip (1971), and Winnicott (1965) played key roles in the development of object-relations schools of psychoanalysis, wherein human beings are construed primarily as embedded in relationships. The object-relations path has continued to a point where numerous relational models of psychiatry have been proposed (e.g., Atwood & Stolorow, 1984; Beebe & Lachman, 1988; Bowlby, 1969, 1973, 1980; Kernberg, 1976; Kohut, 1977; Mitchell, 1988; and Modell, 1984; see Chapter 2).

Finally, the relational self has surfaced as an important theme for today's social-cognitive personality psychologists. In their review of the pluralism that characterized the work of James, J. Baldwin, Dewey, and Mead near the turn of the 20th century, Barone et al. (1997) applaud the resurgence of interest in the social self. It is a defining component of the emergent field of social cognitive psychology, a hybrid interdisciplinary field that views the person as inextricably linked with others. In nearly all spheres of life, we carry with us a host of internal audiences that variously participate in, monitor, and affect our subjective constructions of selves as social creatures. Subjective constructions, almost by definition, are private constructions, and thereby are difficult to probe and represent with standard assessment devices. However, we propose that it is now possible to gain at least partial access to internal worlds of encoded subjective interpersonal experiences and begin the work of mapping out some of their dimensions. The remainder of this chapter addresses this matter.

SELF-WITH-OTHER

Rosenberg (1988) described procedures for gathering individuals' perceptions of self and others and methods for analyzing them. Following his valuable lead and building upon the growing corpus of relational self theory, Ashmore and Ogilvie fashioned a construct, self-with-other, that endeavors to combine "ego" and "alter" into a single unit of analysis (Ogilvie & Ashmore, 1991; Ashmore & Ogilvie, 1992). Instead of focusing on components of self *or* qualities of others or, in a combined fashion, investigating perceptions of self *and* others, this new construct is designed to study individuals' perceptions of self *when-with* other.

Self-with-other belongs in the theoretical company of psychoanalytic self psychologists who propose that individuals form internal representations not only of self and of external objects, but also of self in interaction with significant others (see Ogilvie, 1992). The construct also bears strong resemblance to Stern's (1985) concept of representations of interactions generalized (RIGs). RIGs are defined by Stern as "generalized episodes of interactive experience that are mentally represented" (p. 110). A RIG constitutes a working model that summarizes an individual's subjective experiences of being with a specific "self-regulating other." Mental representations of past self-with-other experiences serve as templates that offer guidance regarding how to be, how not to be, and what to anticipate in subsequent episodes with a particular significant other.

Ogilvie and Ashmore (1991) proposed that it is likely that individuals create unique self-with-other representations for each of their primary relationships. It is also likely that individuals form different mental self-with images of relationships with the *same* person (e.g., me-with-Mom when she is in a good mood, me-with-Mom when she is upset). Even so, it is argued that human beings are as economic with dimensions of self-with-other representations (henceforth SWORs) as they are in forming impressions of others. Kelly (1955) described personal constructs as components of an interlocking construct system. In like fashion, specific SWORs are organized into an overall system of such representations. As detailed by Ogilvie and Ashmore (1991), "Although each self-with-important-other internal representation is unique, the individual develops groupings of similar self-with representations. As the individual experiences self similarly in relationships with multiple specific others, a self-with-other family or constellation develops" (p. 290).

Furthermore, Ogilvie and Ashmore described a method designed to represent implicit clusters of self-with-other experiences. What follows is a restatement of the method described in the context of its application to the case study of an individual referred to as "June." (Portions of this report are drawn from another document, Ogilvie, 1994, and readers interested in some of the clinical implications of the method are referred to that article.) A case study approach has been selected over other options for describing the model because a "real-life" example assists readers in following the logic of the procedures while not compromising various technical details. It also provides several reference points for later discussions of the model's capacity to act as a bridge that links the Apollonian and Dionysian approaches.

JUNE'S QUEST

The circumstances surrounding June's participation in this work were as follows: June was a 22-year-old, white fifth-year senior in college. She had taken a sufficient number of courses to graduate but her low grade point average prevented her from being granted a degree in her major. On the recommendation of an advisor, she contacted her professor (Ogilvie), seeking permission to retake a course from him that she had failed several years earlier. Based on a jumbled history of troubling experiences when similar requests had been approved, June's proposal was denied. As an alternative, June was offered an opportunity to engage in several exercises that held some promise of providing her insight into potential sources of her academic difficulties. This was not an entirely selfless act; June's arrival was perceived as an opportunity to apply a method that until that time had been used to describe normative patterns of SWORs as revealed by nomothetic analyses of collectivities of subjects (see Ashmore & Ogilvie, 1992, for a summary of that work). In short, June's arrival was seen as chance to explore the usefulness of a new method in idiographic (single-subject) research. In her "why not" acceptance of this offer, June stated, "I want a degree more than anything else, but the problem is that something always gets in the way."

PROCEDURES

The procedures June followed had originally been designed by Ashmore and Ogilvie (1989) as components of a longitudinal study of gender identity (see Chapter 16). One facet of that investigation involved the development of a method for gathering data on individuals' self-with-other perceptions. This facet was broken down into two sessions, both of which were implemented in the following manner.

Session One

There are two principal objectives of the first session. One is to compile a list of *targets,* and the other is to compose a list of *features* to be used in subsequent rating tasks.

Targets. The most critical target items for this study were *prominent people* in June's life. The content of this list was so central to this undertaking that June was asked to accomplish some homework that involved preparing a list of 25 or so "important people" in her life. This list was to include individuals who "popped to mind" as having played significant roles in her development (for better or worse), as well as people with whom she was presently engaged in her daily activities.

The first part of the session was devoted to reviewing the list that she brought with her in order (a) to ascertain who these people were, (b) why and when they were important to her, and (c) to assure that no prominent people had inadvertently been left off the list. June was also invited to create two or more people from one in the event that she had experienced a shift in her relationship with a particular person. This resulted in her dividing her mother into "Mom when I was young" and "Mom now." Dad was similarly divided. A final list of 23 individuals resulted from this review. It included family members, childhood friends, a feared third grade teacher, high school acquaintances (including a few past boyfriends), adults influential during adolescence (high school teacher and a gymnastics coach), and several same-aged people significant in her present-day life.

The targets list was expanded to include five *roles* that June identified as important to her and two of her foremost *projects.* The labels June gave to her primary *roles* were *College Student, Tutor, Girlfriend, Daughter,* and *Gymnast.* Two of these roles require brief explanations. Tutor refers to her activities in a part-time job working with a developmentally disabled youngster. June expressed great pleasure in this undertaking, describing in some detail her efforts to teach the child to perform simple self-care operations like zipping her own jacket. Gymnast refers to a former role that, for a span of several years, had been a defining identity. Especially in middle school, she had enjoyed notable success in the sport and was considered to have Olympic potential. She remained competitive in high school, but changes in her physical structure prevented her from progressing into "world class" status. In response to questions about her current personal undertakings, June described two *projects* of particular concern to her: "graduating from college" and "finding better friends."

So far, three types of targets have been described: important people, roles, and projects. All of these items were generated by June. Only three researcher-generated items were added to the list. These entries were *Me At My Best, Me At My Worst,* and *Me As I Usually Am.* These *global items of self-evaluation* are of both theoretical and practical importance. At the conceptual level, Me At My Best pertains to the "ideal-self," a variable that has enjoyed a long history in personality research. Me At My Worst is a self-evaluative category that bears on the concept of the "undesired-self," which has elsewhere been described as a neglected variable in personality research (Ogilvie, 1987). Finally, Me As I Usually Am is intended to capture impressions of the present-day "real-self." At a practical level, these supplemental targets provide assistance in interpreting SWOR structures.

Features. The principal objective of the next portion of this session was to create a list of words and phrases from June's vocabulary that described the various ways she perceived herself to be in different situations and/or with different people. Ogilvie and Ashmore (1991) described alternative ways to gain access to individual's self-descriptive terms. The procedures used with June began with her being asked to describe herself "at the present moment." She stated that she was a bit confused, she hoped she would not come off as stupid, and she was somewhat worried that she did not have a very large vocabulary. *Confused, stupid,* and *worried* were written down as well as additional descriptors she used as she thought about herself outside the immediate setting. For example, as a student she described herself as *hardworking, serious,* and *frustrated.* Bringing to mind her impressions of herself at a recent gathering of friends, she used the words *carefree, happy, accepted,* and *innocent.* Different scenarios elicited more features (e.g., *tense, in-control, angry, caring,* and *well-liked*), and eventually a point was reached when June began to repeat traits, qualities, and feeling states she had already mentioned. She then reviewed the list of 45 features that had been recorded and judged the list to be suitably representative of a wide range of personal attributes.

Session Two

Between Sessions 1 and 2, June's targets and features were entered into a computer program designed to collect individual's ratings of all targets on each feature. The system is programmed so that one target appears on the monitor with one feature listed below it. For June, since the bulk of her targets were important people, the most commonly appearing target was the name of one of these people. When this configuration came to the screen, June was instructed to create an image of a particular interactive episode with the person named and to judge whether or not the feature on the monitor characterized *her* in the episode. For example, when *B. L.* (June's roommate) was shown, June formed a mental image of a me-with-B. L. episode and explored that image to judge if the feature beneath B. L. described how June perceived *herself* to be in that episode. When the feature *caring* appeared, for instance, June consulted her image and determined if that word described her (not B. L.) in the mentally depicted scene. If she perceived herself as caring, a 1 was entered. If caring did not apply to self-with-B. L., she entered 0. After that judgment was made and entered, the feature caring was replaced by feature *competitive* and June referred to the *same* scene to determine if she experienced herself as competitive in the situation she had brought to mind. After June rated self-with-B. L. on all features, a tone announced that target B. L. was being replaced by a new target.

Two matters involved in this exercise need to be emphasized. One is that the rating target is *not* the person whose name is on the monitor, as it would be if the focus of this research followed the tradition of implicit personality theory (IPT) research initiated by Kelly (1955). Rather the name of a person serves as a cue for conjuring up a scene, a representative interactive episode with that person, for the purpose of rating *self* in that scene. Thus, the true target for feature ratings is not the other person, but self-*when-with* that person. Second, instructions used in this exercise ask respondents to operate with the same mental representation of a remembered self-with-other interactive episode when making me-with-that-person ratings. This rule is probably difficult to follow. In fact, it is impossible to know the degree to which the instructions are obeyed. However, June and other people who have participated in SWOR research report that the instruction is particularly useful in resolving instances of uncertainty. That is, when a person has a long history of interactions with another person, it is likely that instances when nearly every aspect of self was activated can be recalled. Instructions to continue to refer to a single scene prevents the rater from conducting a memory search of multiple interactive episodes to determine if a feature *ever* characterized self-with that person. As researchers, it is important to be mindful that we are less interested in *all* the ways that a person can be with a particular person than we are in discovering *different* ways of being with multiple others. For that purpose, staying with a particular interactive scene appears to be effective.

June's 5 roles, 2 projects, and 3 self-evaluative categories (At Best, At Worst, and As Usual) were interspersed among "important people" on the targets list. When any of these items appeared, June was instructed to shift her mental set. Rather than rating these items from a "me-with" perspective (e.g., me-with-me when At Best—an exercise in absurdity), she constructed an image of self based on the target cue and rated that image directly.

June completed the rating exercise in about 70 minutes. The pace with which ratings can be accomplished is remarkable considering that, in this instance, 1,440 separate ratings were involved in completing a 32-targets-by-45-features matrix. Her rate matched the average amount of time it took 72 participants in another study (Ashmore & Ogilvie, 1989) to complete similarly sized matrices.

METHOD OF ANALYSIS

One of the assumptions of this line of investigation is that individuals detect certain commonalities across scenes in ways that enable the formation of "families" of self-with experiences. It is also assumed that the presence of some features and the absence of others assist in determining which targets are members of what families. This is a nontrivial problem that requires a method of analysis capable of recovering the structure of rows (targets), the structure of columns (features), and the manner in which the two structures are joined.

An algorithm dubbed HICLAS (for HIerarchical CLASses) developed by De Boeck and Rosenberg is ideally suited to these tasks. HICLAS recovers the underlying structure of a two-way, two-mode binary matrix in a way that reveals the organization of targets, the organization of features, *and* associated relationships among them. De Boeck and Rosenberg

(1988) described how HICLAS is related to Boolean factor analysis and to additive clustering but differs from both in that it postulates an order relation among rows and among columns, using a set-theoretical framework. Instead of requiring as input the initial computation of proximity measures (a step needed for most other models), HICLAS accepts the raw binary matrix itself and renders a graphic representation of target groupings and feature groupings, the hierarchical arrangements of both, and simultaneously describes the links and associations among target and feature groups.

Terms Used in HICLAS

Before describing the results of recovering the underlying structure of June's ratings, it is necessary for the reader to become familiar with some of the terms applied to the output of the HICLAS algorithm.

Classes. HICLAS begins by identifying two initial target classes and two corresponding feature classes. Targets that match a global pattern of *yes-no* feature ratings are temporarily assigned to one class, and all others are assigned to the second class. This *first-pass* recovery of the structure of a matrix is refined by subsequent iterations that use increasing numbers of classes to form the base upon which a hierarchical structure is built. Each time a new *bottom class* is added, the *rank* of the solution is increased by 1. Selecting the optimal number of ranks to be computed involves a trade-off between parsimony (a low number of ranks producing an interpretable structure) and the goodness of fit of a solution (a value that usually increases at a diminishing rate each time a rank is added).

Figure 15.1 represents all possible classes in a Rank-3 solution. (A Rank-3 solution was selected for June's matrix because its goodness of fit [.874] was increased only slightly [.881] by a Rank-4 solution.) There are seven possible target classes and seven possible feature classes. Target and feature classes are arranged hierarchically, with the hierarchy of target classes depicted right side up and the hierarchy of feature classes shown upside down.

Hierarchies are created by stacking higher order classes upon bottom or "building-block" classes located in the figure at Level 1. Looking first at the top half of the figure, Level-1 target classes are labeled *A, B,* and *C.* Level-2 classes are linked with two bottom classes. For example, Target Class A-C contains some properties contained in both A and C. Any items that appear in Target Class A-B-C, Level 3 at the top of the hierarchy, "share" properties assigned to all target classes.

Feature classes and their hierarchy are formed in a similar fashion. It is important to note again, however, that neither hierarchy is formed without reference to the other. That is, HICLAS alternates between the rows (targets) and columns (features) of a matrix as it computes the best fitting model that describes how classes of targets and classes of features are organized in relationship with each other. These associations are precisely what the present endeavor seeks to determine. The associative target class and feature class links are depicted in Figure 15.1 by squiggly lines.

Bundles. It is tempting to conclude that there is a one-to-one correspondence between target classes and their mirroring feature classes. If that were the case, the items in Feature Class a would fully "define" items in Target Class A. In fact, that is not the case; rather, classes are organized into larger units called *bundles.* A bundle is delineated by beginning with a Level-1 class and including any higher level classes connected to it. Two bundles are outlined in Figure 15.1. They are labeled *Target Bundle-A* and *Feature Bundle-a.* Target

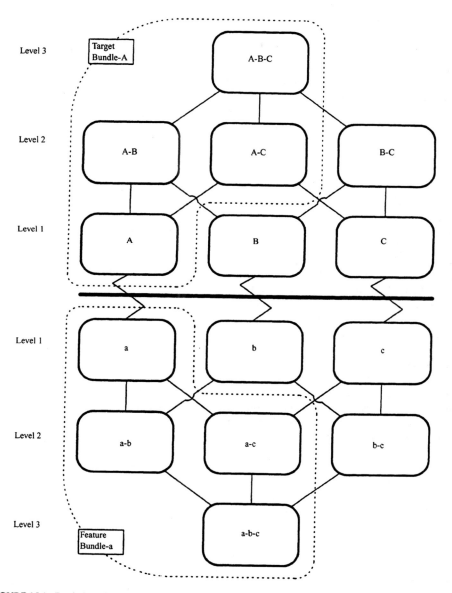

Level 3

Level 2

Level 1

Level 1

Level 2

Level 3

Target Bundle-A

A-B-C

A-B   A-C   B-C

A   B   C

a   b   c

a-b   a-c   b-c

a-b-c

Feature Bundle-a

FIGURE 15.1. Depiction of all possible target and feature classes and outline of two bundles in a HICLAS, Rank-3 solution.

Bundle-A is comprised of Class A and all other classes with an *A* designation (i.e., Classes A-B, A-C, and A-B-C). Similarly, Feature Bundle-a is comprised of Feature Class a and all other higher order classes containing *a* in their labels. The squiggly line connecting these two bundles indicates the presence of associative elements. As will be shown shortly, bundles are essential in providing a comprehensive context for dynamic interpretations of an overall representational model.

Residuals. Residuals refer to targets and features that cannot be contained in a computed model. There are several reasons that an item falls into a residual category. A common reason for features to fall outside the representation is that they were seldom rated as descriptive of a target. Another condition for residual designation, for both targets and features, is that their patterns of scores cannot be contained by the number of ranks computed. Numerous residuals suggest that additional ranks may need to be added in order to break the matrix down into more refined units.

RESULTS

The results of applying HICLAS to June's ratings reveal two primary constellations of self-with experiences that are candidates for being viewed as major players in what Murray (1940, p. 160) referred to as the "full Congress of orators and pressure groups" that constitute an internal household. A useful way to conceptualize these constellations is to think of them as *dynamisms,* defined by Sullivan (1953, p. 103) as "relatively enduring patterns of energy transformation which recurrently characterize the organism." A particular "pattern of energy transformation" is triggered by the presence of cues associated with its enactment.

A Weak-Inadequate Dynamism

The lower portion of Figure 15.2 shows the four classes that constitute the bundle of features that June eventually called her Weak-Inadequate (W-I) self. Note that Feature Class a-b-c containing *serious, feminine, innocent,* and so on connects with both major bundles, meaning that June rated these attributes to be characteristic of her in all, or nearly all, of her relationships, roles, and activities. Items in this class represent her fundamental beliefs about herself. In Allport's terms, these are June's *cardinal* traits (Allport, 1961). Lower in the hierarchy are Feature Class a-b (*scared* and *competitive*) and Class a-c (*unsure of self, tense, frustrated,* etc.). These classes are linked with Feature Class a, a class that contains *weak, inadequate, struggling, depressed,* and so on. Again all four classes are involved in the W-I bundle.

The target class most directly associated with June's W-I is Target Class A. This class contains *with-Mom when I was young, As College Student, with-Ms. B.* (3rd grade teacher), *with-B. L.* (roommate), *At My Worst, with-former boyfriend* (2 of them) and self in the project *graduating from college.* These items represent the targets that evoked June's subjective sense of self as weak, inadequate, depressed, worried confused, and so on.

A Powerful-Strong Dynamism

Evidence of the presence of a qualitatively quite different dynamism came packaged by a second bundle. The patterns of June's ratings revealed its association with her subjective experiences of self *with-Dad* (as a youngster), *At My Best, As Gymnast, with-Mr. N.* (high school teacher), *As Tutor,* and *with-childhood friend* (2 of them). Figure 15.3 shows that June rated self as *powerful, strong, in control, smart, happy,* and so on (Feature Class b); *scared* and *competitive* (Feature Class a-b); and *carefree, accepted, warm,* and so on

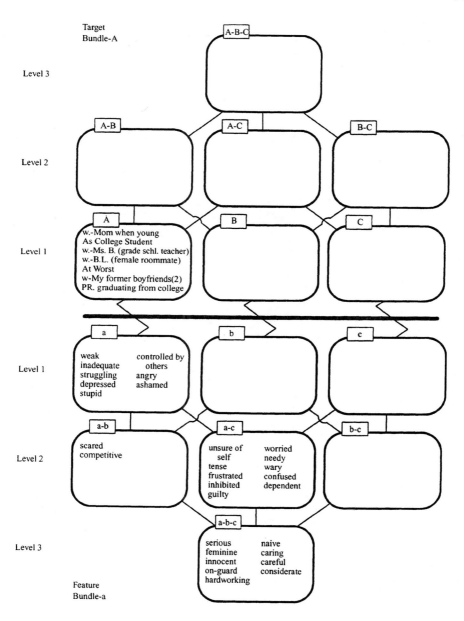

Target
Bundle-A

Level 3

A-B-C

A-B   A-C   B-C

Level 2

A
w.-Mom when young
As College Student
w.-Ms. B. (grade schl. teacher)
w.-B.L. (female roommate)
At Worst
w-My former boyfriends(2)
PR. graduating from college

B   C

Level 1

a
weak   controlled by
inadequate   others
struggling   angry
depressed   ashamed
stupid

b   c

Level 1

a-b
scared
competitive

a-c
unsure of   worried
  self   needy
tense   wary
frustrated confused
inhibited   dependent
guilty

b-c

Level 2

a-b-c
serious   naive
feminine   caring
innocent   careful
on-guard   considerate
hardworking

Level 3

Feature
Bundle-a

FIGURE 15.2. HICLAS representation of June's Weak-Inadequate feature bundle and primary targets associated with it.

(Feature Class b-c) in these roles and relationships. Contributing to this Powerful-Strong (P-S) bundle of attributes are the always present cardinal traits contained in Feature Class a-b-c—*serious, feminine, innocent,* and so on.

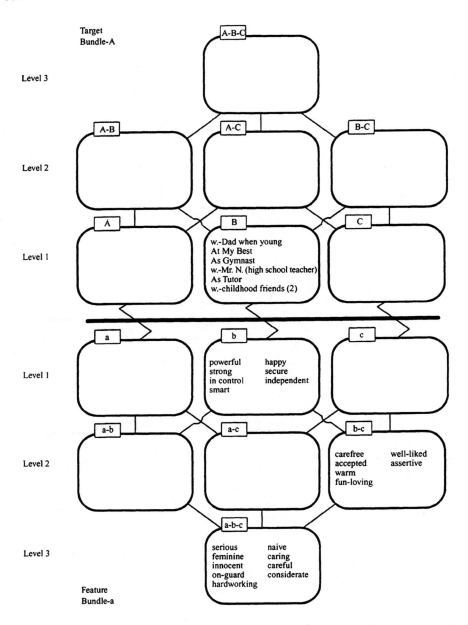

FIGURE 15.3. HICLAS representation of June's Powerful-Strong feature bundle and primary targets associated with it.

The full display of the HICLAS representation of June's ratings is reproduced in Figure 15.4. The figure contains much more information that can be dealt with here without distracting us from the primary results, showing that, in large measure, June has two primary,

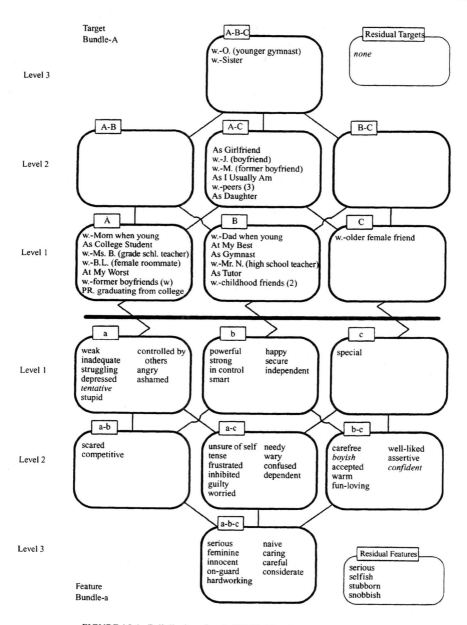

FIGURE 15.4. Full display of rank-3 HICLAS solution to June's ratings.

global, and competing subjective senses of self. On the one hand, she experienced self as weak and inadequate and had developed a role (*As College Student*) through which this dynamism found expression. Other domains of life wherein June subjectively experienced self as weak and inadequate included several "me-with" relationships and the project *graduating from college*. On the other hand, also available to her was a powerful and strong sense of self that had previously been expressed in her activities as a gymnast; when she was "with" her dad, a supportive high school teacher, and two childhood friends; and currently, in her activities as a tutor for a disabled child.

The diagram (Figure 15.4) representing the results of the HICLAS analysis of June's ratings were reviewed with her several times over a three-month period. This review was done as a collaborative undertaking wherein Ogilvie explained the structural aspects of the display, and June interpreted its meaning. A context was established for June to accept the fact that *she*, not the investigator, was the specialist in her life, and that part of her job was to "breathe life" into the diagram. During the course of these discussions, it became evident that the two self-with-other modes of experience depicted in the diagram (i.e., W-I and S-P) brought to the foreground aspects of self that June recognized as familiar. Two pictures were organized into a single frame, whereas in the normal course of events, one tended to obliterate the other. June was particularly inspired by the "way the pieces fit together." Nothing in these sessions suggested anything like a major "split" in her personality. The diagram served as a psychological road map that facilitated her moving back and forth between different styles of coping and articulating the conditions (and the history of conditions) to which she responded by feeling inadequate, strong, or a combination of both. In the language of Hermans, Kempen, and Van Loon (1992), one could detect the back-and-forth movement of two relatively autonomous "I's" in the landscape of self.

The sessions devoted to a collaborative understanding of June's representational structure led to a remarkable outcome. June's name was entered on the dean's list during her final two semesters, and she was certified to graduate. Ogilvie (1994) set forth alternative explanations for this turnaround in academic performance but focused mostly on the effects of June's discovery of two primary and competing "working models" of self. The hierarchical display assisted her in becoming conscious of previously nonconscious patterns of coping and revealed to her some of the arbitrary circumstances that had brought self As Student into the realm of a felt sense of being weak and inadequate. Courageously and cautiously, she began to, as she stated, "step out of character" and approach school-related work from a context of "can-do" confidence.

SCRIPT THEORY

One of the central themes of this chapter is that the study of psychology's tradition of being divided along "hard/quantitative" and "soft/qualitative" lines can be and, for the benefit of personality psychology, should be broken. In the remaining sections of this chapter, we give three examples of how an overall representational structure of families of self-experience can be used in accordance with the preferences and habits of researchers committed to different standards for understanding human behavior. First, we will explore June's structural diagram from a script theory perspective. Then, we will show how predictions can be derived and empirically tested by integrating new information into the computed space. Finally, we will provide an example of how certain structural properties of a single SWOR-HICLAS display can be used in a nomothetic (cross-person comparative) design.

Earlier in this chapter, when presenting the idea that individuals group particular SWORs into larger units, Ogilvie and Ashmore (1991) were cited as declaring that "as the individual experiences of self similarly in relationships with multiple specific others, a self-with-other family or constellation develops" (p. 290). Left unasked and therefore unanswered in that passage was the question, on what basis does one record one self-with-other experience as similar to another? Tomkins (1979, 1987) provided some useful leads in this regard. He proposed that innate *affects* serve as primary filters for linking *scenes* (a term used by Tomkins that, like Stern's RIGs, refer to mental representations of events). Tomkins theorized that individual scenes are sorted and coassembled according to convergences of in-common affects or blendings of affects. Affects of particular prominence in a person's life are those that have been "magnified" during critical, and probably repeated, episodes in childhood. As individual scenes are coassembled by the affective glue that binds them together, a *script* is formed. A script contains the individual's rules for interpreting, responding to, and controlling an affect-laden, magnified set of scenes.

Initially, a set of associated scenes determines a script. For example, a child may learn that seeking sympathy serves to alleviate feelings of shame. Over time, especially when a script becomes an effective strategy for dealing with a magnified set of scenes, an important shift takes place wherein a well-exercised script increasingly determines the scenes to which a person is drawn, and how such scenes are interpreted. This aspect of Tomkins's theory has far-reaching implications for understanding personality. It explains, for example, the puzzling phenomena of people engaging in what, on the surface, appears to be self-defeating activities—why, for instance, the just-mentioned child, as an adult, might gravitate to shame-inducing scenes. The reason offered by Tomkins is that there is a timeless ring of familiarity across affectively magnified scenes that have become associated with a set of rules of conduct and affect management integral to the individual's sense of self. Even in instances when affective experiences are unpleasant, a certain degree of comfort can be derived from knowing what to do when they arise.

Tomkins's theory is so complex that a few paragraphs cannot do it justice. Even so, this brief review of some of its main elements permits us to now consider how certain elements of script theory can be used to structure observations about June's self-with-other structural diagram, and how these observations may be used to inform the theory. We do this by mapping her two working models of self onto two scripts that Tomkins (1987) and Carlson (1988) have described in considerable detail. What has been referred to as June's W-I working model resembles a *nuclear* script; her S-P working model corresponds to a *commitment* script. We will take each up separately.

JUNE'S NUCLEAR SCRIPT

June was in a hopeless frame of mind when she first arrived to participate in this study. She explained that she had made every effort to do well in her courses, but "always, I mean always, something gets in the way." She described the elation she experienced when her application for admission to the university was accepted five years earlier. Over time, however, she began to perceive her acceptance as a "dirty trick." The hallmark of a *nuclear* script is its collection of scenes that have the common element of good things turning bad. The Target Class in Figure 15.2 most directly linked with June's W-I working model contains (among other items) individuals who had been sources of intense excitement followed by great disappointment. The most notable person in this regard is June's mother. June's parents were divorced shortly after her birth, but they remained in hostile contact throughout her childhood and adolescent years. June was under her mother's care during the week, and her father took over on the weekends. June recalled numerous instances when she was compelled to check on her mother's mood state. She described her mother as unpredictable, alternating between being a provider of comfort and reassurance and a source of scorn and rejection. As though quoting from Tomkins, she summarized her early self-with-Mom relationship by stating, "when things started getting good between us, I could count on them to turn bad, very bad."

June's ratings of self *As College Student* and of self engaged in the project of *graduating from college* place those items in the same class as *with-Mom, with-grammar school teacher, with-roommate B. L., with-two former boyfriends,* and *Met At My Worst.* Each of the self-with relationships in this sphere of her life is characterized by cycles of hopefulness followed by disappointment. June's third grade teacher, a woman who she first "worshipped," treated her badly and unjustly accused her of various wrongdoing. Her roommate, B. L., stole from her. One of her former boyfriends had cheated on her, and the other had repeatedly lied to her. According to the results of June's ratings of these targets, the primary affects involved in the coassembly of these scenes were anger, shame, fear, and sadness (the latter being an inferred element of feature *depressed*). June's script for managing such scenes, including numerous good-turned-bad scenes in college, involved actions consonant with perceptions of self as *weak, inadequate, struggling, stupid,* and so on. One can see how such a script could seriously interfere with a person's academic performance. Recall that one of June's first comments about her academic plight was "something always gets in the way." We are now in a position to identify her W-I script as a major culprit.

JUNE'S COMMITMENT SCRIPT

Commitment scripts, like nuclear scripts, begin with an intensely positive series of scenes from childhood. From there, however, these two "species" of scripts part company. Rather than being followed by disappointments, scenes that form the foundation of commitment scripts are coassembled on the experiential grounds of "good things getting even better." The script itself is characterized by a singleness of purpose and steadfast dedication to accomplishing particular goals. June provided evidence of the operation of a commitment script in several areas of her life. For instance, one of the items in the Target Class linked with her S-P working model of self (see Figure 15.3) is the role of tutor. This role refers to her activities in a part-time job assisting a handicapped child in learning simple skills. June was enthusiastic about the youngster's progress and looked forward to new challenges in her work with the child. According to the information contained in Figure 15.3, June experienced a degree of similarity between her tutoring activities and *with-Dad, As Gymnast, At My Best,* and several other past "me-with" relationships. The primary affects linking these scenes were *happiness* and *love* (the latter term summarizing features *secure, warm, accepted,* and *well-liked*). This array of affects was prominent in her memories of weekends with her father. She spoke of numerous adventures that included horseback riding, ball games, and backyard activities. Among her more prominent recollections was the time that her father constructed two balance beams (one for outside and another for indoor use) to encourage her interest in gymnastics. Indeed, it was in the sport of gymnastics that the operation of June's commitment script can be seen most clearly. In middle school and throughout high school, she practiced five to six hours a day. The payoff for her single-minded dedication to the sport was an invitation to participate in pre-Olympic competitions.

June's commitment script was dormant when she sought permission to retake a course that she had previously failed. Her nuclear script prevailed at that time, as it seemed to scream, "Don't you see? The world is against me!" Without the benefit of the representational display of the structure of her self-perceptions, evidence of her past history of successes—evidence of a sleeping giant—might have remained hidden. But it was undeniably displayed on a piece of paper and undeniably available. Her task became one of gradually moving her perceptions of self as student from the accustomed clutches of her W-I (nuclear) script and bringing them within the range of her P-S (commitment) script. It was not easy work, but the mental operations that resisted the transition were weakened by a constant going back to the display and recovering memories of actions and rules of conduct, provided by a script, that heretofore had been experienced as outside the jurisdiction of academic-related matters.

We applied script theory to June's self-representational display to show how a theory can be used in interpreting results. It should be clear, however, that this exercise was not done with an intention of providing "proof" for the theory. One does not prove theories. Rather, we have used a theory as a source of guidance in framing results. The next step involved a reversal of the process in order to discern if the theory can be informed by the results of its application. That seems to be the case in this instance. In our review of Tomkins's extensive writing, we have failed to locate passages that address the operation of multiple scripts in a single person's life. Instead, Tomkins devoted much of his attention in this area to describing affective templates for coassembling scenes that, in turn, lead to the emergence of *a* script that organizes a large share of a person's existence. In June's case, however, we have described the operation of *two* primary scripts that conjointly served to organize her experiences. This results provides an opening for subsequent elaborations of script theory that borrows from recent developments in "self-as-multiplicity" literature. We suspect that this challenge to theory could lead to a more comprehensive framework for understanding the multifaceted nature of personality.

TRACER TERMS

The range of information contained in a hierarchical structure that summarizes the results of numerous self-with-other ratings makes it amenable to different interpretations. Although we have written about its potential for illuminating script theory, that is only one of several perspectives that can be taken. One of the strengths of the approach is that it intersects nicely with a growing consensus about the importance of the "social self" and provides a context for exemplifying theoretical alternatives. Structural displays can serve as centerpiece supplements to more traditional case-study methods and can be put to good use in specifying properties of different theoretical models. For educational purposes, case studies are often the best vehicles for articulating different frames of reference for understanding personality. The method also provides opportunities to test predictions of the usefulness of these alternative models suggested by one or another. One way that testing can be done is by introducing "tracer" items into a rating exercise and subsequently locating these items in the structural space.

Thus far we have stressed the importance of permitting research participants to describe their lives, using their own vocabulary. This is a good rule that for certain research purposes can justifiably be broken. In fact, Ashmore and Ogilvie (1989) created a standard list of gender-related features to supplement self-generated descriptors of the 72 individuals who participated in the first study to use the SWOR system. Pennell and Ogilvie (1995) described how these features were used as marker terms to compute group differences. An issue that also pertains to gender arose in the collaborative work with June. What was done in that instance is described here as a brief example of one of the ways tracer items can be used to inform a structural diagram.

After June's original matrix had been analyzed by HICLAS, and after she had taken advantage of several opportunities to reflect on the results, she spoke one day about her fond memories of weekends with her dad when she was growing up. Horseback riding, attending baseball games, and gymnastic activities were the standard fare of many Saturdays. In her summary of one discussion about her relationship with her father, June said, "I think that I did my best to be the boy that I was pretty sure he always wanted." This statement led directly to her discussing some differences she had noticed between girls and boys when growing up, differences that now operated at the level of stereotypes. She described boys in her grammar school classes as having a great deal more confidence than girls. Boys seemed self-assured. "They either knew more things or thought that they knew more things. It didn't matter, they stood out in that way." Girls were different. June described them as more tentative, less certain about their abilities. Near the end of that conversation, June was asked if she ever thought of herself as masculine. She replied that she did but preferred the term *boyish*.

Prior to her next session, features *confident, boyish, tentative,* and several other "filler" terms were entered into a computer. June was then asked to apply these terms in another round of target ratings. The filler terms were excluded from the analysis, leaving confident, boyish, and tentative as tracer features that were merged into the pre-exiting, larger matrix that was reprocessed by HICLAS. The predictions were simple: boyish and confident would appear as defining elements of June's S-P (Strong and Powerful) bundle; tentative would be situated as a component of her W-I (Weak and Inadequate) working model of self. As shown in italic print in Figure 15.4, these items appear in their predicted locations. *Boyish* and *confident* became residents of Feature Class b-c in the company of *carefree, accepted, assertive,* and other S-P defining features; and *tentative* was integrated into Feature Class-a, locating it as a quality self-experience consonant with a sense of inadequacy.

This was not a particularly striking outcome in that it was so directly inferred from June's portrayals of herself and others. But the results are encouraging for several reasons. They boost one's confidence in the validity of the SWOR-HICLAS approach. And, they underscore the largely untapped potential of using tracer terms to test predictions in single-subject research. Finally, they contribute a degree of credibility to the idea that judicious combinations of participant-generated features and/or targets with researcher-generated items is oftentimes a quite suitable way to preserve unique qualities of the person *and* follow the course of marker items that reflect the researcher's particular interests.

NOMOTHETIC PROSPECTS

Although a great deal can be learned by devoting concentrated attention to the intricacies of a single case, few academic careers are spawned and maintained by such activities. In the face of an overwhelming preference for research using large numbers of participants, major journals routinely reject case study submissions. This is a fact of life for personality psychologists. It requires one to press beyond any insights garnered by intensive investigations of a few individuals and formulate one's interests in ways that meet current standards. Rosenberg, Van Michelen, and De Boeck (1996) described a wide range of studies that serve as models for extracting properties from HICLAS structures for the purpose of making cross-person or cross-group comparisons. The following is an example of how nomothetic research can be based on the process of identifying certain structural properties contained in SWOR-HICLAS configurations in a way that describes group differences.

One of the major problems with case studies is the degree to which any one person is similar to and different from others. Let us take June as an example. We now know a considerable amount about her life, her perceptions of her interpersonal selves, her setbacks and successes, and so on, but this information tells us nothing about how she may or may not be typical of persons or subsets of persons in her cohort. Is she unusual, is she one of a kind, or is she at some level representative of one or another group of same age peers? In order to answer such questions, one must decide on what bases such comparisons are to be made.

In this instance, we will place June in the context of the results of a study of 72 college students who participated in the panel study that spearheaded the development of the SWOR-HICLAS system. All participants (50 females and 22 males) performed self-with-other ratings. One aspect of subsequent data analyses involved the extraction of four categories of self-evaluation into which all subjects were slotted. These all-inclusive categories were derived from the structural locations of the three researcher-generated targets, Me at My Best, Me at My Worst, and Me as I Usually Am. These targets were included as tracers intended to mark the locations of the ideal-self (I), the undesired-self (U), and the real-self (R) within each individual's SWOR-HICLAS diagrams. Interest in the juxtaposition of two of these variables (R and I) follows a long history of research in which real/ideal-self discrepancies have been computed as primary dependent or independent "personality" variables. The undesired self (U) is less fashionable and rarely appears in discrepancy equations. (See Ogilvie and Clark, 1992, for a partial review of the literature that pertains to this topic.)

The four categories of self-evaluation reported by Ashmore and Ogilvie (1992) reflected four distinctive arrangements of I, U, and R in a hierarchical display. They are labeled *Integrated, Unintegrated, Content/Defended,* and *Unhappy.* Integrated occurs when R appears in a superset class that links both I and U. This configuration reveals that the rater perceives the real-self to contain some elements descriptive of the ideal-self *and* the undesired-self. Unintegrated occurs when I, U, and R each appear in separate, disconnected classes. Content/Defended describes a pattern wherein R is linked with I (i.e., they either occur in the same class or one subsumes the other), and U is separated from R and I in an unconnected class. Unhappy is a profile that links R with U, and I is separated from them.

These four arrangements are symbolized in Table 15.1. The table also summarizes the results of using the taxonomy to categorize the self-evaluative patterns of the 72 participants in the panel study. One result is particularly robust: Nineteen of the 22 males in the

TABLE 15.1. Distribution of 72 Young Adults Across Four Categories of Self-Evaluation

Category Label	Description	Example	Frequency (Percentage)	
			Females	Males
Integrated	R links with I and U.	(R) (I) (U)	11 (22%)	1 (5%)
Unintegrated	R, I, and U are in separate and unlinked clusters.	(R) (I) (U)	8 (16%)	2 (9%)
Content/Defended	R links with I; U is isolated.	(R) (I) (U)	23 (46%)	19 (86%)
Unhappy	R links with U; I is isolated.	(R) (U) (I)	8 (16%)	0 (0%)

Note: R = Real Self; I = Ideal Self; U = Undesired Self.

sample were categorized as Content/Defended. This means that 86% of the males rated R and I as similar enough to have them appear either in the same or linked classes. The appearance of U in a separate class means that the vast majority of males attributed few, if any Me At My Worst defining features to images of Me As I Usually Am. This result is an additional source of evidence that males are more likely than females to isolate negative qualities and, in effect, declare that they play no part in their daily "real-self" lives. Ogilvie and Clark (1992) cited research that females, on the other hand, are less likely to deny the presence of "negative" aspects of self in everyday experiences. This was definitely so for June.

As is shown in Figure 15.4, June's real-self (As I Usually Am) is in Target Class A-C, a superset class that connects with Target Class A, the class that contains At My Worst. Her At My Best ratings placed that item in Target Class B. This pattern, R is linked with U while I is isolated, places June in the category Unhappy. There she joins eight subjects in the panel study (all of them females) whose real-self ratings frequently overlapped with undesired-self-attributions, and whose ideal-self descriptors were rarely applied to real-self images.

These data reveal that June is not "one of a kind." She joins a small group of females (16% of them and 11% of the total sample) who fit the Unhappy pattern. She is a member of a subset of individuals who were distressed during the period of their involvement in research. Situating June in this broadened context permits a kind of blending of highly individualized and unique patterns of self-perception with partly "shared" patterns of self-evaluation. Research of this nature holds promise of cracking the hard idiographic-nomothetic nut that haunts the field of personality psychology. One begins at the level of the individual. Structural properties of SWOR-HICLAS results are formulated for the purpose of making cross-person comparisons. These comparisons lead to the distribution of individuals into emergent nomothetic categories. The process can then be reversed by identifying exemplars of a category of persons and studying their lives in greater detail with existing or new case study information. Although June was not in the original sample, she can be considered to be an exemplar of the Unhappy self-evaluative category. The study of her life results in a deeper understanding of some of the experiential factors involved in a particular pattern of self-evaluation. With robust samples, it would be feasible to devise new nomothetic indices for the purpose of testing hypotheses derived from studying the lives of individual prototypes. This back-and-forth movement between idiographic and nomothetic modes of investigation would enrich the research by satisfying the requirements of nomothetic designs and not reducing the individual to a mere point on scatterplot diagram.

CONCLUSION

In an article that addressed the issue of variance and invariance in personality structure, Mischel and Shoda proposed a theory that accepted the idea that, in some respects, individuals can be characterized by trait invariance and, in other respects, by situation specific variability (Mischel & Shoda, 1995, p. 246). Their *both* (decontextualized invariance) *and* (contingently variable) argument is a welcome contribution that softens a conceptual deadlock on trait-driven constructs of personality. It also provides us with an opportunity to summarize the SWOR-HICLAS model in the context of its fulfilling some of the requirements for representing trait invariance and trait variance in a single configuration.

We build upon a long tradition of viewing self as a social construct. (See Barone *et al.*, 1997, for a comprehensive review of our rich heritage in this regard.) It is within the framework of mental representations of specific self-with-other interpersonal experiences that a method has been fashioned to capture and condense situational nuances into patterns that reflect different working models of self. The method not only reveals elements of various working models but also specifies situations that grant access to them. It organizes an otherwise confusing array of personal qualities into a system that identifies subjectively perceived invariant, always present, personal qualities, as well as characteristics that are contingent on the presence of certain "families" of associated others.

We propose that there is a sufficient amount of flexibility in the SWOR-HICLAS method to permit a host of other issues in personality psychology to be addressed more comprehensively than has been customary in the field. For example, one of the most hotly debated issues of the day is the suitability of the Five-Factor Model for describing personality. Accepting for the moment that the Big Five dimensions are sufficiently robust to meaningfully plot and compare personality structures, more knowledge is needed before any functional comparisons can be made. The solution to this problem will not be simple, but the application of the SWOR-HICLAS approach is beginning to shed light on the matter. Here are a few examples of the results that are emerging from a project dealing with this question.

A young adult female obtained a very high score on N (neuroticism) and midrange score on the other four dimensions measured by the NEO-PI-R (Costa & McCrae, 1995). Remarkable by their absence were any of the N tracer terms—*worried, tense, neurotic*—in the HICLAS space computed from her SWOR ratings. However, these tracer terms entered the space as a package when her ratings of her roles and personal projects were added to the rating matrix. They were linked to and fully descriptive of one project in particular, *Losing*

Weight. In this instance, features pertaining to N, rather than being invariant as one might expect from a high score on that dimension, were subjectively experienced in the context of a single preoccupation with weight loss.

Invariance on the feature *introverted* characterized another female who scored very low on E (extraversion). Introverted was the stand-alone item residing at the peak of her SWOR pyramid of features, a result that bore witness to her low E profile. However, features *open, talkative,* and *outgoing,* tracer terms for E, were leading items of a bottom-level class linked with eight self-with relationships. *Shy* appeared in a separate feature class describing self in several other relationships, roles, and projects. Thus, as one might predict from this woman's Five-Factor profile, a sense of self as introverted was decontextualized. But in the overall fabric of this introvert's life resided an extravert who perceived herself as unrestrained in numerous close relationships.

Instead of viewing these sort of results as idiosyncratic anomalies or as noise that disturbs the abstract harmony of personality profiles, the ability to chart patterns within patterns shows promise of uncovering regularities that are easily masked by averaged and comparative scores on major personality instruments.

The field will continue to struggle with the Apollonian/Dionysian dilemma. But there are prospects that the debate can be raised to a more sophisticated level by making use of new models capable of representing perceptions of self across a broad range of human endeavors. Let SWOR-HICLAS and other methods certain to supplant it serve as modern symbols of Hermes (Labouvie-Vief, 1994), whose role in Greek mythology was to serve as a mediator between competing forces. For humanistic psychologists, this may require the suspension of hardened beliefs that no quantitative approaches are suitable for representing the complexities of human experience. Quantitative psychologists, in their turn, might need to become less attached to their nomothetic preferences. Such work will, for some, weaken the ideological boundaries that often distract us from making genuine progress in the understanding of human personality.

REFERENCES

Allport, G. W. (1961). *Pattern and growth in personality.* New York: Holt, Rinehart & Winston.

Ashmore, R. D., & Ogilvie, D. M. (1989). *Gender identity and social action.* Research proposal funded by the National Institute of Mental Health.

Ashmore, R. D., & Ogilvie, D. M. (1992). He's such a nice boy . . . when he's with his grandma: Gender and evaluation in self-with-other representations. In T. M. Brinthaupt & R. P. Lipka (Eds.), *The self: Definitional and methodological issues* (pp. 236–290). Albany, NY: State University of New York Press.

Atwood, G. E., & Stolorow, R. D. (1984). *Structures of subjectivity: Explorations in psychoanalytic phenomenology.* Hillside, NJ: Analytic Press.

Baldwin, J. M. (1973). *Social and ethical interpretations in mental development.* New York: Arno Press. (Original work published 1897)

Barone, D. F., Maddux, J. E., & Snyder, C. R. (1997). *Social cognitive psychology: History and current domains.* New York: Plenum Press.

Beebe, B., & Lachman, F. (1988). The contribution of mother-infant mutual influence to the origins of self- and object-representations. *Psychoanalytic Psychology, 5,* 305–387.

Bowlby, J. (1969). *Attachment and loss: Vol. 1. Attachment.* New York: Basic Books.

Bowlby, J. (1973). *Attachment and loss: Vol. 2. Separation.* New York: Basic Books.

Bowlby, J. (1980). *Attachment and loss: Vol. 3. Loss.* New York: Basic Books.

Carlson, R. (1988). Exemplary lives: The uses of psychobiography for theory development. *Journal of Personality*, *56*, 105–138.

Cooley, C. H. (1902). *Human nature and the social order.* New York: Scribner's.

Costa, P. T., & McCrae, R. R. (1995). *Revised NEO Personality Inventory (NEO PI-R).* Odessa, FL: Psychological Assessment Resources.

De Boeck, P., & Rosenberg, S. (1988). Hierarchical Classes: Model and data analysis. *Psychometrika, 53,* 361–381.

Erdelyi, M. H. (1985). *Psychoanalysis: Freud's cognitive psychology.* San Francisco: Freeman.

Erdelyi, M. H. (1994). Commentary: Integrating a dissociation-prone psychology. *Journal of Personality, 62,* 699–696.

Fairbairn, W. R. D. (1952). *Psychoanalytic studies of the personality.* London: Routledge & Kegan Paul.

Guntrip, H. (1971). *Psychoanalytic theory, therapy, and the self.* New York: Basic Books.

Hermans, H. J. M., Kempen, H. J. G. & Van Loon, R. J. P. (1992). The dialogical self: Beyond individualism and rationalism. *The American Psychologist, 47,* 23–33.

James, W. (1890). *Principles of psychology.* New York: Holt.

Kelly, G. A. (1955). *The psychology of personal constructs.* New York: Norton.

Kernberg, O. (1976). *Object relations theory and clinical psychoanalysis.* New York: Jason Aronson.

Klein, M. (1948). *Contributions to psychoanalysis 1921–1945.* London: Hogarth.

Kohut, H. (1977). *The restoration of self.* New York: International Universities Press.

Labouvie-Vief, G. (1994). *Psyche and eros.* New York: Cambridge University Press.

Mead, G. H. (1934). *Mind, self, and society.* Chicago: University of Chicago Press.

Mischel, W., & Shoda, Y. (1995). A cognitive-affective system theory of personality: Reconceptualizing situations, dispositions, dynamics, and invariance in personality structure. *Psychological Review, 102,* 246–268.

Mitchell, S. (1988). *Relational concepts in psychoanalysis.* Cambridge, MA: Harvard University Press.

Modell, A. (1984). *Psychoanalysis in a new context.* Madison, CT: International Universities Press.

Murray, H. A. (1940). What should psychologists do about psychoanalysis? *Journal of Abnormal and Social Psychology, 35,* 150–175.

Ogilvie, D. M. (1987). The undesired self: A neglected variable in personality research. *Journal of Personality and Social Psychology, 52,* 379–385.

Ogilvie, D. M. (1992). Competing epistemologies. *Psychological Inquiry, 3,* 50–53.

Ogilvie, D. M. (1994). The use of graphic representations of self dynamisms in clinical treatment. *Crisis Intervention and Time-Limited Treatment, 1,* 125–140.

Ogilvie, D. M., & Ashmore, R. D. (1991). Self-with-other representation as a unit of analysis in self-concept research. In R. A. Curtis (Ed.), *The relational self: Theoretical convergences in psychoanalysis and social psychology* (pp. 282–314). New York: Guilford Press.

Ogilvie, D. M., & Clark, M. D. (1992). The best and worst of it: Age and sex differences in self-discrepancy research. In R. P. Liopka & T. M. Brinthaupt (Eds.), *Self-perspectives across the life span* (pp. 186–222). Albany: State University of New York Press.

Pennell, G. E., & Ogilvie, D. M. (1995). You and me as she and he: The meaning of gender-related concepts in other- and self-perceptions. *Sex Roles, 33,* 29–57.

Rosenberg, S. (1988). Self and others: Studies in social psychology and autobiography. In L. Berkowitz (Eds.), *Advances in experimental social psychology* (Vol. 21, pp. 57–95). New York: Academic Press.

Rosenberg, S., Van Michelen, I., & De Boeck, P. (1996). A hierarchical classes model: Theory and method with applications in psychology and psychopathology. In P. Arabie, L. J. Hubert, & G. De Soete (Eds.), *Clustering and classification* (pp. 123–155). River Edge, NJ: World Scientific Publishing.

Stern, D. N. (1985). *The interpersonal world of the infant.* New York: Basic Books.

Sullivan, H. S. (1953). *The interpersonal theory of psychiatry.* New York: Norton.

Tomkins, S. S. (1979). Script theory: Differential magnification of affects. In H. E. Horowitz & R. A. Dienstbier (Eds.), *Nebraska Symposium on Motivation: Vol. 26.* (pp. 201–236). Lincoln: University of Nebraska Press.

Tomkins, S. S. (1987). Script theory. In J. Arnoff, A. I. Rabin, & R. A. Zucker (Eds.), *The emergence of personality* (pp. 147–216). New York: Springer.

Winnicott, D. W. (1965). *The family and individual development.* London: Tavistock.

Wylie, R. (1974). *The self-concept.* Lincoln: University of Nebraska Press.

CHAPTER 16

SEX/GENDER AND
THE INDIVIDUAL

RICHARD D. ASHMORE AND ANDREA D. SEWELL

INTRODUCTION

Freud once asked, What do women want? Long before Freud, and continuing to the present day, many men have wondered, Why do *they* (women) behave as they do? Similarly, many women ask, Why do *they* (men) behave as they do? In a widely read nonacademic volume, Gray (1992) suggested a simple answer with the title of his book, *Men Are from Mars, Women Are from Venus:* Women and men are from "different planets" and are "supposed to be different" (p. 10). From the very beginnings of their discipline in the late 1800s, psychologists have addressed the issue of why women and men think, feel, and behave as they do. At times, the prevailing answers were almost as simple as Gray's suggestion that the sexes come from different planets. At other times, and increasingly so today, the answers concerning the why of men's and women's experiences and actions have involved complex multifaceted frameworks.

RICHARD D. ASHMORE and ANDREA D. SEWELL, Department of Psychology, Livingston College, Rutgers University, The State University of New Jersey, New Brunswick, New Jersey 08903.

Advanced Personality, edited by David F. Barone, Michel Hersen, and Vincent B. Van Hasselt. Plenum Press, New York, 1998.

In this chapter, our primary goal is to provide an overview of the major approaches that psychologists have taken to understanding sex, gender, and the individual. To address these issues, we will proceed as follows: First, we will identify more precisely what this chapter will and will not cover and offer working definitions for the key terms, *sex* and *gender*. Next, we will take a look backward by providing a brief history of psychology's concern with sex and gender. Following this, we will describe in depth three major contemporary paradigms for the scientific analysis of how sex and gender influence the experience and behavior of individuals: sex/gender differences, gender as a personality variable, and sex as a social category. As part of a brief concluding section, we offer a speculative look into the future of this topic.

SPECIFYING COVERAGE AND WORKING DEFINITIONS

Freud was certainly not the first to wonder why women and men think, feel, and behave as they do. Lay, philosophical, and literary explanations for sex, gender, and behavior have a long history. As the social and behavioral sciences emerged from philosophy at the end of the 19th century, sex/gender, while not the most important or central issue, was one topic that some psychologists, sociologists, and workers from related disciplines sought to understand by empirical analysis. As a consequence, sex and gender are not the exclusive province of any one academic field.

In this chapter, we seek to understand this topic at the level of the individual person, hence our title, "Sex/Gender and the Individual." We will draw almost exclusively on material by psychologists. This means that we will not review work by those adopting a level of analysis that is either more molar (e.g., sociologists, anthropologists) or more molecular (e.g., biologists) than that of psychologists. Within psychology, we will focus on the contributions of social and personality psychologists, with some treatment of work by developmental and differential psychologists. As a consequence, we will not review the research conducted by biopsychologists and behavioral neuroscientists (see parts I and II of Reinisch, Rosenblum, & Sanders, 1987). We will also not address clinical issues related to sex and gender, such as gender identity disorders (e.g., Money, 1994).

Having specified the domain of our analysis, it is now necessary to address the issue of the meaning of the central terms, *sex* and *gender*. Their meanings have been a topic of lively debate. The emerging consensus, at least among psychologists who study sex and gender, is that *sex* is best used to refer to biologically determined aspects of men's and women's behavior, whereas *gender* should denote male-female differences that are shaped by sociocultural factors (cf. Unger, 1979). A major reason offered for this terminological specification is that, without this separation, and with the word *sex* being more commonly used to refer to all female-male differences, people might infer that all "sex differences" are genetically given and, hence, not influenced by social conditions and also not alterable. We certainly understand this argument, and we will use *sex* to refer to genetic/biological inputs and *gender* to denote social/environmental inputs to men's and women's experiences and conduct. We will not, however, be slavish in our use of these terms for two reasons: First, it is not easy, and sometimes it is not possible, to partial out genetic/hereditary causes from social and environmental influences. In fact, almost all who study sex and gender acknowledge that both factors operate, and, further, that they interact. To capture this intertwining and interdependence of sex and gender, we used the label *sex/gender* in our chapter title, and we will use this rubric at times in the text. Second, biological sex is not just a matter of one's genetic endowment and biological propensities, it also constitutes a powerful social category. In fact, one of the major current perspectives we will cover is based on the starting assumption that sex is a primary societal sorting device and, as such, influences gender-related thought, feeling, and behavior.

A BRIEF HISTORY OF PSYCHOLOGY'S CONCERN WITH SEX AND GENDER

Although sex and gender have attracted the attention of psychologists from the very start of the field, no single approach has guided work on this topic. Instead, it is possible to identify six historical periods on the basis of the conceptual and empirical tools that were most popular.[1] With approximate dates, these periods are as follows: "(1) 1894–1936: 'sex differences in intelligence'; (2) 1936–1954: 'masculinity-femininity as a global personality trait'; (3) 1954–1966: 'sex-role development'; (4) 1966–1974: 'grand new theories of sex typing'; (5) 1974–1982: 'androgyny as a sex-role ideal'; (6) 1982–present: 'sex as a social category'" (Ashmore, 1990, p. 487).

SEX DIFFERENCES IN INTELLIGENCE (1894–1936)

This first period was inaugurated by Ellis's (1894) *Man and Woman,* which proposed that sex differences should be studied scientifically, and ended with Terman and Miles's (1936) *Sex and Personality,* which is the seminal volume for the second period in psychology's analysis of sex and gender. The primary question asked during this first period was, Are men more intelligent than women?

During the late 1800s, it was widely assumed that it was natural for men to have a disproportionate share of societal power and prestige because they were biologically suited for such positions. The emerging theory of evolution and the development of numerous empirical sciences served to support and rationalize this societal ideology. Psychologists and other behavioral and biological scientists played their roles by seeking to identify the brain differences between the sexes that made men more intelligent and, hence, better suited to run society (Shields, 1975, 1982).

Thompson (Wooley) (1903) was the first to test empirically the crucial link between biological sex and intellectual ability in the implicit causal model depicted at the top of Figure 16.1. With the development and proliferation of intelligence tests during the early years of this century, considerable data on this issue became available. In her comprehensive review of such work, Miles (1935) concluded that the sexes are not different in general intelligence, and this conclusion was endorsed by most workers in the field.

---

[1]The history of psychology's concern with sex and gender is not as neat or simple as here portrayed. For each period, we identify and describe the major *new* approach. The reader should note that when a new period begins it is not the case that the type of work characteristic of the earlier period stops. For example, sex-differences research has been a mainstay of the psychological study of sex and gender from the 1890s to the present; it is not restricted to the first period we discuss. (For a more detailed version of the present history, see Ashmore, 1990; for other histories of sex and gender research, see Carter, 1987; Crawford & Marecek, 1989; Lewin, 1984; Morawski, 1985, 1987.)

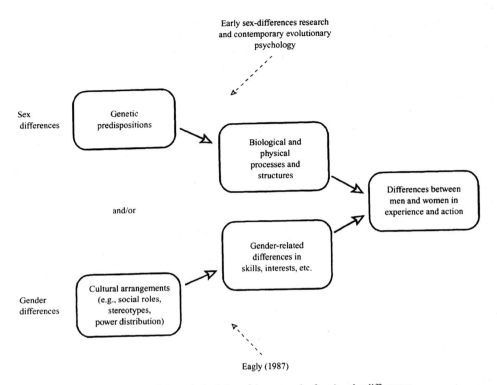

FIGURE 16.1. Schematic depiction of the approach of sex/gender differences.

MASCULINITY–FEMININITY AS A GLOBAL PERSONALITY TRAIT (1936–1954)

Although sex differences work continued after 1936 (a topic to which we return later), publication of Terman and Miles's (1936) book brought to center stage a new variable and approach that captured widespread attention; their work was widely imitated and extended. The new construct was *masculinity/femininity.* Terman and Miles offered no formal definition, perhaps believing that everyone already understood these common language terms. Essentially, they conceived of masculinity/femininity as a global personality trait (involving a broad range of abilities, interests, attitudes, traits, behaviors, etc.) that represented the individual's psychological orientation to her/his sex category. Also, they viewed masculinity and femininity as psychological opposites. Furthermore, they developed a self-report questionnaire to assess this global and bipolar construct, and many other masculinity/femininity (M/F) scales were then constructed by others. Finally, it was assumed that femininity is normal and natural in girls/women, and, in parallel fashion, that masculinity is important to psychological health in boys/men (congruence model, Whitley, 1984). Although Terman and Miles avoided discussing the origins of psychological masculinity/femininity, the causal model implicit in their analysis is depicted in the top path of Figure 16.2.

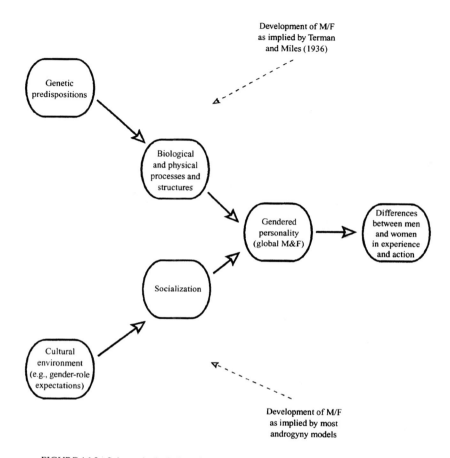

FIGURE 16.2. Schematic depiction of the approach of gender as a personality variable.

Sex-Role Development (1954–1966)

The year 1954 was selected as the boundary between this period and the previous one because Terman and Tyler's (1954) chapter on sex and gender for the *Manual of Child Psychology* featured sex differences (in intellectual abilities and masculinity/femininity), as had been true in the two earlier editions of this major handbook (Terman, 1946; Wellman, 1933), but which would not be true for the next two editions' gender chapters (Huston, 1983; Mischel, 1970). Instead, in the 1950s and 1960s many sex/gender workers shifted their attention to a new construct: *sex role*. In 1936, the sociologist Ralph Linton introduced the notion of *role;* he suggested that each society consists of "positions," and these have associated roles. For example, "boss" at work and "mother" in the family are social positions, and each has associated with it a set of prescribed behaviors (e.g., a mother should take care of and nurture her children). This notion of social role was not restricted to such specific positions as boss and mother; it was generalized to the sex/gender categories as the male and female sex roles. During the 1950s and 1960s, attention also focused on development, especially how boys learned to be men and girls were socialized to be women. For many workers, the answer lay in combining the sociological idea of sex role with the psychoanalytic concept of *identification*. As a consequence, much work during this period sought to explicate the inputs to, as well as correlates and consequences of, sex-role identification (Pleck, 1984).

Grand New Theories of Sex Typing (1966–1974)

Maccoby's (1966) *The Psychology of Sex Differences* contained two major new theories of sex and gender. Mischel (1966) put forth a social learning model of sex typing. Although learning principles had often been used to explain why boys and girls behaved as they did, Mischel's chapter formalized learning principles and substantially extended the S-R learning theory of the 1940s and 1950s by adding such new elements as vicarious reinforcement (hence the label *social learning theory*). One of the central tenets of social learning theory is that enactment of behavior depends on environmental contingencies. An important deduction that Mischel made from this tenet with regard to sex-typed behavior is that boys/men and girls/women will not behave the same way across all situations because not all situations have the same rewards and punishments for sex-typed action. Thus, sex-typed behavior should not be as consistent and homogeneous as previous accounts (via biological sex differences, psychological masculinity/femininity, or sex-role identification) implied. (This notion of variability/inconsistency/nonhomogeneity of gender-related behavior resurfaces in the 1980s, especially in the writing of Spence, 1984; 1985; and Deaux & Major, 1987).

The second "grand new theory" was articulated by Kohlberg (1966), who introduced a cognitive developmental account of gender-linked experience and action. As we are now well into the "cognitive era" in psychology, the idea that cognition is at the center of the relationship between the individual and gender does not seem "new." In the mid-1960s, however, the emphasis was still on behavior (not thought), and the reinforcement principles of learning theory were the preferred explanations for behavior. Nonetheless, Kohlberg argued "that children's gender concepts are constructed, not directly taught" (Maccoby, 1990b, p. 5). Basically, Kohlberg proposed that (a) children acquire their beliefs about maleness and femaleness by observing men and women and especially gender differences in physical size and strength; (b) children at about the age of six develop gender constancy (the understanding that their biological sex is fixed and can't change); (c) this gender self-schema motivates the child to learn about the traits, interests, and the like of same-sex others and to seek out and imitate same-sex models; (d) this active search for information about "people in the same sex category as me" causes gender-related patterns of thought, feeling, and behavior. Indeed, for Kohlberg, imitating same-sex models is an effect of the child's self-categorization, whereas for Mischel imitation was a cause of sex typing. Although some of the details of Kohlberg's account have been revised (e.g., gender constancy does not appear to be a single achievement but a series of cognitive steps), his basic insight that self-categorization is central to understanding gender-related experience and action is alive and well today (e.g., see Bem's, 1981, notion of gender schema discussed later in this chapter).

ANDROGYNY AS A SEX-ROLE IDEAL (1974–1982)

In 1974, Bem introduced a new M/F measure, one that did not assume that masculinity and femininity are psychological opposites. Instead, the Bem Sex-Role Inventory (BSRI) contained separate masculinity and femininity scales. In addition, Bem introduced a new construct, *androgyny,* which she viewed as the blending of masculinity and femininity within the person. She also proposed that contrary to earlier thinking that masculinity is psychologically healthy in males, and femininity essential for adjustment in females, androgyny is positive for both sexes. Hence, we term this period as *androgyny as a sex-role*

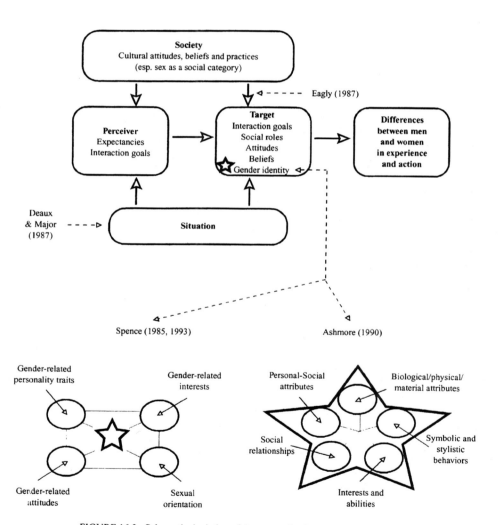

FIGURE 16.3. Schematic depiction of the approach of sex as a social category.

ideal. Bem's Sex-Role Inventory was followed by similar self-report questionnaires (which we label as *M/F/A measures*), and scores on these instruments were related to a wide variety of other variables (Cook, 1985). We will return to this topic later.

SEX AS A SOCIAL CATEGORY (1982–PRESENT)

Sherif (1982) ushered in the next period in the psychological analysis of sex and gender when she proposed that to understand gender-related experience and action, we must start by recognizing that sex is not just a biological fact, but that all societies treat sex as a major social category distinction. That is, all societies categorize people as males and females, and this social categorization is regarded as important (e.g., imagine the consternation of doctors and parents when the "Is it a boy or girl?" question is not easily answered). Furthermore, the social categories *female* and *male* are accompanied by societal-level differences in power and prestige (e.g., in the United States, men occupy more positions of political authority than do women) and a set of institutional practices that serve to maintain this gender status quo. These societal and institutional correlates of sex as a social category are also accompanied by an interrelated set of social psychological variables. These variables include role prescriptions (e.g., "women should make themselves attractive to men"), stereotypes (e.g., "men are more aggressive than women"), and attitudes (e.g., "I am strongly opposed to the Equal Rights Amendment"). In addition, sex as a social category, and the set of societal, institutional, and social psychological factors that accompany this social categorization, means that the individual must somehow take these factors into consideration when she or he constructs a self-concept or personal identity. The influence of societal factors, including sex as major social category, on the individual and sex/gender-related thought and action is schematically depicted in Figure 16.3. The sex as a social category approach has spawned a variety of specific models of sex/gender and the individual, and these will be described in more detail in the sections following.

MAJOR CONTEMPORARY PARADIGMS FOR THE STUDY OF GENDER AND THE INDIVIDUAL

There are three primary contemporary approaches to understanding the issue of sex/gender and the individual: Sex/gender differences, gender as a personality variable, and sex as a social category.

SEX/GENDER DIFFERENCES

As the preceding history indicates, sex/gender differences[2] is the oldest paradigm for understanding sex and gender. This framework has had ups and downs over the past 60 years, but it continues to be one of the major approaches to sex/gender and the individual.

---

[2]We use the terms *sex differences, sex/gender differences, sex-related differences,* and *sex-correlated differences,* as well as the parallel *similarities* constructions, interchangeably to refer to data comparing males with females (see Eagly, 1995, footnote 1). This terminology is not intended to suggest that such differences and similarities are primarily the result of genetic/biological or social/cultural factors.

Thus, we now provide a bit more detail on this topic. We begin by filling in some of the history we neglected earlier. When work on sex differences in general intelligence went into disfavor in the mid-1930s, sex/gender differences research did not stop altogether. Instead, it switched to assessments of male-female differences in more specific mental abilities (e.g., mathematics, verbal intelligence) and other topics (e.g., interests). A steady stream of such work appeared for the next three-plus decades, though it was not center stage. Then, in the late 1960s and early 1970s, sex-related differences work was sharply criticized by many observers, especially feminist psychologists, who argued that such work overestimated male-female differences and, in so doing, helped perpetuate existing sex-role arrangements. The monumental survey of the sex-correlated differences literature by Maccoby and Jacklin (1974) provided support for those who "minimized" sex differences. Maccoby and Jacklin concluded that (a) there are few empirically established sex differences; (b) the size of sex differences are quite small; and (c) male-female differences are often qualified by statistical interactions with other variables (e.g., age). The Maccoby and Jacklin (1974) volume was highly influential and widely cited.

Even though Maccoby and Jacklin (1974) became the established wisdom for most sex/gender workers, the sex/gender differences issue took another turn in the 1980s, as some suggested that there are, in fact, substantial differences between the sexes. This new "maximize" position had two very different facets. (The pros and cons of the minimize and maximize viewpoints are cogently presented in Hare-Mustin & Maracek, 1988.) On one side, some psychologists suggested that, if we "listen to women," we will find that they take very different stances from men with regard to relationships, morality, and knowing. On the other side, a new tool, meta-analysis, came to be used to quantitatively summarize existing sex-differences literatures, and often the conclusion was that sex-correlated differences are non-negligible.

The best known of the "listen to women" authors is Gilligan (1982, 1986). She argued that for too long men had served as the standard against which to measure women; she proposed, instead, to study women in their own right. She did just this and conducted a study using as participants women only. Gilligan (1982) interviewed 29 women, between the ages of 15 and 33, who were in the first trimester of a pregnancy and were considering having an abortion. Gilligan picked the topic of abortion because it represents a very important personal moral decision over which the woman has control. In individual open-ended interviews, participants "were asked to discuss the decision they faced, how they were dealing with it," (p. 72) and related topics. Careful listening to the responses led Gilligan to conclude that women view moral issues from a perspective of "a problem of care and responsibility in relationships" (p. 73) and not from one emphasizing abstract rights, which previous work with males had suggested was the highest level of moral thinking. From the abortion study and other work, Gilligan concluded that men are motivated to separate self from others, while women are motivated to maintain connectedness with others. According to Gilligan, it is this basic difference in self-conception and interpersonal orientation that leads the sexes to different ways of making moral decisions—men concentrating on rules and women focusing on the interpersonal implications of moral choices. Gilligan's work has drawn praise and criticism (e.g., Kerber et al., 1986; Mednick, 1989). A major criticism is that it is not possible to draw sex/gender differences conclusions from single-sex studies.

The other facet of the 1980s approach that emphasized sex-related differences is grounded in meta-analysis. Meta-analysis is a technique for quantitatively combining results of multiple studies to arrive at an overall index of a particular effect. Maccoby and Jacklin (1974) used the narrative approach to summarizing the various sex-differences literatures in their book. They basically identified the relevant studies on a particular topic (e.g., aggression, verbal ability) and counted how many showed significant sex-correlated differences and how many did not. Their "box score" method has several shortcomings, including ignoring sample size and being too conservative. For example, 10 studies showing $p = .06$ would all be counted as "no difference," but combining these 10 studies would reveal that the likelihood of no difference overall would be quite low. Meta-analysis overcomes these difficulties by focusing on the effect size of, for example, the difference between males and females on the dependent variable of interest. The effect size is the mean difference in relation to the pooled within-sex standard deviations. The sex difference of each study, then, is expressed in standard units and, thus, can be combined across studies. This method yields a measure of the size of the overall male-female difference.

The method of meta-analysis and how it can yield different conclusions from a narrative review are illustrated by Eagly and Crowley's (1986) quantitative summary of studies of sex differences in helping behavior. Maccoby and Jacklin (1974, pp. 221–226, Table 6.9) did a box score count of helping studies and concluded that "a person's helpfulness is not consistently related to his sex" (p. 223). Eagly and Crowley (1986), on the other hand, identified 172 studies that included comparisons of helping behavior by males versus females and used meta-analytic procedures to combine these. The mean sex of subject effect size was .34, with men helping more often than women. This effect size was statistically significant and fell into the range often termed *moderate* in size. Eagly and Crowley, however, went well beyond this demonstration that on average men help more than women. In a series of ingenious analyses guided by a social role theory (which is discussed in depth later), they showed, among other things, that most studies of helping behavior involve short-term encounters between strangers, which is precisely the type of helping promoted by the male role ("heroic and chivalrous"; p. 283); there are few studies of the types of helping that follow from the female role (e.g., nurturance in long-term relationships). Thus, the conclusion that males help more than females must be qualified by noting that only male-like forms of helping have been studied from the sex-differences perspective.

Meta-analysis is clearly a powerful and welcome tool. At the same time, like all methodological tools, it must be used with care by the analyst and properly understood by the reader of meta-analytic studies. The issues involved are covered in detail by others (Ashmore, 1990; Eagly, 1987, 1995; Hyde & Plant, 1995), and we will not repeat them here. We will, however, discuss four questions that Eagly (1995) correctly identified as central to the debate about what meta-analysis reveals about sex-related differences. The first is, "Are sex differences small?" (p. 150). But, what is small? There is no one rule for evaluating the magnitude of effect sizes revealed by meta-analysis. Eagly (1987, 1995) had suggested several yardsticks and provided a very balanced and useful guide for the consumer of meta-analyses. Eagly's (1995) conclusion on the size issue was that sex-correlated differences vary considerably, from very small to quite large. She is quite critical of some reviewers, including textbook writers, for asserting that most sex/gender differences are small in size and negligible in personal or societal importance. Hyde and Plant (1995) acknowledged that sex/gender differences show a wide range, but they concluded that "more psychological gender differences (25%) fall in the close-to-zero range than do other effects in psychology" (p. 159). Our view is that, at present, it is impossible to answer the question, "Are sex differences small?" There is clearly a wide range in such differences. We also agree with Eagly (1995) that some sex/gender differences are quite large. Our suggestion is that the size question is best rephrased as, "In what areas are sex-correlated differences relatively large or relatively small in magnitude?" Ashmore (1990) noted that many large gender differences are for biological/physical variables, especially those that involve physical strength. There are also many large effect sizes for symbolic or stylistic behavior, especially nonverbal immediacy (e.g., women exhibit more social smiling).

Eagly's (1995) second question is, "Are sex differences especially inconsistent across studies?" (p. 152). She acknowledged that male-female differences interact with other variables and are context dependent. She differed from others who suggested that such interactions mean that sex differences are unimportant, noting that the context dependencies of sex differences are not random and that interactions are the rule in all of psychology. Eagly argued that sex-differences interactions are about as common as other effects that psychologists regard as well established. We cannot evaluate this claim, but concerning all aspects of human social behavior, we agree that statistical interactions are the rule and not the exception. In fact, Anastasi (1972) listed statistical interaction as an "orienting concept," noting that all psychologists accept that interactions are common, and that it would be a mistake to seek to build a psychology of simple unqualified main effects.

"Are sex-differences findings artifactual?" (p. 153). In addressing this question, Eagly (1995) reviewed several arguments against sex differences that suggest that obtained male-female differences are not genuine but rather the result of some problem with the research. Probably the most widely noted of such artifacts is the possible publication bias in favor of significant differences. And if this is so, there will be fewer "no-differences" results available for meta-analysts to consider in their reviews. Although this bias may be a problem in some areas, Eagly is correct to note that sex differences are often peripheral to the interests of the researcher, and that in such cases publication does not depend on whether sex/gender differences are or are not significant. Concerning other possible artifacts, Eagly notes that meta-analysts can and routinely do code studies for data quality. It does not appear that the non-negligible sex-related differences documented by meta-analysis can be explained away as artifactual.

Eagly's (1995) final question is, "Do sex-difference findings disconfirm gender stereotypes?" (p. 153). Some have claimed that documented sex/gender differences contradict sex stereotypes (e.g., Unger & Crawford, 1992). Eagly, however, argued that the accumulated sex-differences findings paint a different picture, "thematic analysis of demonstrated sex differences in social behavior suggests that they conform to stereotypic expectations that women are communal and men are agentic (see Eagly, 1987, 1993; Eagly & Wood, 1991)" (p. 154). Furthermore, Eagly noted that Swim (1994) directly compared perceivers' estimates of female-male differences in several domains with effect sizes from available meta-analyses of actual sex differences in these domains and found a relatively high match between perceived or stereotypic and actual sex-correlated differences. Although we agree with Eagly that the accumulated data are more indicative of agreement than disagreement between stereotypes and actual sex differences, we caution that assessing the accuracy of stereotypes, whether about sex or other social categories, is not a simple task that yields a definitive accurate or not-accurate judgment (cf. Ashmore & Longo, 1995). We cite just one "complicating factor"—perceivers not only have stereotypes about the superordinate social categories of female and male, but also stereotypes about types of men (e.g., hunk) and types of women (e.g., housewife); sometimes these subtype stereo-types are not consistent with the stereotype of the overarching category (e.g., cultural stereotype of the career-woman type and shared beliefs about women, in general).

We add a fifth question, What do non-negligible sex differences mean? Stated somewhat differently, what can one conclude about sex/gender and the individual if one documents a moderate-to-large sex difference or a set of moderate-to-large sex-correlated differences? The answer is that such differences have little meaning in and of themselves. Even if it were demonstrated that there are a large number of non-negligible sex/gender differences, such a demonstration would not provide an answer to the question we began this chapter with, Why do women and men think, feel, and behave as they do? Quite simply, gender differences do not directly address the *why* of sex/gender and the individual. Even for a sex difference with a large effect size (e.g., social smiling), it is not clear what this means. It may mean that via an evolutionary mechanism females needed to both appease powerful males and nurture males and females, and as a result, women are genetically inclined to smile more than men (the top path in Figure 16.1, p. 380). Or, it could be that the female sex role specifies that women should be pleasant and interpersonally responsive and, hence, they should and do smile rela-tively more often than men (the bottom path in Figure 16.1, p. 380). Or, the greater social smiling by females could result from some combination of these biological/genetic and so-cial/cultural causes (the "and" indicated at the left side of Figure 16.1, p. 380, between the top and bottom paths). Thus, our general conclusion is that the sex-differences approach is not a high priority for the researcher interested in sex/gender and the individual. It can document differences but does nothing to explicate these. We temper this negative conclusion by noting that the sex-differences position can, in the hands of a skilled social scientist, be a powerful tool. For example, Eagly (1987, 1995) has successfully used this paradigm to test multiple facets of her social role model of sex-related behavior, which we discuss later.

Gender as a Personality Variable

In the second major contemporary approach to sex and gender at the individual level, gender is conceptualized as a personality variable, and the focus is on the constructs of mas-culinity and femininity. The underlying premise of this approach is that these constructs summarize one's psychological maleness and femaleness. This section traces the recent de-velopment of this approach. First, the androgyny era (1974–1982) and the contributions of that era's leaders, Sandra Bem and Janet Spence, are described. Then, we describe the di-vergent paths that Bem and Spence have taken since the early 1980s. Bem shifted her at-tention to the construct of *gender schema,* a culturally imposed cognitive structure that predisposes individuals to process information in gender-related terms. Spence, on the other hand, began to espouse the notion that gender at the individual level is best conceived of as a psychological multiplicity rather than as one or a few relatively global constructs. We conclude this section with an evaluation of research efforts based on the conceptualiza-tion of gender as a personality variable.

The Androgyny Era (1974–1982)

The Terman and Miles approach dominated the study of masculinity/femininity until the 1970s, when it was finally abandoned by most gender researchers. First, the assump-tions of the approach were criticized (Constantinople, 1973); a careful review of empirical evidence casts doubt on the assumptions that psychological femininity and masculinity are opposites, and that masculinity and femininity are homogeneous global categories. Shortly afterward, a new view of masculinity and femininity emerged, along with two easy-to-use self-report devices with which to measure these constructs (Bem, 1974; Spence, Helmreich, & Stapp, 1974, 1975). Masculinity and femininity were reconceptualized as independent and not opposite variables, and a new concept, *androgyny*, which referred to some combination of masculinity and femininity, was introduced. This led to the development of similar paper-and-pencil questionnaires by others, and the generation of a large amount of research which linked the reconceptualized masculinity and femininity, as well as the new construct of androgyny, to a variety of other variables (Cook, 1985).

The two major figures during the androgyny era were Janet Spence and Sandra Bem. They shared the following four basic assumptions:

1. Femininity and masculinity can be assessed via self-reports concerning personality traits. Bem developed the Bem Sex-Role Inventory (BSRI) (which continues to be the most widely used measure of gendered personality, Beere, 1990) for this purpose, and Spence and her colleagues constructed the Personal Attributes Questionnaire (PAQ).[3]
2. Masculinity and femininity are not opposite ends of a single psychological continuum but are separate and independent. Thus, the BSRI and PAQ each had separate M and F scales instead of a single M-F scale.
3. Femininity and masculinity are best conceptualized from the outside in (from gender at the societal level to the individual). The Terman and Miles framework, in contrast, implicitly defines masculinity and femininity from the inside out (sex from within the person). Operationally, Terman and Miles defined masculinity and femininity in empirical terms. Thus, M refers to what biological males report thinking, doing, or feeling to a greater extent than biological females, and F was defined in a parallel fashion. During the androgyny era, Bem, Spence, and others defined these constructs in terms of societal ideals and expectations (the bottom path in Figure 16.2, p. 381).
4. In terms of psychological health, it is preferable for individuals not to possess exclusively either masculine or feminine qualities. Prior to the androgyny era, the majority of researchers held the belief that masculine males and feminine females were the most well-adjusted individuals (the congruence model).

Although they agreed on these major points, the work of Bem and Spence and her colleagues rested upon different conceptual and empirical foundations. Motivated by the desire to bring about social reform as well as scientific advancement, Bem proposed the concept of *psychological androgyny* (as did others at about the same time, both in psychology, e.g., Block, 1973, and outside, e.g., Heilbrun, 1973) as a new cultural ideal. She viewed traditional sex roles as restrictive and believed that androgynous individuals, whose personalities represent a balance of masculinity and femininity, are better able to adapt to situational demands and are, presumably, better adjusted psychologically.

While Bem (1974) created a new scale in order to measure androgyny and its building blocks, Spence's work on the topic of masculinity and femininity grew out of a desire to

---

[3]Spence's (1993) most recent position is that it is more appropriate to describe the BSRI and PAQ as measures of desirable instrumental and expressive traits. She views masculinity and femininity as broad concepts that cannot be adequately represented by a collection of personality traits.

construct methodologically sound and standardized instruments, such as the Attitudes Toward Women Scale (AWS; Spence & Helmreich, 1972), in order to examine a variety of
gender concepts. Unlike Bem, Spence and her coworkers regarded the androgyny construct
as a tool for description and data analysis rather than as a distinct and ideal personality type.
Also, Spence and Helmreich (see especially 1978, 1979) viewed masculinity, femininity,
and androgyny as capturing only the personality trait aspect of gender at the individual level
(see footnote 3). Thus, the PAQ, their measuring device for these constructs, was just one
instrument among several that they developed to measure various gender-related variables.

Androgyny research flourished in the late 1970s and continued into the 1980s and
1990s. Unfortunately, the body of work generated is laden with inconsistent findings and
failures to replicate, and it seems that this research may have generated more questions than
it answered. Nevertheless, drawing from a major review by Cook (1985), we briefly summarize and evaluate the research that addresses three basic questions.

1. *What exactly is androgyny?* Although many conceptual definitions of *androgyny*
have been offered, the vast majority of empirical studies on the subject are based on the formulations of Bem and of Spence and her colleagues. According to Bem's (1974) original
usage of the term, an androgynous person is one who endorses approximately the same proportion, or number, of male and female qualities as self-relevant (the "balance" notion). In
1975, however, Spence and her colleagues demonstrated that individuals with low M scores
and low F scores scored low on self-esteem, which challenged the assumption of androgyny
as psychologically healthy. Consequently, androgyny was operationally redefined, and only
individuals with high M and high F scores were classified as androgynous. Bem accepted
this "additive model" of androgyny, which was preferred by Spence and her colleagues
from the start (Bem, 1977; 1979).

Androgynous individuals were identified empirically by splitting the M and F subscales (of the PAQ, BSRI, and similar "androgyny scales" developed in the 1970s and
1980s [Cook, 1985]) simultaneously and independently at their respective medians. The
procedure partitions all participants in a study into one of four categories: high M-high F
(androgynous), high M-low F (masculine; sex-typed males and cross-sex-typed females),
low M-high F (feminine; sex-typed females and cross-sex-typed males), and low M-low F
(undifferentiated). This classification system soon became utilized widely.

There are some major problems with this operational solution to the assessment of androgyny. One is that researchers have not thoroughly investigated the extent to which the redefined construct of androgyny and the new construct of *undifferentiated* are theoretically
meaningful (cf. Sedney, 1989). Another is that it is a crude categorization system; because
it involves the compression of two continuous variable into four discrete categories, much
data is wasted, and the classification of those who score near the median is unreliable. (See
Cook, 1985, especially pp. 104–105 and 135–136, on these and other criticisms.) It has also
been suggested that the BSRI does not reflect current social conceptions of masculinity and
femininity (Ballard-Reisch & Elton, 1992). Finally, this method of assessing androgyny
makes it difficult to determine whether androgyny is a *special* combination of masculinity
and femininity with unique properties, or merely the sum of its constituents. (We will return
to this last issue later.)

2. *What is the relation between masculinity and femininity?* Terman and Miles assumed
that masculinity and femininity were negatively correlated and built their M-F measuring device accordingly. In contrast, androgyny researchers assume that the constructs are essentially

unrelated. However, correlations between F and M scales from the BSRI, PAQ, and other androgyny measures have been shown to be highly variable, depending on the specific instrument and the composition of the sample (Cook, 1985; see also Marsh and Myers, 1986).

3. *How are masculinity, femininity, and androgyny related to other variables?* If M/F/A measures are valid indices of a global trait, we can expect these instruments to be related to indices of other gender-related qualities and behavior. Assessment of such relations has been and continues to be the focus of numerous studies (the most recent of which include Dimitrovsky, Singer, & Yinon, 1989; Evans, Turner, Ghee, & Getz, 1990; Gunter & Gunter, 1990; Jones, Bloys, & Wood, 1990; Jurma & Powell, 1994; Lombardo & Kemper, 1992; Susser & Keating, 1990; Szymanski, Devlin, Chrisler, & Vyse, 1993). In the past five or six years, for example, there have been many studies that examined the relation between M/F/A measures and behavior in social relationships (e.g. personal perception; marital, parent-child, and peer relations; same- and opposite-sex touching) or gender-related attitudes. Across studies, it seems that the strength of these relationships is highly variable, and in studies in which significant relationships were found, it is almost always the case that androgyny is positively associated with socially desirable qualities and behavior (e.g. greater mental, attitudinal, and behavioral flexibility, likability). For example, it was found that androgynous working adults experience less marital conflict over domestic tasks than others (Gunter & Gunter, 1990), and androgynous adolescents smoke less frequently than others (Evans *et al.*, 1990).

As mentioned earlier, the starting point for Bem's (1974) analysis was the assumption that individuals who possess both male and female qualities are better able to adjust to varying situations (the androgyny model, Whitley, 1984). The most common test of this notion is to assess the extent to which PAQ or BSRI scores covary with self-report measures of self-esteem and mental health. Such studies have shown—and recent studies continue to show—that to a great extent androgyny does covary with high self-esteem and psychological well-being. However, the conclusion that androgyny per se is uniquely associated with these variables has been repeatedly challenged. Androgyny as assessed via the PAQ or BSRI means endorsing a high number of positive masculine and positive feminine traits as self-descriptive; this is very similar to the way in which high self-esteem is defined and measured. Thus, as others have suggested (e.g., Brown, 1986; Carson, 1989), it is possible that the correlation between androgyny and self-esteem is due to shared method variance.

In addition, there is evidence that androgyny does not have special properties that contribute to self-esteem and psychological health beyond those of its constituent constructs. It has been demonstrated that while M and F scores independently contribute to reported self-esteem and psychological health, with often a negligible contribution from F, the combined—or interaction—effect of M and F is minimal (cf. Bassoff & Glass, 1982; Cook, 1985; Taylor & Hall, 1982; Whitley, 1983, 1984). In light of such findings, the masculinity model (Whitley, 1984) became the dominant position in the 1980s; according to this model, masculinity alone is positively associated with mental health. Consistent with this model, a few recent studies have shown that depression is negatively related to masculinity and unrelated to femininity (e.g., Bromberger & Matthews, 1996; Whitley & Gridley, 1993), and that self-esteem, although a separate construct, is highly correlated with both masculinity and depression (Whitley & Gridley, 1993).

However, other recent studies have questioned the masculinity model (Aube, Norcliffe, Craig, & Koestner, 1995; Forshaw & Shmukler, 1993). While it is acknowledged that, empirically speaking, this model appears to be more plausible than its predecessors—the androgyny model and the congruence model—it is argued that the relationship between gender-related traits and psychological adjustment is more complex than the model implies. The extent to which masculinity is ideal depends on, for instance, the specific dependent variable and social context in question. For example, as indicated in a recent review (Helgeson, 1994), it has been demonstrated that masculinity (instrumentality/agency) is positively related to well-being in terms of reduced psychological distress, whereas researchers have found either no relationship or a positive but small relationship between femininity (expressiveness/communion) and this aspect of well-being. On the other hand, femininity, to a much greater extent than masculinity, is positively related to aspects of well-being involving interpersonal relations, such as social support and help-seeking behavior. Furthermore, there is evidence that *extreme* masculinity and *extreme* femininity have negative consequences for well-being. Extreme masculinity has been shown to be positively related to poor physical health, and, although less clear, it appears that extreme femininity is positively related to psychological distress.

The "What exactly is androgyny?" question has been addressed in a very creative way by Shaver *et al.* (1996). Shaver and his colleagues investigated how the gender traits of masculinity, femininity, and androgyny are related to the three styles of attachment in romantic relationships hypothesized by Hazan and Shaver (1987): avoidant (distrustful, uncomfortable with psychological intimacy), anxious-ambivalent (insecure, eager for intimacy but afraid of rejection/abandonment), and secure (confident, comfortable with intimacy). Of particular interest was the relationship between the two personality ideals: androgyny and attachment security. It was found that there were significant relationships between the two sets of constructs: Masculine and undifferentiated subjects scored higher than others on the avoidant rating scale; feminine subjects scored higher than others on the anxious-ambivalent rating scale; and androgynous participants scored higher than others on the secure rating scale. However, the gender constructs were found to be significantly related to sex of respondent, whereas the attachment styles were unrelated to sex. The authors suggest that the gender constructs, as opposed to the attachment styles, are based on traditional sex roles, which accounts for their relationship to sex of participant. This analysis reveals an important irony surrounding androgyny—it was intended to connote flexible behavior unconstrained by gender prescriptions, and yet the concept itself is based on traditional gender roles. Shaver and his colleagues, therefore, argued that attachment security may provide a better approximation of the ideal personality than androgyny because the former is not tied to sex roles and the associated personality attributes, such as dominance (part of the male role) and emotional vulnerability (part of the female role), that do not contribute to harmonious interpersonal relationships and self-fulfillment.

Broad (Bem) and Narrow (Spence) Perspectives on Femininity and Masculinity (1982–Present)

Androgyny research continued in the 1980s, but the work of the two leaders of the androgyny era moved off in other directions. Bem (1981, 1985) viewed gender as a global, ubiquitous cultural construct, focused on how the male-female distinction is used to structure virtually all aspects of our social environment, and emphasized the detrimental effects of this practice. Spence (1985), on the other hand, began to espouse a multidimensional views of gender phenomena.

In 1981, a new psychological concept, *gender schema,* was proposed by Bem. According to her, as children receive cultural messages about what maleness and femaleness entail in their society, they develop gender schemas, which are networks of sex-related associations. They then use the gender schemas to process and organize information, including information about themselves. Thus, sex-typed individuals are highly gender-schematic individuals whose self-concepts have become assimilated into a gender schema. For example, a sex-typed male would be more likely than other males to describe himself with respect to such dimensions as physical strength or leadership skills rather than in terms of compassion and cooking skills, and more likely to gravitate toward "masculine" domains (e.g., cars, computers, beer, action/adventure movies) and avoid "feminine" domains (e.g., child-care, aerobic dance, "chick flicks"). Bem has demonstrated that such individuals are more likely than non-sex-typed individuals (androgynous and undifferentiated) to process other information in terms of the gender schema as well. For example, she has shown that sex-typed individuals are more likely than other individuals to mentally organize randomly presented words on the basis of gender (Bem, 1981).

Bem's gender-schema theory has been quite influential. Numerous studies that use her conceptual and empirical definitions of gender schematicity to compare schematic and aschematic individuals with respect to some dependent measure, usually some aspect of information processing, have since been conducted. However, not all gender-schema research is based on Bem's theory. There are two other approaches to gender schematicity that have received attention in the literature. Markus and her colleagues (Markus, Crane, Bernstein, & Siladi, 1982) view gender schemas as one type of self-schema, which they define as a "knowledge structure developed to understand, integrate, or explain one's behavior in a particular domain" (p. 38). Thus, masculine schematics have salient, highly articulated knowledge structures relevant to masculinity that are used to organize information. Such individuals are expected to process information differently than feminine schematics, high-androgynous individuals (those who have masculine and feminine schemas in their self-concept), and low-androgynous, or aschematic, individuals. This approach differs from Bem's conceptualization of gender schematicity. According to Bem, schematicity refers to a readiness to organize information on the basis of gender (including male-linked and female-linked stimuli, and not each separately as in Markus's formulation), and, therefore, the relevant distinction is between sex-typed individuals (masculine males *and* feminine females) and others. A third approach to gender schemas, which represents a sizable portion of the current literature, is the developmental approach (e.g., Carter, 1987; Martin & Halverson, 1981; see Signorella, Bigler, & Liben, 1993; for a meta-analytic review). Developmental studies have attempted to demonstrate the existence of gender schemas in children, and how and to what extent they change over time; there is more emphasis on the content of gender schemas in these studies than in research based on Bem's or Markus's approaches, which focus on the cognitive consequences of schemas.

Unfortunately, not much progress has been made with respect to the conceptual and empirical development of the constructs involved in Bem's gender-schema theory. One undeveloped aspect of the theory, for example, is the status of cross-sex-typed individuals. Conceptually, these individuals have not received much attention; empirically, their behavior has been shown to be quite unpredictable (Cook, 1985). Another undeveloped aspect is the "undifferentiated" category of individuals. Conceptually, it has not been made clear whether all of these individuals have rejected the attributes associated with both sexes, or whether people are placed in this category for different reasons (cf. Sedney, 1989).

Bem has shifted her attention away from such empirical and conceptual issues, choosing instead to focus on the transmission of gender-related messages from society to the individual. More specifically, Bem has proposed a new theory—the enculturated-lens theory of individual gender formation—as an extension and elaboration of gender-schema theory (Bem, 1993). The theory elaborates on the two (often inseparable) processes by which an individual learns and accepts the gender-related norms and beliefs of his/her culture: the structuring of the individual's daily experiences based on these norms and beliefs (e.g., boys are given trucks and girls are given dolls), and the transmission of implicit "metamessages" about how social reality is organized in his/her culture (e.g., being a "tomboy" is acceptable, but being a "sissy" is not). Bem's latest work is noteworthy in that it examines the antecedents of the gender schema rather than treating the schema as a "given." Also, as did some of her earlier work (e.g., Bem, 1985), it makes explicit the bold propositions that gender diversity is completely natural, and that the "cultural requirement that the sex of the body match the gender of the psyche" (p. 4) is not, and should be resisted. However, the theory needs further development in regard to those who *do* resist. While it is made clear that many "gender nonconformists" do exist, the theory does not address the issue of why these individuals were not influenced by the enculturation process.

As Bem was focusing her attention on the cognitive aspect of gender in the 1980s, treating cultural gender-related notions as homogenous and unidimensional, Spence turned her attention to the idea of gender as a multiplicity of elements. Spence's (1985) theory of gender identity proposed that children develop a gender identity, narrowly defined as a fundamental sense of maleness or femaleness, early in life. Then, as they grow older and develop interests, acquire certain traits, and experience many different definitions of maleness and femaleness, they develop a personal sense of masculinity and femininity. Spence argues that gender phenomena are multifactorial, and that gender-related personality traits are just one of the many facets of gender.

We will conclude this section with a critical analysis of gender as a personality variable and the use of this perspective as a general strategy for seeking to understand sex, gender, and the individual (and return to Spence's approach to gender in the next section).

Evaluation of Gender as a Personality Variable

As noted, there are methodological issues that cloud viewing gender as a personality variable (cf. Beere, 1979, 1990; Cooke, 1985, especially pp. 143–150; Huston, 1983, especially p. 395). We do not believe, however, that what is needed is simply better research. Instead, we believe that to date a major shortcoming of this paradigm is that much of the past work tended to be method driven. To a large extent, the BSRI and PAQ have defined the concepts that they were created to measure rather than the other way around. The remainder of this section provides a brief critical analysis of basic conceptual issues underlying this approach.

As Morawski (1985) has argued, the major problem of this research area is the underlying assumption that masculinity and femininity are stable, internal qualities with distinct and separate identities. This assumption seems to account for a related implicit assumption of the androgyny era that masculinity, femininity, and androgyny can be fully represented by a collection of gender-related personality traits. These assumptions need to be reexamined in light of the recent evidence that sex and gender can be incorporated into one's self in multiple ways that are not highly interconnected (see Cook, 1985; Huston, 1983; Spence, 1985).

Prior to and during the androgyny era, the concepts of sex and gender tended to be oversimplified in research. Researchers in the androgyny era moved beyond the conceptualization of femininity and masculinity as opposite ends of a single continuum, which was a major step forward, but gender researchers are still attempting to use a few simple constructs to capture a complex phenomenon. In many cases, the causes of individual-level gender phenomena are also oversimplified; the individual is often assumed to be under the complete control of simple and homogeneous genetics, biology, or societal expectations.

Another criticism of approaching gender as a personality variable pertains to a lack of clarity surrounding the process by which gender is incorporated into self. The relations of causes to content (i.e., the relationship between cultural/environmental influences and individual-level gender constructs) and content to consequences (i.e., the relationship between gender constructs and behavior) have not been clearly described or established.

In addition, presumably because masculinity, femininity, androgyny, and gender schema were assumed to be stable individual qualities, much of the research generated before and during the androgyny era failed to consider social and life-stage context. Recently, however, this has begun to change. Researchers are starting to examine how such variables as situation and life stage influence the ability of these constructs to predict behavior and the desirability of the associated traits (e.g., Carlson & Videka-Sherman, 1990; Green & Kenrick, 1994; Hyde, Krajnik, & Skuldt-Niederberger, 1991; Rewal & Kapur, 1991; Rosenzweig & Daily, 1991; Steenbarger & Greenberg, 1990). Regarding interpersonal context, it has been shown, for example, that males' masculinity and femininity scores (based on the BSRI) differ significantly when they are imagining themselves giving gifts to same- versus opposite-sex friends (Gould & Weil, 1991). Also, although androgynous individuals were found to be the most desirable romantic partners, it appeared that femininity (expressiveness) was relatively important in all types of relationships (especially for males), and masculinity (instrumentality) was more highly valued in the context of marriage than with respect to a date or a one-night stand (Green & Kenrick, 1994). Regarding life stage, it has been shown that girls and boys become more masculine and more feminine from the sixth to eighth grades, but sex differences in masculinity are more pronounced in the eighth grade than they are in the sixth, whereas sex differences in femininity are stable across grades (Galambos, Almeida, & Peterson, 1990).

To summarize, the approach of gender as a personality variable has made a valuable contribution to the study of sex and gender by enabling researchers to abandon biological sex as the primary independent variable in sex-differences research. This change in perspective also brought about the realization that gender is a more complex concept than was previously assumed, thus serving as a catalyst for alternative approaches to the study of gender, such as societal-level and/or multiplicity approaches. However, as discussed earlier, the perspective of gender as a personality variable oversimplifies sex, gender, and the individual by focusing on a small set of narrowly defined constructs with the assumption that there is a simple and direct relationship between these constructs and a small set of antecedent variables (causes) and a large and diverse set of outcome variables (consequences) (cf. Ashmore, 1990).

SEX AS A SOCIAL CATEGORY

The basic idea underlying the sex as a social category paradigm was described thus: Gender-related thought and behavior are not rooted in biological sex differences or a general personality disposition, but in society's categorization of people as males or females and the many cultural, organizational, and interpersonal systems associated with this social categorization. Sex/gender and the individual, thus, is to be understood in terms of the person in a social context.

Four specific models of sex as a social category have been proposed. In terms of increasing emphasis on social context they are (a) Spence's (1985, 1993) multifactorial gender identity theory; (b) Ashmore's (1990) multiplicity model of gender identity; (c) Deaux and Major's (1987) interactive model of gender-related behavior; (d) Eagly's (1987) social role model of sex differences.

The Spence (1985, 1993) and Ashmore (1990) models feature gender identity, but with very different meanings attached to the concept. Both frameworks assume that gender-related phenomena are complex (multifaceted), differentially defined, and organized from one person to the next (in contrast to the gender-as-a-personality-variable approaches, which regard gendered traits as culturally defined, homogeneous, and small in number).

Spence's Multifactorial Gender Identity Theory

Spence (1985, 1993) begins with the child's very personal sense of her/his femaleness or maleness (which she terms *gender identity*). Although she acknowledged a considerable variety of inputs and different developmental histories (and, hence, many different structures of gender-associated qualities for individual men and women), Spence suggested that people are motivated to protect their sense of maleness/femaleness, and that they do so, in part, by adopting attitudes, traits, interests, and the like that personally define their masculinity/femininity. The psychological glue in this multiplicity model, then, is one's sense of gender identity as captured, though far from perfectly, in self-perceptions of being masculine/feminine (see bottom left of Figure 16.3, p. 383). Because Spence features masculinity and femininity, this model is, in some ways, a step back to M/F of the 1930s. At the same time, however, Spence's is a very new and potentially important framework. Spence does not assume that masculinity and femininity are simple, homogeneous, and opposed constructs. To the contrary, she is explicit that American society offers many diverse definitions of maleness and femaleness, and that the individual constructs a personal sense of his/her masculinity and femininity in diverse contexts. That is, each person constructs her/his own "constellation of gender-congruent qualities" (Spence, 1993, p. 625) from a wide set of influences, and there are many such different, multifaceted structures.

Because Spence's is a relatively recent model, there has not been a great deal of work directly testing her ideas. Spence (1993) asked a sample of college students to complete the Bem Sex-Role Inventory (BSRI) and measures of sex-role attitudes (Attitude Toward Women Scale—AWS) and sex-role behaviors and interpersonal preferences (Male-Female Relations Questionnaire—MFRQ). As predicted by the model's core assumption that gender-related phenomena are multifactorial, the expressiveness ("femininity") and instrumentality ("masculinity") scores calculated from the BSRI did not correlate significantly with scores on the AWS and MFRQ (i.e., gendered personality did not covary with gender attitudes or gender-associated interpersonal behaviors and references). At the same time, two items on the BSRI—masculine and feminine as markers of gender identity—did show significant covariation with the measures of other gender phenomena. For example, on the AWS, for males, self-ratings on masculine were positively related to traditional gender attitudes, whereas self-ratings on feminine were negatively correlated with traditional attitudes. Just the reverse was true for females. Thus, there is evidence that masculine and feminine self-ratings, which Spence regards as imperfect yet acceptable markers of gender identity, do serve to bind together an individual's multifaceted and individually constructed gendered self. Koestner and Aube (1995) reported three studies that provided additional support for Spence's theory. Their first study showed that in a sample of 118 thirty-one-year-olds, gender-related leisure interests, occupational choices, child-rearing values, and personality traits were only moderately correlated; that each of these adult gender qualities were associated with different patterns of childhood experiences (which had been assessed when the participants were five years old). This study, then, further documented the multifactorial nature of gender phenomena and also supported Spence's contention that different gender-related qualities have different developmental histories. We look forward to learning the results of other tests of Spence's model and seeing the development of more precise measures of the central construct, gender identity.

Ashmore's (1990) Multiplicity Model of Gender Identity

Ashmore and his colleagues did not begin with masculinity and femininity, but with a general intergroup relations perspective on sex and gender (Ashmore, 1990; Ashmore & Del Boca, 1986; Ashmore & Ogilvie, 1992). They regard female-male relations as parallel to relations between other societal categories in many important ways (e.g., ethnic groups such as Euro-Americans and African-Americans). This intergroup-relations approach, coupled with a social-psychological level of analysis, identifies three individual-level constructs as central. Gender attitudes are the person's evaluations of a variety of gender-related issues and targets (e.g., Ashmore, Del Boca, & Bilder, 1995). Sex stereotypes are the individual's beliefs about the personal qualities of the social categories female and male (e.g., Ashmore, Del Boca, & Wohlers, 1986). Gender identity is "the structured set of gendered personal identities that result when the individual takes the social construction of gender and biological 'facts' of sex and incorporates these into an overall self-concept" (Ashmore, 1990, p. 512). Like Spence (1985), but contrary to those focusing on biologically based sex differences or gender as a personality trait, Ashmore (1990) assumed that sex and gender do not provide simple and univocal inputs into the individual's thinking about self. Instead, the person's biological sex provides multiple influences on self-perception, and not all of these are consistent with one another. The diversity of cultural messages about maleness and femaleness is even greater. Thus, a person confronts a bewildering variety of inputs to her/his sense of being a female or male. In addition, Ashmore and his collaborators assumed that each individual is a creative processor of biological-sex and cultural-gender messages. The person does not simply swallow whole or spit out what biology and culture provide; instead, these messages can be adapted as the person sees fit. An important implication of diverse inputs and creative processing is that each individual has a relatively unique gender identity.

To bring a bit of order to the complexity that this approach entails, Ashmore (1990), building on Huston (1983), identified five general content areas of gender identity (see bottom right of Figure 16.3): (a) Personal-social attributes, such as traits and roles, are relatively enduring and cross-situationally consistent qualities. These are the most widely studied aspects of gender and the individual. The Bem Sex-Role Inventory, for example, uses self-perceived instrumental and expressive personality traits to index the broad-gendered personality trait gender schema. (b) Biological/physical/material attributes refer to the person's body, what he or she does to it and puts on it, as well as the things that the person values as self-defining. (c) Symbolic and stylistic behaviors are ways of walking and talking and include nonverbal behaviors. (d) Interests and abilities are self-definitions that describe what the person likes to do (e.g., preferred leisure activities) and what he or she is good and not so good at (e.g., self-perceived abilities). (e) Social relationships are the way that individuals answer the question, Who am I?. They refer to important people in their lives and how they experience self when with these people.

As with Spence's model, the Multiplicity Model of Gender Identity is quite new; consequentially, it has only begun to be subjected to empirical test. Ashmore and Ogilvie (1992) explored one domain of gender identity, social relationships. More specifically, they investigated individuals' self-with-other representations of how gender-related qualities were incorporated into these representations. Ogilvie and Ashmore (1991) coined the term, *self-with-other representation,* to refer to the individual's structured set of beliefs about how she or he experiences and enacts self when with the important people in her or his life. To assess this hypothetical construct, a sample of college student respondents was asked to identify the 25 most important people in their lives. Ashmore and Ogilvie then asked each participant to rate self when with each of these targets on a set of words and phrases. Most of the descriptors were of the individual's own choosing, solicited via an open-ended interview. To this "personal vocabulary," however, were added a set of words that all participants were asked to use. These words were selected on the basis of research on sex stereotypes (Williams & Best, 1982) and consisted of four traits each for the following categories: male (instrumental)-positive (e.g., *strong*), and female (expressive)-positive (e.g., *gentle*), male (instrumental)-negative (e.g., *hard-hearted*), and female (expressive)-negative (e.g., *fussy*), plus *masculine* and *feminine.* The self-with-other targets by descriptors matrix, separate for each respondent, were then subjected to hierarchical classes analysis (HICLAS; De Boeck & Rosenberg, 1988), which is a hierarchical clustering algorithm that simultaneously clusters the targets (self-with-others) and descriptors and also links these two clustering trees. (See chap. 15 for a more thorough discussion of this research.)

For the present purpose, the crucial findings concern how the participants made the gender-related descriptors part of their overall self-with-other representation system. As expected, there was considerable variation in where the sex stereotypic descriptors appeared in the HICLAS display for each respondent. There were also predicted differences for sex of participant. For males, masculine was significantly higher on the clustering tree diagram (and, thus, presumably more central to overall self-definition) than was the case for females; just the reverse was true for feminine. The results for the sex-stereotypic traits were not so simple. The respondents tended to disavow the negative instrumental and negative expressive qualities. Thus, neither sex claimed the negative aspects of its group's stereotype as self-descriptive. As for positive stereotypical components, participants of both sexes treated the descriptors in a relatively schematic way (operationally defined as three or all four of the instrumental-positive or expressive-positive items ending up in the same cluster). *Feminine* appeared in the same cluster with the expressive-positive items for 50% of the female respondents; at the same time, 25% of the males group expressive-positive with *masculine.* Thus, for one in four males, masculinity was implicitly defined, in part, by culturally stereotypical female qualities, such as affectionate. For instrumental-positive, over 70% of the males grouped *masculine* with these culturally defined male attributes; over 70% of the females clustered *feminine* with societal stereotypes about men, such as independent. Quite simply, the respondents in this study showed that the incorporation of gender into self-concept is not a simple matter of accepting what is appropriate for one's sex and rejecting what is stereotypic of the other sex. Future work on the Multiplicity Model of Gender Identity will need to address other hypothesized facets of gender identity, investigate how the various components are integrated with one another, and identify the psychological glue that individuals and subgroups of men and women use to organize their gendered self-concepts.

Deaux and Major's Interactive Model of Gender-Related Behavior

Unlike most theoretical models of gender, Deaux and Major's (1987) Interactive Model of Gender-Related Behavior emphasized the *display* rather than the *acquisition* of such behaviors. The self-conceptions and past experiences that people bring to a situation are assumed to be only part of what motivates individuals to behave a certain way in a particular situation. Although acknowledging that factors such as biology, childhood socialization, and adult social roles can account for aggregate differences between the sexes, Deaux and Major argued that a more dynamic model is needed to account for the variability in behavior that exists across situations. They, therefore, developed a model that incorporated as causal variables the characteristics of the immediate situation that influence behavior (see the middle left of Figure 16.3).

Deaux and Major's model, although applicable to a broad range of social contexts, is presented as a hypothesized sequence of events that take place during the course of an interaction between a perceiver (or expectancy-holder) and a target (or self). The model proposes that the perceiver has a gender-related expectancy regarding the target's behavior or personal characteristics, and the perceiver's treatment of the target is influenced by this expectancy and by his or her interaction goals. The target's subsequent behavior is influenced by his or her self-conceptions, interaction goals, and interpretation of the perceiver's behavior. This sequence is modified by the characteristics of the expectancy (e.g., the perceived social desirability of the expected behavior) and the target's concerns with self-presentation or self-verification. Lastly, the perceiver interprets the target's behavior, and the target interprets his or her own behavior, which may change the target's self-conceptions. For example, suppose a woman named Sarah (the target) finds herself in a social setting where Steve (the perceiver) is present. Based on his observations of Sarah and his beliefs about women in general, Steve expects her to behave a certain way and to possess a certain set of characteristics; thus, he treats her in a manner that is consistent with these expectations. Sarah's interpretation of Steve's behavior may or may not influence her subsequent behavior; to make a more accurate prediction regarding Sarah's behavior, we would need a bit more information about Sarah, the situational context, and the expected behavior. Sarah is less likely to conform to a gender-related expectancy, for example, if she is low in self-monitoring and if the expectancy is inconsistent with a central aspect of her self-conception.

Deaux and Major's interactive model has been quite influential in gender research. It has contributed to an increased emphasis on situational influences in subsequent work, and it has prompted researchers to empirically test various aspects of the model. For example, recent findings have provided support for the assertions that interpersonal expectancies influence gender-related behavior (Morier & Seroy, 1994; Muehlenhard & McCoy, 1991), and that situational variables can influence gender-related behavior (Heatherington et al.,

1993; Leary *et al.,* 1994) and self-perceptions of masculinity and femininity (Gould & Weil, 1991; James, 1993). One pattern that emerged from this research is that both males and females are more likely to exhibit behavior that conforms to traditional gender roles if they perceive their opposite-sex interaction partner to be traditional in his or her gender-role attitudes. It was found, for instance, that when interacting with desirable females, males changed their expressed gender-role attitudes in order to appear more similar to their inter-action partners (Morier & Seroy, 1994). Another general finding is that self-perceptions of masculinity and femininity can be influenced by gender-associated situational cues. For example, as mentioned earlier, males obtained lower masculinity scores and higher feminin-ity scores on the BSRI when they imagined themselves giving a gift to an other-sex friend than when they imagined giving a gift to a same-sex friend (Gould & Weil, 1991).

The model proposed by Deaux and Major represents an important step toward the recognition of the complexity and variability of gender-related behaviors. Deaux and Ma-jor move beyond normative expectations and environmental contingencies (reward/punish-ment) as explanatory variables and emphasize the cognitive and behavioral factors that account for the cross-situational variability in behavior. They have suggested, however, that there are a number of important unanswered questions with regard to the various compo-nents of the model that need to be addressed in future research (e.g. under what conditions gender-linked schemata are activated and how changes in the self-concept occur). We be-lieve that another useful research direction in which to go would be to explore the link between the display of gender-related behaviors and the gender-related phenomena inves-tigated by other researchers, such as gender identity and gender schema, discussed earlier, and social roles, the topic to which we now turn.

Eagly's Social-Role Theory of Sex Differences in Social Behavior

Adopting the perspective of sex as a social category, Eagly (1987) began to reexam-ine and reinterpret the sex-differences literature. Much of the past work on sex differences focused on children, the assumptions being that sex differences are directly attributable to biology and/or childhood socialization processes, and that adults continue to exhibit the sex-appropriate characteristics and behavior that they developed in childhood. Eagly, on the other hand, argued that adult social roles—gender roles as well as other work- and family-related roles—are much more relevant to sex differences in adult social behavior than the more heavily emphasized, less immediate factors.

In her social-role theory of sex differences in social behavior, Eagly proposed that the division of labor between the sexes in society leads to gender-role expectations and sex-typed skills and beliefs, both of which contribute to sex differences in social behavior (see bottom path in Figure 16.1 and the top right in Figure 16.3). Eagly argues that certain social roles are primarily occupied by members of one sex; for example, women tend to be re-sponsible for a much greater number of domestic tasks than men. This indirectly influences social behavior in two ways. First, role enactment involves exhibiting the qualities and be-haviors that are associated with the role. Therefore, if a role is typically occupied by mem-bers of one sex, then the role as well as the qualities and behaviors associated with the role become associated with that sex. For instance, because the child-care role is associated with nurturant qualities, women, who typically enact this role, became associated with nurturant qualities. In general, "male roles" are associated with agentic qualities (e.g. aggressiveness, dominance) and "female roles" are associated with communal qualities (e.g. nurturance, compassion). Men and women are then seen as being suited to the roles that they typically occupy, and they are expected to occupy these roles; as a result, people tend to adjust their behavior so that it is consistent with these gender-role expectations. Second, because of the different roles that they occupy, men and women acquire different skills, attitudes, and beliefs, which also result in sex-typed social behavior. For example, men are disproportionately represented in settings that involve aggression, such as the military and contact sports, and are therefore more likely to become highly skilled in aggression-related behaviors and likely to hold more tolerant views regarding the appropriateness of such behaviors.

Results of meta-analyses of sex differences in social behavior (e.g. Eagly, 1987; Eagly & Crowley, 1986; Eagly & Karau, 1991; Eagly & Steffen, 1986) have been consistent with Eagly's social-role theory. For instance, compared with women, men tend to be more aggressive and are more likely to help strangers and emerge as leaders in initially leaderless groups; whereas, compared with men, women tend to be more easily influenced, better able to decode nonverbal cues, and more likely to emerge as social facilitators in group settings. Furthermore, these differences are accentuated when the salience of gender-role expectations is increased (e.g., the presence of other people is likely to increase the salience of social norms), and when the degree to which the specific task requires agentic or communal qualities is increased (Eagly & Wood, 1991). For example, men are more likely to help strangers when bystanders are present and when helping requires assertive behavior.

Several recent studies that have applied Eagly's social role theory to a variety of social behaviors have provided additional support for her framework. For example, it has been shown that the sex differences in emotional intensity (Grossman & Wood, 1993), aggression (Lightdale & Prentice, 1994), and attitudes and behavior regarding sexual activity (Muehlenhard & McCoy, 1991; Sacco, Rickman, Thompson, Levine, & Reed, 1993) are consistent with societal norms about the roles of men and women (e.g. agency versus communion). Also, there is evidence that occupational rank significantly influences interpersonal sensitivity (Snodgrass, 1992), gender-role orientation, and gender-related beliefs (Reid, Roberts, & Ozbek, 1990); more specifically, high-ranking women are less likely to exhibit the qualities and behaviors traditionally associated with females than are low-ranking women. Furthermore, findings of recent studies have suggested that sex differences in emotional intensity are eliminated when gender-neutral normative expectations are established (Grossman & Wood, 1993), and that deindividuation (which reduces the influence of social roles) eliminates sex differences in aggressive behavior (Lightdale & Prentice, 1994).

Based on past research, Maccoby (1990a) offered an alternative (though not contradictory) interpretation of sex differences in social behavior. She argued that as children interact with their same-sex playmates, girls and boys develop distinctive interaction styles (characterized by communal and agentic behaviors, respectively) that continue throughout adulthood. In mixed-sex groups, however, behavior is more complex. Maccoby suggested that men and women alter their behavior in order to adapt to this relatively unfamiliar situation, but especially women, because they find that their more agreeable and less assertive interaction style puts them at a disadvantage in such groups. Thus, Maccoby explains cross-situational variability in behavior in terms of the gender composition of social groups rather than in terms of social roles. Consistent with this assertion are those recent studies that have shown that sex differences in the display of gender-related qualities and behaviors are greater in same-sex dyads/groups than in mixed-sex dyads/groups (e.g. Carli, 1989; Leaper, 1991; Moskowitz, 1993).

The social-role theory suggests that women who occupy high-status occupational roles and men who occupy low-status roles (e.g., female executive and male secretary) would exhibit, respectively, fewer communal and agentic behaviors than women and men who occupy more traditional roles. Taking Maccoby's account into consideration, it is also possible that high-status women act in a less stereotypic fashion because they must work closely with men and therefore adopt men's behavioral styles. This issue was addressed in a recent study (Moskowitz, Suh, & Desaulniers, 1994) in which the interpersonal behavior of males and females was monitored in various work settings. The results partially supported both theories. It was found that status of interaction partner (boss, co-worker, supervisee), and not sex, influenced agentic behavior (e.g., voicing an opinion, showing impatience); workers exhibited agentic behaviors more frequently with lower status interaction partners than with higher status partners. However, sex, and not status, influenced communal behavior (e.g., waiting for others to act, listening attentively to others); regardless of status of interaction partner, females exhibited communal behavior more frequently than did males.

Eagly's social-role theory has made a noteworthy contribution to the literature on sex/gender in that it revived the focus of the sex-role development period (1954–1966) but without the simplistic assumptions that children automatically and completely incorporate all sex-related societal norms into their self-concepts and behave according to these norms throughout adulthood. A useful next step would be to expand the model so that it can accommodate the multifaceted nature of male and female roles. For example, Brannon (1976) has identified four components of the male role: avoid femininity (i.e., "No sissy stuff"), be successful (the "Big Wheel"), be strong (the "Sturdy Oak"), and be aggressive ("Give 'em Hell"). Various components of the female role can also be identified (such as nurturing mother, supportive wife, and physically attractive companion).

CONCLUSION

Understanding why women and men think, feel, and behave as they do continues to be a popular albeit somewhat daunting quest for those within and outside of academia. As we have seen in this chapter, multiple approaches to sex/gender have been introduced, and the predominant approach has varied across the 100-year history of the field of psychology.

There are three major contemporary paradigms: The first, sex/gender differences, is an approach favored by differential psychologists. It focuses on average differences between the biological categories *male* and *female*. The second, gender as a personality variable, is an approach favored by personality psychologists. This approach emphasizes the measurement of global gender-related constructs (e.g., masculinity and femininity), the assumption being that these constructs represent stable, internal qualities that individuals "possess." The third, sex as a social category, an approach favored by social psychologists, stresses the importance of female and male as social categories.

A few noteworthy trends seem to be emerging in research on sex, gender, and the individual. One is the integration of the social and personality approaches. There is still a great deal of reliance on concepts established during the androgyny era, such as androgyny and gender schema. Present research, however, focuses on how the activation/manifestation of such constructs is influenced by social context variables, such as interpersonal expectancies, social roles, sex of interaction partner(s), and culture/ethnicity.

Another trend is the change in topics studied in research on sex differences. Domains such as mental abilities and nonverbal behavior received considerable attention in previous years. Currently, the majority of this research examines sex differences in gender-related attitudes and social relationships (behavior, experiences, etc.).

In addition, there seems to be a great deal of research being generated that is motivated by a feminist political/social agenda. A sizable proportion of the studies dealing with attitudes and social relationships, for example, addresses what are often thought of as "women's issues," such as sexual harassment, rape, and employment bias, with the hope that identification of the gender-related attitudes, beliefs, and behaviors fostering these social problems can eventually be used to eliminate them.

Finally, there is a small but potentially important upswing in research and theory on sex/gender from evolutionary-psychological and behavioral-genetic perspectives (Jacklin & Reynolds, 1993, pp. 201–203; Kenrick & Trost, 1993). As this work develops, an important goal for the overall field will be to seek ways to integrate the largely "nurture" views discussed in this chapter with the "nature" perspectives of those who stress evolution and genetics.

In conclusion, though the conceptual simplicity of the notion is appealing, it is evident that men are *not* from Mars, nor are women from Venus. Many factors, from biological substrates to societal messages, contribute to gendered experience and behavior. Interestingly, men and women in the same society are exposed to a variety of messages about maleness/femaleness. In a parallel fashion, our guess is that the genetics and biology of sex will be far from simple. As a consequence, the topic of sex, gender, and the individual is quite complicated. There are, however, models that are beginning to address this complexity. Our look ahead optimistically predicts the continuing improvement and extension of these frameworks and the integration of social and personality perspectives with one another as well as with models that stress genetic/biological and emphasize societal-level variables.

Acknowledgments: For assistance with securing library materials, we express our gratitude to Nelson Cantada, Donn Nungesser, Yvonne Hauch, and Regina Frau. For providing comments on an earlier draft of the chapter, we thank Marc Beebe, Ray Green, and our editors.

REFERENCES

Anastasi, A. (1972). The cultivation of diversity. *American Psychologist, 27,* 1091–1099.

Ashmore, R. D. (1990). Sex, gender, and the individual. In L. A. Pervin (Ed.), *Handbook of personality: Theory and research* (pp. 486–526). New York: Guilford Press.

Ashmore, R. D., & Del Boca, F. K. (Eds.). (1986). *The social psychology of female-male relations: A critical analysis of central concepts.* Orlando, FL: Academic Press.

Ashmore, R. D., Del Boca, F. K., & Bilder, S. M. (1995). Construction and validation of the Gender Attitude Inventory (GAI): A structured inventory to assess multiple dimensions of gender attitudes. *Sex Roles, 32,* 753–785.

Ashmore, R. D., Del Boca, F. K., & Wohlers, A. J. (1986). Gender sterotypes. In R. D. Ashmore & F. K. Del Boca (Eds.), *The social psychology of female-male relations: A critical analysis of central concepts* (pp. 69–119). Orlando, FL: Academic Press.

Ashmore, R. D., & Longo, L. C. (1995). The accuracy of stereotypes: What research on physical attractiveness can teach us. In Y. T. Lee, L. Jussim, & C. McCauley (Eds.), *Stereotype accuracy: Toward appreciating group differences* (pp. 63–86). Washington, DC: American Psychological Association.

Ashmore, R. D., & Ogilvie, D. M. (1992). He's such a nice boy . . . when he's with grandma: Gender and evaluation in self-with-other representations. In T. M. Brinthaupt & R. P. Lipka (Eds.), *The self: Definitional and methodological issues* (pp. 236–290). Albany: State University of New York Press.

Aube, J., Norcliffe, H., Craig, J. A., & Koestner, R. (1995). Gender characteristics and adjustment-related outcomes: Questioning the masculinity model. *Personality and Social Psychology Bulletin, 21,* 284–295.

Ballard-Reisch, D., & Elton, M. (1992). Gender orientation and the Bem Sex Role Inventory: A psychological construct revisited. *Sex Roles, 27,* 291–306.

Bassoff, E. S., & Glass, G. V. (1982). The relationship between sex roles and mental health: A meta-analysis of twenty six studies. *Counseling Psychologist, 10,* 105–112.

Beere, C. A. (1979). *Women and women's issues: A handbook of tests and measures.* San Francisco, CA: Jossey-Bass.

Beere, C. A. (1990). *Gender roles: A handbook of tests and measures.* Westport, CT: Greenwood Press.

Bem, S. L. (1974). The measurement of psychological androgyny. *Journal of Consulting and Clinical Psychology, 42,* 165–172.

Bem, S. L. (1977). On the utility of alternative procedures for assessing psychological androgyny. *Journal of Consulting and Clinical Psychology, 45,* 196–205.

Bem, S. L. (1979). Theory and measurement of androgyny: A reply to Pedhazur-Tetenbaum and Locksley-Colten critiques. *Journal of Personality and Social Psychology, 37,* 1047–1054.

Bem, S. L. (1981). Gender-schema theory: A cognitive account of sex typing. *Psychological Review, 88,* 354–364.

Bem, S. L. (1985). Androgyny and gender-schema theory: A conceptual and empirical integration. In T. B. Sonderegger (Ed.), *Nebraska Symposium on Motivation: Vol. 32. Psychology and gender* (pp. 179–226). Lincoln: University of Nebraska Press.

Bem, S. L. (1993). *The lenses of gender: Transforming the debate on sexual inequality.* New Haven, CT: Yale University Press.

Block, J. H. (1973). Conceptions of sex role: Some cross-cultural and longiudinal perspectives. *American Psychologist, 28,* 512–526.

Brannon, R. (1976). The male sex role: Our culture's blueprint of manhood, and what it's done for us lately. In D. David & R. Brannon (Eds.), *The forty-nine percent majority: The male sex role.* Reading, MA: Addison-Wesley.

Bromberger, J. T., & Matthews, K. A. (1996). A "feminine" model of vulnerability to depressive symptoms: A longitudinal investigation of middle-aged women. *Journal of Personality and Social Psychology, 70,* 591–598.

Brown, R. (1986). *Social psychology* (2nd ed.). New York: Free Press.

Carli, L. L. (1989). Gender differences in interaction style and influence. *Journal of Personality and Social Psychology, 56,* 565–576.

Carlson, B. E., & Videka-Sherman, L. (1990). An empirical test of androgyny in the middle years: Evidence from a national survey. *Sex Roles, 23,* 305–324.

Carson, R. C. (1989). Personality. *Annual Review of Psychology, 40,* 227–248.

Carter, D. B. (1987). *Current conceptions of sex roles and sex-typing.* New York: Praeger.

Constantinople, A. (1973). Masculinity-femininity: An exception to a famous dictum. *Psychological Bulletin, 80,* 389–407.

Cook, E. P. (1985). *Psychological androgyny.* New York: Pergamon Press.

Deaux, K., & Major, B. (1987). Putting gender into context: An interactive model of gender-related behavior. *Psychological Review, 94,* 369–389.

De Boeck, P., & Rosenberg, S. (1988). Hierarchical classes: Model and data analysis. *Psychometrika, 53,* 361–381.

Dimitrovsky, L., Singer, J., & Yinon, Y. (1989). Masculine and feminine traits: Their relation to suitedness for and success in training for traditionally masculine and feminine army functions. *Journal of Personality and Social Psychology, 57,* 839–847.

Eagly, A. H. (1987). Reporting sex differences. *American Psychologist, 42,* 756–757.

Eagly, A. H. (1993). Sex differences in human social behavior: Meta-analytic studies of social psychological research. In M. Haug, R. Whalen, C. Aron, and K. Olsen (Eds.), *The development of sex differences and similarities in behaviour* (pp. 421–436). London: Kluwer Academic.

Eagly, A. H. (1995). The science and politics of comparing women and men. *American Psychologist, 50,* 145–158.

Eagly, A. H., & Crowley, M. (1986). Gender and helping behavior: A meta-analytic review of the social psychological literature. *Psychological Bulletin, 100,* 283–308.

Eagly, A. H., & Karau, S. J. (1991). Gender and the emergence of leaders: A meta-analysis. *Journal of Personality and Social Psychology, 60,* 685–710.

Eagly, A. H., & Steffen, V. J. (1986). Gender and aggressive behavior: A meta-analytic review of the social psychological literature. *Psychological Bulletin, 100,* 309–330.

Eagly, A. H., & Wood, W. (1991). Explaining sex differences in social behavior: A meta-analytic perspective. *Personality and Social Psychology Bulletin, 17,* 306–315.

Ellis, H. (1894). *Man and woman.* London: Scott.

Evans, R. I., Turner, S. H., Ghee, K. L., & Getz, J. G. (1990). Is androgynous sex role related to cigarette smoking in adolescents. *Journal of Applied Social Psychology, 20,* 494–505.

Forshaw, K., & Shmukler, D. (1993). Sex-role orientation and psychological well-being: A critique of the masculinity model. *South African Journal of Psychology, 23,* 81–86.

Galambos, N. L., Almeida, D. M., Peterson, A. C. (1990). Masculinity, femininity, and sex-role attitudes in early adolescence: Exploring gender intensification. *Child Development, 61,* 1905–1914.

Gilligan, C. (1982). *In a different voice: Psychological theory and women's development.* Cambridge, MA: Harvard University Press.

Gilligan, C. (1986). Reply by Carol Gilligan. *Signs, 11,* 324–333.

Gould, S. J., & Weil, C. E. (1991). Gift-giving roles and gender self-concepts. *Sex Roles, 24,* 617–637.

Gray, J. (1992). *Men are from Mars, women are from Venus.* New York: HarperCollins.

Green, B. L., & Kenrick, D. T. (1994). The attractiveness of gender-typed traits at different relationship levels: Androgynous characteristics may be desirable after all. *Personality and Social Psychology Bulletin, 20,* 244–253.

Grossman, M. G., & Wood, W. (1993). Sex differences in intensity of emotional experience: A social role interpretation. *Journal of Personality and Social Psychology, 65,* 1010–1022.

Gunter, N. C., & Gunter, B. G. (1990). Domestic division of labor among working couples: Does androgyny make a difference? *Psychology of Women Quarterly, 14,* 355–370.

Hare-Musten, R., & Maracek, J. (1988). The meaning of difference: Gender theory, postmodernism, and psychology. *American Psychologist, 43,* 455–464.

Hazan, C., & Shaver, P. R. (1987). Romantic love conceptualized as an attachment process. *Journal of Personality and Social Psychology, 52,* 511–524.

Heatherington, L., Daubman, K. A., Bates, C., Ahn, A., Brown, H., & Preston, C. (1993). Two investigations of "female modesty" in achievement situations. *Sex Roles, 29,* 739–755.

Helgeson, V. S. (1994). Relation of agency and communion to well-being: Evidence and potential explanations. *Psychological Bulletin, 116,* 412–428.

Heilbrun, C. G. (1973). *Toward a recognition of androgyny.* New York: Knopf.

Huston, A. C. (1983). Sex-typing. In P. H. Mussen (Ed.), *Handbook of child psychology* (4th ed., Vol. 4, pp. 387–467). New York: Wiley.

Hyde, J. S., Krajnik, M., & Skuldt-Niederberger, K. (1991). Androgyny across the life span: A replication and longitudinal follow-up. *Developmental Psychology, 27,* 516–519.

Hyde, J. S., & Plant, E. A. (1995). Magnitude of psychological gender differences: Another side to the story. *American Psychologist, 50,* 159–161.

Jacklin, C. N., & Reynolds, C. (1993). Gender and childhood socialization. In A. E. Beall & R. J. Sternberg (Eds.), *The psychology of gender* (pp. 197–214). New York: Guilford Press.

James, K. (1993). Conceptualizing self with in-group stereotypes: Context and esteem precursors. *Personality and Social Psychology Bulletin, 19,* 117–121.

Jones, D. C., Bloys, N., & Wood, M. (1990). Sex roles and friendship pattenrs. *Sex Roles, 23,* 133–145.

Jurma, W. E., & Powell, M. L. (1994). Perceived gender roles of managers and effective conflict management. *Psychological Reports, 74,* 104–106.

Kenrick, D. T., & Trost, M. R. (1993). The evolutionary perspective. In A. E. Beall & R. J. Sternberg (Eds.), *The psychology of gender* (pp. 148–172). New York: Guilford Press.

Kerber, L. K., Greeno, C. G., Maccoby, E. E., Luria, Z., Stack, C. B., & Gilligan, C. (1986). On *In a different voice:* An interdisciplinary forum. *Signs, 11,* 304–333.

Koestner, R., & Aube, J. (1995). A multifactorial approach to the study of gender characteristics. *Journal of Personality, 63,* 681–710.

Kohlberg, L. A. (1966). A cognitive-developmental analysis of children's sex-role concepts and attitudes. In E. E. Maccoby (Ed.), *The development of sex differences* (pp. 82–173). Stanford, CA: Stanford University Press.

Leaper, C. (1991). Influence and involvement in children's discourse: Age, gender, and partner effects. *Child Development, 62*, 797–811.

Leary, M. R., Nezlek, J. B., Downs, D., Radford-Davenport, J., Martin, J., & McMullen, A. (1994). Self presentation in everyday interactions: Effects of target familiarity and gender composition. *Journal of Personality and Social Psychology, 67*, 664–673.

Lightdale, J. R., & Prentice, D. A. (1994). Rethinking sex differences in aggression: Aggressive behavior in the absence of social roles. *Personality and Social Psychology Bulletin, 20*, 34–44.

Lombardo, J. P., & Kemper, T. R. (1992). Sex role and parental behaviors. *Journal of Genetic Psychology, 153*, 103–113.

Maccoby, E. E. (Ed.). (1966). *The development of sex differences.* Stanford, CA: Stanford University Press.

Maccoby, E. E. (1990a). Gender and relationships: A developmental account. *American Psychologist, 45*, 513–520.

Maccoby, E. E. (1990b). The role of gender identity and gender constancy in sex-differentiated development. *New Directions for Child Development, 47*, 5–21.

Maccoby, E. E., & Jacklin, C. N. (1974). *The psychology of sex differences.* Stanford, CA: Stanford University Press.

Markus, H., Crane, M., Bernstein, S., & Siladi, M. (1982). Self-schemas and gender. *Journal of Personality and Social Psychology, 42*, 38–50.

Marsh, H. W., & Myers, M. (1986). Masculinity, femininity, and androgyny: A methodological and theoretical critique. *Sex Roles, 14*, 397–430.

Martin, C. L., & Halverson, C. F. (1981). A schematic processing model of sex-typing and stereotyping in children. *Child Development, 52*, 1119–1132.

Mednick, M. T. (1989). On the politics of psychological constructs: Stop the bandwagon, I want to get off. *American Psychologist, 44*, 1118–1123.

Miles, C. C. (1935). Sex in social psychology. In C. Murchison (Ed.), *A handbook of social psychology* (Vol. 2, pp. 683–797). New York: Russell & Russell.

Mischel, W. (1966). A social-learning view of sex differences in behavior. In E. E. Maccoby (Ed.), *The development of sex differences* (pp. 56–81). Stanford, CA: Stanford University Press.

Mischel, W. (1970). Sex typing and socialization. In P. H. Mussen (Ed.), *Carmichael's manual of child psychology* (3rd ed., Vol. 2, p. 3–72). New York: Wiley.

Money, J. (1994). The concept of gender identity disorder in childhood and adolescence after 39 years. *Journal of Sex and Marital Therapy, 20*, 163–177.

Morawski, J. G. (1985). The measurement of masculinity and femininity: Engendering categorical realitites. *Journal of Personality, 53*, 196–223.

Morier, D., & Seroy, C. (1994). The effect of interpersonal expectancies on men's self-presentation of gender role attitudes to women. *Sex Roles, 31*, 493–504.

Moskowitz, D. S. (1993). Dominance and friendliness: On the interaction of gender and situation. *Journal of Personality, 61*, 387–409.

Moskowitz, D. S., Suh, E. J., & Desaulniers, J. (1994). Situational influences on gender differences in agency and communion. *Journal of Personality and Social Psychology, 66*, 753–761.

Muehlenhard, C. L., & McCoy, M. L. (1991). Double standard/double blind: The sexual double standard and women's communication about sex. *Psychology of Women Quarterly, 15*, 447–461.

Ogilvie, D. M., & Ashmore, R. D. (1991). Self-with-other representation as a unit of anlaysis in self-concept research. In R. C. Curtis (Ed.), *The relational self: Theoretical convergences in psychoanalysis and social psychology* (pp. 282–314). New York: Guilford Press.

Pleck, J. H. (1984). The theory of male sex role identity: Its rise and fall, 1936 to the present. In M. Lewin (Ed.), *In the shadow of the past: Psychology portrays the sexes* (pp. 205–225). New York: Columbia University Press.

Reid, P. T., Roberts, C., & Ozbek, I. N. (1990). Occupational status and gender-role orientation among university women. *Psychological Reports, 67*, 1064–1066.

Reinisch, J. M., Rosenblum, L. A., & Sanders, S. A. (1987). *Masculinity/femininity: Basic perspectives* (pp. 13–82). New York: Oxford University Press.

Rewal, V., & Kapur, V. (1991). Sex roles: Masculinity, femininity, and androgyny as a function of age, sex, and city. *Journal of Personality and Clinical Studies, 7*, 67–72.

Rosenzweig, J. M., & Dailey, D. M. (1991). Women's sex roles in their public and private lives. *Journal of Sex Education and Therapy, 17,* 75–85.

Sacco, W. P., Rickman, R. L., Thompson, K. Levine, B., & Reed, D. L. (1993). Gender differences in AIDS-relevant condom attitudes and condom use. *AIDS Education and Prevention, 5,* 311–326.

Sedney, M. A. (1989). Conceptual and methodological sources of controversies about androgyny. In R. K. Unger (Ed.), *Representations: Social constructions of gender* (pp. 126–144). Amityville, NY: Baywood.

Shaver, P. R., Papalia, D., Clark, C. L., Koski, L. R., Tidwell, M. C., & Nalbone, D. (1996). Androgyny and attachment security: Two related models of optimal personality. *Personality and Social Psychology Bulletin, 22,* 582–597.

Sherif, C. W. (1982). Needed concepts in the study of gender identity. *Psychology of Women Quarterly, 6,* 375–398.

Shields, S. A. (1975). Functionalism, Darwinism, and the psychology of women: A study in social myth. *American Psychologist, 30,* 739–754.

Shields, S. A. (1982). The variability hypothesis: The history of a biological model of sex differences in intelligence. *Signs, 7,* 769–797.

Signorella, M. L., Bigler, R. S., & Liben, L. S. (1993). Developmental differences in children's gender schemata about others: A meta-analytic review. *Developmental Review, 13,* 147–183.

Snodgrass, S. E. (1992). Further effects of role versus gender on interpersonal sensitivity. *Journal of Personality and Social Psychology, 62,* 154–158.

Spence, J. T. (1984). Masculinity, femininity, and gender-related traits: A conceptual analysis and critique of current research. In B. A. Maher & W. B. Maher (Eds.), *Progress in experimental personality research* (Vol. 13, pp. 1–97). New York: Academic Press.

Spence, J. T. (1985). Gender identity and its implications for the concepts of masculinity and femininity. In T. B. Sonderegger (Ed.), *Nebraska Symposium on Motivation: Psychology and gender* (Vol. 32, pp. 59–96). Lincoln: University of Nebraska Press.

Spence, J. T. (1993). Gender-related traits and gender ideology: Evidence for a multifactorial theory. *Journal of Personality and Social Psychology, 64,* 624–635.

Spence, J. T., & Helmreich, R. (1972). The Attitudes Toward Women Scale: An objective instrument to measure attitudes toward the rights and roles of women in contemporary society. *JSAS Catalog of Selected Documents in Psychology, 2,* 66.

Spence, J. T., & Helmreich, R. L. (1978). *Masculinity and femininity: Their psychological dimensions, correlates, and antecedents.* Austin: University of Texas Press.

Spence, J. T., & Helmreich, R. L. (1979). On assessing "Androgyny." *Sex Roles, 5,* 721–738.

Spence, J. T., Helmreich, R. L., & Stapp, J. (1974). The Personal Attributes Questionnaire: A measure of sex-role stereotypes and masculinity-femininity. *JSAS Catalog of Selected Documents in Psychology, 4,* 43. (MS no. 617)

Spence, J. T., Helmreich, R. L., & Stapp, J. (1975). Ratings of self and peers on sex-role attributes and their relation to self-esteem and conceptions of masculinity and femininity. *Journal of Personality and Social Psychology, 32,* 29–39.

Steenbarger, B. N., & Greenberg, R. P. (1990). Sex roles, stress, and distress: A study of person by situation contingency. *Sex Roles, 22,* 59–68.

Susser, S. A., & Keating, C. F. (1990). Adult sex-role orientation and perceptions of aggressive interactions between girls and boys. *Sex Roles, 23,* 147–155.

Swim, J. K. (1994). Perceived versus meta-analytic effect sizes: An assessment of the accuracy of gender stereotypes. *Journal of Personality and Social Psychology, 66,* 21–36.

Szymanski, L. A., Devlin, A. S., Chrisler, J. C., & Vyse, S. A. (1993). Gender role and attitudes toward rape in male and female college students. *Sex Roles, 29,* 37–57.

Taylor, M. C., & Hall, J. A. (1982). Psychological androgyny: Theories, methods, and conclusions. *Psychological Bulletin, 92,* 347–366.

Terman, L. M. (1946). Psychological sex differences. In L. Carmichael (Ed.), *Manual of child psychology* (pp. 954–1000). New York: Wiley.

Terman, L. M., & Miles, C. C. (1936). *Sex and personality.* New York: McGraw-Hill.

Terman, L. M., & Tyler, L. E. (1954). Psychological sex differences. In L. Carmichael (Ed.), *Manual of child psychology* (2nd ed., pp. 1064–1114). New York: Wiley.

Thompson (Wooley), H. T. (1903). *The mental traits of sex: An experimental investigation of the normal mind in men and women.* Chicago, IL: University of Chicago Press.

Unger, R. K. (1979). Toward a redefinition of sex and gender. *American Psychologist, 34,* 1085–1094.

Unger, R. K., & Crawford, M. (1992). *Women and gender: A feminist psychology.* New York: McGraw-Hill.

Wellman, B. L. (1933). Sex differences. In C. Murchison (Ed.)., *A handbook of child psychology* (Vol. 2, pp. 626–649. New York: Russell & Russell.

Whitley, B. E., Jr. (1983). Sex-role orientation and self-esteem: A critical meta-analytic review. *Journal of Personality and Social Psychology, 44,* 765–778.

Whitley, B. E., Jr. (1984). Sex-role orientation and psychological well-being: Two meta-analyses. *Sex Roles, 12,* 207–225.

Whitley, B. E., Jr., & Gridley, B. E. (1993). Sex-role orientation, self-esteem, and depression: A latent variables analysis. *Personality and Social Psychology Bulletin, 19,* 363–369.

Williams, J. E., & Best, D. L. (1982). *Measuring sex stereotypes: A thirty-nation study.* Beverly Hills, CA: Sage.

AFTERWORD

Personality psychology has a weighty history and intriguing prospects for the future. Its theories originating in the clinic, survey research, and the laboratory are freely being accessed in integrative contemporary research. Prognostications of the future of personality abound (Sarason, Sarason, & Pierce, 1966a; Van Heck & Caprara, 1992). A few are offered here.

Research in personality will continue to draw on various traditions. As the contemporary research in Part IV demonstrates, researchers now commonly pursue questions and utilize a variety of methods originating in different personality traditions.

Personality psychology will continue its integrative role. While other fields in psychology and related disciplines continue to focus on narrow research topics, personality will continue to draw together various aspects of human functioning. An example is the field's openness to recent work from the psychobiological perspective. This integrative role is ongoing and not dependent on a new big integrative theory (Sarason, Sarason, & Pierce, 1996b).

Personality psychology will be influenced by new models for understanding complexity. Nonlinear dynamic models and the tradition identified as chaos theory provide new conceptual tools for understanding traditional phenomena in personality (e.g., Waller, Tellegen, McDonald, & Lykken, 1996). Informal verbal elaborations of such phenomena, as have occurred in the psychoanalytic tradition, have not met the scientific demand for rigor. The reductionistic formulations of scientific psychologists have not met the clinicians' demands for a theory that adequately represents a complex changing subject matter. The new science of self-organizing systems can be expected to bridge this long-existing chasm in personality, as it is already doing in related fields (Barton, 1994; Fogel, Lyra, & Valsiner, 1997; Robertson & Combs, 1995; Vallacher & Nowak, 1994, 1997).

REFERENCES

Barton, S. (1994). Chaos, self-organization, and psychology. *American Psychologists, 49,* 5–14.

Fogel, A., Lyra, M. C. D. P., & Valsiner, J. (1997). *Dynamics and indeterminism in developmental and social processes.* Mahwah, NJ: Erlbaum.

Robertson, R., & Combs, A. (Eds.). (1995). *Chaos theory in psychology and the life sciences.* Mahwah, NJ: Erlbaum.

Sarason, I. G., Sarason, B. R., & Pierce, G. R. (1996a). The future of personality. *Journal of Research in Personality, 30,* 307–308.

Sarason, I. G., Sarason, B. R., & Pierce, G. R. (1996b). Views of the future. *Journal of Research in Personality, 30,* 447–453.

Vallacher, R. R., & Nowak, A. (Eds.). (1994). *Dynamical systems in social psychology.* San Diego, CA: Academic Press.

Vallacher, R. R., & Nowak, A. (1997). The emergence of dynamical social psychology. *Psychological Inquiry, 8,* 73–99.

Van Heck, G. L., & Caprara, G.-V. (1992). Future prospects. In G.-V. Capara & G. L. Van Heck (Eds.), *Modern personality psychology: Critical reviews and new directions* (pp. 459–471). New York: Harvester Wheatsheaf.

Waller, N. G., Tellegen, A., McDonald, R. P., & Lykken, D. T. (1996). Exploring nonlinear models in personality assessment: Development and preliminary validation of a negative emotionality scale. *Journal of Personality, 64,* 454–576.

AUTHOR INDEX

SUBJECT INDEX

ABOUT THE EDITORS

DAVID F. BARONE is Professor of Psychology and Director of Academic Affairs at Nova Southeastern University's Center for Psychological Studies in Fort Lauderdale, Florida. He received an A. B. (1969) in psychology from the University of Chicago and an M.A. (1970) and Ph.D. (1975) in personality and social psychology from the University of California, Santa Barbara. He was previously on the faculty at the University of Wisconsin–Parkside. He has been involved in textbook publishing since his graduate student days when he authored an instructor's manual for *Psychology: An Introduction* by P. Mussen and others (D.C. Heath, 1973). He recently published with James E. Maddux and C.R. Snyder a text entitled *Social Cognitive Psychology: History and Current Domains* (Plenum Press, 1997), an integration of past and present work in social and personality psychology. His interest in the history of personality and social psychology is exemplified in a recent chapter on John Dewey in *Portrait of Pioneers in Psychology, Volume II* (American Psychological Association, 1996). His interest in work stress resulted in the Work Stress Inventory (*Educational and Psychological Measurement*, 1988), a transactional theory of work stress (a chapter in *Occupational Stress: A Handbook*, 1995), and the study of stress and social support in police officers (*International Journal of Stress Management*, 1994). He currently is interested the self as conceived interpersonally and was the editor of a special issue of *Review of General Psychology* (December, 1997) on this topic. For additional up-to-date information about him, see his webpage at http://www.nova.edu/~barone.

MICHEL HERSEN (Ph.D., State University of New York at Buffalo, 1966) is Professor and Dean, School of Professional Psychology, Pacific University, Forest Grove, Oregon. Past President of the Association for Advancement of Behavior Therapy, he has coauthored and co-edited 111 books, including the *Handbook of Prescriptive Treatment for Adults* and *Single Case Experimental Designs*. He has also published more than 220 scientific journal articles and is coeditor of several psychological journals, including *Behavior Modification, Clinical Psychology Review, Journal of Anxiety Disorders, Journal of Family Violence, Journal of Developmental and Physical Disabilities, Journal of Clinical Geropsychology, and Aggression and Violent Behavior: A Review Journal*. With Alan S. Bellack, he is coeditor of the forthcoming 11 volume work *Comprehensive Clinical Psychology*. Dr. Hersen has been the recipient of numerous grants from the National Institute of Mental Health, the Department of Education, the National Institute of Disabilities and Rehabilitation Research, and the March of Dimes Birth Defects Foundation. He is a Diplomate of the American Board of Professional Psychology, Distinguished Practitioner and Member of the National Academy of Practice in Psychology, the Distinguished Career Achievement Award in 1996 from the American Board of Medical Psychotherapists and Psychodiagnosticians.

VINCENT B. VAN HASSELT is Professor of Psychology and Director of the Interpersonal Violence Program at Nova Southeastern University in Fort Lauderdale, Florida. Dr. Van Hasselt received his M.S. and Ph.D. from the University of Pittsburgh and completed an internship in clinical psychology at Western Psychiatric Institute and Clinic of the University of Pittsburgh Medical Center. His is editor of the *Journal of Family Violence, Aggression and Violent Behavior: A Review Journal, Journal of Child and Adolescent Substance Abuse, Handbook of Family Violence,* and the soon to be published *Handbook of Psychological Approaches with Violent Offenders: Contemporary Strategies and Issues.* He has published over 150 journal articles, books, and book chapters, including several on the assessment and treatment of family violence and substance abuse. Dr. van Hasselt also a certified police officer working with the City of Plantation, Florida, Police Department. Further, he is a lecturer at the Broward County, Florida, Police Academy and the FBI National Academy in Quantico, Virginia, on the topics of police stress, domestic violence, and suicide prevention. In addition, he has served as a consultant to several police departments in South Florida on the utilization of psychological procedures to facilitate homicide investigations.

CPSIA information can be obtained at www.ICGtesting.com
Printed in the USA
237791LV00004B/24/A